33.99

CATIVE STUDIES

OPERATIONS
STRATEGY

To Elizabeth

OPERATIONS
STRATEGY

DONALD WATERS

THOMSON ™

Australia • Canada • Mexico • Singapore • Spain • United Kingdom • United States

Operations Strategy
Donald Waters

Publishing Director	**Commissioning Editor**	**Development Editor**
John Yates	Patrick Bond	Anna Carter
Production Editor	**Manufacturing Manager**	**Marketing Manager**
Stuart Giblin	Helen Mason	Katie Thorn
Typesetter	**Production Controller**	**Cover Design Controller**
International Typesetting and Composition	Maeve Healy	Jackie Wrout
Cover Design	**Text Design**	**Printer**
Claudio Rosas	Design Deluxe, Bath, UK	Zrinski d. d., Croatia

Brief Contents

v

Contents

11 Process planning and improvement 333

Contents of the book

Operations are responsible for creating the goods and services that organizations pass on to their customers. This function is at the heart of all organizations, giving the means of achieving their aims and the reason for their existence. Every student of business and management should understand this central role, and appreciate the aims, methods and activities of operations.

In recent years managers have been looking more closely at their organizations' strategies. There has been a growing interest in the broad area of strategic management and also in the separate functional strategies – which includes the operations strategy.

Operations strategy is a relatively new idea, and this book gives an introduction to current thinking in the area. It discusses the nature, importance, context, design and contents of an operations strategy, and shows how long-term decisions about operations are fundamentally important for every organization.

Distinctive features of the book

We have written the book in an easy, clear and 'reader friendly' style. Its aim is to give a readable and informative review of current thinking on the subject. In common with all strategic management, there is rarely a single best answer to a problem, or even a best way of looking for an answer. Opinions and judgement can be as important as formal analyses, and we hope that the book encourages discussion in the area. Its approach is practical, presenting ideas in a straightforward way, avoiding abstract discussions – illustrating concepts by a series of ideas in practice. We have deliberately concentrated on the underlying ideas rather than getting bogged down in formal analyses or numerical investigations. At the same time, we have avoided the pitfalls of esoteric discussion and abstract argument.

You do not need any previous knowledge of operations strategy to read the book, as it introduces the subject from first principles. The opening chapters give a review of the important elements of strategy and operations, and these give the foundations for the rest of the text. We relate operations to other areas of management, but we do not expect detailed or specialized knowledge in any topic.

The book follows a logical path through the topics of operations strategy, developing a comprehensive view of the subject. To make this easier, we have divided the book into three parts. The first part gives a broad review of strategic management, setting the context and foundations for the more specific operations strategy. The second part shows how the broad principles of strategic thinking can be applied to operations. This develops the concepts underlying an operations strategy. The third part focuses on specific areas where strategic decisions are most commonly made in operations. Together, these three parts cover some of the most important decisions in any organization.

We have taken an inclusive approach to the subject and not emphasized one area at the expense of others. For example, we show that operations strategies are needed in all types of organization – whether they are businesses, governments, charities, or whatever – and whether they make goods, services, a combination of the two, or neither.

The book also recognizes that operations are becoming increasingly global and describes material that is relevant to operations anywhere. The ideas in action give real examples from all around the world, and none of the material is specific to any particular region.

Each chapter follows a standard pattern, containing a number of learning features. The chapters start with a statement of aims and main themes. Then there is the main content divided into coherent sections. At the end of the chapter is a chapter review, case study, set of discussion questions, some useful Websites and list of references. The Websites and references give starting points for finding more information, and there is more material in the associated Website. A list of key terms can be found at the end of the book.

Who should read this book?

The book can be read by anyone who is meeting operations strategy for the first time and wants a comprehensive view of the subject. This includes a student taking a course in business, management, or other subject that needs knowledge of operations strategy – or you might read the book to learn more about a central area of management.

Typical readers are business and management students who are doing:

- a course specifically in operations strategy and want a comprehensive text to cover all the material
- a course in operations management that takes a strategic view of the subject and does not get involved with the operational detail covered in standard operations management texts
- a course in operations management, and who want more information about the specific area of operations strategy than is given in their general course book
- a course in business strategy and want to see how this affects, and depends on, the operations strategy.

Because we do not assume specific knowledge of methods or types of operation, it could also be read by other people, including:

- students doing other courses that need an appreciation of the strategic importance of operations
- practising managers who want to know what is happening in this relatively new subject, and relate it to their own work.

THE AUTHOR

Donald Waters has degrees from the Universities of Sussex, London and Strathclyde. He worked for a variety of organizations in the UK before moving to Canada to become Professor of Operations Management at the University of Calgary. In 1997 he returned to the UK to become Chief Executive of Richmond, Parkes and Wright, a private foundation whose interests are in management research and education. Dr Waters continues working for organizations around the world, using his specialist knowledge of operations and supply chain management. He has written a number of successful books in these areas.

Contacts

If you have any comments, queries, requests or suggestions for the book or associated material, the author and publisher would be very pleased to hear them. You can contact the author at donaldwaters@lineone.net.

Walk through tour

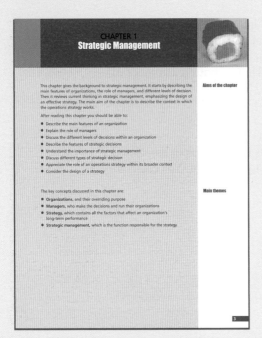

Aims of the Chapter Bullet points at the beginning of each chapter outline the material covered and suggest benefits from reading the chapter

Main Themes A concise statement of the two or three key topics that are discussed in the chapter

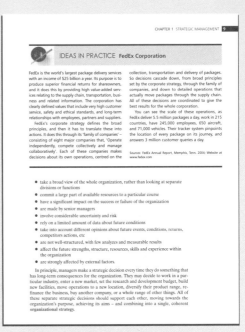

Ideas in Practice Give real illustrations of the ideas discussed, showing how they are used by different types of organisation

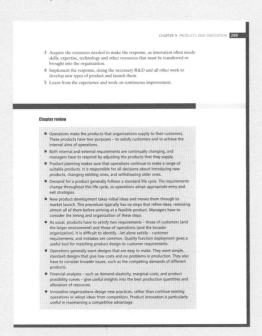

Chapter Summary Bullet points at the end of each chapter review the main findings about the material discussed

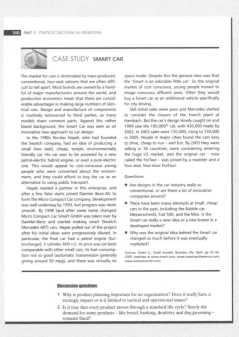

Case study and questions Give practice in applying the ideas described in the chapter to real problems, encouraging readers to think about how to actually use the methods

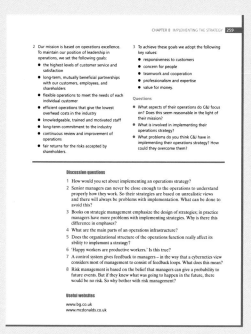

Discussion questions Encourage readers to think more broadly about topics, especially when there is rarely a 'right' answer to a complex problem

Glossary

Achieved quality how good the delivered product is, defined by how it meets specifications and satisfies customers
Action plan gives a timetable for implementing the operations strategy
Activation translation of higher ideas and decisions into operational activities
Aggregate plans medium term plans which show the production of families of products over the next year or so
Agility flexible operations that can deal efficiently with changing conditions
Analyses for operations gives information about the internal operations
Analyses of the environment gives information about the external environment
Appraisal cost costs of monitoring operations to make sure that the designed quality is actually achieved
Attractiveness the extent to which an industry or market can lead to an organization's success
Automation has operations done by equipment without people taking part (compared with manual and mechanized operations)

Balanced scorecard analysis that gives a broad view of operations performance
Batch process makes a few kinds of products in medium sized batches
Benchmarking analysis of the best operations in an industry, looking for ideas to adopt and adapt
Bottleneck the resource or activity that limits the capacity of a process
Bottom-up design where the strategy emerges from the activities of junior managers and passes upwards through the organization
Business environment complex set of external factors that affect an organization
Business process re-engineering the fundamental redesign of a process to give dramatic improvements in performance
Business strategy strategy for a distinct SBU

Capability operations that an organization does – or can do – particularly well
Capacity of process is the maximum amount of a product that it can make in a given time
Capacity management is responsible for all aspects of operations' capacity
Capacity planning aims at finding a long-term match between available process capacity and demand for products

Capacity plans strategic plans that ensure capacity meets the long-term demand
Capacity requirements planning standard approach to planning capacity
Change the inevitable alteration of conditions over time
Choice of strategy choosing the best of the set of feasible strategies considered
Closed-loop MRP adds feedback to basic MRP system
Competencies operations that an organization does particularly well
Competition appears when different organizations supply similar products to the same market sector
Competitive advantage features that make customers prefer one supplier over its competitors
Competitive features product features that customers value and which operations can focus on
Concurrent development reduces the time for product development by running stages in parallel rather than series
Continuous improvement acceptance that a process needs to be constantly updated for operations to remain competitive
Continuous improvement introduction of a continuing stream of ideas for improving quality and operations
Continuous process makes one product in a continuous stream
Control adjusting the strategy to correct any problems
Control system monitors the performance of operations and adjustments the strategy to improve its performance
Core capability key operations that an organization does particularly well
Core functions marketing, operations and finance which exist in every organization
Corporate Strategy strategy for a whole diversified corporation
Corporation an umbrella organization for diversified SBUs
Culture values, norms, beliefs and assumptions that influence the way that people think and behave
Customer relationship management collects and analyzes information about customers

Demand the total amount of a product that customers want
Demand management adjusts the demand for a product to match the available capacity of a process
Dependent demand where there are relationships between individual demands for materials
Designed capacity the theoretical limit on output that can be achieved under ideal conditions
Designed quality the quality that a product is designed to have, defined in its specifications

Glossary Reviews the main terms used in the book, defines specialised terms, and shows how other terms are used in this context (terms included are printed in bold in the text)

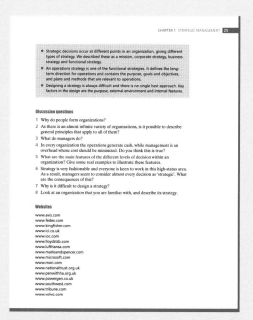

Useful websites Lists websites used in the text, and pointing to further sources of information on the web

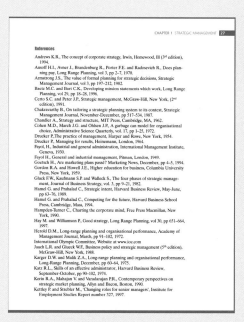

References Show the sources of material used in the text, and give starting points for finding sources of further readings

About the website

Visit the *Operations Strategy* companion website at
www.thomsonlearning.com/waters or www.thomsonlearning.com
to find valuable teaching and learning material including:

- A review of the aims of each chapter
- A review of the key points of the material
- Comments on the case examples
- Comments on the case studies
- Comments on discussion questions
- PowerPoint copies of diagrams
- A selection of further case studies
- Glossary
- References used in text
- Website links
- Answers to ideas in practice
- Case study precis

PART 1

STRATEGIC CONTEXT

Operations are the activities that are directly responsible for making an organization's products. Strategy is concerned with long-term management. When we combine these two ideas, we get an operations strategy, which is concerned with the management of operations. It consists of all the goals, plans, policies, culture, resources, decisions and actions that affect operations over the long term.

It is not easy to visualize an operations strategy. There is nothing tangible to look at, it is difficult to identify – and sometimes it seems little more than the opinions of certain managers. Nonetheless, a well-designed operations strategy is an essential part of any organization. It says how the organization will achieve its aims, what type of products it makes, how it satisfies customers, how it develops a competitive advantage, where it works, how big it is – and just about everything else that determines its long-term success.

It may be difficult to understand the complex web of ideas that forms an operations strategy, but we have to appreciate its role in setting the context and giving a guiding purpose to the operations. The only way that we can manage an organization properly is to get to grips with the operations strategy – and know how to translate its vague concepts into concrete actions.

Despite its central importance, operations strategy is a surprisingly new subject, where ideas are continuing to evolve. This book gives a comprehensive review of current thinking. For convenience, we have divided it into three parts (illustrated in Map 1). The first part describes the general context of strategic management; the second part discusses the aims, contents, design and implementation

1 Strategic management

2 Business environment

3 Strategy design

of an operations strategy; and the third part looks at specific areas for strategic decisions.

There are three chapters in this first part:

- **Chapter 1** reviews the key features of strategic management;
- **Chapter 2** describes the external influences on strategy, including the business, economic and competitive environment;
- **Chapter 3** discusses the design of strategies, emphasizing the internal capabilities that give strategic fit.

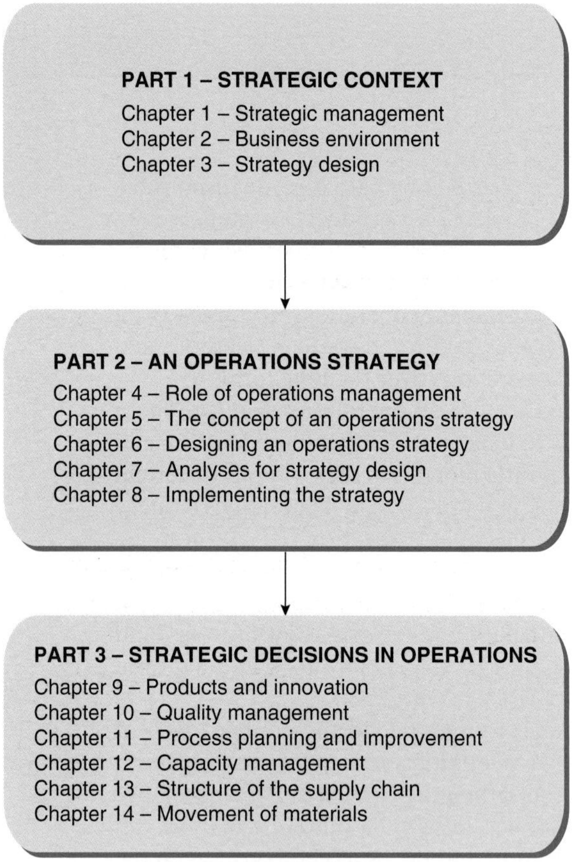

PART 1 – STRATEGIC CONTEXT
Chapter 1 – Strategic management
Chapter 2 – Business environment
Chapter 3 – Strategy design

PART 2 – AN OPERATIONS STRATEGY
Chapter 4 – Role of operations management
Chapter 5 – The concept of an operations strategy
Chapter 6 – Designing an operations strategy
Chapter 7 – Analyses for strategy design
Chapter 8 – Implementing the strategy

PART 3 – STRATEGIC DECISIONS IN OPERATIONS
Chapter 9 – Products and innovation
Chapter 10 – Quality management
Chapter 11 – Process planning and improvement
Chapter 12 – Capacity management
Chapter 13 – Structure of the supply chain
Chapter 14 – Movement of materials

Map 1

CHAPTER 1
Strategic Management

This chapter gives the background to strategic management. It starts by describing the main features of organizations, the role of managers, and different levels of decision. Then it reviews current thinking in strategic management, emphasizing the design of an effective strategy. The main aim of the chapter is to describe the context in which the operations strategy works.

After reading this chapter you should be able to:

- Describe the main features of an organization
- Explain the role of managers
- Discuss the different levels of decisions within an organization
- Describe the features of strategic decisions
- Understand the importance of strategic management
- Discuss different types of strategic decision
- Appreciate the role of an operations strategy within its broader context
- Consider the design of a strategy

Aims of the chapter

The key concepts discussed in this chapter are:

- **Organizations**, and their overriding purpose
- **Managers**, who make the decisions and run their organizations
- **Strategy**, which contains all the factors that affect an organization's long-term performance
- **Strategic management**, which is the function responsible for the strategy

Main themes

ORGANIZATIONS AND MANAGERS

Features of organizations

We all have goals in life – such as getting a degree, buying a house, running a marathon, starting a business, writing a book, getting promotion, or climbing a mountain. Occasionally, we can accomplish one of these goals by ourselves, but usually we need a lot of help from other people. If you want to break the record for sailing single-handed around the world, like Ellen MacArthur in 2005, you need other people to publicize your project, give sponsorship, control finances, design a boat, build and test the boat, plot a route, monitor progress, check weather conditions, give medical advice, and so on. Each individual contributes to the pool of resources and works towards a specific goal – in this case your journey around the world. When people work together in this way they form an **organization**.

> An **organization** is an arrangement of people who pool their resources and work to accomplish a specific purpose.

Morgan says that an organization can appear as a machine, organism, brain, culture, or political system – but the key feature is an overriding **purpose**. If there is no purpose, there would be no reason for the organization to exist. And when we talk about an organization's 'success', we mean that it is actually achieving its purpose.

The purpose of the UK's National Trust is 'to preserve places of historic interest or natural beauty'; the purpose of Penwith Housing Association is 'to provide affordable housing for local people'; the purpose of the Organising Committee of the Olympic Games is 'to organize the Olympic Games' (National Trust; Penwith Housing Association; International Olympic Committee). Each of these purposes refers to the whole organization, which exists in its own right and is distinct from the people who form it. The New York Yankees, for example, is an organization that would continue to exist, even if all the players, managers, owners and employees changed; and a company can go bankrupt while its owners and employees are still solvent. People join an organization when they believe that helping to achieve its purpose is the best way of achieving their own personal aims.

We all belong to many different organizations – a university, company we work for, sports club, professional institute, political party, pension scheme, doctor's practice, motoring service, family, newsgroup, and so on. There is an almost limitless variety of organizations. Some are businesses that try to make a profit; others are governments, charities, institutions and social organizations that are not-for-profit. Some organizations have a rigid structure, such as military forces; others are very informal, such as families. Some provide services, some make goods, and some do virtually nothing. Some have lasted for centuries, while others appear and disappear in an instant. Some are huge with virtually unlimited resources, while others are tiny with almost no resources. To make things more complicated, each large organization contains many smaller organizations within it – so an entire company is one organization, as is a department within the company, a section within the department, a committee within the department, and a working group within the committee.

Despite this diversity, all organizations share common features. To be specific, they all have:

1 a *purpose,* which describes its overall aims
2 a *process,* that works towards achieving the purpose
3 *resources* that are used by the process
4 *managers* who are responsible for running the organization

For example, IotaTech is a company whose purpose is to make a profit for its owners. To achieve this it uses a process that designs, manufactures and supplies state-of-the-art communication equipment. This process uses resources that range from a factory in Singapore to the specialized knowledge of its employees. And a team of managers runs the business.

Role of managers

Managers are the people who run their organizations, making decisions, organizing resources, and getting things done. Van Fleet defines management as 'a set of activities directed at the efficient and effective utilization of resources in the pursuit of one or more goals'. It is difficult to give a detailed description of these activities, as the huge variety of organizations leads to an even greater variety of management jobs. We could use the truism that 'management is everything that managers do' – but in reality they seem to rush around under great pressure spending a few minutes on a series of widely differing tasks (Mintzberg; Stewart). An alternative is to categorize the different types of job that they do, following the lead of Fayol in the 1920s who included 'planning, organizing, commanding, coordinating and controlling'. In this traditional view, managers were commanders who designed work and then tightly supervised and controlled the people doing it. Later, managers found that better results came from an understanding of people's needs and paying more attention to individuality, human issues and interpersonal skills. So the authoritarian 'commanding' softened to 'leading' (Stoner) and then 'influencing' (Certo and Peter). The following list gives a fuller view of the different categories of managers' activities:

● *defining purpose* – describing the reason for their organization's existence
● *setting aims* – translating the purpose into a set of goals and objectives to be achieved
● *planning* – showing how to achieve these aims
● *organizing and designing infrastructure* – giving the best organizational structure and systems to achieve the plans
● *budgeting* – to acquire money and control its expenditure
● *allocating resources* – so that they are available as needed
● *staffing* – so that people are available to do the work
● *coaching* – to make sure that everyone has the training, skills, experience and support that they need
● *motivating* – encouraging people to work productively towards the organization's aims
● *monitoring performance* – to measure progress and compare it with established standards

- *controlling* – adjusting plans to make sure that the organization continues to move towards its aims
- *informing* – distributing information as needed
- *negotiating* – to find compromises between conflicting views.

We could add many other types of activity, but it is already clear that managers do a complex and varied job that needs many different skills. We can summarize these skills as (Katz):

1 *interpersonal* – being able to work with, understand and motivate other people
2 *conceptual* – taking a broad view of the organization, appreciating its aims, the impact of decisions, etc.
3 *analytical* – to define, examine, model and understand situations
4 *technical* – using appropriate methods, tools and procedures.

No-one can have all the skills needed to run an entire organization, so managers specialize in areas where they can use their own particular strengths. For example, someone who has stronger technical skills is more likely to work in accounting, while someone with stronger conceptual skills is more likely to work in planning. Some managers specialize in particular functions, such as finance, human resources, operations or marketing. Some have knowledge and experience in certain industries, such as retailing, education, energy or sport. Some work with specific types of process, such as assembly lines or projects. And a particularly important type of specialization concerns the scope of their decisions, with some managers specializing in long-term decisions for the whole organization and others making short-term decisions for relatively small parts of it.

It is worth mentioning that this division of work into separate specializations leads to a fundamental paradox (Pascale; Hampden-Turner). Even the simplest organization can only work efficiently by dividing the work into smaller parts and creating specializations; but this division creates more work to control the divided parts and integrate them back into a unified whole. So the creation of specializations seems to both increase and decrease efficiency.

Levels of management

Some decisions are very important, with widespread consequences felt throughout the whole organization over many years. Other decisions are less important with consequences felt in a small part of the organization for days or even hours. We can use these levels of importance to classify decisions as, strategic, tactical or operational.

- **Strategic decisions** are long-term decisions that have major consequences throughout the organization.
- **Tactical decisions** are medium-term decisions that have less serious consequences for parts of the organization.
- **Operational decisions** are short-term decisions that have relatively minor consequences for specific activities.

Managers in every organization make decisions at these three levels. In P&O Ferries they made a strategic decision to run a service between Portsmouth and Bilbao, tactical decisions about the frequency of sailing, and operational decisions about crew schedules. Microsoft made a strategic decision to open a research centre in Europe, a tactical decision to upgrade its Word 2003 software, and an operational decision about the number of units of Office to deliver next week. For the University of Sydney, deciding whether to concentrate on post-graduate education is strategic; deciding whether to offer a particular post-graduate course next year is tactical; choosing someone to teach a course next week is operational.

A rough guideline says that strategic decisions have effects over the next three to five years, tactical decisions have effects for around a year, and operational decisions have effects up to a few weeks – but the scale of these decisions varies widely. A strategic decision for Electricité de France considers the number of new power stations it needs over the next thirty years and involves costs of billions of euros. A strategic decision for the New Hambleton village store looks a year or two into the future and involves costs of a few thousand dollars. Whatever the scale, the key point is that organizations need decisions at every level, ranging from broad plans for the distant future to detailed arrangements for tomorrow. Table 1.1 summarizes some of the differences between these levels of decision.

The traditional view has a relatively small group of senior managers – with titles like director, executive, or vice-president – who make the strategic decisions that set their organization's overall direction. They define its purpose and lay down the broad principles of how to achieve this. Middle managers analyse these broad concepts and translate them into realistic activities. They form the link between abstract aspirations and positive actions. Junior managers – typically called supervisors, foremen, first line or first level managers – are responsible for doing the work. They make sure that jobs are actually done according to plans. In Gusthavssen's Nordic Bakery, for example, a senior management team of three decide overall policies, such as the business to work in, type of products, location of facilities and overall financing. Eight middle managers translate these policies into actions by designing the product range, processes to make these products, production targets, marketing effort, supply chain policies, etc. Seventeen supervisors design schedules for production, order materials,

Table 1.1 Some differences between different levels of decision

Type of decision	Strategic	Tactical	Operational
Importance	high	medium	low
Timescale	long	medium	short
Level of manager	senior	middle	junior
Focus	whole organization	parts of the organization	individual activities
Resources used	many	some	few
Risk and uncertainty	high	medium	low
Structure	unstructured	some structure	highly structured
Amount of detail	little	some detail	very detailed
Data available	limited	some	more
Management skills	conceptual	interpersonal	technical

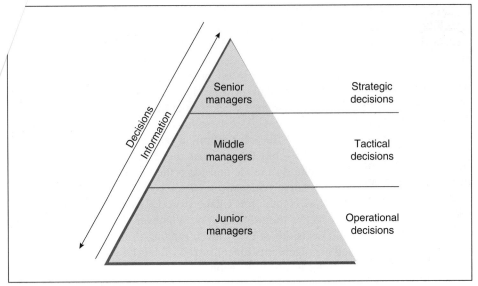

Figure 1.1 Traditional management hierarchy

and make sure that everything runs smoothly so that deliveries are made to customers at the promised times.

This conventional view gives a hierarchy of management, with decisions moving down through the organization and information moving upwards (as shown in Figure 1.1). But new technologies and styles of management have changed this view, and now you will rarely find such a rigid structure. It is increasingly clear that the best people to make decisions are the ones most closely involved – and these are often junior managers who are close to the operations, familiar with conditions, have the necessary information, and can make rapid on-the-spot decisions. Most decisions are discussed, negotiated and agreed rather than simply passed down. This devolution of decisions to lower levels allows organizations to become 'leaner' by removing layers of middle managers. It also reduces the differences between layers of management, with The Institute for Employment Studies (Kettley and Strebler) reporting that, 'the boundaries between different management levels are now blurred'.

Despite these changes, it is worth pointing out that a survey by MORI in 2005 found that 10 percent of managers still made decisions without consulting their staff at all, and a further 14 percent took little or no account of staff views.

STRATEGIC MANAGEMENT

Contents of a strategy

We have mentioned some features of strategic decisions, but a fuller list says that they:

- set the long-term direction of the organization
- define its overall purpose and aims

IDEAS IN PRACTICE FedEx Corporation

FedEx is the world's largest package delivery service with an income of $25 billion a year. Its purpose is to produce superior financial returns for shareowners, and it does this by providing high value-added services relating to the supply chain, transportation, business and related information. The corporation has clearly defined values that include very high customer service, safety and ethical standards, and long-term relationships with employees, partners and suppliers.

FedEx's corporate strategy defines the broad principles, and then it has to translate these into actions. It does this through its 'family of companies' – consisting of eight major companies that, 'Operate independently, compete collectively and manage collaboratively'. Each of these companies makes decisions about its own operations, centred on the collection, transportation and delivery of packages. So decisions cascade down, from broad principles set by the corporate strategy, through the family of companies, and down to detailed operations that actually move packages through the supply chain. All of these decisions are coordinated to give the best results for the whole corporation.

You can see the scale of these operations, as FedEx deliver 5.5 million packages a day, work in 215 countries, have 245,000 employees, 650 aircraft, and 71,000 vehicles. Their tracker system pinpoints the location of every package on its journey, and answers 3 million customer queries a day.

Sources: FedEx Annual Report, Memphis, Tenn. 2004; Website at www.fedex.com

- take a broad view of the whole organization, rather than looking at separate divisions or functions
- commit a large part of available resources to a particular course
- have a significant impact on the success or failure of the organization
- are made by senior managers
- involve considerable uncertainty and risk
- rely on a limited amount of data about future conditions
- take into account different opinions about future events, conditions, returns, competitors actions, etc.
- are not well-structured, with few analyses and measurable results
- affect the future strengths, structure, resources, skills and experience within the organization
- are strongly affected by external factors.

In principle, managers make a strategic decision every time they do something that has long-term consequences for the organization. They may decide to work in a particular industry, enter a new market, set the research and development budget, build new facilities, move operations to a new location, diversify their product range, re-finance the business, buy another company, or a whole range of other things. All of these separate strategic decisions should support each other, moving towards the organization's purpose, achieving its aims – and combining into a single, coherent **organizational strategy**.

But this strategy is more than a set of decisions and it includes all of the factors that affect long-term performance. Walker *et al.* summarize these in their definition of strategy as 'a fundamental pattern of present and planned objectives, resource deployments, and interactions of an organization with markets, competitors, and other environmental factors' (see also Kerin *et al.*). Andrews highlights the three essential parts of a strategy as 'the pattern of objectives, purposes and goals and the major policies and plans for achieving these goals'.

> An **organizational strategy** shows what the organization wants to achieve and how it will achieve it. This includes:
>
> 1 the **purpose** of the organization
> 2 which is expanded into a series of **goals** and **objectives**
> 3 **plans** and **methods** to achieve these goals and objectives

A particular company has a purpose of increasing shareholder value; this leads to more immediate goals of increasing sales and profits; the plans to achieve this include increasing capacity and production. If you compare this picture with the features of an organization that we listed earlier, you can see that the organization's purpose is formalized in the strategy's purpose, goals and objectives; the way the organization's process, resources and management achieve its purpose are described in the strategy's plans and methods (as shown in Figure 1.2).

When discussing management, a common problem is that people give slightly different meanings to words. You can see this with 'aim', 'purpose', 'goal', and 'objective'. In this book, we use the convention that an organization has some overriding **purpose**. We can expand this purpose into a series of more immediate **goals**. These goals are still phrased in rather general terms, so an **objective** gives a more precise – preferably numerical – statement. For example, BKR Sports has a purpose of becoming a major supplier of high quality sports apparel; one goal is to become the leading supplier of certain products; this becomes an objective of gaining a 20 percent market share. A doctor's surgery has a purpose of providing medical care to people living within a specified area; one goal is to give patients prompt service; this becomes an objective of arranging all appointments within two working days. We use 'aims' as more general terms to describe any targets that managers want to achieve.

Strategy as context

The strategy defines an organization's aims and the way that it will achieve these – so it sets the context for all other decisions. The principle is that managers who face any decision should choose the option that gives the greatest contribution to the strategy. When managers throughout the organization follow this thinking, they work consistently towards a common purpose, both supporting and enhancing the strategy.

There are two important points here. The first is that every organization needs a clear strategy, so that everyone knows what they are trying to achieve. This strategy does not just appear, but must be carefully designed through a process of **strategic**

management, which Jauch and Glueck define as 'a stream of decisions and actions which lead to the development of an effective strategy or strategies to help achieve corporate objectives'.

The second point is that everyone concerned should know what the strategy says. Normally, this means that an organization describes its strategy in a written – and well-publicized – document. Southwest Airlines, for example, publish their mission on their Website and confidently state that, 'The Employees of Southwest Airlines understand our mission'.

An organization that fails to design and publish its strategy must expect confusion and managers who lack focus. They cannot consider the broader strategic context and are left to make isolated decisions that do not reinforce each other or work towards a common purpose. As Peter and Hull say, 'If you don't know where you are going, you will probably end up somewhere else'. Toffler adds that, 'A corporation without

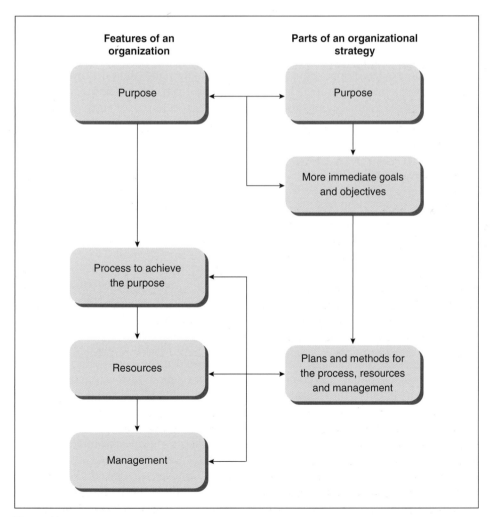

Figure 1.2 Relationships between the features of an organization and its strategy

a strategy is like an airplane weaving through stormy skies, hurled up and down, slammed by the wind, lost in the thunderheads. If lightning or crushing wind don't destroy it, it will simply run out of gas'.

When there is no explicit strategy, the best that managers can do is make inferences from prevailing patterns of decisions and actions. If, for example, you work for a company that advertizes its bargain offers, gives big customer discounts and has regular sales, you can assume that low prices form a part of its strategy. Unfortunately, different people might interpret this apparent strategy in different ways. A marketing department might assume that the company wants to increase its market share; an operations department might assume that it focuses on efficiency; a research and development department might look for new, lower-cost products; a finance department might look for ways of generating cash quickly. Each department bases its decisions on different interpretations and assumptions, and these inevitably lead to conflict. And there may be other parts of the strategy that are just as important, but less obvious.

Growth of strategic management

Of course, you might argue that a formal strategy can be a hindrance as it inhibits flexibility and fast reactions. Without a strategy, managers are freer to move quickly and follow unexpected opportunities without having to relate their decisions back to a rigid, bureaucratic structure. However, research from the 1970s found that this argument is flawed, and organizations with formal procedures for strategic management are generally more successful than organizations without them (for example, Ansoff *et al.*; Thune and House; Herold; Schoeffler *et al.*; Karger and Malik). More recently there has been growing support for the view that good strategic management leads to a good strategy, and this in turn is a dominant factor in organizational performance (Armstrong; Goetsch; Walker *et al.*). When managers design a strategy that sets an organization moving in the right direction they open the road to – but do not guarantee – future success; but if they move the organization in the wrong direction, it cannot possibly succeed and no amount of good middle and lower management will help.

Despite this obvious importance, strategic management has a relatively short history. With some imagination, we could argue that the subject originated at a distant point in history – but the truth is that it has only really developed since the 1950s. Then both Penrose and Chandler argued that the performance of an organization depends more on the broad decisions made for the whole organization than on the narrower decisions made within specific functions. At the same time, Gordon and Howell suggested that management education should include a broad, integrating course on business policy, and companies began to look more seriously at their strategic management. Often they started by manipulating budgets – assuming that the best way to achieve some desired long-term goal was to increase funding for activities that led to the goal, and decreasing funding to activities that moved in other directions. This was a useful starting point, but it had limited success as the achievement of goals clearly depends on more than the allocated budget.

The subject broadened under the influence of Drucker who asked, 'What is our business now?' and the related question, 'What should it be in the future?' His conclusion was that companies need careful planning – certainly beyond simple budget manipulation – to move efficiently from their actual current positions to desired future ones. Managers started to talk about 'business planning', and in the 1960s the subject broadened again to allow for different types of organization with 'corporate planning', and then into the even more general 'strategic planning'.

At the heart of this planning were long-term forecasts of economic conditions, business cycles, product trends, consumer behaviour, competition, and so on. Managers could analyse the implications of these forecasts and design their strategic plans accordingly. But by the 1970s, there was a growing belief that the whole approach of 'planning' was too rigid (Gluck *et al.*). It suggested a regimented procedure that gave a timetable for activities – but which could not deal with uncertainty and unexpected events. 'Strategic management' grew as a more flexible approach that is less concerned with formal planning and more concerned with creating the conditions in which an organization can succeed. Strategic planning would say, 'We will increase production by ten percent over the next three years', while strategic management turns this into, 'We will identify opportunities and create conditions for increased sales'. Strategic planning tried to fit the organization into fixed future conditions; strategic management tries to create new opportunities and even change the shape of the future. This does not mean that strategic planning has disappeared, but it has become more of an administration function, providing support for strategic managers, collecting relevant information, identifying key issues, doing background analyses, presenting options, administering periodic reviews, and so on.

Some problems with strategic management

Despite many years of progress in strategic management, there are still some basic problems. Some of these are conceptual, such as the absence of a definitive model for strategic decision-making, and disagreement about the 'best' approach to strategic management. Other problems are practical, commonly arising from managers who:

- are not prepared for their strategic roles
- do not appreciate the purpose or aims of strategic management
- cannot take a broad view of their organization
- do not recognize or understand the issues that could affect them in the long term
- are unwilling to take a rigorous and disciplined approach to strategic management
- do not appreciate the amount of uncertainty in long-term plans
- do not recognize the assumptions that underlie their decisions.

Another practical problem comes from finding the resources for strategic management. This needs a combination of knowledge, time, effort, money and other resources that many organizations – particularly smaller ones – are unable or unwilling to provide.

A basic problem is that strategic management needs a distinct approach that is difficult to fit into normal management activities. Normal management is highly unstructured and discontinuous, with managers spending a short time on each task. They cannot find – or are not in the habit of finding – substantial blocks of time to mull over long-term options. And they spend most of their time responding to unexpected events and crises, so they habitually look for small adjustments to the current situation that will solve their immediate problem, but rarely generate innovative new ideas or find dramatically new solutions.

In these circumstances, it is not surprising that managers often fail to design real strategies, but wait until circumstances force them to take some kind of action. Then they quickly make intuitive decisions that do not form a coherent strategy or really contribute to the organization's purpose. Cohen *et al.* investigated this phenomenon in state-run organizations and found that managers often avoided, deferred, made by oversight, or never implemented strategic decisions. MacCrinnon suggests that managers only really think about strategy when there is a noticeable gap between their organization's desired state and its actual one, and they are motivated to take the actions that they believe will reduce this gap.

Unfortunately, the lack of a real strategy can be hidden behind statements of lofty and aspirational aims. 'To be recognized as the leading supplier of . . .' is an impressive aim, but without more explanation we have no idea of what it means or how to achieve it. This kind of bold statement might be one-step towards a strategy, but it is only a minor part of strategic management. Such problems become more acute when there are fundamental differences between the stated aspirational aims, and a more realistic unstated one. A government whose stated aim is 'to work in the best interests of the whole population' may have a more prosaic, real strategy of staying in power. Usually the difference is more subtle, such as a company with a stated strategy of innovation and new products – but with a research and development budget that is actually below industry norms. Or a university with a stated strategy of putting equal emphasis on teaching and research, but which spends almost its entire budget on teaching. As Stacey says, 'Managers frequently say that they are doing one thing when they are really doing another. . . . This clearly makes the study of strategic management a tricky business'.

LEVELS OF STRATEGIC DECISION

Four main levels

We have said that strategic decisions refer to the whole organization, but this is rather a simplification. If you take a large organization, such as Wal-Mart, some parts of its strategy clearly refer to the whole organization, such as the policy on low prices, efficiency, international operations and growth. But other decisions only affect part of the organization, despite having all the other characteristics of a strategy. For example, Wal-Mart owns the Asda chain of supermarkets in the UK and some long-term decisions here seem to have little impact on the parent company. In the same way, a strategic decision about marketing might have a long-term impact on a marketing department, but not directly affect other functions. So strategic decisions are rather more diverse than we have suggested, managers can make them at different points in an organization, and they can have more limited effects.

A standard model has three levels of strategic decision – corporate, business and functional (Vancil and Orange). For convenience, we can add an overriding **mission** and **vision** to give the four levels shown in Figure 1.3. In principle, we could use more levels, such as the six proposed by Hay and Williamson, but there is no real benefit in this and the whole process of strategic management becomes fragmented.

Four levels of strategic decision are:

1 **Mission and vision**
2 Corporate strategy
3 Business strategy
4 Functional strategies

Mission and vision

The **mission** gives a concise, unambiguous statement of an organization's purpose and aims. It shows what the organization is going to do and achieve – and by implication, what it is not going to do. Lloyds TSB Group has a mission of 'Maximising shareholder value   by dividend increases and by share price appreciation'

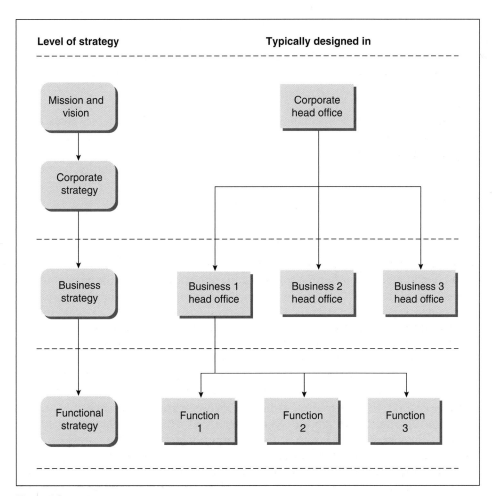

Figure 1.3 Different levels of strategy

[www.lloydstsb.com]. The mission of the Kingfisher Group is 'to be the world's best international home improvement retailer' [www.kingfisher.com]; Avis 'will ensure a stress-free car rental experience by providing superior services that cater to our customers' individual needs' [www.avis.com]; Microsoft 'enable people and businesses throughout the world to realize their full potential' [www.microsoft.com]; Tribune Company, 'build businesses that inform and entertain our customers in the ways, places and at the times they want' [www.tribune.com].

A mission gives stability and shows how an organization is going to act over the long term. It typically includes statements about:

- The organization's purpose and reason for existing;
- what the organization does now and what it wants to do in the future;
- responsibilities to stakeholders, including shareholders, employees, customers, suppliers and competitors;
- underlying values, beliefs, ethical standards and behaviour;
- long-term aims and measures of success;
- business the organization works in, its type of products, attitude towards innovation, processes, technology, etc.;
- its competitive advantages and positioning;
- corporate citizenship, protection of the environment, responsibility to society;
- and a whole range of other information.

A well-designed mission statement serves four purposes. Firstly, it forces managers to think about the strategic direction of the organization, exploring options, encouraging debate and analyzing the fundamental aims. Secondly, it develops a consensus within the organization about its direction and principles. Thirdly, it communicates the agreed results, making sure that everyone is working towards the same goals, that they do not move in the wrong direction, or in too many directions at once, or are so confused that they do not move in any direction at all. Fourthly, it gives a platform for the next levels of decisions – as managers expand the mission to give more details of the organization's operations.

The mission statement should be a clear statement that everybody understands. But we could argue that there is some benefit in phrasing it in rather vague terms, as it allows more flexibility and need not be changed for an extended period. A open-ended mission of 'offering the best products in the industry' can remain unchanged for decades, while a more precise statement would need adjusting every time there is a change of circumstances. If the mission gives stability and continuity over many years, a certain amount of fuzziness is inevitable. This seems to be the view of many managers who find it difficult to design a short, clear statement, and end up with some meaningless cliché about 'being the best' or 'being a world leader'. One way around this is to make a distinction between a mission, which gives a realistic target for the future, and a **vision**, which says what the organization ideally wants to become. Then a vision is more aspirational – giving a view of an ideal future – while the mission focuses more on the achievable. Parikh and Neubauer define a vision as, 'an image of a desired future state', which has the attributes of idealization, uniqueness, future orientation, and imagery (Kouzes and Pozner). Hamel and Prahalad (1989, 1994) prefer 'strategic intent' to show a desired leadership position

IDEAS IN PRACTICE E.ON UK plc

In 1988 the British government announced the sale of the state-owned Central Electricity Generating Board. By 1991 a new company, Powergen, had been formed with 60 percent of the shares privately owned, and the remaining 40 percent sold by the government in 1995. Since then it has expanded into a leading producer, distributor and retailer of electricity and gas in the UK. It owns Central Networks which runs the electricity distribution network for the Midlands and delivers electricity to 4.8 million customers through a network of 133,000 km of cables. It generates enough electricity for eight million homes, and sells electricity and gas to nine million customers.

In 2004 the company changed its name to E.ON UK plc, with the following vision and mission.

'Our Vision

E.ON UK will be the recognised leader in UK power and gas industry.

Our Mission is to provide value for:

- **Our customers** through innovation and delivering our promises on service and quality
- **Our employees** by helping them achieve their full potential
- **Society** by taking responsibility for the impact we have today on future generations
- **Shareholders** by delivering superior financial returns'

Sources: Powergen, Annual Report, London, 2004; Website at www. powergen.co.uk

and Van de Heijden suggests the more general 'business idea' to describe a mental model of the organization. When Baetz and Bart asked organizations for their mission statements they received documents with many different titles. The important point is not the labels we use, but that organizations work with some overriding sense of their purpose and direction.

Corporate strategy

The next level of strategy adds details to the mission, leading to a corporate strategy. Many organizations are diversified **corporations** or conglomerates, which means that they have distinct divisions – perhaps working in different industries, markets, products, or in some other way that makes their activities span traditional boundaries.

A typical route towards a diversified corporation starts with a single business that serves a local market. This business adopts a strategy of growth, but there comes a point where it exhausts opportunities for growth in its existing market. Then it has three options: it can try to take more market share from rivals, it can move into new markets, or it can diversify into other types of products. All of these can encourage diversification, but the third option of moving into new types of products is the most common. Often the new products do not fit into existing operations, so managers set-up a new business unit. Repeated expansion of this type gives a series of distinct business units, all working under the umbrella of the corporation. Essentially, then, an organization moves towards diversification when it runs out of opportunities for growth in its core business.

A corporate strategy contains all the strategic decisions that affect the whole diversified corporation. In general, a strategy consists of a purpose, a series of goals and objectives, and the plans and methods to achieve these – so the corporate strategy contains these elements for a diversified organization. It considers such broad questions as the amount of diversification, acquisitions, structure, relationships between subsidiaries, typically answering questions like:

- How can we best achieve the organization's mission?
- What values does the organization have, and how do we interact with stakeholders?
- How can we keep the organization growing and improving?
- How much diversification or integration should there be?
- Which industries and product segments do we work in?
- Which business should we maintain, grow or contract?
- Which businesses should we start, acquire, close or sell?
- What is the organizational structure and relationships between the separate businesses?
- What is the best allocation of investment and resources among businesses?
- How can we find synergies among the businesses to boost their combined performance?
- How do we coordinate the strategies of different businesses?

The corporate strategy shows how the whole organization achieves its mission. It includes a series of qualitative goals for the corporation and these, in turn, lead to a series of quantitative objectives. A company with a mission of achieving low costs might have a goal of reducing operating costs and an objective of reducing production costs by five percent over three years. The objectives give targets for the organization, and they also measure progress – and if production costs have only fallen by one percent in the first two years there is still a lot to do in the third year.

Each division of a diversified corporation forms a **strategic business unit (SBU)**. Each SBU makes a particular type of product, works in a particular industry, is limited to a country or geographical region, has its own customers, or is in some other way distinct. The corporate strategy defines its portfolio of SBUs, their features and the interactions between them. Sometimes each SBU has virtual autonomy and operates almost as an independent body: at other times the activities are closely controlled, enforcing corporate policies and standards down to the lowest levels.

Business strategy

Each SBU has its own **business strategy**, which contains all the long-term decisions that affect the whole business. In particular, each SBU has its own purpose, series of goals and objectives, and the plans and methods to achieve these. So the Virgin Group has an overall corporate strategy, and then Virgin Atlantic, Virgin Trains, Virgin Mobile, Virgin Megastores, Virgin Credit Cards and all the other businesses in the group each have their own related business strategies.

IDEAS IN PRACTICE Volvo, ICI and Lufthansa

- The mission of the Volvo Group says that they use their, 'expertise to create transport-related products and services of superior quality, safety and environmental care for demanding customers in selected segments'. The whole Group is divided into separate businesses, for trucks, construction equipment, buses, aeronautics, Mack trucks and Penta powerboats. Up until 1999 they also included cars, when a change of corporate strategy led them to concentrate on commercial vehicles and sell their car division to Ford.

- ICI used to be a leading supplier of bulk chemicals. Over the past few years their strategy changed, selling the bulk business and moving into consumer products. They bought a number of companies (including Unilever's Speciality Chemicals, Acheson Industries, Williams Home Improvement, and National Starch) and formed a corporation based on five new businesses – National Starch, Quest, Uniqema, Paints, and

Regional & Industrial. Their vision is, 'to be a genuine leader in formulation science', with a strategy based on 'knowledge of customer needs, leading edge technology and superior products'.

- Lufthansa Aviation Group is an airline, whose corporate mission says that, 'the basis for our activities is the management of international passenger and cargo flights'. The corporation has six distinct SBUs responsible for passenger business, logistics, catering, leisure travel, IT services, and aircraft maintenance, repair and overhaul. Each of these, 'make a significant contribution to sustainable value creation in the Group by focusing consistently on their core business. They all target on market leadership in their business segment'.

Sources: Annual reports Volvo Group, ICI plc and Lufthansa Aviation Group, Websites: www.Volvo.com; www.ICI.co.uk; www.lufthansa.com

A simplified view has the corporate strategy showing which industries and markets a business works in, and then the business strategy shows how it competes within these designated areas. So it typically answers questions like:

- How can we best contribute to achieving the organization's mission and corporate strategy?
- What type of products do we make?
- Who are our customers and how can we satisfy them?
- Who are our competitors and how can we get a competitive advantage?
- In what geographical areas are our markets and operations?
- How much vertical integration should we have?
- What are our long-term targets for profitability, productivity and other measures of performance?
- How innovative are we, and how do we change over time?
- How do we coordinate the strategies of different functions?

The business strategy defines the aims and methods that the business will use to support the corporate strategy, and hence the organization's mission. It shows how the business will succeed in its chosen market, and this means finding exactly what customers want and supplying products that satisfy them.

So the business strategy clearly includes long-term plans for the types of products and processes used to make them. But the operations in an organization consist of all the activities that combine to make its products – thus there is a clear link between the business strategy and operations. In particular, operations become the means by which an organization achieves its business strategy. We will return to this theme in chapter 4.

Functional strategies

Each SBU is likely to contain core business functions of operations, marketing, finance, human resources, IT, customer relations, etc. Each of these functions makes long-term decisions to plot their course into the future and show how they will contribute to the business strategy – in other words, each function has its own **functional strategy**.

Every organization has three core functions: marketing to see what customers want, operations to make the products, and finance to control the money. So each of these has its own functional strategy – corresponding to a marketing strategy, operations strategy and finance strategy. The contents of each of these functional strategies follows the usual pattern, so an operations strategy, for example, defines the long-term direction for operations and contains the purpose, goals and objectives, and plans and methods that are relevant to operations. But the functional strategies have a narrower focus, as their effects are more contained within a single function. Although the operations strategy has a clear impact throughout the whole organization, its focus is clearly on the operations.

Of course, you could ask about strategies for other functions, such as human resource, procurement, logistics, information technology, sustainable development, and so on. The obvious answer is that there are more than three core functions, and an organization can have any appropriate number of functional strategies. A second possibility is that these other strategies form part of the three core strategies – with, say, procurement and logistics strategies included within the operations strategy. A third alternative is that these other strategies form yet another layer of strategic decisions below the functional strategies. Then as well as an operations strategy, an organization might have a lower procurement strategy, logistics strategy, product development strategy, and so on.

It does not really matter what we call the strategies or where we draw boundaries between them, but the important point is that managers have to make long-term decisions for all business functions. These should work together to achieve the business strategy. Sometimes this cooperation is surprisingly difficult. For example, a business strategy might aim for high profits, and this encourages operations managers to develop a low-cost strategy that concentrates on a narrow range of products; at the same time marketing managers might develop a high-sales strategy that concentrates on increasing sales by offering a wide range of products. The clear message is that functional strategies cannot work in isolation, but they must cooperate to achieve the higher aims of the business strategy. Each has some impact on other functions, and managers must negotiate, compromise, and balance competing aspirations to find the best solution for the business as a whole. The resulting strategies can owe as much to internal political compromise as to impartial analysis.

Bringing the strategies together

In principle, strategic management starts at the top with the mission and then progressively adds more details to each of the lower levels. Table 1.2 shows how the different levels of strategy fit together in a typical company.

The division of strategy into different levels has several benefits. An obvious one appears with implementation, which translates the vague principles of a mission into positive actions within each function. This is much easier when there is a series of smaller steps to guide progress, rather than one major hurdle. A second benefit is that strategies can allow for different conditions in different parts of the organization.

Table 1.2 Features of different levels of strategic decision

Level	Responsible	Focus
Mission	Board of directors	Overall purpose and aims of the corporation
Corporate strategy	Senior corporate managers with decisions reviewed by the Board of directors	Building a successful corporation Relations between SBUs, acquisitions and disposals Establishing the industries and markets for each SBU Creating synergies from businesses Setting priorities for investment and resources Reviewing and revising the strategies proposed by each business
Business strategy	General manager of the SBU and its senior managers, with decisions reviewed by senior corporate managers	Building a successful business Policies for competing in their market Choosing the type of products to supply Developing distinctive capabilities Responding to changing conditions Reviewing and revising the strategies proposed for each function
Functional strategies	Senior functional managers, with decisions reviewed by senior business managers	Setting long-term objectives for the functions Decisions about a range of strategic issues for each function, including operations, finance and marketing Reviewing and revising strategies proposed by lower managers
Others strategies	Lower managers within each function, with decisions reviewed by senior functional managers	Designing more specific strategies within each function Setting departmental and other objectives to support functional strategies Reviewing tactical decisions made within each department

IDEAS IN PRACTICE Poseidon–Lanhoff Communications

Poseidon–Lanhoff is a private company that specializes in supplying communications systems for logistics companies. They define several layers of strategic decision, which correspond to their organizational structure. These strategies are designed during a series of meetings but – as you would expect from a communications company – these are virtual meetings that invite contributions from a broad spectrum of managers. The following list illustrates one thread through the layers of strategy.

- **Mission** – to earn returns for investors that are above the norms for the communications industry.
- **Corporate strategy** – to provide customers with outstanding communications systems and services.

- **Business strategy for Poseidon Software** – to design innovative communications software.
- **Operations strategy within Poseidon Software** – to write communication software that is specially tailored to individual customer needs.
- **Human resources strategy within Poseidon Software** – to reward skilled people who can analyze customer problems and produce specialized software that meets their needs.

There are many of these parallel threads down through the layers of strategy, each ending in a set of strategic aims for a particular function. These aims lay the foundations for lower tactical and operational decisions.

Source: Company records

For example, one business might be in a declining industry, encouraging strategies of diversification, cost minimization and eventual closure; another business might be in a growing sector, with optimistic strategies based on expansion, new products and growing sales. A third, less striking, benefit is that more managers are involved in making strategic decisions. Ultimately, all managers have to accept, work with, and implement the strategies, and this is much easier if they are involved with the design.

DESIGNING A STRATEGY

Strategies do not just appear in an organization, but have to be carefully designed by managers. Unfortunately, there is no single best way to approach this design. Some organizations – particularly small ones – have virtually no formal methods for strategic management and seem to rely on the judgement of the owner or entrepreneur. Others have very rigid procedures that use formal and inflexible planning. We look at this problem in chapter 3, but can introduce some underlying ideas here.

A traditional model assumes that the starting point for strategic management is at the top of the organization, with the aims summarized in an agreed mission. Then strategic managers show how the organization will achieve these long-term aims. For this, they must consider the future conditions in which the organization will work, and then define the type of organization that will succeed in these conditions. The next step is to design policies that move the organization from its present state to this desired future one. We can summarize this procedure in the following five steps:

1 *Define the organization's overall purpose* – which is summarized in a mission and expanded into a set of goals and objectives.

2 *Analyze the environment in which the organization works* – including the present and likely future conditions, emphasizing apparent opportunities and threats.

3 *Analyze the organization* – including its current state, capabilities and particularly its internal strengths and weaknesses.

4 *Design the strategy* – to identify the best future state of the organization, and design policies for moving from its present state to this desired future one. Usually several strategies could move the organization forward, and managers have to compare the alternatives and choose the best.

5 *Implement the results* – taking related decisions and actions through all levels of the organization, monitoring progress, checking results, and making adjustments.

This approach is traditionally summarized as 'analysis, choice and implementation' or 'discovery, choice and action'. Then steps 2 and 3 form the analysis, steps 1 and 4 form the design, and step 5 forms the implementation.

This procedure raises some interesting questions. For example, how do managers get an accurate view of future conditions, generate alternative strategies, or compare them? And is it sensible to start with a fixed mission and then see how to achieve this – or would it be better to work the other way around and look for opportunities in the future and then define a mission that takes advantage of them? And should we passively accept future conditions and look for ways of working within them (with strategic planning), or should we try to influence future conditions and make changes that suit our purpose (with strategic management)?

Unfortunately, there are no simple answers to these questions – or a whole range of similar ones. Designing a strategy is always difficult, and nobody has yet designed a universal approach that always leads to a good result. To put it simply, there is no best way of designing a strategy. But this is not an insurmountable obstacle, as managers can use different methods to reach equivalent solutions. The key element of design does not seem to be the details of the method, but that managers tailor the strategy to the organization's internal capabilities and conditions in its external environment (Chakravarthy). In other words, strategy design needs a thorough understanding of three main factors (shown in Figure 1.4):

1 *The organization's overall purpose* – as summarized in its mission

2 *Its external environment* – defined by its industry, market, economic conditions, competition, and other factors over which it has little control

3 *Its internal features* – including operations, structure, distinctive capabilities, competitive advantage, and other factors that allow it to succeed in its environment, and which it can control.

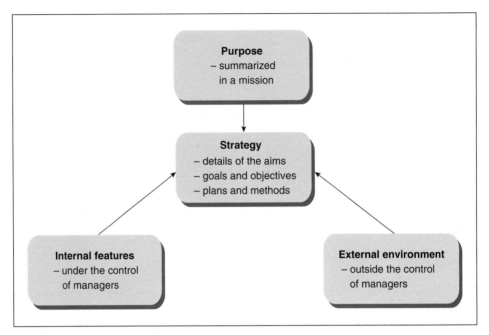

Figure 1.4 Key factors in strategy design

These factors are at the heart of strategic management, and we will look at them in more detail in the next two chapters. In particular, chapter 2 discusses the external environment, while chapter 3 looks at the internal factors.

Chapter review

- People form an organization whenever they pool resources and work together to achieve a common purpose.
- An organization is a distinct entity whose main features are a purpose, a process to achieve the purpose, resources to support the process, and a management structure.
- Managers are the people who run their organizations, making decisions and doing a variety of tasks to ensure the organization achieves its purpose.
- We can describe levels of management as strategic, tactical and operational. Strategic decisions have a long-term impact and set the overall direction of the organization.
- All the long-term decisions and actions combine to form an organization's strategy. Strategic management is the process for designing this strategy. Key elements of the strategy are the organization's purpose, goals and objectives, together with its policies and methods for achieving these.

- Strategic decisions occur at different points in an organization, giving different types of strategy. We described these as a mission, corporate strategy, business strategy and functional strategy.
- An operations strategy is one of the functional strategies. It defines the long-term direction for operations and contains the purpose, goals and objectives, and plans and methods that are relevant to operations.
- Designing a strategy is always difficult and there is no single best approach. Key factors in the design are the purpose, external environment and internal features.

CASE STUDY Marks and Spencer plc

In the 1890s Michael Marks and Thomas Spencer started selling textiles and clothing from a market stall in the North of England. By the 1930s their company had expanded to become a national chain selling clothes only under its St Michael label. Their dramatic growth continued and by the 1960s they were acknowledged as the country's leading retailer. This success was founded on the principles of attractive products, high quality, reasonable prices, efficient operations and good relationships with customers, suppliers and staff.

Unfortunately, by the late 1990s their performance was causing concern. Competitors were taking their market share and profits were falling. The company seemed to lose direction as it moved from its core business of own-label clothing into branded clothes, food retailing, international operations, home furnishings and finance. It introduced a stream of initiatives, including the 'Salon Rose' range of underwear in 1999, 'Count On Us' range of food in 2000; 'Per Una' clothes for women and 'Simply Food' stores in 2001; 'Blue Harbour' clothes for men, 'View From' sportswear and 'DB07' clothes for boys in 2002; '& More' credit cards and 'Sp' clothes for men in 2003; and a new 'Lifestore' in 2004.

By 2004 the company had a turnover of £7.3 billion (half from clothes), 375 stores in the UK and 155 franchised stores in 28 countries. But its performance had stagnated or declined for some years, and the company narrowly escaped a hostile take-over. To survive as an independent company, the senior managers (including many new recruits) had to do some serious rethinking. They recognized that the business had become too complicated, inward looking, inefficient, out of date, and lacking leadership and direction. So they changed their strategy away from expansion and diversification, to concentrate on their traditional core activities. For this they reaffirmed their:

- **Vision** – to be the standard against which others are measured
- **Mission** – to make aspirational quality accessible to all
- **Values** – quality, value, service, innovation and trust.

And they developed a strategy that focused on core capabilities, better products, improved purchasing, more efficient supply chains, better stock control, better customer service and communication, improved stores and lower operating costs. This was implemented in a three-year plan, with priorities of:

- **2004/05:** Re-establishing basic retail standards and satisfying core customers.

(continued)

CASE STUDY Marks and Spencer plc (continued)

- **2005/06:** Getting substantial improvements in product, service, store layout and supply chains.
- **2006/07:** Broadening their appeal to a wider UK customer base and building successful international franchises.

Questions

- Describe Marks and Spencer's strategy and show how it has evolved.

- How has the business environment changed for Marks and Spencer?
- To what extent were Marks and Spencer's problems caused by poor strategic decisions rather than changes in the business environment?
- Do other retailers face similar problems?

Sources: Website at www.marksandspencer.com; Press Release, Marks and Spencer, London 12th July 2004; Annual Report, London, 2004

Discussion questions

1 Why do people form organizations?

2 As there is an almost infinite variety of organizations, is it possible to describe general principles that apply to all of them?

3 What do managers do?

4 In every organization the operations generate cash, while management is an overhead whose cost should be minimized. Do you think this is true?

5 What are the main features of the different levels of decision within an organization? Give some real examples to illustrate these features.

6 Strategy is very fashionable and everyone is keen to work in this high-status area. As a result, managers seem to consider almost every decision as 'strategic'. What are the consequences of this?

7 Why is it difficult to design a strategy?

8 Look at an organization that you are familiar with, and describe its strategy.

Useful websites

www.avis.com
www.fedex.com
www.kingfisher.com
www.ici.co.uk
www.ioc.com
www.lloydstsb.com
www.lufthansa.com
www.marksandspencer.com
www.microsoft.com

www.mori.com
www.nationaltrust.org.uk
www.penwithha.org.uk
www.powergen.co.uk
www.southwest.com
www.tribune.com
www.volvo.com

References

Andrews K.R., The concept of corporate strategy, Irwin, Homewood, IL (3rd edition), 1994.

Ansoff H.I., Avner J., Brandenburg R., Porter F.E. and Radosevich R., Does planning pay, Long Range Planning, vol 3, pp 2–7, 1970.

Armstrong J.S., The value of formal planning for strategic decisions, Strategic Management Journal, vol 3, pp 197–212, 1982.

Baetz M.C. and Bart C.K., Developing mission statements which work, Long Range Planning, vol 29, pp 18–28, 1996.

Certo S.C. and Peter J.P., Strategic management, McGraw-Hill, New York (2nd edition), 1991.

Chakravarthy B., On tailoring a strategic planning system to its context, Strategic Management Journal, November–December, pp 517–534, 1987.

Chandler A., Strategy and structure, MIT Press, Cambridge, MA, 1962.

Cohen M.D., March J.G. and Ohlsen J.P., A garbage can model for organisational choice, Administrative Science Quarterly, vol 17, pp 1–25, 1972.

Drucker P., The practice of management, Harper and Row, New York, 1954.

Drucker P., Managing for results, Heinemann, London, 1964.

Fayol, H., Industrial and general administration, International Management Institute, Geneva, 1930.

Fayol H., General and industrial management, Pitman, London, 1949.

Gluck F.W., Kaufmann S.P. and Walleck S., The four phases of strategic management, Journal of Business Strategy, vol 3, pp 9–21, 1982.

Goetsch H., Are marketing plans passé?, Marketing News, December, pp 4–5, 1994.

Gordon R.A. and Howell J.E., Higher education for business, Columbia University Press, New York, 1959.

Hamel G. and Prahalad C., Strategic intent, Harvard Business Review, May–June, pp 63–76, 1989.

Hamel G. and Prahalad C., Competing for the future, Harvard Business School Press, Cambridge, MA, 1994.

Hampden-Turner C., Charting the corporate mind, Free Press Macmillan, New York, 1990.

Hay M. and Williamson P., Good strategy, Long Range Planning, vol 30, pp 651–664, 1997.

Herold D.M., Long-range planning and organisational performance, Academy of Management Journal, March, pp 91–102, 1972.

International Olympic Committee, Website at www.ioc.com

Jauch L.R. and Glueck W.F., Business policy and strategic management (5th edition), McGraw-Hill, New York, 1988.

Karger D.W. and Malik Z.A., Long-range planning and organisational performance, Long-Range Planning, December, pp 60–64, 1975.

Katz R.L., Skills of an effective administrator, Harvard Business Review, September–October, pp 90–102, 1974.

Kerin R.A., Mahajan V. and Varadarajan P.R., Contemporary perspectives on strategic market planning, Allyn and Bacon, Boston, MA, 1990.

Kettley P. and Strebler M., 'Changing roles for senior managers', Institute for Employment Studies Report number 327, 1997.

Kouzes J.M. and Pozner B.Z., Envisioning your future, The Futurist, May–June, pp 14–19, 1996.

MacCrinnon K., Managerial decision making, pp 445–495 in Contemporary management edited by McGuire J., Prentice Hall, Englewood Cliffs, NJ, 1974.

Mintzberg H., The manager's job, Harvard Business Review, July–August, 1975.

Morgan G., Images of organisation, Sage, Thousand Oaks, CA, 1996.

MORI, UK management styles, London, 2005.

National Trust, National Trust Handbook, London, 2005.

Parikh J, and Neubauer F., Corporate visioning in Hussey D.E. (editor) International review of strategic management, John Wiley, Chichester, 1993.

Pascale R.T., Managing on the edge, Penguin Books, London, 1991.

Penrose E., The theory of the growth of the firm, Basil Blackwell, Oxford, 1959.

Penwith Housing Association, Annual Report, Penzance, 2005.

Peter L. and Hull R., The Peter Principle, Bantam Books, New York, 1969.

Schoeffler S., Buzzell R.D. and Heany D.F., Impact of strategic planning on profit performance, Harvard Business Review, March–April, pp 137–145, 1974.

Stacey R.D., Strategic management and organisational dynamics (4th edition), Financial Times Prentice Hall, London, 2002.

Stewart R., The reality of management (3rd edition), Butterworth-Heinemann, London, 1999.

Stoner J.A.F., Management, Prentice Hall, Englewood Cliffs, NJ (5th edition), 1997.

Thune S.S. and House R.J., Where long-range planning pays off, Business Horizons, August, pp 81–87, 1970.

Toffler A., The adaptive corporation, Gower, London, 1985.

Van de Heijden K., Scenarios, John Wiley, Chichester, 1996.

Van Fleet D.D., Contemporary management, Houghton Mifflin, Boston, MA (3rd edition), 1994.

Vancil R.F. and Orange P.F., Strategic planning in diversified companies, Harvard Business Review, January–February, pp 81–90, 1975.

Walker O.C., Boyd H.W. and Larreche J., Marketing strategy (4th edition), Irwin McGraw-Hill, New York, 2002.

CHAPTER 2
Business Environment

In the last chapter we saw that the design of a strategy depends on the organization's purpose, its external environment and its internal features. In this chapter we discuss the concept of a business environment. This includes all the external factors that affect an organization, but which it cannot control. Important aspects of the business environment include the overriding economic system, the industry in which it works, and the market that it serves.

Aims of the chapter

After reading this chapter you should be able to:

- Understand the importance of a business environment
- Describe the factors that form an environment
- Appreciate the economic context of operations
- Discuss the concept of an industry and the features that make it attractive to an organization
- Discuss the concept of a market and the features that make it attractive to an organization
- Consider the ways that managers respond to changes in the environment

Main themes

The key concepts discussed in this chapter are:

- **Business environment**, which is the external setting in which an organization works
- **Economic system**, which defines the basic rules of the environment
- **Industry**, in which an organization works
- **Market**, whose customers it serves
- **Changes** in the environment

FEATURES OF THE ENVIRONMENT

The business environment

To design a successful strategy, managers need a thorough understanding of three areas:

1 the organization's overall purpose
2 its external environment
3 its internal features.

In this chapter we discuss the environment in which an organization works, while the next chapter looks at the internal features that allow it to compete in this environment.

The **environment** is the external setting in which an organization works. People tend to think of this in terms of the physical environment, or the physical surroundings. Here, though, we are interested in the broader scope of the **business environment**, which includes complex interactions of the economic system, political system, legal restraints, society, industry, labour relations, customer expectations, markets, competition, technology, culture, history, infrastructure, state of the economy, shareholder demands, natural environment, labour conditions, and so on. The important point is that these external factors are almost completely outside the organization's control. Some organizations – particularly very large ones – can influence or make changes, but most have to accept their environment and work within its confines.

- The **environment** is the external setting in which an organization works.
- It consists of all the external factors that affect the organization, but which it cannot control.

The environment affects virtually every aspect of an organization's activities, to the extent that Ansoff (1984) defines strategy as, 'the positioning and relating of the organization to its environment in a way which will assure its continued success'. A useful model of the environment has a set of **stakeholders**, each of which puts pressure on the organization to work in certain ways, and tries to constrain its activities. These stakeholders are all the people and other organizations that have any interest in the organization, including shareholders, financiers, customers, suppliers, employees, past employees, competitors, neighbours, pressure groups, governments, regulators, community and society in general. The obvious problem is that different stakeholders try to push the organization in different directions. Society wants it to be socially responsible and work towards legitimate objectives; owners want some kind of profit from their investment; employees want fair returns for their work; competitors expect it to compete vigorously but fairly; governments see it as a resource that brings economic and social returns; customers want it to satisfy their needs.

This view of the environment seems rather negative, with stakeholders restr. trying to control, and even threatening the organization. A fairer view also shows itive aspects of the environment, as it gives opportunities, encourages organizatic to pursue valid aims, and allows them to succeed. Government regulations on a. industry, for instance, might prevent certain actions, but they also ensure that all competitors maintain the same standards and work in a socially acceptable way. So the environment is really a complex and far-reaching concept that contains both threats to the organization and opportunities that it can exploit.

Components of the environment

The environment can include a huge variety of factors, all of which interact and continually change. We can classify these factors in several ways, with a useful one considering the physical environment, political or legal factors, economic factors, social or socio-cultural factors, and technological factors.

Physical environment The natural and built environment in which the organization works. This often has a dominant impact on the operations, as you can imagine with a company drilling for oil in Alaska, where the temperature drops below minus forty degrees centigrade; or a bank headquarters in the financial centre of Tokyo; or a copper mine in the Outback of Australia. To some extent organizations can choose where to work, but their choice is often limited and they have to accept prevailing conditions. Stockbrokers, for example, have to work in the expensive and crowded financial areas that inevitably surround stock markets, and companies often have to work near to their sources of materials or their customers.

A serious concern with the physical environment is that uncontrolled human activity is causing escalating damage. Deserts are growing, forests are shrinking, global warming is increasing, animal species are disappearing, groundwater is scarcer, seas are increasingly polluted, air quality is lower, natural resources are disappearing, cities cover more land, the population rises exponentially, and so on (Sanderson; United Nations). In response to these problems there are movements – more noticeable in certain parts of the world – towards green products and sustainable operations. Managers often see these as threats, and do not see the opportunities they create. As Hart says, organizations that do not recognize the strategic benefits of environmental protection are missing the 'biggest opportunities in the history of commerce'. Porritt *et al.* report that the output from 'environmental industries' will rise from $280 billion in 1999 to $640 billion in 2010, and that this will create half a million jobs in the European Union alone.

Political or legal factors The laws and regulations that affect an organization. They include governments that make laws, courts and officials who interpret laws, departments that enforce them, and other groups – such as pressure groups – that have political power. Organizations want political conditions that allow – and ideally encourage – them to achieve their aims. But perhaps more importantly, they want political stability, as they can adapt to slowly evolving conditions, but find it difficult to deal with very rapid changes.

On a global scale, there are many areas where government regulations have decreased – such as transport, telecommunications, broadcasting, utilities, and the movement of materials around free trade areas like the European Union and North American Free Trade Area. But most people feel that there is a trend towards increasing political intervention and regulation. They also claim that these stifle innovation, distort markets, inhibit competition, reduce flexibility and increase costs. In reality, this case is often overstated and many organizations find that regulations create opportunities – typically encouraging new products, making competition fairer, and even using new services to enforce the regulations (Porter and Van der Linde; Carey and Regan). For example, more stringent regulations on the disposal of household waste have created a growing industry in the uses of rubbish as a raw material.

Economic factors The financial and monetary conditions that affect an organization. All organizations have some financial goals – typically making a profit, working within a fixed budget, reducing costs, or increasing income – so they are all affected by prevailing economic conditions. These conditions range from the overall type of economy, down to pricing policies of competitors. There are three particular economic concerns: the general economic system, the nature of industries, and the nature of markets. We consider each of these later in the chapter.

Social or socio-cultural factors These define the relationships between an organization and the society in which it exists. They are concerned with the written and unwritten rules and assumptions about the behaviour of individuals, organizations and society in general. These include considerations of health, welfare, education, language, culture, use of resources, elimination of waste, pollution, impact of opening or closing facilities, responses to societal expectations, balance of stakeholders' interests, and requirements for being a good corporate citizen.

At any time, there are major social trends. One of the most obvious is the growing internationalization of operations, so that companies like McDonald's, Coca-Cola and Microsoft have a dominant presence throughout the world. The United Nations described 7,000 companies as 'transnational' in 1975, but this figure had risen to 60,000 by 2000, and the top 500 of these account for 70 percent of world trade and 30 percent of global GDP (Time). Another strong trend appears in demographics, with developing countries having increasing populations and declining average age, while developed countries have more stable populations and increasing average age. Hart says that between 1997 and 2020 the total economic activity of the world will have to increase by a factor of ten to provide a minimum living standard for the increasing population.

Social factors also include ethical and moral responsibilities that managers have because of their humanity and not because of any legal or economic forces. There are many debates about business ethics. One view says that if an action is sufficiently harmful there will be laws against it, so ethical questions do not arise in business. As Friedman says, 'There is one and only one social responsibility of business – to use its resources and engage in activities designed to increase its profits so long as it stays within the rules of the game, which is to say engages in open and free competition without deception or fraud'. Of course, this raises questions about the meaning of 'deception', the limits of competition, the efficiency of legal systems, and so on. And it ignores the point that many organizations are aware that something is 'wrong' and, even illegal but they continue to do it until stopped – such as releasing pollutants into rivers or the air.

An opposing view says that organizations should care about what is 'right' and 'wrong' – so they should have a social conscience that protects the long-term interests of different stakeholders, rather than just doing what is expedient. More organizations are adopting this view and including a positive ethical stance as part of their strategy. This is obvious in charities, and has been a long-established principle in other businesses, such as the Body Shop, Co-operative Bank, Prudential, 'fair trade' goods, and ethical investment trusts. Many companies follow PepsiCo's example and publish a Corporate Citizenship Report. Surveys in Europe (Ipsos) suggest that around 85 percent of people think that large companies should use some of their resources to help solve societal problems – both in countries where they operate and countries where they sell products.

Technological factors (These include all the applications of science, engineering and related knowledge that might affect an organization.) More specifically, they refer to the actual and potential technology that can be put into an organization's products, or the operations that are used to make these products. (Improved technology in products either makes existing products more attractive to customers, or else it creates entirely new products; improved technology in operations can reduce costs, improve efficiency, guarantee quality, increase capacity, give more flexibility, and generally allow change and improvement.)

In recent years, the most obvious impact of technology has been in electronics, which have revolutionized computing, communications, data management, control, and many aspects of operations (Gates). Perhaps the other area of technology that has received most attention is biology, primarily through gene therapy, genetic modification, pharmaceuticals and agricultural products.

Inherent and competitive factors

Another useful view of the environment draws a distinction between inherent factors that are fixed by a location, and competitive factors that are set by the actions of other organizations (Daft).

1 *Inherent or macro factors* give the infrastructure and framework within which an organization works. These are largely fixed by location and include the political, legal, economic and social systems, climate, technological development, demography, natural environment, transport system and all the other conditions that are determined by the geographic position.

2 *Competitive or micro factors* are the more variable aspects that are set by the industry and market that an organization chooses to work in. They include the industry attractiveness, market size, customer features, suppliers, competitors, employees, changing conditions, and anything else that affects operating conditions.

When a company works in a particular location, it cannot change the type of economy, climate, transport system, or tax rates, which are fixed, inherent factors. But the features of the industry, market, suppliers and competitors are more variable, competitive factors that are largely set by competitive forces. The inherent factors form a rigid framework, and the competitive factors come within this, as illustrated in Figure 2.1.

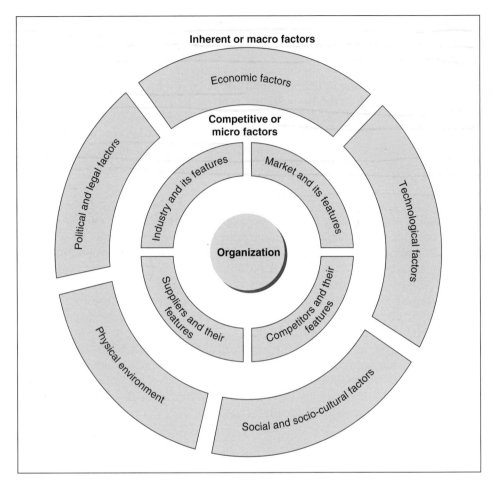

Figure 2.1 An organization's inherent and competitive environment

ECONOMIC ENVIRONMENT

Supply and demand

A dominant factor in an organization's macro environment is the type of economy that it works in. Economics studies the **supply** and **demand** for products, and the way that governments manage these to achieve their broader aims. Their methods depend on political ideology and form a spectrum. At one end of this are centrally planned economies, where the government manages every aspect of economic activity. It analyzes the supply and demand for products and then makes central decisions about the type of products made, organizations that supply them, ownership of these suppliers, quantities, prices, and so on. At the other end of the spectrum, there is no central planning and all economic activity is left to free market forces. Suppliers and customers arrange their own transactions without any involvement of other bodies, and the whole economy is self-regulating.

IDEAS IN PRACTICE AstraZeneca

AstraZeneca is one of the world's leading pharmaceutical companies, with 64,000 employees in 100 countries and annual sales of over $21 billion. They take their corporate responsibility seriously, with aims that include the creation of 'enduring value for society' and making 'a real contribution to human health'. They recognize that their 'reputation and continued long-term success depend on our ability to integrate successfully our financial obligations with our social and environmental responsibilities'. This leads to a strategy that is based on sales growth, increasing productivity, developing new products, effective risk management, corporate responsibility and valuing people.

Their concern for the business environment appears in almost every aspect of operations. The corporate strategy explicitly states that they 'set, promote and maintain high standards of corporate responsibility worldwide', and their core values are:

- Integrity and high ethical standards;
- Respect for the individual and diversity;

- Openness, honesty, trust and support for each other;
- Leadership by example at all levels.

A Corporate Responsibility Priority Action Plan shows how the company responds to a series of key issues, including human rights, safety, employee health and well-being, diversity, relations with suppliers, legislation and government policies on chemicals, marketing and sales practices, animal use and welfare, clinical trials, access to medicines, diseases in the developing world and community support.

The company's concern for the physical environment is summarized in its view that, 'Our challenge is to sustain improvement in our environmental performance as we continue to grow our business'. And this means continual improvements in performance related to climate change, ozone depletion, energy use, effects of transport, sustainable production, biodiversity, and unplanned emission of chemicals.

Sources: AstraZeneca company report, 2004; AstraZeneca Corporate Responsibility Summary Report, London, 2004; www.astrazeneca.com

---

In practice, no governments work at either of these extremes, but they adopt a mixed approach that balances market forces and central planning. Even the most market-oriented government has some central planning – typically for education, national defence, law and health; and the most centrally planned economies allow some level of market activity. This means that virtually every organization has to respond – at least to some extent – to market forces. Even organizations working with the most rigid central planning, and the most blatant monopolies, have to consider market forces to some extent.

Market forces mean that organizations have to identify products that customers want, and then supply products that satisfy these demands. Figure 2.2 shows this cycle, which starts with customers demanding a product. In fact, they want the product so much that they are willing to pay a price above the production costs, and this premium is the supplier's profit and incentive to make the product. In general terms, the operations add value. Some of this value passes to customers, when it satisfies their demand; and some remains with the supplier, where it contributes to profit. The difficulty, of course, is to design products that customers really want, and operations that add enough value. These are the fundamental problems of operations management.

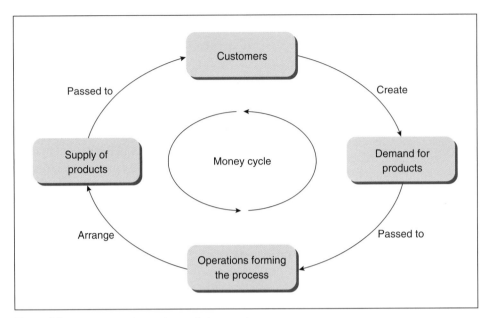

Figure 2.2 The cycle of supply and demand

Effects of price

Operations use a variety of resources to make their products, including raw materials, facilities, equipment, money, time, information, people, and anything else that they need. All of these resources come at a price. If there is an abundant supply, like sand in the desert or seawater at the coast, the resource is virtually free. But most resources are in short supply and cost more – with greater shortage usually meaning higher price. When organizations sell the product, they have to cover the cost of all the resources, plus any other operating costs. So the lowest price they can accept is the **marginal cost** – which is the cost of producing the last unit. Any price below this minimum gives a loss, while any price above it gives a profit. Higher prices obviously give more profit, and encourage suppliers to make more units – and they also attract new competitors into the market. So a high price tends to increase the supply of a product.

The total demand for a product depends on many factors, including the number of customers, their tastes, size and distribution of income, availability, marketing effort, alternative products, and so on. But customers have limited amounts of money, and price is usually a major factor in their decision to buy something. When we buy one product we have to forego another – in the way that when you buy a new car you cannot also afford an exotic holiday. So a low price raises demand by attracting new customers, encouraging existing customers to buy more, and encouraging customers to move to this product from alternatives.

Figure 2.3 shows these effects of price on supply and demand (with straight lines indicating general trends rather than realistic values). The obvious problem is finding a reasonable price that satisfies both customers and suppliers. In theory, when markets are left to their own devices they reach an equilibrium where demand equals supply. At this point customers pay a price that they are relatively happy with, and suppliers receive an amount that gives a reasonable profit. Sometimes there are constraints on the price, such as legal restrictions, and it is impossible to work with the equilibrium

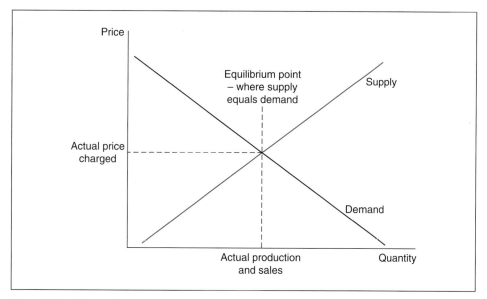

Figure 2.3 Effects of price on supply and demand

value. Economists view these constraints as distorting the market. If, for example, the government imposes a maximum price for some product – such as health care for the elderly – there is a price ceiling and then the supply of the product does not meet the demand. Then there must be some kind of rationing, achieved by queues, lotteries, discrimination (so that certain people are prohibited from buying), changes in the product (perhaps with lower cost alternatives), or unofficial markets. Similarly, if minimum prices are fixed – perhaps for agricultural products – there is a price floor and supply of the product exceeds demand. Then there has to be some mechanism to remove the excess production (shown in Figure 2.4).

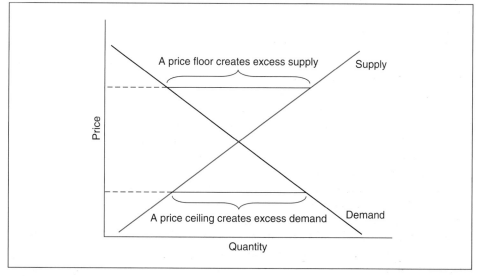

Figure 2.4 Effects of price controls

IDEAS IN PRACTICE Balakrishnan and Sons

In the summer of 2004 Franklin Balakrishnan was thinking about making a new type of product in his factory in Munchen, Germany. An initial estimate showed that he could make 10,000 units a year of the product with a variable cost of €26 a unit, and he wanted to know if this would be worthwhile.

A firm of consultants ran a series of interviews with potential customers and focus groups, and estimated the demand for the product at various prices. In parallel with this, they studied the trading results of potential competitors and used these to get an idea of likely supply. These results are summarized in Figure 2.5. As you can see, the likely equilibrium point comes with sales around 7,000 units a year at a price between €25 and €30. This was not encouraging. With sales of only 7,000 units a year Franklin would have spare capacity and increased variable costs. After a short deliberation, he decided that this type of product and market was not attractive, and he would look elsewhere for opportunities.

Source: Internal Report, Richmond, Parkes and Wright, Berlin, 2005

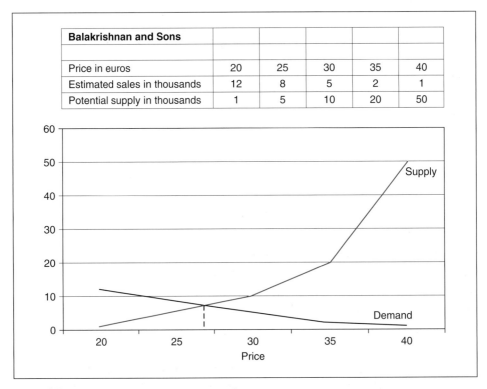

Balakrishnan and Sons					
Price in euros	20	25	30	35	40
Estimated sales in thousands	12	8	5	2	1
Potential supply in thousands	1	5	10	20	50

Figure 2.5 Results from Balakrishnan and Sons

Of course, these models give idealized views and some weaknesses are obvious – do sales inevitably fall with rising price, what happens when the cost of production is higher than the price customers are willing to pay, what happens when there is limited competition, can customers collaborate, can suppliers force artificially high prices, will suppliers be happy with a 'reasonable' profit, why should the price reach an equilibrium, are circumstances stable, and so on? More sophisticated analyses answer many of these questions, and they go a long way towards showing the type of products that an organization should make, and the financial returns expected.

Economic development

Another important economic factor is the overall state of development. All things being equal, you would not expect to see the same type of operations in, say, Switzerland and Sudan. A high technology manufacturer, for example, would find it difficult to justify working in a predominantly agricultural area where it would meet problems with the infrastructure, skills, suppliers, services, and general support.

A traditional view describes three categories of industry:

- **Primary or extractive** – which are the basic economic activities of agriculture, fishing, mining, quarrying, etc.
- **Secondary or industrial** – which are manufacturing and construction.
- **Tertiary or services** – which are all the services to industry and individuals.

A problem with this classification is that the tertiary industries form a very broad group. Apart from the fact that they are both services, there is virtually no similarity between the operations of Sarah Williamson (who is a self-employed management consultant) and Carrefour (which is Europe's largest supermarket chain). An obvious answer is to sub-divide services into more groups. In the 1950s Foote and Hatt described services as either domestic (hotels, restaurants, laundries, hairdressers, etc.), commerce (retailing, transport, banking, insurance, government, etc.), or personal (health, education, recreation, etc.). Thirty years later Riddle suggested five sub-divisions, but a fuller list includes:

- **public services** – local, national and international governments;
- **shops** – retailers, wholesalers, restaurants, repair services, etc.;
- **logistics** – including transport, distribution and communications;
- **non-profit organizations** – such as charities, clubs and NGOs;
- **other business services** – including finance, accounting, consulting, legal and professional services for industry;
- **other personal services** – including education, health, leisure, banking and domestic services for individuals.

A common view says that economies move through these industries in a natural progression (Clark). As productivity rises in one sector the number of people employed declines and they move on to the next sector. Then economies move in sequence from extraction to industry and then on to services – with stages often described as pre-industrial, industrial and post-industrial. A typical 'developed' country has around 20 percent of its population working in manufacturing, over 70 percent in services, and the rest in the primary industries. Of course, there are exceptions to this, and some highly developed economies have major primary industries, notably Australia, Canada and the USA. At the same time, countries like Switzerland and Dubai move directly from primary to tertiary industries without developing a significant manufacturing base.

INDUSTRIES

Choice of industry

If you think about BMW, you probably imagine a car maker. Similarly, Heinz is a food processor, Microsoft delivers software, Exxon Mobil is an oil company and AOL is an internet service provider. When an organization decides to supply a particular type of product, it chooses the **industry** that it works in. So the software industry includes Microsoft and all the other suppliers making similar products. In many ways 'industry' is an unfortunate name as it suggests manufacturers, but we mean all kinds of activity and could equally talk about the banking industry, healthcare industry, or any other kind of service.

> An **industry** is a group of organizations that use similar resources to make equivalent products to satisfy the same customer demand.

Industries with different characteristics appeal to different types of organization. An organization that is strongly innovative and constantly working on new ideas will have little interest in working in a conservative and unchanging industry. But what factors make a particular industry attractive or unattractive? In 1965 Ansoff gave a checklist of important factors, which include product-market structure, growth, profitability, technology, investment, marketing, competition and strategic perspective. We can expand this to give a fuller list of questions that organizations normally ask before deciding to work in a particular industry.

- How big is the market the industry supplies?
- How good is the industry's financial performance, and is this likely to change?
- What are the main products and where are they in their life cycles?
- Who are the customers, and what are their main features?
- What factors influence demand for products, and is this static, growing or falling?
- Who are the competitors and how big are they?
- What is the basis of competition and is this likely to change?
- What are the financial, capacity and resource requirements?
- How efficient is the industry in terms of capacity, productivity, utilization, etc.?
- Are there economies of scale, learning curves or other key affects?
- What are the current levels of technology, and is this likely to change?

- Does the industry have seasonal variations?
- Are there barriers to entering or leaving the industry?
- What are relations like in the supply chain, and how much forward and backward integration is there?
- What are the risks, uncertainty or potential problems for the industry?
- Can the industry be broken down into smaller segments?

This kind of checklist is useful, but it only gives broad guidelines and managers need more specific details of the industry. Fortunately, there is rarely a shortage of information, and managers usually become swamped by the huge amounts of data. So much data is available about any industry that it is impossible to do a complete analysis – and there would be no point as only a fraction of the available data is relevant to a particular organization and its strategy. So managers have to identify a few of the most relevant features of an industry and concentrate on these, looking to see if the industry gives an attractive environment for their operations. If the environment seems attractive, they can move forward and adjust their strengths – or potential strengths – to the requirements of the industry, with the aim of becoming active and successful members.

But if managers analyze an industry and find that it does not give an attractive environment, they have four alternatives:

1 Accept that their operations would not succeed in this industry, and move on to find another more suitable industry to work in.

2 Make internal changes to operations, developing new products and processes that would be more successful in the industry.

3 Develop innovative new ideas, use their dominant size, or have some other influence that actually changes the industry.

4 Look for a smaller attractive **segment** in an otherwise less attractive industry.

Industry segments

It is often difficult to draw a convincing boundary around an industry. Nintendo make computer games – so are they in the computer industry, the software industry, the home entertainment industry, or a separate computer games industry? Another problem comes when the industry is very large and too diverse to consider in one part – like the fast food industry. The way around both of these problems is to divide whole industries into smaller segments that have similar characteristics. For example, we can divide the fast food industry into pizza restaurants, hamburger restaurants, coffee shops, sandwich bars, and so on.

These segments are normally based on related types of product, but they might also consider the types of customer, perhaps using their age, gender, education, family size, hobbies, and so on. Spa Lady, for example, works in the women's fitness industry, while Saga provides services for retired people.

These segments might still be very big, so we can divide them into smaller **sectors**. For example, we can describe the vehicle manufacturing industry as follows:

- **Industry** – vehicle manufacturers:
  - *Segment 1* – manufacturers of vehicles to carry people

- *Sector 1* – manufacturers of cars
- *Sector 2* – manufacturers of buses
- **●** *Segment 2* – manufacturers of vehicles to carry goods
  - *Sector 1* – manufacturers of delivery vans
  - *Sector 2* – manufacturers of trucks

If these sectors are still too big we can divide them into yet smaller parts, with the car sector divided into companies making sports cars, luxury cars, family cars, small cars, F1 cars, and so on.

There are two benefits of dividing an industry in this way. Firstly, it gives a more precise picture so that managers can examine the features of the specific area they will be working in. Secondly, it identifies new opportunities where a segment or sector currently has few, or no, competitors. For example, BedRock Lager works in the lager brewing industry, but it cannot compete with huge, international companies. By analyzing the industry, managers identified a sector for microbreweries supplying specialized lagers around Melbourne, and found that they could fit in – and compete – very effectively. So managers analyze the capabilities of their organization and find the type of industry where it can succeed, looking for the best match between capabilities and industry requirements. Then they home-in on a particular sector that is most suited to their operations. They find the specific requirements of this sector, and fine-tune their operations to get the best results (we return to this theme in the next chapter).

Industry life cycle

An industry does not remain static, but it is constantly changing. The changes include long-term growth (like small car production) or decline (like tobacco products), new products, technological developments, new customers, evolving customer demands, entry or exit of major suppliers, new processes, increasing globalization, new regulations, societal concerns, evolving lifestyles, and a whole range of other factors. The overall effect of these changes gives industries a characteristic life cycle with the five stages shown in Figure 2.6:

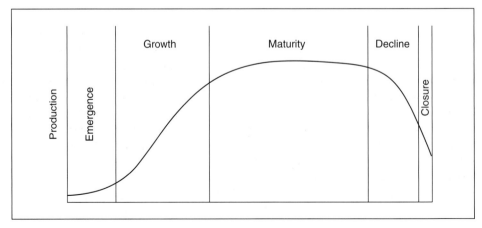

Figure 2.6 Industry life cycle

- **emergence** – developing and producing new products, with innovative suppliers starting and expanding a new industry;
- **growth** – as competitors enter the industry, increasing capacity to meet customer demand for products that are seen as new and attractive;
- **maturity** – with capacity stabilizing to meet a level demand, standardized products and processes, supply consolidated into fewer, larger mass-producers;
- **decline** – capacity falls as producers leave the industry to concentrate on newer products;
- **closure** – when the last organizations move out of the industry.

To a large extent, the industry life cycle is driven by the life cycles of its leading products. Blackberry devices are currently emerging, low cost airlines are growing, electricity generation is mature, tobacco products are declining and black-and-white television plants have been closed. Some industries remain stable for long periods, such as sugar refining and insurance; others move very quickly, such as mobile telephones and computer software.

Of course, there are variations in this basic pattern, and a common option is to regenerate a mature or declining industry and extend its life. For example, cinema attendance, travel by train, and newspaper publishing all had a period of decline before suppliers changed their strategies and moved to a period of growth.

It is always faster, easier, cheaper and less disruptive for an organization to adjust its operations in the same industry, rather than move to a completely new one. Ideally, then, an organization remains in the same industry for a long time, evolving to meet new conditions. But the constantly changing environment might force it to move in a direction that it does not like. Until the 1990s airlines invariably gave a high value – and expensive – service, competing through their schedule, network and quality. Then new, low-cost operators changed the direction of the industry to focus on price. Many

IDEAS IN PRACTICE **Baileys**

Diageo is one of the world's leading producers of alcoholic drinks. It owns many leading brands, including Guinness, Smirnoff Vodka, Archer, Gordons, Haig, J&B, Johnnie Walker, Blossom Hill Wines, Moët and Chandon, Piat d'Or, Harp – and Baileys.

Baileys is a cream-based liqueur that has been produced in Dublin, Ireland since the 1970s, using the local surplus milk production. But by 1998 sales of Baileys had grown to 4.2 million cases – and this needed the same amount of milk as the city of Dublin itself. Diageo was now facing a shortage of local

milk, and the obvious solution was to import it from somewhere else. However, this would be contrary to Diageo's strategy of supporting local communities. Instead, they gave technical help and management training to local dairy farmers. This brought production from the fragmented dairy industry up to European Union standards, ensured a long-term supply of milk for Diageo, maintained low costs, and kept the support of the local community.

Sources: Diageo, Corporate Citizenship Guide, London, 2001; Website at www.diageo.com

traditional airlines could not cope with this change and either closed-down or were taken over, and the industry divided into low-cost and full-service segments. The lesson is that organizations should evolve to continue their good performance in the same industry, but they should do periodic reviews to check for more attractive alternatives.

MARKETS

Market segments

When talking about an industry, we generally take the view of the producer looking for an attractive type of business; when taking the viewpoint of a consumer, we talk about the **market**.

> The **market** is the set of customers who buy – or might buy – a particular type of product.

The market for shoes is all the people who buy, or who might buy, shoes. In the same way that we can divide an industry into smaller parts, we can divide a market into segments and sectors. Then we can look at the market segment for women's shoes, and within this the sector for women's sports shoes, and within this the smaller sector for women's running shoes. Dividing the whole market into smaller pieces gives the same two advantages that we mentioned when dividing the industry. Firstly, it allows organizations to target specific types of customers who share similar features – perhaps buying certain types of products, living in the same area, buying similar quantities, being in the same age-group, having similar preferences, etc. Secondly, it identifies opportunities when there are no, or few, competitors meeting the demands of a particular sector.

And in the same way that managers look for attractive industries to work in, they also look for attractive markets. Managers start by analyzing their organization's capabilities, and identifying the type of market where it could succeed. Now they are looking for a good match between the organization's capabilities and the market requirements. Then they divide the market into smaller segments and sectors, to identify the most attractive, find its specific requirements, and adjust their operations to satisfy these. Kotler summarizes this approach as 'segment, target, position'.

This approach depends on managers having a clear idea of what customers want – and this depends on market research. There is so much information available that managers cannot possibly analyze it all, and they have to concentrate on certain features. In particular, they have to identify the factors that customers really value, and which affect their choice of products and suppliers. Then managers can rate the importance of these factors, and identify a small number – typically between four and six – of the most important **key success factors** (KSFs). There are many possible types of KSF, with some common ones based on technology (using the latest developments, innovation, research strength, expertise, etc.), operations (giving low costs, high quality, high productivity, flexibility, etc.), logistics (convenient locations, easy purchasing, fast delivery, efficient stocks, etc.), organizational abilities (product design, reputation, customer service, skills, etc.), and finances (financial strength, return on investment, payment options, etc.).

To succeed, an organization must perform all the KSFs well, and it must excel in at least one of them – giving a better overall performance than competitors. This means that managers must analyze the performance of their competitors, see how strong the competition is, and identify gaps where other organizations are failing. The next step is to design a strategy to meet customer expectations better than competitors and gain a competitive advantage, and we return to this aspect of design in the next chapter (see also Faulkner and Bowman).

There are obviously close links between market and industry sectors, and it often seems pointless to distinguish between the two – the industry sector of breakfast cereal producers meets the demands of the market sector for breakfast cereals. But because of the relative numbers of consumers and producers, there are far more market sectors than industry sectors. So a single organization can meet the demands of many market sectors, and is continually looking for opportunities in untapped market sectors that are close to sectors that it already works in.

Competition

There is **competition** when different organizations supply similar products to satisfy customers in the same market sector. Then an organization can only succeed by delivering products that customers in this sector want – and in particular, they must want its products in preference to similar products from competitors. To achieve this, the organization must have some kind of **competitive advantage** that sets it apart from competitors and makes it the supplier of choice. There are many ways of developing a competitive advantage – low price, high quality, product features, innovation, availability, convenient location, customized products, reliability, customer service, guarantees, and so on. By definition, the difficulty of actually gaining this advantage depends on the performance of competitors – and when competition is weak, it is relatively easy to gain a competitive advantage; when competition is fierce, it is very difficult. But the level of competition depends on the market's features, including its size, growth potential, stability, profitability, significant trends, risks, number of competitors, relative size of competitors, barriers to entry and exit, etc. Porter (1979; 1980; 1985) summarizes these in his model of 'five forces of competition' below (also illustrated in Figure 2.7).

1 *Rivalry among existing organizations.* This is usually the strongest of the five forces, and originates from the desire of every organization to gain a competitive advantage. This competition is stronger with:

- a lot of organizations of similar size and capabilities supplying the market
- no single organization dominating the market or controlling market conditions
- organizations that use diverse strategies to improve their market position
- high exit barriers, so it costs more to get out of a market than to stay in and compete
- customers who have no loyalty to a particular supplier, and can change to another supplier with little cost or inconvenience

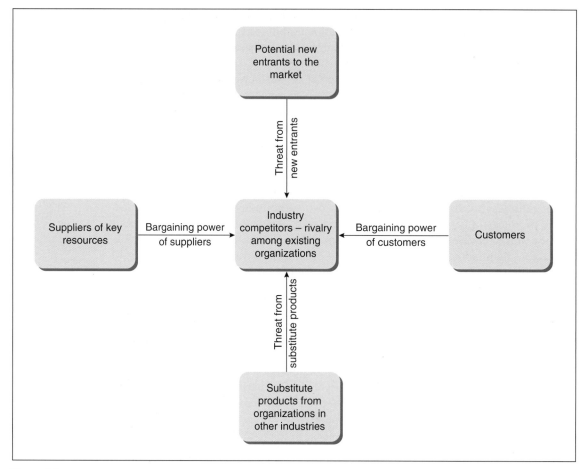

Figure 2.7 Porter's model of 'five forces of competition'

- customers who are knowledgeable and informed about prices and conditions
- stable demand for products
- excess capacity, often found when capacity can only be increased in large steps, and it needs high investment
- high fixed costs or perishable products, giving strong incentives to cut prices when demand slackens
- some organizations that are dissatisfied with their current position and are willing to make a move for change.

Exit barriers are the costs of leaving a market, and these can be both economic (liquidation costs, severance pay, discounted stock, etc.) and social (employee protests, local community pressure, government intervention, etc.). When the exit barriers are low, an organization can easily change its strategy and move on to another market; but high exit barriers mean that the organization has to stay in the market even when it is no longer attractive, and look for a strategy that limits damage.

2 *Suppliers of key inputs*. Every organization needs reliable suppliers for its materials – where we use 'materials' as a general term to cover all of the raw materials, resources, services, utilities, and other things that it buys. These suppliers can play a direct role in competitiveness. At a basic level, an unreliable supplier can reduce the availability of some key resource, making it impossible for an organization to complete customer orders – thereby reducing its competitiveness. On a broader level, suppliers affect the cost of operations, quality, performance of products, production quantities, delivery times, terms and conditions of supply – and the very feasibility of an organization. This effect is particularly strong when:

- reliable deliveries are critical for smooth operations
- materials have a major effect on the final quality of products
- purchased materials account for a large part of operating costs
- it is cheaper for an organization to buy materials than make them itself
- there are no substitute materials
- it is difficult or expensive for an organization to change suppliers
- a few suppliers dominate the industry
- there is little fear of backward integration
- the industry is not an important customer of the suppliers.

Most organizations find it best to develop stable, long-term relationships with suppliers, and these often come from strategic alliances or partnerships (which we discuss in chapter 14).

3 *Customers*. Customers prefer competitive markets as they can shop around to get the best deals and switch to suppliers that offer the best terms. Of course, strong customers can always exert pressure – in the way that supermarkets use their huge buying power to force their suppliers into giving the best possible deals. But customers are not always in a strong position. The UK water companies, for example, have monopolies of an essential commodity, so they have all the power and their customers have none at all. In general, customers are in a strong position when:

- they are big and buy large quantities
- they buy a large proportion of a particular organization's output
- products are standardized or commodities with little to differentiate them
- there are many competing suppliers and customers can move between them with little cost or inconvenience
- there are low cost substitutes or alternative products
- customers can integrate backwards and establish their own sources of supply
- the materials are relatively expensive, making customers more careful in their choices.

4 *Potential new entrants*. At any time, only some of the organizations that could supply products to a market are actually doing so, and there is also a pool of organizations that do not currently supply competing products, but will start if the conditions are right. These new entrants bring extra capacity, either building new facilities or acquiring and reorganizing operations that already supply the market. And they typically adopt strategies of aggressive competition to build market share at the expense of existing suppliers.

Potential new entrants to a market usually face some kind of entry barrier, which consists of the obstacles that put them at a disadvantage compared with organizations already in the market. The sources of these barriers include:

- the need for large initial investments
- economies of scale that make it difficult for new entrants to start small and build up their operations
- effects of experience and the learning curve
- need to access specialized knowledge or technology
- customer loyalty and brand preferences
- access to logistics channels that might be reluctant to take on new products
- vertically integrated competitors that limit access to parts of the supply chain
- regulatory barriers, such as licenses, tariffs and international trade restrictions.

The threat from new entrants is strongest when entry barriers are low, the industry is attractive, and there are many potential new entrants. The success of these new entrants largely depends on the reactions of existing competitors. If existing producers decide to compete strenuously with the new entrants, they can take advantage of their experience and knowledge of the market. The result can be fierce competitions and difficult trading conditions. Sometimes, though, existing organizations are unwilling or unable to compete with new entrants and their own performance quickly declines. This is particularly noticeable when the entrants bring new operations, technology or methods that make the existing competitors obsolete.

5 *Substitute product.* These occur when customers can replace one product by another that comes from organizations in a different industry. For example, a mail service can substitute printed letters by telephone, e-mail or text messages. Similarly, customers can substitute contact lenses for glasses, artificial sweeteners for sugar, and internet news services for newspapers. These substitutes put an upper limit on the prices an industry can charge, as higher prices encourage customers to move to the substitutes. Substitute products are a strong force when:

- they are relatively cheap compared with the product
- other costs of moving to the substitute are low
- they are readily available
- they have equivalent performance and features
- producers of the substitute are keen to increase their sales
- producers of the substitute can easily add new capacity.

Attractiveness of a market

As a rule, organizations do not like working in markets that are aggressively competitive – so they are not happy when all five of these forces are strong, with aggressive competition between existing organizations, powerful suppliers and customers, and high chances of substitute products and new entrants. A market is much more attractive when there is little competition from existing organizations, weak suppliers and customers, and low chance of substitute products and new entrants. But the market does not have to look like this, and a well-designed strategy can allow an organization to succeed in even the most hostile market. For example, retail competition in the United States has always been strong, but Wal-Mart designed a successful strategy that guided it to become one of the world's largest and most successful companies.

If a market is generally attractive, it is reasonable to assume that new organizations will try to enter – and if it is generally unattractive, existing organizations will try to leave. But barriers to both entry and exit limit this movement. If there are high entry barriers and low exit barriers, existing competitors can leave but new entrants cannot arrive. This is likely to reduce competition in the market and allow the remaining organizations to earn high and stable profits. On the other hand, low entry barriers and high exit barriers mean that new entrants can easily arrive but it is difficult for any of them to leave. This increases competition and leads to low, uncertain profits. Figure 2.8 summarizes the effects of entry and exit barriers on likely profits.

Managers are generally happiest when their organizations are working in markets with high entry and low exit barriers. They are also happiest when their organizations have large shares of rapidly growing markets. But what happens when there are other conditions? We can begin to answer this by looking at the four combinations of market share and market growth shown in Figure 2.9 (Henderson).

- **Stars** are organizations with a large share of a growing market. Managers like this area, as it gives the best profit growth and opportunities for the future. Large investment may be needed to maintain market share, but returns are high from the price premiums that come with a growing market – so the overall cash flow should be roughly in balance. Demand often outstrips supply, but managers must maintain their competitive advantage during this inevitably short period of rapid growth.

- **Cash cows** are stable performers that have a high share of a mature market. There is no need for heavy investment, as the operations are already established, run smoothly, and give economies of scale. Aggressive competitors have already

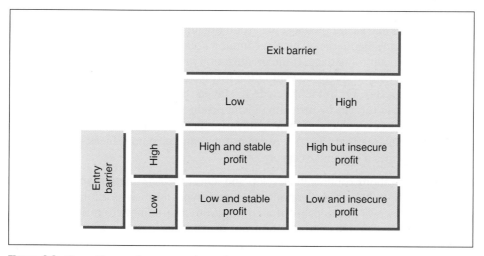

Figure 2.8 The effects of entry and exit barriers

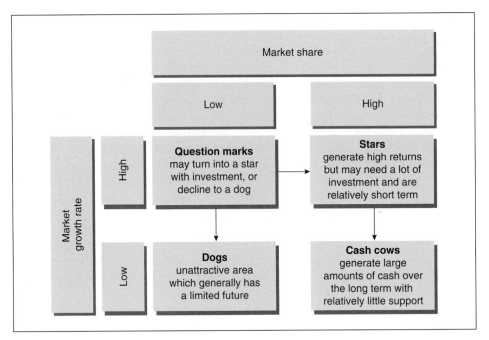

Figure 2.9 Attractiveness of markets

moved on to higher growth areas, and with considerable experience of the market, there is no need for expensive campaigns. The result of high market share and low support costs give high cash flows and profits.

- **Dogs** are poor performers that have a small share of a stable or declining market. This is the worst type of organization and is often a drain on resources. Occasionally a dog can be revitalized, perhaps by creating a niche product. Usually, though, there is little hope of restoring fortunes, and dogs tend to hang around until their products are withdrawn and they are sold or closed down.

- **Question marks** are the most uncertain organizations, with a small share of a rapidly growing market. This is a common area for new products, and it is the most difficult to manage. If the organization invests enough to increase its market share, it might do well in the future, get a bigger market share and become a star. Or it might decide to stay in the same position and get reasonable returns by providing niche products. Or the market might not develop as expected and the organization becomes a dog. This is a very uncertain area that can soak up investment and give no returns, or it can develop into a star and cash cow.

Most corporations continually develop and adjust their businesses, and at any time they are likely to have organizations of all four types in their portfolio. Hopefully, there are cash cows at the heart of a corporation. The money from these can fund both the consolidation needed by stars until they become cash cows, and attempts to turn some question marks into stars. Money is also needed to cover the cost of dogs. Although they drain resources, there is nothing wrong with having some dogs, as their absence suggests the corporation has not been adventurous enough in trying new ideas.

IDEAS IN PRACTICE Huang Sho Lan Industries

Huang Sho Lan Industries originated in Hong Kong, but expanded to mainland China, particularly the rapidly growing area around Shanghai. They are now a diversified corporation that starts – or more usually buys existing – companies and develops them until they contribute to the group. Their current interests range from agriculture through to electronics, but their core business is in testing and measuring equipment.

Before entering a new market they do a detailed analysis of its attractiveness. Part of this includes a scoring model, with the following figures taken from a possible acquisition. Both the weights and scores are agreed by the acquisitions team, and the weighted scores are the products of these two.

Criterion	Weight (1 to 20)	Score for DSF Limited (1 to 10)	Weighted score
Market size	9	17	153
Expected market growth rate	8	11	88
Variation in demand	3	4	12
Industry profitability	10	10	100
Amount of concentration	2	2	4
Strength of existing competition	8	18	144
Presence of a dominant competitor	4	5	20
Entry barriers	8	12	96
Exit barriers	6	4	24
Threat of substitute products	6	12	72
Threat of new entrants	5	4	20
Supplier relations	4	16	64
Customer relations	7	10	70
Possibility of product differentiation	3	4	12
Technological changes	2	3	6
Total			**885**

The score here is 885 points, which by itself does not have much meaning. But with a maximum possible score of 3,000 it does not seem very optimistic, and it compares unfavourably with several other markets that Huang Sho Lan were considering. In the event, the company did not proceed with this acquisition.

Source: Internal company records

This analysis suggests that a corporation should have a balance of business types, with enough cash cows to cover the costs of the others. But there are obvious weaknesses in the approach (Slatter; Walker *et al.*). It really tries to link market attractiveness and competitiveness – but a single figure for market growth (inevitably related to the stage in a product life cycle) does not show how attractive a market really is, and a single figure for market share does not give an adequate view of competitiveness. Managers really have to take a more considered view of market conditions.

RESPONDING TO ENVIRONMENTAL CHANGES

Alternative responses

An organization's environment is constantly changing. Sometimes, the change is slow, with many features remaining constant over long periods and the environment steadily evolving over time. At other times there are very sudden changes, perhaps when a single issue becomes critical, such as a major customer going bankrupt, new government regulations, new logistics channels, a major technological breakthrough, a natural disaster disrupting the supply chain, and so on. Organizations have to respond to every significant change in the environment. There are two ways of doing this. Firstly, we have already said that managers should do periodic reviews to make sure that their industry is still attractive, and they should do equivalent checks on their markets. But this is a retrospective view, responding to circumstances that have already changed. Managers need time to implement changes, so they should really be more proactive. Then the second approach is to look for events that might occur in the environment and prepare for them in advance.

This proactive approach needs more skill and experience, but it prepares an organization for possible events, rather than waiting to see what happens before doing anything. Of course, waiting may be the best answer, but this is only one of the alternatives that managers can adopt. They should really identify possible events, analyze the potential consequences, and then take the appropriate action (Waters; Walker *et al.*), which might be to:

1 *Ignore it* – assuming that the event is unlikely, or that the consequences are minor, or that any positive action could make the situation worse. This wait-and-see approach delays all actions until after events occur – or do not occur – when managers have a better idea of the consequences and alternatives.

2 *Avoid or reduce the risk* – taking actions to reduce the probability that an event will occur.

3 *Reduce or limit the consequences* – changing the strategy to limit the effects of risky events.

4 *Share or deflect the risk* – passing the risk onto someone else more able or willing to handle it, such as an insurance company or financial institution.

5 *Make contingency plans* – which show what the organization will do if an event actually does occur. These are often referred to as 'plan B', which is only activated when the event occurs.

6 *Adapt to it* – accepting the event as inevitable and taking whatever action is necessary to remain competitive within the same environment. The weakness with this reactive approach is that the environment, and not the organization, controls the rate and direction of change.

7 *Treat it as a new opportunity* – as any change to the environment will affect all competitors, those that are more flexible and innovative can gain a competitive advantage.

8 *Oppose it* – trying to prevent an event, but this generally has limited results as, by definition, an organization has little control over factors that occur in its environment.

9 *Move to another environment* – recognizing that a change will make the environment less attractive, an organization can move into another market and industry that is relatively more attractive.

Obviously, the best response depends on many factors, with an important one being the likelihood that a particular event will actually happen. Managers can foresee some events with virtual certainty and they have time to prepare their best strategy. For example, governments usually signal that they will change regulations some time in advance, while many technological innovations are developed years before they become widely available. Other events are completely unforeseen, such as the tsunami that devastated Indonesia and surrounding countries in 2004. Then managers can only be reactive, and respond quickly to an event that has already happened but could not be predicted.

IDEAS IN PRACTICE Decisions under strict uncertainty

Suppose you hear that a new competitor is considering entering your main market and is likely to reduce your profit by €1 million a year. If you increase promotion now by €200,000 a year you can avoid this loss and maintain your current position. You can describe this problem in the following table, where entries are costs in millions of euros.

	New competitor enters market	New competitor does not enter market
Increase promotion now	0.2	0.2
Do not increase promotion now	0.0	1.0

There is no obvious best policy. If the new competitor enters the market it is better to have prepared and spent the extra money on promotion; if the new competitor does not enter the market it is better to have done nothing. When faced with such problems, managers usually use simple decision rules to guide them. For example, they might choose the option with the lowest average cost – which is to increase promotion; or they might avoid the greatest cost – again by increasing promotion; or they might use some other decision rule that best suits their purpose.

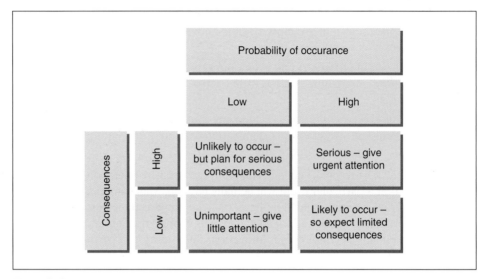

Figure 2.10 Attention needed by different types of event

Usually managers find themselves between these two extremes, and know that an event might occur, but do not know whether it actually will or will not. Then the best that they can do is list events that might occur and describe the consequences. This is decision making under strict uncertainty, and methods for analyzing these problems are usually based on simple decision rules (Waters; Golub; Lindley).

Expected values

Sometimes we know a bit more about events that may occur in the environment and, in particular, we can estimate a probability for them. These probabilities may be calculated, but they are more likely to be subjective estimates. However they are obtained, these probabilities give an idea of the likelihood of an event and they allow some analyses. In particular, we can calculate the expected value, where:

> Expected value = probability of the event × value of the outcome. If an event has a probability of 0.6 of occurring, and the estimated cost is £1 million, then expected value is a cost of 0.6 × £1 million = £0.6 million.

Expected values are highest for events with high probabilities and high values, and these are the ones that managers should give their most urgent attention (as shown in Figure 2.10). On the other hand, expected values are lowest for events with low probabilities or values, and managers can give these less attention – either because they are unlikely to happen, or if they do happen the consequences are relatively minor.

Analyses with expected values make a number of assumptions, with the obvious one being that managers can estimate the probability of an event and value of the outcome. But there are other, more basic assumptions. For example, we assume that managers know what they want to achieve and make rational decisions to move in this direction. This may seem a strange comment, as we know that managers want to achieve the aims

IDEAS IN PRACTICE Expected values

In 2005 a major Chinese company announced that it would bid $50 a share for a small company in Mexico. The directors of the Mexican company estimated that there was an 80 percent chance that the bid would be successful at this price and that the Chinese company would buy the core 200,000 shares. But they felt that the bid really undervalued the company. If they spent a million dollars doing some promotion and buying more shares themselves, there was a 60 percent chance that the deal would go through at a share price of $70.

The directors calculated the following expected values.

- The original bid valued the company at 200,000 × 50 = $10 million. As there is only an 80 percent

chance that the deal will succeed, the expected value is 0.8 × 10 million = $8 million.

- Spending money would raise the value of the company to 200,000 × 70 = $14 million. But there is only a 60 percent chance that the deal will go through, so the expected value is (0.6 × 14 million) = $8.4 million. This seems more attractive, but now the directors have to subtract the million dollars they spent defending the company, to give a final expected value of $7.4 million.

On this evidence, if the Mexican directors want the deal to go through, they should recommend the initial bid.

---

of their organization, which are presented in the mission. But in the complex real world, there might be differences between stated aims and actual ones – and managers may have their own aims that are not completely aligned with the organization's. So there can be some uncertainty about the real aims.

And there are almost certainly going to be different views on how to achieve any specified end. You can see this with political parties who often agree about broad aims, but disagree vigorously about the way to achieve them. The problem, of course, is that there is almost never a clear link between a decision and its consequences. There are so many factors working in the environment that it is generally impossible to assign an effect to one specific cause. So managers might do something one year that leads to a notable success – but if they repeat exactly the same thing the following year it can lead to complete failure. And random circumstances in the environment often seem to have as much effect as informed decisions. For example, in 2004 global oil prices rose sharply and even oil companies whose management was of questionable competence made bumper profits – industry analysts explained that 'when the tide comes in, even the worst boats rise'.

So managers can face uncertainty in both aims and cause-and-effect relationships. Not surprisingly, these different conditions suggest different approaches to decisions as illustrated in Figure 2.11 (Turton). If both the aims and cause-and-effect relationship are clear then managers can use rational analysis to get the best solutions. But if there is uncertainty in the cause-and-effect relationship, managers have to use judgement to see if the aims will be achieved; if there is uncertainty in the aims they have to look for compromise and negotiate agreed solutions. If neither the aims nor cause-and-effect

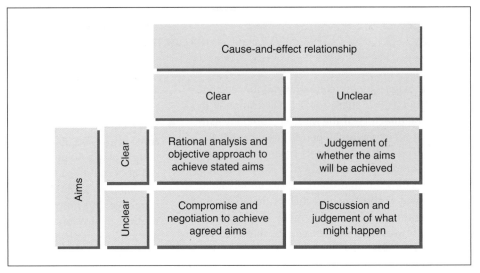

Figure 2.11 Approaches to different situations for change

relationship are clear, managers do not really know where they want to go or how to get there. This is not an ideal position, but it is surprisingly common.

An idealized view has managers analyzing situations, making informed decisions and implementing the results. But this ignores the fact that they work in an intuitive rather than analytical way; they do not know many of the important facts; they do not understand all aspects of their decisions; they are often surprised by circumstances; they make decisions based on emotions and power; these decisions can be reflex reactions to unfolding events; they implement the results tentatively, often using trial and error; the consequences are often a matter of chance.

As Stacey says, 'Strategy is a deadly serious game . . . it is in many ways amusingly bizarre . . . it is this sometimes bizarre aspect that makes the game so interesting to reflect upon and so difficult to draw conclusions about'.

Chapter review

- To design a successful strategy, managers need to understand three key factors – the organization's purpose, its external environment and internal features. This chapter describes the business environment.
- The environment is the external setting in which an organization works. It consists of all the external factors that affect an organization, but which it cannot control.

- A useful classification of factors in an environment describes them as the physical environment, political or legal factors, economic factors, social or socio-cultural factors, and technological factors.

- The economic environment is particularly important for operations. Almost inevitably, some form of market forces drives the supply and demand for products.

- The general state of economic development affects the predominant type of operations.

- An industry consists of all the organizations that produce the same, or similar, products. Managers have to identify an attractive industry, segment and sector in which their organization can succeed. This needs a match between the organization's strengths and the industry requirements.

- A market consists of the customers who buy, or might buy, a particular product. Managers have to identify attractive markets, segments and sectors, looking for a match between the market requirements and the organization's capabilities.

- Many factors affect the attractiveness of a market, especially the amount of competition. This, in turn, depends on a variety of features, including existing competitors, potential new competitors, substitute products, customer and supplier strengths.

- There are continual changes in the environment. Managers have to respond to these, and their response can range from ignoring the changes through to moving to other markets.

CASE STUDY Royal Dutch/Shell Group

From 1907 until its reorganization in 2005, the Royal Dutch/Shell Group has been a complicated amalgam of the Royal Dutch Petroleum Company in the Netherlands and The Shell Transport and Trading Company in the UK. It is one of the world's major companies employing 120,000 people in 145 countries, with a turnover approaching $275 billion a year. Shell companies produce about 3 percent of the world's oil and 3.5 percent of the world's gas.

Shell is probably best known for its service stations – which is understandable as 300 cars a second use Shell service stations around the world. But the Shell group of companies has much wider interests, which include marketing, transporting and trading oil and gas; providing oil products for industrial uses, including fuel and lubricants for ships and planes; generating electricity, including wind power and solar panels (having made 20 percent of the solar panels installed around the world); providing energy efficiency advice; producing petrochemicals that are used for plastics, coatings and detergents; investing in making renewable and lower-carbon sources of energy competitive for large-scale operations; and developing technology for hydrogen vehicles.

Shell is very concerned with its broad environment and they 'work in partnership with industry, government and society to deliver what is expected of us – economically, socially and environmentally'. Their

(continued)

CASE STUDY Royal Dutch/Shell Group (continued)

Business Principles include 'a commitment to support human rights and to contribute to sustainable development' as well as policies about business integrity, their responsibilities to stakeholders and the broader community, political activities, health and safety, the environment, competition, and communication. As well as financial performance, their annual report reviews environmental and social performance.

But the oil industry is always controversial. The global use of energy is set to double between 2002 and 2050 and oil companies are expected to satisfy much of this increase. So they are expanding operations into new geographical areas, and facing increasingly complex problems. Along with other oil companies, Shell often works in difficult circumstances, and the following examples give a tiny indication of these.

- Shell is the largest oil and gas company in Nigeria. Major production facilities in the Niger Delta have more than 1,000 wells and 6,000 kilometres of pipelines. Some concerns include damage to the physical environment, limited benefits returned to local communities, disruption by dissatisfied locals, and ethical standards of business.

- Shell, along with partners, has invested $10 billion in the second phase of the Sakhalin II integrated oil and gas project on Sakhalin Island in the Russian Far East. This is the largest single foreign investment, and reinforces Shell's position as the leading foreign direct investor in the Russian energy sector. Concerns include difficult operating conditions and political and economic uncertainty.

- Shell's oil sands mine in Athabasca, Canada, needed an initial investment of $5.7 billion to reach full production of 155,000 barrels of bitumen a day. This is 10 per cent of Canada's oil needs and joins other major oil sands developments at Peace River and Fort McMurray. Concerns are technical difficulty of working with oil sands, remote locations and difficult operations.

- A $4.3 billion joint venture to build a petrochemical complex in Daya Bay, Southern China set new environmental standards, and has improved living conditions of the 2,500 families forced to move away from the site.

- Many oil wells also contain natural gas. If this gas cannot be delivered economically to a market, it is burnt (flared) as waste. This is clearly a waste of a natural resource, the flares produce carbon dioxide and other emissions, and they disturb local communities. Shell has a target of eliminating flaring, and gathering this gas to generate electricity or to produce liquid natural gas.

- Greenhouse gas emissions (carbon dioxide, methane, nitrous oxide and hydrofluorocarbons) from Shell's own operations represented approximately 0.5 percent of global manmade greenhouse gas emissions in 2003. This was 10 percent below the 1990 level and the company has a target of reducing this by a further 5 percent.

- Spills of crude oil, oil products and chemicals from Shell's operations and shipping occur through accidents and sabotage of pipelines. These have high costs for environmental damage, lost production, loss of reputation, and cleaning up the damage.

Questions

- What are the main elements in Shell's business environment?

- How would you summarize the environmental concerns facing Shell? What strategies does it have to deal with these concerns?

- How does the environment of oil companies compare with that of major companies in other industries?

Source: The Shell Report, London, 2004; Annual Report, Shell Transport and Trading Company plc, 2004; Website at www.shell.com

Discussion questions

1 What factors should managers consider in their organization's environment?

2 Do you agree with the view that business should not be concerned with ethics, as any action that is sufficiently harmful will be illegal, and any action that is legal must be acceptable?

3 Some people say that organizations do not succeed by fitting their strategy to opportunities in an existing environment, but by developing strengths to create entirely new opportunities. What does this mean?

4 Economic analyses, like the models for supply and demand, are usually so simplified that they are of little practical value to organizations. Do you think this is true?

5 What is the difference between an industry and a market?

6 An organization has to match its operations to both the industry that it works in and the market that it satisfies. How can it satisfy both of these requirements?

7 Organizations only succeed by satisfying market requirements. Does this mean that marketing is the only really import function?

8 If you ask senior managers what they do, they say that they analyze circumstances to design and implement strategies. If you watch what they do, they spend most time reviewing past performance and justifying their previous decisions. Why is this?

Useful websites

www.astrazeneca.com
www.diageo.com
www.ipsos.com
www.pepsico.com
www.pepsicola.com
www.shell.com

References

Ansoff H.I., Corporate Strategy, McGraw-Hill, New York, 1965.

Ansoff H.I., Implanting strategic management, Prentice Hall, Englewood Cliffs, NJ, 1984.

Carey J. and Regan M.B., Are regs bleeding the economy, Business Week, June 17, p 75, 1995.

Clark C., The conditions of economic progress (3rd edition), Macmillan, London, 1957.

Daft R.L., Organization theory and design (8th edition), South Western, St Paul, MN, 2003.

Faulkner D. and Bowman C., The essence of competitive strategy, Prentice Hall, Englewood Cliffs, NJ, 1994.

Foote N.N. and Hatt P.K., Social mobility and economic advancement, American Economic Review, May, pp 364–378, 1953.

Friedman M., Capitalism and freedom, University of Chicago Press, Chicago, IL, 1962.

Gates B., The road ahead, Viking Penguin, New York, 1995.

Golub A., Decision analysis, John Wiley, New York, 1997.

Hart S.L., Beyond greening, Harvard Business Review, January–February, p 71, 1997.

Henderson B.D., The product portfolio, Boston Consulting Group, Boston, MA, 1970.

Ipsos, European attitudes toward corporate community investment, Paris, 1999.

Lindley D.V., Making decisions, John Wiley, Chichester, 1985.

Kotler P., Marketing management (12th edition), Prentice Hall International, Englewood Cliffs, NJ, 2005.

PepsiCo, Annual Report, Purchase, NY, 2004.

Porritt J. et al., A new vision for business, Committee of Enquiry into a New Vision for Business, London, 1999.

Porter M.E., How competitive forces shape strategy, Harvard Business Review, March–April, 1979.

Porter M.E., Competitive strategy, Free Press, New York, 1980.

Porter M.E., Competitive advantage, Free Press, New York, 1985.

Porter M.E. and Van der Linde C., Green and competitive, Harvard Business Review, September–October, p 123, 1995.

Riddle D.I., Service-led growth, Praeger, New York, 1986.

Sanderson G., Climate change, The Futurist, March–April, p 34, 1992.

Slatter J., Common pitfalls using the BCG product portfolio matrix, London Business School Journal, Winter, 1980.

Stacey R.D., Strategic management and organizational dynamics (4th edition), Financial Times Prentice Hall, London, 2002.

Time, Supplement to Prince of Wales International Business Leaders Forum, London, 1999.

Turton R., Behaviour in a business context, Chapman and Hall, London, 1991.

United Nations, Review of population trends, policies and programs, New York, 2004.

Walker O.C., Boyd H.W. and Larreche J., Marketing strategy (3rd edition), Irwin McGraw-Hill, New York, 1999.

Waters D., A practical introduction to management science (2nd edition), Addison-Wesley, Harlow, 1998.

CHAPTER 3
Strategy Design

The last chapter discussed the business environment, which includes all the external factors that affect an organization. In this chapter we focus on the internal features of an organization. In particular, we see how managers can design a strategy that allows their organization to succeed, and this calls for a strategic fit between the organization and its environment. Here we discuss some general principles, and the next part of the book shows how to apply these to an operations strategy.

After reading this chapter you should be able to:

- Discuss the purpose of strategy design
- Appreciate the concept of strategic fit
- Describe a general approach to strategy design
- Consider the design and contents of a mission
- Consider the expansion of a mission into goals and objectives
- List the different people who may design a strategy
- Outline the effects of management styles on design
- Discuss the differences between top-down and bottom-up design
- Describe different types of generic strategy

The key concepts discussed in this chapter are:

- **Requirements of a strategy**, which shows what a strategy should achieve
- **Strategy design**, which considers the way that managers design a strategy
- **Strategic managers**, who are responsible for the design of a strategy
- **Generic strategies**, which are widely used types of strategy

REQUIREMENTS OF STRATEGY DESIGN

Strategic fit

To design a successful strategy, managers need a thorough understanding of three main factors – the organization's overall purpose, its external environment and its internal features. In the last chapter we looked at the business environment. This is largely fixed and there is little that managers can do to change it. But they can change the purpose and internal features of the organization. So the essence of **strategy design** is that managers design the aims and internal features that enable an organization to succeed within its environment.

When an organization's aims and internal features are designed properly, it can work well within its environment, it is said to have good **strategic fit**. This suggests a certain harmony between an organization and its environment.

- Strategy design sets the long-term aims and internal features of an organization.
- There is strategic fit when the strategy gives harmony between the organization and its environment.

The presumption behind 'fit' is that an organization is more likely to succeed when everything works smoothly together. As Stacey says, 'organizations are successful when they intentionally achieve internal harmony and external adaptation to their environment'.

Strategic fit is the fundamental requirement of smooth operations; without it, there are continuing problems and managers spend all their time dealing with the latest emergency rather than planning long-term progress. In particular, strategic fit allows operations to evolve over time, so that the organization develops its strengths. Prahalad and Hamel describe the operations that an organization does particularly well as its **competencies**. We will use the term **capability** as it is slightly more general, and also suggests the potential for doing operations well.

If a capability is one of the key activities that directly affects an organization's performance and competitiveness, it becomes a **core capability**. Prahalad and Hamel suggest that a core capability should:

- open access to a wide variety of markets
- contribute significantly to operations performance, and
- be difficult for competitors to imitate.

When an organization performs a core capability better than its competitors, it becomes a **distinctive capability**. In 1957 Selznick established the principle that an organization can succeed by developing distinctive capabilities. This simply means that it does key activities better than competitors – or maybe it does completely different activities. Porter (1996) says, a successful strategy has an organization 'choosing to perform activities differently or to perform different activities than rivals'. Intel's distinctive capability is developing new chips for personal computers; Toyota's is mass production of high-quality cars; Coca Cola's is marketing of its brand. An organization can develop a distinctive capability in many areas, such as production skills, features of the product, high quality, rapid development of new products, systems for processing customer orders, after sales service, better locations, expertise in important technology, service in particular locations, and so on.

A distinctive capability means that an organization has a **sustainable competitive advantage**. This means that customers appreciate the superior performance and prefer one organization's products to those of competitors – and this position is so entrenched that it will continue over the long term.

To summarize:

- A successful strategy gives a strategic fit where the organization's internal features are in harmony with its environment.
- This gives stability that allows it to build distinctive capabilities, with performance in key operations that is superior to competitors.
- This gives a sustainable competitive advantage.

Requirements of a strategy

To put it simply, managers have to design a strategy that gives a sustainable competitive advantage. They set the aims and internal features that lead to continuing, long-term success. Some basic requirements of this strategy are that it is:

- **Focused on the long-term purpose of the organization**, putting resources into the areas that are critical to success.
- **Realistic**, giving aims and operations that are reasonable, bearing in mind the organization's resources and capabilities.
- **Appropriate**, to the organization's features and environment, giving a good strategic fit.
- **Achievable**, so the strategy can be implemented to give a high probability of success.
- **Comprehensive**, covering the broad range of organizational activities and plotting a consistent route towards the aims.
- **Responsible**, considering the views of major stakeholders.
- **Agreed**, known and understood by everyone concerned.
- **In tune with corporate culture**, so that the strategy does not conflict with values shared by employees.

IDEAS IN PRACTICE Shokisumai Industries

Shokisumai Industries are continually searching for ways to improve their operations and gain an advantage over their competitors. They identify five types of factor where they can develop such an advantage.

1 *Market features and relations with customers,* including:

  a market size and share

  b nature, size and frequency of sales for each product

  c size, locations and characteristics of customers

  d reputation and customer loyalty

  e channels of distribution

  f barriers to entry.

2 *Product features,* including:

  a types of products

  b distinctive features – price, quality, customer acceptance

  c range offered

  d costs of production

  e product technology and likely developments

  f research and development leading to new products.

3 *Availability of resource* – their ability to acquire resources for present and future operations, including:

  a facilities owned by the company

  b bought-in resources, including critical resources

  c sources and stability of supply

  d relationships with suppliers, alliances, joint ventures, etc.

  e competition in the market for resources

  f organizational factors, such as monopoly or government suppliers, restrictions, etc.

4 *Use of resources,* including:

  a efficient and high utilization of facilities

  b low-cost, flexible capacity

  c areas of operational excellence

  d process technology

  e efficient movement through supply chains

  f availability of capital.

5 *Relationships with stakeholders,* through contracts, agreements, joint ventures, alliances, favoured treatment by customers, preferred suppliers, etc.

Source: Waters C., Report on competitive position, Shokisumai Industries, Tokyo, 2005

STEPS IN STRATEGY DESIGN

Overall approach

There is no single, best approach to designing a strategy. In principle, we can simply ask, 'What is the problem? What are the alternatives? Which is the best alternative?' But in practice, Gooderham confirms that 'No one "right" way to develop and implement strategy exists'.

But we can give some guidelines. We have outlined a general approach with managers looking at their organization's purpose, and then studying the environment to find attractive industry and market segments. Then they analyze their operations and adjust them to give a strategic fit – following Kotler's advice to 'segment, target, position'. This approach seems to emphasize the industry and market sectors – or more broadly finding an attractive environment – and then adjusting operations to fit its requirements. But this would have drawbacks, particularly encouraging organizations to make radical changes to their operations, and then working in an environment to which they are not really suited. The chosen industry and market segment might be inherently attractive, but they could need skills and capabilities that the organization simply does not have.

An alternative is to work the other way around and build an organizational strength into a distinctive capability. Then managers could look for segments where this expertise would lead to success. But the obvious problem is that nobody might be interested in the particular expertise of the organization or its products.

Neither of these approaches is completely satisfactory, and managers are more likely to use an iterative approach that balances internal operations and the environment, without giving predominance to either. Effectively, they make decisions in parallel rather than in series. So we can adjust the general approach to strategy design that we mentioned in chapter 1. This has five steps that fit into the broad pattern of 'analysis, choice and implementation' as shown in Figure 3.1. Effectively steps 1 and 4 involve choice, steps 2 and 3 use analysis, and step 5 considers implementation.

1 *Define the organization's overall purpose* – which is summarized in a mission and possibly a vision that describes its aspirations. Extend this mission into a set of goals and objectives. We look at this step in the next section.

2 *Analyze the environment in which the organization works* – including the present and likely future conditions, and emphasizing opportunities and threats. As we saw in the last chapter, key elements here are the economic system, industry and market. These, in turn, influence the broader conditions in which the organization works.

3 *Analyze the organization* – describing the details of its current state, examining its resources, core capabilities and distinctive capabilities. This analysis particularly looks for strengths that the organization can build into distinctive capabilities, and weaknesses that have to be improved.

4 *Design the best future state of the organization* – which will best achieve its aims in the future conditions. Ideally, managers would consider all possible future states for the organization, select the best, and then design a strategy to reach this. But this is unrealistic. How could a manager identify all possible future states for an organization, let alone choose the best? The usual approach is much more limited and has managers only considering the broad principles of a future state. Then they design a small number of feasible strategies that move in the right direction, and choose the one that seems to give the best results. So they:

a develop principles for the future state of the organization based on its overall aims
b consider the results of analyses from steps 2 and 3
c generate a small set of feasible strategies
d choose the best strategy – which is the one that comes closest to satisfying the organization's aims.

5 *Implement the strategy* through all levels of the organization. This translates the chosen strategy into actions, moving from goals and objectives, through plans and methods, to positive actions. There are two parts to implementation:

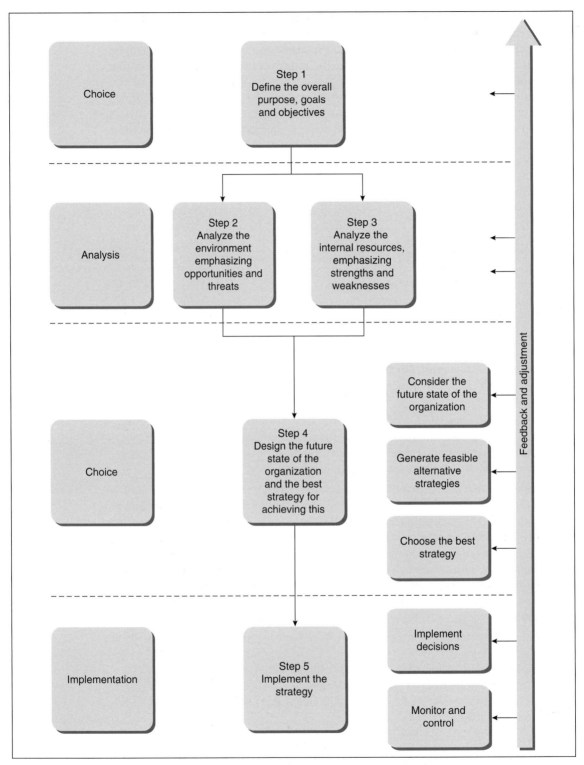

Figure 3.1 Steps in designing a strategy

- The first part starts the cascade of decisions and actions in the organization. Implementing the corporate strategy leads to the design of a business strategy; then implementing the business strategy leads to the design of functional strategies; then implementing the functional strategies leads to tactical and operational decisions that define actual operations. These decisions (shown in Figure 3.2) give the route through which the aims and values of senior managers pass down to the rest of the organization.
- The second part of implementation monitors performance to make sure that the planned results are actually achieved – with adjustments to the mission, objectives, strategy or implementation to correct any divergence. These adjustments also allow for continually changing conditions in the environment and organization.

As you can imagine, designing the strategy it is not as straightforward as these steps suggest (Thompson and Strickland). At the simplest level, there is likely to be a lot of feedback and cycling. For example, managers may start to implement a strategy but see that it does not have the desired effects, so they return to an earlier step; or they might not be able to design a strategy that achieves the organization's mission, so they have to rethink the overall aims. Strategic design is inevitably an iterative process, with managers revising aims and reviewing options until they home-in on a solution that everyone can work with.

Assumptions of this approach

This approach to strategy design is based on a series of assumptions about the overall approach, the people doing the design, the results, the implementation, and so on. These do not affect the reliability of the general approach, but you should bear them in mind and be prepared to discuss their validity.

The basic assumption is that organizations actually follow some formal procedure for strategy design. As we mentioned in chapter 1, there is general agreement that organizations using some formal method generally do better than organizations without them (Walker *et al.*). We have given the outline for an approach, but the details vary widely and it is difficult to go beyond the rather vague advice to use a method that is best suited to particular circumstances. But there may be reasons for an organization to use a completely different approach, or not to use a formal method at all.

If an organization uses a rational approach to design, the next assumption is that there is someone to do the design. These designers are the strategic managers who are willing and able to follow the formal procedure. Again, we assume that they are rational people with reasonable goals, and they have the necessary skills, experience, knowledge, information and motivation. In practice, there are many ways of assigning responsibility for strategy design, and these largely depend on organizational culture and management style.

Now we have a formal method and the people to use it. They will presumably start by considering the organization's overall purpose – and may discover that is has changed, it may not be achievable, there may be more important unstated aims, people may disagree about the precise interpretation of aims, they may have their own individual aims, and so on. And if they get over these problems, they may find that people disagree about future conditions, the effects of alternative strategies, likelihood of success, ability to achieve aims, benefits – and virtually everything else.

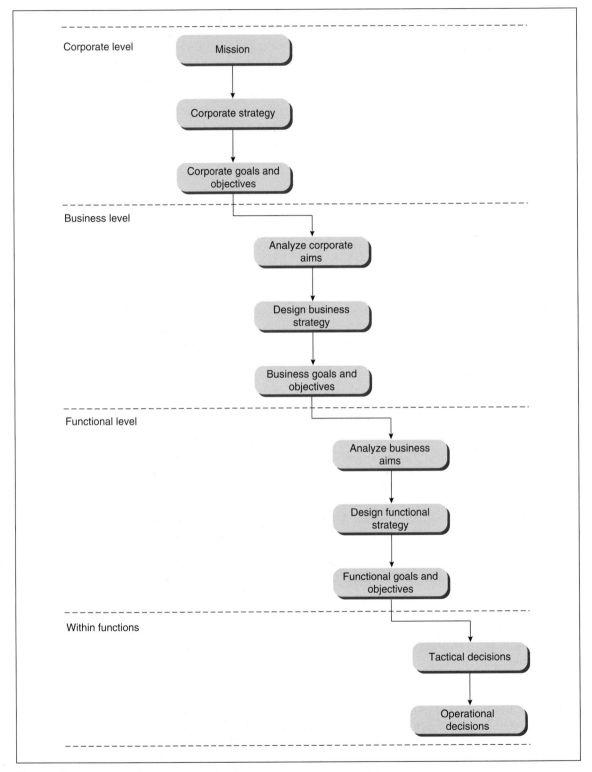

Figure 3.2 Sequence of decisions to implement the strategy

We could continue arguing in this way, but the picture already seems clear. We described a general approach to strategy design, but recognize that it is based on a series of assumptions. Real circumstances are so complex that there is never a straightforward result, and the design can never be reduced to a simple analysis that identifies an optimal solution. Even if it were possible to identify a technically optimal strategy, this would rarely gain the support of all managers, who have their own views and feelings. So we acknowledge that within our general approach, there are countless variations to allow for subjective views, diverse opinions, internal politics, differing aims, negotiations, uncertainty, compromise, ignorance – and just about every other kind of complexity.

DEFINING THE PURPOSE AND AIMS

Mission statement

An organization succeeds when it achieves its purpose, which is summarized in a mission. So an obvious starting point for strategy design is to agree a mission. Here we use the term 'mission' in its broad sense to include the concept of a vision or 'strategic intent' (Hamel and Prahalad; Collins and Porras). O'Brien and Meadows suggest that over 90 percent of organizations work with a statement of their purpose. No two organizations are the same, so it is not surprising that they all have different mission statements.

A mission sets the long-term direction of an organization, but this itself raises questions about the organization's real purpose and who defines this. In principle, the mission is designed by people who appreciate the purpose of the organization, can phrase this in a clear statement, and communicate it to the rest of the organization. In reality, it reflects the views of the most powerful lobby within the organization. When the shareholders are powerful, the mission is likely to focus on rewarding investment; when employees are powerful, the mission talks about treating them fairly; in competitive markets the mission talks about customer satisfaction. Of course, there are problems when the views of people with the most power do not match, or support, the views of other stakeholders. An aim of 'increasing shareholder value' is not likely to encourage someone who works for the organization but does not hold any shares.

This is a basic paradox of organizations, that members are always pulled in two directions – one to conform to the requirements and expectations of the organization, and in another to retain individuality and achieve personal aims. As Stacey says, 'The first force leads people to develop a common set of beliefs, a paradigm or mission for their organization. The second force leads them to pay lip service only to that common mission, to try to undermine it, or to change it.' This paradox can lead to differences between the stated mission and an espoused one that people actually work to (Argyris and Schon).

The views of people within an organization – as well as the business environment and just about everything else – are continually changing, so the mission will also evolve. You can imagine its changing focus with a company that is founded to give its owners some level of income; as the company expands, new shareholders might be interested in continuing growth; then with maturity, the focus might switch to maintaining a leading position in their industry. These adjustments must be handled carefully as the mission should give long-term stability to the organization, rather than continually change in response to short-term variations.

There is a tendency for a mission to expand over time to include duties to more stakeholders. Initially it reflects the aims of owners, but can evolve to include a statement of responsibilities to shareholders, employees, customers, suppliers, competitors and other stakeholders. Eventually it might extend to include their responsibilities to society in general, fundamental values, ethical conduct, environmental protection, health issues, charitable contributions, and so on. This reflects the pressure on organizations to include a broader range of opinions when making decisions. For example, when Stansted Airport wants to build a new runway it cannot base its decisions on pure economics, but must also take into account a whole range of opinions ranging from local employment through to environmental conservation.

Of course, this does not mean that the interests of the owners are forgotten. In fact, the owners often form the dominant lobby, as it is considered more difficult to find replacement owners than customers, employees, and other stakeholders. This is an interesting point, as organizations often claim that their customers or employees are their most important concerns. The reality is that both customers and employees are a means to an end, with their interests secondary to the primary interests of the dominant lobby – typically shareholder returns. You can see the signs of this repeatedly – customers would be happiest with very high quality products at very low prices; employees would be happiest with high pay, more benefits and better conditions; but the organization does neither of these as it puts more weight on owners' demands for higher returns.

Contents of the mission

The 'Ashridge Mission Model' (Campbell and Tawady; Campbell and Yeung) says that a mission focuses on:

- *purpose* – why the organization exists
- *values* – what it believes in
- *strategy* – competitive position and distinctive capabilities
- *behaviour standards* – policies and behaviour patterns.

These four factors – or some of them – include the contents of most mission statements, but some organizations add other points including:

- long-term survival and independence
- improving performance phrased in terms of financial, operational, competitive, entrepreneurial, societal, or other targets
- accomplishment of specific goals set by senior managers or other stakeholders.

In reality, few organizations explicitly include survival as an aim – even though it is often an overriding concern. On the other hand, many organizations include some aspect of performance – particularly financial performance. All organizations are financial entities to some extent, as they all generate income, buy resources, live within budgets, pay people, and so on. So it seems reasonable for a mission to include financial targets, often concerning profits. But many organizations – including government, charities, social organizations, etc. – do not aim at making a profit, so we should

IDEAS IN PRACTICE Tarmac

Tarmac is a major engineering and construction company that is best known for its work on roads. Their mission statement has three parts:

- **Vision** – to be the most successful and rewarding heavy building materials company, offering the best value and service to customers within a safe working and sustainable environment.

- **Purpose** – to create shareholder value by increasing the returns from the current business, and growing the business to earn higher returns.

- **Values** – about quality and customer care. Offering the best value products to customers, controlling costs, giving a high level of customer care, and continuing product innovation.

Source: Website at www.tarmac.com

phrase the financial targets in terms of maximizing benefit, utility or returns. In practice, of course, managers rarely aim at maximizing anything. They usually want some reasonable level of performance that is acceptable and satisfies – or 'satisfyces' (Simon). If a 5 percent increase in sales seems reasonable, managers are likely to set this as an arbitrary target.

You can still see many mission statements that talk of 'maximizing profits', but this is questionable for even a business. It raises questions about the definition of 'maximum', measure of profit, role of ethics, conflicting aims, period over which profits are measured, accounting conventions, and so on. Organizations essentially measure profits over the short term to appear in their annual accounts, so there are always doubts about their use to assess long-term performance. They are also unreliable, as at times of recession companies concentrate on survival rather than profit, and reported profits can change markedly because of prevailing conditions rather than actions by the organization. An interesting point is that people often react with hostility towards companies that make large – perhaps excessive – profits. MORI surveys find that, 'stakeholders want companies to make a profit but not at the expense of their staff or the community'. Perhaps more realistic financial targets should consider the return on investment, performance benchmarks, share price, market share, competitive advantage, reputation, global perspective, technological superiority, or innovation.

Organizations inevitably have more than one aim and they typically aim at simultaneously increasing market share, reducing operating costs, and having higher share value. Even when the mission focuses on a small number of the most important aims, it can be difficult to encapsulate these in a single statement.

Expanding the mission to goals and objectives

After agreeing a mission, managers set about expanding it into a series of goals and objectives. The **goals** give targets for the organization, but are still expressed in general terms; the **objectives** translate these into more positive – preferably quantitative – statements. To put it simply, the mission gives the purpose, goals show the areas

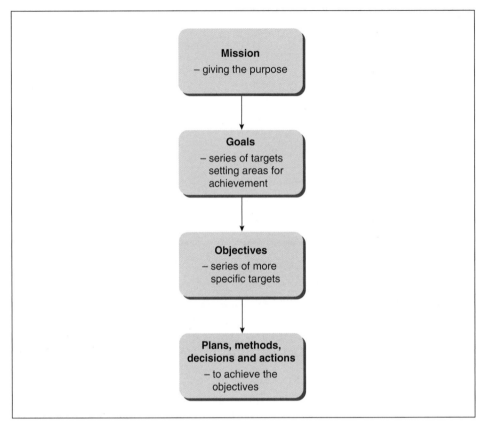

Figure 3.3 Setting aims within the organization

where targets are needed, and objectives show the actual targets to be reached (as illustrated in Figure 3.3).

The next stage, of course, is to develop the plans, methods, decisions and actions to achieve these objectives. These, in turn, lead to targets for lower levels of the organization – so we have a mechanism for implementing the strategy. A direct line downwards from the mission gives progressively more detailed objectives and decisions about how to achieve them – and these, in turn, lead to more detailed objectives for the next level of decisions.

At the highest level, the set of strategic goals should:

- refer to the organization's overall purpose and support the mission
- remain stable over the long term
- refer to the whole organization and its proposed future state
- relate specifically to actions needed to move the organization to its future state
- consider the future environment
- build on and develop distinctive capabilities

- be mutually supportive
- be specific and clear.

For example, managers could look at a mission that includes 'market leadership' and decide that they can achieve this by efficient operations and improved marketing. Then they could set specific goals that move the organization in the right direction. For example, they might expand the aim of efficient operations into goals of increasing productivity and lower operating costs; and they might expand the aim of improved marketing into goals of great market share and greater customer loyalty.

These goals, in turn, lead to a corresponding set of objectives. These are more specific, preferably use quantitative measures, give a target performance level, and a time in which to achieve this target. So objectives have a general format along the lines of, 'increasing return on investment by 5 percent over the next three years'. The goal of increasing productivity might lead to an objective of 'increasing productivity by 10 percent over the next four years', while the goal of greater market share might give an objective of 'gaining a 10 percent market share within five years'.

Ideally, the objectives should support each other, all working towards the mission, but there can be conflicts. For instance, Exeter City Football Club may have goals of being the leading club in the region, and making a profit (or not making too much of a loss). Expanding these goals into objectives shows the problem, as a leading club needs star players that come at a high cost, which is in conflict with the profit that needs low costs. This is a common problem with objectives in different areas. Common areas for goals and objectives are given in the following list:

1 *Finance:*
   a from long-term investment – such as return on investment, internal rate of return and net present value
   b higher profit – increasing margins, turnover, higher revenues, lower costs
   c generating cash – improving cash flow, reducing debt, managing current assets, reducing fixed asset value
   d organizational value – share price, earnings per share, improved bond and credit ratings, dividends
   e expansion through acquisition and mergers.

2 *Markets:*
   a value of sales
   b prices relative to competitors
   c market share, penetration, leadership, dominance, improve position
   d customer characteristics and distribution of orders
   e customer satisfaction, differentiation, perceived value to customers
   f brand awareness, reputation.

3 *Operations:*
   a size measured by output, capacity, number employed, etc.
   b product range, quality, unit costs, patents
   c leadership in innovation and new product development
   d process features, including technology, resource capability
   e productivity, efficiency and utilization of resources
   f achieving technological superiority in the product or process

g being faster to take advantage of new opportunities

h control of the supply chain through integration, partnerships and alliances.

4 *Relations with employees:*

a wage rates, benefits and equity

b personal development, training, promotion

c stability of employment, culture.

5 *Geographical scope* – becoming regional, national, international or global.

6 *Personal aims of managers* – such as the image of the organization and ethics.

7 *Conforming to external controls* – such as government regulations or industry standards.

There are no analyses to identify appropriate objectives, so managers usually set them by judgement, discussion and agreement. And they are typically based on previous objectives that were (or were not) achieved, industry standards, and competitors' performance. Often the objectives are based on key success factors (KSFs), which as we saw in the last chapter are the small number of factors that customers really value, and which affect their choice of products and suppliers. To be competitive, an organization must be competent in all the KSFs, and it should excel in at least one of them. A brewery, for example, might do market research that identifies its KSFs as low costs, recognized brand, and efficient logistics. Managers could then expand these three KSFs into a series of related goals and objectives.

The resulting objectives should be 'demanding but achievable', so that they are sufficiently above the existing performance to need some effort, but they are still attainable. When objectives are set at a demanding level, the organization will not always achieve them, either because of changing circumstances or because the goals actually turned out to be too demanding. By implication, an organization can only achieve all of its objectives if they are too easy. An organization that just misses a very demanding objective is probably doing a better job than a competitor that always achieves less demanding ones.

The progression from mission through goals and into objectives is not always straightforward. For example, it can be difficult to translate a mission that refers to values and standards of behaviour into achievable goals. Microsoft's mission is 'to help people and businesses throughout the world realize their full potential', and it is not obvious how this can be translated directly into objectives. But managers can progressively expand the mission until objectives become clearer. Disneyland has the informal mission of 'making people happy'. Managers understand that this means providing entertainment in a major theme park; the entertainment consists of presentations, rides, restaurants, etc.; each of these has specific features, operations, costs, etc. – and managers can set long-term objectives for these.

Of course, managers can still set goals and objectives that are inappropriate or clearly wrong. Perhaps they set targets that look good and may be highly desirable, but they do not directly contribute to the mission. For example, some universities aim at taking students from a broad range of backgrounds, but others ask whether this contributes to their mission of providing academic excellence. And you can often see goals that are simply impossible to achieve. If LatGas had a goal of being 'a world leader in gas exploration' it would have no chance of achieving this in competition with the existing market leaders. More commonly, managers put too much emphasis

IDEAS IN PRACTICE Lufthansa Aviation Group

Lufthansa Aviation Group has a mission that is in three main parts. The first part outlines their business, which is centred on international passenger and cargo flights, and includes services in supply chain management, aircraft maintenance and overhaul, airline catering and IT. This business is stable, but managers adjust operations to take advantages of changes in their environment.

The next two parts of the mission balance performance and value with responsibility. In particular, they look for performance in all areas, with businesses:

- working in the market under the Lufthansa brand
- focusing on core business operations
- making a significant contribution to the sustained creation of value
- aiming for market leadership in their business segment
- being committed to serving customers, with emphasis on safety, reliability, punctuality, technical competence, quality, flexibility and innovation.

At the same time they accept their broader responsibilities:

- acknowledging that staff are their most important asset
- being an attractive employer, offering employees job security, good working conditions, career opportunities
- having convincing corporate ethics
- being leaders in service provision, with customer-friendly service underpinning future growth
- creating sustainable value for investors
- giving financial performance that is a benchmark for the European airline industry
- protecting the environment with sustainable development.

These aims set clear directions for the company, and managers expand them into more immediate objectives. These, in turn, set the scene for the next levels of decision.

Sources: Lufthansa press releases, Hamburg, 2005; Lufthansa Annual Report, Hamburg, 2004; Website at www.lufthansa.com

---

on easily measured factors, to give objectives like, 'increasing sales by 5 percent over the next financial year'. This sounds convincing, but it is probably an arbitrary figure that cannot be justified by any rational analysis, or realistic expectations. Conversely, managers can put too much emphasis on subjective goals – such as 'improving customer relations' – where there is no way of saying whether they have been achieved.

From goals to decisions

It is notoriously difficult to judge the quality of a strategy. An organization only implements one strategy, so it is impossible to make internal comparisons of different ones, and no two organizations are the same so it is difficult to make comparisons across organizations. We can make retrospective judgements and say that, 'if we had used this alternative strategy we would have had better results' – and managers spend a lot of time reviewing past performance and justifying their previous decisions.

But conditions change so quickly that it is difficult to apply lessons from the past. In the 1960s Tilles suggested six criteria for evaluating business strategies, and these still give reasonable guidelines:

1 internal consistency between components of the strategy
2 consistency within the environment
3 appropriateness in the light of available resources
4 satisfactory degree of risk
5 appropriate time horizons
6 workability.

'Workability' concerns the implementation of the strategy and the way that it can lead to useful results. We have already described the mechanism for this, with managers at each level expanding the objectives of the higher level, turning them into more detailed objectives, and making decisions about how to achieve them and the resources needed. These, in turn, set the objectives for the next level of managers (shown in Figure 3.4). As decisions move downwards through the organization, each level moves further away from abstract principles and towards positive actions. So the most intense planning and design is done at the strategic level and most work organized at tactical and operational levels.

This mechanism for implementing the strategy by progressively moving objectives down each level of the organization, is not the only approach – and it is not always the

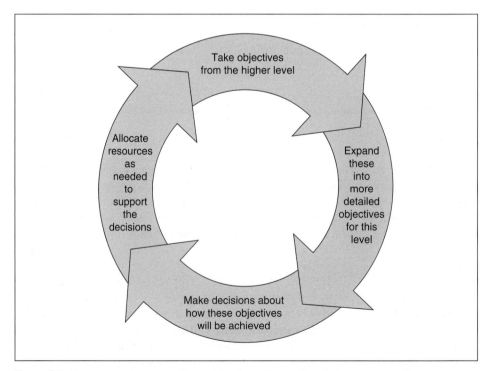

Figure 3.4 Progressively expanding objectives throughout the organization

best. But since Drucker described it as **management by objectives** in the 1950s it has remained the most widely used. The formal structure of management by objectives needs agreement between two levels of managers – a superior and a subordinate. The superior sets objectives for the subordinate, and the subordinate is rewarded for achieving these objectives. Management by objectives has these two collaborating and jointly setting objectives that are acceptable to them both. As everyone has some responsibility for setting their own objectives, they should be more committed to achieving them, and realistic and agreed objectives can be set for all levels of management.

Updating a strategy

An important point about strategic design is that managers rarely sit down to devise an entirely new strategy from scratch. More usually, there is already a strategy in place, and they have to review its performance and make adjustments. Some specific reasons for updating a strategy include:

- appearance of new and unexpected opportunities
- errors in long-term forecasts, so that actual events are different from those expected
- changing customer demands and preferences
- changes in the structure of the market
- moves by competitors
- availability of new technologies
- new operations and means or production
- new managers with different ideas
- political or regulatory changes
- a crisis of some kind.

We have already said that managers should be careful when updating a strategy, as it gives long-term stability and should not change too often. On the other hand, without adjustments to the strategy, an organization can become trapped in a declining industry, miss new opportunities, and generally be left behind by more innovative competitors. The stability argument usually wins, and an existing strategy can gather momentum and offer surprising resistance to any kind of change, even when it is clearly failing. Managers still prefer to make selective adjustments rather than throw away the whole strategy and start again. These iterative adjustments are certainly easier to absorb and less traumatic than major changes that throw the organization into a completely different direction. But they also mean that organizations become inflexible and slow to change.

The usual practice has periodic reviews – perhaps annually – to see how well a strategy is working. If this identifies gaps between the organization's goals and its actual performance, managers must look for the most efficient way of overcoming them. Unfortunately, it is often difficult to judge exactly how well the current strategy is working. If an organization is not achieving its goals the strategy might certainly be at fault – but the strategy might actually be good, and problems come from conditions in the environment, or other factors within the organization. Similarly, if an organization is doing well it is tempting to stick with the existing strategy – but the organization might be succeeding despite the strategy rather than because of it.

IDEAS IN PRACTICE Microsoft

Microsoft Corporation was founded in 1975 and now dominates the world's software markets. By 2005 its revenue reached $40 billion, and its assets approached $100 billion (primarily intangible assets such as knowledge, culture, brand, and information). Their mission is to 'help people and businesses throughout the world realize their full potential'. This mission is supported by values of:

- 'Integrity and honesty.
- Passion for customers, for our partners, and for technology.
- Openness and respectfulness.
- Taking on big challenges and seeing them through.
- Constructive self-criticism, self-improvement, and personal excellence.
- Accountability to customers, shareholders, partners, and employees for commitments, results, and quality.'

These are practised in Microsoft's seven core business units:

- **Windows Client** – Windows XP, Windows 2000, and Windows Embedded operating system.
- **Information Worker** – Microsoft Office, Microsoft Publisher, Microsoft Visio, Microsoft Project, and other freestanding applications.

- **Microsoft Business Solutions** – Great Plains and Navision business process applications, and bCentral business services.
- **Server and Tools** – Microsoft Windows Server System, software developer tools, and MSDN.
- **Mobile and Embedded Devices** – mobile devices including Windows Powered Pocket PC, Mobile Explorer, and Windows Powered Smartphone.
- **MSN** – the MSN network, MSN Internet Access, MSNTV, MSN Hotmail and other Web services.
- **Home and Entertainment** – Microsoft Xbox, consumer hardware and software, online games, and TV platform.

Then within each business managers make decisions for each product. Goals for Windows NT, for example, include 'robustness, extensibility and maintainability'. In this way, a huge corporation progressively expands its mission to give achievable goals and objectives. But Microsoft work in a rapidly changing environment, explicitly saying, 'Just as we constantly update and improve our products, we want to continually evolve our company to be in the best position to accelerate new technologies as they emerge and to better serve our customers.'

Source: Microsoft Annual Report, 2004; Website at www. Microsoft.com

WHO DESIGNS THE STRATEGY?

Top-down approach

All managers have their own styles, preferences, assumptions, viewpoints, beliefs, and so on – and they make decisions that reinforce their own views. So the choice of people to design the strategy has an impact on the final result. An obvious question, then, is 'Who designs the strategy?'

The picture that we have been developing has senior managers doing the strategic design, as they can take a broad view of the organization, and have the relevant information and skills. But there are really four options:

1 *An individual or very small group of senior managers* who plot the future of the organization according to their own vision. This has the advantage of being fast and easy to get agreement on – and it reflects the views of important stakeholders. But it has the disadvantage of relying on limited knowledge, experience and skills, and being dominated by the personal preferences of a small group.

2 *A wider team of senior managers* drawn from the organization to work on strategic design, alongside their other work. This has the advantages of cutting across departmental barriers, tapping into expertise from different backgrounds, and having a broader range of people with ownership of the strategy. But it has the disadvantages of needing agreement between people with diverse views, and still only involving a few senior managers.

3 *A permanent, dedicated department* set up for the sole purpose of strategic management. These people form a group of in-house specialists whose only job is to design and update the strategy. This has the advantage of developing a core of expertise, but the disadvantage of leaving key decisions to a remote group who are not involved with the other activities of the organization.

4 *Outside specialists* who can take an objective view of the organization and use their broader experience to plot a realistic future. This has the advantage of using expertise, but it can be expensive and relies on people who know very little about the organization or its environment.

The choice of option depends on many factors, including the size of the organization, industry, degree of centralization, management style, and culture. In a small organization, one or two people usually make all the strategic decisions; in a major company there is likely to be a strategic management group. A small survey by O'Brien and Meadows found that 15 percent of organizations have a mission (or in their terms a vision) designed by a single person, 67 percent designed by a small team and 18 percent had wider involvement from the organization. In practice, organizations are increasingly reluctant to entrust their long-term future to a single person, a small group, or remote specialists, so the trend is towards broader-based strategy teams that cross traditional boundaries. But the **top-down** model is still dominant, where senior managers have most responsibility for strategy design, and pass their thoughts downwards through the organization.

A survey by The Institute for Employment Studies (Kettley and Strebler) confirms that most senior managers are involved in strategy design by:

- setting the organization's goals and policies
- managing resources and controlling the business
- directing their part of the business.

Saunders says that the responsibilities of senior managers include a thorough understanding of the organization and communicating its aims, but he puts less emphasis on the actual design of the strategy. Interestingly, he warns that senior managers should not exaggerate the importance of their role in strategy design, but should accept that more junior managers have a significant input. This is in line with a growing recognition that strategic decisions permeate the whole organization and all managers contribute – at least to some extent. Certainly all managers are involved in the implementation of a strategy, so it seems reasonable to assume that they can play a significant role in its design. Perhaps it is fairer to say that senior managers make the biggest contribution to strategy design, and they have the final say in its contents, but lower level managers can play an important role (Evered). The exact nature of this role depends largely on the prevailing corporate culture and management styles.

Management styles

In the 1970s Mintzberg (1973) suggested that managers use three styles of strategy design: planning (which is based on rational analysis), entrepreneurial (where a strong leader does the design), and adaptive (where managers wait to see what happens before making a decision). An entrepreneurial approach can take many different forms, but Table 3.1 shows some differences between planning and adaptive styles.

Other views of **management styles** have developed, but we can usefully expand Mintzberg's model into four styles of strategy design.

1 *Rational decision makers*. We have been emphasizing this style, as it uses some formal approach to strategy design. It assumes that there is a best strategy – or probably several satisfactory ones – that we can find by doing rationale analyses, comparing alternatives, and choosing the best. The systematic and structured process foresees problems before they arise and uses proactive decisions to get the best long-term results. This gives a strong sense of purpose and direction. But it assumes that skilled and knowledgeable managers always

Table 3.1 Some comparisons between adaptive and planning managers

Management style	Planning	Adaptive
Overall approach	Rational	Pragmatic, administrative
Goals	Defined by managers during strategy design	Not clearly defined, but usually based on survival
Design of strategy	Comes from mission and goals	Depends on current conditions and affected by immediate opportunities and threats
Environment	Analyzed in detail and considered during the design of strategies	Source of short-term threats and opportunities
Strategic inputs	Purpose and goals, strengths, weaknesses, opportunities, threats	Current circumstances
Stability of strategy	Adjusted at periodic reviews	Changes whenever there are significant changes to conditions
Organization structure	Designed to achieve strategy	Changes with circumstances

make rational decisions to maximize benefits to their organization, based on perfect information, and without problems of communications, perception, or personality. Unfortunately, this idealized view does not explain why managers' often make irrational decisions.

2 *Administrators*. This view sees managers more as administrators, who have limited information, knowledge and experience, do not know or understand all their options, have inconsistent values, and can behave irrationally. They have little control and generally respond to pressures from stakeholders. Decisions are made through negotiation, agreement and compromise – often accepting the first solution that gets general agreement rather than looking for an optimal, or even good, decision. Strategies designed by administrators are usually limited to the areas where it is easy to get agreement, and they tend to ignore more contentious issues.

3 *Entrepreneurial*. Here a strong leader – often the founder or owner – relies on their own judgement and experience to make decisions. Powerful individuals pursue their own aims, usually looking for rapid growth and continually looking for new opportunities. This is an irrational style as managers tend to make decisions quickly, based on intuition rather than any analyses – and then they might go through the motions of generating and evaluating alternatives as a way of justifying their original choice. Such strategies are usually limited to those areas where the managers have a particular interest, and where they feel confident in making fast decisions. As there is no underlying theme, the organization typically moves forward in a series of large steps, often into an uncertain future.

4 *Pragmatist*. This is often described as 'incremental pragmatism' – or 'muddling through'. Managers do no proactive strategy design, but wait to see what actually happens before making decisions. Then they make small adjustments to the existing strategy, moving the organization forward in a series of small, disjointed steps without any overriding aims, guidelines, analyses or priorities. This approach sees managers as doing their best to work on very complex problems, where it is almost impossible to know or understand all the conditions, with too many stakeholders applying pressure, too many goals to achieve, and too short a time for decisions. There is so much uncertainty about the future and so many possible events, that no analyses can possibly take all of these into account – so it is not worth doing analyses based on hypothetical futures that will inevitably be wrong. A better approach is to simply wait and see what actually happens, and then make decisions to deal with known problems. This approach leads to defensive organizations that are always reacting to changes and negotiating ways of surviving current problems. There is little overriding direction, but the fragmented approach can be very flexible in dynamic conditions.

Most organizations use some combination of all four styles, trying to get the best mix for their particular circumstances. At different times, each style might be more appropriate, and better suited to different parts of the organization. A growing R&D department might use an entrepreneurial style, a new marketing department might be more pragmatic, a mature operations department might be more rational, and a finance department might prefer an administrative style.

IDEAS IN PRACTICE Oakland Bay Investment Trust

Tom Spiegel is the Vice-President of Finance for Oakland Bay Investment Trust (OBIT). This is a private company whose clients want secure, long-term investments. OBIT looks for small companies that have good prospects of growing and giving high returns to investors. Tom explains their approach as follows.

'We tend to become major shareholders in smaller companies, so we are careful to invest in companies that have good management and know where they are going. We put a lot of store in our assessment of the senior management team. We want a good return on shareholder equity, so we look for companies whose mission includes an aim of high profits and increasing shareholder value. There are two ways of making high profits. The first is to work in an industry that is currently attractive and allows

players to earn high returns. So we look for a corporate strategy of working in one of these attractive industries. The second is to work efficiently within an industry and gain a sustainable competitive advantage. So we look for a business strategy of competing aggressively. Then, of course, we look for an operations strategy that can actually deliver the competitive advantage. The strategies must all work together to give a positive view of the company's likely performance.'

This approach seems to work as OBIT has achieved 'superior' investment performance for four out of the six years.

Source: provided by Tom Spiegel, based on OBIT Annual review to investors, New York, 2004

In many respects the pragmatic approach to strategy design is particularly interesting. It accepts that we cannot know all circumstances in advance, or design a strategy that will take all eventualities into account. So any plans for the future will inevitably be, at least to some extent, flawed. As circumstances emerge over time, it might be sensible not to waste so much time developing flawed plans for a distant future, but to wait and let a strategy for dealing with actual events also emerge. Perhaps the best approach is a combination of the two, so that some parts of a strategy are designed proactively, while other parts emerge in response to developing circumstances. Then the whole idea of 'designing' a strategy is too simple, and Mintzberg (1987) proposed 'crafting' as giving a better view.

Bottom-up design

The idea of an **emerging strategy** is that senior managers start with some basic ideas, but circumstances alter these and influence the final shape of the strategy. For instance, managers might base a strategy on likely sales of a new type of product; but if the product is unexpectedly successful, a strategy will emerge of concentrating more effort onto it and ensuring its long-term future. This was not a prior choice, but a result that emerged from learning, experience – and a certain amount of experimentation. But this learning has not emerged with senior managers, but has occurred lower down the organization during implementation of the strategy. So aspects of the design occur at all levels of management – and it makes no sense to have one isolated group of senior managers designing a strategy and another group of more junior managers implementing it.

This is not really a new view, but is an extension of the normal view that strategy designers must consider the effects at lower levels. A strategy of high quality products is only realistic if operations can actually produce the quality needed; a strategy of expansion only works if all levels of the organization can increase their capacity. So the traditional top-down approach accepts that all levels of the organization have some input to the strategy, even when it is limited to supplying information. The idea of an emerging strategy is that this contribution is not limited to information, but includes the actual form and contents of the strategy.

Some people go further and say that senior managers cannot be aware of the impact of their decisions at lower levels, so their designs can never be realistic. Instead, the dominant force must be an emerging strategy fuelled by the day-to-day decisions of more junior managers. For example, a company will focus on a particular market not because senior managers identify this as the best strategy, but because a protracted series of small iterative decisions made at lower levels has moved it slowly in this direction. A salesperson might start by meeting a single new customer in the market; and if the product is well received they may look for other customers and pass-on the message to other salespeople. The market grows and eventually becomes an area of strategic importance. A relatively disorganized process of *ad hoc* decisions, perhaps little more than informed trial and error, has moved the organization to focus on this market, and over time this has emerged – largely in retrospect – as its strategy.

Junior managers' more detailed knowledge of operations is the driving force behind a **bottom-up**, emerging strategy. They set the scene, and their findings pass upwards to senior managers who observe, discuss, negotiate and consolidate the best practices into a formal strategy. The senior managers may start with a view of what the strategy should be, but this contributes relatively little to the result that finally emerges.

Most organizations use a combination of top-down design and bottom-up emerging. An interesting question concerns the balance between these two. Recent opinion puts more emphasis on a bottom-up approach, with senior managers often doing little more than confirming and formalizing the emerging strategy (Mintzberg and Waters). Quinn reinforces this view, describing five features of successful strategic management:

1 Senior managers have a clear idea of what they are trying to achieve and where they are trying to take the organization.
2 They recognize the inevitable uncertainty and do not design all the details of a comprehensive strategy from the outset.
3 The strategy largely emerges from the interactions of different groups within the organization; these interactions are monitored, assessed and integrated by senior management.
4 The strategy emerges in small incremental steps that move towards the agreed purpose, steered by senior management.
5 The organization effectively feels its way towards its aims, continually learning as it progresses.

Collingridge confirms that the idea of an iterative, emerging strategy is particularly important when conditions are uncertain. Then managers cannot hope to use analytical methods to find the 'best' solution, but they try something, see if it works, and then correct any mistakes and learn from their experience. Again, the strategy emerges from a process that is little more than trial and error.

GENERIC STRATEGIES

Strategic themes

As every organization is unique, you might assume that each develops its own unique strategy. To some extent this is true, but organizations in similar circumstances tend to think along similar lines. For example, most supermarkets sell products at the lowest possible prices; car manufacturers compete on reliability; PC manufacturers use the latest technology; fast food restaurants compete on convenient locations. To a large extent these organizations are making similar products to satisfy the same customer demands, so it is not surprising that they move along similar lines. And the result is that they adopt similar strategies – giving **generic strategies** that share a common theme (Miller). These generic strategies include low costs, low prices, high quality, fast delivery, convenient locations, high technology, flexible production, and so on.

An organization does not choose a generic strategy as such, but it recognizes that a particular focus is important. Other organizations also recognize that this focus is important, and then it develops into a generic strategy. This focus brings together a bundle of related ideas. For example, a generic strategy of low cost brings together related ideas about efficient operations, reduced overheads, economies of scale, standard products, mass markets, and all the other factors that contribute to low costs.

There are many types of generic strategy, some of which are more relevant to corporate strategies, while others refer to business strategies. At a corporate level, some common generic strategies are based on:

- **Development of a single business** – where an organization continues to specialize in a single type activity, such as Coca-Cola, Dell computers and Bic pens. They develop considerable expertise in their areas and can exploit a dominant position.
- **Growth** – which maintains the same core businesses, but looks for continuing expansion in each of them. This can be difficult to achieve through organic growth, so it often involves acquisition of competitors.
- **Diversification** – where the organization expands into other business areas that are not parts of its core businesses. This is the approach used to build conglomerates.
- **Vertical integration** – where an organization progressively buys its key suppliers and customers to gain greater control of its supply chains.
- **Retrenchment** – which cuts back operations to focus on core activities and make better use of resources. You often see this with organizations that have run into some kind of trouble.

At a business level, we can describe three generic strategies for responding to market conditions (Miles and Snow). Firstly, defensive strategies are the most conservative, where an organization builds a clear place for itself in a market and then defends this position against competitors. An organization with a defensive strategy tries to maintain the status quo, avoiding trends and changes, preferring to continue as efficient suppliers of the same products to the same set of customers. Secondly, entrepreneurial strategies are the opposite of defenders, as organizations continually search for new opportunities, repeatedly changing industries and markets to follow new opportunities. Thirdly, analytical strategies come in between the first two extremes. Organizations here look for new markets and opportunities, but at a planned and more deliberate rate. They keep a core set of products and customers to provide stability, but systematically look for new opportunities.

Porter (1980, 1985) described another set of generic business strategies, with competition through:

- **Cost leadership** – supplying the same or equivalent products as competitors at a lower price. This works best when price is the dominant competitive force, products are readily available, there are few ways to differentiate them, customers have similar needs, they can easily switch to another product, and they can negotiate terms. It has the benefits of emphasizing efficient operations, putting pressure on competitors, discouraging new competitors, and discouraging substitute products.

- **Product differentiation** – supplying products that are somehow different from those offered by competitors. This works best when there are many ways of differentiating a product, customers are aware of – and value – the differences, they have diverse needs and uses for the product, few competitors follow a similar differentiation approach, and product features are evolving. It brings the benefits of brand loyalty, entry barriers to new products, a price premium, patent and copyright protection, and having sales less vulnerable to price fluctuations.

- **Market niche** – specializing in some way, perhaps dealing with a limited part of the market, specialized products, or specific customer needs. The organization develops unique capabilities to satisfy this niche better than any competitor. This works best when there are many different market segments, it is expensive or difficult for one organization to meet the needs of all – or even many – segments, the segment chosen is big enough to be profitable, the organization has special skills and resources, the segment is not crucial to the success of major competitors, no competitors are focusing on the same segment, and the organization does not have enough resources to satisfy more of the market.

Amazing Cake Corporation are cost leaders who make standard cakes so efficiently that their unit costs are low; La Patisserie Française use product differentiation to make different types of cakes at much higher prices; Tiers at Weddings have a niche strategy and make wedding cakes. Skoda and Fiat are cost leaders who make large numbers of inexpensive cars; Land Rover use product differentiation to make noticeably different cars; Morgan have a niche market.

You might think that a compromise between the two major strategies of cost leadership and product differentiation would give the benefits of both and lead to better

IDEAS IN PRACTICE PepsiCo, Inc

Pepsi-Cola was first produced in 1898, and has become one of the world's best-known brands. In 1965 the company merged with Frito-Lay to form PepsiCo, and then merged with the Quaker Oats Company in 2001. The result is the world's fifth-largest food and beverage company, with 15 brands that each earn more than $1 billion a year. The company's principal businesses now include Frito-Lay snacks, Pepsi-Cola beverages, Gatorade sports drinks, Tropicana juices, and Quaker Foods.

PepsiCo's overriding objective is 'to increase the value of our shareholders' investment through integrated operating, investing and financing activities'. The associated strategy concentrates resources on growing businesses, both through internal growth and acquisitions. Some distinctive capabilities are implicit in the company's statement that their 'success is the result of superior products, high standards of performance, distinctive competitive strategies and the high level of integrity of our people'. This strategy is continually updated in the light of emerging opportunities and risks, and some of the adjustments have led to major changes in direction. For example, reorganizations changed the relations between businesses, moving towards decentralized management in the 1990s, and then back to centralized decisions in the 2000s. A particularly important change was its move into restaurants, with its purchase of Pizza Hut in 1977, Taco Bell in 1978, and Kentucky Fried Chicken (KFC) in 1986 – along with East Side Mario's Restaurants Inc, D'Angelo's Sandwich Shops, California Pizza kitchen, and others. At this time diversification was seen as a good way of spreading risk, reducing the effects of seasonality, and using 'cash cows' to expand areas that have potential long-term growth. But the combination of beverages, snack foods and restaurants was difficult and stock market analysts were generally pleased when PepsiCo sold its restaurant companies in 1997, with the three main ones forming Tricon Global Restaurants Inc. (In 2002 Tricon, which then also owned Long John Silver's and A&W Restaurants, changed its name to Yum! Brands.)

After this, PepsiCo limited its acquisitions to companies in the snack food business, including its biggest acquisition of Tropicana Products selling fruit juices around the world, as well as Walker and Smith's Crisps in the UK, Hostess Foods in Canada, Smith's Snackfood in Australia, Alimentos del Valle in Spain, Smartfood popcorn, South Beach Beverage Co., etc. To concentrate on its core businesses, it even sold off a large part of its bottling operations in 1998, forming The Pepsi Bottling Group.

Sources: PepsiCo annual reports, Purchase, NY, 2005; Websites at www.pepsi.com; www.pepsicola.com; www.yum.com

overall results. In practice, this does not seem to work. Companies with 'average' products and 'average' costs usually have worse performance than those concentrating on either low costs or specialized products. For example, in 2001 analysts suggested a reason for the declining sales of Marks & Spencer was customers moving away from their mid-price clothes to buy either expensive, designer clothes or cheap, discount ones. As Porter (1980) says, 'cost leader, differentiators, or focusers will be better positioned to compete in any segment'.

Impact on operations

You can see that Porter's classification of business strategies begins to consider the type of products that organizations make. When an organization chooses a particular generic strategy it implicitly defines the type of products it will make. For example, cost leadership usually involves standard products, that are mass-produced, using automated processes, with few features, in narrow ranges. So the business strategy directly affects the operations that make the products. We can see this effect in every type of strategy. A company might adopt an aggressive, entrepreneurial strategy, supplying innovative products to a growing market – but this relies on operations to develop new ideas, turn these into viable products and launch them quickly onto the market. A strategy of product differentiation relies on flexible operations that can make a variety of different products. We consider such links between business and operations strategies in the next section of the book.

Chapter review

- A strategy shows what an organization wants to achieve, and how it will achieve it. This strategy does not just appear, it must be designed.
- When an organization's internal features and aims are aligned with its external environment, there is a good strategic fit. Strategic fit allows an organization to function well.
- The external environment is largely fixed, so strategy design focuses on the aims and internal features to achieve these. In particular, it develops distinctive capabilities that give a sustainable competitive advantage.
- There is no single, right way to design a strategy, but a useful approach has five steps – to identify purpose, analyze the environment, analyze the organization, design a new strategy and implement it. In practice, this is an iterative procedure that homes in on a reasonable result.
- The starting point for strategy design is the mission. This statement of purpose summarizes the long-term direction of the organization.
- The mission is expanded into a series of strategic goals and objectives. These may cover a variety of areas, often dictated by key success factors.
- The strategic objectives are progressively expanded, into objectives for all other levels within the organization, giving a mechanism for achieving the mission.
- Strategy design might be done by individuals, teams, specialized departments and consultants. Different people, with different management styles, adopt different approaches to strategy design and get different results.
- With top-down strategy design, senior managers play the leading role. But a strategy always needs inputs from more junior managers. When these become dominant, a strategy emerges from the bottom-up. In practice, organizations use some combination of top-down design and bottom-up emerging.
- Organizations in similar circumstances often follow a common theme and adopt a generic strategy. There are several types of generic strategy.

CASE STUDY Carrefour

Carrefour is best known for its French hypermarkets. Certainly 50 percent of the group's sales are in France, and 59 percent are in hypermarkets – but when annual sales are €90 billion this leaves a lot of room for other activities. The Carrefour group is the largest retailer in Europe, and the second largest in the world (following Wal-Mart). It has 10,500 stores in 29 countries, 420,000 employees, is the leading retailer in nine countries, and is the world's leading operator of hypermarkets.

The group has five store formats:

1 *hypermarkets* with floor areas ranging from 5,000 to over 20,000 square metres, offering an average of 70,000 food and non-food products at low prices, and attracting customers from very large catchment areas;

2 *supermarkets* with floor areas between 1,000 and 2,000 square metres, offering a wide selection of mostly food products, at competitive prices, and trading under the names Champion, GS, Norte, Gb and Marinopoulos;

3 *hard discounters* operating under names such as Dia, Ed and Minipreço, small stores (between 200 and 800 square metres) selling 800 food products at unbeatable prices;

4 *convenience stores* including the Shopi, Marché Plus, 8 à Huit and Di per Di chains of stores;

5 *cash-and-carry and food service* outlets meeting the needs of restaurants and the food industry.

Carrefour's corporate strategy is to expand rapidly its three main types of store – hypermarkets, supermarkets and hard discounters – internationally. It aims to build market share in each country in which it works by 'expanding the type of retailing best suited to the local market and by taking advantage of the way the three formats complement one another'. This strategy has different store formats working closely together to cover a range of market segments. Under this corporate umbrella, each business has its own strategy to compete in its defined market, and then the functional strategies work to achieve the business strategies.

Food retailing is a particularly competitive area, where customers are keen to get the best deals. Retailers react by giving a combination of low prices and the best possible service to customers. Carrefour says that, 'Regardless of the business or country in which they work, Carrefour employees share one major focus: the customer. Our personnel aim to satisfy each and every customer expectation with professionalism and to offer the best possible prices for high-quality products and services.'

Questions

● How would you describe the Carrefour group's strategy? How do the different levels of strategy fit together?

● How do the strategies affect the operations in their stores?

● What are Carrefour's distinctive capabilities and competitive advantages?

● How do the strategies compare with those of other retailers?

Sources: Carrefour annual report, Paris, 2005; Website at www.carrefour.com

Discussion questions

1 As competing organizations work in the same business environment, are there significant differences in the strategies that are open to them?

2 The aim of every business is to make as much profit as possible. Anything else is playing with words. What do you think of this view?

3 The design of a strategy starts with purpose, and then moves on to strategic goals and objectives, and then downwards through other layers of the organization. Is this a sensible approach, or are there better alternatives?

4 What are 'key success factors' and why are they important?

5 With at least three levels of strategy above people actually doing the work, organizations are clearly top-heavy with unproductive planners. What can organizations do to reduce these overheads?

6 The key factor in strategy design is to put the right people in charge. Who might these people be, and how might they approach the design of a strategy?

7 Senior managers are paid a lot of money. Their main job is to design a strategy that steers the organization in the right long-term direction. But if strategy really emerges from the bottom-up, what are the senior managers doing, and why are they paid so much?

8 Managers know what their own organization can achieve, and a strategy must be based on its internal strengths. But they can never understand every aspect of the business environment, or even the likely actions of competitors, so they should not waste time trying. Do you agree with this introspective view?

Useful websites

www.carrefour.com
www.lufthansa.com
www.microsoft.com
www.mori.com
www.pepsico.com
www.pepsicola.com
www.tarmac.com
www.yum.com

References

Argyris C. and Schon D., Organisational learning, Addison-Wesley, Reading, MA, 1978.

Campbell A. and Tawady K., Mission and business philosophy, Heinemann, Oxford, 1990.

Campbell A. and Yeung S., Creating a sense of mission, Long Range Planning, vol 24, pp 10–20, 1991.

Collingridge D., The social control of technology, Open University Press, Milton Keynes, 1980.

Collins J.C. and Porras J.I., Building your company's vision, Harvard Business Review, September–October, pp 65–77, 1996.

Drucker P.F., The practice of management, Harper and Row, New York, 1954.

Evered R., So what is strategy, Long Range Planning, vol 16(3), pp 57–72, 1983.

Gooderham G., Debunking the myths of strategic planning, CMA magazine, May 1998.

Hamel G. and Prahalad C., Strategic intent, Harvard Business Review, May–June, pp 63–76, 1989.

Hamel G. and Prahalad C., Competing for the future, Harvard Business School Press, Cambridge, MA, 1994.

Kettley P. and Strebler M., 'Changing roles for senior managers', Institute for Employment Studies Report number 327, 1997.

Kotler P., Marketing management (12th edition), Prentice Hall International, Englewood Cliffs, NJ, 2005.

Miles R.E. and Snow C.C., Organisational strategy, structure and process, McGraw-Hill, New York, 1978.

Miller D., Configurations of strategy and structure, Strategic Management Journal, vol 7, pp 234–249, 1986.

Mintzberg H., Strategy making in three modes, California Management Review, vol 16(2), pp 44–53, 1973.

Mintzberg H., Crafting strategy, Harvard Business Review, July–August, pp 54–63, 1987.

Mintzberg H. and Waters J.A., Of strategies, deliberate and emergent, Strategic Management Journal, July–September, pp 257–272, 1985.

MORI, Britain's change of heart on profit, MORI, London, 2001.

O'Brien F. and Meadows M., Corporate visioning, Journal of the Operational Research Society, vol 51(1), pp 36–44, 2000.

Porter M.E., Competitive strategy, Free Press, New York, 1980.

Porter M.E., Competitive advantage, Free Press, New York, 1985.

Porter M.E., What is strategy, Harvard Business Review, November–December, pp 61–79, 1996.

Prahalad C.K. and Hamel G., The core competencies of the corporation, Harvard Business Review, May–June, pp 79–91,1990.

Quinn J.B., Strategic change, Richard D. Irwin, Homewood, IL, 1980.

Saunders C.B., Setting organisational objectives, Journal of Business Policy, vol 3(4), 1973.

Selznick P., Leadership in administration, Harper and Row, New York, 1957.

Simon H.A., The new science of management decisions, Harper and Row, New York, 1960.

Stacey R.D., Strategic management and organisational dynamics (4th edition), Financial Times Prentice Hall, London, 2002.

Thompson A.A. and Strickland A.J., Strategic Management (12th edition), McGraw-Hill, New York, 2001.

Tilles S., How to evaluate corporate strategy, Harvard Business Review, July–August 1963.

Walker O.C., Boyd H.W., Mullins D. and Larreche J., Marketing strategy (4th edition), Irwin McGraw-Hill, New York, 2004.

The first part of this book reviewed the foundations of strategic management. We introduced the idea that organizations have a purpose, and strategic management works towards this over the long term. We described four layers of strategic management, with a mission leading to a corporate, business and functional strategies. If these strategies are to work successfully, they need to be carefully designed. There is no single best approach to this design, but the three most important factors to consider are the organization's purpose, its internal features, and its business environment.

The business environment is a complex mixture of all the external factors that give the setting in which an organization works, but over which it has no control. Some of the key factors in the environment are the economic system, industry and market.

Managers have little say over the business environment, so strategy design concentrates on the aims and internal features of an organization. In particular, managers look for a strategic fit with the environment, and this allows them to build distinctive capabilities that lead to a sustainable competitive advantage.

The mechanism to implement the mission has progressively more detailed layers of objectives and decisions. In practice, the whole procedure is so complicated that parts of a strategy inevitably emerge from lower levels of the organization.

Figure R1.1 gives a summary of the process of strategic management.

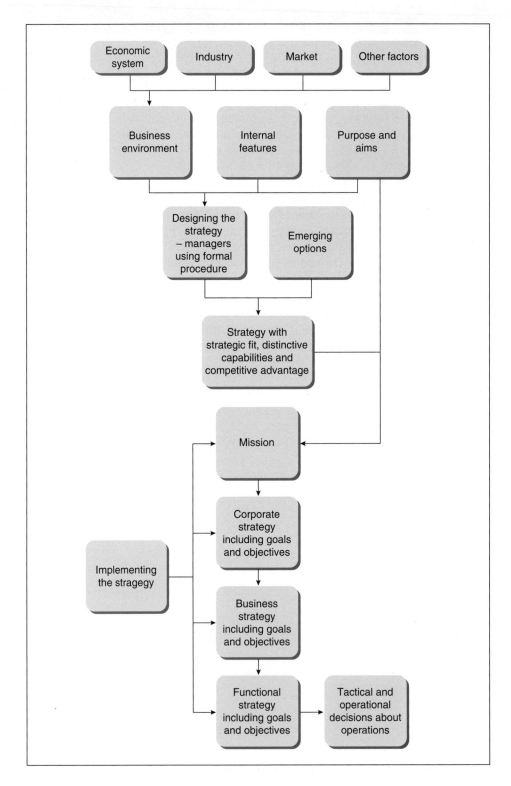

Figure R1.1 Overall view of strategy design and implementation

PART 2

AN OPERATIONS STRATEGY

The operations of an organization are all the activities that are directly concerned with making its products. The operations strategy consists of all the long-term goals, plans, policies, culture, resources, decisions and actions that affect the operations.

We cannot consider an operations strategy in isolation, so the first part of the book described the context. It reviewed the concept of strategic management, and discussed the design of a strategy that balances the needs of an organization's aims, internal features and external environment. The requirements of higher strategies pass downwards from the mission, through an operations strategy, and on to operations. The operations strategy is a complex web of interrelated parts that gives a guiding purpose to the operations. It shows how the organization will achieve its purpose, what type of products it makes, how it satisfies customers, what distinctive capabilities and competitive advantages it has, where it works, how big it is – and pretty much everything else that determines its long-term success. This second part of the book focuses on the design of an operations strategy.

There are five chapters in this part,

- **Chapter 4** outlines the role of operations in making a product
- **Chapter 5** gives more details of the purpose and contents of an operations strategy
- **Chapter 6** sees how to design an operations strategy
- **Chapter 7** describes a range of analyses that are used in strategy design
- **Chapter 8** considers the implementation of the strategy

The third part of the book looks at some specific types of strategic decision in operations – particularly relating to the product, process and supply chain.

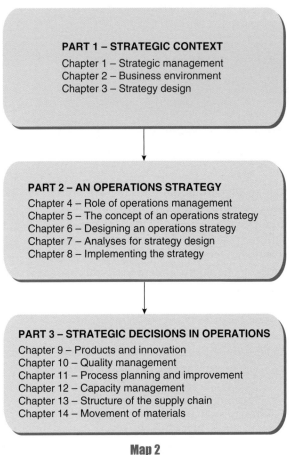

Map 2

CHAPTER 4
Role of Operations Management

An organization achieves its aims by supplying a product to customers. Operations are the activities that it uses to make this product, and taken together they form its process. A general systems view has an organization collecting a series of inputs, performing operations, and producing outputs – which include the product package that is passed to customers. This chapter outlines the role of operations managers and their responsibility for operations.

Aims of the chapter

After reading this chapter you should be able to:

- Understand the role and importance of operations
- Describe the relationship between operations, products and processes
- Outline the role of operations managers
- Discuss the areas in which operations managers make decisions
- Understand the process as a series of value adding operations
- Consider the relationship between operations management and other core functions
- Discuss some trends in operations

The key concepts discussed in this chapter are:

Main themes

- **Operations**, which are all the activities directly concerned with making an organization's products
- **Operations management**, which is the function responsible for operations
- **Process**, which consists of all the activities that make a particular product
- **Product**, which is the complete package of goods and services that is passed to customers

SUPPLY OF PRODUCTS

Product package

All organizations supply **products**. This is obvious with manufacturers like Toyota, Dell, Carlsberg and Nike – but it is also true for organizations that provide services, like AOL, HSBC, Vodafone and Ryanair. The difference is that manufacturers supply tangible goods that you can pick up, look at and store, while services supply the intangible benefits that we experience. We mentioned in chapter 2 that a typical industrialized country has around 20 percent of its workforce in manufacturing, over 70 percent work in services, and the rest in primary industries. The bulk of people work in services, but this forms such a diverse group that it is easier to consider it in smaller parts. A useful classification divides the broad service sector into public services, shops, logistics, non-profit organizations, other business services, and other personal services.

Manufacturing and services form the great bulk of economic activity, and at first you might imagine that the activities of manufacturers are fundamentally different to those of service providers. But this would be misleading. If you go into a McDonald's restaurant you see a combination of manufacturing (when they make the hamburgers) and service (when they serve them). General Motors is the world's biggest car manufacturer, but it gives services through warranties, after-sales service and finance packages; Vodafone gives a communications service, but it also supplies telephones, exchanges and other equipment; Langdon Bay Winery is a primary industry when it grows grapes, a manufacturer when it makes wine and a service industry when it delivers to customers.

The reality is that every product is a complex package that contains a mixture of both goods and services. This package – or 'offer' – contains all the benefits that an organization passes to customers. In the 1960s Lancaster developed this theme of a product as a 'bundle of attributes' and Kotler reinforces the view of a product as 'something that is viewed as being capable of satisfying a need or want'. This broad view of a product can include many intangibles, such as the feeling of satisfaction and pride you get after buying certain things.

Different products have different mixes of goods and services, forming the spectrum shown in Figure 4.1. At one end of this spectrum are products that are mainly goods, such as cars, washing machines and furniture. At the other end of the spectrum

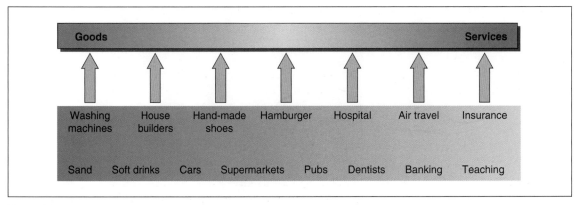

Figure 4.1 Spectrum of products

are products that are mainly services, such as insurance, education and travel. The products of, say, Pizza Express and Specsavers opticians come in the middle, with a more even balance of goods and services.

> ● A **product** consists of everything that an organization passes to its customers.
>
> ● Every product is a **package** of benefits that includes some combination of goods and services.

Operations make the product

The **operations** in an organization are all the activities that make its products. If the product is a mobile phone, the operations are all the activities that make the phone; if the product is a holiday, the operations are all the activities that provide the holiday. Operations form the core of an organization, and they usually define what the organization does. Operations at Ford make cars; operations at Qantas fly aeroplanes; at Norwich Union they give insurance; at CNN they make television programmes; at Real Madrid they play football.

> **Operations** are the activities that are primarily concerned with making an organization's products.

At the heart of every organization is a set of operations that manufacture, serve, transport, sell, refine and do everything else needed to make the products. Everything that you own, use, buy or borrow is a product of some organization, and has been made by the operations. And all organizations – whether they are charities, governments, social clubs, universities, or anything else – use operations to make products that they supply to customers. It is worth emphasizing again that when we talk about 'making products' this does not only mean manufacturing, but we take a completely general view that includes every type of product and every kind of operations.

A standard description of operations takes a simple systems view. This has organizations collecting a variety of **inputs**, using operations to transform them, and producing a range of **outputs** (as shown in Figure 4.2). The inputs include raw materials, money, people, machines, time, and all other resources. Operations include manufacturing, serving, transporting, selling, training, and all other activities. The outputs are goods, services, wages, waste material, etc. To give some specific examples:

● Ford's assembly plant in Cologne takes inputs of components, energy, robots, people, etc.; it performs operations of pressing, welding, assembly and painting; the main outputs are cars and spare parts.

● When Persimmon build houses, they take inputs of land, bricks, plans, equipment, etc.; perform operations of laying bricks, carpentry, plastering, plumbing, etc.; and outputs include houses, gardens and investments.

● La Paella y Vino Tinto in Malaga has inputs of food, chefs, kitchen, waiters, and dining area; it does operations of preparation, cooking and serving; outputs include meals and (hopefully) satisfied customers.

There can be many types of input. For simplicity, we will often refer to these as **materials** – but again we are using this as a general term to include all sorts of raw materials, resources, information, equipment, and anything else that is used by the process. Some of these inputs are changed during the operations, and these are the **transformed inputs** that are mainly raw materials, components, information and customers. Other inputs do not change themselves, but bring about transformations, and these are the **transforming inputs** that are typically the assets, people employed, equipment and facilities. For example, Pringle make a range of knitwear and their transformed inputs are wool, cotton, dyes, and other materials, while their transforming inputs are knitting machines, sewing machines and other factory facilities. As well as the tangible inputs, there are also intangible ones, such as reputation, experience, skills, financial strength, knowledge, etc. (Godfrey and Hill).

There are also different types of output, with the primary ones being the goods and services that form the product. But there are also secondary outputs that are not part of the product, such as wages for employees, profit, waste material, cultural identity,

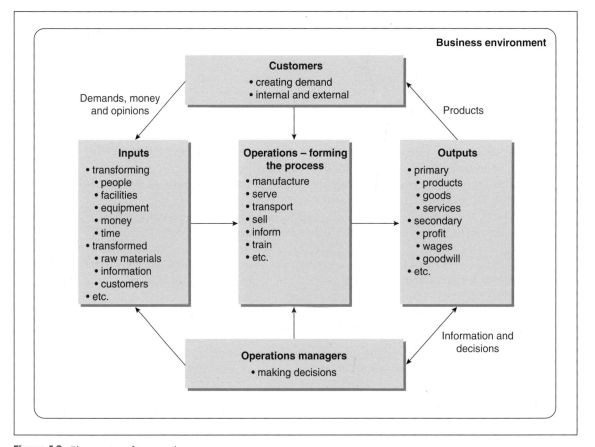

Figure 4.2 Elements of operations

corporate citizenship and networks of contacts. Some of these are clearly benefits that the organization wants to encourage – but others are harmful that it positively wants to avoid, such as scrap, waste and pollution.

The products are passed to customers who create demand for the product and give other inputs of money, opinions, etc. These might be external customers from outside the organization, or internal customers from another part of the organization. For example, a petrol refinery will sell fuel to its own transport fleet, and it then becomes an input to their logistics activities. The operations managers form another element in this picture, and they are – not surprisingly – the people who manage the operations, and are responsible for all aspects of an organization's products. The final part is the business environment in which the operations work.

In chapter 1 we said that organizations were compound entities, where an entire company is one organization, as is a department within the company, a section within the department, a committee within the department, and a working group within the committee. As each of these organizations has its own operations, we also have different levels of operations. A whole company has operations, when it buys materials from suppliers and sells products to customers. Within the company are the various divisions, so manufacturing has its own assembly operations, along with operations in accounting, marketing, finance, HRM, and so on. Then within each of these major divisions, each department, section, office, committee, etc. has its own set of operations. Each of these has the same structure of converting inputs to outputs and, as we shall see later, faces a similar set of problems.

Operations form the process

All the operations that make a particular product combine to form its **process**. This process starts with the collection of initial inputs and finishes with the delivery of products to final customers. The process for the Guardian newspaper, for example, starts with the planning of articles; it continues with sending reporters to collect stories, writing, editing, composing and printing, and finishes when copies are sold to

IDEAS IN PRACTICE Langdon Bay Winery

Langdon Bay Winery produces high quality red wines in Sonoma County, California. It uses a traditional process for making wine. Every vineyard uses a similar process, but details vary with the variety of grape, type of wine, region, climate, and so on. The process has the following operations:

1 pick the grapes and take them to the vineyard;

2 crush the grapes and remove the stems to form the must;

3 treat the must and let it ferment in vats;

4 first racking to filter the wine into containers;

5 second racking to clarify the wine and age it in barrels;

6 blending and bottling;

7 ageing in bottles;

8 packing bottles in cases;

9 delivery to customers.

Source: Publicity material from Langdon Bay Winery, Langdon Bay, 2005

customers. The process at Mars starts with picking cocoa beans and includes all the operations needed to deliver bars of chocolate to hungry customers. So a process consists of a series of connected operations, all contributing to the final product (as illustrated in Figure 4.3).

Langdon Bay Winery illustrates a typical process, as it collects materials, performs a series of operations, and delivers products to customers. It is unusual, though, for the entire process to be within one organization. Usually, there are many different organizations contributing to the final product. When you buy a computer, for example, Intel might make the processor, Fujitsu the disc drives, Canon the scanner, Hewlett-Packard the printer, Microsoft the operating system, and so on. As well as these manufacturers, there are other organizations supplying transport, finance, communications, marketing, accounting, utilities, and all the other resources needed to get the finished product to your door. Each of these organizations has its own operations, inputs and outputs, and they all contribute to the final product.

There are different terms for an extended process that spans several organizations, especially when we want to emphasize different activities. The term 'process' emphasizes the operations, but when we want to emphasize the flow of materials we refer to a supply chain or supply network; when we want to emphasize value added we refer to a value chain or demand chain; when we want to emphasize marketing we refer to a marketing or distribution channel; when we want to emphasize the movement of materials we refer to a logistics system, and so on.

Often there is one dominant organization that has most control over a process. For example, when you buy a car, there are hundreds of organizations that have contributed to the final product – but the dominant one is the major assembler, like Ford or Toyota. And when you buy a bottle of milk, many organizations have contributed to it, but the dominant one is the retailer that you bought it from. The position of the dominant organization shows where power is in the process, and it shows which organization can use its muscle to dictate terms to the others.

Adding value

All the operations contributing to a process must add value to the final product – or else there is no point in having them in the process. Porter (1980, 1985) says that an organization adds value by performing both primary and support activities. The primary activities are:

- **Inbound logistics** – moving all the inputs from suppliers into the operations.
- **Operations** – which are all the activities that transform the inputs to outputs.
- **Outbound logistics** – moving outputs to their destinations, including finished products to customers.
- **Marketing and sales** – which promote the product and give the means of buying it (such as availability in retail shops).
- **Service** – which enhances the value of the product (through installation, maintenance, repair, etc.).

Support activities are those that are still essential, but are not linked directly to operations, such as human resource management, public relations, technology development, and organizational systems.

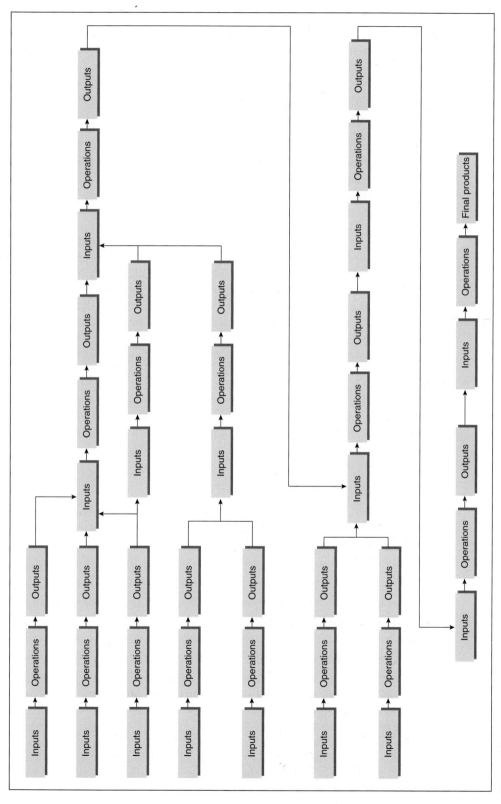

Figure 4.3 Combination of operations into a process

There are several weaknesses in Porter's description. For example, he tends to look at each organization in isolation rather than as one member of a continuous chain. The current trend is to integrate steps in the process, to give a smooth flow of materials from initial suppliers right through to final customers. Porter's model also suggest clear differences between functions within each organization, again giving the impression that each works separately in a disjointed process. Operations really span the whole range of activities that make the product but this model gives them a much more limited role. And we can question the separation of activities into primary and support. All activities in an organization should be concerned with supplying its products – or else managers should question the reason why they are being done. And saying that purchasing, for example, is a support function does not acknowledge its central role in moving materials through the process.

So a fairer view of operations has a continuous chain – or network – of activities, all adding value to the final product that is delivered to customers. There are many different ways of adding value; perhaps adding features to the product, moving it nearer to customers, storing it until its value increases, presenting it in a better way, adding packaging, arranging finance, giving information to the customer, and so on. The key point is that customers ultimately pay for all the operations, so they must view a product as having more value after an operation than it had before. If an operation adds no value, the process is inefficient as it incurs unnecessary costs.

When we describe a process as a series of related, value-adding operations, we have to be a bit careful. The problem is that this bald statement only considers the customers' view, without taking into account the requirements of the organization. Any organization can add value if it spends a lot of money on operations, but there are two further considerations. Firstly, organizations want operations to cost less than the value they add, so that they make a net profit. Secondly, there is a limit to the amount that customers will pay for a product, and this sets the maximum amount that an organization should pay for operations. Even if additional operations appear to add more value, customers will not pay for them, so they make a net loss.

As we have already seen, organizations perform their operations and satisfy customers, not as a noble end in itself, but as a way of achieving their own aims. A company looks for customer satisfaction not for the glow they get from a job well done, but for the profit that they can make. So operations always have to consider two viewpoints:

1 *an external view of customers,* supplying a product that satisfies some need of customers; making an attractive product that customers are willing to pay for;
2 *an internal view of the organization,* making products as a way of achieving their overall aims; using resources efficiently.

To put it simply, operations want to make a product that customers want so badly that they are willing to pay a price that is above the cost of production. This means making a very attractive product so that customers will pay a relatively high price (emphasizing the external view) or making it very efficiently so that the price is relatively low (emphasizing the internal view). Of course, there is likely to be some conflict between these two views. At a basic level, customers want a lot of added value but a low price, while organizations want a price that is much higher than the production costs. So

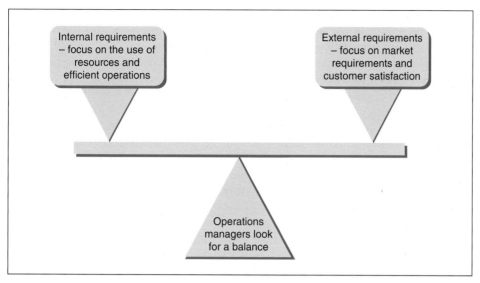

Figure 4.4 Operations managers balance internal and external factors

managers have to look for a point of balance that satisfies both parties, as illustrated in Figure 4.4.

The cost calculations behind this balance are illustrated in Figure 4.5. Producers have to cover all of their costs – traditionally classified as material, labour, operations overheads, general overheads and administration – so this sets the lowest acceptable

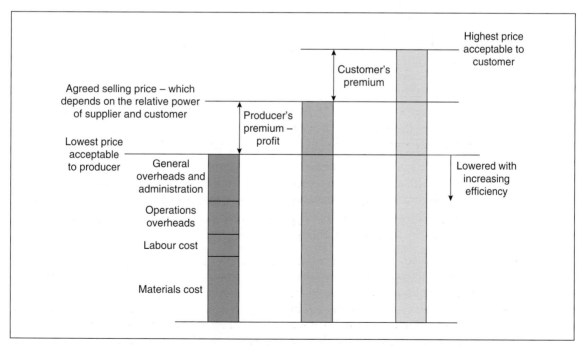

Figure 4.5 Range of acceptable selling price

price to the producer. Any price above this gives a profit or producer's premium. The product has a value to the customer, and this sets the highest price that the customer will pay, and any price below this gives a customer's premium.

The problem is agreeing a price that gives a fair balance between the two. This largely depends on the relative power of the supplier and customer. In very competitive markets the customer is normally at an advantage, which is the reason why supermarkets work on very small margins. Organizations here look for efficient operations that lower costs, and either raise profits or increase competitiveness. In less competitive markets the price tends to favour suppliers, who can charge a premium. But there is still an incentive to improve operations as this will make profits even higher. Monopoly suppliers can dictate the price they charge, up to the maximum that customers are willing to pay. In extreme cases, like the water companies in the UK, there is a monopoly supplier of an essential product. Then customers are forced to pay any price asked – arguably beyond the highest price that they are reasonably prepared to pay – and the result is very high profits. Such monopoly suppliers have little incentive to increase efficiency, as they simply pass on costs to customers.

MANAGEMENT OF OPERATIONS

Operations managers

Not surprisingly, the people who manage operations are the **operations managers**, and their function is **operations management**.

- **Operations managers** are responsible for all the activities that make an organization's products.
- **Operations management** is the management function that is responsible for all aspects of operations.

Organizations always use different titles for their employees, so it is not surprising that people who are actually operations managers have many different labels. Whenever you look at an organization, the people who are responsible for making its products are the operations managers – even if their actual title is production manager, plant manager, site manager, materials controller, shop manager, matron, postmaster, chef, supervisor, headmaster, transport manager, factory superintendent, maintenance manager, production engineer, or any other alternative. At first sight, you might imagine that these people do totally unrelated jobs. Operations in Airbus Industries, for example, seem completely different from operations in AOL, which are completely different from operations in the Copper Kettle Tea Shop in Almondsbury. Obvious differences include:

- **Size** – broadly measured in terms of capacity, output, investment, number of employees, or some equivalent measure that affects almost every aspect of operations.

- **Finances** – including cash flows, costs, assets, investment, profitability, debts, share value, market capitalization, etc.
- **Purpose and aims** – which depend on the type of organization, its industry, ownership, etc.
- **Variation in demand** – particularly seasonality and long-term trends.
- **Type of products** – and the balance between goods and services.
- **Continuity of operations** – whether they are continuous (like electricity production) or sporadic (like organizing the Olympic Games).
- **Range and variety of products**.
- **Amount and type of customer contact**.
- **Type and severity of competition**.
- **Use of technology and sophistication of equipment and systems**.
- **Constraints on operations**.

There is clearly an enormous range of operations, so it seems likely that operations managers do completely different jobs. However, this is not true. Despite apparent differences, there are fundamental similarities among all processes. If you look at the three organizations we mentioned above, managers in Airbus Industries, AOL and The Copper Kettle Tea Shop all have to find the best location for their operations; they all choose suppliers and buy raw materials; they use a defined process to turn the raw materials into products; they forecast customer demand and organize the capacity needed to meet this; they employ staff and schedule their time; they organize resources as efficiently as possible; they measure productivity, quality and profit. In fact, they face a wide range of similar problems. The reality is that operations managers in these three organizations – and every other one – have to solve a range of surprisingly similar problems. This set of common problems allows us to define a broad, coherent and widely applicable subject of operations management.

Operations decisions

We know that operations managers are responsible for making products, but exactly what kind of decisions do they make? In chapter 1 we said that managers set objectives, plan, organize, allocate resources, schedule activities, staff, direct, budget, monitor performance, control progress, and so on. So operations managers clearly do these jobs for operations – and they also do some more specific jobs that are directly concerned with operations. The following list is by no means exhaustive, but it gives an idea of the range of issues that they tackle.

- **Objectives** – what are the purpose, goals and objectives for operations? How can operations best help to achieve the overall purpose of the organization?
- **Organizational structure** – what is the best structure to support the operations?
- **Management systems** – what associated management systems do operations need?
- **Products** – what type of products do they make and how do they guarantee customer satisfaction?

IDEAS IN PRACTICE Centaur Communications

Centaur Communications is a small but rapidly growing company in East Africa. It has been planning an expansion into an adjacent market and made some comparisons between its own operations and those of the current market leader. Figure 4.6 illustrates some of the differences. This graph clearly shows that the market leader has much higher volume, and it also highlights other differences. For example, Centaur puts much more emphasis on customer contact, which reflects their aim of 'giving customer service that goes

beyond satisfaction'. This might be developed into a competitive advantage, but it seems at odds with an objective that puts more emphasis on costs than quality.

Comparisons of this type showed how Centaur might compete in the new market, and what areas of its operations might need adjusting.

Source: Richmond D.H., Analysis of competitive positioning, Centaur Communications, Johannesburg, 2005

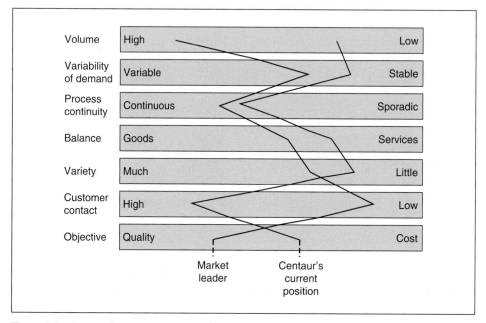

Figure 4.6 Comparison of processes for Centaur Communications

- **Demand** – how do they forecast and stimulate demand for these products?
- **Quality** – how can they measure quality and deliver products with guaranteed high quality?
- **Pricing** – what prices should they charge customers?
- **Technology** – what levels of technology should they use in the products and process?

- **Process** – what kind of process is best for making the products and what facilities does this need?
- **Capacity** – how much capacity does the process need and how does this vary over time?
- **Location** – where is the best place to perform the operations?
- **Planning** – what is the best timing for operations and how do they schedule resources?
- **Layout** – how do they arrange facilities in the process?
- **Performance** – how do they measure performance and set appropriate targets?
- **Materials** – what materials and other resources do operations need and where should they get them?
- **Logistics** – how do they organize an efficient flow of materials through the supply chain?
- **Stocks** – what do they keep in stock and how do they manage the stores?
- **People** – who do they employ and how do they motivate employees?

It is probably easiest to imagine these decisions in a particular organization, such as a supermarket, where managers have to make a whole series of decisions to keep their store running smoothly. And every other organization needs a similar range of decisions whether it is HSBC running the world's largest banking operation or Graham Barnet deciding how to run his painting and decorating business in Derby.

When making these decisions, operations managers follow the principles that we have already laid down and they reconcile the external demands of customers with the internal requirements of operations. All operations managers could supply products that customers want and get very high customer satisfaction if they used enough resources. But they also have to use internal resources efficiently, so that they neither waste resources nor raise cost above the level that customers are willing to pay. But, again, this is not the whole story. Operations managers help the organization achieve its overriding purpose – and this is unlikely to be either satisfied customers or efficient use of resources. Both of these are admirable aims, they are really ways of achieving the organization's broader purpose. So we should broaden our views and say that operations managers consider three types of factor in their decisions (illustrated in Figure 4.7).

1 *Internal factors for operations* – including efficient use of resources, types of products, design of the process, capacity, productivity, cost control, etc. These factors are under the direct control of the operations manager who can adjust them to get the best results.

2 *Broader factors within the organization* – including overall purpose, objectives, attitude towards risk, marketing, finances, HRM, etc. These factors are outside the direct control of operations managers, but they are controlled by other managers within the organization. These factors should be generally supportive, as all parts of the organization are working towards the same overall purpose. This purpose is passed down from higher strategies, as the normal means of control, so many of the factors are routed from the business strategy, through the operations strategy and on to operations.

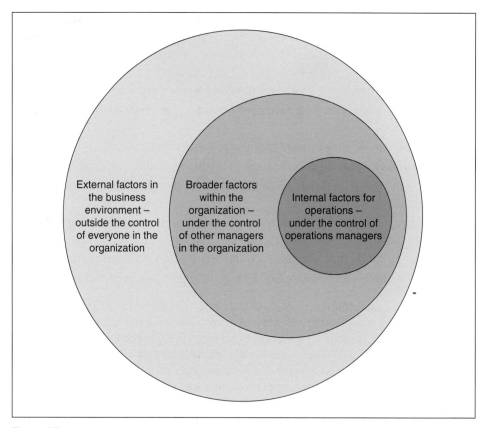

Figure 4.7 Factors for operations managers to consider

3 *External factors in the business environment* – including customer satisfaction, market conditions, demand, competition, suppliers, legal controls, etc. These factors are outside the control of all managers in the organization. As such, they are not necessarily supportive of the organization and, particularly in competitive markets, are more likely to be hostile.

By considering these three types of factors, operations managers are in a position to make informed decisions. We can imagine them facing a series of problems and making the best decisions to overcome them. In principle, they can use a standard approach to solving problems, based on the questions, 'What is the problem? What are the alternatives? Which is the best alternative?' To be more specific, a useful approach has the following seven steps (Waters).

1 *Describe the problem properly* – finding the exact problem, its cause, the context, effects, stakeholders, seriousness and variables.

2 *Define the objectives* – showing what operations want to achieve by solving the problem and giving priorities to different objectives.

3 *Collect and analyze data* – getting all relevant information about the problem, and associated internal and external factors.

4 *List the alternative solutions* – defining all the options, including those that are not immediately obvious.

5 *Compare alternatives and find the best* – examining the consequences of each alternative, and finding the one that best achieves (or comes closest to achieving) the declared objectives.

6 *Implement the decision* – doing whatever is necessary to carry out the chosen alternative, translating ideas and plans into actions.

7 *Monitor progress* – checking what actually happens over time and making necessary adjustments or new decisions.

This gives an analytical approach that assumes there is a best way of tackling problems, and using it inevitably leads to the best solution. This is typical of the scientific approach of operational research and management science. The problem, though, is that most scientific analyses are too simplistic to deal with real problems, and they cannot tell managers what to do in a particular situation, or predict the precise consequences of their actions. If the analytical approach were entirely accurate, people would be able to make infallibly rewarding investments in the stock market, or place winning bets on a horse race. Real problems are so complex that managers rely on less analytical approaches and more on judgement, maintaining the view of 'management as an art' rather than 'management as a science'.

Importance of operations management

It is easy to see why operations management is important. Operations make the products that an organization uses to achieve its purpose. So without operations managers, there are no operations, no products, no achievement of purpose – and soon no organization.

The quality of the operations management is also important. When operations managers do a good job, the organization makes products that customers want, they achieve high customer satisfaction, and can prosper. Next time you are particularly pleased with a product, it is a sign that operations managers have done a good job. On the other hand, when operations managers do a bad job, customers do not like the product for some reason, and they do not buy it. When you cannot find shoes that you like, or there is a long queue for service in a shop, or your train is cancelled, or you cannot connect to your Internet service provider, or a kitchen gadget breaks the first time you use it, or your water bill rises at twenty times the rate of inflation, you know that operations mangers have done something wrong.

To summarize, operations management is:

- **essential**, because it is at the heart of every organization, responsible for making the products;

- **important**, because it has a real effect on the organization's performance.

Organizations rely on good operations management to achieve their aims. So the pressure is on operations managers to deliver results – and this means supplying better products than competitors and using resources more efficiently. It means building distinctive capabilities that set the organization apart from its competitors with unique products, a process that no other organization has, low operating costs, customized products, flexible response to changing demand, rapid development of new products, fast service, convenient locations, high quality, or a wide range of other options. As always, the purpose of these distinctive capabilities is to gain a sustainable competitive advantage.

Now we can bring together these ideas and summarize the aims of operations management, which are to:

- help achieve the overall aims of the organization
- by making products that customers want;
- using resources efficiently
- and developing distinctive capabilities that give a sustainable competitive advantage.

IDEAS IN PRACTICE Nissan Motor Manufacturing (UK) Limited

In 1914 Nissan produced its first cars in Tokyo, Japan and by 1970 the company was exporting a million cars a year. Then production costs were rising in Japan, and the policy of meeting overseas demand by direct exports was becoming less acceptable. In 1985 they started production at their major facility in Sunderland, UK. This had the aim of 'building profitably the highest quality vehicles sold in Europe, to achieve the maximum possible customer satisfaction and thus ensure the prosperity of the company and its staff'.

Operations in the Sunderland plant can be summarized as 'making cars'. There are seven key types of operation:

1 *Panel pressing* – forming the panels for car bodies from steel sheets.

2 *Body assembly* – welding panels together to form the body on an automated assembly line.

3 *Paint* – painting finished bodies several times in a clean air environment.

4 *Plastics injection and blow moulding* – making parts from plastic, including fuel tanks, bumpers, radiator grills and facia parts.

5 *Aluminium casting* – moulding engine parts.

6 *Engine machining and assembly* – finishing engine parts and assembling them into a range of different models.

7 *Final assembly* – bringing together all the components to make finished cars.

Operations in this plant are extraordinarily complex, and managers make the whole range of decisions needed to keep a huge factory working smoothly and producing a new car every few seconds. The distinctive capability of the Sunderland plant is its efficiency. It is the most productive plant in Europe, and one of the most productive in the world. In 1999 the plant produced its millionth Micra, and its success brings continuing expansion. In 2006, the latest investment of £125 million will allow production of 100,000 units a year of the new Tone. As well as 5,000 people employed directly at the plant, there are twice as many people employed in a network of 200 suppliers, often with dedicated facilities near to the main site.

Sources: Anderson G., 2000 jobs secured by Nissan, The Journal, 24/9/2004, Newcastle; Websites at www.nissan.co.uk; www.nissan-europe.com; www.icnewcastle.co.uk

CORE FUNCTIONS

Operations management is a core function in every organization, but it clearly does not work alone. A traditional view says that every organization has three **core functions** (shown in Figure 4.8).

- **Marketing** – identifies customer demand, stimulates new demand, analyzes customer needs, organizes product information, takes orders, delivers products, gives after-sales service, etc.
- **Operations** – is responsible for all aspects of the process that makes products from sourcing materials through to delivery to customers.
- **Finance** – raises capital, invests funds, records financial transactions, arranges transfers of money, collects cost information, maintains accounts, etc.

These core functions are directly concerned with the product. You might say that an organization needs many other functions, such as human resources, research and development, catering, information, and public relations. But these can either be included in one of the core functions, or they are support functions that are not directly concerned with the product. Research and development, for example, considers the continuing supply of products and, therefore, forms a part of operations management. Catering might be an important function within an organization, but it is not directly concerned with the product – as no matter how well or badly the catering is done, it does not have a direct effect on the product. As usual such arguments depend on the precise definitions rather than principles. In reality, there are no clear boundaries between the three core functions and the various supporting ones. Purchasing, for example, may be an independent support function, or part of logistics within marketing, or part of the process within operations, or a cost centre

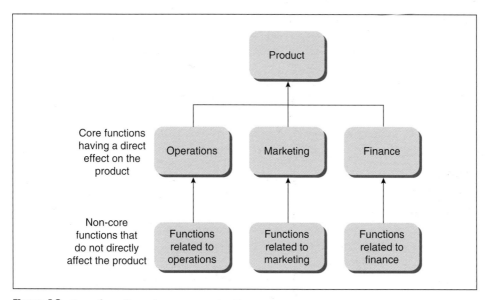

Figure 4.8 Core functions in an organization

within finance. The important thing is not to draw boundaries around activities, but to make sure that they all work together to achieve the organization's goals. Organizations are increasingly taking a broad view of the process and removing internal boundaries to give a set of diverse activities that work together to achieve the organization's purpose. Then the description of different functions is only for convenience and does not reflect actual divisions within the organization.

The three core functions should work together to achieve the purpose of the organization. The amount of emphasis given to each function varies between organizations. As a manufacturer, Airbus Industries might highlight its operations, but must still market its products and control its finances; Budweiser might emphasize its marketing, but still needs efficient operations to produce its beer and control its finances; American Express might focus on its financial performance, but still has to deliver products to customers.

In the 1960s companies tended to emphasize marketing, while the 1980s saw a move towards stronger financial management. More recently there has been a shift

IDEAS IN PRACTICE Schenfeld Industries

Until 2004 Schenfeld Industries (SI) was a division of a large international conglomerate, but it was then floated on the Frankfurt Stock Exchange as an independent company. It now makes a small range of domestic electrical equipment, including CD, DVD, computer and video equipment. In the second half of 2004 its sales grew by 5 percent and profits increased by 7 percent. This healthy performance was a welcome relief after years of financial troubles.

The problems started in the 1970s, when the company began to notice the effects of Japanese imports, and they made their first trading loss of $1 million in 1976. Senior managers felt that the best way to fight the competition was by improved marketing. In the following year they tripled the advertising budget, but this had no significant effect and SI's losses rose to over $4 million.

A consultant's report identified the main problem as high costs, as Japanese products were 20 percent cheaper than equivalent ones from SI. The company started a severe cost-cutting programme, including a reduction of 60 percent in the research and development budget. In such a fast moving market it is not surprising that SI's products soon became outdated.

In 1988 they tried to restructure the operations, closing two plants and selling another in Western Europe, and opening a new factory in Indonesia. But the hard times continued and losses reached a new peak in 1996.

After this, SI appointed a new Chairman, who immediately saw that despite cosmetic changes, the company had been making the same products and using the same process for 20 years. To meet the new competition it had to concentrate on operations, developing new products, improving quality and reducing costs. The company started a 'customer focus' campaign, which found out exactly what products customers wanted, and set out to supply this. Research and development designed new products and a state-of-the-art manufacturing centre was built in Munich, Germany.

By 2002 SI was making a profit for the first time in 25 years and was preparing to become an independent company. The Chairman said of his success, 'It was all very easy. We designed products that customers wanted – and then made them using the best operations.'

Source: Internal company records

towards operations. This is partly a response to major changes in the area, but it also recognizes that the operations of most organizations employ the majority of people, use most of the assets and generate all the income.

TRENDS IN OPERATIONS MANAGEMENT

Ideas about operations management are continually evolving. Some of these ideas lead to dead-ends and are quickly forgotten. Other ideas develop into movements that change the shape of whole industries. Since the 1980s Total Quality Management and just-in-time operations have changed the way that many industries work; communications and e-business did the same in the 1990s; now virtual enterprises and efficient supply chains are continuing the changes. It is worth giving a brief outline of the way that operations management has developed in the past, as this gives the background to current trends and gives some ideas of how the function may develop in the future.

Historical development

Operations management is an essential function in every organization, so it has been around since organizations started to make products. But most of the formal analyses have been done within the last hundred years, and the term 'operations management' has only been widely used since the 1960s.

In the pre-industrial age – often called the 'craft era' before large-scale manufacturing – most operations were done by hand. Typically, individual craftsmen worked in cottage industries, using their skills to produce small quantities of a wide variety of products. This was the standard pattern until the industrial revolution of the eighteenth century, when large-scale manufacturing and mass production moved operations into factories. Division of labour separated the whole process into a series of small parts, each of which could be done by unskilled people, and increasing automation made large numbers of standard products at low costs. Henry Ford is often described as the driving force behind mass production, and his enthusiastic use of new methods meant that by 1916 three quarters of cars bought in America were Fords (Bryson).

The principles used in these factories were developed by the **scientific management** school of thought, which used scientific methods to study operations and improve performance (Taylor; Gilbreth; Gantt). With the universal availability of cheap computing for the analyses, this approach has had a rebirth since the 1960s and often appears with titles like management science, operational research, operations research and decision science.

A second school of thought started rather later and concentrated on 'human relations' to show that motivation and inter-personal relationships are as important as technical design (Mayo; Fayol; Weber). This has developed into the broad area of human resource management.

Since the 1960s computers have been the driving force behind change, improving communications, information flows, process control, quantitative analyses and just about every other aspect of operations. Their impact on manufacturing has been dramatic, allowing widespread automation and huge increases in productivity. This, in turn, allowed more people to move into services, which became the clearly dominant type of industry in developed countries. People have used many terms to describe this new economic era, including post-industrial society (Bell), service economy (Fuchs), service society (Lewis; Gersuny and Rosengren; Gartner and Riessman) and age of mass customization (Pine *et al.*). Whatever we call the age, it is characterized by a dominant service sector, along with manufacturing that is both flexible and efficient.

Current trends

In recent years many significant trends in operations management have continued to bring change. Some of these trends look certain to continue, and will determine the directions of operations management long into the future. For example, operations have become increasingly global, and unless there is some major upheaval it is difficult to imagine this changing. You can get some idea of the scope of these changes from the following list. This is by no means exhaustive – and the list is in no particular order – but it illustrates some directions in which operations are heading. These trends are clearly at different stages of adoption, and they range from minor adjustments through to major breakthroughs.

- **Global operations** – with organizations trading in a single world market, and competition not limited to other local organizations but appearing from anywhere in the world.
- **Mass customization** – bringing a combination of high volume operations and flexibility to meet individual customer demands.
- **Lean operations** – removing all waste from operations (Womack *et al.*).
- **Agile operations** – focusing on the ability to change quickly from one type of produce or market sector to another (Kidd; Dugay *et al.*).
- **Integration of operations** – extending cooperation, and managing operations for the whole process rather than dividing it into separate bits.
- **e-business** – improving communications allowing all kinds of electronic business, particularly B2B and B2C.
- **Just-in-time operations** – which has every operation done just at the right time, thereby reducing stocks and improving flows through the process.
- **Total Quality Management** – where products are made with guaranteed perfect quality.
- **Quick response or efficient customer response** – pulling materials quickly through a supply chain (Suri).
- **Outsourcing** – where organizations concentrate on their core operations and use other organizations to do the periphery operations.
- **Strategic view** – emphasizing the importance of setting long-term directions.
- **Time-based competition** – reducing delays throughout the process and rapidly delivering new products to customers (Stalk; Stalk and Hout; Hum and Sim).

The importance of these trends is that they show the directions in which operations are moving – and the likely shape of operations in the future. Operations managers must take this changing environment into account when making their decisions. For example, if managers decide to expand capacity it might take several years before

IDEAS IN PRACTICE Sleep Inn

Choice Hotels International is one of the world's largest hotel chain franchises with more than 5,000 hotels in 44 countries. They operate chains under the names Comfort Inn, Comfort Suites, Quality, Sleep Inn, Clarion, Manestay Suites, EconoLodge and Rodeway Inn. Most of the company's 400,000 rooms are in America, where they are a leading name in low cost hotels.

Most of the employees of economy hotels do the cleaning and general maintenance – generally referred to as housekeeping. But when the economy picks up, these people tend to move to other industries that are better paid or have less demanding conditions. This happened in the 1990s, when Choice Hotels International found that their chains were hit by a combination of labour shortage and declining employee productivity. They responded by developing their Sleep Inn brand as giving no-frills rooms at a bargain price.

Sleep Inns were designed specifically for efficient cleaning, with smaller rooms, fewer contents and smooth surfaces everywhere. To fully service a room took two-thirds of the time needed for an average room – with other savings meaning that Sleep Inns typically employed half as many staff as other economy hotels.

The operations are based on:

- a standardized, well-designed and low-cost product
- high quality delivery, measured in terms of reliability and consistency
- standard operations with efficient, well-designed procedures
- high staff productivity, with appropriate training, flexibility, motivation and rewards
- good design, maintenance and upkeep of facilities
- effective monitoring of all facilities and operations.

This efficiency is accompanied by high customer service, with 97 percent of guests ranking their stay as either excellent or good, and 99 percent saying that their rooms were good value for money. The company also achieve their profit targets, with returns that are significantly higher that industry averages, and a profit approaching $100 million a year.

Sources: Choice Hotels International, Annual Report, Silver Springs, MD; Schember J., Sleep Inn wakes up to new labour, Personnel Journal, vol 70(8), pp 71–73, 1991; Website at www.sleepinn.com

this expansion is complete – so their decisions must be based on likely conditions in several years time. During this period, operations will have become more international, communications will have improved, automation will have increased, the service sector will have grown, more will be spent through e-business, manufacturing will become more productive, operations will be more flexible, materials will move faster through the process, and so on. Of course, we cannot say exactly how operations will develop – but it is safe to say that they will certainly be different in the future, and we have to plan these changes now. This brings us to an operations strategy, which sets the long-term direction for operations. We discuss this in the next chapter.

Chapter review

- Every organization makes a product, which is a complex package that contains a mixture of goods and services.
- Operations are all the activities (designing, serving, manufacturing, transporting, etc.) that are directly concerned with making an organization's products. They take a range of inputs (largely the transformed or transforming resources) and produce outputs (largely products, but including others).
- A process consists of the series of related operations, often spread over several organizations, that are used to make a product. Each operation in the process should add value to the final product.
- Operations managers are the people responsible for operations. They make all the decisions that affect an organization's products.
- Operations managers have to balance the competing requirements of operations (particularly efficient use of resources), the organization (particularly its purpose and aims) and the business environment (particularly customer satisfaction).
- Operations management is an essential function in every organization. Despite obvious differences in operations, all operations managers face a range of similar problems. The way managers tackle these problems has a direct impact on organizational performance.
- A traditional view has three core functions in an organization – operations, marketing and finance – working together to achieve the overall aims.
- There are clear trends in operations, many of which are likely to continue for the foreseeable future. Managers must take these into account when making decisions.

Discussion questions

1 What is a product?

2 Operations are the activities that make an organization's products. But the only thing that organizations really do is make products – so what is the point of the other functions?

3 Do the operations in different organizations really have so much in common that we can talk about a single, unified subject of operations management?

4 What are the main operations decisions at Real Madrid Football Club? How are these different from the decisions at the Channel Tunnel, the Red Cross, the White Hart Pub in Bedale Avery and Gillette?

5 What do operations managers do?

6 What do we mean by 'adding value'?

CASE STUDY Amazon.com

In 1995 Jeff Bezos founded Amazon.com in his garage as an on-line book retailing business. Its mission was 'to use the Internet to transform book buying into the fastest, easiest, and most enjoyable shopping experience possible', and it quickly grew to become the world's largest bookseller. In 2003 the company began to make a profit, and in the following year, sales passed $6 billion.

Amazon gives access to huge stocks that are not available in local bookshops. And they can give low prices because of their efficient operations, low overheads, economies of scale, and discounts from publishers. This combination of customer service, wide choice, efficient delivery and low costs has been very successful. The company expanded beyond its original operations in Seattle, and now has Websites in the UK, Germany, France, Japan and Canada. It expanded beyond selling books – firstly into associated areas of CDs and videos, and then into games, electronic and office equipment, garden furniture, sporting goods, clothes, jewellery and gifts, tools and hardware, kitchen equipment and food, pharmaceuticals, auctions, and just about everything else. The company now has millions of products, advertising that it 'offers Earth's biggest selection' and it 'seeks to be Earth's most customer-centric company, where customers can find and discover anything they might want to buy on-line, and endeavours to offer its customers the lowest possible prices'.

On its busiest day over Christmas 2004 the company shipped 2.8 million deliveries or 32 a second. Its main site made two million deliveries to 217 countries, was visited by 700,000 visitors in an hour, sold a million units a week from the music store, and sold a watch every second from the jewellery store.

Amazon.com obviously has a winning formula and its strategy and operations are clear. But other booksellers now have to ask how they can compete against such a dominant presence. Amazon.com says that 'The environment for our products and services is intensively competitive' – but all other retailers have to compete against a clear market leader that continues to improve and expand. Many traditional booksellers have gone out of business, and others have followed Amazon.com into e-business – a selection including www.books.com, www.whsmith.com, www.worldbooks.com, www.buybooksontheweb.com, www.delbergbooks.com, www.thesimplestway.com, and www.ukbol.com.

Questions

● What are the main operations at Amazon.com?

● How has Amazon.com developed these operations into distinctive capabilities and what are its competitive advantages?

● How can other booksellers compete against Amazon.com?

● Amazon.com was the first company to use a new type of process to sell books. Is it always an advantage to be the first in the market?

Source: Press Releases, Seattle, 2004/2005; Amazon.com Annual Report, Seattle, 2005; Websites at www.amazon.com; www.amazon.co.uk

---

7 A series of mergers and takeovers has concentrated car assembly in fewer companies (for example, Jaguar-Ford, Daimler-Chrysler, Volvo-Ford and Renault-Nissan). What operational factors do you think encourage these mergers?

8 How have operations changed over the past 20 years? What changes are likely over the next 20 years?

Useful websites

www.amazon.com
www.amazon.co.uk
www.books.com
www.buybooksontheweb.com
www.delbergbooks.com
www.icnewcastle.co.uk
www.nissan.co.uk
www.nissan-europe.com
www.sleepinn.com
www.thesimplestway.com
www.ukbol.com
www.whsmith.com
www.worldbooks.com

References

Bell D., The coming of post-industrial society, Basic Books, New York, 1973.

Bryson W., Made in America, Minerva, London, 1994.

Dugay C.R., Landry S., and Pasin F., From mass production to flexible/agile production, International Journal of Operations and Production Management, vol 17(12), pp 1183–1196, 1997.

Fayol H., Industrial and general administration, International Management Institute, Geneva, 1930.

Fayol H., General and industrial management, Pitman, London, 1949.

Fuchs V.R., The service economy, National Bureau of Economic Research, New York, 1968.

Gantt H.L., Industrial leadership, Yale University Press, New Haven, CT, 1916.

Gartner A. and Riessman F., The service society and the consumer vanguard, Harper and Row, New York, 1975.

Gersuny C. and Rosengren W., The service society, Schenkman Publishing, Cambridge, MA, 1973.

Gilbreth L.M., The psychology of management, Sturgis and Walton, New York, 1914.

Godfrey P.C. and Hill C.W.L., The problems of unobservables in strategic management research, Strategic Management Journal, vol 16(7), pp 23–45, 1995.

Hum S.H. and Sim H.H., Time-based competition, International Journal of Operations and Production Management, vol 16(1), pp 75–91, 1996.

Kidd P., Agile manufacturing, Addison-Wesley, Reading, MA., 1994.

Kotler P., Principles of marketing, Prentice Hall, Englewood Cliffs, NJ, 1980.

Kotler P., Marketing management (12th edition), Prentice Hall International, Englewood Cliffs, NJ, 2005.

Lancaster K.J., A new approach to consumer theory, Journal of Political Economy, vol 14, pp 132–157, 1966.

Lewis R., The new service society, Longman, New York, 1973.

Mayo E., The human problems of an industrial civilisation, Macmillan, London, 1933.

Pine B., Bart V. and Boynton A., Making mass customisation work, Harvard Business Review, September–October, pp 108–119, 1993.

Porter M.E., Competitive strategy, Free Press, New York, 1980.

Porter M.E., Competitive advantage, Free Press, New York, 1985.

Taylor F.W., The principles of scientific management, Harper and Row, New York, 1911.

Stalk G., Time the next source of competitive advantage, Harvard Business Review, July/August, pp 41–52, 1988.

Stalk G. and Hout T., Competing against time, The Free Press, New York, 2003.

Suri R., Quick response manufacturing, Productivity Press, Portland, OR, 1998.

Waters D., Operations management (2nd edition), Financial Times Prentice Hall, Harlow, 2002.

Weber M., The theory of social and economic organisation, Free Press, New York, 1947.

Womack J., Jones D. and Roos D., The machine that changed the world, Rawson Associates, New York, 1990.

Aims of the chapter

This chapter outlines the features of an operations strategy. It discusses the definition of an operations strategy, along with the aims, contents and relationships with other strategies. Different views put more emphasis on either the internal operations or the external environment, and the strategy has to reconcile these competing needs over the long term. This chapter lays the foundations for designing an operations strategy, which we discuss in the next chapter.

After reading this chapter you should be able to:

- Define 'operations strategy'
- Discuss the aims of an operations strategy
- Say how an operations strategy is likely to develop over time
- Outline the contents of an operations strategy
- Describe a market view of operations strategy
- Compare this with a resources view
- Discuss measures of operations performance
- Appreciate the need for strategic fit to match operations to their environment

Main themes

The key concepts discussed in this chapter are:

- A **definition** of operations strategy, discussing its role in the organization
- **Aims and contents** of the strategy, showing what it tries to do
- **Market and resources views** of an operations strategy
- **Strategic fit**, which matches the operations to their external environment

DEFINITION

In the last chapter we looked at the role of operations management as a core function in every organization, directly responsible for making its products. Operations managers make all the decisions related to operations, starting with the original design of products and processes, continuing through production, and ending with delivery of products to final customers. Some of their decisions are strategic, with consequences felt over many years – such as deciding whether to build new facilities, choosing a location for operations, developing an entirely new type of product, and extending into new geographical areas. Some decisions are tactical with consequences felt over months, such as designing the layout for a process, employing people with new skills, replacing equipment, and sub-contracting work. Some decisions are operational with consequences felt over the short term, such as scheduling people to do jobs, deciding when to order new materials, timetabling routine maintenance, and setting daily production.

Table 5.1 gives an idea of the scope of these decisions (Waters). In reality, the different levels of decision are not as distinct as this table suggests. For example, there is no magic cut-off time that automatically separates types of decision – and any way some short-term decisions are very important for an organization.

If we collect all the strategic decisions about operations, we have the basis of an **operations strategy**. Slack and Lewis describe this as, 'the total pattern of decisions which shape the long-term capabilities of any type of operation and their contribution to overall strategy'. But the operations strategy is more than a set of decisions, and we can broaden this view to include other long-term effects.

> The **operations strategy** of an organization consists of all the ...... term goals, plans, policies, culture, resources, decisions and actions that rela............ ......tions.

Other definitions of operations strategy emphasize i.......
and internal requirements. The external requirement......
organization (from market, industry, customer dema.......
but still within the organization (typically set by ...
requirements of operations relate to capabilities, ...
etc.). Slack and Lewis describe this balance, in p......
market requirements with operations resource......

Another approach to a definition focuses on ......
egy, such as Wheelwright's view that an opera......
areas of capacity, facilities, vertical integrati......
ine, there are many variations on this list ......

Perhaps it is easier to look at the typ......
to answer, such as:

- What kinds of customers do ......
- What type of products do ......
- What types of process do ......

- What level of technology do we use, and how innovative are our products and processes?
- What are our distinctive capabilities that we do better than competitors?
- How do we guarantee high quality?

Table 5.1 Different types of decisions made by operations managers

Strategic decisions
- *Aims* – setting the long-term purpose, goals and objectives
- *Operations structure* – choosing the best way to organize operations
- *Type of product* – deciding the type of products to make and timing the introduction of new products
- *Quality management* – showing how to ensure high quality products
- *Type of process* – showing how to make the products
- *Capacity* – setting the size of facilities
- *Structure of the supply chain* – showing how materials are moved from suppliers to customers
- *Location* – choosing where to make products
- *Vertical integration* – deciding how much of the supply chain to own
- *Alliances, partnerships and outsourcing* – describing relations within supply chains

Tactical Decisions
- *Planning* – giving a timetable for operations in the medium term
- *Product development* – designing and introducing new products
- *Technology* – using the best level of technology for the process
- *Layout* – designing the way operations are arranged
- *Logistics* – organizing the flow of materials through supply chains
- *Quality assurance* – implementing quality improvement systems
- *Replacement* – finding the best time to replace facilities
- *Staffing* – employing people with the right skills
- *Make/buy* – deciding whether to make or buy materials
- *Performance* – defining measures of performance
- *Systems* – designing systems to support, check and monitor operations

Operational Decisions
- *Scheduling* – setting the order in which operations are done
- *Staffing* – designing staff schedules
- *Inventory control* – deciding how much stock to hold
- *Ordering* – placing orders to acquire resources
- *...ility* – finding ways to improve equipment reliability
- *...e* – scheduling maintenance periods
- *...* checking that products reach designed quality
- *...* the best way to do an operation
- *...* how long operations take

- How do we manage capacity?
- What is the structure of the supply chain, and type of relationships within it?
- Where do we locate facilities?
- What is the best organizational structure for operations?

This kind of list shows the type of problems covered in an operations strategy, but it has the drawback of suggesting that an operations strategy can be reduced to a simple series of statements. But it is much more than this – and it forms a complex web with many facets, few defining features, and no clear boundaries around it. Sometimes it is easiest to imagine an operations strategy as a set of strategic decisions – and at other times we have to focus on its role in supporting higher strategies, or supplying products that customers want, or using resources effectively, or achieving customer satisfaction, or interacting with other functions, or developing an operations culture, or a host of other things. The important point is that an operations strategy does all of these – and everything else that is concerned with the long-term performance of operations. To put it succinctly, the operations strategy combines all the long-term aspects of operations. This means that it can appear in many different forms. Sometimes, particularly in smaller organizations, the operations strategy is just a vague notion of what senior managers imagine the organization will be doing in the future; at other times, it is a rigorous set of procedures covering every aspect of operations and presented in a formal document. The important point is the thinking behind the operations strategy, and not how this strategy is presented.

AIMS OF AN OPERATIONS STRATEGY

Supporting higher strategies

The overriding aim of an operations strategy is to help the organization achieve its purpose. This purpose is passed down from the mission, through the corporate and business strategies, on to the operations strategy and then to operations. So the operations strategy forms a link between the more abstract and fuzzy higher strategies and more precise details needed by operations (Krajewski and Ritzman). EasyJet have a business strategy of running a low price airline; the related operations strategy defines a no-frills, low-cost service using secondary airports, with no meals or entertainment, and a simplified booking system; then the operations are the activities that actually provide this service. The business strategy of UPS calls for outstanding service to customers, which translates into an operations strategy of delivering parcels quickly and reliably to almost any point in the world, and operations that actually make the deliveries.

When we describe an operations strategy as the link between a business strategy and operations we use an internal focus, but as usual we also have to consider its broader effects outside the organization. Then the main concern is to develop a competitive advantage, and this comes from the superior performance that emerges from the distinctive capabilities. So operations managers look at the higher strategies and they see how operations can help achieve these, through distinctive capabilities. Then they design an operations strategy that moves operations in this direction over the long term. This suggests a path to designing the operations strategy that we expand in the next chapter.

- The **overall aim** of an operations strategy is to support the higher strategies in achieving the organization's purpose
- It does this by providing **superior performance** in operations

We can break down these overriding aims into more immediate ones, suggesting that the operations strategy should:

- be vertically consistent with higher strategies to help achieve their broader goals and objectives;
- be horizontally consistent with strategies in other parts of the organization – making sure that all parts work together to achieve the organization's aims;
- define the overall direction of operations, describing their purpose, goals and objectives – with realistic targets that operations can actually achieve;
- establish efficient, value-adding operations in a process that gives a positive contribution to the organization;
- make products that continue to satisfy customer demand over the long term;
- develop internal strengths to give superior performance and distinctive capabilities in operations;
- identify internal weaknesses in operations and take appropriate measures to overcome them;
- identify and exploit opportunities in the environment, while supporting the societal, ethical and broader values of the organization;
- identify potential threats in the environment and take actions to avoid their effects;
- focus resources on areas that are critical for operations' success – and conversely prevent scarce resources being diverted to less important areas;
- take into account the views of stakeholders, gaining support both within the organization and from external bodies;
- be executable, so that the strategy can be implemented properly to achieve the planned results.

This list might suggest a rather passive role for the operations strategy, accepting the higher strategies and circumstances set elsewhere, and then working to get the best results within these fixed conditions. But this is a false view, as operations managers do not simply respond to prevailing conditions, but actively participate in forming them (Skinner, 1969 and 1978). For example, they do not just accept a fixed business strategy that other people design, but they make a positive contribution towards it. Even at a basic level, operations managers have to say what operations can and cannot achieve, and this becomes an important input to the business strategy. So there is feedback (illustrated in Figure 5.1) with the business strategy giving the context for the operations strategy – which, in turn, provides an important input for the business strategy.

The size of operations' contribution to the higher strategy varies widely between organizations. At one end of a spectrum are organizations where the operations

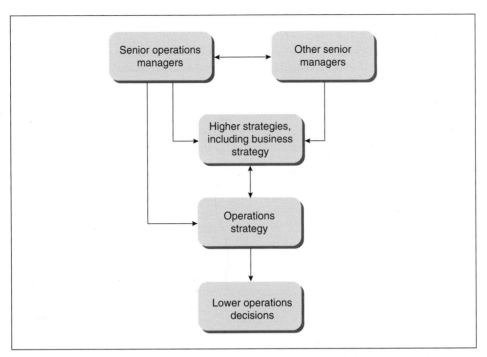

Figure 5.1 Role of operations managers in designing higher strategies

managers contribute little and respond to the conditions imposed on them. At the other end of the spectrum are organizations whose operations are dominant and dictate the higher strategies. For ease, we can describe three levels of interaction between the operations strategy and the higher strategies (Slack).

1 *Operations strategy implements the higher strategies.* Here the main role of the operations strategy is to provide a path for transmitting the organization's aims downwards from its corporate and business strategies. Operations managers interpret these aims from an operations perspective and design an operations strategy that will achieve them. This is a purely supporting role, assuming that the higher strategies have already been fixed, and the operations strategy is only concerned with designing operations and organizing resources to achieve them (Miller and Roth). The higher strategies give a statement of intent, and this is only realized when appropriate decisions and actions are taken at lower levels – so the basic role of the operations strategy is to 'operationalize' the higher strategies.

2 *Operations strategy supports the higher strategies.* This is a more active role for the operations strategy, as it makes sure that the higher strategies are actually achievable before considering their implementation. Here operations managers have a role in designing the higher strategies, reviewing their practicalities, and then a more active role in their implementation (Skinner, 1985). The key point is that operations are not just responding, but are positively assessing the requirements of higher strategies and developing capabilities needed to achieve them.

3 *Operations strategy drives the higher strategies*. An organization can only succeed in the long term if customers perceive its products as somehow better than those of competitors'. So the operations must be doing something better than competitors – and they develop distinctive capabilities that gives them a competitive advantage. Strategic managers recognize this superior performance and include it in their business and corporate strategies. At an extreme, the operations performance may become so dominant that it effectively defines the higher strategies. Operations at Rolls Royce, for example, made very high quality cars, and this became the basis of their business strategy.

Distinctive capabilities

The third level of support has distinctive capabilities in operations driving the business strategy. As we saw in chapter 3, an organization's capabilities are the activities that it does particularly well, with core capabilities being the key activities that affect performance and competitiveness, and distinctive capabilities being core capabilities that it does better than competitors. Distinctive capabilities are the key activities that set an organization apart from its competitors. They allow FedEx to deliver parcels quickly, at Intel they design state-of-the-art computer chips, at Stephen Baxter's garage they repair cars cheaply, at Tesco they sell a wide range of products at low prices.

Distinctive capabilities give a sustainable competitive advantage, so they are an important input to business strategies. Again there is feedback, with an operations strategy leading to distinctive capabilities – and these, in turn, being important inputs to business strategies. FedEx have a business strategy of fast service, and this leads to an operations strategy of delivering parcels quickly – so they put resources into rapid delivery and develop a distinctive capability, which becomes an input to their operations strategy. Common sources of distinctive capabilities in operations come from:

- **products** – quality, reputation, innovation, differentiation, range
- **facilities** – capacity, flexibility, location, age, reliability
- **processes** – uniqueness, experience, flexibility, economies of scale, quality
- **technology** – in products, proprietary technology, R&D, in processes, expertise
- **performance** – low costs, productivity, utilization, continuous improvement
- **employees** – availability, skills, expertise, loyalty, motivation
- **managers** – knowledgeable, experienced, entrepreneurial
- **finances** – cash flows, turnover, profit, profitability, ROI, capital available
- **customers** – growing customer base, knowledge of their demands, loyalty, size of orders, long-term relationships
- **markets** – large share, leadership, experience, reputation, sales procedures
- **suppliers** – access to raw materials, relationships, flexibility, partnerships, arrangements for procurement
- **logistics** – locations, channels, ownership through integration, speed of delivery, stocks, transport operations
- **organization** – structure, relationships, flexibility
- **other assets** – knowledge, innovation, patents.

It is important to identify distinctive capabilities, as even the smallest advantage can give benefits in competitive markets. But this can be surprisingly difficult and managers are tempted to use vague generalities, such as 'our distinctive capability is in providing mobile communications'. This could be true, but it does not give any practical guidance for allocating resources or making related decisions – and it will largely be ignored. A more useful format could follow Ace Dairy's statement of, 'our distinctive capability is to provide an efficient, low cost daily delivery of milk to households in Hayle'.

Once operations have established a competitive advantage, they have to set about defending it, and this means putting up barriers that restrict competitors (Porter 1979). The principle of defending a position is that operations go further than preparing for an inevitable future, and play a role in shaping it. Suppose that a company works in an industry where e-business is growing quickly. You would expect an operations strategy to extend the use of e-business, perhaps developing new methods and capabilities, and certainly raising competitiveness. But by doing this, the company has itself changed the business environment by raising the level of e-business and making competitors face more difficult conditions. Of course, the impact of an individual organization is usually small, but the effects are cumulative – or a small number of organizations may dominate an industry.

In practice, operations can adopt several ploys to defend a competitive position, including:

- improving some aspect of the product package, such as features, quality, service, lead time, warranties, etc.;
- broadening the product range to close gaps or niches in the market;
- introducing specific new models with the same features as those proposed by competitors;
- keeping prices low, especially for models that are similar to competitors';
- giving big price discounts, especially for large volumes;
- offering additional services, such as finance or training;
- signing exclusive agreements with suppliers, purchasers or other parts of the supply chain;
- defending proprietary elements with patents and copyright.

As well as giving an advantage over current competitors, such measures raise the barriers facing potential, new competitors. We saw in chapter 2 that entry barriers to markets include large capital investments (for R&D, equipment, production facilities, advertising, customer credit, stocks, and other start-up costs), economies of scale (that make it difficult for new entrants to start small and grow), customer loyalty (arising from product differentiation and brand preferences), experience (with learning curve and related cost disadvantages), need for specialized knowledge (with proprietary technology, patents, etc.), limited access to the supply chain (with vertically integrated companies, limited capacity, long-term agreements, partnerships, restricted locations, shortage of raw materials, etc.), and regulatory barriers (such as licenses, planning restrictions, standards, quotas, tariffs and international trade restrictions).

There are obvious benefits to defending a competitive advantage but, surprisingly, this defence can become too rigorous, and prohibit normal development. When an organization develops a distinctive capability that gives a significant advantage, it becomes very difficult to change, even when conditions change – becoming a 'core rigidity' (Leonard-Barton). Imagine a clothes retailer that has a strategy of providing low cost, basic clothing. This strategy might work very well during a period of economic stagnation, and the retailer might grow very quickly. But the strategy gathers momentum and operations managers will be reluctant to change this winning formula, even when the economy picks up and customers are looking for higher quality products. Then the strategy that gave them initial success will lead to their eventual downfall. You can see countless examples of highly successful companies that fail to update their distinctive capabilities and eventually become victims to changing circumstances.

However hard an organization defends a competitive advantage, it is only likely to be short term, as there are always other organizations who can see the success and try to duplicate it (Williams). They might even benefit by avoiding the mistakes of earlier producers, and making their own improvements. The duration of any advantage depends on the original source of advantage – whether it gives a real benefit to core strategic issues – and how easy it is for other organizations to copy or develop alternatives (Peteraf). But the clear message is that an organization cannot stand still, but has to update its operations, continually looking for further improvements and reacting to changes in its internal working and external environment (Teece *et al.*). You would probably expect new operations to be rather passive and concentrate on implementing the higher strategies and not making too many mistakes. But as the operations mature you might expect them to build on their strengths to give a superior performance and work towards supporting and then driving higher strategies. Hayes and Wheelwright give more details of these changes, which they expand into four stages (summarized in Figure 5.2).

- **Stage 1 – Internally neutral.** This is the first stage of development, where operations are relatively new. They make a limited contribution to the organization and struggle not to hinder progress by making too many

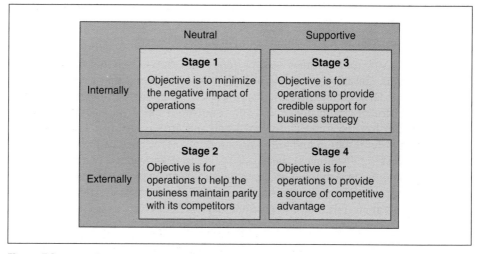

Figure 5.2 Four stages in operations strategy development

mistakes. The main aim is to minimize the negative impact of poor operations. Managers from other functions see operations as limiting their ability to work and compete effectively and, as there is little expertise within operations, they largely design the operations strategy. Operations managers generally look for improvements by tackling the causes of the biggest problems.

- **Stage 2 – Externally neutral.** Operations have now improved to the point where their performance is comparable with competitors. The guiding forces are industry standards, benchmarking and 'best practices', with an aim of maintaining parity with competitors. This means that the operations do not give a significant competitive advantage, but at least they allow the organization to compete effectively. Operations management has developed into a distinct function within the organization and has taken responsibility for the process and all questions of production. The process often needs capital investment to bring it up to the standards of main competitors and maintain this parity.

- **Stage 3 – Internally supportive.** Operations have now overtaken competitors and have reached the point of being the best in their industry. Operations have become a strength and developed distinctive capabilities. Operations management is well established as a core function, and interacts on equal terms with other functions. It gives credible support to the business strategy and clearly contributes to the organization's aims. This means that managers have to review proposed changes to both operations and business strategies to see how proposed changes in each would affect the other.

- **Stage 4 – Externally supportive.** This is the final stage of development, where operations are not only the best in their industry, but they have moved on to new levels, establishing a clear lead over competitors. This lead is so pronounced that it gives a major source of competitive advantage for the foreseeable future. The main aim is to redefine industry standards and customer expectations – thereby forming a barrier to potential competitors. Operations must continuously anticipate new practices, technologies and other developments so that they can maintain their pre-eminent position. Operations managers are largely responsible for their organization's continuing success, so they are involved in major decisions of other functions.

The benefit of this model is that managers can describe the current state of their operations, and advocate a direction in which they should move forward. If operations are comparable with industry standards, they are already in stage 2 and should look for a move to stage 3. Ideally operations managers should always aspire to improve and progress to following stages. But the model is clearly idealized and many organizations do not have the resources to leave the first stage, let alone achieve the pre-eminence suggested by the fourth.

CONTENTS OF AN OPERATIONS STRATEGY

We know that an operations strategy consists of all the decisions, policies, culture, goals, resources, actions etc., that relate to the long-term direction of operations. We also know that it can provide distinctive capabilities that give a competitive advantage. But how does it actually do this, and what type of decisions does it include?

To answer this we can use the model of an organization's strategy that we developed in chapter 1, but adjusted for operations. This gives us three elements.

An operations strategy contains:

1 the **purpose** of the operations, summarized in an operations mission
2 an expanded series of **goals and objectives**
3 **plans and methods** to achieve these goals.

Operations in a SemiGame BhP have a purpose of making products with the industry's lowest costs; goals include reducing the cost of defective units; corresponding objectives include a reduction of the cost of defects by 60 percent over two years; plans and methods show how to achieve this, including a new quality management programme. Beneath this operations strategy comes the range of tactical and operational decisions that turn the plans and methods into actual operations.

Operations mission

An operations mission gives a statement of the overall purpose and aims of operations. It defines the long-term direction of operations, and can describe related issues such as distinctive capabilities, values, expertise, skills, relationships, processes, ethics, and other relevant factors. It typically answers questions like:

- How do we support the business strategy?
- What markets do we work in?
- What type of products do we make?
- What type of process do we use?
- What are our distinctive capabilities?
- How do we measure success?
- What values do we have?

Sometimes the operations mission is a visionary statement of aspirations and beliefs; sometimes it is much more down to earth and says how products are made and delivered to customers. There is a tendency for operations missions to err in the direction of aspirations and give general ambitions rather than more concrete targets. An operations mission of 'developing operations excellence in core activities' is commendable – but it gives no direction and more useful mission statements might include down-to-earth ideas like 'making fault-free products' or 'eliminating stocks of work in progress'. Useful operations missions give a more precise statement of what the operations will achieve, typically mentioning performance in core capabilities, values, expertise, abilities, relationships, processes, and other relevant areas.

The idea of an operations mission is not new, but they are nowhere near as common as broader organizational missions. Nonetheless, they can serve a useful purpose, defining the overall direction and aims of operations, consolidating ideas into a single statement, telling everyone about these ideas, making sure that everyone is working towards the same goals, and generally giving the context for all other operations management decisions. Without such an explicit statement we have to infer its contents from past behaviour – or agreed policies, aims, methods and procedures that relate to operations.

Goals and objectives

The operations mission gives the broad aims of operations, and managers have to expand this into a series of more detailed goals and objectives. The goals give a series of more immediate, largely qualitative targets, and the objectives convert these into more specific, practical, quantitative ones. A mission of 'low cost operations' becomes a goal of continually reducing costs and an objective of reducing operating costs by 3 percent a year. Eriksson Systems has an operations mission that includes efficient operations; this leads to a series of goals, which include a target of increasing productivity; in turn, this leads to objectives that include an increase of labour productivity by 20 percent over the next four years.

As well as giving targets, goals and objectives also allow managers to monitor progress and check on actual progress. An increase of productivity of 2 percent in a year might show operations moving towards their target, but it might also show that some kind of action is needed to speed up progress.

The specific goals and objectives obviously depend on the type of operations, and in different circumstances almost any aspect of operations can become critical. Common goals relate to cost, capacity, output, quality, speed, flexibility, customer satisfaction, productivity, efficiency, and reliability.

Plans and methods to achieve the goals

The goals and objectives show what the operations want to achieve, so managers now have to design the methods that will best achieve them. The details of these methods depend on the type of organization. A goal of improving productivity encourages a call centre to look for ways of increasing the number of phone calls answered by each person, while a power station looks for ways of getting more electricity from each tonne of fuel, a theatre wants to fill more seats, and a chiropractor wants to treat more clients.

Sometimes the methods are straightforward, almost mechanical, such as 'using an improved method of scheduling that increases equipment utilization by 10 percent'. Sometimes they are fairly straightforward in principle, but more difficult in practice, such as 'introducing a new quality management programme' (which we discuss in chapter 10). Sometimes they are conceptually more complex, such as 'encouraging a culture of fast delivery'. Despite this variety, we can give broad suggestions for achieving the aims, and we discuss these in the next chapter.

IDEAS IN PRACTICE Bessinger Associates

Senior managers at Bessinger Associates believe that unless something is clearly written down there will inevitably be misunderstandings. So when they do an annual review of their operations strategy they present the results in a structured format. This has the following sections.

1 Executive summary.

2 Analysis of the higher strategies and the implications for operation.

3 Operations aims, goals and objectives.

4 Financial situation.

5 Analysis of the environment:
- Economic situation
- Market situation
- Competitive situation
- Opportunities and threats.

6 Analysis of the operations:

- Main processes
- Products
- Distinctive capabilities
- Strengths and weaknesses.

7 Choice of strategy:
- Review of key operations and alternatives
- Choice of operations strategy
- Rationale for this choice
- Effects of the strategy on products, processes, capacity, quality, flexibility, speed, etc.

8 Action plan:
- What is needed to implement the strategy
- What is the timetable for these activities
- Who is responsible for each activity
- What budget is allocated.

Source: Company records; Bessinger K., Strategy to action, Presentation to the German Academy of Operations Management, Berlin, 2005.

APPROACH TO DESIGN

We now have a model for the contents of an operations strategy, and can start thinking about its design. In chapter 1 we said that there were three main influences on the design of an organization's strategy – its purpose, the external environment and internal features. We can use the same model for an operations strategy, but adjusting these influences to the operations. In other words, we have to consider the purpose of operations, the operations environment and internal features of operations (illustrated in Figure 5.3).

1 *Operations' purpose* – shows what the operations want to achieve. We know that the overall aim of operations is to contribute to the organization's aims, and this breaks down into a series of more immediate aims, usually transmitted through the business strategy. This purpose can usefully be summarized in an operation's mission.

2 *External environment for operations* – defines all the factors that affect operations, but which operations managers cannot control. There are two parts to this.

   a Features that are outside the operations function, but still within the organization. For example, decisions about finance are made within the organization, and they certainly affect operations, but they are largely under the control of finance managers. Operations managers can play a part in these decisions and influence the outcomes, but they rarely have much control. Nonetheless, these features should provide a supportive environment, with all parts of the organization cooperating and working together to achieve the same overall purpose.

b Features that are completely outside the organization. These include all the external factors that affect operations, such as the market, customer demands, competition, economic conditions, regulations, legislation, social conditions and all the other factors that contribute to the broader environment. This defines a more competitive environment that constrains and affects activities, and over which operations managers have little influence.

3 *Internal features of operations* – which are the strengths, experience, knowledge, skills, expertise, etc., of operations that currently exist within the organization, or which can be developed for the future. These factors are all under the control of operations managers.

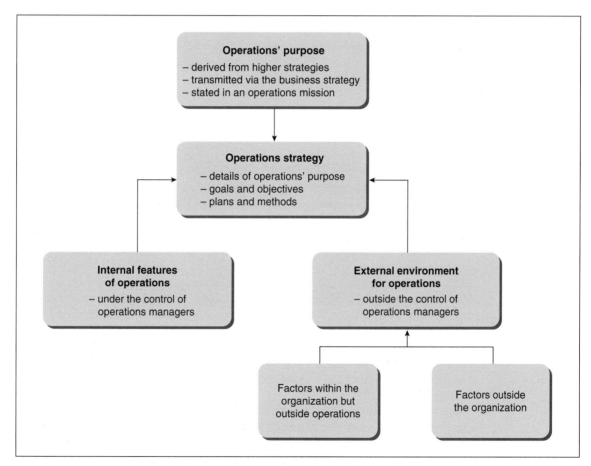

Figure 5.3 Influences in the design of an operations strategy

The design of an operations strategy should achieve its aims, while balancing the requirements of internal operations and their environment. This is an interesting observation, as it leads to two views of an operations strategy, depending on which of the two factors gets more emphasis. The first – a **market view** – emphasizes the external view of the environment, particularly the market. It says that operations managers should start by identifying customer demands and opportunities in the market, and then adjust the operations to supply products to satisfy these demands. Distinctive capabilities come from the activities that effectively and efficiently meet market demands.

The second – a resource-based view – emphasizes the internal operations. The **resources view** sees operations as using a collection of resources, and says that these should be used as well as possible. So operations managers build on their strengths to develop excellent performance, and then look for market sectors where this will give a significant advantage. Distinctive capabilities come from activities that are clearly better than competitors (Wernerfelt; Hayes *et al.*).

An operations strategy looks for distinctive capabilities.

- With a **market view** this comes from matching products closely to customer demand.
- With a **resources view** it comes from superior performance in operations.

MARKET VIEW

Product features

The market view of an operations strategy starts with managers analyzing the market, dividing it into coherent segments and identifying the most attractive segments in which to compete. Then they identify the precise requirements of customers in this market, design products with features that will meet this demand, and then design the best operations to make these products. This approach (which we mentioned in chapter 3) is described as **positioning**, with Kotler summarizing strategic design as 'segment, target, position'.

Distinctive capabilities come from the operations that precisely match products and processes to customer demands, with flexibility to satisfy different and varying demands (shown in Figure 5.4). And when an organization has established a competitive advantage, the market view's best way for defending it is to keep monitoring customer demands and adjusting products to meet their needs. As Porter (1996) says, 'A company can outperform rivals only if it can establish a difference that it can preserve. It must deliver greater value to customers or create comparable value at a lower cost, or do both.'

The market view has operations supplying products that customers view as better than rivals', but we know that Porter (1979, 1980, 1985) says that there are only three ways in which organizations can compete – product differentiation (making different products), cost leadership (making the same products at a lower price) and market niche (satisfying a small sector of the market). Some people add other categories,

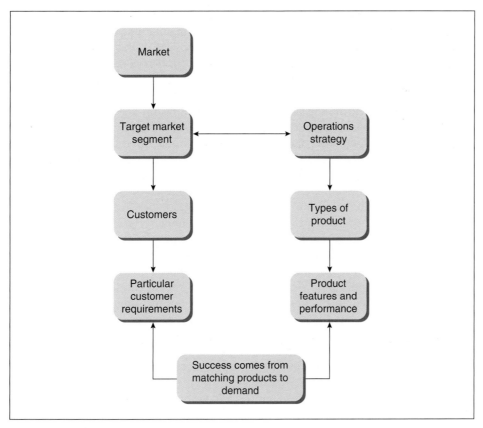

Figure 5.4 Market view of operations strategy

often dividing a niche strategy into those with a cost focus (supplying a niche market at low cost, such as a regional, low-cost supermarket) and those with a differentiation focus (producing a superior product to a narrowly defined market, such as country house hotels). The important point here is that the market and means of competing are defined in the business strategy. Then operations managers have to translate these requirements into an operations strategy, which includes the general features of products and the process that is used to make them. If the business strategy specifies a market segment and competing through price leadership, the operations strategy focuses on low-cost operations and products; if customers want fast delivery, the operations strategy emphasizes speed; if customers want convenient locations, managers carefully choose the places where operations are performed.

But there is an obvious problem in an operations strategy that focuses on meeting customer demand, as almost every customer – even in the smallest market segment – wants a different product. Each uses different criteria to judge a product and they will rarely agree about which really is best. Some people value a brand image and buy Leonidas Abelmann jeans; other people look at value for money and buy PriceRight jeans; others buy Levis because they fit; others buy any jeans they can find in a convenient shop. Even dividing the market into smaller and smaller segments does not really solve this problem, as people would really like products that are always customized to their individual needs. Organizations can rarely make such customized products – and they certainly cannot make them at the same time as maintaining any reasonable level of operations performance. The best that they can do is to make a range of similar – but different – ones that satisfy most customer needs. But now managers have to ask what features customers want in their products?

In principle, organizations should do everything well, giving customers all the features that they want, including good design, high quality, low cost, fast delivery, good customer service, reliability, and so on. In practice, they simply cannot deliver all of these complex and competing requirements, as they would put too many demands on operations. Instead, they have to compromise and focus on certain competitive features that appeal to enough customers, but still allow efficient operations. Rolls Royce, for example, made a strategic choice to emphasize the quality of their cars, Amazon focus on the breadth of their product range, FedEx focus on the speed of delivery, and O_2 focus on the price of their mobile phone services.

An operations strategy that focuses on specific competitive features, allows a realistic development of operations. But there is always the risk of focusing on features that customers do not really care about, or giving too little attention to features that customers view as important. This decision obviously needs careful market research. At the same time, managers can spread their risk by not focusing on a single feature, but on a bundle of related features, typically under a broader heading such as 'customer satisfaction' or 'customer service'. You can see this with PC manufacturers who focus on 'latest technology', which means that they design products that are simultaneously faster, more powerful, smaller, cheaper, more reliable, more attractive, and so on.

A operations strategy normally identifies a focus on certain types of feature. A traditional view of marketing says that the most important competitive features are the 'four Ps' – product, place, promotion and price. A broader view would add many other features, but for convenience we will classify these around five areas:

1 *Price* – usually low price, based on an operations strategy of low unit costs through efficient operations, economies of scale, eliminating waste, low overheads, etc.

2 *Quality* – with an operations strategy of supplying products that are always fault free, perform properly and meet – or exceed – customer expectations.

3 *Speed* – with operations that give short delivery times, fast flows of materials through supply chains, rapid design of new products, etc.

4 *Flexibility* – with operations that adjust to different customer tastes (giving mass customization) or work efficiently through rapid changes in demand.

5 *A whole range of other factors* – including style, design, availability, reliability, convenience, durability, technology, after sales service, location, financial arrangements, and so on.

Other people have proposed variations on this list of **competitive features**. Slack and Lewis, for example, add dependability (which we view as a part of quality), while Hayes and Wheelwright see speed as part of flexibility.

Each of these five competitive features is really a bundle of issues that we bring together under a convenient heading. When we say that an organization competes by, say, price, we really mean that it has an acceptably low price, gives value for money, has a price advantage over substitute products, customers accept the price as reasonable, operating costs are lower than industry norms, the price is high enough to give a profit, and so on.

And when operations focus on one of the competitive features, it obviously does not mean that they ignore all of the others. A baker might focus on low cost bread, but must still give high quality, deliver the bread quickly so that it is fresh, and so on. These broad categories of features still allow organizations to differentiate their products. For example, most supermarkets focus on price, but they still offer widely different services.

Qualifying and order-winning features

In principle, we can find the best features to put in a product by looking at the way that customers buy it. When you decide to buy something, you usually approach the purchase in three steps. Firstly, you decide what features you want in the product; then you look around to see which products can satisfy these needs, forming a shortlist of alternatives; then you look down this shortlist and choose the best one. This suggests three different types of feature (Hill).

- **Qualifying features** – are the features that a product must have before customers consider it, so these are the features needed to get onto the shortlist. Public transport, for example, must be fast, convenient and cheap, or people will not think of using it as an alternative to their own cars. The qualifying features define a threshold that products must reach, and if they fail to reach this standard, they will not win many customers. On the other hand, once a product reaches this threshold it gets on to shortlists – and raising the performance of qualifying features any higher is unlikely to affect sales.
- **Order-winning features** – which determine the product that customers choose from their shortlist. These are the key factors that make a customer view one product as superior to others. If several computers all have the qualifying factors, then price and reliability might be the order-winning factors that make a customer choose a particular one. Raising a product's performance in an order-winning factor means that it is more attractive to customers, and is likely to be more successful.
- **Less important features** – which do not significantly affect customers' views of a product's attractiveness, and affect neither the products ability either to reach a shortlist, or to be selected from the shortlist. Superior performance in these factors has little affect on sales, and is simply a waste of resources.

Qualifying features are usually more general, while order-winning factors are more specific. When you choose to open an account in a high-street bank, the qualifying factors might be broad security, reputation, efficiency, low fees and helpful staff. Then order-winning factors might be more specific and include a convenient location for the nearest branch, interest rates on current accounts, overdraft charges, and so on. An organization only remains competitive by having products with all the main qualifying factors (so that it gets on to most shortlists) and many of the order-winning factors (so that it wins a reasonable number of orders).

Relating product features to purchasing habits in this way gives a useful view, but it can be criticized. An important objection is that it only considers a single purchase, while many purchases occur as a series of transactions over an extended period. When a long-term relationship has grown between a seller and a buyer, each may overlook the occasional lapse to preserve the relationship. Suppose that a company has been happily buying materials from a local supplier for the past five years, but is approached by a competing supplier who offers a temporary, promotional price. The company might ignore this offer and continue using its usual supplier to preserve its harmonious relationship (of course, this does depend on the conditions and offer being made). So the relationship between supplier and buyer is more important than either qualifying or order-winning factors.

Another criticism of the description of qualifying and order-winning features is that organizations target products in more than one market segment, and they should focus on different features in each. It is difficult enough to match one product (or variations of the same product) to different market segments, and treating features in different ways makes this even more complicated.

A more basic criticism of the classification rejects it as unrealistic, saying that customers rarely adopt such a formal method of buying, but simply take a broad view of all products that they know about and see which one seems to have the best overall features. The suggestion of a shortlist and selection from this is, at best, a justification of a decision that is largely made by intuition and judgement.

While we are talking about criticisms, we should mention a more general criticism of the whole market view of an operations strategy. This says that a strategy based

IDEAS IN PRACTICE Rio Cosmetico

Many personal services give high levels of customization, with operations that are flexible enough to tailor products to the needs of individual customers. Nowhere is this more obvious than in medical treatment – particularly plastic surgery. This also demonstrates that customized service comes at a high cost.

Dr Raol Villablanca, opened a surgery in Rio de Janiero, Brazil in 1994. He is a leading practitioner of aesthetic facial plastic surgery, and is described as an innovator of modern oculoplastic, facial plastic and reconstructive surgery techniques. Most of his work is described as reconstructive surgery (which is loosely described as medical treatment) and cosmetic surgery (loosely described as improving patient appearance). Some of the most common procedures are:

Reconstructive surgery	Cosmetic surgery
Eyelid lift	Facelift
Eyelid Ptosis	Brow lift

Mohs skin cancer
Thyroid eye disease
Tumours and trauma
Facial / Bells Palsy
Tear duct surgery
Ectropion / entropion

Neck lift
Facial implants
Eyelid lift
Fat transfer
Lip augmentation
Laser resurfacing
Chemical peels

Most of the clinic's patients come from the greater Rio area. The first step in treatment is an interview at the clinic to see what the patient wants. At the same time the clinic explains what it can – and is prepared to – do. This is followed by a series of consultations, where the patient and clinic come to an agreement about the work to be done. At the end of this consultation Dr Villablanca performs the actual procedure.

Source: For obvious reasons, the details of this example have been changed

on customer demands inevitably leads an organization to become a follower rather than a market leader (Christensen; Christensen and Rayner). Listening to customers, making the products they want, and carefully recording market trends, means that organizations satisfy established needs and follow existing practices – but they ignore radical new products and processes, innovation or substantially new ideas. Eventually, the operations become too conservative, losing their competitive advantage and being overtaken by more innovative and adventurous competitors. For example, a postal service that kept listening to its customers would develop a faster, cheaper more reliable postal service – but it would have missed the move to electronic mail.

RESOURCES VIEW

Strategic resources

The market view of an operations strategy was dominant until the 1990s, when managers increasingly began to question an approach that always adjusted operations to fit a fixed environment. One motive for questioning the approach was that the market view does not explain why some organizations get good results in poor market conditions. If the market is poor, an organization can adjust its operations to fit in, but it can only get correspondingly poor results. In practice, though, many organizations seem to enter poor markets and then get good results (Rumelt). Issues like these encouraged managers to take another view of operations strategy, and they homed-in on a **resources view**, which shows how operations excellence can create new opportunities. This is not a new idea (see, for example Penrose in 1959), but it has only gained prominence relatively recently.

> A **resources view** says that an organization's success comes from the way that it owns and uses resources.

Often possession of a resource is enough to guarantee – or at least raise the probability of – success in the way that a management consultant succeeds because of their special knowledge and experience, a ferry company gains a competitive advantage from its fleet of ships, a bank uses its financial resources, a diamond mine owns mining rights, a manufacturer owns patents, and an electricity company owns a comprehensive supply network. There are, of course, many different types of resource and ways of classifying them. In the last chapter we mentioned one view of resources as transforming, transformed and intangible (Godfrey and Hill):

- **Transforming** – resources that actually do the work, but themselves remain largely unchanged, such as machines, equipment, software, people, systems, buildings, etc.
- **Transformed** – inputs that are changed in some way during the operations, usually raw materials, components, work in progress, products or customers.

- **Intangible** – which might be:
  - impersonal resources, such as reputation, financial strength, contracts, patents, and brands, or
  - human resources, such as experience, knowledge, skills, contacts, relationships with suppliers.

A more direct classification (Craig and Grant) lists resources as:

- **Physical** – plant and equipment, facilities, locations, access to raw materials.
- **Financial** – cash flow, borrowing power, sources of capital, debtors and creditors.
- **Technology** – in products and processes, illustrated by patent, copyrights, trade secrets, R&D, etc.
- **Human** – number and type of employee, their experience, knowledge, skills, loyalty, flexibility, adaptability, management skills, etc.
- **Relationship** – with customers, suppliers, distributors and other stakeholders.
- **Reputation** – goodwill, brands, trademarks, market acceptance.

Resources that are particularly important to an organization and have a strategic impact are its **strategic resources**. These can include any type of resource, but they are usually the ones needed for core operations. Slack and Lewis say that they tend to share four common properties of being:

1 *Scarce* – so that not every organization can get the same resources (such as knowledge, specialized production facilities, and many natural resources).
2 *Difficult to move* – so that competitors cannot simply acquire the resources by buying them or recruiting staff (with major facilities, loyal employees, culture, infrastructure, etc.).
3 *Difficult to copy* – so that competitors cannot simply copy products and operations (perhaps involving patented products, proprietary operations, specialized information, etc.).
4 *Difficult to substitute* – so that competitors cannot bypass their lack of certain resources by using substitutes (with leading brands, efficient supply chains, detailed knowledge, etc.).

The essential features of strategic resources are that their possession gives a long-term advantage, and that competitors cannot acquire equivalent resources. This is why R&D is a traditional source of strategic resources, as it gives unique products that are protected by patents. In the same way, specialized knowledge is difficult to acquire and detailed information about, say, individual customer preferences becomes a strategic resource for an airline. In different circumstances, a secret recipe for a drink, large-scale facilities that need huge capital investment, patented inventions, copyright material, employees with unique skills, formats for software, technology that has become an industry standard, brand loyalty, specialized knowledge, research findings, and almost anything else, can become a strategic resource.

Resources audit

It seems strange, but many managers have little idea of the resources they have available. They can probably list the raw materials needed by products, but may not appreciate the role of less tangible resources, such as knowledge, information, experience and culture. The way to get an understanding of all available resources is to run a **resource audit**. This identifies the resources that an organization already has, and those that could be available if needed. It answers more detailed questions like, 'What resources do we have?', 'Which of these are unique?', 'Which have a strategic impact?', 'What is their condition (quality, quantity, age, etc.)?' and 'How do we use them?'

A resource audit also identifies the resources that are needed for a particular operations strategy, and identifies gaps between availability and needs. Then managers have to devise plans for overcoming these shortages. This is easy for some resources that are simply bought on the open market, but it can be more difficult for others that are in short supply or only come at an unacceptable price. Perhaps it is generally more difficult to acquire intangible resources, such as knowledge and experience that develop over time.

Of course, managers always have to balance the cost of resources with their benefits. And they always have limited funds, so if they decide to buy more of one resource, it inevitably means that they can afford less of another. If managers decide to buy more of resource A it means that they can buy less of resource B, and by implication the benefit from having more of A is greater than the loss from having less of B. But they still give up some benefit from having less of B, and this lost benefit is measured by the **opportunity cost**.

Suppose that operations managers could acquire three resources but they only have enough funds for two. They must clearly give up the least attractive resource. If the three resources have expected benefits of €1 million, €2 million and €3 million, the managers should acquire the last two. The opportunity cost is €1 million, as this is the amount given up by not acquiring the third resource. Of course, if it costs less than €1 million to acquire the third resource, the economic argument says that managers should acquire it anyway as they will get a net benefit. So the opportunity cost is the maximum reasonable price to pay for resources. If the actual cost of acquiring resources is lower than the opportunity cost of not buying them, the difference shows the organization's incentive to buy. When the actual cost is higher than the opportunity cost, there is a disincentive to buy.

Management of resources

Although we have been emphasizing the ownership of resources, strategic resources might not necessarily be in short supply. The supply of vegetables is a strategic resource for Campbell's soup, but anyone can buy these on the open market. Campbell's success comes from the way that it uses its resources. So it is generally not just the possession of resources that is important, but also the way that they are managed. You might be lucky enough to own a warehouse or similar facility – but this has no value when it is unused and deteriorating, and it only becomes a benefit when you use it properly. So there are three basic decisions about resources:

- What resources to acquire.
- How to allocate resources between competing operations.
- How to manage resources and use them effectively and efficiently.

IDEAS IN PRACTICE e-Management Principles

e-Management Principles is a firm of consultants based in Northern Europe. They have many years of experience in running resource audits for businesses, for which they have developed a standard format. This analyzes ten types of resource:

1 *Financial* – everything to do with money including sales, cash flow, profit, profit margins, overheads, operating costs, debt, etc.

2 *Human* – everything to do with human resources including number of people, skills, costs, training, recruitment, morale, motivation, etc.

3 *Management* – everything to do with the managers and decision makers, including number of people, skills, costs, experience, motivation, etc.

4 *Organizational structure* – everything to do with responsibilities, reporting and relationships.

5 *Purchase and acquisition* – everything to do with the inward flow of materials,

including suppliers, transport, raw material stocks, etc.

6 *Facilities* – everything to do with available facilities, including buildings, equipment, types, amounts, ownership, quality, flexibility, etc.

7 *Operations* – everything to do with making the product, including processes, technology, efficiency, R&D, innovation, etc.

8 *Distribution* – everything to do with the outward flow of products, including supply chain structure, facilities, transport, finished goods stocks, etc.

9 *Markets* – everything to do with customers and sales, including sales, market share, brands, image, reputation, etc.

10 *Information* – everything to do with information flows through the organization, including the information system, technology, levels of information, availability, etc.

Sources: Internal company reports

This is the basis of a resources view of operations strategy (illustrated in Figure 5.5). Success comes from both ownership and proper management of resources. In particular, resources are used so efficiently that they build distinctive capabilities – with **operations excellence** giving superior performance that sets an organization apart from its competitors. For example, a company that is excellent at designing new products very quickly can develop a distinctive capability based on innovation; the distinctive capability of the Cooperative bank is based on operations excellence in its responsible, friendly and personal service; the distinctive capability of Wal-Mart is selling goods at the lowest possible price; BMW mass produces high quality cars; Whizz Air has low cost flights.

Operations excellence can occur in almost any activities, but Katz gave a list of the ten most common sources, and we can expand this to include:

1 R&D, new product development and innovation

2 design and performance of products

3 design of the process used to make products

4 low costs, efficiency and high productivity

5 in-depth knowledge of technologies

6 skills, knowledge, experience and abilities of employees

7 customer service

8 fast response to changing demands and needs

9 supply chain management and flows of materials

10 relationships with customers, suppliers and others in the supply chain

11 procurement and trading in commodities

12 marketing, promotions and merchandizing

13 ability to influence legislation.

The aim of operations excellence is to give distinctive capabilities that set an organization apart from its competitors. By definition, there is no point in doing minor or peripheral activities well, so managers should aim for excellence in their core operations. These are the relatively small number of operations that are central to their success – in the way that playing football is central to Manchester United

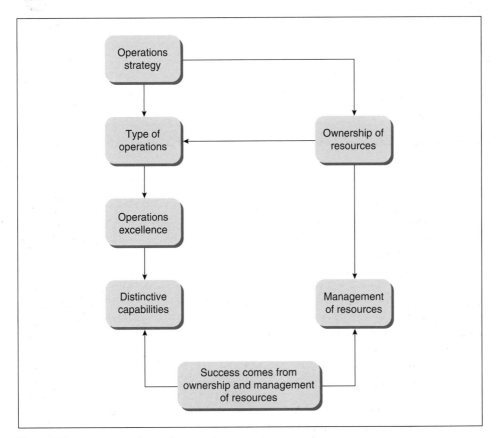

Figure 5.5 Resources view of operations strategy

Football Club and selling clothes is central to Next. To succeed, an organization must do these core operations well – giving core capabilities – and it should look in these areas for operations excellence to give distinctive capabilities (a concept discussed by Selznick in 1957).

We can connect the use of resources to the product's competitive features described in the market view above, and suggest that useful areas for operations excellence relate to price, speed, quality, flexibility or a range of other relevant areas. Then the product features demanded by customers are paralleled by performance areas for operations; a customer demand for cheap products has the same effect as a resources demand for low unit costs, and so on. Table 5.2 illustrates these links between concerns in market and resource views.

Wherever managers try to build a distinctive capability, it will not come from copying other organizations in the same industry. There are obvious benefits from benchmarking other operations and adopting best practices, but this only gives the same performance as competitors. To get superior performance, operations have to do things better, and this means focusing on their own resources and developing their own strengths. This route to a distinctive capability is usually steady and evolutionary rather than dramatically fast. It can start by identifying individuals with particular skills and expertise, and forming them into groups to create organizational ability. With experience, this ability grows into a competence and capability, and when performance is better than rivals it emerges as a distinctive capability – built on a 'centre for excellence'. And with a resources view, the best way to defend this advantage is to continually improve operations, so that competitors are always having to catch up.

Table 5.2 Examples of concerns in the product features/performance areas

	Market view	Resources view
Price	Cheap to buy, low running costs, high added value, fees, associated costs	Low cost operations, low unit costs, high productivity, efficient operations, quantity discounts
Quality	Customer satisfaction, high specifications, no faults, reliable service, accuracy of information	No errors in operations, no disruptions, conformance to specifications, quality programmes
Speed	Short lead time, short queues, response time, total time in the system	Fast throughput, low stocks, efficient flow of materials, utilization of capacity
Flexibility	Customization, response to varying demand, consistent product despite uncertainties	Efficient new product development, wide range, variable capacity, variable operating speed
Other features	Aesthetic value, helpfulness, colours, intellectual content, status, etc.	Staff training, intellectual property, proprietary content, associated advice, etc.

IDEAS IN PRACTICE McDonald's

Two brothers, Dick and Mac McDonald, opened their first fast food restaurant in 1940. Their first franchisee was Ray Kroc, who opened a restaurant in Des Plaines, Illinois in 1955. In 1959 the corporation adopted the motto of 'Quality, Service, Cleanliness and Value', which it still maintains. In 1962 Ray Kroc bought the McDonald's concept from the brothers and guided the McDonald's Corporation to become one of the world's most recognized symbols with a revenue approaching $20 billion a year.

The company takes a resources view, with operations excellence as the foundation for its success. The original concept had efficient operations to give very fast service for a limited menu. People who had been accustomed to long delays for waiter service, suddenly found that they could be served within seconds of entering the restaurant. McDonald's offered another way of eating out – rather than a long, formal process with lots of waiting, they could drop into a restaurant and be eating a meal faster than they could buy a bar of chocolate. The limited menu was designed to make standard operations

easier and faster, with restaurants around the world serving the well-known mixture of Big Mac, Quarter Pounder, Chicken McNuggets, Egg McMuffin, French Fries, McFlurry and so on.

McDonald's take a resources view of their operations strategy. They work in almost every significant economy of the world, but maintain virtually the same format for operations. You can walk into a McDonald's anywhere and know what the restaurant will serve, what it will taste like, what its colour scheme will be, what everything will look like, and how everything is done. The distinctive capabilities are based on very efficient operations for preparing and serving meals quickly.

Their formula clearly works, as McDonald's has expanded to become one of the world's best-known brands, with a leading share of the branded quick-service restaurant industry. It has more than 30,000 restaurants in 119 countries, serving 50 million people a day.

Sources: Websites: www.mcdonalds.com; www.mcdonalds.co.uk

Operational performance

We have talked about operations excellence, but an assumption here is that managers can gauge – and preferably measure – the **performance** of their operations. If they cannot take these measures, they have no idea how good the operations really are, whether they are improving, whether they meet targets, or how they compare with competitors. An old maxim says, 'what you can't measure, you can't manage'. The problem, of course, is finding what to measure and how to measure it.

There are many possible measures of performance – gross profit, profitability, return on investment, return on assets, share price, price to earnings ratio, productivity, sales, market share, stock turnover, output per employee, and so on. Many of these relate to finance. These financial measures can give a broad view of the organization and allow direct comparisons for judging management skills – and they also sound convincing and are easy to measure. On the negative side, they concentrate on past rather than current performance, are slow to respond to changes, rely on accounting conventions, and do not record important aspects of operations. And they might show overall performance, but give no idea of how to improve things. This is like doctors taking your temperature – a fever shows that you are unwell, but does not show how to get you better.

A resources view of strategy needs a more direct measure of operations. It typically searches for areas where resources are wasted, and then looks for ways of removing this waste – with the aim of operational excellence achieved by reducing the use of resources to a minimum. This is often phrased in terms of working effectively and efficiently. Being effective means using the resources for the right purpose, so that they contribute to operations' goals; being efficient means using a minimum amount of resources to achieve the goals. Being effective is 'doing the right thing', while being efficient is 'doing the thing right'.

Figure 5.6 summarizes the possible combinations of efficiency and effectiveness. As you can see, being efficient is not enough in itself, as operations might be moving efficiently in the wrong direction. This is rather like motivation, which again is not enough in itself, as people can be highly motivated to do the wrong things.

Two measures of performance that are related to efficiency are capacity, which measures the potential output from a process, and utilization, which shows how much of this capacity is actually used (we return to these themes in chapter 12). Perhaps the most widely used measure of operations performance is productivity. There are several kinds of productivity, with the broadest picture coming from total productivity, which is:

$$\text{Total productivity} = \frac{\text{total output}}{\text{total input}}$$

In principle, any value of total productivity above one – usually reported as 100 percent – shows that the operations have added value. Unfortunately, this measure has several serious problems. To start with, the input and output must use consistent

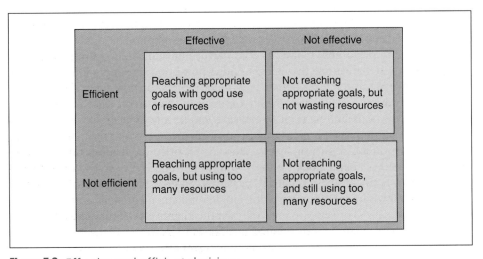

Figure 5.6 Effective and efficient decisions

units, so they are normally translated into units of currency. Then values depend on the accounting conventions used and we no longer have an objective measure. Another problem is finding values for *all* the inputs and outputs. Some inputs are difficult to value, such as sunlight and reliability – as are some outputs, such as pollution and reputation. We could say that we are only interested in the important factors – but then someone has to decide which these are, and again the measure loses its objectivity.

Because of these difficulties, most organizations measure partial productivity, which relates the outputs to a single type of input. Also, they are primarily interested in the output of products, so they ignore all secondary outputs, such as waste, by-products and intangibles. Then partial productivity measures the volume of products made by each unit of a chosen resource used.

$$\text{Partial productivity} = \frac{\text{Amount of products made}}{\text{Amount of a single resource used}}$$

The four main types of partial productivity are:

1 *Equipment productivity* – such as the number of units made per machine hour, miles flown per aeroplane, or customers served per petrol pump.

2 *Labour productivity* – such as the number of units made per person, tonnes produced per shift, and order shipped per hour worked.

3 *Capital productivity* – such as the number of units made for each pound of investment, sales per unit of capital, or production per dollar invested in equipment.

4 *Energy productivity* – such as the number of units made per kilowatt-hour of electricity, units made for each euro spent on energy, and value of output per barrel of oil used.

The example of Parkvale Logistics Center shows how different measures of productivity can give conflicting views. They are measuring different things, so you would expect some to rise while others fall – in the same way that driving a car faster than usual increases the miles per hour, but reduces the miles per litre of fuel; refurbishing a shop increases sales per square metre, but reduces sales per pound invested; automating a process increases labour productivity but reduces capital productivity.

You can also see why it is not always a good idea to raise productivity. We might improve one type of productivity that has little relevance to overall performance, and actually damage the wider organization. When Pradesh Gupta replaced old knitting machines in his factory with sophisticated new ones, his labour productivity rose sharply. But wages only accounted for 7 percent of his costs, and the more critical measure was capital productivity. His income did not cover the increased debt charges and he soon went out of business.

Each measure of performance looks at one thing, and to get a broader view we have to balance several measures that look at different aspects of operations. Managers might set a range of targets that are phrased in terms of productivity, utilization, cost, efficiency, quality, capacity, use of processes, geographical cover, technology, or a host of other terms. Heizer and Render take an optimistic view and say that every organization must achieve at least:

- **High product quality** – measured by customer satisfaction.
- **High capacity utilization** – showing the proportion of available capacity that is actually used.
- **High operating efficiency** – giving the ratio of actual output to expected output.
- **Low investment** – measured by the amount of capital needed to produce a unit of sales.
- **Low direct unit cost** – relative to competitors.

Some of these are more difficult to measure than others. For example, if you look at the productivity of a school it is easy to calculate the ratio of pupils to staff, but it is almost impossible to get equivalent measures for the academic standards, learning skills, teaching quality, and so on. Unfortunately, people tend to concentrate on the easier measures and forget the other factors that may be more important. An authority might measure the performance of a police force by counting the number of crimes solved per employee – but this opposes the preferred solution of preventing all crime and having none to solve.

Improving performance

These measures often relate to performance in the shorter term, so it is worth emphasizing their long-term significance. The point of measuring performance in the last month, say, is to monitor progress and see how operations are moving towards their longer-term objectives. The efficient use of resources certainly has a strategic impact and determines the long-term success of any organization. So the general aim is for continually improving performance.

Rather like quality management (which we discuss in chapter 10) performance improvement has moved from its largely technical roots to a much broader role. It has moved from asking basic questions like, 'How well are we doing work?' to the more important, 'How do we compare with competitors, are we continuing to improve, and how can we get even better?'

In practice, there are many ways of improving performance, and managers have to evaluate the alternatives and choose the approaches that best match their company's culture, capabilities and competitive needs. The usual approach starts by describing current operations, analyzing them in detail, finding ways of overcoming problems, making comparisons with other operations, and generally trying to make things better. This typically makes changes to:

- **Operations** – with improved ways of doing activities in the process.
- **Facilities and equipment** – with upgrades, automation, improved layouts, more efficient material flows, new premises, etc.
- **Systems** – providing information, monitoring performance, setting new standards, etc.
- **People** – through education, training, incentives, participation, work redesign, etc.

We return to this theme of improvement in chapter 11.

IDEAS IN PRACTICE Parkvale Logistics Center

Joan Mitchell is the operations manager at Parkvale Logistics Center in Seattle, Washington. The company has a business strategy of continuously improving performance, and each year Joan prepares a report to show how the operations support this. In 2004 some raw figures for performance of the 'A Facility' showed the following results.

	2003	2004
number of units processed ('000s)	50	65
added value per unit	$20	$21
raw materials used	10,100 kg	13,100 kg
cost of raw materials ('000s)	$141	$180
hours worked	12,300	12,500
direct labour costs ('000s)	$615	$681
energy used	10,000 kWh	14,000 kWh
energy cost ('000s)	$58	$83
other costs ('000s)	$122	$117

The total productivity in 2003 was (working in thousands of dollars):

$$\frac{\text{total outputs}}{\text{total inputs}} = \frac{50 \times 20}{141 + 615 + 58 + 122} = 1.07$$

By 2004 this had risen to 1,365 / 1,061 = 1.29, showing that volume throughput, value added and productivity had risen. This overall figure hid some interesting variations. For example, the energy cost per unit had risen by 10 percent from 58/50 = $1.16 to 83/65 = $1.28. Some other measures are:

	2003	2004	percentage increase
total productivity	1.07	1.29	21
units/kg of raw material	4.95	4.96	–
units/$ of raw material	0.35	0.36	3
units/hour	4.07	5.20	28
units/$ of labour	0.08	0.10	19
units/kWh	5	4.64	–7
units/$ of energy	0.86	0.78	–9

In general, labour productivity has risen, raw materials productivity has stayed about the same, and energy productivity has fallen.

Source: Mitchell J., Measuring operations performance, Presentation to the Western Operations Forum, Calgary, 2005

COMBINING THE TWO VIEWS

Strategic fit

Now we have described an operations strategy in terms of its markets, emphasizing the external view of gaining a competitive advantage by supplying products that closely match customer demands. And we have described it in terms of its use of resources, emphasizing the internal view of operations excellence giving distinctive capabilities. Of course, these views are not mutually exclusive, and the reality is that managers have to design operations strategies that achieve both of them. To put it simply, they have to make products that customers want, while ensuring effective and efficient use of resources. This long-term match between the internal operations and the external environment is the **strategic fit**.

> ● A **strategic fit** occurs when managers design internal operations that are in harmony with their external environment.

We introduced the idea of strategic fit for corporate and business strategies in chapter 3, and can now extend the concept to an operations strategy. And we can illustrate its principles with a simple model that considers only one factor. Suppose we rate the environmental, or market's, requirement for this factor on a linear scale of 0 to 100 – and then we rate the organization's actual performance on the same scale. If the market demands a value of, say, 30 and the organization's actual performance is also 30, there is a perfect strategic fit (shown as point X in Figure 5.7) – and any other point on the diagonal also represents a perfect strategic fit. If the organization achieves a score of less than 30, it is not meeting environmental demands (shown as any point above the line of perfect fit, such as point A). Then there is a risk that competitors will move to give better customer satisfaction. If the organization achieves more than the environmental demands it has excess capability and is probably wasting resources (shown as any point below the line of perfect fit, such as point B). Then there is a risk that internal operations are not being used to capacity and resources are being wasted.

Customers generally become more demanding over time, so their demands move vertically upwards in Figure 5.7. As organizations want to maintain an advantage over the long term, they must look for continuous improvement and move to the right. The result is a long-term movement up the diagonal, say from point X to point Y.

We have assumed that managers always want the best fit between their operations and the environment. But there is an argument that the fit can be too good. An organization with a worse fit will keep looking for changes so that its operations get better through continuous improvement. But when there is a near perfect fit there is no incentive to change operations or look for improvements. For a time, this does not matter, but eventually the demands of the environment change while the operations have inertia and remain fixed, and eventually the organization falls behind more flexible

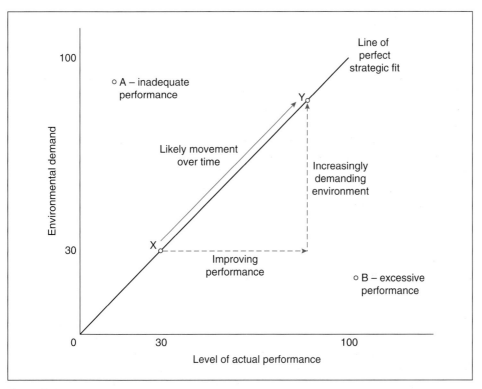

Figure 5.7 Concept of strategic fit

competitors (Leonard-Barton). This is not an entirely convincing argument, but it might have some validity.

Balance and reconciliation

With strategic fit operations make products that customers want (satisfying the market view) and are efficient (satisfying the resources view) as shown in Figure 5.8. Sometimes these two views are balanced and both can be satisfied equally by the same operations. For example, customers want high quality products, while operating costs are lowest when they make products with no defects – so the requirements of both are satisfied by ensuring high quality. Similarly, when a market view suggests faster customer service and a resources view suggests lower stocks, then just-in-time operations can satisfy both requirements.

Often, though, the two views give different requirements and it is impossible to satisfy both of them completely. There is a fundamental conflict between the aims of customers who want to pay less than a product is worth, and suppliers who want to charge more than it is worth. This conflict appears in many – usually more subtle – forms, perhaps with operations preferring long production runs of a standard product, while customers prefer a wide range of distinctive products tailored to their specific needs. And even if there is a good strategic fit, there is no guarantee that this inevitably

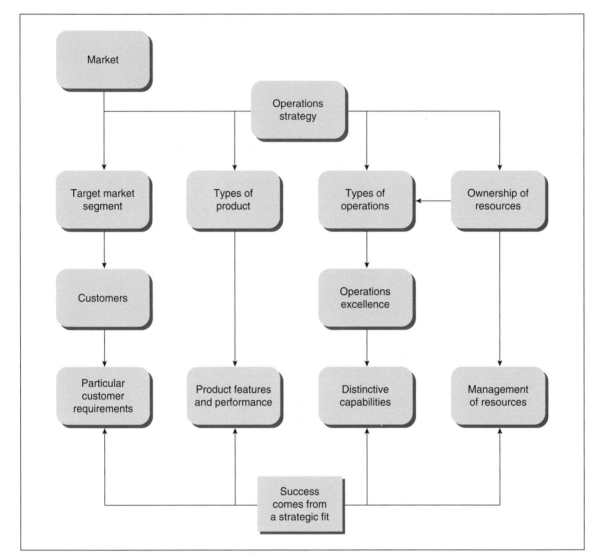

Figure 5.8 Concept of strategic fit

leads to distinctive capabilities that give an advantage over competitors. In reality, there are many organizations that work in harmony with their environments, but have no features that really distinguish them from competitors.

So the operations strategy must look for a compromise that gives acceptable levels of both customer satisfaction and resource use. Wild (2002, 2003) refers to this as 'balancing the customer service objective with the resource utilization objective'. This compromise might, for example, employ enough people to give good service during busy periods, and accept that their productivity is lower during quieter times; or making a loss on some activities that are needed to boost long-term relations with customers. This kind of compromise is such a fundamental part of management decisions that it is difficult to understand Skinner's comment in 1969 that, 'Few executives realize the existence of trade-offs.'

A basic problem with finding the best compromise is that managers have to understand the requirements of both operations and their environment, and these can be very complex. If we consider the environment, it is difficult for managers to get a detailed understanding of all its intricate features, unravelling the structure of the market, finding exactly what customers want, analyzing possible actions of competitors, identifying all the stakeholders, considering the effect of legislation, and every other aspect of external influences. Then they have to monitor, analyze and respond to rapidly changing conditions – which might occur because of sudden moves by competitors, or customers, or for no apparent reason at all. And the difficulties are more pronounced because each organization works in many different markets, each with different features and requirements.

Managers also face difficulties with operations, as many do not really understand their own operations or their capabilities and potential. This is obvious in many high technology industries, where managers do not really understand the underlying science, but is apparent in other industries. For example, the managers of Sedgefield Bus Company ran a standard service for many years until protracted financial problems in the 1990s caused them to close the company. But during their problems, they only ever looked for adjustments to their operating schedules, and never considered adding related services, or revising working practices to improve productivity, or considered their social function, or developed new opportunities for expansion. They understood their existing operations, but not their potential for development. This is common, as managers generally spend their time dealing with immediate problems and have little opportunity to step back and consider broader issues or radical new alternatives.

So managers have a limited understanding of both their operations and environment, so it is not surprising that they often cannot see how to achieve a strategic fit. But our assumption is that an organization is more likely to succeed when everything works smoothly together. As Stacey says, 'organizations are successful when they intentionally achieve internal harmony and external adaptation to their environment'. But there are really two ways of getting strategic fit. The first is the one that we have assumed, where managers adjust their operations to fit into a fixed environment; but the other is to assume some flexibility in the environment and allow operations to make some changes, even if these are limited in scope. Hamel and Prahalad describe this effect as **strategic stretch** (see also Prahalad and Hamel).

The argument behind strategic stretch is that managers should not just look for a good fit in an existing environment, but they should develop new capabilities that can actually change conditions. For example, they might develop products that change existing markets and even create new ones. When Macintosh developed iPod they did not just create a product for an existing market, but they created an entirely new market. So managers should define an operations strategy that stretches both the operations and their environment into new shapes.

There are arguments in favour of both fit and stretch, and the real picture is usually somewhere in between (illustrated in Figure 5.9). Managers start by analyzing

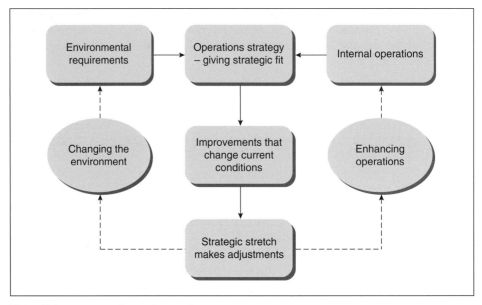

Figure 5.9 Strategic fit and stretch

IDEAS IN PRACTICE BT

BT is one of the world's leading suppliers of communications to customers in Europe, the Americas and Asia Pacific. It employs over 100,000 people around the world, has more than 20 million customers, and has a turnover approaching £20 billion.

This is a huge company with long experience in meeting customer demands and running efficient operations, so it is not surprising that its strategy considers both of these. Their continuing growth is 'fuelled by eight strategic imperatives', most of which seem to include elements from both market and resource views. The imperatives are:

- **network IT services** – using excellent networking skills to find innovative ways of meeting customers' IT needs;
- **mobility solutions** – offering mobile services through a partnership with Vodafone giving a mobile virtual network operator;
- **delivering broadband** – with 5 million lines installed by 2005;

- **twenty-first century network** – to update the network, giving a radically simplified structure, better performance and lower costs;
- **cost efficiency** – continuing to look for cost reductions, with annual savings between £300–400 million;
- **relentless customer focus** – valuing each customer and focusing on improving satisfaction;
- **defend traditional business** – fixed-voice telephone calls are in a relative decline, but they are still fundamental to BT's business and they compete aggressively;
- **employees** – the company relies on its employees and has values of being trustworthy, helpful, inspiring, straightforward and caring.

Sources: Annual Report, BT, London, 2005; Website at www.bt.com

operations capabilities and the environment, and then design a strategy that gives a reasonable fit. Then they look for improvements that move away from the current conditions and both enhance performance and open new opportunities – stretching both the environment and operations. We will look at this approach to design in the next chapter.

Chapter review

- The operations strategy of an organization consists of all the long-term goals, plans, policies, culture, resources, decisions and actions that relate to the operations.

- An operations strategy forms a link between higher strategies and more detailed operations. It can contribute to the higher strategies at several levels, ranging from simple implementation through to being a driving force.

- The overall aim of an operations strategy is to contribute to the business strategy – and hence the corporate strategy and mission. This leads to a series of more immediate aims. None of these are static but continually evolve over time.

- The contents of an operations strategy include an operations mission, goals and objectives, and plans and methods for achieving these. These can be presented in many different forms.

- Major influences on the design of an operations strategy are the purpose of operations (usually transmitted through the business strategy), internal features of operations and external operations environment. Operations managers generally emphasize the last two points, reconciling the different requirements of the market and resources.

- A market view of the operations strategy focuses on its ability to meet customer demand, with competitive advantage coming from designing products with the features that customers want.

- A resources view of the operations strategy focuses on its ability to manage operations well, developing operations excellence. This superior performance gives a distinctive capability and competitive advantage.

- Operations must use their resources effectively and efficiently. There are several related measures of performance, with the most common based on productivity.

- An operations strategy has to satisfy both the market and resources view, giving both acceptable customer service and acceptable resource use. When the operations are in harmony with the environment, there is strategic fit.

CASE STUDY **CNN**

In the 1980s, most countries had a small number of broadcast television networks. But markets were becoming less regulated and new services were broadly encouraged. Anyone starting a new channel could look for a strategic fit for their operations, analyzing the environment and designing operations that would achieve their goals. Because of the high start-up costs, this inevitably meant appealing to a wide audience and adapting strategies that had proved successful for other television companies. In the UK, for example, the five broadcast networks all offered similar services, with differences in detail rather than fundamental concepts.

Then cable television – and later satellite broadcasting – reduced the cost of creating a television network. The result has been a huge increase in the number of networks, with most catering to more specialized interests.

In the mid-1970s Ted Turner decided to form Cable News Network (CNN) as a specialized news service that gives 24-hour coverage of news to cable viewers. Initially, there was considerable uncertainty about whether there was enough demand for such a service, but it has clearly been a success. The service is coordinated from the CNN Center in Atlanta, Georgia and is now available in almost a million US hotel rooms and 100 million US households – and boasts of 1.5 billion viewers in over 212 countries and territories around the world. Ted Turner extended the ideas of CNN to form other networks, including, TBS Superstation, Turner Network Television, Cartoon Network, Boomerang,

Turner South, Turner Classic Movies, and the WB Network. These companies formed the core of The Turner Broadcasting System. In the complex world of media companies, The Turner Broadcasting System is now part of Turner Entertainment, which was bought by Time Warner in 1996.

The news service has extended to more specialized forms, such as CNN Headline News, CNN en Español, CNN Turk, CNBC, CNN International, CNN Plus, CNN Sports – and also extended to other formats, such as CNN.com and CNN Airport Network. Since its formation the CNN format has inspired many other television news services, including Al Jazeera, BBC News 24, CBC Newsworld, Newsnet, Euronews, FOX News, ITV News Channel, Le Canal Nouvelles, NewsWorld International and Sky News.

Questions

- How would you describe the operations strategy of CNN? Does this take a predominantly market or resources view?
- Why did CNN adopt these strategies, and what are the benefits?
- To what extent did CNN change its markets, rather than match its operations to existing markets?
- What options does this leave for other television networks?

Sources: TimeWarner Inc annual report, New York, 2004; Websites at www.cnn.com; www.edition.cnn.com; www.wikimirror.com

Discussion questions

1 Does every organization have an operations strategy?

2 Customers are only interested in products. If they like a product, the supplier does well: if they do not like a product, the supplier is in trouble. Any talk about strategy, process, human resources, and other peripherals is just diverting the organization's attention away from making products that customers like. Do you agree with this?

3 What would you expect to see in an operations strategy? How does an operations strategy fit in with other strategies?

4 What are the main differences between a market view and a resources view of operations strategy? Does this distinction make sense?

5 How does an organization decide which features to add to its products?

6 How can you measure the performance of operations?

7 All organizations in the same industry are likely to have similar operations and they work in the same environment. So managers looking for a strategic fit will inevitably design the same – or at least very similar – strategies. How can one organization get an advantage over its competitors?

8 Operations managers have to accept the environment in which they work, as they have no control over it. But the basis of strategic stretch is that the environment can be changed. How is this possible?

Useful websites

www.bt.com
www.cnn.com
www.edition.cnn.com
www.mcdonalds.co.uk
www.mcdonalds.com
www.wikimirror.com

References

Christensen C.M., The innovator's dilemma, Harvard Business School Press, Boston, MA, 1997.

Christensen C.M. and Rayner M.E., The innovator's solution, Harvard Business School Press, Boston, MA, 2003.

Craig J.C. and Grant R.M., Strategic management, Kogan Page, London, 1993.

Godfrey P.C. and Hill C.W.L., The problems of unobservables in strategic management research, Strategic Management Journal, vol 16(7), pp 23–45, 1995.

Hamel G. and Prahalad C., Competing for the future, Harvard Business School Press, Boston, MA, 1994.

Harrison M., Operations management strategy, Pitman, London, 1993.

Hayes R.J. and Wheelwright S.C., Restoring our competitive edge, John Wiley, New York, 1984.

Hayes R.H., Pisano G.P. and Upton D.M., Strategic operations, The Free Press, New York, 1996.

Heizer J. and Render B., Operations management (7th edition), Prentice Hall, Englewood Cliffs, NJ, 2004.

Hill T., Manufacturing strategy (third edition), Palgrave Macmillan, Basingstoke Hants, 2000.

Katz R.L., Skills of an effective administrator, Harvard Business Review, September–October, pp 90–102, 1974.

Kotler P., Marketing management (12th edition), Prentice-Hall International, Englewood Cliffs, NJ, 2005.

Krajewski L.J and Ritzman L.P., Operations management (7th edition), Prentice Hall Reading, MA, 2004.

Leonard-Barton D., Core capabilities and core rigidities, Strategic Management Journal, vol 13, pp 111–125, 1992.

Leonard-Barton D., Wellsprings of knowledge, Harvard Business School Press, Boston, MA, 1995.

Lowson R.H., Strategic operations management, Routledge, London, 2002.

Miller J.G. and Roth A.V., A taxonomy of manufacturing strategies, Management Science, vol 40(3), pp 285–304, 1994.

Penrose E., The theory of the growth of the firm, Blackwell, Oxford, 1959.

Peteraf M.A., The cornerstones of competitive advantage, Strategic Management Journal, vol 14(2), pp 37–46, 1993.

Porter M.E., How competitive forces shape strategy, Harvard Business Review, March–April, pp 86–93, 1979.

Porter M.E., Competitive strategy, Free Press, New York, 1980.

Porter M.E., Competitive advantage, Free Press, New York, 1985.

Porter M.E., What is strategy, Harvard Business Review, November–December, pp 61–79. 1996.

Prahalad C.K. and Hamel G., The core competencies of the corporation, Harvard Business Review, May–June, pp 79–91, 1990.

Rumelt R., How much does industry matter?, Strategic Management Journal, vol 12(3), pp 167–185, 1991.

Selznick P., Leadership in administration, Harper and Rowe, New York, 1957.

Skinner W., The missing link in corporate strategy, Harvard Business Review, May–June, pp 136–145, 1969.

Skinner W., Manufacturing in the corporate strategy, John Wiley, New York, 1978.

Skinner W., Manufacturing: the formidable competitive advantage, John Wiley, New York, 1985.

Slack N., The manufacturing advantage, Mercury Business Books, London, 1991.

Slack N. and Lewis M., Operations strategy, FT Prentice Hall, Harlow, 2002.

Stacey R.D., Strategic management and organisational dynamics (4th edition), Financial Times Prentice Hall, London, 2002.

Teece D.J., Pisano G. and Shuen A., Dynamic capabilities and strategic management, Strategic Management Journal, vol 18(7), pp 509–533, 1997.

Waters D., Operations management (2nd edition), FT Prentice Hall, Harlow, 2002.

Wernerfelt B., A resource-based view of the firm, Strategic Management Journal, vol 5(2), pp 171–180, 1984.

Wheelwright S.C., Japan, where operations really are strategic, Harvard Business Review, July–August, pp 67–74, 1981.

Wild R., Essentials of operations management (5th edition), Thomson Learning, London, 2002.

Wild R., Operations management (6th edition), Thomson Learning, London, 2003.

Williams J., How sustainable is your competitive advantage?, California Management Review, vol 34(3), 1992.

CHAPTER 6
Designing an Operations Strategy

In the last chapter we looked at the features of an operations strategy and its contents. This chapter discusses the design of an operations strategy. In particular, it develops a general approach to design and outlines the choices that managers have to make. Often the strategy focuses on a particular aspect of operations, so we discuss the most common options. The next two chapters consider strategic analyses and implementation.

After reading this chapter you should be able to:

- Discuss approaches to the design of an operations strategy
- Describe a general approach consisting of eight related steps
- Consider the differences and balance between top-down design and bottom-up emergence of strategy
- Appreciate the role of an operations mission
- See how to expand an operations mission into a series of goals and objectives
- View alternative strategies as consisting of different choices about strategic aspects of operations
- Consider the evaluation of different strategies
- Appreciate the idea of focused operations strategies and describe some types of focus

The key concepts discussed in this chapter are:

- **Operations strategy design**, which shows the steps that managers take when designing a strategy
- **Purpose, goals and objectives of operations**, which show what the operations have to achieve
- **Strategic choice**, which concerns the choices available to an operations strategy
- **Strategic operations focus**, where a strategy focuses on a particular aspect of operations

APPROACH TO DESIGN

Progress so far

We have already come a long way to describing the design of an operations strategy. For a start we know that it contains all the factors that affect operations over the long term, particularly the purpose of the operations stated in a mission, an expanded set of goals and objectives, and plans and methods to achieve these goals. We also know the aims of the strategy, which are to support the higher strategies and help the organization achieve its aims. More specifically, the operations strategy looks for operations excellence that comes from the management of resources and builds on operations' strengths. At the same time it aims at customer satisfaction by making products that match their demands. So the strategy looks for a compromise that achieves a strategic fit between internal operations and their external environment – conventionally 'balancing the customer service objective with the resource utilization objective', Wild (2002, 2003).

In this chapter, we see how managers consider all of these factors and set about the actual design of an operations strategy. Perhaps we should say right at the start that there is no single best approach to **strategy design**, but we can give some useful guidelines and general advice. One important point is that there are usually several strategies that could give reasonable solutions, so managers have to consider these and choose the best. Figure 6.1 gives a summary of the overall procedure for designing an operations strategy.

Adjusting an existing strategy

An important point is that managers rarely design an operations strategy from scratch. Instead, they start with an existing strategy and make periodic adjustments. These typically come with annual reviews that assess the performance of the current

IDEAS IN PRACTICE Avis

Avis is one of the world's leading car rental companies. Its vision is to, 'lead our industry by defining service excellence and building unmatched customer loyalty'. This statement sets the scene for the operations strategy, which must clearly set the scene for operations that provide an excellent service as a way of getting customer satisfaction.

The vision of Avis is expanded into a mission, 'We will ensure a stress-free car rental experience by providing superior services that cater to our customers' individual needs . . . always conveying the "We Try Harder" spirit with knowledge, caring and a passion for excellence.' And this leads to a set of values based on integrity, respect for the individual, quality,

teamwork, growth, profitability and community responsibility.

The company has already defined its broad requirements (which are expanded in a corporate and business strategy) and the operations strategy must show how it will contribute to achieving these. For example, Avis aims at providing 'an individualized rental experience that assures customer satisfaction' – so the operations strategy must provide a customized, high quality service; with growth, the company strives for 'continuous innovation' which must be supplied by an inventive operations strategy.

Source: Website at www.avis.com

strategy, identify problems and opportunities, consider alternative adjustments to allow for these, choose the best and implement it (Hofer and Schendel).

These periodic reviews have to be timed carefully. The whole point of an operations strategy is that it gives long-term stability, so it should be changed relatively infrequently. As the operations strategy typically looks beyond five years in the future, it would be nonsensical to change the strategy every few months. On the other hand, reviews that are too far apart would allow the strategy to become dated, fail to notice changes in the environment, and miss opportunities to improve performance. Many organizations feel that they need an annual review of strategy, often coinciding with their financial reports; others prefer a cycle that covers two or three years.

The benefit of periodic updates of an existing strategy is that they allow managers to make a series of relatively small adjustments. These can be absorbed by the operations without major disruptions, and are easier and less traumatic than making major changes that move in completely new directions. They can also be more tentative

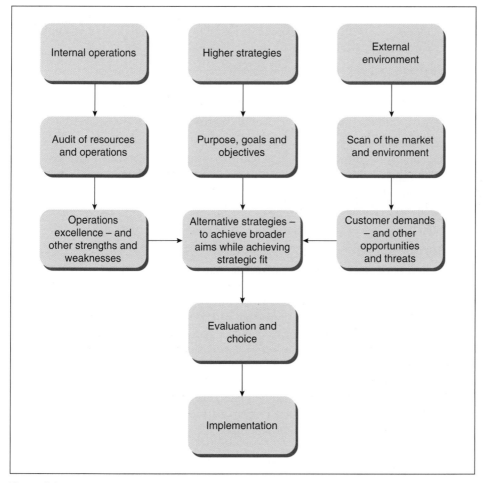

Figure 6.1 Summary of the operations strategy design procedure

and experimental. Managers may not really know the consequences of a proposed change, but they can try it in one period and if the adjustment gives an improvement they can consolidate it and repeat the changes in the next period. On the other hand, if there is no improvement – or even positive harm – they can easily reverse the change without too much damage.

On the other hand, the problem with this iterative approach is that changes follow no coherent pattern or rationale. Managers seem unsure of what to do, and they give the impression of tinkering with the present strategy, trying a few options, but with no overall direction. An alternative to the iterative adjustment is to make more dramatic changes. When there are serious problems with an existing strategy managers may feel that it needs a major overhaul to move the operations in radically new directions. This is the approach recommended by re-engineering (Hammer and Champy; Hammer). Hopefully, the major changes may bring dramatic improvements, but they can be very disruptive and difficult to implement. And there is always the risk of something going seriously wrong.

Approach to design

If we want a more radical redesign, there are several suggested approaches, all of which build on the connections between different levels of strategy. For example, Hill describes a five-step approach to the design of a manufacturing strategy.

- **Step one** analyzes the corporate objectives and sees how the operations strategy can contribute to these.
- **Step two** analyzes the marketing strategy – which defines the type of products, ranges, volumes – and sets the overall type of operations that make them.
- **Step three** looks at the features that customers want in their products, defining the qualifying and order-winning features. This more firmly defines the competitive features and operations needed to supply them.
- **Step four** designs the best process to supply these, making decisions about technology, capacity, quality, etc.
- **Step five** provides the infrastructure to support the process, including the organizational structure, control and support systems.

This approach seems to emphasize the market view, and sees operations as responding to the conditions imposed by the marketing strategy. Actually, Hill saw marketing and operations as working closely together to develop cooperative strategies (Teece *et al.*; Spring and Bowden). This reflects the views of Skinner who argued that operations managers should have a bigger input to other strategies.

In chapter 3 we outlined an alternative approach to designing strategies, based on 'analysis, choice and implementation'. Now we can adapt this for an operations strategy, with 'analysis' describing the current position of operations, 'choice' saying where they should be in the future, and 'implementation' showing how they will move from one to the other. We can get a clearer picture of operations strategy design by expanding this basic approach into five steps:

1 *define the operations' overall purpose*
2 *analyze the operations environment*

3 *analyze the features of the operations*

4 *design the best future state for operations and the strategy to achieve it*

5 *implement the operations strategy.*

Step 4 is the main design element, but it includes a range of complex questions that managers struggle to answer. How can they really design the best future state for operations? Should they identify all possible future states – which must be an almost limitless number? How could they compare all their different features, and then identify a single 'best'? How could they consider all the strategic options for moving from their current position to this best state? These questions suggest that this approach to design is impossibly difficult, so managers generally work the other way round. In other words, they design alternative, **feasible strategies** and then compare the consequences of each. Then they choose the strategy that seems to give the best results – which they now identify as the best future state for operations. The choice of strategy and future state becomes a single, joint decision.

Even this approach has to be limited, as it is impossible to consider all feasible strategies, and even if managers could list them all they could not possibly take into account all the conflicting issues and choose a single 'best'. So managers inevitably limit their considerations to a small list of reasonable alternatives, and choose the one that seems to give the best overall results.

So the view of managers doing rational analyses to find the best operations strategy is replaced by a simplified view where they generate a few reasonable alternatives and choose the one that seems to give the best overall results. Kinnunen confirms that, particularly in large organizations, strategies evolve from compromise and negotiation among the concerned parties, with managers looking for 'satisfycing' rather than optimal results. And there are few analyses that really help with the design of an operations strategy (which we describe in the next chapter), so managers generally have to use a mixture of analysis, reasoning, experience, judgement, intuition – and often informed guesswork.

In the light of these comments, we can adjust the list of five steps for strategy design to give a more realistic approach with the following eight steps.

Steps in designing an operations strategy:

1 Assess the current strategy;

2 Define the purpose of operations, including goals and objectives;

3 Analyze the operations environment;

4 Analyze the internal operations;

5 List alternative new operations strategies;

6 Evaluate these alternatives and choose the best;

7 Add details to the chosen strategy;

8 Implement the strategy.

Details of the eight steps

Each organization is unique and adopts a different approach to these eight steps, but the following factors are usually most important.

Step 1. Assess the current strategy Apart from entirely new operations, there must be some operations strategy in place, even if it is implicit rather than formally recorded. So an obvious starting point is to analyze the current strategy and see how well it is working. So this first step concentrates on four factors:

a The contents of the current operations strategy – including the purpose, goals and objectives, how these are achieved, types of products and processes, environmental conditions, level of strategic fit, distinctive capabilities, etc.

b Apparent problems with the current strategy – which are the symptoms that things could be improved. Typically the strategy does not achieve its aims, it is missing trends in the environment, it is it difficult to implement, there is poor use of resources, it is falling behind competitors, there is low customer satisfaction, etc.

c Real problems with the strategy – which are the underlying faults with the strategy. Perhaps it needs capabilities that the organization does not have, fails to develop operations excellence, gives no real competitive advantage, is not flexible enough to adapt to changing conditions, does not fit in with other strategies, etc.

d Amount of adjustment – which depends on the performance of the current strategy. Managers only need to design a completely new strategy when operations are entirely new or when there are severe problems with the current strategy. Otherwise, they can evaluate the current strategy, and see how much of it can be used as the basis of a new strategy and how much reworking is needed (illustrated in Figure 6.2).

Step 2. Define the purpose of operations perhaps summarized in an operations mission. This gives the overall direction of operations, typically showing how they support the organization's mission through its corporate strategy and, most directly, through its business strategy. The operations mission must be expandable into a set of goals and objectives for operations, so for this step managers:

a Analyze the business strategy – and other strategies – from an operations viewpoint. Define the overall aims of operations, and phrase this as an operations mission that supports the higher strategies, gives a statement of purpose, shows direction, and sets the context for operations. This is likely to include both efficient use of resources and customer satisfaction.

b Expand the operations mission into a series of specific strategic goals that show exactly what operations must achieve.

c Translate these goals into more precise – preferably quantitative – objectives.

Step 3. Analyze the operations environment which consists of a complex picture of business, economic, political, technological, cultural, historical and social factors. All of these – and the numerous other factors – interact and are constantly changing. An operations environmental scan analyzes:

a   Current conditions within the organization, but outside operations – including finance, marketing, HR, etc. – and their relations with operations.

b   Forecast future conditions within the organization.

c   Current conditions in the organization's external environment – markets, competition, stakeholders, economy, regulation, constraints, etc.

d   Features of the industry and segment in which operations work.

e   Features of the market, segments and potential customers.

f   Features of customer demand and the type of products that can best meet this.

g   Actions of competitors – and how operations can get a competitive advantage.

h   Forecasts of likely future conditions in the broader environment.

i   Opportunities – being factors that operations can exploit to gain some kind of advantage.

j   Threats – being factors that might harm operations, and the likelihood of their occurrence.

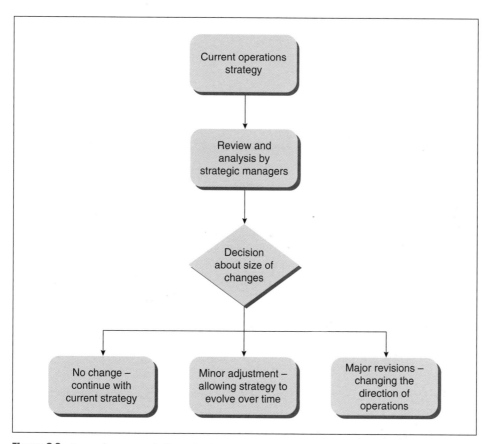

Figure 6.2 Assessing an existing strategy

Step 4. Analyze the internal operations doing an operations audit that includes:

a Details of all current operations including core capabilities.

b Ability to make the type of products demanded by customers.

c The best type of operations to supply these products – along with levels of technology, capacity, resources, etc.

d Changes needed to move from current operations to the best ones.

e Use of resources – with a resources audit to identify strategic resources.

f Measures of operations performance, with relevant comparisons and methods of improvement.

g Areas for key operations decisions, such as type of product, capacity, locations, technology, quality, etc.

h Strengths in operations that can develop into operations excellence and distinctive capabilities.

i Weaknesses that have to be overcome.

Step 5. List alternative new operations strategies giving a relatively small number of feasible alternatives. So managers:

a Consider an ideal future state of operations, with the features that would contribute most to the business strategy.

b Generate a set of feasible, alternative operations strategies that would move in some way towards this ideal.

c Assess the consequences of each strategy and likely performance over a range of factors.

Step 6. Evaluate these alternatives and choose the best finding:

a Which alternative contributes most to achieving the operations aims – and hence the business and higher strategies.

b Which comes closest to achieving the ideal future state for operations.

c Which gives the best strategic fit between operations and their environment.

d Which develops superior performance in customer satisfaction, competitive advantage, operations excellence and distinctive capabilities.

e How the organization's capabilities or resources limit the alternatives that are feasible.

f How management preferences, standards, views on risk, opinions, etc. limit the alternatives.

Step 7. Add the details to this strategy which means that managers:

a Describe general features of products that meet customer expectations.

b Describe general features of the process that can best deliver these products.

c Describe the capacity, technology, quality, logistics system, etc., that the operations need.

d Design the best organizational structure, controls and functions to support the process.

e Define performance targets to measure progress towards the purpose.

f Design all the other features included in the operations strategy.

Step 8. Implement the strategy which translates the chosen strategy into actions and actual operations, with managers:

a Planning the implementation throughout the operations, including changes to organizational structure, methods and systems.

b Setting targets for other levels of operations decisions.

c Initiating decision-making throughout the operations, starting the cascade that turns ideas into actions through all levels of management.

d Monitoring actual performance of operations to make sure that they are producing the planned results.

e Controlling the strategy, continually looking for improvements and making necessary adjustments.

f Keeping the strategies up to date, reviewing circumstances and making adjustments in the light of changing conditions, new ideas and new opportunities.

This daunting list is summarized in Figure 6.3. But it still only gives advice on some central concerns, and is a long way from a recipe for designing a complete operations strategy. At the very least, strategy design is an iterative search for an acceptable solution, so managers will loop through these steps until they find a compromise that gives broadly acceptable results.

Top-down or bottom-up design

There are many variations on the design procedure, and these often reflect the aims, values and style of the people involved. With a corporate strategy we identified several types of people who could be involved in the design, but the choice is much smaller for an operations strategy. Generally, designers have to be people who have expertise in both the operations and strategic management – and this means senior operations managers.

When senior operations managers design a strategy we get the standard **top-down** approach that we mentioned in chapter 3. Such formal, top-down approaches have several advantages. Above all, they give a structured procedure that managers can follow, and if they follow these steps – with the necessary adjustments for real circumstances – they get a good strategy. As a clearly identifiable group of senior operations managers makes the decisions, there is also clear responsibility for these decisions and their consequences. These managers are, arguably, the best qualified to make the decisions, as they have the necessary information, experience, long-term view of operations, analytical skills, and so on. And the resulting strategy can be passed on through clearly defined, and well-established, channels of communication.

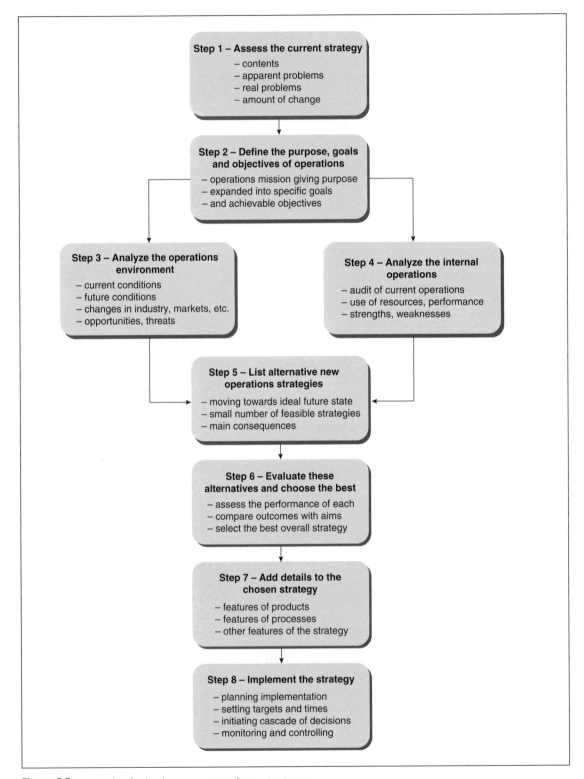

Figure 6.3 Steps in designing an operations strategy

These benefits are so convincing that this is how strategies should be designed under ideal circumstances. But there are also problems (Hamel and Prahalad), including:

- The circumstances around a strategy – both external and internal – are so complicated that managers cannot be aware of them all, let alone understand all the ramifications.

- Designers do not have the necessary skills, knowledge and experience – particularly being ill-prepared to make strategic decisions and unable to see the whole picture.

- Senior operations managers cannot be aware of the detailed impact of their decisions at lower levels.

- Decisions are based on assumptions about likely conditions far into the future.

- Designers get bogged down in analyses, particularly looking for a cause-and-effects relationship for every aspect of performance.

- The strategy becomes too detailed and gives too many results and too much information.

- The process of strategy design becomes so time-consuming and burdensome that people lose interest.

- A strategy is designed by one group of people, and then it is implemented by a different group, with different aims, priorities, ideas, etc.

- A strategy that is designed by a group of senior managers may not have credibility or 'ownership' by other people in operations or the rest of the organization.

- The people responsible for implementing the strategy are too busy with day-to-day operations to give it much consideration.

- People in the rest of the organization have little interest in the strategy, and give it lip-service when necessary, but little actually happens.

- Organizational culture and politics are important, but these are not taken into account by formal procedures.

The alternative **bottom-up** approach assumes that senior managers do not design a strategy in a single step, but it emerges over time from the actions of managers lower down the organization. These lower managers continually respond to actual conditions, making practical decisions to cope with new problems as they arise. They have to keep the organization moving, and the sum of their decisions eventually emerges as a strategy.

Imagine a less senior operations manager who is under pressure to supply an order quickly, and finds a way of saving some time in delivery. The new method may improve customer service and be more convenient for operations, so the manager repeats it for all future deliveries. This improves the general speed of delivery and eventually fast service becomes a key feature – and even a distinctive capability – of operations. In due course fast service becomes a part of the operations strategy – not because it was initiated by senior managers, but because the capabilities and improved results filtered up from lower levels. A relatively disorganized process of *ad hoc* decisions, perhaps little more than informed trial and error, made operations focus on speed and add it – largely in retrospect – as a part of the operations strategy.

Even the most rigid top-down approach to strategy design uses some information from lower in the organization, as it must take into account the capabilities, experiences, skills, etc. found in lower levels. An operations strategy based on, say, high product quality, must have assurances from lower operations managers that they can deliver the necessary results. This recognizes that the people nearer the operations have a clearer view of what is feasible and appropriate. Bottom-up design goes a step further, and says that they are also in the best position to make decisions – even for the long term.

At the same time, there must always be some top-down design, as senior managers have to make sure that the emerging strategy really does achieve the aims of operations. They have to make sure that it supports the business strategy, contributes to the organization's purpose, is consistent, and so on. So senior managers must, at least, analyze the emerging strategy, formally accept it as part of the operations strategy, add guidance to coordinate the strategies emerging from different sources, and allocate necessary resources.

In reality, designing an operations strategy involves a mixture of both top-down design and bottom-up emerging, as shown in Figure 6.4. The best point of balance

IDEAS IN PRACTICE Sanyo Electric Co. Ltd

Sanyo Electric Co., Ltd, was incorporated in 1950 and is now the third largest manufacturer of consumer electronics in Japan. It 'is committed to becoming an indispensable element in the lives of people all over the world' and has the strategic priorities of 'Customer satisfaction and harmonizing with the environment.'

In 1975 the executive vice president gave a directive to the home refrigerator business to aim for substantial reductions in stocks of both raw materials and work in progress. Manufacturing managers considered this as an important strategic aim and adjusted their operations to:

- standardize parts and components
- increase the frequency of materials deliveries from one to four times a month to one to four times a day
- merge production of low-volume models into a single assembly line
- modify procedures and equipment to reduce setup times

- reduce production batch sizes to have production runs every one or two days
- reduce the amount of warehouse space needed
- get everyone's commitment to the new policies.

Over the next five years stock levels declined from an average of ten days down to 1.5 days, warehouse space declined from 8,000 square metres to 2,000, production rose by a factor of three, and production runs were reduced from two or three days to one. Sales more than doubled, while profits rose by a factor of seven.

The adjustments and focused changes to operations developed into distinctive capabilities, and were important enough to have an effect at strategic level, eventually being incorporated into the corporate strategy.

Source: Wheelwright S.C., Japan – where operations really are strategic, Harvard Business Review, July/August, pp 67-74, 1981; Websites at www.sanyo.com; www.sanyo.co.jp

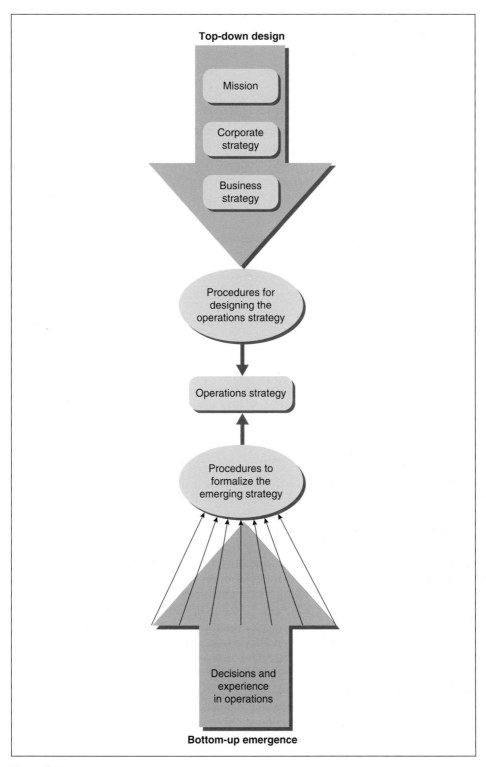

Figure 6.4 Balancing top-down and bottom-up approaches to designing an operations strategy

between these two depends on a whole variety of factors loosely described as the corporate culture. Mintzberg and Waters suggest eight styles of management that home-in on different points of balance:

- **Planned** – where senior managers design the operations strategy and control its implementation.
- **Entrepreneurial** – where the strategy is dictated by a single, dominant leader.
- **Ideological** – where people in operations have collective beliefs that senior managers express in inspirational terms.
- **Umbrella** – where senior managers define the principles and overall targets for the strategy, but leave lower managers to add details and formulate the content.
- **Process** – where senior managers control the process of strategy design, but leave the contents to lower managers.
- **Unconnected** – where there are no central strategy designers, so the strategy flows from a synthesis of unconnected strategies of different groups.
- **Consensus** – where people converge on a common theme.
- **Imposed** – where the environment dictates the strategy.

DEFINING THE PURPOSE OF OPERATIONS

We know that an operations strategy has three main parts – **purpose**, expanded into goals and objectives, with methods of achieving these (shown in Figure 6.5). In this section we discuss the purpose, goals and objectives, while the next section looks at the methods, plans, decisions and actions to achieve these.

Designing an operations mission

An **operations mission** gives a broad statement of the purpose and aims of operations, giving overall intent and long-term direction. We could use the 'Ashridge Mission Model' (Campbell and Tawady; Campbell and Yeung) to describe its contents as purpose, values, strategy and behaviour standards – or we could use some other model. But the operations in every organization are in some way unique, so there is a corresponding variety of operations missions. They usually start with the operations' purpose and show how the operations strategy will support the organization's overall mission through its corporate and business strategies.

The business strategy is a fundamental input to the design of an operations mission, as it defines the overall conditions in which operations work, setting the industry, market, and even the type of products and key goals. So an initial step must be to analyze the business strategy – and other strategies – from an operations perspective. But managers have to be careful here and go beyond published statements, as an organization's publicity can give one view of its objectives, but its actions give a completely different view. A water company, for example, might publish a business strategy that boasts of giving customers low costs and value for money, when it regularly raises prices by the highest amount that it can get away with. There are really three views of an organization's aims. The first is its published statement of objectives, the second is the purpose that emerges from its actual behaviour, and the third is an outsider's view of what the objectives are, could or should be. When moving on to design an operations strategy, managers have to be sure that they have the appropriate version of the purpose. A mistake at this initial stage would make the rest of the strategy of little value.

From their analysis of higher strategies, managers should search for an overall purpose for operations, and then summarize this in an operations mission statement. So the key steps in defining an operations mission are to:

- analyze the business strategy – and other strategies – from an operations point of view
- form an understanding of the long-term purpose of operations
- phrase this as a clear operations mission statement
- communicate this mission to the rest of the operations function
- know when to adjust the mission to allow for changing conditions

This mission is necessarily vague, outlining principles and giving a general direction rather than describing positive actions. Unfortunately, this means that it sometimes becomes a rather meaningless cliché based on 'leadership', 'excellence' or some other undefined terms. This gives no guidance at all to show operations managers what they should be doing. On the other hand, we could argue that a fuzzy mission can have the

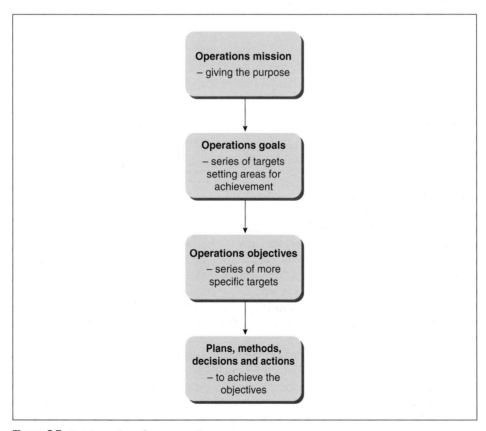

Figure 6.5 Setting aims for operations

IDEAS IN PRACTICE Project Management Group

Management is usually viewed as a continuous process that moves forward over time without a break. Some managers find that their work is not really continuous, but consists of a series of discrete projects. This often needs a different style of management, based on the distinct methods and techniques that have been developed for project management.

The Project Management Group in the University of Southern Alberta was formed to improve the practice of project management. Its mission was to 'be world leaders in research, teaching and practice of project management'. This led to an ambitious operations strategy which included research in four

key areas – developing degrees in project management, contributing to a range of university and professional courses, building strong links with the business community, and using their skills on real projects.

Unfortunately, there were only three people in the Project Management Group, and they spent most of their time teaching and doing the related administration. Their published mission described dreams rather than realities, and the operations strategy based on it was unachievable and pointless. Operations managers should have identified the real purpose of the group and designed a more appropriate strategy that would achieve this.

advantage of stability, giving basic values that remain unchanged over many years. McDonald's has an operations mission based on 'quality, cleanliness, service, and value', and they have not changed this for more than 50 years. A more positive mission could give clearer guidance, but need adjusting every time there is a significant change to competition, broader environment, product, process, technology, or anything else.

Despite the need for stability, an operations mission usually evolves over time, and we might link this adjustment to Hayes and Wheelwright's model of the changing role of operations. With new operations – that are internally neutral – the operations mission will probably focus on raising performance to acceptable levels and eliminating mistakes. As operations move to become externally neutral, the mission will move to being comparable with competitors or achieving industry standards. Then as operations become internally supportive, the mission will move on to achieving operations excellence and developing distinctive capabilities. The few operations that become externally supportive will have a mission of redefining customer expectations, industry standards, or some other level of outstanding performance.

Designing operations' goals and objectives

Now managers have to take the operations mission and expand it into a set of appropriate **goals** and **objectives**. A mission might include an aim of 'achieving the lowest cost operations in our industry', which leads to a goal of 'continually reducing operating costs' and an objective of 'reducing real operating costs by 2 percent a year'.

The specific goals and objectives obviously depend on the type of operations. Almost any aspect of operations can become critical enough to warrant a strategic target, so managers have two jobs. Firstly, they have to decide which areas are important enough to be assigned targets; secondly they have to set the actual targets. Some obvious areas for operations goals relate to the competitive features of price, quality, speed, flexibility and a range of other factors. Then there can be many types of objective, as suggested by the following list.

- **Price**, and related costs, are probably the most common objectives for operations. Low operating costs give obvious benefits to both the organization (increasing its competitiveness and allowing higher profits) and customers (who pay low prices). Organizations can reliably measure their costs, so objectives are commonly phrased in terms of low unit costs, prices, total operating costs, asset value, profitability, interest rates, transaction charges, discounts, terms of payment, and many other financial ratios.

- **Quality** shows how good the products are, and making products with no defects again brings benefits to both organizations and their customers (as we discuss in chapter 10). Contrary to the traditional view, high quality usually reinforces the aims of low costs. Quality objectives are commonly phrased in terms of percent defective, percent conforming to specifications, number of customer returns, cost of reworking, customer complaints, warranty costs, surveys of customer satisfaction, usefulness of product, and a range of similar measures.

- **Speed**, with organizations generally aiming to do operations faster or to meet specified targets such as 'delivery at 10:00 on Tuesday'. There can be trade-offs here, with a faster service perhaps costing more and increasing errors. Common objectives for speed relate to the lead time from ordering to receiving a product, proportion of on-time deliveries, time to develop new products, time that customers have to wait in queues, number of people in queues, fast payments, time to complete administrative transactions, and so on.

- **Flexibility** is more difficult to measure and covers broader areas such as volume, customization, and new product development.
  - *Volume flexibility* shows an organization's ability to deal with variations in demand. It might approach this in several ways, perhaps hiring temporary staff, holding stocks, forming queues, and so on. Related objectives refer to the utilization of capacity, proportion of sales lost, variable cost per unit, peak production, variation in capacity, waiting times, etc.
  - *Customization* shows how well an organization can deal with individual demands for specific features in its products. Objectives might refer to the width of product range, number of features, proportion of customers satisfied, variety of features (sizes, colours, etc.), time needed to customize products, average size of order, etc.
  - *New product flexibility* shows how innovative operations are and how they bring new products from concept to market. Related objectives refer to the number of new products introduced, time to develop new products, new technologies used, response to customer demands, etc.

- **Other objectives** include all the other types of aims for operations, such as technology (with operations always using the latest technology, such as computer manufacturers, Internet services, or mobile phones), dependability (with operations that reliably deliver products, honouring delivery dates, having products in stock, being able to answer queries, and generally giving no surprises) and customer service (with customers generally more interested in how well they are treated than the technical details of products).

Obviously, this list only gives an idea of possible objectives, and in different circumstances there is a virtually limitless number of possibilities. Many of these are general, such as 'increasing output by 5 percent', but others are specific to a particular organization. For example, a nuclear power station might have an objective of eliminating leaks of radioactive material into the environment, a water company reducing leaks from its pipes, a delivery service eliminating lost mail, and so on.

IDEAS IN PRACTICE T. Jones Industrial

T. Jones Industrial is a manufacturer of springs and mechanical parts for the home furnishing industry. Although they have been in business for over fifty years, they have never had a formally presented operations strategy. However, several members of the family who run the business are thinking of retirement, and they decided to put their ideas onto a more formal footing before their replacements take over.

Simon Jones was in charge of preparing an operations strategy. One of his concerns was to see how customer requirements affect strategic decisions in operations. He described five areas for strategic

operations, and six aspects of customer requirements, and showed the relationships in Table 6.1. He felt, for example, that there is a strong link between the capacity of the company's facilities and the final price of the product, but there is no significant link between capacity and product reliability. This table showed how the company's operations strategy could consider customer requirements. For example, when market research shows that customers value technology, the company's strategy can be adjusted to put more emphasis on product innovation.

Source: Internal company reports

Table 6.1 Links between strategic decisions and product features

		Customer requirements of the product					
		Price	Quality	Availability	Customization	Reliability	Technology
Strategic decisions for operations	Capacity	***		*			*
	Quality	**	***			**	
	Product innovation	*	*	*	**		***
	Process design	**	**	*	***	*	*
	Supply chain management	*	*	***			

*** critical
** important
* some influence

Guidelines for goals and objectives

Sometimes managers set absolute targets, such as 'no customer complaints' or 'delivery within 24 hours'. Often they use comparative performance, such as achieving industry norms, or matching competitors' performance. Another type of objective looks for an improvement over previous performance, perhaps base targets that were – or were not – achieved. There are no rules for choosing the types of objective, and few guidelines beyond the bland statement to 'use the most appropriate for the particular circumstances'. In practice, this means that targets usually emerge from discussion, compromise, agreement and subjective views about what managers feel is reasonable.

An obvious point is that managers have to be careful about the way that they phrase objectives. If someone does not understand a target, they will simply ignore it, or possibly divert efforts in the wrong direction. For instance, a goal of 'minimizing operating costs' would be misleading, as operations can reduce their costs to zero simply by closing down; a goal of 'minimizing customer queuing time' can be achieved by not allowing any customers to wait. So managers have to set clear objectives, that are well thought-out and SMART:

- *Specific* – giving a precise and exact description of the target to reach, such as 'raise productivity by 5 percent'.
- *Measurable* – that can be accurately measured, or at least has some quantitative element, avoiding vague terms like 'customer satisfaction' or 'morale'.
- *Achievable* – so they are realistic and sufficiently above the current level of performance to stretch the operations and need some effort; or alternatively *Assignable* – with someone clearly responsible for achieving the objective.
- *Relevant* – making a real contribution to the achievement of broader operations and organizational aims; or alternatively *Realistic* – being achievable.
- Timely – achieved within a specified time period, such as 'over the next two years'.

As we have mentioned before, these goals and objectives give targets and not requirements. Therefore, you should not expect operations always to achieve them. If the goals are demanding enough, it is quite reasonable to occasionally miss them – either because of changing circumstances, or because the goals actually turned out to be too demanding. Managers should only expect to meet their goals all the time if they are too easy. Operations with demanding goals that they just miss, are probably doing a better job than operations that always achieve their easier goals.

Problems with goals and objectives

If operations have a single, overriding purpose they can build a concentrated strategy that has the advantages of (Thompson and Strickland):

- Focusing on doing one type of operation very well, and building this into a distinctive capability.
- Focusing on a particular market segment and always meeting its demands.
- Knowing how to differentiate themselves from competitors to gain a competitive advantage.

- Encouraging the use of specialized resources that are efficient and fully used.
- Having specialized knowledge, identifying changes early and responding quickly.
- Responding efficiently to competitive threats and opportunities.

In practice, though, operations rarely have a single, dominant aim. Even those that seem to focus on one area, such as 'quality' are really using this as a convenient umbrella to include a range of other factors, such as speed, reliability, costs, productivity, and so on. Operations are much more likely to have a set of different aims, all of which they have to achieve at the same time. For example, they might be aiming simultaneously for a 2 percent reduction in operating costs, an increase of 5 percent in output, elimination of returned goods, and many other objectives. Ideally, these aims should all reinforce one another, so that moving towards one goal automatically moves closer to the others. For instance, making higher quality products can also bring lower costs, while faster delivery can also increase service quality.

Generally, though, there is likely to be some conflict between goals with, say, increased flexibility coming at a higher cost, or higher output needing more people to be employed. Then managers might set conditional goals, such as, 'reducing costs while maintaining high customer service'. More usually, they use their judgement to decide the priority of each goal and assign a rank that shows its relative importance. Or they may use a more structured scoring model that assigns a weight to each goal. Occasionally managers find the best balance of goals with more sophisticated analyses, such as goal programming and decision analysis, but the complexity of real problems means that such analytical methods are not yet widely used.

Another problem is that the emphasis on each goal changes over time. It might, for example, be affected by the stage in the product's life cycle – with new products the emphasis is on delivery speed and flexibility, but as the design stabilizes the emphasis moves to quality, and then on to cost for mature products. And there are also more general trends. For instance, the widespread use of Total Quality Management means that customers have got used to products with very high quality and are reluctant to accept anything less; and this means that any lower goal becomes unacceptable. In consequence, the other competitive features of price, timing, flexibility, and other features have become relatively more important. We could also argue that common technology and similarity of operations have narrowed production cost ranges, so managers must focus more on the remaining competitive features of timing and flexibility.

A benefit of assigning priorities to goals is that managers can allocate resources to the most useful areas. But suppose that there are simply not enough of the right resources? In other words, managers define a set of goals that operations simply cannot achieve with their available resources. They might, for example, design a strategy based on innovation and new product development, when the organization does not have the necessary skills, expertise or budgets for R&D.

Managers with a strong preference for a particular strategy, often find it difficult to accept that it can never succeed. A common reaction is to argue that operations can achieve the objectives if everyone puts in enough effort, and displays originality and flexibility in using new practices. Often, though, the real result is that resources are stretched beyond sensible limits and cannot cope. An alternative reaction is to assume that they can quickly get resources that are in short supply. Unfortunately, the availability of many resources is strictly limited, such as people with certain skills, patented products, copyright material, fixed production quantities of some resources, limited amounts of natural materials, legal restrictions, and so on. Sometimes the constraints are more subtle. If, for example, you want to open an independent petrol station, you might find it difficult to get deliveries at reasonable prices, as major oil companies own all the supply chains.

Such shortages of resources can put real constraints on strategic choices. When they are likely to be a problem, managers should do a resources audit of the type we mentioned in the last chapter, emphasizing the questions:

- What resources are currently available?
- What resources does a proposed strategy need?
- How many of these resources have potential shortages?
- How big are the gaps between current and required resources?
- How hard will it be to fill these gaps and assemble the necessary resources?

Obviously, resources are more of a problem when there are major shortages and the gaps are difficult to fill.

IDEAS IN PRACTICE Game theory

The strategic choices of an organization inevitably affect the results of a competitor. For example, when Southwest Airlines adopted a low price strategy for internal flights in America, all other airlines were affected – generally losing market share while they looked for a suitable response.

Game theory is a way of studying simple interactions between competitors' actions. Suppose two competitors (called X and Y) are working in a fixed market, and each has essentially three strategic options. The following matrix shows the consequences of alternative choices of strategies, with entries showing payment from Y to X – or net benefits to X and net losses to Y. For example, when competitor X chooses strategy A and competitor Y chooses strategy K, the consequence is a net benefit of 13 to X and a net cost of 13 to Y. This benefit is typically phrased in terms of cash or market share.

This example shows a stable position – called a saddle point – where both competitors adopt a strategy and stick to it. The best result has competitor X choosing strategy B and competitor Y chooses strategy L. This seems unfair, as Y always pays 4 to X. But if X changes its strategy, it would gain less (either 2 or 3); and if Y changed its strategy, it would pay more (either 5 or 10).

Normally, games do not have such clear strategies, and the best option is found by linear programming and involves random changes. (You can check this effect by simply changing the 4 in the saddle point to 8 – then competitor Y could do better by switching to option K; and then competitor X can retaliate and do better by switching to option A, and so on.)

		Competitor Y		
		K	**L**	**M**
	A	13	2	0
Competitor X	**B**	5	4	10
	C	11	3	9

The problem of multiple, conflicting, changing and interacting goals is very complex, giving what Hampton describes as a 'network of objectives'. We have mentioned potential problems with deciding the areas for goals, setting actual targets, phrasing them clearly, conflicting aims, setting priorities, changes over time, and the availability of resources. This might seem complicated enough, but there can be many other practical difficulties, with common ones including:

- Managers setting the wrong or inappropriate goals – typically ones that do not contribute to the organization's purpose, such as an operations goal of reducing the number of people employed when the business strategy is looking for expansion.

- Managers set unrealistic or impossible goals – they should be challenging, but they must be achievable. Doubling of profit next year would be an impressive goal, but it is rarely feasible.

- Quantitative or easily measured factors are given too much emphasis – for example, equipment productivity is easy to measure, but it may not be important for a service company.

- Qualitative or subjective goals are given too much emphasis – such as abstract targets of 'improving the corporate image' or 'improving employee motivation'.

- There is no link between goals and rewards – so people do not gain any benefit from achieving the targets.

- Objectives change quickly over time – so nobody knows what the current targets are.

ANALYSIS AND CHOICE

Strategic aspects of operations

Now we are at the point where managers have defined the purpose of operations and expanded this into a set of more immediate goals and objectives. The next stage is to design the methods, plans, decisions and actions for achieving these. In terms of our eight step procedure described above, we have finished the first two steps, and have reached steps 3 and 4, which are concerned with analyses of the operations environment and operations capabilities. Analyzing the operations environment gives a snapshot of the relevant external conditions and their impact on operations. Analyzing the current state of operations shows their activities and capabilities. These analyses give us a clear picture of the conditions in which operations work, but they need more explanation and we will discuss them in the next chapter.

This brings us to steps 5 and 6, which generate a list of alternative new operations strategies, evaluate these and choose the best. At this point managers have to start looking at specific aspects of operations. For example, they might consider strategic aspects of capacity, perhaps looking for ways of ensuring a process has enough capacity over the next few years. There may be several ways of organizing this capacity, each of which involves different options for the process, such as the level of automation, location, suppliers, etc. In turn, each option for the process leads to different options for the layout of facilities, quality of products, supply chain, etc. We could continue in this way, but the point is already clear that managers consider a whole series of options for strategic operations. Each combination of these options identifies one potential strategy, with its particular configuration of capacity, process, layout, quality, etc. The whole set of possible configurations of these strategic operations identifies all the potential strategies.

- To **design** an operations strategy, managers consider options for a series of strategic operations – capacity, process, location, quality, etc.
- Different strategies have different configurations of these strategic operations.

An obvious question asks, 'Which aspects of operations are important enough to have a strategic impact?' Heizer and Render say that there are ten areas for strategic decisions in operations – product design, quality, process design, location, layout design, human resource, supply chain management, inventory, scheduling and maintenance. We will look at these key areas in more detail in the third part of the book. Wheelwright takes an alternative view and identifies eight areas for operations decisions, four of which are traditionally considered as having a strategic impact:

- **Strategic operations decisions:**
    - *capacity* – amount and type
    - *facilities* – location and size
    - *vertical integration* – direction and extent
    - *process technology* – levels and type.
- **Non-strategic operations decisions:**
    - *work force* – training, pay, etc.
    - *quality* – control, specifications
    - *planning* – operations and materials
    - *organization* – structure and support.

This classification gives a very limited view of operations, and Wheelwright argues that it implicitly delegates decisions in key areas to less senior managers and broadcasts the message that they are less important. But you can imagine circumstances in which the 'non-strategic' decisions actually have a strategic impact. If a company cannot employ people with the skills that it needs, or is losing sales because of poor quality, then these become strategic issues. A more sensible approach – which evolved largely in Japanese companies – considers all decision areas as potentially strategic. So strategic decisions are not limited to certain types of activity, but can occur in any area.

So the basis of an operations strategy is the configuration of decisions about strategic operations. But there are likely to be many areas for these decisions, each of which has many options. So there is a huge number of different configurations – and potential operations strategies. There are so many of these that it is impossible for managers ever to form a complete list of all possible strategies, let alone analyze and compare them. Instead, they limit their considerations to a reasonable number of feasible alternatives. They consider the few aspects of operations that are likely to have the greatest strategic impact (rather than the large number of possible areas for strategic operations) and a few of the most important options for each of these (rather than the large number of possible alternatives).

This raises questions about how strategic managers choose the small number of strategies to consider. Ideally, they will always choose a few good strategies – while disregarding the huge number of inferior ones. But there are no analyses that guarantee this will happen and little guidance. It remains one of the essential skills for strategic managers.

Choice of options

When managers have identified a reasonably small set of feasible operations strategies, their next job might seem straightforward. They compare these alternatives and choose the best. Of course, things are not really this easy. Typically, they start with some key goals that the strategy must achieve, and then an initial screening rejects the alternatives that do not reach these goals. Then they can give more attention to the remainder. In principle, managers can evaluate the alternatives purely on their contribution to the operations mission, but this has practical problems. Most obviously, each strategy is likely to give different levels of performance in the different areas of concern – so that one achieves high quality but poor productivity, another gives high productivity but low capacity, a third has high capacity but high costs, and so on.

Managers might use some analyses like weighted scores, expected utilities, cash flows, ratings or a range of other methods to compare these results. But these can give useful guidelines and the final choice is generally based on experience, judgement, discussion, agreement and intuition. This, in turn, assumes there is some broad agreement about what actually forms a good result and how much it contributes to organizational aims. When faced with identical problems people inevitably have different views about the best solution – as you can see in any political election.

As there is no formal analysis for identifying the best strategy, managers often make mistakes. They might follow a good procedure for designing a strategy, but there are so many areas of uncertainty that they still get the wrong answer. An obvious problem is that the operations strategy should consider prevailing conditions for some point in the distant future. Knowledge of these conditions depends on forecasts, but these can simply be wrong. Or the organization and its environment change so that the designed strategy is no longer appropriate. Whatever the cause, there is always some level of **risk** associated with a strategy. This means that when the strategy is implemented, it may not give satisfactory results – because of either faulty forecasts or changing conditions.

Of course, the inevitable uncertainty might mean that a strategy gives reasonable results, or even better ones than expected – but the problem comes when the results are worse than expected. Different styles of management view this risk in different ways. Some organizations are entrepreneurial risk-takers, who look for the high rewards that come with uncertainty; others are risk averse and look for more certain strategies. This is why you would not expect pension fund managers to choose the same strategies as e-companies.

IDEAS IN PRACTICE Shang Hu Games

When Shang Hu Games made an annual review of their operations strategy, they identified capacity as a key aspect of operations. They currently had one assembly line making 10,000 units a year with an average profit of $8 a unit, and their main options were to keep this or install a second line. A second assembly line would increase operating costs by $100,000 a year, but economies of scale would raise the average profit to $11 a unit. Unfortunately, there was only a 60 percent chance that they could sell all the production. A more likely scenario had normal demand of 15,000 units. Then there was a 50:50 chance that a trading partner would take the excess production with a token profit of $2 a unit.

This is a simplified description of a small part of the choices for an operations strategy, and managers summarized it in the decision tree in Figure 6.6. Then they calculated expected values as the basis for discussions.

At node B, they keep current production with an annual profit of:

$$10,000 \times 8 = \$80,000$$

At node D, they increase production and sell it all, giving an annual profit of:

$$20,000 \times 11 - 100,000 = \$120,000$$

At node G, they increase production but only sell 15,000 units, giving an annual profit of:

$$15,000 \times 11 - 100,000 = \$65,000$$

At node F, they increase production, sell 15,000 units normally and pass the rest to a trading partner, giving an annual profit of:

$$(15,000 \times 11) + (5,000 \times 2) - 100,000 = \$75,000$$

At node E the expected value from nodes F and G is:

$$(0.5 \times 65,000) + (0.5 \times 75,000) = \$70,000$$

At node C the expected value from nodes D and E is:

$$(0.6 \times 120,000) + (0.4 \times 70,000) = \$100,000$$

At node A managers have a choice between nodes B and C, and the expected values suggest that it is better to go for the expansion. This raises expected annual profit from $80,000 to $100,000. Managers can use this information to help with their decision.

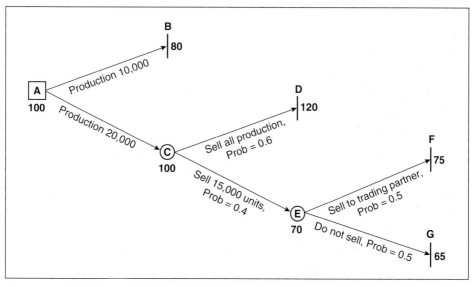

Figure 6.6 Decision tree of capacity decision at Shang Hu Games (node values are in thousands of dollars)

FOCUSED OPERATIONS STRATEGIES

Meaning of focus

The operations in every organization are different, so it is reasonable to assume that each will design a unique strategy that best fits its own circumstances. But we saw in chapter 3 that businesses are likely to think along similar lines and follow common strategic themes, in the way that supermarkets follow a common theme of low prices. They might follow Porter's model and focus on cost leadership, differentiation or a market niche. Or they may be more specific and focus on low costs, low prices, high quality, fast delivery, convenient locations, high technology, flexible production, and so on. But the business strategy sets the context for the operations strategy, so each of these themes translates into a focus for the operations strategy. The relatively small number of generic business strategies leads to a relatively small number of focuses in the operations strategies.

> An operations strategy has a particular **focus** if it concentrates on one aspect of operations.

A focus on, say, quality means that managers concentrate on quality so much that it is the overriding aim of operations and affects all other decisions. Operations cannot do all activities equally well, so some focus is inevitable in a strategy, but a focus is really a positive decision to develop some aspects of operations into distinctive capabilities that give the primary means of competing.

A focus for the operations strategy is a way of achieving the operations' purpose – but it is not the purpose itself. A company might have a purpose of making reasonable profits, and they choose a focus of low costs in their operations strategy as a way of achieving this. Sometimes this obvious point is lost, and managers get carried away by their enthusiasm for a particular focus. Some organizations that adopted TQM in the 1980s put so much effort into achieving high quality products that they seemed to forget this was a means of achieving their aims and not an end in itself, and they pursued a 'relentless quest for quality' to extraordinary lengths. The underlying problem is the difficulty of separating a strategy from its effects. When an organization adopts a strategy of 'producing high quality products' this affects almost every issue of the type of products and process used to make them. But where are the boundaries – if they exist – between the strategy and its consequences? Kim and Arnold found that managers have difficulty distinguishing between strategy and programmes that implement it. And Mills *et al.* ask, 'What is a manufacturing strategy nowadays – is it world-class, lean production, JIT, cells or TQM? Is it none of them, some of them or all of them?' The answer, of course, is that the operations strategy shows the overall direction, and the programmes are designed to achieve this. A strategy of low costs shows the direction that the operations should move in and lean operations give a mechanism for achieving this.

There are many possible areas for a strategic operations focus. We can start with Porter's generic business strategies and see how they give strategic focus in operations, but there are many other options. For example, a strategy might focus on the five competitive performance features of price, quality, speed, flexibility, or other factors. We can outline the effects of some of these foci, starting with the three factors suggested by Porter.

Focus on cost

Porter's generic strategy of price leadership aims at supplying the same or equivalent products as competitors, but at lower prices. This works best for commodities where price is the determining factor in sales and customers can move easily between suppliers. Price leadership translates into a strategic focus in operations of low unit costs – but without sacrificing quality or other competitive features.

Low cost is an almost universal objective for operations. It means reducing operating costs (of actually making the products), capital costs (of buying facilities), and working capital (to fund the delays between expenditure and income). The result is a bigger gap between the price that customers are willing to pay and the cost of production. This might mean higher profits, but organizations generally use a low cost strategy to gain a competitive advantage by selling at low prices.

A problem with focusing on costs is that the results often depend on the accounting conventions used. It is notoriously difficult to allocate overheads fairly, or to assign specific costs to operations, so redistributing the overheads between operations can radically change the apparent costs of a product, but without affecting the organization's overall performance. Another concern is that when costs become a dominant factor, other measures of performance may be sacrificed. For example, reducing costs almost inevitably reduces flexibility to respond to changing conditions. This is, of course, a problem with any focus, that it diverts attention away from the other competitive factors.

There are really three variations on cost objectives:

- **Lowest costs** – where cost is a dominant factor in success and operations aim at having the lowest costs possible, and certainly lower than competitors.

- **Competitive costs** – where cost is relatively important, but is not the dominant factor. Operations aim for costs that are comparable with other organizations in the industry, and rely on other factors to give a competitive advantage.

- **Acceptable costs** – where cost is not a major factor, such as luxury goods, manufacturing prototypes, health products, works of art, fashion accessories, etc. Then organizations use other factors to make their products attractive to customers, often supplying a unique product or one that is perceived as having a high value for customers. Organizations charge premium prices and do not have to control prices so carefully.

So low costs do not always mean low prices, and there often appears little relationship between the two. With many luxury goods, it seems that the higher the price the better the sales – and there is a proverb from somewhere that says, 'If your product is not selling, then raise the price.'

A strategy of low cost means efficient operations, with Porter (1996) saying that, 'Ultimately, all differences between companies in cost or price derive from the hundreds of activities required to create, produce, sell, and deliver their products.' Usually low-cost operations are characterized by large-volume, automated production, high productivity, continuous improvements to the process, concentration on a few main products, limited product ranges, simple designs, waste reduction, locations near to customers, shorter supply chains, high product quality, and any other means of reducing costs. Again quoting Porter (1996), 'Cost is generated by performing activities, and cost advantage arises from performing particular activities more efficiently than competitors.'

Effectively, low costs are achieved by eliminating all waste, and this approach has become increasingly known as **lean operations**. Cost reduction and lean operations are not entirely the same, but they follow the same general reasoning. The aim of lean operations is to do every operation using less of each resource – people, space, stock, equipment, time, etc. It organizes the efficient flow of materials to eliminate waste, give the shortest lead time, minimum stocks and minimum total cost.

Toyota did a lot of early development of lean production, and their methods were so successful that they spread to other areas, eventually developing a 'lean enterprise' (Ohno; Womack *et al.*). Their work identified seven major areas of waste in operations, numbered 1 to 7 in the following list (Monden). Etienne-Hamilton added two more to give 'nine mortal wastes of production', and we can add some more to give the following general list.

1 *Overproduction* – making units that are not currently needed giving too high stocks of finished goods.
2 *Waiting* – with resources sitting idly waiting for operations to start or finish, materials to arrive, equipment to be repaired, etc.
3 *Transportation* – moving materials and products over too long distances between suppliers and customers.
4 *Poor process* – with unnecessary, too complicated or time-consuming operations.
5 *Work in progress* – with too many materials held and moving slowly through operations.
6 *Movement* – with products making unnecessary, long, or inconvenient movements during operations.
7 *Product defects* – with too poor quality giving scrap and wasting resources.
8 *Overbuying* – giving too high stocks of raw materials.
9 *Spare capacity* – that is not used and gives low utilization and productivity.
10 *Waste of human resources* – not using people to their full potential.
11 *Bureaucracy* – giving inefficient flows of information.
12 *Excessive overheads* – adding unnecessary costs to operations.

When waste builds up in a process it can be difficult to identify and remove. A useful approach starts with a detailed analysis of operations – and then removes all activities that add no value, eliminates delays, simplifies movements, reduces complexity, integrates operations, uses standard operations and materials, organizes workloads, introduces concurrent working, uses higher technology, looks for economies of scale, locates near to customers to save travel, and removes unnecessary links from the supply chain, reduces variance and increases quality. Womack and Jones say that such an approach should concentrate on five principles:

- **value** – designing products that customers value
- **value stream** – designing the best process to make the products
- **value flow** – creating efficient flows of materials through supply chains
- **pull** – only making products when there is customer demand
- **aim of perfection** – looking for continuous improvements to get closer to perfect operations.

One warning is that low costs do not automatically mean lean operations. Lean operations maintain customer service while using fewer resources – they do not just minimize costs. A greengrocer could minimize its inventory costs by having no stock, but it would not generate many sales or much customer satisfaction. Another weakness suggested by opponents is that lean operations work well in mass production, but not so well in other types of operations. In particular, lean operations might not work when there are variable and uncertain conditions, and a more flexible strategy would be better.

Focus on product differentiation

Product differentiation supplies products that are somehow different from those offered by competitors, so customers cannot find equivalents anywhere else. This leads to an operations strategy that focuses on innovation in developing new products or variations on existing ones. And this needs strength in research and development, product design, speed in bringing new products, flexibility in responding to customer demands, wide product range, communicating product features in a credible way, and so on.

A rule of thumb has large organizations developing inertia and being more conservative, with dramatic innovation usually found in smaller, low-volume operations. But there are exceptions to this and you can find many large, innovative organizations that strive for dramatically new ideas.

Focus on niche or specialized products

Niche products are aimed at a particular set of customers with distinct demands – perhaps being in a restricted geographical area, or demanding a specialized product. This leads to an operations strategy that focuses on flexibility, identifying precise customer needs, designing customization products, using a specialized process, with flexible operations, convenient location, and so on. Long-term success comes from having an operations strategy that continues to focus on the niche and serve it better than competitors – and not being tempted away from this focus to expand into new types of product or markets.

A niche focus – along with a focus on product differentiation – depends on product flexibility, with operations making products that are tailored to specific customer needs. This is one aspect of an agile strategy, which focuses on flexibility and changes operations to adapt to prevailing conditions. **Agility** means that operations can respond quickly to demands for new products (product flexibility), new patterns of demand for existing products (volume flexibility) and general changes to the product mix, delivery times, terms of trade, transport, the broader environment, internal operations, and anything else that affects the operations. The benefit of this agility is that it allows organizations to deal with – and even prosper in – changing and unexpected conditions.

Focus on material management

A common focus is on the movement of materials through supply chains (which we discuss in chapters 13 and 14), particularly getting a smooth flow without breaks that cause material to accumulate as stocks of work in progress. These stocks can account for a surprisingly high part of operating costs, often quoted at more than 20 percent (Waters).

Managers can use several approaches to reducing stocks, with the earliest based on the models of inventory control. These consider the features of the inventory system and calculated optimal values for stock levels and corresponding order size, timing, probability of shortages, variable costs, and so on. These methods have remained the standard means of controlling the flow of materials for almost a century. However, alternatives have appeared for certain types of operations. In the 1960s material requirements planning (MRP) appeared, with a series of schedules to exert rigorous control over the movement of materials. These schedules are found by 'exploding' production plans to find precise demands for materials, and then organizing the supply to match these demands.

MRP can only be used in certain circumstances, and it relies on large systems to manage the flows of information. In the 1970s an alternative approach grew under the general name of just-in-time (JIT). The basis of JIT is that it organizes all activities to occur at exactly the time they are needed. They are not done too early (which would leave materials hanging around until they were actually needed) and they are not done too late (which would give poor customer service). This seems an obvious idea, but it can have a dramatic effect on the way that materials are organized. The traditional approach buys materials early and keeps them in stock until they are needed. MRP reduces stock by coordinating the arrival of materials with the demand. But JIT aims at delivering materials directly to operations at exactly the time they are needed and virtually eliminating stock. To organize this it has operations sending a signal backwards down the supply chain and pulls materials forward every time they are needed. We will discuss this approach in more detail in chapter 14.

Focus on timing

Just-in-time operations clearly focus on the timing of activities, but this is just one aspect of 'time-based competition' (Stalk; Stalk and Hout). Services have always emphasized delivery speed – largely because they cannot store products and have greater customer contact – so a focus on timing extends their ideas into other areas.

A strategic focus on timing generally means designing operations to do things faster than competitors. There are two main aspects of this. Externally, it means minimizing the time between customers asking for a product and having it delivered, increasing both availability and customer service. This usually means short delivery times from stocks of standard items, but it can also mean rapid development of new products, or delivering at the time specified by a customer. Internally, it means moving materials faster through the supply chain, reducing stocks, eliminating queues and reducing obsolescence.

Focus on productivity improvement

All managers want to improve the performance of operations, but some emphasize it so much that it becomes a strategic focus. This is usually phrased in terms of increasing productivity. Although this seems a straightforward aim, we have already mentioned that different measures of productivity can give conflicting advice, and raising some measures will inevitably lower others. So managers can disagree about the measure to improve – let alone the amount of improvement, or the best way to achieve it.

Like quality, productivity has been viewed historically in narrow tactical terms. Both were confined to manufacturing, used as an excuse to reduce the number of people employed, the subject of short-term programmes for improvement, used to pursue quick cost savings by attacking symptoms rather than causes of problems, and used to justify questionable investments. Now, both have emerged as strategic issues that affect the competitiveness and very survival of every organization.

A strategic focus on productivity improvement involves a continuing drive to improve agreed measures of performance (linked to the broader organizational aims), involving all parts of the organization, based on broad performance of operations (not just the number of people employed), looking for long-term benefits (not quick cost reductions), and enhancing skills and capabilities.

Focus on human resource management

Most organizations say that, 'our most valuable asset is our people'. Despite this boast, the truth is that many organizations treat their employees badly. When it is time to reduce costs most companies immediately start sacking people – thereby getting rid of their most valuable assets, while keeping the office furniture, equipment and other peripherals. Harvey-Jones says, 'There is practically no area of business where the difference between rhetoric and actuality is greater than in the handling of people.' But if an organization does not treat its employees properly, why should it expect its employees to work conscientiously in return?

A strategic focus on human resource management (HRM) develops employees and uses their abilities to the full. An obvious way of doing this is to reward people for their performance, so that the aims of the employees coincide with the aims of the organization and everyone pulls in the same direction. Starting points for this can be profit sharing, bonus payments, rewards for suggestions, promotion, pay increments, and so on. But not all rewards involve money, and you can see many schemes for recognizing 'the employee of the month', or something equivalent. Other rewards are less specific and typically have organizations treating all employees with courtesy, respect and consideration – treating each as an individual, with jobs that match their abilities and responsibility to make as many of their own decisions as possible. This reinforces the view that decisions should made by those most closely affected and at the lowest possible level – giving empowered employees.

Empowerment gives people control over – and responsibility for – their own work. It allows them to use their own judgement, skills and experience for the benefit of the organization. This has a considerable effect on operations, removing the traditional roles of supervisors, and freeing people from the instructions and control of remote managers who have no feel for the practical details of operations. Benefits include:

- better decisions by those with most knowledge and information
- faster decisions made close to operations
- lower costs by reducing layers of management
- giving everyone more control and responsibility for their own jobs
- greater employee satisfaction, sense of achievement and commitment
- releases skills, knowledge and creative abilities of employees
- encourages continuous improvement of operations
- more time for senior managers to concentrate on strategic issues.

Focus on other factors

We have now outlined strategic operations focus on cost and waste, product differentiation, niche products, materials management, timing, productivity improvement and human resource management. We could continue with this list giving a long string of alternative foci (see, for example, Miller and Roth). Frequently used foci would include:

- *Aspects of the product*
  - Type of product – focusing on a particular range of products, typically specializing in a niche market.
  - Product design – with features that customers demand.
  - Product technology – incorporating the latest developments.
  - Product innovation – continually developing new products.
  - Product quality – guaranteeing levels of quality that customers demand.
  - Customer satisfaction – always giving customers the service that they want.
- *Aspects of the process*
  - Type of process – using particular operations, often that no other organization can duplicate.
  - Process technology – using the latest methods to supply products.
  - Process costs – looking to minimize operating and unit costs.
  - Process capacity – having enough capacity to deal with all foreseeable circumstances.
  - Process performance – typically looking for high productivity or appropriate production targets.
  - Process flexibility – reacting quickly to changing conditions, level of demand, type of product, etc.
  - Speed of operations – looking for short lead times, fast flows of materials through a supply chain, rapid development of new products, etc.
- *Related factors*
  - Geographical region – supplying demand to a limited area.
  - Supply chain strategies – efficient customer response, supply/demand management, outsourcing.

- Strategic resources – particularly raw materials that are in short supply.
- Employee skills – with training and retention to keep skilled people.
- Knowledge – developed by a research group.
- Finances – giving financial security, like a bank.

In reality, though, there is an almost endless list of possible foci. Many bring together a range of different factors under a common umbrella – in the way that a focus on low cost includes considerations of waste, productivity, timing, quality, material movement, etc. And different foci often come to common conclusions – in the way that foci on timing and material management both move materials quickly through the supply chain. The foci that we have mentioned give an idea of the issues, and shows that each puts different requirements on operations. Table 6.2 suggests the differences that a sample of strategic foci make to operations.

An obvious point is that a strategic focus on one aspect of operations does not mean that all the other factors are forgotten. Operations may focus on one factor – but they still have to perform well in the others. RyanAir, for example, has a strategic focus on cost, but it must reach acceptable standards for comfort, reliability, efficiency, and so on. UPS has a strategic focus on speed, but it must still have competitive costs, reliability, product range, etc. But we can argue that putting more effort into one factor inevitably means putting less effort into another, so managers must find a balance between conflicting factors. But this argument ignores the point that there is not necessarily a trade-off and efficient operations can improve performance in several areas at once.

Table 6.2 Effects of some foci in operations strategies

Focus	Competitive advantage	Type of products	Types of operations
Cost	low prices	basic products, commodities	large scale production, automation, high productivity, standard products, low overheads
Product differentiation	meeting customer demand, satisfaction	unique, different to competitors	strong in R&D, product leaders, knowledge of customers
Quality	guaranteed high quality products	high quality low variability	reliable, total quality management, quality at source, zero defects
Speed	fast response, short lead times	delivered when wanted	efficient and responsive, adequate capacity, efficient schedules
Flexibility	responsiveness, customization	customized	versatile and responsive operations, rapid adjustments to the process, customer involvement
Technology	most advanced design	innovative	investment in research and development, stream of new products, exploiting new ideas
Service	'pampering' customers	customized	close customer relations, sharing information, flexibility, openness to suggestions

Benefits of focus

A strategic focus has the benefit of giving a unified approach to operations. It gives managers guidance for their decisions, showing that they should support the focus in preference to achieving other aims. The cumulative benefits from a focus can be substantial, as illustrated by Japanese manufacturers in the 1960s. Many had a strategic operations focus on narrowing the product range, giving focused factories that concentrated on making a single product. All their efforts went into this product, giving

 IDEAS IN PRACTICE **Rybinsk Country Club**

Rybinsk Country Club was founded in 1876, and after several changes in fortunes, now provides a country retreat for 800 members. Most of these are businessmen from Moscow, and it gives them a chance to take their families out of the city and spend some time in the countryside. The club has always focused on very high quality (and expensive) service, and members can take advantage of its policy of pampering members.

Every year a management committee considers suggestions for strategic changes, and their recommendations are voted on at the annual meeting of members. Last year, the strategic operations issues facing the management committee were:

- **Capacity** – membership of the club is limited to 800, and there is always a long waiting list. Existing members continually want to get memberships for more of their family, friends and contacts.
- **Private status** – the club is privately owned by its members, but it could generate more income and get tax concessions by allowing public access.
- **Land development** – the club owns a large area of land that it maintains as a nature reserve, prohibiting all activities other than rambling and horse riding. Some members want to open this for more active sports, such as car rallying and motocross.
- **Entertainment** – the club has a fitness centre, swimming pools, restaurants, tennis courts,

golf course, and the usual facilities of a country club, but some members want more entertainment, such as a casino and concert hall.

The management committee considered the strategic issues and alternatives, and recommended that the existing operations strategy remained. This includes the following points:

- **Operations mission** – To manage the Rybinsk Country Club, providing the highest quality services and facilities that our members expect.
- **Operations aims:**
  - To preserve our identity as a private country club, with limited membership;
  - To fit into and carefully manage our parkland, preserving its natural flora and fauna, and maintaining it in good condition for the benefit of future generations;
  - To provide a peaceful and hassle-free experience for our members, taking advantage of our rural location, traditions and customs;
  - To identify appropriate services and facilities for our members, which fit in with our ideals;
  - To provide the highest possible quality in all our services.

Source: Internal reports

benefits of specialization, becoming leaders in understanding their product, and designing very efficient operations. The efficiency of factories is sensitive to the range of products offered, and a rule of thumb suggests that cutting the range of products in half increases productivity by 75 percent and cuts costs by 30 percent.

On the negative side, though, an organization with a strong focus becomes vulnerable to changes – in the way that a strong focus on a particular type of product becomes a disadvantage when customer tastes change. And managers can become too focused. Porter (1996) says that, 'Overall advantage or disadvantage results from all a company's activities, not only a few.' In other words, an organization can never really succeed by concentrating on a few of its operations, but it should aim at performing them all well – or at least as well as possible.

Chapter review

- We have already touched on several aspects of strategy design. This chapter brings these ideas together and considers the design of an operations strategy in more detail.

- Chapter 3 described a general approach to strategy design based on 'analysis, choice and implementation'. We can adapt this to the design of an operations strategy. In particular, we described a general approach with eight related steps.

- Operations strategies usually involve a combination of top-down design and bottom-up emerging. The balance between these two varies in different circumstances.

- An operations mission describes the purpose and long-term direction for operations. This is usually based on its overall contribution to the business strategy.

- Managers expand the operations mission into a set of related goals and objectives. These give more immediate targets for operations.

- In principle, managers can design strategies by considering the options for key aspects of their operations. In practice, there are so many different configurations that this is impossible, and they limit their consideration to a reasonable number of feasible alternatives.

- There are so many competing factors, views and considerations that it is impossible to choose 'the best' strategy. Managers make their decisions after discussion, agreement, and compromise to get an acceptable design. This always has some associated risk.

- Operations strategies often have a particular focus. There is a large number of possible foci, including cost and waste, product differentiation, niche products, material management, timing, productivity improvement, human resource management, etc. Each of these has different requirements of operations.

CASE STUDY Beta OpStratMan Limited

Beta OpStratMan Limited is a firm of management consultants based in Toronto, Canada and owned by a major firm of accountant's. In the fifteen years since they were formed, they have developed considerable expertise in operations management, particularly in the area of strategic options.

Their own strategy includes an operations mission of, 'working with clients in the best possible ways to help them achieve their goals'. Their operations strategy focuses on a unique product – which comes from the corporation's combination of knowledge, experience and skills. Their operations goals include:

- 'maintaining our position as an industry leader in the practice of operations management
- 'working with diverse organizations to secure major improvements to their performance
- 'building relationships with clients based on trust, integrity and the highest professional standards
- 'providing timely and cost effective advice
- 'continually searching for new opportunities and improvements to the way we work.'

Over the years Beta OpStratMan have helped in the design of operations strategies for many companies. They have developed a standard approach which starts with ten basic questions.

1 What is the overall purpose of your operations?

2 What specific goals and objectives must you achieve?

3 Who are your customers?

4 What type of products do they want, and how many will they buy?

5 What type of products can you make, and how well do these match customer demands?

6 What are your competitors doing and how can you gain a competitive advantage?

7 What type of operations will you use to make your products?

8 What strengths and distinctive capabilities do you have, or can you develop?

9 How do you measure performance?

10 How do you keep up to date with changes?

Based on the answers to these, Beta OpStratMan can start discussing strategy with clients. They identify the key, long-term issues for operations, define options, evaluate these and choose the best, and combine these into an acceptable operations strategy. Then they give assistance with the implementation of this strategy.

Questions

- What is the basis of Beta OpStratMan's own operations strategy? How does this compare with other management consultants?

- How do they set about designing an operations strategy for clients?

- Imagine that you work for a competing management consultant, and have been asked to write a report on 'A general approach to designing an operations strategy'. What would you say in your report?

Source: Company promotional material; private correspondence

Discussion questions

1 How would you set about designing an operations strategy?

2 Several of the problems with top-down strategy design refer to weaknesses in senior managers – with them typically having inadequate knowledge, understanding,

skills, credibility, etc. Why do organizations generously reward such people when they do not seem capable of doing their job?

3 No single group of managers can ever have enough knowledge of both the broad scope of the organization and the details of operations. So an operations strategy must inevitably emerge from the day-to-day experiences of lower managers. Do you agree with this?

4 What is the point of designing an operations mission? Is this simply a more detailed view of the organization's mission?

5 What aspects of operations are likely to have a strategic impact? Are these the same for all types of organization?

6 The factors affecting an operations strategy are so complex that it is impossible to understand them all. Does this mean that strategy design is little more than haphazard guesswork?

7 How can managers compare alternative strategies?

8 What are the likely areas of focus for an operations strategy? How do these affect operations?

9 An organization should not focus on one aspect of its operations, like customer service or quality, but it should try to do everything as well as it can. What are the problems with this approach?

Useful websites

www.sanyo.co.jp
www.sanyo.com

References

Campbell A. and Tawady K., Mission and business philosophy, Heinemann, Oxford, 1990.

Campbell A. and Yeung S., Creating a sense of mission, Long Range Planning, vol 24, pp 10–20, 1991.

Etienne-Hamilton E.C., Operations strategies for competitive advantage, The Dryden Press, Montreal, 1994.

Hamel G. and Prahalad C., Competing for the future, Harvard Business School Press, Boston, MA, 1994.

Hammer M., Beyond reengineering, HarperCollins, New York, 1996.

Hammer M. and Champy J., Reengineering the corporation, HarperCollins, New York, 1993.

Hampton D.R., Contemporary management, McGraw-Hill, New York, 1981.

Harvey-Jones J., All together now, Heinemann, London, 1994.

Hayes R.J. and Wheelwright S.C., Restoring our competitive edge, John Wiley, New York, 1984.

Heizer J. and Render B., Operations management (7th edition), Prentice Hall, Englewood Cliffs, NJ, 2004.

Hill T., Manufacturing strategy (4th edition), Macmillan, Basingstoke, 2000.

Hofer C.W. and Schendel D., Strategy formulation, West Publishing, St Paul, MN, 1978.

Kim J. and Arnold P., Operationalising manufacturing strategy, International Journal of Operations and Production Management, vol 16(12), pp 45–73, 1996.

Kinnunen R.M., Hypotheses relating to strategy formulation in large diversified companies, Academy of Management Review, October, pp 7–14, 1976.

Miller J. and Roth A., Taxonomy of manufacturing strategies, Management Science, vol 40(3), pp 285–304, 1994.

Mills J.F., Neeley A., Platts K. and Gregory M., A framework for the design of Manufacturing design processes, International Journal of Operations and Production Management, vol 15(4), pp 17–49, 1995.

Mintzberg H. and Waters J.A., Of strategies, deliberate and emergent, Strategic Management Journal, July–September, pp 257–272, 1985.

Monden Y., Toyota production system, Industrial Engineering and Management Press, Atlanta, GA, 1983.

Ohno T., Toyota production system, Productivity Press, New York, 1988.

Porter M.E., Competitive strategy, Free Press, New York, 1980.

Porter M.E., Competitive advantage, Free Press, New York, 1985.

Porter M.E., What is strategy, Harvard Business Review, November–December, pp 61–79, 1996.

Skinner W., Manufacturing – the missing link in corporate strategy, Harvard Business Review, May–June, 1969.

Skinner W., Manufacturing in the corporate strategy, John Wiley, New York, 1978.

Spring M. and Bowden R., One more time: how do you win orders, International Journal of Operations and Production Management, vol 17(8), 1997.

Stalk G., Time – the next source of competitive advantage, Harvard Business Review, July–August, pp 41–52, 1988.

Stalk G. and Hout T., Competing against time, The Free Press, New York, 1990.

Teece D.J., Pisano G. and Shuen A., Dynamic capabilities and strategic management, Strategic Management Journal, vol 18(7), pp 509–533.

Thompson A.A. and Strickland A.J., Strategic management (12th edition), McGraw-Hill, New York, 2001.

Waters D., Inventory control and management (2nd edition), John Wiley, Chichester, 2003.

Wheelwright S.C., Japan – where operations really are strategic, Harvard Business Review, July–August, pp 67–74, 1981.

Wild R., Essentials of operations management (5th edition), Thomson Learning, London, 2002.

Wild R. Operations management (6th edition), Thomson Learning, London, 2003.

Womack J. and Jones D., Lean thinking, Simon & Schuster, New York, 1996.

Womack J., Jones D. and Roos D., The machine that changed the world, Rawson, New York , 1990.

CHAPTER 7
Analyses for Strategy Design

Aims of the chapter

The last few chapters have been developing the theme of an operations strategy, and we know that the design needs a detailed knowledge of higher strategies, operations and their environment. In this chapter, we look at some analyses that give this knowledge. In particular, we consider an environmental scan to collect information about the operations environment, and an operations audit to show the details of operations. Then we outline some further analyses that use this information

After reading this chapter you should be able to:

- Discuss the types of analyses needed to design an operations strategy
- Describe the types of information needed about the environment
- Collect data through an environmental scan
- Outline a number of analyses for environmental factors
- Discuss the type of information needed about internal operations
- Collect data through an operations audit
- Use a number of analyses for internal operations
- Do a SWOT analysis

Main themes

The key concepts discussed in this chapter are:

- **Analyses**, to collect information and investigate conditions of the environment and operations
- **Environmental scan**, which describes the operations environment
- **Operations audit**, which describes the operations used in an organization

ENVIRONMENTAL SCANS

In the last chapter, we described a general approach to designing an operations strategy, based on the traditional view of 'analysis, choice and implementation'. This approach has the eight steps shown in Figure 7.1. The three important areas for analysis concern the higher strategies, the operations environment and features of the operations (corresponding to steps 2, 3 and 4). Earlier chapters have described the way that higher strategies – particularly the business strategy – lay down the context for operations, effectively defining the way in which they work. In this chapter, we look at analyses of the other two areas.

We are going to start by looking at the environment, concentrating on the industry and market. Information about the environment comes from an **environmental scan** (as illustrated in Figure 7.2). When we have this information we can do another series of analyses. With something as complicated as an operations strategy, many analyses might be useful for the design, but we will focus on the most common. This separation of the collection of information from its more detailed analysis is somewhat artificial, but it helps to describe the procedure.

The next stage is to look at the operations, where information is collected through an **operations audit**. Here we concentrate on the product, process, resources and management. And again we look at some common analyses that can be done with the information.

Definition of an environmental scan

An operations environment consists of all factors that are external to operations, and which they cannot control. As we saw in chapter 5, the two main areas of this environment are:

- **Within the organization, but outside the operations function** – such as finance, marketing, HRM, etc. These should provide a supportive environment, with all parts of the organization cooperating and working together to achieve the same overall purpose.

- **Completely outside the organization** – including all the external factors that affect operations, such as the market, economic conditions, customer demands, competition, regulations, legislation, social conditions, and all the other factors that contribute to the broader environment. These give a harsher, more competitive environment that is likely to constrain the operations strategy, limiting the strategies available and their likely success.

An **environmental scan** gives managers a clear view of this environment, collecting information about all the important features that surround operations. Because the environment within the broader organization should generally support the operations strategy, an environmental scan focuses on features outside the entire organization.

- An operations environmental scan collects all relevant information about the operations environment.
- It allows analyses of the effects of the environment on current and proposed operations.

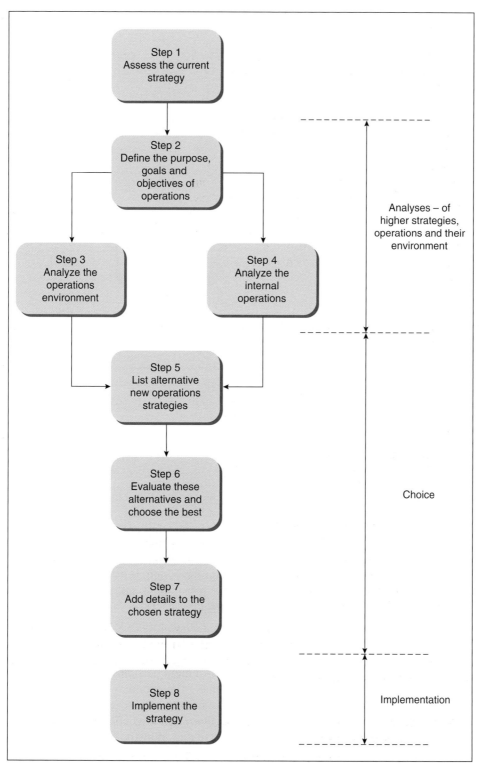

Figure 7.1 Steps in designing an operations strategy

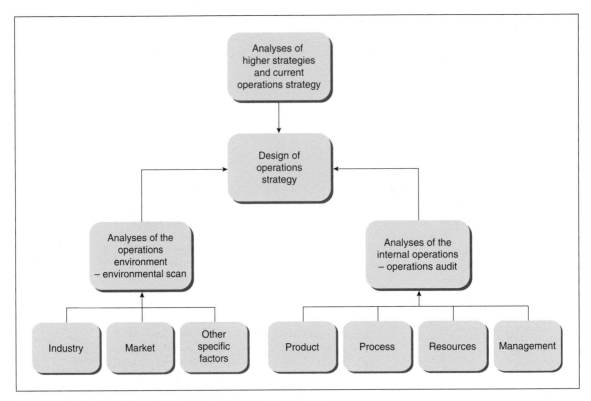

Figure 7.2 Analyses for the design of an operations strategy

Areas of main concern

Only certain strategies can succeed in a particular market and industry. So an environmental scan identifies the main features that exist, and then managers can define the type of strategy that is most likely to succeed. But what are the main features in the environment? In chapter 2 we classified them as the physical environment, political or legal factors, economic factors, social or socio-cultural factors, and technological factors. Each of these affects operations, but the extent of the impact varies with circumstances. BNFL recycle radioactive waste at Sellafield, UK and they work with very tight legal restrictions; The Lavender Residential Home for the Elderly has fewer legal constraints but it responds to strong social issues; American Express is largely affected by economic conditions, and so on. Sometimes one factor is – or becomes – dominant. When there is an earthquake in Kobe, a hurricane in Miami, or a tsunami in the Indian Ocean, the physical environment becomes dominant. In a less spectacular way, an economic downturn can make the economy dominant, while a new law brings the legal system to the fore. An environmental scan has to identify the features that are currently important, and also those that might become important in the future. A company working in a highly regulated industry, for example, has to look carefully at the existing restraints on its actions – and at likely or potential restraints in the future.

Despite obvious examples of rapidly changing environments, most operations work in environments that evolve in a relatively controlled way. The underlying economy remains stable for long periods – and there are unlikely to be rapid changes in the physical environment, political and economic system, social conditions or even developments in technology. Other factors can change more quickly, such as customer demands, market conditions, the actions of competitors, etc. This relative stability is aligned to the two types of environmental factor that we mentioned in chapter 2 (Daft).

1 *Inherent or macro factors* give the infrastructure and framework within which an organization works. These are the more stable factors largely fixed by location and include the political, legal, economic and social systems, climate, technological development, demography, natural environment, transport system and all the other conditions that are determined by the geographical position.

2 *Competitive or micro factors* are the more variable aspects that are set by the industry and market that an organization chooses to work in. They include the industry attractiveness, market size, customer features, suppliers, competitors, employees, and so on.

When managers choose a location for their operations, the inherent factors in the environment are largely fixed – they cannot change the type of economy, weather, tax rates, etc. Perhaps they have more flexibility in the competitive factors, as they can adjust these by their choice of industry and market segments. But it is these competitive factors that change more quickly and generally cause more concern. In particular, operations are affected by changing patterns of customer demand and the actions of competitors, so an environmental scan focuses on three features:

1 *The industry in which the operations work*, which is defined by organizations that use – or might start using in the future – similar resources to make equivalent products to satisfy the same customer demand.

2 *The market for the operations' products*, which is defined by the customers who buy – or might buy – a particular type of product.

3 *Any other relevant external factors, including economic conditions, legal requirements, market conditions, etc.*

A scan reviews the current state of the industry, market and other relevant factors, and particularly looks at ways that the environment will constrain operations. These constraints may come from bodies that have direct power – such as governments, regulators, trade organizations, consumer groups, pressure groups, suppliers and competitors. Or they may be more subtle pressures from prevailing social, cultural, political and ethical standards that restrict the types of activities that are acceptable.

But the scan does not just identify constraints and, conversely, it shows where there are opportunities for the operations to exploit. So its broad thrust is to identify the **opportunities** and **threats** in the environment.

● **Opportunities** show areas where operations can take advantage of prevailing conditions to improve their position. Such opportunities come from many sources, but specific ones are the failure or withdrawal of a current competitor from the market, changing patterns of demand for products, availability of new products, improving economic conditions, societal changes that create unmet demand, and creation of new needs and desires.

● **Threats** are potentially adverse effects that may hinder the long-term survival, integrity, or performance of operations. Again, they come from many sources, but obvious ones are competition, a breakthrough in technology, changing regulations, changing customer tastes, etc. As we saw in chapter 2, there are many responses to environmental threats, ranging from ignoring them through to moving to a new environment (Waters, 1998; Walker *et al.*).

The balance of opportunities and threats shows how successful operations are likely to be. If opportunities predominate we would expect managers to create operations strategies that take advantage of them and be successful; if threats predominate even the best strategy might be unsuccessful. But this balance changes over time, so managers must be prepared to update the operations strategy after an environmental scan, as suggested in Figure 7.3.

Industry analysis

The purpose of an **industry analysis** is to study actual and potential competitors, their characteristics, strategies, objectives, performance, strengths and weaknesses. This gives managers a detailed understanding of the industry, and the likely moves of competitors. Industry analyses tend to concentrate on five questions.

1 *What are the main features of the industry?* This typically starts with a description of the industry's structure, its ownership, supply chains, amount of forward and backward integration, barriers to entry and exit, geographical boundaries, any other specific features that shape the industry. From this

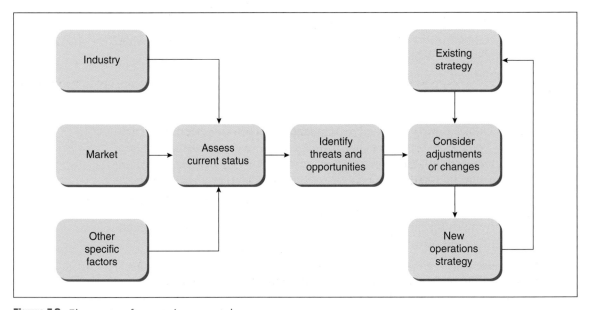

Figure 7.3 Elements of an environmental scan

IDEAS IN PRACTICE Ratner Group

An operations environment can sometimes change very quickly. Sometimes the cause of the change is obvious, such as a leading competitor's change of strategy, or new legislation. Occasionally the source of the change comes from within the organization itself, and you can see many examples of senior managers making mistakes that seriously affect the performance of their organization.

In 1984 Gerald Ratner became managing director of the family jewellery business. It had 130 shops in the UK, but made a loss of £350,000 in the last year. Things obviously needed to change. Gerald Ratner looked at the threats facing his company and designed strategies to convert them into new opportunities. In particular, he moved away from the traditional, high-cost operations of jewellers and developed a new low cost alternative – effectively changing the strategy from product differentiation to price leadership. Then he replaced the cold, aloof and unwelcoming shops by bright, brash, modern ones that sold goods at very low prices. The 'pile 'em high, sell 'em cheap' approach was successful and the company soon bought the competing chains of H. Samuel, Zales, Salisbury, Sterling, Ernest Jones, and Kay Jewellers of America. By 1991 Ratner Group was the world's biggest chain of jewellers, employing 25,000 people in 1,300 stores in the UK

and 1,000 stores in the USA, its value had risen from £11 million to £680 million, its profit had doubled every year for seven years to £120 million.

On 23rd April 1991, Gerald Ratner was giving a talk at the annual convention of the Institute of Directors in London, with 3,000 senior managers meeting in the Albert Hall. He was explaining how he could sell goods so cheaply, and said that it was because 'they're total crap'. A pair of earrings from Ratners costs less than a prawn sandwich from Marks and Spencers, but 'the earrings probably won't last as long'.

Not surprisingly, customers were not impressed by these comments – despite a half million pound advertising campaign to limit the damage, and rebranding the different chains in the Group. Then the UK was hit by a recession, which hit the sales of luxury goods, and made Ratner's strategy of continuing rapid expansion seem reckless. By October sales had fallen alarmingly, the share price fell 42 percent in five weeks, and the company was making a loss. In 1992, it closed 326 shops, shedding over 2,000 staff, and Gerald Ratner left the company, which was then valued at £49 million.

Source: Tibballs G., Business blunders, Robinson Publishing, London, 1999

---

broad view of the structure of the industry, the analysis moves on to look at more details – typically, key processes, strategic resources, power in the supply chains, economies of scale, specialized expertise needed, point of main products in their life cycle, underlying economic performance, what organizations have to do to be successful in the industry, and so on. This part of the analysis gives a general view of how attractive the industry is.

2 *Where is the industry heading and what forces are driving it?* This identifies dominant trends and the reasons for their existence. There might, for example, be rapid developments in technology or changing customer demand that are pushing the industry to be innovative and develop new products. Common driving forces are growth, changes in customer characteristics, changes in product use, product innovation, technological change, marketing innovation,

entry or exit of major organizations, diffusion of knowledge, increasing globalization, changes in costs and efficiency, moves to differentiated products instead of standard ones, new regulations, government policies, changes in societal concerns, attitudes and lifestyles, changes in uncertainty or business risk.

Industries, like their products, move through a life cycle of emergence, growth, maturity, decline and closure. At each point in this life cycle there are different pressures on operations. For example, the driving force in a new industry is likely to be product innovation; but with a mature industry there is likely to be more pressure from process innovation. By extrapolating trends, this part of the analysis gives a view of what the industry will look like – and how attractive it will be – in the future.

3 *Who are the competitors?* This gives a broad picture of competition within the industry, including the type of competitors, their number, size and performance. Useful information includes market performance (sales, market shares, prices, trends, etc.), financial performance (profitability, costs, cash position, ROI, price/earnings ratio, etc.), products (range, features, age, etc.), operations (locations, process technology, capacity, productivity, etc.), significant successes or failures, major commitments, regulatory constraints, and any other relevant information. Particular concerns here might be potential entrants to the industry and possible leavers.

4 *What are their strategies?* This shows the objectives of the competitors, how they look for competitive advantages, whether their strategies are working, and what moves they might make in the future. In many industries there is a dominant strategy – like low costs in supermarkets – and managers can decide whether to adopt this strategy for direct competition, or develop an alternative. This decision depends on how successful the strategy is. If an apparently strong competitor is focusing on low costs, but has poor financial results, we might think twice before following the same route. On the other hand, we would be tempted to adopt other strategies that are clearly leading to success.

If we compare the objectives of competitors with their actual performance, we can see how well they are achieving their objectives. This comparison shows whether they are likely to be satisfied with their current performance, or are likely to make moves to improve their position in the future. For example, a competitor who is currently the third largest in the industry with an aim of being the leader, is inevitably going to look for further expansion.

5 *What are competitors' strengths and weaknesses?* This sees what each competitor does particularly well or badly, their distinctive capabilities, how this affects competition and whether there are any gaps in current offerings. An organization would find it difficult to compete on costs, if the main competitors were all very strong in their use of efficient processes. A better strategy would be to focus on some other area of operations, perhaps customized products. On the other hand, if no competitors were strong in, say, fast delivery, this would be a potential strategy that is at least worth considering.

The answers to these five questions give the details of the industry, identify opportunities and threats, and show managers how they might develop their strategies (as indicated in Figure 7.4).

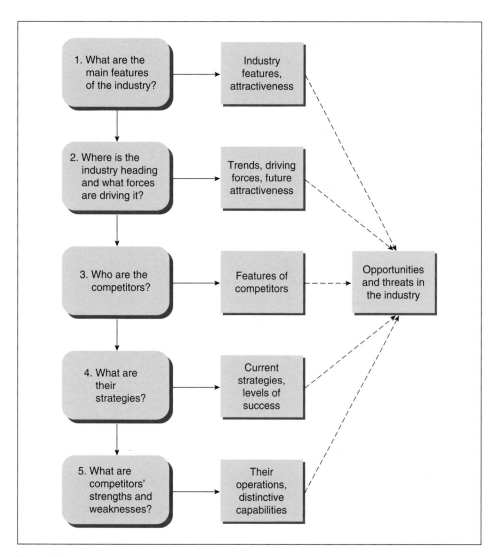

Figure 7.4 Basis of an industry analysis

Market analysis

A **market analysis** shows the state of the market, giving a description of customers, their main characteristics, and type of products they want. It tends to focus on the following four questions.

1 *What are the main features of the market?* – the sales volume, sales value, distribution of sales value, geographical spread of sales, channels of distribution, supply chains, trends in demand, ease of market entry and exit, seasonality and trends.

2 *Who are the customers?* – number, size, common features, products they really want, satisfaction with current products, loyalty, etc.

3 *What are their buying habits?* – the probability of repeat orders, distribution of order size, reasons for buying, incentives, etc.

4 *What are the products?* – important features, where are they in their life cycle, delivery frequency, quality, lead time, stocks, substitutes, potential new products, customer service, etc.

The answers to these questions give a detailed view of the market, showing who the customers are, what they really want, and if their needs are currently being satisfied (illustrated in Figure 7.5). The aim is to identify gaps that operations can exploit – and highly competitive areas that might be avoided. If, say, customers want a customized Internet service, while all suppliers are competing on cost, there may be an opportunity to exploit.

Collecting information

At the heart of an environmental scan is the need to collect information. There are several ways of organizing this, with an important distinction between primary and secondary data (Waters, 2001). Primary data is collected for a specific purpose – in this case it is collected by operations for the environmental scan. Secondary data is

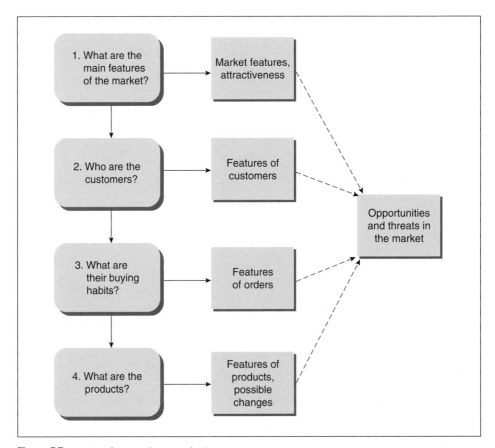

Figure 7.5 Basis of a market analysis

collected by other people or for other purposes, such as reviews conducted by trade organizations or surveys of consumer tastes run by marketing departments.

The benefits of primary data are that it fits the need exactly, is up to date and is reliable. Market analyses are more likely to use primary data, to give details of specific segments and keep up to date with changing attitudes. Despite problems and well-known mistakes, market surveys remain the most important way of collecting information about demand. Another useful source is internal sales records, which give a complete breakdown of all customers and sales, allowing:

- a better understanding of individual customer needs and the operations that are needed to meet them (Walker *et al.*)
- identification of opportunities to sell more to each customer, including individual marketing plans
- a broader picture of the lifetime value of a customer (Blattberg and Unglaub)
- generally improved effectiveness and efficiency of marketing.

Secondary data is much cheaper, faster and easier to collect. It also has the benefit of using sources that are not generally available, with governments, trade organizations, professional institutes, trade unions, universities, research units, international bodies, etc., collecting statistics from a wide range of sources. This often relates to industry, and is used most commonly for industry analyses. There is often a huge amount of secondary information available – as you can see from any search of the Web – and managers should look for this first. There is no point in spending time and effort to collect data that somebody already has sitting on a shelf. If you just search the Web for information about, say, the fast food industry, you can find thousands of sites, with millions of pages of data that might be relevant. The problem is not usually finding secondary data, but sorting through everything available to identify the small part that might be relevant. And annoyingly, the secondary data is often not exactly what you want, is in slightly the wrong form, or is out of date.

In practice, it is often best to use a combination of primary and secondary data, perhaps using secondary data to give the overall picture and then adding details from primary data. A UK logistics company, for example, might get a broad view of industrial prospects from secondary data collected by the UK Government and European Union; then it can get more details about the transport industry from secondary data collected by the Road Haulage Association and Chartered Institute for Logistics and Transport; then it can collect primary data from its customers to get a detailed view of their future plans.

There is a huge amount of secondary data available, and if managers have the resources they can collect another huge amount of primary data. The problem is not getting enough data, but sorting through everything, seeing what it means, analyzing it, interpreting the results – and then using it properly for the operations strategy. And the environment is so complex that even when they have as much information as possible, managers still cannot get a complete picture of it. They can never hope to understand all the minutiae, and it is usually impractical to get more than an overview of the main features. So managers have to decide the most important features of the environment and concentrate on these. A motor insurance company, for example, might decide that their most important considerations are the types of policy offered by competitors, market price structures, future traffic conditions, and driving habits. Then managers in the company can put most effort into analyzing these. Unfortunately, most analyses for strategy present information, but do not give much guidance on what to do with it. So this is where the skills of managers are important. Strategic managers have to review the information and use it as the basis for informed decisions – and here they need experience, judgement and intuition. Napoleon liked his generals to be lucky – and luck always plays a part in strategic success.

ANALYSES OF THE ENVIRONMENT

Having collected information, managers now have to use it – and this means doing appropriate analyses to help with the design of an operations strategy. There are many possible analyses, and possibly the most common is a **PEST analysis**.

PEST analysis

A **PEST analysis** concentrates on four important factors in an environmental scan – **P**olitical, **E**conomic, **S**ocial and **T**echnological factors. By taking a broad view of these categories, managers can bring together related ideas, and see how they can design a strategy to give an appropriate fit. Typical considerations in a PEST analysis are:

- *Political factors* – which include government laws, regulations and legal issues that set the formal rules under which the organization must work:
  - Existing laws and new ones likely to be passed.
  - Industry regulations, norms and acceptable behaviour.
  - Government spending and priorities.
  - Tax levels, policies and likely changes.
  - Free trade zones, trade barriers, tariffs and quotas.
  - Employment laws, with health and safety considerations.
  - Environmental regulations.
  - Different views of political parties.
  - Political stability.
- *Economic factors* – affect the cost of operations and the purchases of potential customers:
  - Strength of the global, national and regional economy.
  - Position in economic cycle.
  - Economic growth.
  - Taxation and likely changes.
  - Exchange rates and relative strengths of currencies.
  - Interest rates.
  - Inflation rates.
- *Social factors* – demographic and cultural aspects of the environment, which affect the products that customers demand and their pattern of purchases:
  - Demographics.
  - Trends and changes to the population structure such as movements, growth, age distribution, ethnic mix.

- Social trends, such as attitudes towards carers, increasing leisure, use of IT and mobile communications.
- Changing lifestyles, such as flexible working arrangements, health consciousness, convenience shopping.
- Changing purchasing habits, such as branding and purchasing over the internet.
- Emphasis on safety and increasing litigation.

- *Technological factors* – can change products and the process, increasing productivity, lowering entry barriers to industries, giving more flexibility, and so on:
  - Technologies recently available or still being developed.
  - R&D and new types of product.
  - New purchasing mechanisms (internet, intranet, extranet).
  - Automation and new production technologies.
  - New supply chain mechanisms.
  - Increasing developments in computer technology, IT and mobile communications.
  - Incentives to use new technology and rate of change.

Other analyses

There are many other analyses for different aspects of the environment. Because of the complex circumstances and the essentially subjective nature of the data, these almost invariably take a qualitative view. They do not look for 'optimal' solutions, but they summarize findings and help managers organize their thoughts. Sometimes they do little more than give standard formats for presenting ideas and making comparisons. There are so many possible analyses that we can do little more than illustrate some of the most common.

Industry attractiveness is difficult to gauge, but depends on factors like the size, growth rate, demand variability, profitability, competitiveness, global opportunities, and so on. We cannot define a convincing measure of industry attractiveness, so managers tend to summarize it as 'high, medium or low'. This is clearly a very coarse measure, but it does give some structure. A useful extension adds a similar measure of the operations' performance – that might include capacity, output, market share, growth, logistics, costs, profit margins, etc. – to give the matrix shown in Figure 7.6.

This is an extension of the market growth/market share matrix that we described in chapter 2, but with the market growth expanded into a broader view of industry attractiveness, and market share expanded into a broader view of operations performance. And this matrix can suggest strategic moves. The most attractive area has good operations in an attractive industry, and managers should actively develop these areas and make them even stronger. At the other extreme are poor operations in an unattractive industry, and managers here should consider radical changes or selling the operations. Between these two extremes is the option for 'holding' or keeping things as they are. This matrix obviously gives a limited view, but it can give a useful synopsis.

Market attractiveness is, again, difficult to summarize in a single measure, but economists do attempt to give figures for industry 'concentration'. For example, the

IDEAS IN PRACTICE Polish television

In 1989 Poland began its transition from a centrally planned economy, to a free market. The whole economic structure of the country has now changed, with the government actively encouraging competition and privatizing most nationalized industries. Thousands of new domestic companies have been formed, and foreign companies have been quick to invest in a large, stable economy that has relatively low operating costs. Poland became a member of the European Union in 2004.

An interesting area for development is the television service. Until the 1990s the state ran a limited service, but now the privately owned networks are far more extensive. Nonetheless, there is still room for expansion, particularly in specialized services delivered through cable and satellite. For a company considering entering this market, a PEST analysis could start by identifying the opportunities and threats posed in each category.

- **Political**
  - *Opportunities* – government commitment to an independent television service, integration with the European Union, security of private investment.
  - *Threats* – political rivalry between emerging parties, uncertainty about satellite services, possible new regulations.
- **Economic**
  - *Opportunities* – fast growing economy, growing private sector, increasing consumer spending, declining unemployment, free trade in the European Union, export of specialized language services.
  - *Threats* – potential instability in economy, high taxation, needs of social security funds, impact of foreign services.
- **Social**
  - *Opportunities* – growing consumerism, tastes for new ideas, international viewpoint, transfer of successful ideas from other countries.
  - *Threats* – diverse tastes give market segmentation, potential growth of nationalism, limited interest in television, competing activities, increasing acceptance of foreign language services.
- **Technology**
  - *Opportunities* – adoption of European standards, import of latest technology, educated and knowledgeable workforce, new production facilities.
  - *Threats* – inconsistent formats, outdated operations, other forms of media distribution (internet, mobile phones, DVDs, etc.).

Sources: Waters D., Report on the Polish television industry, Richmond, Parkes and Wright, Warsaw, 2005

'concentration ratio' shows the combined percentage share of a market held by the four largest producers (or sometimes the largest 8, 25 or 50 suppliers). A high concentration ratio shows that the market is dominated by a few producers – which suggests that it is less competitive or even close to a monopoly. A low concentration ratio shows that there are many rivals.

A better view of market attractiveness comes from Porter's five forces that shape market competitiveness – rivalry among existing organizations, suppliers of key inputs, customers, potential new entrants, and substitute products. When an organization

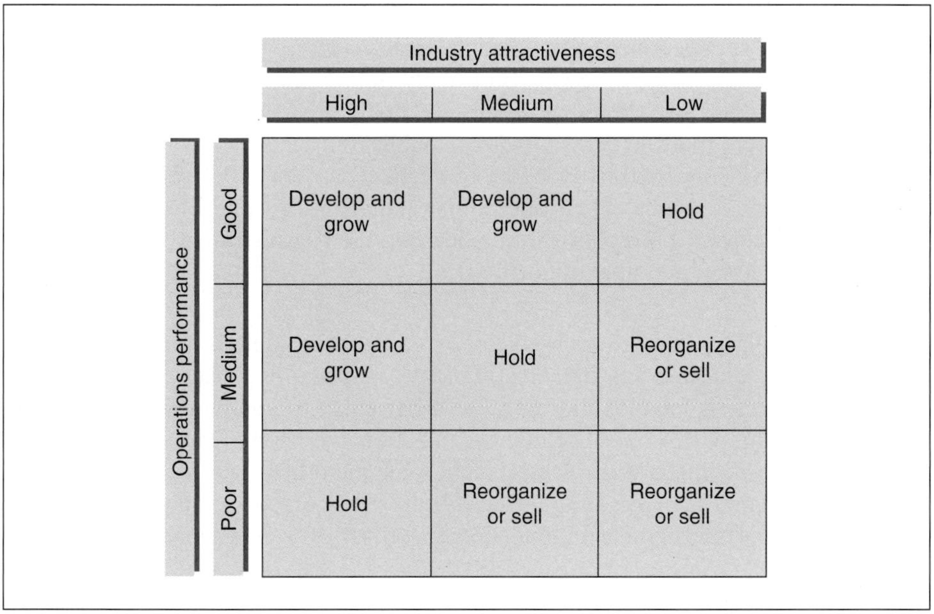

Figure 7.6 Industry attractiveness/operations' strength matrix

takes a specific action to gain an advantage, a competitive market has rivals responding, with the strength of their reaction showing the level of competition (usually described as cut throat, intense, moderate or weak).

Key success factors identify the critical elements that operations must deliver if they are to succeed. Typically the KSFs are the small number – usually between four and six – of factors that customers really value, and which affect their choice of products and suppliers. A beer company, for example, must brew a beer whose taste customers like, have enough advertizing to make the brand known, have efficient logistics to get the product to customers, and low operating costs to keep the price down. In the same way, a management consultant must have a clear sense of purpose, specialized knowledge, a focus on results, clear communications, and be able to produce valuable and timely results.

KSFs show the areas where operations must concentrate – and to succeed they must perform all the KSFs well – and get a competitive advantage by excelling in at least one. A problem, though, is that the operations environment is so complicated that it is difficult to identify cause and effects. In other words, managers cannot hope to understand the environment fully, and they may not even be able to identify the factors that lead to success. So the ability to identify KSFs is one of the skills that operations need from their strategic managers.

Competitor analysis looks for a thorough understanding of competitors, describing what competitors are doing now and what they are likely to do in the future. It identifies the main competitors, describes their characteristics, identifies their operations and strategies, sees how successful these are and how they evolve, looks at their strengths and weaknesses, and identifies any vulnerable areas.

Perhaps the key point of a competitor analysis is that it anticipates competitors' likely future actions. Sometimes this is easy, as many organizations are happy to distribute their future plans in press handouts, public announcements, rumours, acquisitions, research efforts, and so on. More often, likely moves have to be inferred from past actions and decisions. Then operations managers can plan their reactions to these moves in advance, preparing and modifying their own strategy to avoid potential threats and grasp potential opportunities.

Competitor profiling is more focused than a competitor analysis and gives a direct comparison of some aspects of performance. The usual approach is to identify a series of key success factors, and then use a bar chart to compare two operations. Alternatively, the performance of one organization can be compared with standard targets, industry norms, historic achievement, or some other measure.

Figure 7.7 shows the basis of a typical profile. This compares the performance of an organization's operations and its main competitor over eight key success factors.

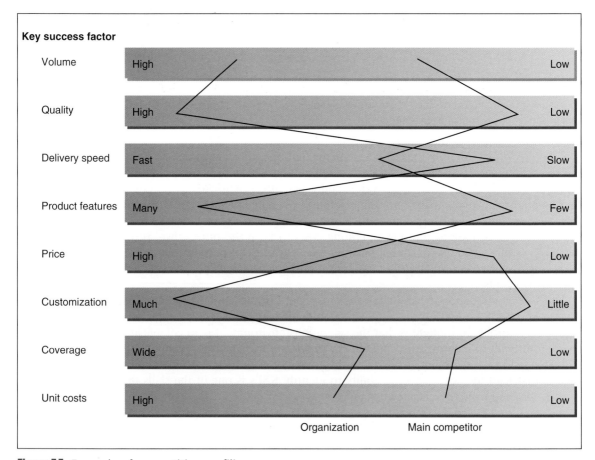

Figure 7.7 Example of competitive profiling

From this, managers can identify differences, discuss reasons and suggest possible changes. In this example the organization seems to be lagging behind in quality and product features, while giving much more emphasis to customization.

Group map compares the competitive characteristics of different groups or organizations within the same industry. An industry may consist of groups of rivals that compete using a similar strategy, typically having the same type of product, appealing to the same customers, emphasizing the same features, and so on. Then we can draw a graph to compare the features of different groups, with axes showing key details – usually the most important competitive factors. Figure 7.8 shows an example from the Hungarian beer industry, showing the position of key groups according to price and geographical coverage. The size of circle around each location shows the market share.

Driving force analysis assumes that industries change because of driving forces that move them inexorably in a particular direction. To design a reasonable strategy, managers have to identify the strength and direction of these driving forces, and then adjust the operations strategy to fit the consequent new conditions. This analysis identifies the three or four factors that are most likely to influence change over the next few years, then assesses the impact of each, and the effects on the operations strategy.

This can also monitor the way that conditions change over time. An environmental scan describes conditions at a single point, but managers must know how the key factors change over time so that they can update the results of previous environmental scans, interpret the new findings, identify trends, forecast likely conditions in the future and update their strategies.

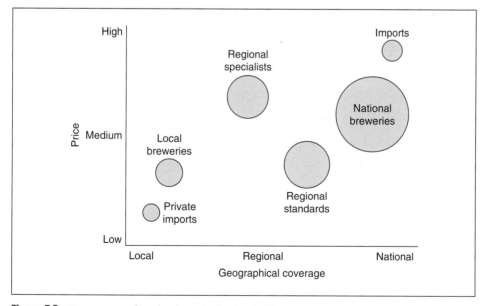

Figure 7.8 Group map for the beer industry in Hungary

OPERATIONS AUDIT

The design of an operations strategy must be based on a realistic evaluation of their operations. This seems obvious, but many managers – even those who can give a detailed description of the current operations – do not really appreciate their scope or potential. To get this appreciation, they need an **operations audit.**

> ● An operations audit gives a detailed description of the operations used by an organization.

Waller describes an operations audit as, 'a detailed analysis of the firm, the operation, or the supply chain to obtain an in-depth understanding of current performance'. It concentrates on the **strengths** and **weaknesses** of operations, and looks at four key areas of concern – the type of product, process used, resources and management.

The product

At the heart of an operations audit is a review of the products. This review looks at the type of product, its general design, features, quality, image, age, point in its life cycle, components, costs, resources used, and so on. The aim is to get an intimate knowledge of the product, that allows managers to compare it with the demands of customers, and with the products made by competitors. Then they can build on its relative strengths, identify any weaknesses and take actions to overcome them.

Traditionally, research and development plays an important role in the long-term supply of products. It is difficult to judge the quality or performance of R&D, but we can start by asking whether their activities help achieve the organizations objectives, are properly managed in the interests of the organization, have a reputation for competence, and produce results. Presumably, if R&D provide a series of new products that continues to satisfy customer demand, then it is doing a reasonably good job. Of course, many organizations do not need any formal R&D facilities, as they either do no fundamental research for new products, or else they can get the results from other sources. There are many research centres, industry collaborations and universities that do research and then widely publish their results.

We develop the ideas of product design in chapters 9 and 10.

The process

The next part of an operations audit asks how the products are made – giving the details of the operations and wider process. The main information here concerns:

- details of operations, showing exactly what is done, facilities available, capacity, bottlenecks, level of technology, age of facilities, etc.
- performance of operations, including productivity, comparisons with competitors, efficiency, operating costs, and unit costs

- structure of the supply chain, including location of facilities, stocks, relations with suppliers, and transport
- the types of raw materials, amounts, costs, suppliers, reliability of supply relationships with suppliers
- financial support, amounts spent on buying new equipment, funds available for modernizing and improving existing facilities, R&D budget, education and training budget
- the skills, experience and knowledge of people working in operations, staff turnover, morale, etc.

We discuss the design of the process in chapters 11 and 12, and then move on to supply chain management in chapters 13 and 14.

Resources

The third part of an operations audit concerns the various resources that are needed by the process. This information comes from a resource audit, which we described in chapter 5. This identifies the resources that an organization already has available, recognizes the ones that are in some way unique, describes their condition, shows how they are used – and lists the resources that could be available if needed.

As well as giving a snapshot of the availability and use of resources, an audit also identifies more productive ways to use resources – by either supplying more products with the same resources, or supplying the same products using fewer resources. The aim is to improve the use of resources until it becomes a strength and then a distinctive capability.

Resources cost money, so their use is invariably linked to financial performance, with managers balancing the cost of acquiring resources with their benefits. In principle, managers should pay up to their opportunity cost for resources, but this assumes that managers can put a value on the possession of resources and, by implication, their absence. It is fairly easy to put a notional value on, say, a piece of equipment, as we can find a depreciated value, sales value, or replacement cost. It is much more difficult to put a value on intangible resources – as who can say how much the knowledge and skills of employees, reputation, ongoing research, intellectual capital, etc. is really worth? Nonetheless, some kind of estimate often must be made, if only to put a fair value on the organization and reliable annual accounts.

The share price of public companies gives its perceived market value, which is a combination of its tangible and intangible assets. As the annual accounts give a value for the fixed assets, we can subtract this from the share value – with adjustments for liabilities and investments – to get a value for the intangible assets. These are often many times greater than the tangible assets, and research by Interbrand (Grayson and Hodges) suggests that 90 percent of the market value of some companies – such as Coca-Cola, Kellogg's and American Express – comes from intangibles. Stewart gives a more rigorous version of this calculation, but all variations on this basic method put too much weight on the share price, which varies quickly and for no apparent reason. This means that the value of intangible assets also varies for no reason.

Intangible assets include a variety of factors, such as brand, corporate culture, customer loyalty, innovation, sustainability, knowledge, skills, and so on. It seems inevitable that some of these will continue to grow, such as the value of brands.

IDEAS IN PRACTICE mmO$_2$

BT Wireless was the mobile phone division of BT, which was launched as a separate company, mmO$_2$, in 2001. By 2004 it had become a successful company with 20 million customers in the UK, Germany and Ireland, 12,000 employees and an annual turnover of £6 billion. A reorganization in 2004 left mmO$_2$ as a wholly owned subsidiary of the O$_2$ group.

The whole mobile phone industry continues to grow quickly, particularly data services. When more than 11 billion text messages were sent through mmO$_2$'s networks in 2004, this accounted for 20 percent of their business. Like all mobile phone companies, mmO$_2$ has substantial resources, some of which are classified as fixed assets, but leaving the majority as intangibles. We can get a notional value for these from mmO$_2$'s 2004 balance sheet, with the following figures in millions of pounds. Then the two basic calculations are:

Fixed assets = tangible assets + investments + intangible assets
Shareholder value = fixed assets + current assets − total liabilities

Tangible assets	£ 3,996	
Investments	£ 5	
Intangible assets	£ 7,354	
Fixed assets	£ 11,355	£11,355
Current assets		£ 2,043
Total liabilities		(£ 3,307)
Shareholder value		£10,091

This suggests that the intangible assets are valued at almost twice the tangible assets. This is by no means unusual for the communications industry, and the intangibles often account for much more than this.

Sources: mmO$_2$ Annual report, London, 2004, O$_2$ Information for shareholders, London, 2004; website at www.mmo2.com

However, these values can change very quickly, and some people suggest that traditional accounting methods are unable to give a realistic response (Schwartz). For example, owners of brands are increasingly being held accountable for the wider effects of their operations, with fast food restaurants responsible for environmental damage caused by logging and factory farms, electronics companies and car manufacturers having to buy back discarded models, cigarette companies responsible for health care, and so on. And mistakes happen quickly and take a long time to repair – with a rule of thumb that, 'it takes twenty years to build a reputation and five minutes to destroy it'.

Management

The fourth part of an operations audit concerns the management. However, it is clearly difficult to give a convincing description of the capabilities and competencies of senior managers. If the organization prospers – or fails – is it because of the skills of managers, or because of some broader effect in the environment? Buchele suggests some questions that can begin to answer this:

- seeing whether senior managers work collectively, or if there is one dominant person or clique
- reviewing the quality of the plans that managers design
- examining their record in meeting their objectives
- seeing how plans are considered and implemented in the organization
- measuring the turnover in senior managers.

Although these are all vague requirements, it is difficult to be more precise. A lot of work has been done on the assessment of senior managers, but it is still difficult to give convincing measures of performance – as you can see when an executive tries to justify an enormous pay rise.

ANALYSES FOR OPERATIONS

As with the environment, there are many analyses that can help with an operations audit. Waller lists 25 useful analyses ranging from an ABC analysis through to Taguchi methods, but this is still only scratching the surface. Obviously, we cannot describe many of these, but the following list shows the scope of some of the most common.

Financial analysis is the traditional way of judging the performance of operations. Often these are simple values such as income, profit, value added, operating costs, unit costs, assets, payback period, etc. More usually, these simple figures are used in financial ratios for funding (such as debt ratio and gearing), liquidity (such as current ratio), cash flows (such as turnover), profitability (such as profit margins), and use of assets (such as return on investment). Sometimes the measures are more complex, such as cost/benefit analysis (which compares the total benefits of a strategy with the costs of achieving it), benchmark performance (comparing financial performance with other operations), gap analysis (finding the gap between projected future performance and competitors' (Argenti)), financial models (to simulate future performance (Shim and McGlade; Rowe *et al.*)).

Financial measures give objective values that are easy to understand, allow comparisons with other organizations, follow trends over time, focus on important issues and are phrased in terms that stakeholders understand. But they have drawbacks of concentrating on past rather than current performance, being slow to respond to changes, ignoring operational issues, relying on accounting conventions, emphasizing symptoms rather than actual features, and giving a very limited view. It may be bad news to see that profitability is declining, but financial measures ignore any underlying reasons – such as changes in the environment – and they do not suggest any remedy.

Performance analysis takes a broader view than finances and looks at other aspects of performance. Managers can use a huge range of measures, some of which relate directly to operations – such as capacity, utilization, production, productivity and efficiency (Neely). Others refer to the five competitive features of price, quality, speed, flexibility or other factors. In the last chapter we listed some objectives for these, each of which is based on a corresponding measure of performance. For

IDEAS IN PRACTICE Scoring models

Managers use performance measures to compare different operations. One way of organizing this uses a scoring model, as illustrated in Figure 7.9. This lists the main measures and gives each a weight to show its relative importance. Then for each operations we can give a score for each measure to show the actual performance (out of ten in this case). Multiplying this score by the weight gives a weighted score. The sum of the weighted scores for each operations give a direct comparison of overall performance. In this example operations B give the best overall performance, followed by operations C.

Performance measure	Weight	Operations A		Operations B		Operations C	
		Score	Weighted score	Score	Weighted score	Score	Weighted score
Price							
Unit cost	16	5	80	6	96	8	128
Fixed cost	8	7	56	8	64	8	64
Profit margin	5	8	40	9	45	7	35
Quality							
Cost of scrap	5	9	45	7	35	5	25
Customer complaints	9	10	90	7	63	4	36
Warranty costs	5	9	45	6	30	7	35
Speed							
Lead time	8	7	56	5	40	10	80
Queue length	7	5	35	5	35	9	63
Cycle time	4	3	12	8	32	6	24
Flexibility							
Product range	5	2	10	8	40	7	35
Variation of capacity	6	3	18	7	42	8	48
Time to change	6	1	6	4	24	7	42
Other							
Productivity	4	5	20	9	36	3	12
Capacity	6	5	30	9	54	1	6
Utilization	6	5	30	8	48	2	12
Totals	100	84	573	106	684	92	645

Figure 7.9 Scoring model for comparing operations' performance

instance, we listed some common objectives for quality as percent defective, percent conforming to specifications, number of customer returns, cost of reworking, customer complaints, warranty costs, surveys of customer satisfaction, usefulness of product – and each of these is based on a measure of operations performance.

As well as such general measures, there are specific ones for particular industries, such as the utilization of airline seats, weight of goods transported by rail, and number of calls answered in a call centre. A supermarket will do the usual financial measure, and then it has a huge number of other options for measuring the operation – starting with area, shelf space, brands, number of products, back-room space, unloading bays, etc. – and relating these to sales, stocks, costs, profits, employees, customer views, management overheads, etc.

The aim of these measures is to make comparisons, identify problems, show strengths that can be developed, indicate areas for improvement, direct resources to the most useful areas – and they can monitor performance over time to show trends. On the other hand, the main problems are knowing what factors are important enough to measure, deciding how to measure them, and what is a reasonable level of performance. As Reichheld says, 'The choice of what a business measures communicates values, channels employee thinking and sets management priorities. . . . Measures define what a company will become.'

Performance – importance relates some measure of actual operations performance to customers' views of its importance. The principle is that if customers put a lot of importance on a measure, then operations should achieve good performance here, or at least better performance than competitors. On the other hand, if customers do not put much importance on a measure, then operations need not pay it so much attention, and they need not necessarily be worried if their performance is worse than competitors'. Figure 7.10 shows a useful matrix to illustrate this. Here customers' view of importance – ranked as low, medium or high – is compared with actual performance – ranked as worse than competitors, the same as, or better. The body of the matrix shows an appropriate response. For instance, when some measure of performance is worse than competitors' and customers rate this measure as highly important, then operations must take urgent action to improve things. At the other extreme, when some measure of performance is better than competitors' but customer rate this measure as unimportant, then operations might be giving excess performance and wasting resources.

Balanced scorecard recognizes that no single measure of performance can give a broad picture of the organization's health, so managers need to consider a range of measures

		Importance to customers		
		Low	Medium	High
Performance relative to competitors	Worse	Monitor and possibly improve	Improve	Urgent action to improve
	Same	OK	Monitor and possibly improve	Improve
	Better	Possibly excess	OK	OK

Figure 7.10 Performance–importance matrix

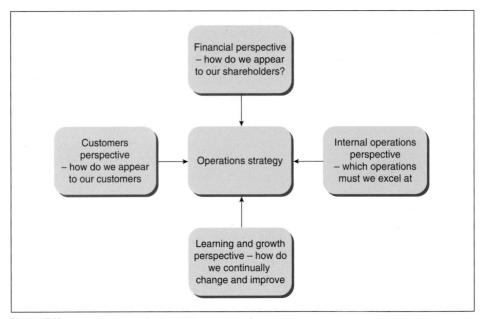

Figure 7.11 Elements in a balanced scorecard

for different aspects of operations. For convenience, these measures are often clustered into a number of distinct categories, in the way that a PEST analysis considers four categories of environmental factor. There are many versions of this, but a popular one is the **balanced scorecard** described by Kaplan and Norton (and illustrated in Figure 7.11). This used four 'perspectives' to describe the impact of different factors:

1 *Financial perspective* – which considers financial performance (profits, return on investment, income, operating costs, sales value, etc.). This asks how the organization appears to its shareholders, and how it can create value and further gains from its operations.

2 *Customer perspective* – which considers competitive advantage (customer satisfaction, number of product returns, customers moving to competitors, service time, waiting time, reliability, etc.). This asks how the organization appears to its customers, what they value, and how the organization can serve them better.

3 *Internal operations perspective* – which considers distinctive capabilities (productivity, number of defects, unit cost, time to produce a unit, materials waste, etc.). This asks what operations the organization must excel at, how it can best achieve its aims, and what systems and processes it needs.

4 *Learning and growth perspective* – which sees how the organization reacts to changing conditions (number of new products, sales of new products, research and development effort, development time, training of employees, qualifications of employees, training programmes, etc.). This asks how the organization can continually change and improve, what capabilities and tools people need to continue the growth, and how these can be developed into distinctive capabilities.

Benchmarking compares operations performance with the best of its competitors. The basis of **benchmarking** is that managers build on the experience of other organizations in their industry. To be specific, the procedure starts with managers identifying areas where the performance of their own operations should be improved, and finding the competitor with the best performance in this area. Then they analyze the competitor's operations to see how it achieves its superior performance, and look for ideas that they can adopt and adapt to their specific conditions. This procedure is summarized in Figure 7.12.

Benchmarking originally made comparisons with direct competitors, but it now looks at any other organization that can give benefits (Pickering and Chambers; Lebfried and McNair). For example, Movers International and PetroCanada are not direct competitors, but they both run transport fleets, and can learn lessons from each other. Similarly, rail companies can learn lessons from the operations of airlines, or even from companies that give good customer service, such as fast food restaurants.

An interesting consequence of benchmarking is that operations tend to converge into common patterns. When one organization gains an advantage, then its competitors will notice this and do some benchmarking to look for ideas that they can adopt – and so the whole industry is soon working along common lines. As Porter (1996) says, 'The more benchmarking companies do, the more they look alike.' This in itself gives opportunities for managers to gain an advantage by following a more differentiated strategy.

Value chain analysis is based on the view of a process as a series of operations, each of which adds value to the product. Value chain analysis looks at the sequence of

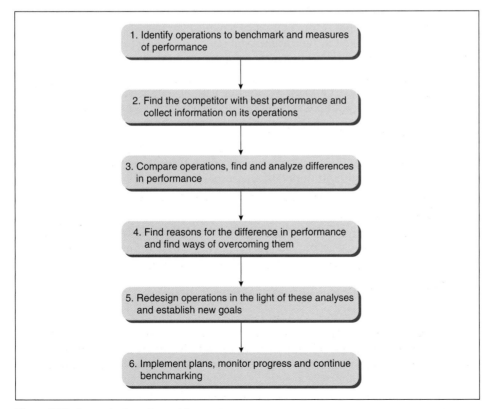

Figure 7.12 Steps in benchmarking

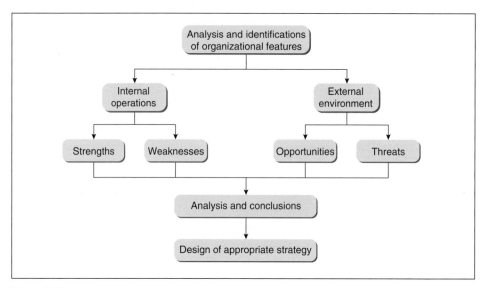

Figure 7.13 Feasible performance with constrained resources

operations, compares the costs and benefits, and makes sure that each actually is adding value. If there are operations that add no value they should be removed and the process redesigned. On the other hand, some key operations add most value and managers should put most effort and resources into these.

A well-known example of the benefit of value chain analysis is Häagen-Dazs ice cream. When they looked at their value chain, they found that more value could be added to retailing – so they opened a chain of their own shops.

Cost analysis is similar to a value chain, but with an emphasis on costs. In other words, it sees all the operations in a process as incurring costs and looks for ways of reducing them. Excessive costs can occur at three points in the supply chain:

1 *Backwards from the organization*, incurred because of prices paid for the inputs, inbound transport, foreign exchange rates, etc. Ways to reduce these costs include negotiation with suppliers to get more favourable prices, backward integration to get control of supply, use of lower priced substitute inputs, savings in inbound transport costs, etc.

2 *Internal to the organization*, caused by the age of plant and equipment, outdated technology, economies of scale, effects of learning, low productivity, administration overheads, tax rates, inflation, etc. Ways to reduce these are to tighten budgets, raise productivity, look at outsourcing high cost operations, invest in cost-saving technology, improve operations, redesign the product, redesign the process, etc.

3 *Forward in the supply chain*, caused by the costs of advertising and marketing, sales and promotion, outwards transport, margins of distributors, cost of wholesalers, etc. Ways to reduce these include negotiating more favourable terms with distributors, change to a less expensive distribution strategy, forward integration, etc.

SWOT ANALYSIS

So far in this chapter we have outlined some analyses for the environment – emphasizing external opportunities and threats – and operations – emphasizing internal strengths and weaknesses. Now we can bring these two together into a single review, and the usual way of doing this is with a **SWOT analysis**. This is the most widely used analysis for operations strategy, and it lists:

- *Strengths* – what the operations do well, giving superior performance over competitors that can be built into distinctive capabilities.

- *Weaknesses* – problems within the operations, showing areas that need improvement. In particular, the operations that put the organization at a disadvantage, as they do not compare well with competitors.

- *Opportunities* – openings that can help the organization. These are the combinations of circumstances that allow an organization to gain significant benefits.

- *Threats* – hazards that can cause damage. These are the events that might occur – at least with reasonable probability – and if they did occur would cause significant damage to the organization.

IBM might start a SWOT analysis by listing its strengths as brand recognition, high reputation, expertise and large resources; its weaknesses as slow innovation, bureaucracy and high costs; its opportunities as growing demand for new technology products; its threats as low cost competitors copying their products. Managers can plan their reactions to these – and if slow innovation is a weakness for IBM, they can look for ways of becoming more innovative; if low cost imitators form a threat, they can look for ways of overcoming this.

The details of SWOT analyses vary widely with circumstances. Some are very brief to give a review of current status; others are very detailed when the operations need significant changes. It is difficult to give a general procedure for a SWOT analysis, but they start by identifying the most significant factors in each of the four categories. Managers can always give a long list of these that covers all aspects of operations, but

IDEAS IN PRACTICE Synergistic Consultants

In 2003 four junior partners in a major firm of management consultants left to form their own company called Synergistic Consultants. They specialized in tailoring software for supply chain management in the sports clothing industry.

Two years later their review of progress included a SWOT analysis. This listed their strengths as expertise, innovation and local contacts; weaknesses as small size, gaps in experience and local operations; opportunities from the increasing use of information technology, new management methods, and growing local economy; threats from larger competitors, high overheads and a possible take-over.

Source: Company records

IDEAS IN PRACTICE Orange River Project

Much of South Africa consists of a plateau more than 1,200 metres above sea level, bordered by steep escarpments. A large part of this plateau is drained by the Orange River, which is South Africa's longest river and it flows for 2,200 km generally westwards from the Drakensberg Mountains in Lesotho to Oranjemund on the Atlantic coast.

In this arid region, water is a valuable commodity and there are conflicting views of how it should be used. Assorted stakeholders want to achieve different aims, and governments are generally responsible for the strategic use of water, and they have to balance these competing aims. The original Orange River Project was one of the largest in South Africa, with dams built to use excess flow of the river, representing 14 percent of the total runoff in South Africa. The main objectives of the project were to stabilize the river flow, generate hydro-electric power, provide a reliable water supply for users in the Orange river basin, and to irrigate water-deficient areas in the eastern Cape.

But the development of the river is a continuing process, considered under the umbrella of the Orange River Project, which is a grouping of interested bodies. A recent PEST analysis for potential strategic uses started with the political aims of central government, who want economic development, good international relations (the river forms a border with Namibia), limited pollution, diversified industry, and so on. Local governments also have political concerns of ownership, availability of drinking water, uses of the river, etc. Economic questions concern the use of the river for agriculture, power generation, recreation, fishing; social questions look at the stakeholders, public pressures, the environment, access, transport, etc.; technology looks at potential developments for power, fish farming, maintaining its condition, etc. A SWOT analysis for the group identified the following points.

Strengths

International interest
Increasing environmental concerns
Large number of interest groups
Health concerns
Improved agricultural practices
New moves in wetland and agricultural
    development

Weaknesses

Conflict between interest groups
Conflicts and inconsistencies in
    regulations
Limited water available
Limited funds for changes
No long-term plans in place
Major size of problems

Opportunities

Growth of tourism and recreation
Improving state of the economy
Popular opinion favours projects
Availability of international assistance
Potential for new developments
Diversification from extractive industries

Threats

Complacency
Conflicting interests
Difficulty of funding projects
Increasing population
Introduced flora and fauna
Irreversible degradation
Too many demands

IDEAS IN PRACTICE Orange River Project (continued)

Managers can look at the SWOT analysis and plan their reactions. With the strengths, for example, they could build on international interest and look for partners to introduce new projects; with weaknesses, they could look for ways of overcoming the conflicts between different interest groups; with opportunities they could look for ways of increasing income from tourism; with threats they could try to overcome complacency by increasing involvement.

For each point, managers can look at available alternatives and choose the best. For example, they could consider the weakness of limited funding, and look for ways of overcoming this – by increasing the

amount of money from the government, private industry, or other donors. Then they could choose the best solution. The sum of these decisions forms the nucleus of the strategy for the Orange River Project. And then implementing this strategy looks for ways of moving from the current position to the preferred future one. With the funding question, for example, implementation means actually getting more money from the identified sources.

Sources: Richmond D., Opportunities for the Orange River, Report to ORP, Johannesburg, 2005; Websites at www.southafricanplaces. co.za; www.orp.com

this just gets bogged down in detail. It is better to list the relatively small number of key factors – typically six to eight. This is enough to identify the main points, but not too many to lose focus.

The next step is to identify sensible strategies – that clearly build on the strengths, overcome weaknesses, exploit opportunities and avoid threats. So managers consider a series of options for dealing with these, and their choices form the nucleus of the strategy. Each strategic decision can make progress in more than one area. For example, deciding to expand sales into a new country might both exploit an opportunity for increasing sales and overcome a weakness in global operations; reducing prices to new industry lows might both build on a strength of cost leadership and avoid a threat from increasing competition. When these strategic changes have been identified, the next steps move towards implementation, and we develop this theme in the next chapter.

Chapter review

- Analysis is an important part of designing an operations strategy. There are three particular areas that need analyzing – the higher strategies, internal operations and the external operations environment. This chapter looked at analyses for operations and their environment.

- The operations environment includes all factors outside the control of operations managers. An environmental scan collects all relevant information about the operations environment, concentrating on the industry, market and other key factors. It particularly looks for threats that might harm operations and opportunities that they can exploit.

- An organization works within an industry that consists of all organizations that supply competing products. An industry analysis gives a detailed description of this industry.

- A market consists of all customers who buy products. A market analysis gives a detailed description of the market.

- A PEST analysis gives an overall view of the operations environment, describing political, economic, social and technological factors. Many other analyses focus on different aspects of the environment, and we illustrated these by industry attractiveness, market attractiveness, key success factors, competitor analysis, competitor profiles, etc.

- Information about internal operations comes from an operations audit. This focuses on the key areas of the product, process, resources and management.

- Many analyses can give information about different aspects of operations, and we illustrated these by financial analysis, performance analysis, performance – importance matrix, balanced scorecard, benchmarking, value chain analysis, etc.

- A SWOT analysis gives a broad view of both operations and the environment, describing the strengths, weaknesses, opportunities and strengths of operations.

CASE STUDY Jonquille Barrenboem

Jonquille Barrenboem runs a specialized business that finds, buys and trades seventeenth-century French books and prints. She conducts most of her business at private viewing rooms in Paris, London and New York, but is now considering a move to put some lower-valued trade on the Internet.

Jonquille is aware of the importance of her proposed move, and the need for careful preparation. She has some experience in the area (from her previous work as an IT advisor in the financial futures markets), so she designed the following five steps for developing a strategy for e-business. Each step contributes to a final strategy document.

- **Step 1 – analyse the current operations:**
  Assess the company's operations and products, its strengths and weaknesses. Assess its potential for e-business and its IT infrastructure.

Deliverables: Operations audit; Part 1 of the strategy document – summary of the company's current business.

- **Step 2 – assess the company's market:**
  Do a customer analysis and competitor analysis. Identify opportunities and threats. Prepare a SWOT analysis. Describe the state of e-business among related organizations, outlining the benefits they achieve.
  Deliverables: Market analysis; competitor analysis; SWOT analysis; Part 2 of the strategy document – the business' market position.

- **Step 3 – assess the potential for e-business:**
  Describe the company's aims for e-business and consider its alternatives. Do financial analyses (ROI, cost-benefit analysis, funding, etc.) and other measures (competitiveness, critical success factors, expansion, etc.).

Deliverables: Statement of aims for e-business; budget and investment appraisal; performance analyses and requirements; Part 3 of the strategy document – potential for e-business within the company.

- **Step 4 – define and finalize the preferred solution:**
  Consider all the options for e-business and make a reasoned choice of the best. Justify these strategic decisions and summarize their benefits. *Deliverables:* Statement of the defined e-business strategy; reasons for decisions and benefits; Part 4 of the strategy document – description of the e-business strategy.

- **Step 5 – plans for implementing the strategy:**
  Describe the actions needed to implement the strategy, defining the responsibilities, times, cost, risks, criteria for success, etc.

Deliverables: Implementation plan; Part 5 of the strategy document – implementation, summary and conclusions.

Questions

- Why is Jonquille Barrenboem considering a move towards e-business?
- What factors does she have to consider in this move?
- Do you think her proposed approach will work? Can you suggest any improvements?
- What will her final strategy document look like?
- Are there comparable companies that already use e-business? What lessons can Jonquille learn from them?

Discussion questions

1 Is management more of an art or a science?

2 What do managers need to analyze when they design an operations strategy?

3 An operations environmental scan describes the main features of the related industry and market. Is this true?

4 The operations environment is too complicated for any manager to understand properly – and they probably cannot even identify the most important features. So what is the point of trying to use simple, standard analyses of the environment?

5 What are the most widely used analyses for internal operations?

6 Balanced scorecards have become increasingly popular in the past few years. Why?

7 SWOT and similar analyses only describe present conditions. They do not show whether this is good or bad, and they do not show how to improve things. What, then, is their purpose?

8 How would you start a SWOT analysis for a public company? What type of factors would you include?

Useful websites

www.mmo2.com
www.computerworld.com
www.orp.com
www.southafricanplaces.co.za

References

Argenti J., Practical corporate planning, Allen and Unwin, London, 1980.

Blattberg R.C. and Unglaub L.C., Database marketing, in Levy S.J. (editor), Winning marketing plans, Dartnell, Chicago, IL, 1996.

Buchele R.B., How to evaluate a firm, California Management Review, pp 5–17, Fall, 1962.

Daft R.L., Organization theory and design (8th edition), South Western, St Paul, MN, 2003.

Edelman PR Worldwide, StrategyOne, New York, 2000.

Grayson D. and Hodges A., Everybody's business, Dorling Kindersley, London, 2001.

Kaplan R.S. and Norton D.P., The balanced Scorecard, Harvard Business Review, January–February, pp 71–79, 1992.

Kaplan R.S. and Norton D.P., Putting the Balanced Scorecard to work, Harvard Business Review, September–October, pp 134–147, 1993.

Kaplan R.S. and Norton D.P., Using the balanced scorecard as a strategic management system, Harvard Business Review, January–February, 1996.

Kaplan R.S. and Norton D.P., The balanced scorecard, Harvard Business School Press, Boston, MA, 1996.

Lebfried K.H.J. and McNair C.J., Benchmarking, HarperCollins, New York, 1992.

Neely A.D., Measuring business performance, Economist Books, London, 1998.

Pickering I.M. and Chambers S., Competitive benchmarking, Computer Integrated Manufacturing Systems, vol 4(2), 1991.

Porter M.E., Competitive strategy, Free Press, New York, 1980.

Porter M.E., Competitive advantage, Free Press, New York, 1985.

Porter M.E., What is strategy, Harvard Business Review, November–December, pp 61–79, 1996.

Reichheld F.F., The loyalty effect, Harvard Business School Press, Boston, MA, 2001.

Rowe A.J., Mason R.O., Dickel K.E. and Snyder N.H., Strategic management and business policy, Addison-Wesley, Reading, MA, 1989.

Schwartz M., Intangible assets, Computerworld, February 28, 2000.

Schwartz M., Intangible assets, quick study, www.computerworld.com

Shim J.K. and McGlade R., The use of corporate planning models, Journal of the Operational Research Society, vol 35(10), pp 885–895, 1984.

Stewart T.A., Intellectual capital, Nicolas Brearly, Naperville, IL, 1998.

Tibballs G., Business blunders, Robinson Publishing, London, 1999.

Walker O.C., Boyd H.W. and Larreche J., Marketing strategy (3rd edition), Irwin McGraw-Hill, Boston, MA, 1999.

Waller D.L., Operations management (2nd edition), Thompson International, London, 2002.

Waters D., A practical introduction to management science (2nd edition), Addison-Wesley, Harlow, 1998.

Waters D., Quantitative methods for management (3rd edition), Financial Times Prentice Hall, Harlow, 2001.

CHAPTER 8
Implementing the Strategy

The last two chapters have described the design of an operations strategy. So we know what the strategy contains, the type of decisions that form the nucleus of the strategy – and we can do some analyses that can help with these decisions. In this chapter we move on to the next step, which is to implement the strategy. This involves a series of activities to provide the operations infrastructure, activate the lower decisions, and then control the results.

After reading this chapter you should be able to:

- Understand the concept of implementing an operations strategy
- Discuss the infrastructure needed to support an operations strategy
- Describe the different types of organizational structure
- Outline the systems, human resources and culture needed for the infrastructure
- Discuss the activation of an operations strategy
- List areas for strategic operations decisions
- Appreciate the role and structure of a control system
- Consider the schedule for implementation

The key concepts discussed in this chapter are:

- **Implementation**, of the operations strategy
- **Infrastructure**, needed to support the operations strategy
- **Activation**, initiates the avalanche of decisions and actions needed by the operations strategy
- **Control**, of the strategy

MEANING OF IMPLEMENTATION

Definition

Even the best designed strategy is no use unless it is actually used. So as well as designing a strategy, operations managers also have to implement it. Implementing an operations strategy involves taking the ideas, decisions, plans, policies, objectives and other aspects of the strategy and translating them into actions.

- Operations strategies only become effective when they are **implemented**.
- **Implementation** means that the strategic plans are carried out and translated into positive actions.

The design of an operations strategy shows the long-term aspirations and intent – implementing the strategy makes sure that these are realized. When an operations strategy calls for new production facilities to be built within five years, implementation means arranging everything so that the facilities are actually built.

Thompson *et al.* (2004) describe implementation as, 'an internal, operations-driven activity involving organising, budgeting, motivating, culture-building, supervising and leading to "make the strategy work as intended"'.

When operations managers do not – or cannot – implement a strategy properly, it means that it does not achieve its goals. Unfortunately, it may not be clear whether a failure is due to a fault in the strategy itself or in the implementation. Managers often assume that any fault lies in the strategy itself, so they start making changes. But it might be that the strategy was actually the best available, and the implementation was at fault – so any change inevitably moves to a worse strategy.

On the other hand, a good implementation can compensate for some weaknesses in a poor strategy. During the implementation people may notice obvious defects and make changes so that the final results are reasonable, effectively hiding the underlying problem. The only reliable combination comes from a strategy that is both well designed and well implemented (as shown in Figure 8.1)

Stages in implementation

In chapter 3 we outlined a general approach to implementation, which had two parts; the first starts the cascade of decisions and actions down through the organization, and the second monitors performance to make sure that planned results are actually achieved.

Starting with the first, we have to route the aims of the mission down to all levels of the organization, and the mechanism for this has a series of progressively more detailed goals and objectives. At each level of decisions, managers look at the goals and objectives of the higher level and design actions to achieve them. These actions, in turn, define their own goals and objectives, which become targets for the next level down. We saw this with corporate, business and functional strategies, where managers analyze, say, the corporate strategy to see what the business strategy has to achieve, then they design a business strategy, and this gives more detailed goals and objectives that are passed down to functional strategies.

The same mechanism works with a more detailed point of view. Within operations, each level of managers looks at the requirements of the higher level, makes decisions, and sets goals and objectives that set the requirements of lower levels (as show in Figure 8.2). So there is a direct line downwards from the operations mission, through the operations strategy and on to tactical and operational decisions.

This gives the broad framework for implementing an operations strategy. Managers have to take the broad principles and translate them into positive actions – allowing for the huge number of decisions, tasks, interactions to consider, changing conditions, complex activities, initiatives to be launched, people needing different skills, resistance to change, and so on. And, there are always problems with resources, budgets, bureaucracy, inertia, social pressures and political considerations.

This is a complex job, and as usual with strategic management, there are no formulae or procedures that inevitably lead to the best solutions. Implementation is probably the most open-ended part of strategic management, and it is often difficult to give even convincing guidelines. However, there are four common requirements that we describe in the rest of the chapter:

1 *Designing the infrastructure for operations* – to give the right structure to the operations function and add the systems, budgets, policies, etc.

2 *Initiating decision-making at lower levels* – or 'strategy activation' which starts the cascade of decisions and actions through all levels of operations.

3 *Monitoring and controlling actual performance* – making sure that operations are producing the planned results and the strategy is achieving its goals. As the environment and the operations are constantly changing, managers have to continually adapt, review and revise the operations strategy.

4 *Designing an action plan* – giving a schedule for all the activities needed for implementation.

These four activities are specific tasks to be completed, but there are other less well defined jobs that can be grouped under the heading of 'exercising strategic leadership'. These include motivating groups within operations, building a consensus

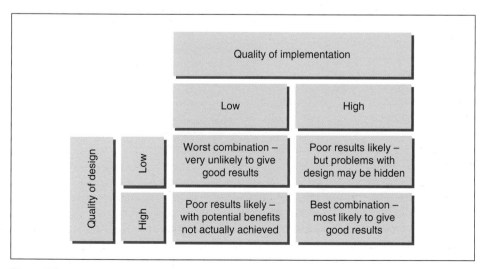

Figure 8.1 Alternatives for strategy design and implementation

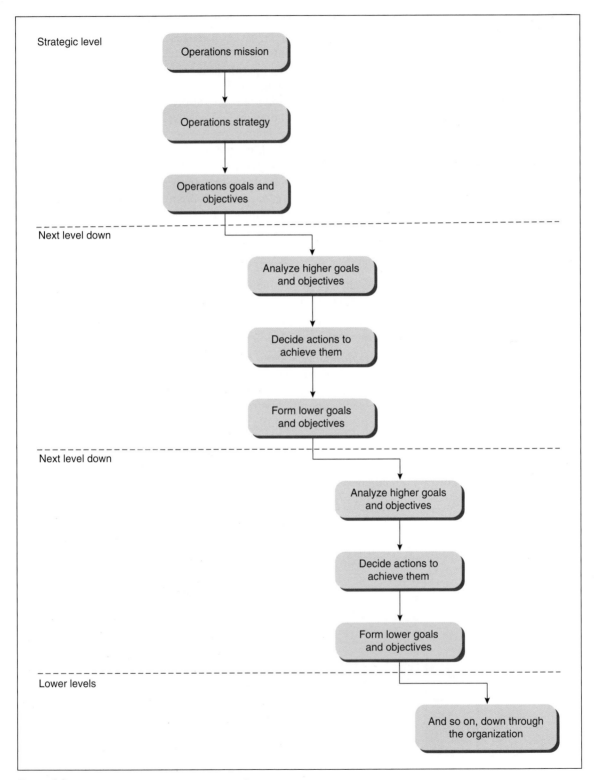

Figure 8.2 Mechanism for implementing the operations strategy

IDEAS IN PRACTICE **North Island University**

Like many universities around the world, North Island University is looking for ways of using its limited resources more effectively. Some of its traditional science and engineering subjects are becoming less popular, and there is growing competition from other educational providers. The university set up a steering committee to consider their strategic options, and this found that North Island University had an international reputation, was considered academically strong, did well-respected research, student demand was high and its finances were in good shape. A more detailed SWOT analysis included the following factors, with corresponding responsibilities.

Strengths	*Responsibility*
Staff performance and morale	HRM Policy
Student quality	Recruiting Exercise
Research quality	Enterprise Zone
Infrastructure and university park	Estates Office
Entrepreneurial culture	Fundraising and Enterprise Zone
Science and engineering strengths	Technology Group

Weaknesses	*Responsibility*
Few long-term endowments	Fundraising
Limited external influence	Public Relations and Governors
Lack of dynamism	Culture change
Strains of recent expansions	Fundraising and HRM Policy
Internal communications	Public Relations and HRM Policy

Slow decision making, such as introduction of new subjects	Governors and Faculty Councils

Opportunities	*Responsibility*
Growing demand for higher education	Recruiting Exercise
Appreciation of technology and entrepreneurs	Enterprise Zone
New technologies for delivery	e-strategy and Faculty Councils
Strategic alliances with other institutions	Faculty Councils and Governors
Growing interest in new subjects	Faculty councils
Increased awareness of funding issues	Fundraising

Threats	*Responsibility*
Decline in government funding	Fundraising and Governors
Targeted government funding	Fundraising and Faculty Councils
Competition from other universities	Public Relations and Recruiting Exercise
Electronic providers	e-strategy
Declining career prospects for staff	HRM Policy
Decline in media profile	Public Relations

The next stage was to have the groups responsible consider actions and choose the most appropriate. These decisions formed the nucleus of the operations strategy, which was formalized by the steering committee, who also started the process of implementing the strategy.

about aims, and moulding the culture needed to support the strategy. Within this culture managers usually have to encourage innovation, entrepreneurship, ethical standards, focus on results, and so on. And they also have to provide figureheads that can deal with the politics and power struggles of the strategy. These type of imprecise jobs are the most difficult for managers to complete, and it is very difficult even to give useful guidelines. This is an area where the personal skills of managers come very much to the fore.

DESIGNING THE INFRASTRUCTURE

The first part of implementing an operations strategy is to build an organization that is capable of doing it. To a large extent, this means designing an appropriate structure for operations and assigning clear responsibilities – but it also adds the systems, human resources, culture and resources that support this structure. Together these factors form the operations **infrastructure**.

> ● The operations **infrastructure** consists of the organizational structure and the systems, human resources, culture and resources to support it.

When designing an infrastructure, the main concerns of managers are to:

- show how the operations function fits into the broader organization
- design an internal structure for the operations function
- install information, communication, financial, control, and other support systems
- create internal policies, methods – and general culture – that support the implementation
- allocate budgets and resources to activities that are most important for strategic success
- build integrated supply chains to ensure the flow of materials
- motivate people to pursue targets, linking rewards to the achievement of goals
- give leadership to drive implementation forward and to continually look for improvements.

We can start by reviewing some options for the structure of operations, and the way that this fits into the broader organization.

Organizational structure

An **organizational structure** divides a whole organization into distinct parts, and defines the relationships between them. It shows who has responsibility for what, who has authority over whom, and who reports to whom. The result is described in an organization chart that shows the place of operations within the broader organization, how it is related to other functions, and how it is organized internally. This structure also determines the broad nature of internal systems. For instance, an information system must be designed to collect all relevant information from sources within the organization and transfer them to the point where they are needed. So designing the structure of the organization goes beyond a definition of the relationships between parts, and also shows the resources, systems, culture and other features needed to support the structure. And superimposed on the formal structure are the informal relationships that emerge over time. This informal structure gives the links between individuals and departments that really allow operations to work smoothly.

To design a structure, managers have to start by deciding the key functions needed to implement the operations strategy, and assign these as organizational 'building blocks' that divide the organization into coherent sections. Then the details of the structure come from the relationships between these blocks, the level of independence, and authority of each unit (Hosmer). Five main concerns are:

1 *Defining the units* – which divides the activities needed to implement the operations strategy into coherent units and establishes their position in the organization. The guideline here is to identify activities that are critical for achieving the strategy, form building blocks from these activities, and give them prominent positions in the organization chart.

2 *Formality* – which is the extent to which formal rules and standard procedures govern decisions and working relationships – in other words, the amount of authority and independence given to each unit. Very formal and structured organizations have clear lines for reporting, so people know exactly what to do in any circumstances. But they can be very slow and bureaucratic, and they are unlikely to be either innovative or flexible. In practice, it is often the informal systems that exist in even the most rigid power structure which ensure things get done. Delegation and empowerment mean that the trend is towards less formal structures, even in traditionally rigid organizations like the army and police service.

3 *Centralization* – refers to the location of authority and control within an organization's hierarchy, and particularly the extent to which decision making is kept within the higher levels. In highly centralized organizations, a few top managers hold all decision-making authority. The argument for this is that people are promoted for their ability to make decisions, and when promoted they have access to more resources and information. So centralized decision-making puts decisions in the hands of those most capable of making the best decisions. Decentralized organizations allow lower level managers more autonomy. The argument for decentralization is that lower level managers have more specialized knowledge, more incentives to do a better job, and can react quickly without referring to remote headquarters. The current trend is clearly towards decentralization.

4 *Specialization* – which is the extent to which an organization's activities are separated into distinct functions. A highly specialized organization puts all of one type of specialist, say accountants, into one group which performs a narrow set of activities. Groups are formed for each type of specialist, and these act as consultants when needed.

5 *Rigidity* – extent to which organizational relationships remain constant and unchanged over time. A rigid organization has the advantages of stability, but it is inflexible and does not respond to changing conditions.

Types of structure

Decisions about these five concerns lead to common organizational structures. These are usually described in terms of headquarters or head office staff, below whom are the various groupings that make up the rest of the organization. The headquarters group is usually described as an overhead to the core functions, but it can add value in several ways, not least being the formulation of strategies (Goold *et al.*; Hamel *et al.*). The following organisational structures are the most common.

Functional organization – the traditional view, where groups are defined by the function that they perform, giving different divisions for operations, finance, human resources, marketing, and so on. A functional organization is the simplest, with each manager reporting to a more senior manager within the same function (see Figure 8.3). This has the benefits of forming stable groups that work together, pooling expertise and sharing knowledge, being easy to administer, with clear authority, no duplication of effort and continuity. On the other hand it has the disadvantages of encouraging a 'silo mentality' where each function concentrates on its own work rather than the broader good of the organization, developing bureaucratic procedures that become aims in themselves, diverting attention away from customers and products, and having conflicts when a department works on several different product areas. There are particular problems when the organization grows and makes many products for different markets, and a single functional manager cannot keep up-to-date with, or coordinate, activities across the whole range of different products and markets.

Product organization – where the groups are responsible for making a particular type of product, as illustrated in Figure 8.4. This has the advantages of concentrating specialized knowledge for each product, developing and retaining special expertise, giving clear authority, and simplified communications. Its main strength is a focus on the whole process that creates products and satisfies customers (Keen). Unfortunately it can also duplicate effort, have people reporting to managers with no knowledge of their functional skills, no-one with responsibility for an entire function, unclear loyalties, and difficulty in transferring skills between products.

Variations on this theme divide the organization by geographic area of operation, project, or some other division based on the use of resources. Another variation comes with diversified organizations, where there would be too many individual business units reporting to the headquarters, so related businesses are clustered into strategic units. This gives another layer of administration, with each business reporting to the head of their business unit, who in turn reports to the headquarters. Multinational companies often arrange this with a layer of vice-presidents in charge of strategic units.

Hybrid organization – which combines aspects of both functional and product structures. There are many forms of hybrid structure, which makes it the most common

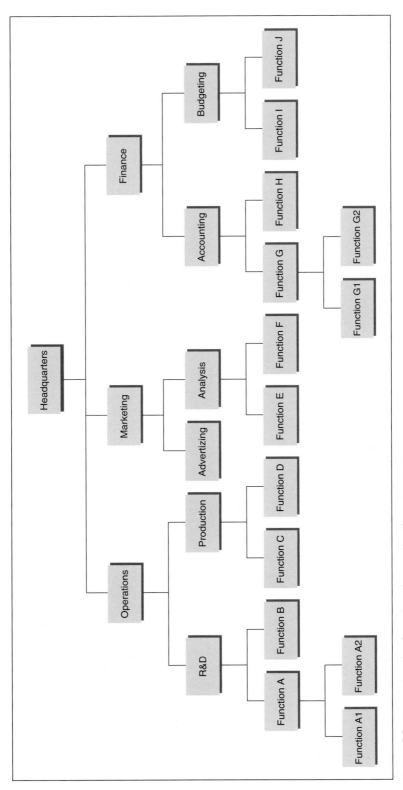

Figure 8.3 Example of a functional organization structure

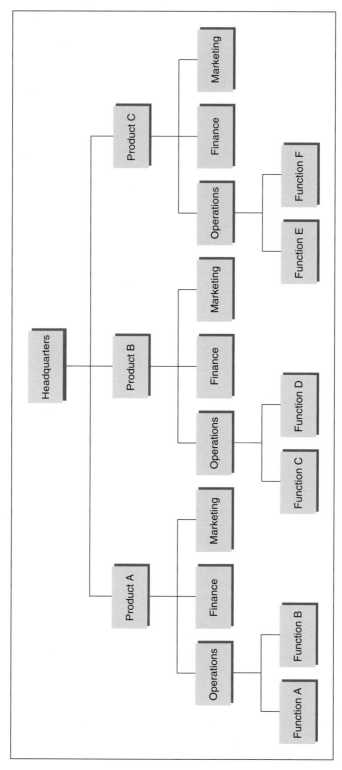

Figure 8.4 Example of a product organization structure

type in practice. A common example has an organization with a functional structure, but one important product plays such a major role that it is worth having a distinct group to look after it. Then the groups reporting to headquarters become a mixture of functions and products. Another option is to have a functional structure at the top of the organization with function heads reporting to headquarters, but a product structure lower down with the groups reporting to function heads divided by product. And the reverse has a product structure at the top of the organization, changing to a functional structure lower down.

Matrix organizations – are a particular type of hybrid, where each group reports simultaneously to two superiors. You can imagine this in an organization that works with a number of key products. Then a particular group, say accountants, report to the head of the accounting division, but also work on a product and report to the product manager (as shown in Figure 8.5). This structure has the advantages of focusing on key operations, being flexible and adapting to needs, allowing easy transfer of skills and easier information flows. On the other hand there are problems with built-in conflicts, extra management overheads, complex authority relationships, and the inherent problems of everyone having several bosses with conflicting interests.

There are several variations on the matrix structure, with differing balances of authority between functions and products. A functional-matrix keeps most authority within the functions, and product managers have less responsibility, primarily planning and coordinating activities. A product-matrix has most of the authority with the product manager, while the functional manager has less responsibility, primarily assigning staff and providing expertise when needed. A balanced-matrix has both functional and product managers of equal status working together to get work done.

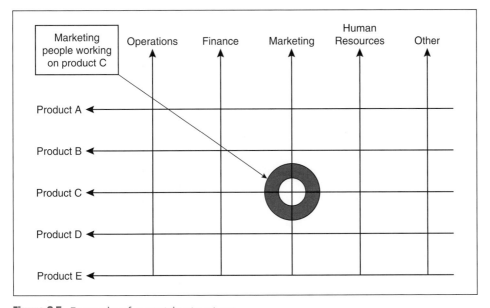

Figure 8.5 Example of a matrix structure

Sometimes the matrix structure is even more complicated when, for example, there is also a geographic structure. Then people might find that they have to report to the head of their function, the product manager, and the head of the geographic division.

Self-managed groups – where authority is delegated down to groups working within the organization. Traditional organization structures assume some kind of rigid hierarchy, with reporting upwards through the hierarchy and control downwards. Self-managed groups have almost all of the decisions and control delegated to lower levels, with each group working, to a large extent, independently. Strategic managers set goals which they pass to lower levels, but they do not say how these should be achieved. They establish overall principles, give guidance, build a unifying culture, encourage actions that benefit the organization as a whole – but have little direct control over the lower operations. The result is a network of groups, all working to a large extent independently, for the good of the organization. The benefits of this structure are that it encourages the development of expertise, is very flexible and delegates authority to appropriate levels. The disadvantages include a loss of overall coordination and control, difficult communications, problems with defining authority, reconciling different objectives of the groups, and general complexity. Because of the practical difficulties, it is more common to find self-managed groups working at some point within a more formal structure – and networks of linked groups are the apparent route to virtual organizations (Manki *et al.*; Blucker; Byrne *et al.*).

Table 8.1 gives some ideas of the different features of the 'pure' structures.

Choice of structure

Managers should design an organizational structure that best achieves their aims – so they are looking for the best match between strategy and structure. In 1962 Chandler identified an empirical link between structure and successful strategy implementation. In particular, he found that changes in a strategy bring new administrative problems that can only be solved by changing the organizational structure. Unfortunately, there is a delay in this process, as the new structure is not introduced until the problems have become severe enough to be noticed, and managers have enough incentive to make the necessary changes.

Table 8.1 **Properties of different organizational structures**

		Factor					
		Centralization	Specialization	Efficiency	Cost	Flexibility	Relationships
Type of structure	Functional	High	High	Medium	High	Low	Formal
	Product	High	Low	Medium	High	Medium	Formal
	Matrix	Medium	Medium	Low	Medium	Medium	Medium
	Self-managed	Low	High	High	Low	High	Informal

In principle, we can describe a procedure for designing an organizational structure. This starts by identifying the key operations. Some of these are best outsourced to other organizations, and when these are subtracted, the remainder form the critical internal operations – the building blocks of the structure. Now assign one person responsibility for each building block, avoiding fragmentation, and deciding how much authority to delegate. Then establish the means of coordinating different operations, usually by having related operations report to a single, senior manager. This gives the skeleton for the structure, and managers can expand this and supplement it by cross-functional task forces, special project teams, self-contained work teams, contact managers, relationship managers, and many other adjustments.

Of course, such advice only scratches the surface of design, and you can look at different organization's structures to see that there are many alternative forms. There is certainly no single best structure for specific conditions, and the usual practice is to choose a basic design, modify it as necessary, and then supplement it with coordinating, communication and control mechanisms. In practice, small single business organizations usually have a centralized, functional structure; organizations with broad geographic coverage typically have regional operating divisions; most larger organizations have some form of hybrid structure.

There are clear trends in organizations, towards decentralized structures with devolved authority and self managed groups. These groups are becoming smaller and leaner, with fewer managers, more technology, and more open communications. Probably the biggest move is to reduce boundaries between functions and operations, emphasizing that all parts of the organization should be working towards common goals (Volberda; Mohrman *et al.*).

IDEAS IN PRACTICE General Electric

One of the classic business reorganizations appeared in the US in the 1980s with General Electric. In the 1980s this was an organization that was clearly struggling, noted for being bureaucratic, cumbersome, slow to react and wildly underperforming. In 1981 they appointed Jack Welch as chief executive with the aim of turning the company around. He achieved this by massive reorganization.

By 1990 the number of senior executives had been reduced from 700 to 500 (and this fell by another hundred over the next four years); headquarters staff had been reduced from 2,100 to less than 1,000; the average number of management layers between the chief executive and day-to-day operations was reduced from nine to four; the average number of people reporting to each manager was raised from five or six to nearer 15; the total workforce was reduced from 404,000 to 220,000. During this period the company prospered, and its revenue more than doubled from $27 billion to $60 billion.

Sources: Crainer S., Key management ideas, Financial Times Pitman (3rd edition), London, 1998; Moody F., I sing the body electronic, Hodder and Stoughton, London, 1995; Flater R., The new GE, Business One Irwin, Homewood, Illinois, 1993; Website at www.ge.com

Supporting the structure

After designing the organizational structure, the next step is to add the systems to support it. Most organizations need various systems for accounts, communications, information, order processing, customer relations, and other basic operations that support operations. There can also be specialized systems, such as reservation systems in airlines, parcel tracking in logistics companies, maintenance systems for service companies, and so on.

These systems basically collect data, analyze it and move the results around the organization. They obviously come in a huge variety of forms ranging from 'post it' stickers through to artificial intelligence systems that automate decisions. Their essential structure consists of hardware that delivers information to all parts of the operations, rules and procedures for deciding what information is actually delivered to each person, and statements of how they should respond to the information.

If we add the human resource aspects of the organization, and the intangible culture, we have the infrastructure needed for implementing an operations strategy (as illustrated in Figure 8.6).

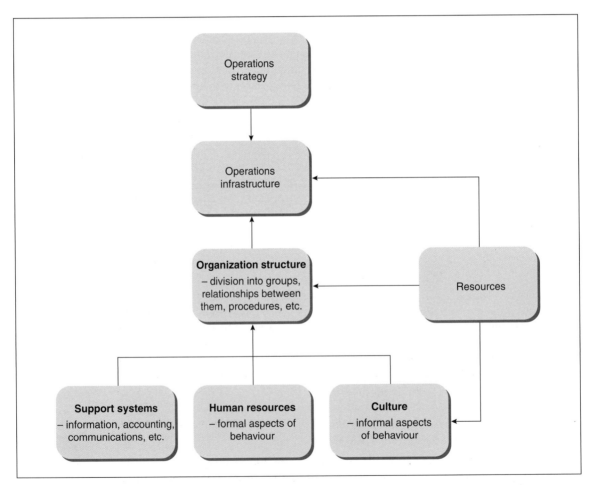

Figure 8.6 Elements in forming an operations infrastructure

It is all very well to design the organizational structure and supporting features, but nothing can actually be done until they get resources, and this is arranged through budgets. The size of budget for each area should be set to give the easiest implementation of the operations strategy. This means giving resources to support areas that can make a positive contribution, encouraging the development of capabilities – and moving resources away from activities that are no longer justified.

Zero-based budgets determine the amount needed for each area, usually each year. This allows a rational allocation of resources to match needs and priorities. However, it does not give continuity as each group can only guarantee its funding for the current period. Almost all organizations give continuity – and give easy procedures that avoid conflicts – by basing next year's budget on last year's budget, with some modifications to reflect changing conditions. But this is not necessarily a rational approach, as it allows old operations to continue long beyond their useful life, and it starves new initiatives.

Human resources

Different organizational structures delegate authority in different ways. Traditional structures tend to keep most authority at the top of the organization – harping back to the idea of managers as controllers rather than enablers. They saw people as a cost, whose contribution came from working as directed. More recent self-managed groups devolve decisions to the lowest level, reflecting developments in human resource management. Current thinking emphasizes the central contribution that people make to operations success, and the belief that they really are the most important resource. Studies by Pfeffer (1998) and Pfeffer and Veiga show the clear benefits of good HR practices across the whole range of industry in the US – with similar findings reported by the DTI for the UK and Blimes *et al.* for Germany. Managers have found that we all respond better to motivation than discipline – the carrot works better than the stick in getting what Joynson described as 'extraordinary efforts from ordinary people'.

Motivation is difficult to define, but a person is motivated if they keep working hard to achieve an appropriate goal. There are three points in this observation. The first point concerns effort, with a motivated person working hard. The second point concerns perseverance, with a motivated person continuing their efforts for as long as needed. The third point concerns effectiveness, with a motivated person working towards an appropriate goal. The question, of course, is how to get people motivated. There has been a huge amount of work looking for an answer to this, with Maslow describing a hierarchy of needs, Hertzberg describing internal and external motivators, Etzioni and Schein both building frameworks for categorizing motivation, Pascale and Athos considering organizational culture, and Galbraith and Kazanian confirming the intuitively obvious result that an organization's reward system can be a powerful motivator. There is clearly no general agreement about a single best approach. However, there is more agreement that no methods give dramatic results overnight and managers have to adopt a systematic view that builds on the value of employees over a long period. This view should include several key ideas (Pfeffer, 1996; DTI) which Brown *et al.* summarize as:

- **Commitment to people** – recognizing that they are a key strategic resource and having clear policies about employees, job security, selection of employees and appropriate rewards.

- **Shared purpose** – through strategic leadership, distribution of information, participation in decision-making and employee ownership.
- **Enabling structures** – including the organizational structure, communications, devolved management and informal structures.
- **Learning and development** – with a commitment to training, upgrading skills, continuous improvement and broader organizational learning.
- **Involvement** – with team working, removal of internal boundaries, participation and recognition of stakeholder needs.

When these are practised over the long term, they become a part of the organization's broader culture – giving a culture that values people within the organization. We need hardly say that this is difficult to achieve when an organization moves through a period of dramatic change, like the illustration of General Electric above. Few people can feel motivated when they are soon likely to lose their job. Dramatic downsizing exercises can reduce costs quickly, but they have long-term consequences. When there are fewer people in an organization it can, by definition, do less work and cannot respond to opportunities. People who can get new jobs are likely to move-on quickly, so the organization loses the experience and knowledge of key people (and it might be left with those who do not have the skills to get other jobs). And while it is difficult to deal with people who are made redundant, it can be even more difficult to manage those who are left.

Operations culture

Operations culture – which forms a part of the broader organizational culture – is a particularly fuzzy and ethereal concept.

- An **organizational culture** is defined by the values, norms, beliefs and assumptions that influence the way that people within the organization think and behave.

There are many facets of culture within an operations function, but they start with some shared, basic assumptions about the organization, work, principles, human relationships, beliefs, aims, ethics, and so on. These form a framework, within which a series of norms and standards develops about rules, authority, behaviour, rewards, legends, taboos, etc. Together these two form the first two levels of culture, illustrated in Figure 8.7. A third level adds visible signs of operations identity, product designs, logos, uniforms, ceremonies, rituals, etc.

These three levels of culture form an important context, and affect all aspects of operations. But they are elusive and particularly difficult to describe. In general they show, 'how we do things' and determine the way that people work, how they feel about the organization, how they treat customers, what they think of people they work with, what they do, and every other aspect of their work. When you see operations with a positive culture, everyone works energetically to achieve the goals – and operations are characterized by high performance, working to clear, shared and agreed principles, with managers spending a lot of time reinforcing these principles, careful selection of new employees who fit into the pattern, and rewards for those who follow the norms. On the other hand, when you see operations with a negative culture, no-one seems to be interested in doing anything for the organization. These operations have either not developed a cohesive culture, or else it is a negative one that is actually harmful. Then operations are characterized by low performance, no sense of identity, few shared values, many sub-cultures, internal political wrangling and hostility to change.

The question, of course, is how to develop a culture that supports and sustains the strategy, rather than working against it? Many cultures develop from founders of the organization, or emerge from later influential individuals or groups. They are sustained through continuity of leadership, new employees who are screened to fit in, systematic coaching of employees – along with stories, legends, ceremonies and rewards.

As the operations and culture evolve, they may well move in different directions. What was once a supportive culture, no longer helps to achieve operations' aims. Then managers – as the people who largely create and maintain the culture – have to take corrective steps. In particular, they have to:

1 examine the present culture and identify the elements that do not support the operations strategy

2 discuss and agree those aspects of the present culture that have to be changed

3 take actions to make the changes.

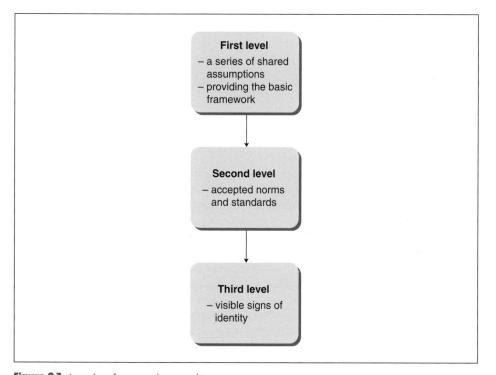

Figure 8.7 Levels of operations culture

IDEAS IN PRACTICE McDonald's and Wal-Mart

Dick and Mac McDonald, opened their first fast food restaurant in 1940. In 1959 the corporation adopted the motto of 'Quality, Service, Cleanliness and Value', which it still maintains. This motto has given the core of the McDonald culture for fifty years. Despite enormous changes as they developed into one of the world's most recognized brands, their culture has remained rooted in these four values, which were formulated by the company founders.

There is a similar story at Wal-Mart. Sam Walton opened a discount store in Rogers, Arizona in 1962 and since then Wal-Mart has grown into the world's biggest retailer with an annual turnover of US$200 billion. But the company culture is still based on the values that Sam Walton originated – of dedication to customer service, treating employees as partners, zealous pursuit of low costs, frugality, ritualistic Saturday morning meetings and executives who visit stores, talk to customers and solicit employees' suggestions.

Sources: Websites at www.mcdonalds.com; www.mcdonalds.co.uk; www.walmartstores.com

Occasionally, it is surprisingly easy to change operations culture, perhaps by replacing an autocratic manager with one who has a more participative style. Usually, though, it is very difficult, slow, time-consuming and without even the reassurance that things are actually moving in the right direction. The actions to change a culture include both real changes and symbolic ones. Real changes include adjustments to the organizational structure, bringing in new people, setting new targets, changing the rewards system, reallocating budgets, and increasing the amount of training. Symbolic changes include visible rewards, senior managers spending more time talking to customers and employees, elimination of unearned perks, new events and ceremonies.

INITIATING DECISIONS

Having put the infrastructure in place, the next part of implementation initiates the lower levels of decisions and actions. We have described the route for this as moving down through the operations mission, strategy, tactics and operational levels (Craig and Grant refer to the move through **m**ission, **o**bjectives, **s**trategy and **t**actics as the **MOST** approach). We have also described the mechanism for this move from vague aspirations through to detailed activities. This has each layer of managers analyzing the requirements of the higher level, designing operations to achieve these, and hence setting objectives for the lower level. In this way, decisions cascade down through the organization, so that an operations mission of 'providing the world's most reliable package delivery service' eventually has someone delivering a parcel to your door. And an operations mission of 'being a low cost supplier of soft-drinks' leads to all the activities that make sure that there is a bottle of orange juice nearby when you are thirsty.

We know that operations managers face a range of similar problems, and in chapter 5 we gave some examples of these:

- **Strategic Decisions** – setting objectives, operations structure, type of product, type of process, capacity, quality management, location, vertical integration, alliances, partnerships and outsourcing.
- **Tactical Decisions** – planning, product development, level of technology, logistics, quality assurance, replacement, staffing, make/buy, performance, systems.
- **Operational Decisions** – scheduling, staffing, inventory control, ordering, reliability, maintenance, quality control, job design, work measurement.

Ansoff points out that this **activation** of the strategy needs different skills from its design, saying that, 'While in strategic management the individual is a change-seeker, risk responsive divergent problem-solver, skilful in leading others into new and untried directions, the (lower) operations manager is a change absorber, cautious risk-taker, convergent problem-solver, skilful diagnostician, coordinator, and controller of complex activities.' In this view, there is a difference between senior operations managers who design the strategy and lower managers who implement it. As we have seen, this is not really a valid distinction and everyone in the organization shares some responsibility for both the design and implementation of the strategy. And there are not really such clear distinctions between strategic, tactical and operational decisions. Quality, for example, is a strategic issue when managers are considering their strategy, perhaps aiming for very high quality products. It becomes a tactical issue when middle managers decide how to measure quality and set reasonable targets for performance. Then it becomes an operational task when junior managers test production to see if they are meeting quality targets. Similarly, inventory is a strategic issue when deciding whether to build a new warehouse for finished goods, a tactical issue when deciding how much to invest in stock, and an operational issue when deciding how much to order this week.

Apart from the indistinct boundaries between different types of decisions, it is also noticeable that different organizations put different emphasis on each. For example, reliability is a strategic issue for NASA, but it is less of an issue for plumbers; durability is a strategic issue for manufacturers of replacement heart valves but little concern for newspaper editors; cleanliness is more important for a hospital than for a coal mine. So within the overall structure of decisions, managers face their own unique problems. Operations managers at Exxon have to decide the capacity for a new oil refinery in the Gulf of Mexico, and managers at Fairmont Dental Practice have to set their capacity for treatment; there are similarities between these two capacity problems, but there are obvious differences in detail.

Not surprisingly there is some disagreement about what decisions areas are generally 'strategic'. Slack and Lewis suggest the four areas of capacity, supply networks, process technology, and organization of the process. Brown *et al.* extend this by adding location of facilities, buyer–supplier relationships, new product development. Others have extended or modified this list again, typically including vertical integration, quality management, human resources, inventory, maintenance, and production planning (for example Fine and Hax; Harrison; Heizer and Render).

Here we describe strategic decisions in six areas of operations:

- **Product development** – including types of products, innovation, breadth of range, new product development, flexibility (discussed in chapter 9).
- **Quality management** – including the aims, tools and programmes for ensuring customer satisfaction (discussed in chapter 10).

- **Process design** – including type of process, technology, measuring and improving performance (discussed in chapter 11).
- **Capacity management** – including measures of capacity, capacity planning, the size and timing of capacity changes (discussed in chapter 12).
- **Structure of the supply chain** – including design options, integration of operations along the supply chains, and location of facilities (discussed in chapter 13).
- **Movement of materials** – including procurement, inventory management, and transport (discussed in chapter 14).

This classification is largely for convenience, as decisions in any area can have far-reaching consequences and become strategic. Nonetheless, these six categories give a useful platform for discussing strategic decisions in operations. We expand this theme in the third part of the book.

IDEAS IN PRACTICE Shell Canada Limited

Shell Canada is a subsidiary of Royal Dutch Shell plc, responsible for the group's activities in Canada. It is guided by the Group's business principles which include their responsibilities to shareholders, customers, employees, trading partners, and society. As the President and Chief Executive Officer says, 'Whatever activities we engage in now or in the future, we will continue to integrate the economic, environmental and social dimensions into everything we do.' But how does this translate into actual operations?

It means that Shell Canada delivers gas and oil to its customers in North America. In particular it:

- produces from sour gas fields in Alberta and the foothills of the Rockies. Some of these fields have been producing natural gas for over fifty years, but improving technology means that they continue to offer new opportunities
- processes gas for other producers in its strategically located gas plants, thereby increasing the return on these expensive facilities
- increases oil and gas exploration in the foothills of the Rockies and British Columbia
- develops offshore energy fields, with interests in exploration licenses for 473,000 hectares off the

Nova Scotia Shelf, and three exploration licenses in deeper water

- develops interests in the Northwest Territories, particularly the Mackenzie Gas Project. This includes facilities for the Niglintgak field which has reserves of 1 trillion cubic feet of natural gas
- operates the Peace River oil sands facility in Northern Alberta, processing 12,000 barrels of bitumen a day. Reserves in the Peace River deposit are estimated at eight billion barrels of bitumen, so this is an important long-term investment
- works the new Oil Sands mining operation in Northern Alberta. Officially opened in 2003, the Athabasca Oil Sands Project needed an investment of $5.7 billion, and will produce 155,000 barrels of bitumen a day, supplying the equivalent of 10 percent of Canada's oil needs and increasing Shell Canada's hydrocarbon production by more than 50 percent. Plans are to substantially increase this output over the longer term.

Sources: Cook L., A Producer's Perspective of the Natural Gas Business Globally and Offshore Canada's East Coast, Canadian Offshore Resources Conference, Nova Scotia, 2003; Shell Transport and Trading Company, The Shell Report, London, 2004; Website at www.shell.com

CONTROLLING THE STRATEGY

Control systems

When managers design an operations strategy they make a series of assumptions about the long-term future. Inevitably, the future does not turn out exactly as forecast. And there are likely to be differences between the designed strategy, and the one actually implemented – perhaps caused by poor implementation, unrealistic goals, conflict with organizational culture, or details that were left out of the design. So there are always differences between the operations imagined by managers and actual performance.

Even if their planning was perfect, there would be changes over time to conditions, requirements, expectations and actual operations. If managers do not recognize these effects, but assume that operations are going as planned, there would be a growing gap between the required and actual performance. To avoid this, managers have to continually monitor operations and adjust the strategy to bring its performance back into line. This is the purpose of a **control system**.

- A **control system** monitors the performance of operations.
- Then it adjusts the strategy to improve its performance.

There are five elements of a control system, shown in Figure 8.8:

- **Part 1** reviews the goals, objectives and constraints of the operations strategy.
- **Part 2** monitors conditions and changes to the operations and their environment.
- **Part 3** measures actual performance of operations in key areas.
- **Part 4** compares this actual performance with plans from the strategy and identifies gaps.
- **Part 5** adjusts the strategy to improve performance, moving or adding resources, revising plans, or in the extreme changing the whole strategy.

It is common to summarize the role of a control system as 'monitor and control'. Then 'monitor' covers parts 2 and 3, while 'control' is step 5.

The monitoring function is fed by the operations information system, which collects and processes all the data needed to keep operations working properly. This must include the key measures defined by the control system – rather than working the other way around and designing a control system that uses information already available. It is easiest to monitor progress towards numerical objectives rather than more nebulous goals, so control systems usually monitor a set of numerical measures. Of course, there can be a huge number of potential measures, but the control system should concentrate on a few key areas of operations, perhaps looking at productivity, efficiency, capacity, utilization, and so on. In practice, they often use surrogate measures, such as financial performance. Unfortunately,

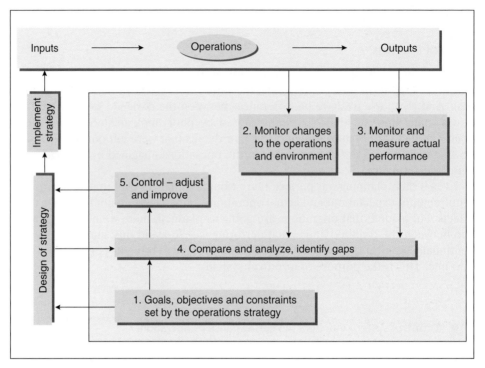

Figure 8.8 Structure of a control system

this raises the problems that we mentioned in chapter 5, particularly their reliance on accounting conventions. A control system that monitors return on investment, for example, could find an apparent improvement in performance by redefining 'investment'.

Adjusting the strategy

Now the control system has the objectives from the operations strategy, and has monitored actual performance, so the next step is to identify gaps between the two and adjust the strategy to overcome any problems. This might suggest a series of small adjustments to the strategy, but this seems to lack an overriding direction, and follows no coherent pattern or rationale. The strategy was originally designed for long-term performance and stability, and control seems to tinker with this and make small *ad hoc* adjustments. Sometimes these adjustments give long-term improvements, but this is not inevitable, and unless managers are careful they can give short-term improvements but long-term deterioration.

The best response to a gap depends largely on its size. If the gap is small, managers can accept it as a normal variation and take no remedial action at all. But if the gap is very large, they may have to completely redesign the operations strategy. Between these two extremes are a number of alternatives including changing goals and objectives

IDEAS IN PRACTICE McKlusky-Ure

Many control systems monitor financial performance, with the most widely used measure of financial performance being the return on investment (ROI). McKlusky-Ure noticed that many of their clients make long-term decisions almost exclusively on the basis of ROI – so they give the following advice about the wisdom of putting too much reliance on this measure.

ROI Strengths:

- easy to find from accounts
- gives a single comprehensive figure that is affected by all aspects of operations
- is phrased in familiar terms and is easy to understand
- measures how well operations use resources
- allows comparisons with other operations
- gives an incentive to use existing resources efficiently
- shows which additional resources would increase returns
- identifies significant trends over time.

ROI Weaknesses:

- there are several different ways of calculating the ROI

- sensitivity to accounting conventions (for depreciation, discounting, book values, transfer pricing, etc.)
- gives historical rather than current view and is slow to respond to changes
- gives a very limited view of operations performance
- is short term, largely considering annual returns
- discourages new investment, as higher investment lowers the ROI
- does not take into account the operations environment
- does not allow for business cycles or other factors over which managers have no control
- does not allow for the levels of assets needed in different industries (for example, a car assembly plant needs much higher fixed assets than an advertising agency).

Although they specifically consider return on investment, McKlusky-Ure make the point that similar arguments hold for almost every other financial measure.

that were too optimistic, improving operations to achieve the targets, changing budgets to redistribute resources, adding new aspects to the existing strategy to overcome deficiencies, deleting parts of the strategy that are unachievable, reviewing the implementation of the strategy, using political or other action to overcome problems, seeking cooperation of customers and suppliers, or a wide range of other options.

Suppose operations have a target lead time for delivering a product of 30 days. If the actual delivery time is 31 days, managers will probably make some adjustments to operations, and they will make more radical changes if the actual lead time is 60 days. But what happens if the lead time is 25 days? Managers still have to review operations to see why there was such a variance – perhaps because of a more favourable environment, or new logistics companies, or some other change in the environment – and whether they can maintain this performance, improve it further, or transfer lessons to other operations.

This approach of identifying a gap and then taking action to correct it makes a number of assumptions. To start with, we assume that there is a recognizable connection between the performance gap and its cause. In practice, this is often not true, and it is difficult to identify the real cause of a problem – and when we cannot identify the causes of a problem, we cannot correct it. Suppose that we suddenly find too many units of a product have faults. It is easy to say that the problem lies with quality management – but it might be difficult to go beyond this to find a more precise cause, such as the way that a particular job is done, defective material, faulty equipment, human errors, etc. This problem is made worse by the delay between a problem occurring and managers noticing its effects. For example, when operations introduce a new design for a product, there is some time-lag before they can identify customer reactions – and then if demand falls it may not be clear that this is due to the new design or some of the other changes that have occurred.

Even when managers can identify the real cause of a problem, it may not be obvious how to solve it. If the problem is too low utilization of capacity, what can they do to improve this? The idea that control systems have a straightforward procedure for identifying problems and then taking corrective action is an idealized rarity (Jaworski).

Risk and contingency planning

The approach to control that we have described is reactive, in that it waits to measure the performance of the strategy and then managers decide what to do. Control is usually more proactive than this and does some planning for possible future conditions. In particular it considers the **risk** associated with a strategy.

There is risk whenever managers cannot be sure of the outcomes from their decisions – and as everything in the future is uncertain, there is always some risk associated with an operations strategy. The essence of risk is that some events may or may not occur, and their occurrence may affect the performance of operations. This rather vague statement shows the problems with risk – we do not know what will happen, and we do not know what the effect will be. But this is still not the same as ignorance. You do not know whether or not your house will burn down next year – but you can assess the risk, you know the consequences, and you can make some plans, such as taking out insurance. In the same way, managers can list the things that might affect a strategy, assess the probable consequences and make appropriate plans.

Risk comes from a number of sources. Operations managers can control some of these, such as the likely variations in output from a process, and they can make decisions to minimize the effects. Some risks are under the control of other people, such as the likely amount invested in a project, and operations managers can influence, coerce, sell or deal with the risk in some other way. Much risk is not under anyone's control, such as the likely weather conditions, and there is little that operations managers can do to affect it. Such options are considered under the general heading of **risk management**, which aims at minimizing the harmful effects of risk. It is based on six steps:

1 Identify the risks – which shows events that might affect the strategy, and is generally described as risk assessment.

2 Estimate the probability of each event.

3 Measure the likely consequences of each event – estimating the likely impact in terms of expected value or utility.

4 Consider ways of dealing with these consequences – such as preventing the event, reducing the impact, or making contingency plans.

5 Compare the alternatives and choose the best.

6 Implement and control the best solution.

Some events cannot be foreseen, such as earthquakes, floods, or other 'acts of God'. These are totally unexpected and managers cannot make detailed proactive decisions, but have to see what actually happens and then make the best decisions to move forward. But operations can make some kind of general 'disaster plans' that prepare them for serious consequences from any source. Usually operations work with events that are more predictable – such as staff leaving, prices drifting upwards, and new products emerging. The basis of risk is that managers can estimate the likelihood of an event occurring – even if this is a broad, subjective estimate. For example, managers do not know whether oil prices will rise next year, but they can give an informed probability. In the same way they can suggest the probabilities for winning an order, that customers will pay their bills, delivery vehicles will have accidents, share prices will rise, and almost every other type of event. This assessment of risk can be difficult and it might be little better than informed opinion – but it is an essential function in every organization, and is at the heart of the insurance, foreign exchange, financial future, betting, stock market, and many other industries.

This situation is similar to the one that we described in chapter 2, considering ways of responding to changes in the environment. Here, though, there are other things to consider, particularly changes that are internal to the operations. Nonetheless, we have the same options for dealing with risk (Waters, 1998; Walker *et al.*):

1 *Ignore it* – do nothing now but wait and see what actually happens, and then take appropriate action.

2 *Avoid or reduce the risk* – taking actions to reduce the probability that a change will occur.

3 *Reduce or limit the consequences* – changing the strategy to limit the effects of risky events.

4 *Share or deflect the risk* – passing the risk onto someone else more able or willing to handle it, such as an insurance company.

5 *Make contingency plans* – commonly referred to as 'plan B', which makes arrangements that are only activated after the event occurs.

6 *Adapt to it* – accepting the event as inevitable and taking whatever action is necessary to maintain performance.

7 *Treat it as a new opportunity* – as any change to the environment will affect all competitors, those that are more flexible and innovative can gain a competitive advantage.

8 *Oppose it* – exerting influence to try and reduce the likelihood that an event occurs.

9 *Move to another environment* – accepting that a change will make the current operations environment less attractive, and moving to another more attractive one.

The best response depends on a range of factors, with important ones being the likelihood that an event will actually happen, the seriousness of its consequences, and managers' attitudes towards risk. An expected value gives a simple measure to help with this:

Expected value = probability of the event × value of the outcome

The expected value is higher when the probability and value are both high, and these are the risks that managers should give most attention. They should probably modify their strategies to avoid them (as shown in Figure 8.9) – unless they are risk takers who look for the high potential gains associated with high risk. Events with low probabilities or values have low expected values, and managers need give them little attention – either because they are unlikely to happen, or because if they do happen the consequences are relatively minor. Managers can probably accept these risks and not worry too much about them.

Contingency plans give an interesting option that is common with unlikely events that have a high cost – which is why they are often called 'disaster plans'. They form a set of general arrangements that can deal with a variety of circumstances. Then managers set some kind of trigger that will activate the contingency plan and specify the appropriate response. Without this trigger, operations continue normally without any interruptions. The problem is that contingency plans need a lot of effort, so it is impractical to design them for all eventualities and they must be limited to the most significant risks.

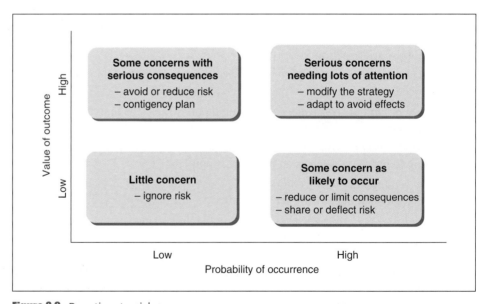

Figure 8.9 Reaction to risk

IDEAS IN PRACTICE BG Group

BG Group is a major supplier of gas. With the world's demand for energy continuing to rise sharply, BG has raised its annual turnover to £5 billion. It is an integrated business that has activities across the whole range of gas operations; its exploration and production business finds and develops gas reserves; it delivers natural gas to customers either through its own transmission and distribution business, or by its fleet of liquefied natural gas ships; its power business generates electricity using gas-fired power stations.

The gas industry has some features that are particularly important for investment decisions:

- It is capital intensive with strategic decisions typically involving expenditure of several hundred million pounds
- There are long lead times between the start of a project and generating cash, typically over five years
- The taxation and contract structure is complex
- Gas is a strategic resource so there is considerable government influence – along with pressures from other stakeholders.

Governments own the rights to minerals in their countries, and they divide the ground into 'blocks' and invite energy companies to bid for the exploration rights. So BG Group makes continual decisions about whether to apply for the right to explore new gas fields, and how much to bid. To make these decisions it considers risks:

- Geologists and geophysicists evaluate the probability of finding gas in a block and the likely amounts

- Engineers examine the facilities, wells, costs, and production problems for extracting the gas
- Health and safety managers assess health, safety and environmental risks
- Economists analyze market demand, price, government requirements, partners and commercial terms.

The overriding goal of the company is to create shareholder value. So any investment must give a combination of optimal growth with acceptable risk. But financial returns are not the only consideration. To start with, the investment must give a strategic fit with current business, skills and expertise. And there are environmental factors. Gas is the cleanest fossil fuel, but energy production always has some environmental cost, such as the release of greenhouse gases when burning fossil fuels, treatment of waste from nuclear power stations, and despoiling the landscape with windfarms. Social issues are also important, and BG's Statement of Business Principles sets out its fundamental values and ethical principles. It will only work in areas where the company can operate in accordance with its Business Principles. This is sometimes difficult as natural gas resources can be located in difficult areas, sensitive environments, war zones and territories where land rights are contested or inadequately protected.

Sources: BG Group Annual Review, London, 2005; Websites at www.bg.co.uk; www.tt100.biz

ACTION PLAN FOR IMPLEMENTATION

An **action plan** gives a timetable for implementing the operations strategy. So the basic elements of an action plan are a list of the activities needed for implementation, and a timetable showing when each of these activities is performed. Many managers view an action plan as a crucial factor for proper implementation, as it gives a formal view, making sure that all the necessary activities are done and that none are overlooked. But an action plan is more than a calendar for operations, as it gives a broad range of information (Katz; Thompson and Strickland, 2001). This typically includes:

- A review of the strategy's aims, scope, performance requirements, etc.
- A review of decisions and policies for operations areas, such as product, quality, process, capacity, supply chain and materials management.
- A 'to do' list that includes all the activities needed to implement the strategy.
- List of responsibilities for each activity.
- Timetable for activities showing when each will be done.
- Budgeted cost and expected flow of funds.
- Resources needed and timing.
- Any other relevant information needed to support the implementation.

A benefit of a good action plan is that it can identify potential problems with implementation. For example, it might reveal that the activities needed to implement a particular strategy are simply not possible. This is an interesting problem, as many managers assume that designing the strategy is the hard bit, and once this is done they can sit back and harvest the rewards. In practice, implementing a strategy is always difficult, as there is a huge number of interactions, many complex activities, no standard methods for doing them, a variety of initiatives to be launched, people needing different skills, overcoming resistance to change, and so on. But there are problems above and beyond the sheer complexity of the problems. One of these is more historical, as before the importance of operations managers was recognized they were largely absent from senior positions (Lazonick and West). Then managers from diverse areas would design an operations strategy without much relevant knowledge or reference to the operations that were going to implement it and deliver the results. Even when operations managers were in senior positions, they were often not involved in the design of higher strategies, but were seen as technical specialists who could be called upon when needed (Kenney and Florida; Hayes and Wheelwright). This attitude has changed, but there can still be problems with implementing an operations strategy, including:

- a rigid hierarchy that has one group of senior managers designing the strategy and another group of more junior managers implementing it
- setting the design of a strategy as the ultimate aim, with no thought given to its implementation
- strategies that are badly designed – typically not relating to actual operations, being unrealistic, ignoring key factors, etc.
- ignoring or underestimating the importance of key assumptions underlying the strategies
- lack of commitment with people only giving the appearance of supporting or having any interest in the strategy
- enthusiasm for the strategy declining over time

- not planning in advance but waiting for crises to occur and then solving problems – perhaps because this is more enjoyable than preparing for problems that might, or might not, occur

- use of subjective views and experience rather than analyses and rational approaches

- failure to recognize that strategic management is not about decisions made in the future, but is about the long-term consequences of decisions that are made now.

One surprisingly common mistake is to design an operations strategy and then think about its implementation. So the design of the strategy pays no attention to implementation, and this becomes correspondingly more difficult. The obvious way to avoid this is to consider implementation all the way through the design, always considering the practical effects of decisions. This is easier when there is widespread participation in the design process, particularly from those most closely involved with its implementation. Other factors that help with implementation include (Waters, 2002):

- an organizational structure that is flexible and allows innovation

- formal procedures for translating the strategy into reasonable decisions at lower levels

- effective information and related systems to support decisions

- acceptance that strategies evolve and operations keep changing

- efficient control systems to monitor progress

- convincing everyone that the strategy is beneficial, so they conscientiously play their part in implementation

- developing an organizational culture that supports the strategy.

Chapter review

- Even the best designed operations strategy serves no purpose until it is implemented. Implementation means that the strategic plans are actually done – turning the aspirations and intent of the strategy into positive actions.

- There are four steps to implementation – designing the infrastructure, initiating decisions, monitoring and controlling the operations, and giving a timetable of activities needed for implementation.

- The infrastructure consists of the organizational structure along with budgets, systems and policies to support it. The design of the infrastructure starts with decisions about the best type of organizational structure.

- The organizational structure gives the infrastructure a skeleton to which must be attached resources in the form of supporting systems, human resources and culture.

- Implementation of an operations strategy includes activation, which starts the cascade of decisions and actions down through the organization, moving from the vague aspirations of a strategy through to operational activities. The mechanism for this has each level meeting the requirements of higher levels, and setting targets for lower levels.

- Operations managers have to make strategic decisions in several areas. We classify these as deciding the type of product, quality management, process, capacity, design of the supply chain and movement of materials.

- A control system monitors actual performance of operations, compares this with objectives, and identifies gaps between the two. Then it adjusts the strategy, looking for improved performance.

- An action plan assists implementation of the operations strategy, giving a schedule for activities and a range of other related information.

CASE STUDY Copeland and Johnson

Copeland and Johnson (C&J) is a well-established company which specializes in arranging marine insurance. Their business centres around three core activities.

1 The first part is an 'insurance shop' which arranges insurance for clients. These operations start when a client approaches them to discuss details of their insurance needs. Then C&J prepare a suitable policy, agree the details and finalize arrangements with the client. The operations here look for a balance between price to the customer and expected benefit to C&J.

2 The second part is 'backroom financing' which sorts out the financial arrangements for the insurance. If the risk and value are relatively small, then C&J will cover the insurance themselves. If the risks are greater, they work with other companies – always established partners – to share the insurance. For big risks they work through Lloyds of London, transferring the risks to interested syndicates. Here the operations look for a balance between the risk and returns to C&J.

3 The third part is a 'claims office' for when things go wrong and clients submit a claim.

C&J discuss the claim with the client and agree the basic information. Then they do follow-up work with claims agents, assessors, and any other involved parties. These consider the circumstances and details of the claim, and decide the amount due to the client. When agreement is reached, C&J arrange settlement of the claim. Sometimes, though, it is impossible to reach an agreement and then C&J follow standard procedures to take the claim to arbitration or court. Their precise role depends on whether they are acting for clients who feel they have a valid claim that has not been met properly, or acting for insurers who feel that clients are making unjustified claims.

The mission of C&J is in three parts:

1 Our mission is to be an acknowledged leader in the supply of marine insurance on the international market. We shall achieve this by using the highest professional standards and integrity to provide our customers with the best possible service.

2 Our mission is based on operations excellence. To maintain our position of leadership in operations, we set the following goals:

- the highest levels of customer service and satisfaction
- long-term, mutually beneficial partnerships with our customers, employees, and shareholders
- flexible operations to meet the needs of each individual customer
- efficient operations that give the lowest overhead costs in the industry
- knowledgeable, trained and motivated staff
- long-term commitment to the industry
- continuous review and improvement of operations
- fair returns for the risks accepted by shareholders.

3 To achieve these goals we adopt the following key values:

- responsiveness to customers
- concern for people
- teamwork and cooperation
- professionalism and expertise
- value for money.

Questions

- What aspects of their operations do C&J focus on? Does this seem reasonable in the light of their mission?
- What is involved in implementing their operations strategy?
- What problems do you think C&J have in implementing their operations strategy? How could they overcome them?

Discussion questions

1 How would you set about implementing an operations strategy?

2 Senior managers can never be close enough to the operations to understand properly how they work. So their strategies are based on unrealistic views and there will always be problems with implementation. What can be done to avoid this?

3 Books on strategic management emphasize the design of strategies; in practice managers have more problems with implementing strategies. Why is there this difference in emphases?

4 What are the main parts of an operations infrastructure?

5 Does the organizational structure of the operations function really affect its ability to implement a strategy?

6 'Happy workers are productive workers.' Is this true?

7 A control system gives feedback to managers – in the way that a cybernetics view considers most of management to consist of feedback loops. What does this mean?

8 Risk management is based on the belief that managers can give a probability to future events. But if they knew what was going to happen in the future, there would be no risk. So why bother with risk management?

Useful websites

www.bg.co.uk
www.mcdonalds.co.uk

www.mcdonalds.com
www.shell.com
www.tt100.biz
www.walmartstores.com

References

Ansoff H.I., The concept of strategic management, Journal of Business Policy, 2(4), p 7, 1972.

Blimes L., Wetzker K. and Xhonneux P., Value in human resurces, Financial Times, 10th February, 1997.

Blucker S.E., The virtual organisation, The Futurist, March–April, p 9, 1994.

Brown S., Lamming R., Bessant J. and Jones P., Strategic operations management (2nd edition), Butterworth Heinemann, Oxford, 2004.

Byrne J.A., Brandt R. and Port O., The virtual corporation, Business Week, Feb 8, p 98, 1993.

Chandler A., Strategy and structure, MIT Press, Cambridge, MA, 1962.

Craig J.C. and Grant R.M., Strategic management, Kogan Page, London, 1993.

DTI, Competitiveness through partnerships with people, Department of Trade and Industry, London, 1997.

Etzioni A., Complex organisations, Holt, Reinhart and Winston, New York, 1961.

Fine C.H. and Hax A.C., Manufacturing Strategy: a methodology and an illustration, Interfaces, vol 15(6), November–December, pp 28–46, 1985.

Galbraith J.R. and Kazanian R.K., Strategy implementation, West Publishing, St Paul, MN, 1986.

Goold M., Campbell A. and Alexander M., Corporate level strategy, John Wiley, New York, 1994.

Hamel G., Prahalad C.K., Thomas H. and O'Neil D., Strategic flexibility, John Wiley, New York, 1998.

Harrison M., Operations management strategy, pitman, London, 1993.

Hayes R. and Wheelwright S., Restoring our competitive edge, Wiley, New York, 1984.

Heizer J. and Render B., Operations management (7th edition), Prentice Hall, Englewood Cliffs, NJ, 2004.

Hertzberg F., Work and the nature of man, World Publishing, Cleveland, OH, 1966.

Hosmer L.T., Strategic management, Prentice Hall, Englewood Cliffs, NJ, 1982.

Jaworski B.J., Towards a theory of marketing control, Journal of Marketing, July, p 24, 1988.

Joynson S., Sid's heroes – uplifting business performance and the human spirit, BBC Books, London, 1994.

Katz R.L., Management of the total enterprise, Prentice Hall, Englewood Cliffs, NJ, 1970.

Keen P.G.W., The process edge, Harvard Business School Press, Boston, MA, 1997.

Kenney M. and Florida R., Beyond mass production, Oxford University Press, Oxford, 1993.

Lazonick W. and West J., Organisational integration and competitive advantage, Industrial and Corporate Change, vol 4(1), pp 229–269, 1995.

Manki D., Cohen S.G. and Bikson T.K., Teams and technology, Harvard Business School Press, Boston, MA, 1996.

Maslow A., Motivation and personality, Harper, New York, 1954.

Mohrman S.A., Galbraith J.R. and Lawler E.E., Tomorrow's organisation, Jossey Bass Wiley, San Francisco, CA, 1998.

Pascale R.T. and Athos A., The art of Japanese management, Simon and Schuster, New York, 1981.

Pfeffer J., Competitive advantage through people, Harvard Business School Press, Boston, MA, 1996.

Pfeffer J., The human equation, Harvard Business School Press, Boston, MA, 1998.

Pfeffer J. and Veiga J., Putting people first for organisaional success, Academy of Management Executive, vol 13(2), pp 37–48, 1999.

Schein E.H., Organisational psychology, Prentice Hall, Englewood Cliffs, NJ, 1988.

Slack N. and Lewis M., Operations strategy, Financial Times Prentice Hall, Harlow, 2002.

Thompson A.A. and Strickland A.J., Strategic management (12th edition), McGraw-Hill, New York, 2001.

Thompson A.A., Strickland A.J. and Gamble J.E., Crafting and implementing strategy (14th edition), McGraw-Hill, New York, 2004.

Volberda H.W., Building the flexible firm, Oxford University Press, Oxford, 1999.

Walker O.C., Boyd H.W. and Larreche J., Marketing strategy (3rd edition), Irwin McGraw-Hill, New York, 1999.

Waters D., A practical introduction to management science (2nd edition), Addison-Wesley, Harlow, 1998.

Waters D. Operations management (2nd edition), FT Prentice Hall, Harlow, 2002.

The first part of this book discussed the broad principles of strategic management. This second part showed how these principles can be applied to an operations strategy.

Operations management is based on the view that every organization makes products, and operation managers are the people directly responsible for creating them. They design products to achieve their aims, continually balancing the internal needs of operations (typically expressed in terms of efficient use of resources) and the external needs of the environment (typically expressed in terms of customer satisfaction).

If we collect together all the long-term goals, plans, policies, culture, resources, decisions and actions that relate to operations, we get the basis of an operations strategy. This forms the link between higher strategies and more detailed operations – but the reality is an intricate network of connected elements that is ill-defined, nebulous, and without any clear boundaries. At its core are the decisions for key areas that set the long-term direction of operations.

Managers design elements of an operations strategy to best achieve their long-term aims – which are largely derived from the aims of higher strategies. We described a general approach to designing an operations strategy. In practice, there are so many different factors that it is impossible for managers to consider all of them, so they only look at a reasonable number of alternatives. Their choice of best is made after discussion, agreement, and compromise – and the results from this top-down design are combined with bottom-up emerging strategies. The result often has a particular focus, such as cost, waste, product differentiation, material management, timing, productivity improvement, etc.

Analysis is an important part of designing an operations strategy. An environmental scan collects relevant information about the operations environment, concentrating on the industry, market and other key factors. Information about internal operations comes from an operations audit. Perhaps the most common format for summarizing results is a SWOT analysis to describe the strengths, weaknesses, opportunities and threats.

Even the best designed operations strategy serves no purpose until it is implemented. This means that the strategic plans are set in motion – turning the aspirations and intent of the strategy into positive actions. This involves designing the infrastructure, initiating decisions, monitoring and controlling the operations, and giving an action plan for implementation.

Figure R2.1 gives a summary of the main factors in designing and implementing an operations strategy.

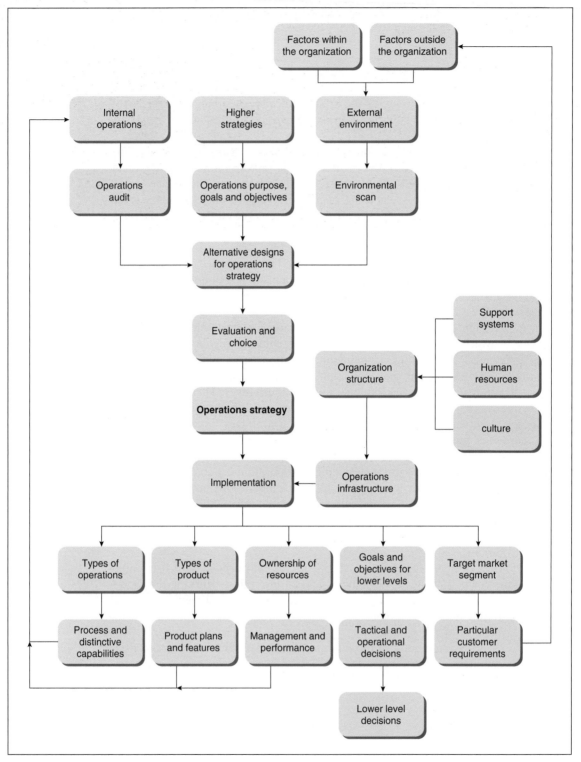

Figure R2.1 Review of operations strategy, design and implementation

PART 3

STRATEGIC DECISIONS IN OPERATIONS

The first part of this book described the context of an operations strategy, outlining the principles of strategic management. The second part showed how these general principles can be applied to an operations strategy. It outlined the function of operations, and then described the role of an operations strategy, its purpose, contents, design, and implementation. The result is a complex web of interrelated parts that gives a guiding purpose to the operations.

At the core of the strategy are decisions about key areas that set the long-term direction of operations. In the third part of the book we look at some of these specific areas where operations managers make strategic decisions. In different circumstances almost any area of operations can have a strategic impact, but we focus on the most common. Together these form some of the most important decisions made in every organization.

There are six chapters in this part:

- **Chapter 9** discusses the type of products made by operations, the design of new products and approach to innovation
- **Chapter 10** shows how quality management ensures that products are free from defects
- **Chapter 11** looks at decisions about the type of process used to make a product
- **Chapter 12** considers the capacity of the process and shows how operations can make enough products to satisfy demand

● **Chapter 13** discusses the structure of the supply chain through which products move
● **Chapter 14** considers the movement of materials through the supply chains

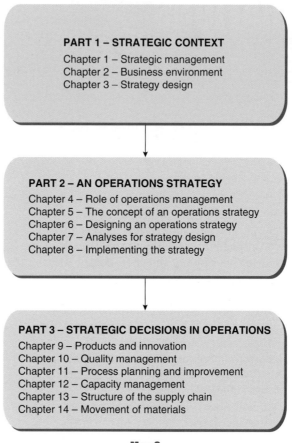

PART 1 – STRATEGIC CONTEXT
Chapter 1 – Strategic management
Chapter 2 – Business environment
Chapter 3 – Strategy design

PART 2 – AN OPERATIONS STRATEGY
Chapter 4 – Role of operations management
Chapter 5 – The concept of an operations strategy
Chapter 6 – Designing an operations strategy
Chapter 7 – Analyses for strategy design
Chapter 8 – Implementing the strategy

PART 3 – STRATEGIC DECISIONS IN OPERATIONS
Chapter 9 – Products and innovation
Chapter 10 – Quality management
Chapter 11 – Process planning and improvement
Chapter 12 – Capacity management
Chapter 13 – Structure of the supply chain
Chapter 14 – Movement of materials

Map 3

CHAPTER 9
Products and Innovation

Operations make the products that organizations supply to their customers. For this, they have to supply a continuing stream of products with features that both satisfy customer demand (the external requirements), and allow operations to achieve its aims (the internal requirements). This is the role of product planning, which is responsible for all decisions about the introduction of new products and changes to existing ones. Innovation describes the extent to which product planning is willing to adopt new ideas.

Aims of the chapter

After reading this chapter you should be able to:

- Understand the purpose and aims of product planning
- Describe the stages in a product life cycle
- List the stages in new product development
- Consider the timing and organization of product development
- Discuss the role of product design
- Show how designers give products the features that customers want
- Discuss the features that operations want designed into products
- Appreciate the use of price elasticity, marginal values and production possibility curves
- Outline the role of product innovation

The key concepts discussed in this chapter are:

Main themes

- **Product planning**, which organizes the continuing supply of products that allows an organization to meet changing demands
- **New product development**, to design new products
- **Product design**, which considers the features that products need to satisfy the requirements of customers and internal operations

PRODUCT PLANNING

At the core of an operations strategy is a set of decisions made by managers about key areas of operations. Around this are the other parts of the strategy, including culture, informal structure, infrastructure and so on (illustrated in Figure 9.1). In this chapter we start looking at these core decision areas, by considering the type of products made. This theme is developed in the next six chapters.

Changes to products

We have consistently developed the idea that the operations in an organization make its products, where each '**product**' is the complete package of goods and services that the organization supplies to its customers. Organizations do not want to satisfy customer demand out of the goodness of their hearts, but because this gives a mechanism for achieving their own aims. A company wants to make a profit, and it can do this by selling its products for more than they cost to make. With this view, the supply of products becomes the main function of an organization. And its products have to be designed to achieve their double purpose – being attractive enough to satisfy customer demand, and allowing operations to achieve their internal aims.

Products do not just appear, but every aspect of their design and development needs careful planning. Not surprisingly, this function is called **product planning**.

- **Product planning** is responsible for the design and introduction of new products, changes to existing products and withdrawal of old ones.
- It ensures that an organization continues to supply products that achieve both its internal and external aims.

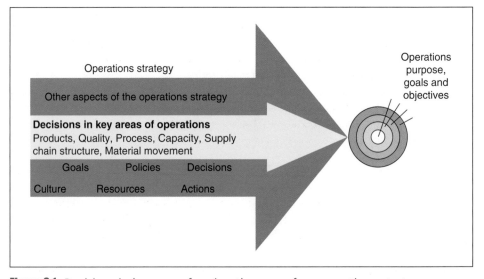

Figure 9.1 Decisions in key areas forming the core of an operations strategy

Product planning is not concerned with the details of design – such as putting a knob on the front of a kettle rather than the side – but on the broad principles about the type of product – such as making high quality electric kettles. It makes the long-term, strategic decisions about the type of product to make. Product planning at Airbus Industries, for example, makes sure that they have a range of passenger air-lines available for the long-term future; at Citigroup they plan their range of financial services; at Vodafone they plan their communications services. The details are added to these broad plans in later tactical and operational aspects of **product design**.

In principle, product planning and design seem rather straightforward. Operations managers assess their own requirements for a product, and they assess customer requirements, then they design products that satisfy both of these. Unfortunately, this simplistic view conceals a complex web of related decisions. When there is a virtually infinite number of options for an organization's products, how does it decide on the one that it will actually make? And the consequences of such decisions can be severe. If an organization gets its product planning right, customers want its products and this lays the foundations for future success; but if it makes a mistake and supplies products that customers do not like, or that fail to achieve the internal requirements, it has serious problems. Most companies fail because of poor sales, and the only real option then is to have another go and improve their products.

In practice, this idea of improving products is the norm, as operations managers continually look for new ideas and enhancements. There are several reasons for this, but the main one is to continue meeting customer demand that changes over time. This year we want clothes of a particular colour, a certain type of car, PDAs and a particular flavour of drink. Next year we will want different coloured clothes, another type of car, some new electronic gadget and a different flavour of drink. It is notori-ously difficult to forecast customers' demands for the long-term future. Perhaps the only certainties are that customers will want new things, they will become more demanding, and they will be less willing to compromise.

Operations keep tuning their products to meet the latest demands, and gain an advantage over competitors who are offering similar products. A small variation in products can be enough to create a substantial difference in demand, so managers tend to make frequent adjustments. But it is worth repeating the warning we gave in chapter 5 – an organization that only responds to customer demands inevitably becomes a follower rather than a market leader (Christensen). The organization can listen carefully to customers, monitor market trends, and make products that exactly match current demands – but it only satisfies established needs and does not consider radically new products and processes, innovation, or substantially different ideas. Eventually, the organization becomes too conventional and old-fashioned, loses its competitive advantage and is overtaken by more innovative and adventurous com-petitors.

Apart from the market, the other pressure for changing the type of product comes from the internal requirements of operations. For example, operations might adjust an existing design to reduce production costs, or research and development might identify a new type of product, or there may be changes to production methods, tech-nology, materials, delivery method, quality, or some other feature that affects the product.

Operations respond to pressures – both external and internal – by continually updating product plans, but most of the changes are relatively minor adjustments,

IDEAS IN PRACTICE McDonald's

In the fifty years since it was founded, the golden arches of McDonald's have become one of the most recognized advertising symbols in the world. By 2002 its revenues from 9,000 company owned restaurants and 22,000 franchisees and licensees were over $15 billion a year, making it twice as big as its next global competitor (Yum! Brands that own Kentucky Fried Chicken, Pizza Hut and Taco Bell).

Despite continuing growth, not everything was going well, and the company ended 2002 with its first ever quarterly loss. There were several explanations for this. The philosophy of quality, service, cleanliness and value was not so convincing as it had been; competitors were offering similar products, often with more variety or lower prices; in parts of the world anti-American feeling was directed at the icon of McDonald's. And there was an underlying concern that McDonald's was seen as encouraging people to eat unhealthy diets of high-fat, junk food (subsequently illustrated in Morgan Spurlock's film, 'Super Size Me', and the unsuccessful attempts of some people to sue McDonald's for making them fat). The company was losing out to sandwich bars, local delis and other restaurants that were seen as offering healthier alternatives.

McDonald's responded to its problems in several ways. It concentrated on increasing revenue from existing restaurants rather than opening more new locations, and by 2004 this organic growth raised sales by 13 percent a year to $20 billion, with profits back up to $2 billion. This was achieved by renovating and smartening restaurants, improving operations, putting even more emphasis on core values – and by adjusting the food on offer. McDonald's became the world's biggest seller of salads – backed by free range eggs, bottled water, fruit and yoghurt. The menus include lighter options that are seen as healthier. They are also taking more notice of local variations, so that Japan has a Teriyaki burger, Europe is expanding its toasted sandwiches, Australia sells gourmet coffee in McCafés, and the company bought a stake in Britain's Prêt a Manger chain of coffee, sandwich and salad bars. The result is that people who never visited McDonald's when their options were limited to 'burger and fries' are happy to go in for the wider range of 'healthier' options.

Sources: The Economist, Big Mac's makeover, 16th October 2004, pp 63–65; Websites at www.mcdonalds.com; www.mcdonalds.co.uk

and are often little more than cosmetic modifications. American Express adjust the conditions on their credit cards; Ford update a model of car, Qantas flies to new destinations, and the BBC replaces a show whose ratings have fallen. Few make radical new products, in the way that digital cameras changed photography, McDonald's changed the way we eat out, DVDs changed the way we watch films, or Dyson changed the way we vacuum carpets. Nonetheless, all changes – even the smallest – can have significant affects and need careful planning.

Product life cycle

The demand for a product usually follows a standard pattern over its life. This **life cycle** has the five stages shown in Figure 9.2 (Waters).

1 *Introduction*. The product is new, and demand is low while people learn about it, try it and see if they like it.

2 *Growth*. New customers buy the product, it becomes more popular and demand rises quickly.

3 *Maturity*. Demand stabilizes as most potential customers know about the product, and they buy it in steady numbers.

4 *Decline*. The product is now getting old, and sales fall as customers start buying new alternatives.

5 *Withdrawal*. Demand declines to the point where it is no longer worth making the product.

This life cycle occurs in general types of products — such as newspapers, credit cards, and low cost airlines — as well as specific brands — such as Le Figaro, American Express and RyanAir. It also occurs in whole industries and sectors – tobacco products and cigarette sales are declining in much of the world for example. These life cycles are not synchronized, and an individual product might be in a decline while the broader market is rising (and vice versa). Superimposed on these cycles are business cycles, economic trends, effects of marketing, market distortions, and general random variations, which mean that actual demand rarely follows such a clear pattern. Nonetheless, the life cycle gives a useful framework for discussing different effects. In particular, we can use it to describe the different requirements of operations during the life cycle, in terms of the scale of operations, type of process, changing costs, marketing strategies, etc. It is easiest to consider this by following a hypothetical product through its life cycle.

1 *Introduction*. The cycle really starts with the research, development, design, testing, economic analysis and market analysis needed to get the product to market (which we describe later in the chapter). When it is ready to sell to customers, the product is launched and moves though an introduction stage. Customers are not sure of the new product, so initial demand is low and can be

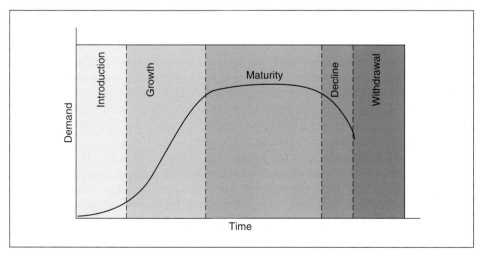

Figure 9.2 Demand over a product life cycle

met by small-scale operations – perhaps making units for specific orders. Production costs are high, but these are covered by a price premium charged for new products when there is limited competition (an alternative view offers a low price to recover costs through rapid market growth). The design of the product is adjusted as customers give their reactions, so the operations must be flexible enough to deal with changing specifications and customization. The main competitive element is product differentiation, with flexibility. This early stage sets the image of the product, so operations must gain a good reputation by meeting quality targets and delivery dates.

2 *Growth*. There is increasing product awareness, and if customers like it, demand increases and the product moves into the growth stage. Promotion extends knowledge of the product to broader audiences. The scale of operations increases, but it is difficult to get accurate forecasts of demand in rapidly changing conditions – so managers find it difficult to plan production, organize resources, develop the supply chain, make sure that there is enough capacity, and use facilities efficiently. The product design becomes more fixed as less popular variations are dropped. Increasing standardization means that units are no longer made for specific orders, but demand is met from a stock of finished goods. Costs become more important as the price falls with new competitors entering the market.

3 *Maturity*. At some point demand stabilizes and the product moves into its mature stage. Forecasting and production planning is much easier with routine operations. Some early competitors have moved on, leaving the market to a few larger organizations that are now making similar products and largely competing on price. Managers look for a competitive advantage by designing efficient operations and improving productivity – typically with an automated process making a standard product in long production runs. At this point, innovation is more likely in the process than in the product.

4 *Decline*. Eventually demand falls, and organizations are left with spare capacity. More competitors drop out of the market, some adjust operations to reduce capacity, and others change the product design to extend its life. When these adjustments are no longer worthwhile, they design termination procedures and stop production.

This is obviously a simplified view, but it shows how operations might evolve during a product life cycle. At the start they emphasize research, development and design; then they may move on to forecasting, capacity management, resource scheduling and developing the supply chain; then on to cost reduction, increasing technology and improving the process; then on to reducing capacity and extending the life. Table 9.1 shows a summary of such effects (Waters).

An obvious question concerns the length of the life cycle. Each edition of a newspaper goes through its life cycle in a few hours; fashion garments have life cycles of months or even weeks; consumer durables have life cycles of five or ten years; some basic commodities like soap and coffee remain in the mature stage for decades. Unfortunately, there is no way of forecasting the length of a life cycle. Some products have an unexpectedly short life, and are quickly withdrawn; others stay at the mature stage for a surprisingly long time. Some products, like full cream milk and beer stayed

Table 9.1 Features of the product life cycle

Stage	introduction	growth	maturity	decline
Demand	low	rising	steady	falling
Product design	evolving	some change	standard	adjustments
Planning	basic	difficult	easy	contracting
Process	small scale	larger scale	mass production	adjustments
Efficiency	low	improving	high	declining
Focus of operations	flexibility, reliability	scheduling, capacity	cost reduction, productivity	cost control, closure
Number of competitors	few	rising	stable or falling	falling
Unit costs	high	falling	low	variable
Price	high	fairly high	low	very low
Total revenue	low	rising	peaks	falls
Profit	low	rising	peaks	falls

at the mature stage for a very long time and are now in a decline. Some products appear to decline and then grow again, like cinema attendance.

Entry and exit strategies

The life cycle might suggest that organizations follow a product through its entire life cycle. They spend a lot of money on research and development to find completely new products, and then continue to make the product during all of its useful life until the demand dies away. Leading pharmaceutical companies work this way, spending huge amounts to find entirely new drugs, regaining their investment while the drugs are still within their patents, and continuing to make them until demand falls as replacements appear. But we have already said that most 'new' products are really minor modifications of old ones. So the reality has a few operations starting with basic research to develop entirely new products, and the majority looking around at existing products to see what they can borrow and adjust to give their own new versions. In other words, most operations look at their existing products, or those of competitors, to identify ideas that they can adopt and adapt. And organisations do not continue making a product throughout its entire life, but they stop when conditions change. For example, Mac do not wait until demand for a model of computer dies before introducing their latest concept; and innovative pharmaceutical companies tend to withdraw from a market when their patents expire and generic manufacturers appear.

The point in product life cycles where operations start – and later stop – making a product defines their **entry** and **exit strategy**. Four common options include:

1 *Research driven operations* – are very innovative and do basic research to find ideas for new products. Often they lack the resources and production skills to

manage a growing demand, so they leave before the growth stage. Their main products are likely to be the ideas, concepts, patents and intellectual property that other organizations exploit and develop into their own products. This is common in the computer industry, where hundreds of small companies develop new ideas that are adopted by the major manufacturers.

2 *New product exploiters* – do less basic R&D themselves, but are good at identifying new ideas that have commercial potential and exploiting them during the growth stage. They aim for the high prices available during the growth period, and exit when profit margins begin to fall. Their strengths are in identifying useful ideas, developing these into attractive products, marketing new ideas, organizing for a growing demand, nursing products through difficult times, and expanding processes through periods of increasing output.

3 *Cost reducers* – do little R&D on products, but concentrate on improving processes. They can design very efficient operations, focusing on high volume, low cost production. This generally comes at high capital cost, and they can only justify the investment by making products that are already successful. So they enter the market at the mature stage and produce large quantities with costs that are low enough to compete with existing suppliers. Then they exit when demand begins to fall and utilization of the facilities declines.

4 *Life extenders* – when demand for a product begins to fall, it generally does not just suddenly stop but declines over some time. During this time, mass producers are leaving the market, and their spare capacity may be available at low prices. Some operations take advantage of this to buy the spare capacity, and use a combination of marketing, efficient operations and adjusted design to extend a product's life. This approach can give short-term profits before a continued decline – but there are many examples of products recovering and returning to a strong position.

The best choices of strategy depend on an individual operations' expertise and resources, as well as their longer term goals. Operations that are strong in research and development and have an aim of expansion, are unlikely to be life extenders; those that have limited resources and an aim of product innovation will not be cost reducers.

Ansoff's matrix

Ansoff looked at various entry and exit strategies – and the underlying attitudes towards new products – and discussed their effects on operations strategies. He described the alternatives in a matrix of operations' current and future products and markets (illustrated in Figure 9.3).

This model gives four different strategies for growth:

1 *Market penetration* – where operations look for growth through existing products in current markets. When demand for a product is growing, simply maintaining market share will give growth; but when the life cycle reaches maturity operations must look for more positive ways to grow, effectively increasing market share. To achieve this, they can reduce prices, increase advertising, or make adjustments to differentiate the product. This is the least

risky strategy as it largely continues current operations. But variations include horizontal integration, or buying a competitor. This gives a very quick increase in market share and at the same time reduces competition.

2 *Market development* – where operations look for growth by selling existing products to new customers. This typically looks to sell products to new market segments, new geographical regions, or for new purposes. For example, sportswear producers, such as Nike, used this approach to sell their existing range of sports clothes in the fashion market.

3 *Product development* – where operations develop new products targeted at its existing markets. At its basic level, this is the most common strategy, where established operations update their product range for existing customers. But expansion really has to sell more products, and this works best when an organization's strengths are related to its customers rather than to a specific product. You can see this with football clubs, films, bands, and so on, who sell a wide range of associated products to an established set of followers.

4 *Diversification* – where operations grow by diversifying into new businesses that make new products and sell them to new markets. This is the most risky of the four strategies as it needs changes in both the product and the market, and these might not build on core capabilities. However, this risk is worth taking when there is a reasonable probability of getting high rewards. Diversification can also give a foothold in an attractive industry, and it can reduce overall risk by spreading operations into more industries. 'Related diversification' slightly reduces the risk, by moving into a new product and market that has some relation with existing products and markets. A common way of achieving this is through vertical integration, where an organization gains control of more of its supply chains by taking over its suppliers (backward integration) or its customers (forward integration).

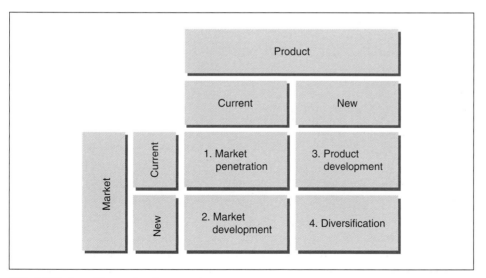

Figure 9.3 Ansoff matrix of strategies

IDEAS IN PRACTICE BlackBerry

Research In Motion Limited (RIM) was founded in 1984 in Waterloo, Canada. It is a designer, manufacturer and marketer of innovative wireless solutions for the mobile communications market. Its research focus is clear from its annual budget of $63 million on a turnover of less than $600 million.

RIM's best known product is probably BlackBerry, which is essentially a wireless, hand-held, e-mail device. Its difference is that it does not wait until users log-on to check their e-mails, but it automatically finds them and pushes e-mails down to their mobile device. This original idea has been expanded to give integrated hardware, software and services, that allow mobile access to e-mail, phone, SMS messaging, Internet, Intranet, browsers, organisers – and any information that people may want from any source.

In 2005 RIM was looking for continuing expansion of its BlackBerry range. This had originally been seen as an executive toy with limited sales, but it was becoming very popular and was moving into mass sales. Unfortunately, this success brought problems, particularly from the throng of competitors who saw a winning idea and were keen to enter the market. Seventy percent of RIM's revenue came from devices, while the rest came from software and services, but it would be difficult to compete in a mass market against big handset makers such as Nokia, Motorola and Samsung. So RIM licensed its BlackBerry software to them. Now RIM technology is used by many third party developers and manufacturers, who enhance their products and services with wireless connectivity. This allows RIM to focus more on research, software and services.

But this move also has problems, as other competitors – such as Good Technology, Visto, Intellisync, Seven and Smartner – began to offer wireless e-mail software that worked on a broader range of computers and smartphones. And Microsoft saw the potential and moved its huge resources into the area, including similar technology in its new mailserver and PocketPC software.

Sources: The economist, Attack of the BlackBerry Killers, March 19th, pp 68–69, 2005; Research in Motion, Annual Report, Waterloo, Canada, 2004; Websites at www.rim.com; www.blackberry.com

NEW PRODUCT DEVELOPMENT

Stages in development

Before a new product is brought to the market, operations have to do a lot of research and development, all of which is considered as **new product development**.

- **New product development** is responsible for taking initial ideas for products and developing them into products that are launched in the market.

There are two views about the best way to get new products. The first considers the whole process as a creative exercise – you give people enough time and resources to think about products, and over time new ideas emerge. There is no formal procedure here, but people are encouraged to share ideas, work on individual projects, and not be hindered by current operations, or rigid ways of thinking. This approach is widely used in software and high technology companies that want entirely new, innovative ideas. The second view says that the only way of guaranteeing results is to use a formal procedure that moves forward in a series of well-defined steps. This more traditional approach is the common model in most R&D departments (Bruce and Biemans; Wheelwright and Clark). The details of the procedure differ widely, but a general approach has six stages, the first of which generates initial ideas, while the next five refine these into viable products.

1   *Generation of Ideas.* Ideas for new products come from many sources, both internal (basic R&D, opportunities identified by marketing, operations suggesting changes to an existing product, suggestion boxes, etc.) and external (customer suggestions, focus groups, competitors' products, government regulations, etc.). At this point we are talking about concepts rather than detailed products, and new ideas of this kind are easy to find. The difficult part is to examine these ideas, choose the best, and turn them into viable products that satisfy both customers and internal requirements.

2   *Initial screening of ideas.* This quickly rejects ideas that have obvious flaws, such as being impossible to make, technically too difficult, have been tried before and failed, duplicate an existing product, use expertise or skills that the organization does not have, do not fit into current operations, obviously would not sell or make a profit, are too risky, etc. This screening might remove 80 percent of the original ideas (as shown in Figure 9.4).

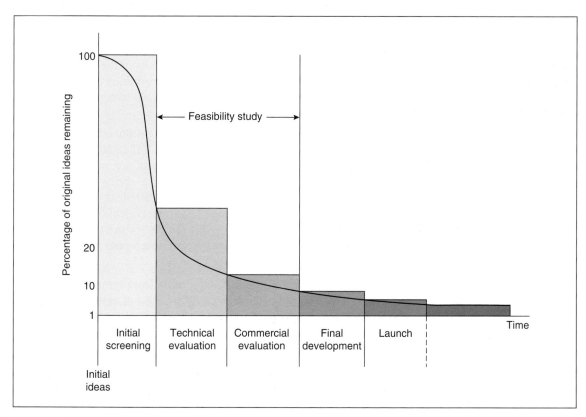

Figure 9.4 Stages in new product development

3 *Technical evaluation – initial design, development and testing.* At this point the idea seems feasible, so details are added to take it from a general concept through to initial designs or prototypes. This allows a technical evaluation, which asks two types of questions. Firstly, it asks general questions about the concept – is the idea based on sound principles; does it work; is it safe and legal; is it a new idea or a variation on an old one; if it is an old idea why have operations not made it before; are there problems with patents; are other developments likely to overtake the product? Secondly, it asks specific questions about the initial design – is it technically feasible; can it be made with available technology; does it fit into current operations; do operations have the necessary skills and experience; do they have the necessary facilities; is there enough capacity?

4 *Commercial evaluation – market and financial analysis.* The technical evaluation makes sure that operations can make the product, and now a commercial evaluation sees if it will achieve its aims. This removes products that customers will not buy, are too similar to existing products, are so different to existing products that customers will not accept them, are in a rapidly declining market, do not fit into existing strategies, will not make enough profit, need too much capital, have poor returns on investment, have too high operating costs, and so on. This stage builds a commercial case for continuing development.

5 *Final development.* Now the product has passed both the technical and commercial evaluation – which together form a feasibility study – it moves on to final design and testing, giving the product that customers actually see. These final designs describe the whole product package, and also give a description of how the product is made, including details of the process, quality measures, materials used, supply chain, and everything else that might affect the final product. At this stage the operations have complete specifications for the product and can start production.

6 *Launch the product.* Now operations start making the product, launch it, and test customer reactions. This is the first chance to see if the planning has worked and the product is actually a success. Very few of the initial ideas reach the point where they are launched on the market, and even fewer become commercial successes. A rule of thumb suggests that 250 ideas lead to one product, and 25 products lead to one success. Pharmaceutical companies routinely examine 10,000 chemicals to find one that they can market – which goes some way to explain the billion dollar costs of developing a new drug.

Because so many trial products are lost during the development stages, operations do not test one product at a time, but they simultaneously work on many ideas. This often means that there are several likely products in final development at the same time – but operations probably only have enough resources to market and supply one of them. Then the real problem is not to identify potential new products, but to compare the alternatives and see which is likely to give the best results.

At the start of this process we are talking about product planning and general concepts that set the type of product operations might make far into the future. At the end, we are talking about product design and more detailed features that appeal to customers. Somewhere between these, there is an uncertain boundary where we move from long-term concepts to shorter term designs. As with all such boundaries, there is no agreement about where it is. Some people say that strategy only considers the broadest views – 'we will provide banking services' or 'we are an entertainment company'. Others say that even the details of design are important for a product's success, and there are many examples of companies that have gone out of business because of a poorly designed product – so product design clearly has a strategic impact. In different circumstances, both of these can be convincing, so we will not assume rigid boundaries in our discussion.

Time for development

The six stages of development give a useful – but simplified – model. In different circumstances products may not go through all of these stages, or they may loop backwards, or they may go through additional stages. If, say, the results from a commercial evaluation are unclear, managers might decide to drop the project and simply write-off their investment; or they might repeat the commercial evaluation to check the results; or they might extend the commercial analyses to include other tests; or they might adjust the designs of the product and return to screening and technical evaluation. Most product development has a lot of cycling and repetition of this kind. At every step the designs get more firmly defined and the amount of uncertainty declines.

All of this work takes a long time. A car manufacturer typically takes five or six years to develop a new model; a new kind of insurance policy can take several years to set up, and even a chocolate bar needs years of testing to finalize its details. But there are obvious benefits from speeding up the development. Getting a new product to market before competitors allows a price premium, earns revenue for longer, gains a dominant market position, and sets standards for later entrants. A shorter development time also frees-up cash and resources, and speeds the generation of income needed to recover development costs. Perhaps a less obvious benefit is that operations can delay work on a new type of product until competitors are already working on their own versions – and then it can learn from their experiences, avoid mistakes, and still reach market at the same time (see also Thomke and Reinertsen).

Concurrent development gives a way of reducing the development time. Rather than take the six stages in strict order, waiting until each stage is finished before moving on to the next, concurrent development starts each stage as soon as possible so that they work in parallel rather than series. The initial screening of ideas need not wait until all ideas have been generated, but can quickly remove non-starters while other ideas are still being considered; similarly, the commercial evaluation can run in parallel with the technical evaluation. The more overlap that there is between stages, the shorter the overall development time, and companies have reported reductions of up to 70 percent (Smith and Reinertsen; Stalk; Stalk and Hout).

Organizational changes

The usual way of organizing a new type of product has everything done within the organization. Development is done by existing R&D departments, production and marketing use internal resources, either transferred from older products that are now discontinued, or through organic expansion. But there are many variations on this model, often needing changes to the organizational structure (Pisano; Trott), and increasingly out-sourcing or contracting-out some of the development work to other organizations.

A variation on internal expansion has a parent organization forming an entirely new business to supply a new product. This is particularly attractive when the new product is innovative and does not fit easily into current operations. Often managers find it difficult to keep changing their current operations, so they prefer to start new businesses specifically to pursue emerging opportunities (Gersick). The new business increases diversification within the corporation, and this can be achieved in several ways. The obvious one is an internal start-up – where a corporation starts a new business from scratch and assigns it a position alongside its other business divisions. This is most attractive when there is enough time, the organization has the necessary resources, it has or can acquire necessary skills and experience, the extra capacity will not adversely affect supply chains, there are no powerful rivals for the new business, there are low entry barriers, and existing businesses are slow to respond to their opportunities. If these conditions are not met, managers might take a more direct route of acquiring an existing business that is already making products similar to the proposed one. This has the advantages of being quick, avoiding entry barriers to the new market, gaining technological experience, using established operations and supply chains, building on proven success, and establishing a size that matches rivals' efficiency and costs.

Keeping all development work for new products within the same organization has the benefits of retaining control of the process, involving people who are familiar with current operations, having free flows of information, using established systems, increasing the utilization of overhead facilities, and reducing the risk that information is passed on to competitors. But new product development may need resources, knowledge and expertise that is not available within normal operations, and then they have to use outside people. They might simply hire them or used fixed-term contracts, effectively increasing the capacity of in-house operations. Or they might out-source all the development and design to specialists, allowing operations to concentrate on their own core capabilities of actually making products. And there are other more flexible arrangements between these two extremes, which somehow share development between the organization and outside specialists. At a simple level, an organization can divide the development work into separate packages, and assign each to either an outside specialist or internal department. More usefully, customers and suppliers can work together, perhaps sharing information to make sure that they are both satisfied with a new product. At a more sophisticated level, staff can be seconded from one organization to work temporarily in another. Slack and Twigg describe approaches of this kind using 'guest engineers' who are temporarily transferred from, say, a customer to a supplier.

If the collaboration between organizations is likely to continue for the long-term, customers and suppliers often form joint ventures with the specific purpose of working on areas of mutual interest. This pools the capabilities of each organization and ensures that the benefits of their work continue to accumulate and are shared by all partners. This is often the best way of moving into foreign markets, where one company has expertise in making and delivering a product, and another has expertise in local conditions and markets. It also avoids problems with import quotas, tariffs, national political interests and different cultures. Of course, there can be difficulties with joint ventures, such as deciding the precise role of each partner, division of activities, effective control, cash flows, and use of profits.

IDEAS IN PRACTICE Feng Shang Industries

Feng Shang Industries is based in the industrial centre of Shanghai, and is increasingly involved in the international market for generic spare parts for cars. In 2005 it was considering a new range of products, primarily aimed at the Australian market. If they went ahead with this product, the next stages were two years of technical development that would cost around $6 million a year, followed by two years of market development that would cost around $4 million a year. At this stage they could assess likely sales as high, medium or low, and possibly move on to making the product. These decisions are summarized in Figure 9.5.

It was fairly easy for managers at Feng Shang to calculate the expected values and use these to help in their decisions. But they were troubled by some assumptions in this analysis. To start with, sales vary over time, so the estimates of $12 million,

$7million or zero were mean figures, about which there would be some random variation, and some underlying patterns, such as product life cycles dictated by the motor manufacturers, and economic cycles. Another problem came with discounting rates. Expenditure was concentrated over the next four years, with development costs in Yuan, and marketing costs in a mixture of Yuan and Australian dollars. Then income would be generated in later years, priced largely in Australian and US dollars. Managers had some difficulty agreeing reasonable discounting rates for these future amounts. And there were problems with the whole approach of expected values, which represent the expected return over the long term if a decision is repeated many times – but gives no idea of the return from a single decision that is never repeated.

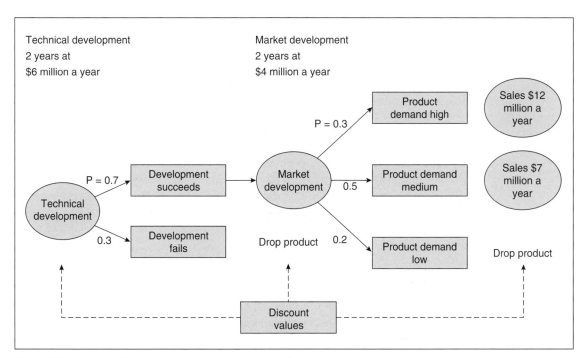

Figure 9.5 Product development for Feng Shang Industries

MARKET DEMANDS

Satisfying customers

As they move from product concepts to more detailed designs, managers have to describe the complete product package, including goods that customers buy, associated goods that support the main product, services that are part of the product specifications, associated services that support the product, surroundings in which customers receive the product, items changed by modifications, and so on. They also describe the broader issues of the process used to make the product, materials, design of the supply chain, customer service, and so on. The end of this development and design is a complete description of the product, how it is made, and how it reaches customers. As usual, the designs have to satisfy the two requirements of customers (and the broader environment) and operations (and broader internal concerns).

From a customer's point of view, the basic requirement is that a product should be functional – which means that it does the job it is designed for. This seems obvious, but you can see many products – ranging from investment services through to bottle openers – that simply do not work. Being functional is, of course, only the start and it often does little more than identify the intended market segment. The next step is to find exactly what type of product customers within this segment want. In Hill's terminology, a functional design gives the qualifying features, and the next stage is to identify the order winning features.

Not surprisingly, the most common way of finding what customers want is to do **market research** and ask them. This seems fairly straightforward, but the process often seems to be plagued by difficulties. There is a long history of managers apparently doing everything properly but ending up with products that nobody wants. Some products have been spectacular failures, with the Ford Edsell giving a classic example (Brough) – followed by 'New Coke' (Pendergast), Sinclair C5, IBM PC jr, Laker Airways, DeLorean Cars (Levin), and a virtually limitless list of others (Tibballs). The problem is that a mistake can occur anywhere in the chain of activities between an initial idea and delivering a final product to a customer – and a single mistake means that the operations do not supply products that customers actually want. Figure 9.6 shows where such gaps or misunderstandings can occur. At the start, there may be a gap between what customers actually want and what they say – and even believe – they want. This may seem strange, but customers often do not really understand what they want – in the same way that when you feel ill and go to a doctor, you do not really know what treatment you want, but you just want to feel better; and when a company goes to an advertising agency, it does not know what kind of campaign it wants, it just wants to sell more.

Market research can make mistakes in identifying the apparent demand, interpreting the results, and passing information to operations. Operations may misunderstand the results from market research, and make mistakes translating these into product features, designing products, and then making them. The overall result can be significant differences between real customer demand, and the product actually delivered (see also Zeithami *et al.*).

As well as straightforward market surveys, most organizations now use some kind of **customer relationship management** (CRM). Essentially, this collects information about customers, and analyzes it to see how the organization can develop the relationship, earn more from existing customers, and find profitable new customers. At the heart of CRM is a customer database that can be analyzed to highlight buying patterns, and identify new sales opportunities. At a simple level, a bookshop might know that a customer buys books by a particular author, so it telephones to say when the latest book is available. More sophisticated systems look for 'cross-selling,' which looks for relationships between previous purchases by customers and the likelihood that they will buy different types of products. Unfortunately, CRM does not recognize the features that customers would really like in products. They may have bought some products in the past, but there is no guarantee that they were happy with them – and it does not identify unmet demands, or potential purchases in the future. After all, customers might have bought a particular product because they had no choice, or they found it to be the best of a bad lot. A common example of this effect is the vacuum cleaner. Nobody seemed to realize that customers were not happy with the standard cleaners they had been buying for decades, until Dyson introduced a revolutionary, bagless machine that soon dominated the market. The traditional market leaders then had to redesign their products, after recognizing that their apparently loyal customers had really been waiting for something better to come along.

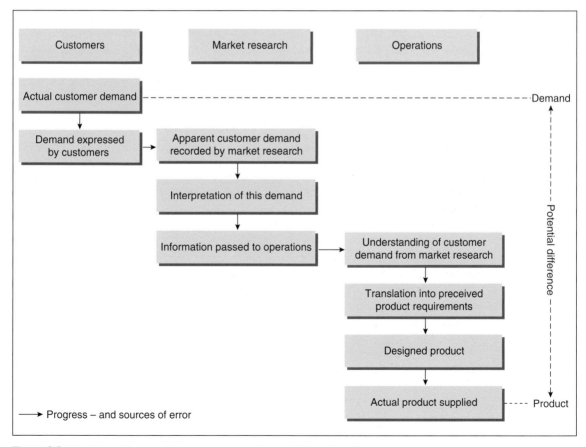

Figure 9.6 Problem of translating customer demand into products

The obvious conclusion is that operations must do careful market research to give an accurate picture of product features that customers want – and they must do the development and design to translate this demand into actual products. As a starting point, they might look at product features related to the five competitive features that we have already described – price, quality, speed, flexibility and a whole range of other factors – and then they can extend these broad categories to include taste, service, reliability, engineering design, performance, spare parts, availability, technological leadership, image, reputation, and so on.

Quality function deployment

Of course, identifying customer demand is only one step, and the remaining difficulties can be summarized as supplying a product to satisfy these demands. In other words, translating customers' requirements into actual product features. **Quality function deployment** (QFD) gives a useful approach to this problem, providing a mechanism for matching the features available in a product to the demands of customers. It can compare alternative designs and see which gives the best results, or as Cohen says,

		Product design features								
		Processor	RAM	Hard drive	Operating system	DVD/CD, etc.	Type of battery	Type of keyboard	Type of screen	Case material
Features customers demand	Small size	2		1		3	2	1	1	
	Lightweight						2	2	1	2
	Fast	3	1		1	1				
	Large memory		3	3		1				
	Durable							2	2	3
	Comfortable keyboard							3		
	Long lasting battery			1		1	3			
	Readable screen								3	
	Compatible with desktop	1			3	2				

Key
1 – some relationship
2 – medium relationship
3 – strong relationship

Figure 9.7 Quality function deployment for a portable computer

it allows operations to, 'specify clearly the customer's wants and needs, and then to evaluate each proposed product . . . in terms of its impact on meeting these needs'.

In its basic form, QFD uses a matrix with customer demands listed down one side, proposed design features listed across the top, and an indication of how these two are related in the body. Figure 9.7 shows a simple QFD matrix for a laptop computer. Here customer demand for a fast computer depends strongly on the processor used; the demand for small size depends to some extent on the type of battery, and so on. Managers can see how closely a particular design meets customer requirements – with a laptop design that includes a very fast processor that satisfies customer requirements for high speed. In particular, they can identify requirements that are not being met, and adjust the designs accordingly.

'Value analysis' gives another view of this matching design features to customer requirements, as it asks whether customers see a product as giving good value. Essentially, it compares the cost of production (and hence the price) with the perceived benefits to customers (and hence the amount they are willing to pay). Operations can compare these two views for different features, removing features where the production cost is greater than customers' perceived value, and focusing effort on the features where perceived value is much greater than production cost. Essentially, they are looking for lower production costs and better value for money.

There is also a more complex format for QFD, illustrated in the 'house' in Figure 9.8. This diagram has seven sections:

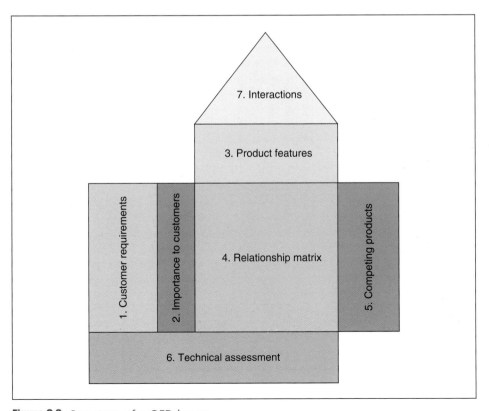

Figure 9.8 Structure of a QFD house

1 *customer requirements* – lists the features that customers want in the product, generally identified by market research
2 *importance to customers* – shows the weight or relative importance that customers put on each factor (typically given as a score out of ten)
3 *product features* – shows the features that designers have put into the product
4 *relationship matrix* – links customer requirements and product features, showing the strength of relationship, typically with a score out of ten
5 *competing products* – shows how customers perceive the proposed design compared with competitors, typically giving each a score out of ten
6 *technical assessment* – giving targets and technical details of the product features

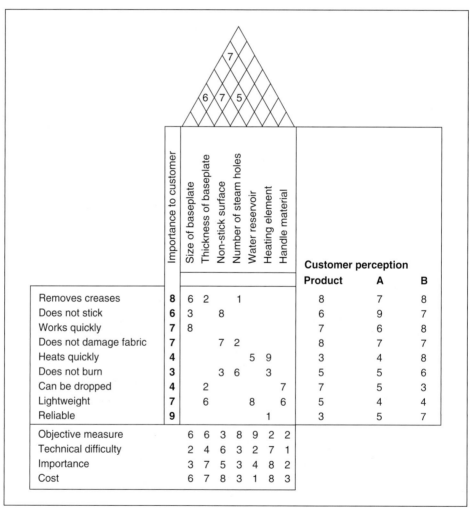

Figure 9.9 Example of QFD for a steam iron

7 *interactions* – shows relationships between product features, perhaps conflicting features that need trade-offs, or supporting features that reinforce each other.

Figure 9.9 shows the start of a QFD for a steam iron. This only lists a few features demanded by customers and design features, but you can see how it forces designers to think about the details needed and the consequences of their decisions. Then they can extend this approach to consider more details in overlaid matrices. The product features included in the first layer can become the requirements demanded in a second layer, perhaps specifying the features needed in components to satisfy the requirements of the final design. Then the component designer adds features to satisfy demand in this second layer. And these component features in the second layer can become the requirements in a third layer, perhaps specifying the features needed by the process to make the components. Then the process designer adds features to satisfy demands of the third layer.

IDEAS IN PRACTICE Polish vodka

After five years of making a loss, the Polish vodka industry returned to profits in 2004, largely because of growing demand in the international market. The growing popularity of vodka led to considerable interest in 2005 when the government offered a stake in the state owned Polmos Bialystok. Twenty companies expressed an interest in buying the vodka producer, including France's Pernod Ricard, America's Central European Distribution Corporation and Sweden's Vin and Spirit.

Poland is often considered the home of vodka, but its industry is fragmented with products of variable quality. The image of Polish vodka is of a rough drink, and its brands never had the same attention as Russian and Swedish counterparts. And there were certainly no premium brands of the type that developed with Scottish whisky and French cognac.

But this changed in 1996 when Millennium Import LLC introduced Belvedere rye vodka (made by Grupa Sobieski) to the US market, followed the next year by Chopin potato vodka (made by Polmos Siedlce). These sold at double the price of existing premium vodkas, and they established new and rapidly growing market segments. In particular, Belvedere appealed to younger trendier drinkers,

while Chopin became established as a connoisseur's drink. This position was enhanced in 2002 when Moët Hennessy purchased 40 percent of Millennium Import, putting the two vodkas in the same portfolio of luxury goods as Louis Vuitton, Christian Dior, Tag Heuer, Dom Perignon, Moët Chandon and Hennessy Cognac.

US sales of the two high premium brands rose from nothing to 1.5 million bottles in 1997, and then four million bottles by 2004, when they accounted for 70 percent of Polish vodka exports. Wyborowa joined the high premium market, with half of its production now exported to Europe and, increasingly, Asia. The Vodka Companion gives both Chopin and Wyborowa their highest four star rating; Wyborowa was named best vodka in the 2001 World's Spirits Competition; all three vodkas won gold medals in the International Review of Spirit Tasting; Forbes' includes the three in its list of the top ten vodkas; and the New York Times put both Wyborowa and Belvedere in its top three.

Sources: Pakulniewicz M., A taste of things to come, Warsaw Business Journal, vol 11(13), pp 6–7, 2005; Karwowski B., CEDC has its shots in a row, Warsaw Business Journal, vol 11(16/17), p 4, 2005

OPERATIONS' REQUIREMENTS

Product design

The operations' requirements of a product are rarely the same as customers' – but they can be just as difficult to identify and satisfy. Customers generally want things like low price, high quality, customization, attractive appearance, and so on – operations essentially want operations that are simple and standard. Simple designs are ones with a small number of parts, no unnecessary features, few variations, that are easy to make on an efficient process, without disruptions, and at low cost. For example, this could mean a limited menu in a hamburger restaurant, or replacing metal parts that need welding together by moulded plastic ones that snap together. Standard designs have routine operations making a range of similar products from common parts and materials. This gives easier planning, purchasing of materials, discounts for larger orders, smaller stocks of parts, and longer production runs for components. Although it may seem contradictory, standardization does not necessarily reduce the choice of products. The same materials can be used in a wide variety of ways – in the way that a pizzeria can use the same ingredients and methods to serve a standard pizza in hundreds of different disguises.

Conversely, operations managers do not like designs that have a lot of work, a long or complicated process, jobs that must be done manually, non-standard procedures, expensive materials, too high specifications, too many product variations, interference with the production of other items – or anything else that can give disruptions, problems and higher costs.

Many operations go beyond simplification and standardization, and positively focus on designs that are easy to make. This is the basis of 'design for operations' – which evolved from earlier versions of 'design for production' and 'design for manufacture' – and is most common with operations that focus on low costs. These designs look for a minimum number of parts, modular designs, common parts across the product range, off-the-shelf materials, easily assembled components, and any other features that can ease operations.

Sometimes the best way of designing a product is not clear. An option is to look at the details of designs from successful competitors. This is the basis of 'reverse engineering', which systematically takes a competitor's products apart to learn everything about them. This includes features of the product itself, how it works, materials used, components, and so on. More importantly, it also shows how the product is made. So managers get ideas for both the designs of products and how to make them.

Financial returns

The choices for operations managers really go beyond a list of features that they add to products, and they have to consider the broader implications of their products. For instance, a decision to make one product may inevitably mean that operations do not have enough resources to make another. We mentioned this effect with the opportunity cost of resources in chapter 5, and can describe it again, in terms of the opportunity cost of not making a particular product.

IDEAS IN PRACTICE Hewlett Packard

As well as being a leading supplier of computer hardware, Hewlett Packard (HP) is one of the most innovative information processing companies. It develops the idea of flexibility and being an 'adaptive enterprise' which it defines as 'business and IT synchronized to capitalize on change'. To become an adaptive enterprise, HP say that organizations have to take, 'a good hard look at your processes, applications and infrastructure to find new ways to simplify, standardize, modularize and integrate'.

- **Simplifying** means reducing the number of IT elements in networks, eliminating customization, automating change – and generally simplifying everything.

- **Standardizing** means using standard technologies and interfaces, creating reusable components, implementing consistent procedures that can interact with any system.

- **Modularizing** means building architectures modularly, breaking-down vertically stacked IT, 'virtualizing' systems, and being able to change one element without affecting the entire network.

- **Integrating** means building a dynamic link between business and IT, connecting both internal and external applications and processes, checking that everything works together.

Source: Website at www.hp.com

Suppose that operations have developed two new products, that we can call A and B. Product A has a net present value of €2 million, while product B has a net present value of €1 million. If operations only have enough resources to make one product, then the obvious choice is product A. However, by not making product B, they are giving up a net benefit of €1 million, so this is the **opportunity cost** they incur by deciding not to make it.

In purely economic terms, if it costs less than €1 million to get the extra resources needed to produce product B, then operations should go ahead and make it. The difference between the cost of acquiring the extra resources and the €1 million opportunity cost is additional profit, or incentive to produce. If it costs more than €1 million to acquire the resources, operations should not make the product, as the difference between the €1 million opportunity cost and the cost of acquiring resources is a loss, or disincentive to produce.

So the opportunity cost is the maximum reasonable price for operations to pay for resources – and a decision to make a product depends on the balance between opportunity cost and cost of resources. When an opportunity cost shows the revenue lost by not making a product this, in turn, depends on the price and sales volume. So operations managers have to take into account the supply and demand curves that we mentioned in chapter 2. These have the general form shown in Figure 9.10, following the principle that higher prices attract more competitors to supply a product, but fewer customers to buy it.

In theory, the equilibrium point identifies the expected price and sales of a product, and so the potential revenue and opportunity cost. But the supply and demand curves are rarely this simple, and an obvious point is that the curves are unlikely to be straight lines. A clearer picture comes from the **price elasticity of demand**, which measures the relationship between the demand for a product and its price, and is defined as the percentage decrease in demand that comes from each percentage increase in price.

$$\text{Price elasticity of demand} = \frac{\text{percentage decrease in demand}}{\text{percentage increase in price}}$$

- When the price elasticity of demand is greater than one the price is *elastic*, meaning that a change in price causes a bigger change in demand. When a 10 percent increase in price causes a 20 percent reduction in demand the price elasticity of demand is $20 / 10 = 2$. A perfectly elastic demand is one where any increase at all in price reduces the demand to zero.

- When the price elasticity of demand is less than one it is inelastic – a rise in price causes a smaller fall in demand. When a 10 percent increase in price reduces demand by 5 percent the price elasticity of demand is $5 / 10 = 0.5$. A perfectly inelastic demand curve has no change at all in demand with a change in price.

- When the price elasticity of demand is negative, it shows that a rise in price actually increases demand. When a 10 percent increase in price raises demand by 5 percent the price elasticity of demand is $-5 / 10 = -0.5$. This may seem strange, but there are many examples, particularly in luxury products, where a rise in price actually increases demand.

An important point about elasticity is that it shows not only the changes in demand, but also the changes in revenue. Consider the simplified linear change in demand with price shown in Figure 9.11. At a maximum price, P, there is no demand, and there is a maximum demand of Q even when the price is zero. The price elasticity

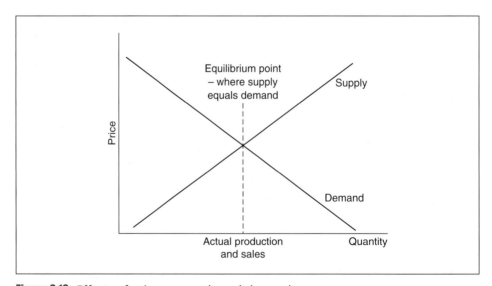

Figure 9.10 Effects of price on supply and demand

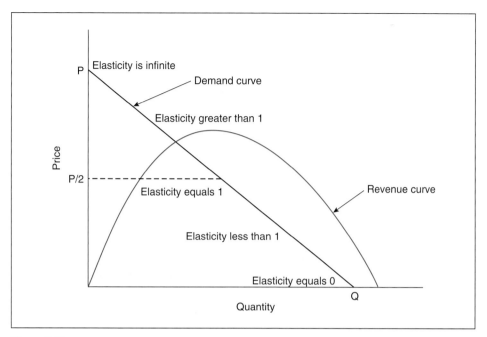

Figure 9.11 Price-demand and revenue curves

of demand changes along the line. At the top of the line any increase in demand from zero is, by definition, an infinite growth, so the elasticity is infinite; at the bottom of the line there is no further change in demand price, so the elasticity is zero. With prices ranging from P to P/2 the elasticity is greater than one, and an increase in price has more effect on demand; with prices in the range point P/2 to 0 the elasticity is less than one, so an increase in price has less effect on demand. When we translate these demands and prices into revenues, there is a distinct peak in revenue corresponding to an optimal price. With lower prices than this optimal, the low unit price reduces the revenue: with higher prices, the lower demand reduces revenue.

The main factor that affects price elasticity is the availability of substitute products. When more substitute products are available, customers can easily change to another and demand is elastic; with fewer alternatives the price becomes less elastic. Other important factors include the proportion of income spent on the product (a higher proportion gives more incentive to look for substitutes), the status of the product (luxuries tend to be less elastic than necessities), ease of finding substitutes (if they are easy to find elasticity is higher), and time taken to adjust prices (more time to find substitutes increases elasticity).

Marginal analysis

In practice, of course, the relationships between demand, price and revenue are rarely as simple as suggested in Figure 9.11. This problem becomes obvious when we look at the unit cost. A simple model separates costs into fixed costs, or overheads, and variable costs per unit produced. Then the average unit cost is:

Unit cost = fixed costs / number of units made + variable cost per unit made
$$UC = FC / N + VC$$

So the unit cost varies with demand, even when there are no changes to operations. Another interesting effect has the amount customers are willing to pay also varying with production. There are several reasons for these two effects.

1 *Fixed costs.* As we have just showed, increasing production spreads the fixed costs over more units and reduces the average unit cost.

2 *Economies of scale.* Larger scale operations can afford more efficient processes, make larger batches, use more automation, and gain experience – all of which tend to raise efficiency and lower unit costs. This is why supermarkets charge less than corner shops, and colour supplements to newspapers are cheaper than limited edition prints. Economies of scale suggest that it is always better to increase production as much as possible, but this argument only holds up to a certain point. Beyond this point, the difficulty of management, more complex communications, and a host of other problems combine to give diseconomies of scale. In other words, it is only possible to get economies of scale and reducing unit costs up to a certain point, and beyond this there are diseconomies of scale and rising unit costs.

3 *Diminishing returns.* Suppose that customers get some benefit or utility from buying a product. Their total utility is the total benefit from all their purchases of the product, while their marginal utility is the benefit from buying one more unit. The law of diminishing marginal utility says that the marginal utility declines as the amount bought increases. If you eat a meal it has some marginal utility; if you eat two meals, the second has a lower marginal utility; if you eat three meals the third has a still lower marginal utility. As customers' marginal utility declines, they are prepared to pay less for each unit of the product, and the profit margin of the producer also falls.

4 *Difficulty of selling more units.* An extension of the diminishing returns argument says that higher levels of production are more difficult and expensive to sell. In essence, the producer has to put more effort into marketing and logistics to reach the extra people.

5 *Different value of inputs.* As more resources are put into increasing production, the cost of resources used for each extra unit rises. Suppose you have operations that need some particular skills. You will probably start production planning by setting the most skilful people to do these operations; but as production rises you will have to use increasingly less skilful people, and unit costs will rise. This effect occurs with many types of resources, and it tends to increase unit cost with higher production levels.

Now we have a more complicated picture, where both costs and prices vary with production. If we look at the costs, we can define a marginal cost, MC, which is the cost of making one extra unit and an average cost, AC, which is the overall mean unit cost. Figure 9.12 shows how these are related. For low levels of production the economies of scale dominate, so increasing production reduces the marginal cost. And it is intuitively obvious that:

- When MC < AC making an extra unit will reduce the average cost.
- When MC = AC making an extra unit will have no effect and AC stays the same.
- When MC > AC making an extra unit will increase the average cost.

Beyond some production quantity, other effects dominate, and the marginal cost begins to rise. As long as it remains below the average cost, the average cost continues to fall. When the marginal cost rises above the average cost, at point X, the average cost also begins to rise. So the average cost reaches a minimum when it is equal to the marginal cost, and this identifies an optimal production quantity.

Now we can compare this cost with the revenue. The marginal revenue, MR, is the income generated by selling one more unit, and if this is higher than the marginal cost, an extra unit makes a net profit:

Increase in net profit = marginal revenue − marginal cost

Alternatively, if the marginal revenue is lower than the marginal cost, the extra unit makes a loss. The marginal utility – and hence marginal revenue – falls with increasing production, so a rule of thumb says that operations should keep increasing production until the marginal revenue falls to the level of the marginal cost. With any production less than this, operations are losing potential profit; at any point beyond, they are making a loss. So the optimal production level has:

Marginal cost = marginal revenue = average cost
MC = MR = AC

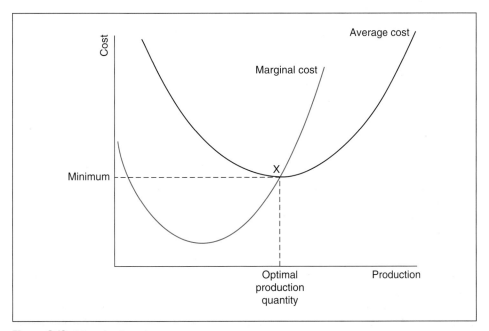

Figure 9.12 Marginal and average costs

As the marginal revenue is generally the market price, operations should increase production until their marginal cost equals the market price.

Production possibility curve

If resources are in short supply, their marginal cost increases and this limits production. But there is another way of looking at this, which puts less emphasis on cost and more on the amounts of resources available. Suppose that operations only have enough of some resource to make a certain number of products. Making more of one product inevitably means that they have to make less of another. Then managers have to arrange production not to get the maximum benefit from one product, but to find the mix of products that gives the greatest overall benefit. They can do this using a **production possibility curve**. It is easiest to see how this works with an example (below).

IDEAS IN PRACTICE Lethbridge Fashion Icons

Lethbridge Fashion Icons make a range of clothes that sell on the West Coast of America. They have limited production facilities, but are reluctant to expand or change their product image. The following table illustrates their problems, when two products compete for a limited resource.

Product A

Units of resource	Production
0	0
1	60
2	100
3	125
4	140
5	150

Product B

Units of resource	Production
0	0
1	80
2	140
3	190
4	210
5	230

If the company have, say, five units of the resource, they could make either 150 units of A, or 140 units of A and 80 units of B, or 125 units of A and 140 units of B, or some other combination. These options are shown in the production possibility curve in Figure 9.13(a) . Any point under the line gives an achievable production plan and forms a feasible region for solutions; any point above the line gives an unachievable plan and forms an unfeasible region. The graph itself shows extreme points, and the optimal solution is somewhere on this line, but its exact position depends on the profit from each product. With a profit of $200 for each unit of product A and $100 for each unit of B, you can see that the best solution comes with around 3 units of the resource allocated to product A (making 125 units) and 2 units to product B (making 140 units).

(continued)

IDEAS IN PRACTICE Lethbridge Fashion Icons (continued)

Lethbridge Fashion Icons

	Product A			Product B			
Solution	Resources	Production	Profit (at $200 a unit)	Resources	Production	Profit (at $100 a unit)	Total profit
0	0	0	$0	5	230	$23,000	$23,000
1	1	50	$10,000	4	210	$21,000	$31,000
2	2	90	$18,000	3	190	$19,000	$37,000
3	3	120	$24,000	2	140	$14,000	$38,000
4	4	140	$28,000	1	80	$8,000	$36,000
5	5	150	$30,000	0	0	$0	$30,000

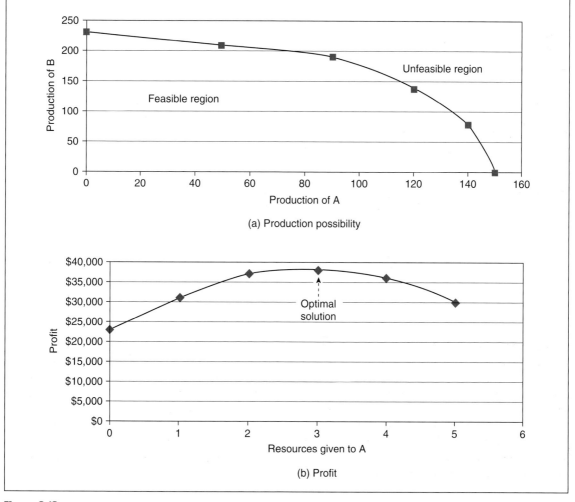

Figure 9.13 Production possibility curve for Lethbridge Fashion Icons

PRODUCT INNOVATION

Definition

People often say that organizations have to be innovative to survive (Brown *et al.*; Bessant *et al.*; Utterback; Tidd *et al.*). They argue that operations must continually introduce new products, and to do this successfully they must be innovative. **Innovation** is probably most obvious in product design, but it can appear in many different forms, such as the latest technology, novel use of supply chains, new markets for established products, improved processes, improved materials, more efficient use of resources, different organizational structure, new approach to marketing, and so on.

> ● The key feature of **innovation** is that it does something new and original, rather than continuing existing practices, or copying the activities of competitors.

In terms of products, the characteristic feature of innovators is that they invest in R&D, and update their products early, before they move into a decline. This maintains product leadership, and puts pressure on competitors. Innovators typically look for some unique selling point – such as new technology or designs – and aim for the premium prices from dramatically new products, while protecting their advantage with patents. An obvious problem is that the most innovative operations are often in small organizations, and they do not have the resources to move a new product to maturity. To get around this, they tend to license the production, leaving themselves free to concentrate on their distinctive capabilities in innovation.

Operations that are not innovative follow the alternative path of being imitators. They wait until they can see that a product is successful, and then adopt and adapt it to their own requirements. Some of the most successful versions of this have supermarkets producing their 'own brands' of breakfast cereals, shampoo and clothing. Similarly, when innovators want to move on, they may license or sell the designs for older products that they no longer want to make. For example, when car companies introduce new models, they can sell the designs for earlier models – as well as the equipment for making them.

Most organizations like to think of themselves as innovative, but the reality is somewhat different. Operations inevitably develop a certain momentum and it is much easier to continue on a present course than change to a new one. This is particularly true of large and successful organizations – which have a combination of less incentive to change and more difficulty in making changes. This is why hugely successful organizations like IBM, General Motors, ICI, RCA and Kodak, seem to continue for too long with existing operations and get left behind by more innovative competitors. We mentioned this effect in chapter 5, with Leonard-Barton describing how core capabilities eventually become 'core rigidities', inhibiting new ideas and stifling innovation.

Rate of innovation

You might imagine innovative products as being completely new ideas or giving dramatically better performance. There are certainly products of this type, such as the CD, Dyson vacuum cleaner, jet engine, mobile phone, Apple iPod, and credit card. But these are rare extremes, and most organizations – even the most innovative – really move forward with a continuing series of relatively small changes. The development of laser printers for PCs in the 1980s was very innovative, but since then their development has been fairly modest. This is the common pattern, with a huge leap forward, followed by continuing smaller improvements over the years. Innovation means that these small improvements keep coming in a continuing stream.

Small incremental changes have a lot of advantages over radical ones. They are less risky, can be reversed if things go wrong, build a culture of continuous improvement that gains its own momentum, can be absorbed by operations without major disruption, and over time they build significant improvements. On the other hand, we can criticize this approach as it appears to tinker with current products, suggests lack

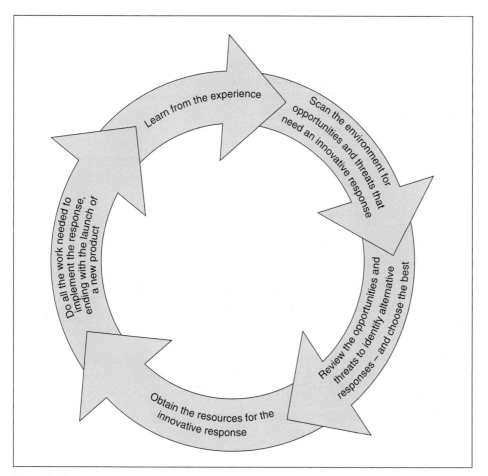

Figure 9.14 Stages in the innovation cycle

IDEAS IN PRACTICE Southwest Airlines

In 1972 Rollin King and Herb Kelleher decided to start a new kind of airline. They began with the idea that passengers want to fly to their destinations, at convenient times, arriving punctually, at the lowest possible cost – and they want to have fun while travelling. With this simple idea they created the original 'budget airline' that started the move away from 'full service' airlines, and is largely responsible for the consequent mushrooming in demand for air travel.

Southwest Airlines adopted an innovative, low cost approach that was not a few dollars less than existing flights, but was a fraction of the price. They achieved this by a mixture of efficient operations, and redesigning their basic product to remove the traditional 'luxuries' of meals, entertainment, boarding cards and printed tickets. They also used smaller, low cost airfields. Explaining their move away from Houston International to Houston's Hobby Airport Herb Kelleher asked, 'why should our customers have to drive 45 minutes to take a 40-minute flight?'

In 1974, Southwest carried its one millionth passenger and remodelled their terminal at Houston's Hobby Airport. By 2004 it had grown to become one of the largest airlines in America, flying more than 65 million passengers a year to 59 cities on 2,800 flights a day – and 31 consecutive years of profits.

According to the US Department of Transportation, Southwest has the airline industry's best consumer satisfaction record, which is in keeping with its mission of, 'dedication to the highest quality of customer service delivered with a sense of warmth, friendliness, individual pride, and company spirit'. This 'highlights our desire to serve our Customers and gives us direction when we have to make service-related decisions. It is another way of saying, "we always try to do the right thing!"' They summarize their customer focus by saying that, 'we are in the Customer Service business – we just happen to provide airline transportation'.

Source: Website at www.southwest.com

of long-term direction and leadership, is too conservative, is satisfied with current performance, and does not get to the root of any problems.

We have suggested that long-term survival is the real incentive for innovation, but there are more immediate pressures from two sources:

- internal research and development creating opportunities – and these are more likely to be completely new ideas, and
- external demands from customers, new regulations, acts of competitors, etc. – which tend to be adjustments to existing products.

These two forces encourage innovation, but there are many views on how to accomplish it (for example, Cooper; Cowell; Scheuing and Johnson). A simple suggestion, illustrated in Figure 9.14, has five steps that form a continuing cycle (Tidd *et al.*) to:

1 Scan the operations environment for opportunities and threats that suggest an innovative change.

2 Consider these opportunities and threats from a strategic viewpoint, see what can be done to respond, consider alternative responses and choose the best.

3 Acquire the resources needed to make the response, as innovation often needs skills, expertise, technology and other resources that must be transferred or brought into the organization.

4 Implement the response, doing the necessary R&D and all other work to develop new types of product and launch them.

5 Learn from the experience and work on continuous improvement.

Chapter review

- Operations make the products that organizations supply to their customers. These products have two purposes – to satisfy customers and to achieve the internal aims of operations.

- Both internal and external requirements are continually changing, and managers have to respond by adjusting the products that they supply.

- Product planning makes sure that operations continue to make a range of suitable products. It is responsible for all decisions about introducing new products, changing existing ones, and withdrawing older ones.

- Demand for a product generally follows a standard life cycle. The requirements change throughout this life cycle, so operations adopt appropriate entry and exit strategies.

- New product development takes initial ideas and moves them through to market launch. This procedure typically has six steps that refine ideas, removing almost all of them before arriving at a feasible product. Managers have to consider the timing and organization of these steps.

- As usual, products have to satisfy two requirements – those of customers (and the larger environment) and those of operations (and the broader organization). It is difficult to identify – let alone satisfy – customer requirements, and mistakes are common. Quality function deployment gives a useful tool for matching product design to customer requirements.

- Operations generally want designs that are easy to make. They want simple, standard designs that give low costs and no problems in production. They also have to consider broader issues, such as the competing demands of different products.

- Financial analyses – such as demand elasticity, marginal costs, and product possibility curves – give useful insights into the best production quantities and allocation of resources.

- Innovative organizations design new practices, rather than continue existing operations or adopt ideas from competitors. Product innovation is particularly useful in maintaining a competitive advantage.

CASE STUDY Smart Car

The market for cars is dominated by mass-produced, conventional, four-seat saloons that are often difficult to tell apart. Most brands are owned by a handful of major manufacturers around the world, and production economics mean that there are considerable advantages in making large numbers of identical cars. Design and manufacture of components is routinely outsourced to third parties, so many models share common parts. Against this rather bland background, the Smart Car was seen as an innovative new approach to car design.

In the 1980s Nicolas Hayek, who had founded the Swatch company, had an idea of producing a small (two seat), cheap, simple, environmentally friendly car. His car was to be powered by a new petrol-electric hybrid engine, or even a pure electric one. This would appeal to cost-conscious young people who were concerned about the environment, and they could afford to buy the car as an alternative to using public transport.

Hayek needed a partner in this enterprise, and after a few false starts joined Daimler Benz-AG to form the Micro Compact Car company. Development was well underway by 1993, but progress was never smooth. By 1998 (and after some name changes) Micro Compact Car Smart GmbH was taken over by Daimler-Benz and started making Smart (Swatch Mercedes ART) Cars. Hayek pulled out of the project after his initial ideas were progressively diluted. In particular, the final car had a petrol engine (turbocharged, 3 cylinder, 600 cc), its price was (at best) comparable with other small cars, its fuel consumption not so good (automatic transmission generally giving around 50 mpg), and there was virtually no space inside. Despite this the general view was that the 'Smart is an adorable little car'. So the original market of cost conscious young people moved to image conscious affluent ones. Often they would buy a Smart Car as an additional vehicle specifically for city driving.

Still initial sales were poor and Mercedes started to consider the closure of the French plant at Hambach. But the car's design slowly caught on and 1999 saw the 100,000th car, with 430,000 made by 2002. In 2003 sales were 120,000, rising to 150,000 in 2005. People in major cities found the cars easy to drive, cheap to run – and fun. By 2005 they were selling in 36 countries, were considering entering the huge US market, and the original car – now called the ForTwo – was joined by a roadster and a four seat, four-door ForFour.

Questions

- Are designs in the car industry really so conventional, or are there a lot of innovative companies around?

- There have been many attempts at small, cheap cars in the past, including the Bubble car, Messerschmitt, Fiat 500, and the Mini. Is the Smart Car really a new idea or a new brand in a developed market?

- Why was the original idea behind the Smart Car changed so much before it was eventually marketed?

Sources: Green G., Small wonder, Business Life, April, pp 55–56, 2005; Websites at www.smart.com; www.smartcarofamerica.com; www.wintonsworld.com

Discussion questions

1 Why is product planning important for an organization? Does it really have a strategic impact or is it limited to tactical and operational issues?

2 Is it true that every product moves through a standard life cycle? Surely the demand for some products – like bread, banking, dentistry and dog grooming – remains fixed?

3 Product development depends on getting an innovative new idea. If this is true, where can operations get such ideas?

4 Suppose that operations develop ten apparently useful products that it can start making. How can it decide which of these actually to produce and market?

5 To what extent do operations managers and their customers want different features in their products? How can these differences be reconciled?

6 'If you ask customers what they want, they will tell you exactly what they think you want to hear.' So how can operations find out what customers really want, and then turn these demands into products?

7 The best production level occurs at the point where marginal revenue, marginal cost and average revenue are all equal. What does this mean and why is it an important result?

8 Innovative organizations look for dramatic improvement to products and processes. If this is true, how can an organization develop a culture that provides these?

Useful websites

www.blackberry.com
www.hp.com
www.mcdonalds.co.uk
www.mcdonalds.com
www.rim.com
www.smart.com
www.smartcarofamerica.com
www.southwest.com
www.wintonsworld.com

References

Ansoff H.I., Corporate strategy, McGraw-Hill, New York, 1965.

Bessant J., Caffyn S. and Gilbert J., Learning to manage innovation, Technology Analysis and Strategic Management, vol 8(1), 1996.

Brough J., The Ford Dynasty, Octopus, London, 1982.

Brown S., Lamming R., Bessant J. and Jones P., Strategic operations management (2nd edition), Butterworth Heinemann, Oxford, 2004.

Bruce M. and Biemans W.G., Product development, John Wiley, Chichester, 1995.

Christensen C.M., The innovator's dilemma, Harvard Business School Press, Boston, MA, 1997.

Cohen L., Quality function deployment, Addison-Wesley, Reading, MA, 1995.

Cooper R., The new product process, Journal of Marketing Management, vol 3(3), pp 238–255, 1988.

Cowell D., New service development, Journal of Marketing Management, vol 3(3), pp 296–312, 1988.

Gersick C.J.G., Revolutionary change theories, Academy of Science Review, vol 16, pp 10–36, 1991.

Hill T., Manufacturing strategy (4th edition), Palgrave Macmillan, Basingstoke, Hants, 2000.

Leonard-Barton D., Core capabilities and core rigidities, Strategic Management Journal, vol 13, pp 111–125, 1992.

Leonard-Barton D., Wellsprings of knowledge, Harvard Business School Press, Boston, MA, 1995.

Levin H., John de Lorean, Orbis, New York, 1983.

Pendergast M., For God, country and Coca-Cola, Weidenfeld & Nicolson, London, 1993.

Pisano G.P., The development factory, Harvard Business School Press, Boston, MA, 1997.

Scheuing E.E. and Johnson E.M., A proposed model for new service development, The Journal of Services Marketing, vol 3(2), pp 25–34, 1989.

Slack N. and Twigg D., The organisation of external resources through guest engineering, International Journal of Innovation Management, vol 3(1), 2000.

Smith P.G. and Reinertsen D.G., Developing products in half the time, Van Nostrand Reinhold, New York, 1991.

Stalk G., Time – the next source of competitive advantage, Harvard Business Review, July–August, pp 31–41, 1988.

Stalk G. and Hout T., Competing against time, The Free Press, New York, 1990.

Thomke S. and Reinertsen D., Agile product development, California Management Review, vol 41(1), 1998.

Tibballs G., Business blunders, Robinson, London, 1999.

Tidd J., Pavitt K. and Bessant J., Managing innovation, John Wiley, Chichester, 1997.

Trott P., Innovation management and new product development, Financial Times Prentice Hall, Harlow, 1998.

Utterback J., Mastering the dynamics of innovation, Harvard Business School Press, Boston, MA, 1994.

Waters D., Operations management (2nd edition), Financial Times Prentice Hall, Harlow, 2002.

Wheelwright S.C. and Clark K.B., Leading product development, The Free Press, New York, 1995.

Zeithaml V.A., Berry L.L. and Parasuraman A., Communication and control processes in the delivery of service quality, Journal of Marketing, vol 52, pp 36–46, 1988.

This chapter discusses the strategic role of quality. It discusses different views of quality, and shows how these come together under the general umbrella of quality management. Total Quality Management has the whole organization working to produce the perfect quality that benefits both operations and customers. This approach has developed from its concern for product quality into a broad management philosophy.

After reading this chapter you should be able to:

- Define quality and appreciate its importance
- Discuss different views of product quality
- Define 'quality management'
- Examine the costs of quality management
- Describe Total Quality Management and its effects on an organization
- Discuss the implementation of TQM and the role of standards
- Understand the role of quality control

The key concepts discussed in this chapter are:

- **Quality**, which is the ability of a product to satisfy customers and other stakeholders
- **Quality management**, which is responsible for all aspects of quality
- **Total Quality Management**, which has the whole organization working to achieve perfect quality

STRATEGIC IMPORTANCE OF QUALITY

Meaning of quality

In the last chapter we looked at product planning and design, which enable operations to make products that continue to satisfy their requirements. They have to satisfy the requirements of customers (and the broader environment) and operations (and the broader organization). In principle, this seems quite straightforward – operations managers identify the requirements of customers, they identify their own require-ments, they design products to satisfy both of these, and then they make the products. Unfortunately, this simplistic view hides a lot of complexities. We have already men-tioned the difficulty of identifying real customer demand, and Figure 9.6 showed the sources of gaps or misunderstandings between real customer demand and products made to satisfy it. There are equivalent problems in assessing internal requirements, again with ample opportunities for misunderstanding. So the reality is that managers cannot really say in advance which designs, or specific features, actually come closest to satisfying their requirements.

There are more opportunities for errors when planners and designers develop products to satisfy their perceptions of requirements. And the problems continue again, when operations interpret the designs and make the products they think have been designed. Figure 10.1 illustrates some of these gaps (see also Zeithaml *et al.*).

If anything goes wrong in this chain of activities, the final product is unlikely to meet all expectations. And when a product does not meet expectations, we are talk-ing about its quality.

Definitions of quality

It is difficult to give a general definition of **quality** – as Garvin (1992) says, 'quality is an unusually slippery concept'. Many people have trouble giving a formal definition, but 'recognize quality when we see it' – agreeing with Pirsig that , '. . . even though qual-ity cannot be defined, you know what it is'.

Despite the difficulty of giving a convincing definition, you probably think of high quality in terms of goods without defects and services that make no mistakes. This is certainly a good starting point, and we can generalize the view to say that a product has high quality when it satisfies both customers and operations. So there is no absolute measure of quality, it means different things to every organi-zation, and the key determinant of high quality is that a product meets stakeholder requirements.

- In its broadest sense, **quality** is the ability of a product to meet stakeholder requirements.
- It should meet – and preferably exceed – customer expectations.
- It should meet – and preferably exceed – the needs of operations.

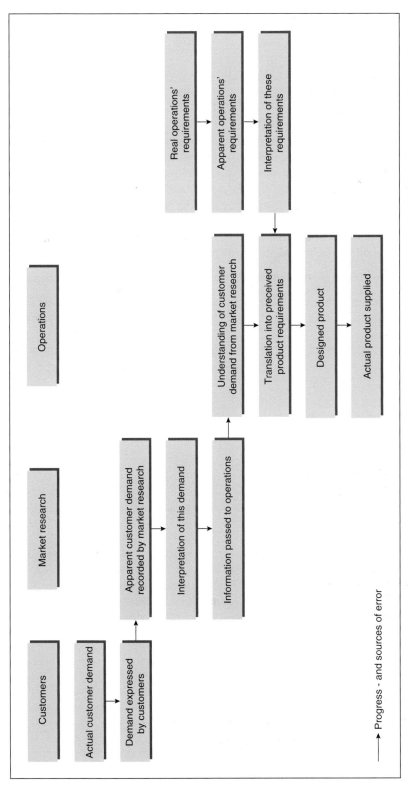

Figure 10.1 Problem of translating requirements into products

There are essentially two views of quality:

- An **external view** of customers – which focuses on how well a product meets their expectations and does the job they bought it for. Customers consider a bar of chocolate as high quality if it tastes good, looks good, satisfies hunger, and so on. This emphasizes the design of the product, and when there is a failing here, it suggests a mistake in product design – with customers who simply do not like the product.

- An **internal view** of the producer – which is more likely to focus on how well the product is made, and how closely it matches designed specifications. Then a bar of chocolate is high quality if it is close to the specified weight, contains the right amount of cocoa, has the right number of calories, is the right colour, and so on. This emphasizes the way that the product is made, and when there is a failing here it suggests a mistake in production. The design of the product may be good, but the product actually made does not match specifications, giving a difference between design and actual results.

As you can see, we are developing three aspects of quality (illustrated in Figure 10.2):

- **Designed quality** – is the quality that a product is designed to have, and comes from the specifications and features that are designed to satisfy customers and

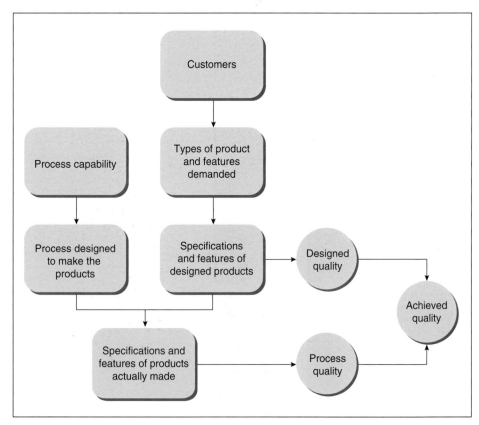

Figure 10.2 Designed, process and achieved quality

operations. Designed quality is good when the product, when made properly, satisfies customers and operations.

- **Process quality** – shows how good the process is at making products, how much variability it introduces – and generally how closely the products match their designed specifications. Process quality is high when the completed product matches its designed specifications.

- **Achieved quality** – shows how good the overall quality is, with its combination of design and process. Achieved quality is high when a product's design meets customer expectations, and it is made according to specifications.

Operations can only get good results (i.e. good achieved quality) when they both design products that satisfy customers (good designed quality), and make the products according to specifications (good process quality). Mistakes in either of these – or both of them – give poor achieved quality (illustrated in Figure 10.3). An airline that aims for 97 percent of flights arriving on time has a high designed quality; if only 20 percent of flights are actually on time it does not meet these specifications and its process quality and achieved quality are low. A water company that aims at exceeding all regulations for drinking water has a high designed quality; if they are prosecuted several times a year for polluting water, their process quality and achieved quality are low. A music CD might be made exactly according to specifications, giving good process quality, but nobody likes the music and it does not sell because of poor designed quality.

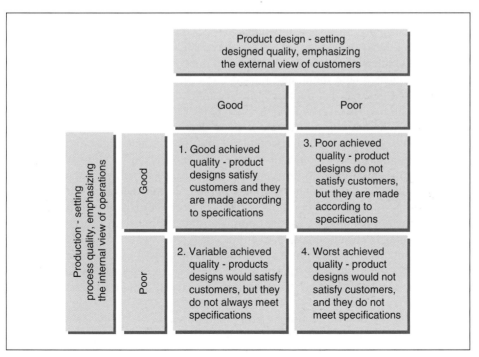

Figure 10.3 The need for both good design and process quality

IDEAS IN PRACTICE Constar pork plant

Smithfield Foods Inc is the world's largest pork producer, based in Virginia, USA. Since 1999 their strategy has included expansion into the major pork markets of central and Eastern Europe. As part of their strategy, Smithfield bought local companies, including Animex in 1999 and Morliny in 2004. This gave them the two most-recognized meat brands in Poland, along with subsidiaries in Romania.

This was a risky move, as Poland was still moving away from its communist past, and going through a period of great social change. The two companies recorded good sales, but there have been some problems with combining different practices and evolving ideas. These came to a head when it was reported that employees at Animex's plant at Constar were 'refreshing' old meat by scraping mould off sausages and sending them back to retailers.

Needless to say, consumers were horrified – as were managers at Smithfield. Constar's director was suspended, all production at the plant was stopped, the parent company sent in a team from America to take control, Polish government food inspectors are investigating, the European Union is considering action. Officials from Animex said that the company is in a 'crisis situation' and directors from Smithfield are taking the situation 'very, very seriously'.

Source: Kureth A., Damage control, Warsaw Business Journal, vol 11(16/17), p 3, 2005.

Balancing external and internal views

Designed quality tends to focus on the external view, putting more emphasis on customer requirements; process quality tends to focus on the internal view, showing that specifications have been reached. In the past, organizations tended to put more weight on the internal view. After all, they had done their market research, designed suitable products, made them, and passed them on to customers – who should be pleased to accept them. They ignored the possibility of misunderstandings within this procedure, and were surprised when customers were not happy with the results. People who felt that a product was of poor quality might complain and get the answer, 'We have considered your complaint, but the product reached our demanding quality standards, so we can find no basis for your grievance.' Unfortunately, you can still find many organizations that have little regard for their customers' views. Local governments, bus companies, water companies, train operators, and many others seem to pay little attention to the opinions of people they notionally serve.

In general though, things are more optimistic, and competition ensures that organizations ranging from supermarkets to airlines take much more notice of the external view of quality. But this returns to the problems of finding exactly what customers want – and what they mean by high quality. You can see the difficulty when you try to describe the features of a film you have seen, and try to explain why its quality was good.

Essentially, we describe a film as being high quality if we enjoy the whole experience of watching it; an airline gives a high quality service if we get to our destination on time and without too much hassle; an electricity supplier gives high quality if we never have to worry about supplies or costs. But this approach is still very vague, and it relies on 'customer satisfaction' which is notoriously difficult to measure. And there is the obvious problem that different customers have different expectations, so one might describe a product as very high quality, while another views it as very low quality.

The problem is that we do not judge quality by a single factor, but by a whole range of different ones. Garvin (1988) lists 'eight dimensions of quality' as performance, features, reliability, conformance, durability, serviceability, aesthetics and perceived quality. We could broaden this view by adding innate excellence, fitness for intended use, safety, convenience, level of technology, availability, lead time, uniformity, with small variability, value, customer service before and during sales, on-time deliveries, after sales service, and a whole series of other factors. Then, when you look at the quality of a television set, you might consider its price, how attractive the cabinet is, how big it is, how easy it is to use, how clear the picture is, how accurate the colours are, how often it needs repairing, how long it will last, how many channels it can pick up, how good the sound is, what additional features it has, and so on. Any reasonable view of quality must take into account many such factors, and it is foolish to judge a product by some factors and ignore others. But, again, customers all choose different factors, put different weights on each, and have different expectations.

An important consequence of this broader view is that customers rarely demand products with the highest technical specifications, but they look for a balance of features that gives a reasonable overall result. Rolls Royce probably makes the best engineered cars in the world, but when we consider buying a car we look at other factors – including price – and almost invariably buy another make. To put it simply, organizations do not design products with the highest possible quality, but with the quality demanded by their customers. For example, manufacturers could make clothes that are so durable that they virtually last a life-time – but few people would buy them as (apart from the high cost) we do not necessarily change clothes because they are worn out, but because of fashions, seasons, tastes, changing body shape, mood, and so on.

When organizations try to match product features closely to customer requirements, they have a particular problem with factors that cannot be measured but rely on judgement – such as appearance, taste, style, comfort, feel, attractiveness, courtesy and helpfulness of staff, reputation, understanding of customer needs, security, comfort of surroundings, communication between participants, and so on (Parasuraman *et al.*). Then customers may put great store on clothes that 'look good', but have difficulty in explaining exactly what this means.

Fortunately, we can usually measure some factors – such as weight, size, number of breakdowns, repair costs, delivery time, length of queue, etc. Then it is easier to see what customers want, design specifications, make products and test them to make sure they actually achieve the specifications. But we have to be careful even with these quantifiable factors. For example, most people would consider large classes in schools to give lower quality education – but it is almost impossible to prove this and there are many debates about correlations between class size and educational quality. And a government that admires efficiency could describe large classes as high quality, as they give excellent value for money. You can see many examples of the 'quality' of a product reduced to a single number, such as the waiting time for appointments in a health service. Obviously, such measures give an easy measure of one factor rather than a meaningful measure of quality.

IDEAS IN PRACTICE Avis

In chapter 6 we saw the emphasis that Avis put on their customers, with a vision of, 'We will lead our industry by defining service excellence and building unmatched customer loyalty.' Their aim is clearly for a high quality service that gives customer satisfaction.

This is explicitly stated in their values, which include:

● placing the interests of customers first

● providing 'an individualized rental experience that assures customer satisfaction and earns the unwavering loyalty of our customers' and

● ensuring that 'the "We Try Harder" philosophy underlies everything we do and shines through in our service to customers'.

Source: Website at www.avis.com

QUALITY MANAGEMENT

Quality revolution

All decisions about quality form the broad area of **quality management**.

> ● **Quality management** is the management function responsible for all aspects of quality.

It seems obvious that when operations makes poor quality products, customers will simply move to a competitor who is better at meeting their expectations (assuming that there is some competition). So high quality products do not guarantee an organization's success, but low quality ones certainly guarantee its failure. Recognition of this basic principle has come surprisingly late. We can argue that this is a consequence of history, as the supply of products has almost universally lagged behind demand, and competition has often been muted.

In 1922 Radford suggested that organizations pay more attention to quality, and proposed the standard model of a separate quality control function to monitor operations. Shewhart added more rigorous statistical analyses in the 1930s, and for many years this remained the accepted approach to quality management. But in the 1950s some people began taking more notice of quality, such as Juran (1951) and Deming. These pioneers found a receptive audience in Japan, where industry had been disrupted by wars, plant and equipment were out of date, productivity was low, raw materials were scarce, and their markets had been destroyed. To rebuild its industry, Japan needed some kind of competitive advantage, and they developed this by simply making better products. Over the next few years, Japanese companies developed their operations to supply products with a quality and price that could not be matched anywhere else. Studies in the early 1980s found that air conditioners made in the United States had 70 times as many defects on the assembly line as those made in Japan, and had 17 times as many breakdowns in the first year of operation. A US manufacturer of television sets had 150 defects per 100 completed sets, and was trying to compete with Japanese companies that averaged 0.5 defects. US manufacturers of car components had warranty costs ten times higher than their Japanese counterparts. In 1977 Hertz reported that its fleet of Chevrolets needed 425 repairs per 100 vehicles in the first 12,000 miles of operation, while its Toyotas needed 55 repairs. Not surprisingly, Japanese companies came to dominate world markets in motor cycles, consumer electronics, cars, machine tools, steel, computer equipment, ship building, banking, and so on.

But by the 1980s organizations around the world began to learn their lessons, and realized the strategic importance of quality. By the 1990s quality management had broadened into a complete business philosophy – where high quality becomes a way of improving reliability, delivery time, flexibility, costs, productivity, profitability and just about every other measure of performance. These changes were so profound that people started to talk about a 'quality revolution'. Unfortunately, this now brings images of expensive consultants, buzz words, and management fads – but underlying all of this has been a significant change in the way that operations see their products (DTI). They no longer look at product quality as an expense to be minimized, but as a benefit that should be maximized. This change came about for three main reasons – improved processes can guarantee high quality, this gives a competitive advantage, and it reduces costs.

Improved processes can guarantee high quality The main problem with achieving high quality products has traditionally been the variability inherent in the process. Differences in materials, weather, tools, employees, moods, time, stress, and a whole range of other things combine to give apparently random variations. When a bottling plant wanted to fill bottles with a litre of liquid, it accepted that some variation was inevitable. Customers could not notice a tiny variation away from a litre, but they would not accept a bottle that was clearly underfilled. The traditional way of dealing with this was to specify tolerances that defined an acceptable range of performance – and provided a unit's performance was within these it was considered acceptable. Our litre bottle of liquid might actually contain between 999.8 cl and 1,000.2 cl and still be considered acceptable, but anything outside this range was rejected as faulty.

Taguchi pointed out the inherent weakness of this approach. Suppose a bank sets the acceptable time to arrange a loan as between 30 and 45 minutes. The traditional view says that any time between these two limits is equally acceptable – the process is achieving its target so there is no need for improvement. But customers would probably not agree that taking 45 minutes is as good as taking 30 minutes. And there might be little real difference between taking 45 minutes (which is acceptable) and 46 minutes (which is unacceptable). The answer, of course, is that there is not such a clear cut-off. If you are aiming for a target, then the further you are away from the target, the worse your performance is. This result is summarized in the Taguchi Loss Function shown in Figure 10.4.

The clear message is that operations should aim at getting actual performance as close to the target as possible, and this means reducing variability in the process. It is only fairly recently that operations have taken this advice to heart, and now improved technology, designs, methods and general performance give processes with very little variation. This does not mean that every unit is identical – as it is still impossible to eliminate all variability – but it does mean that the range is very narrow.

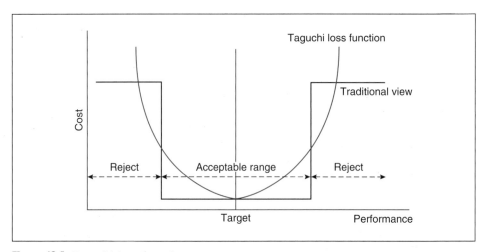

Figure 10.4 Taguchi loss function

High quality gives a competitive advantage We have talked about competitive features such as price, quality, speed, flexibility and a whole range of other factors, so we have acknowledged that organizations can use product quality to gain a competitive advantage. But the competitive advantage comes by supplying products that customers view as being better than competitors' – so this is largely a question of perceived relative quality. And as most suppliers have been conscientiously improving their quality, customers have got used to high quality products and will not now accept anything less. Quality has become a necessity rather than a desirable factor, and in Hill's terminology has moved from being an order winning factor to being a qualifying factor.

An organization can still get a competitive advantage by improving the quality of their products, adding features, improving specifications, giving associated services, etc. But if this move is successful, competitors will presumably react by improving their own products. So a sustainable competitive advantage does not come from a single change, but from a long-term drive to improve quality continuously. This idea of **continuous improvement** is at the heart of quality management.

High quality reduces costs The traditional view had high quality invariably associated with high costs. This is still largely true, which is why a Rolls Royce car is considerably more expensive than lower quality competitors. But the important difference here is between designed quality and process quality – most car manufacturers are good at reaching their specifications and have good process quality – Rolls Royce have a higher designed quality.

So designed quality might come at higher cost, but process quality can actually reduce costs. Imagine a company making washing machines. They might try to reduce production costs by rushing machines through the process, using unskilled people, eliminating quality checks, and so on. The resulting machine probably has lower costs – and lower process quality giving more variability. But this takes a limited view of both quality and costs. Suppose now that you buy the lower quality washing machine and find that it has a fault. You complain, and the manufacturer arranges for someone to repair the machine under its guarantee. This repair is expensive, and the company could have saved money by finding the fault before the machine left the factory. And it could save even more by making machines that do not have faults in the first place. To be specific, it could reduce the administrative costs of dealing with customer complaints, warranty costs, liability for defects, work done to repair defects, work done on units that are later scrapped, extra capacity needed to allow for faulty products, hassle and irritants for managers, and so on (Evans and Lindsay; Ho; Kehoe; Whitford and Bird). As well as lower costs, high quality has the benefit of improving reputation which can lead to higher sales and revenue. In other words, high quality can both reduce costs and increase sales, as suggested in Figure 10.5.

Of course, not all costs fall with increasing quality and common sense tells us that some must rise. We can identify these by separating the total cost of quality into four components.

- **Prevention costs** – are the costs of preventing defects occurring. They include some aspects of designed quality (such as the use of better materials, inclusion of features to ensure good quality, and extra time to make the product) together with costs of easing production and reducing the chance of making a defect (including employee training, pilot runs, testing prototypes, designing and maintaining control systems, improvement projects, etc.). All things being equal, prevention costs rise with product quality.

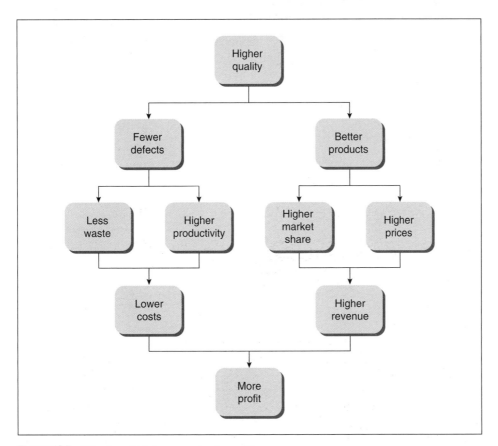

Figure 10.5 Effects of higher product quality

- **Appraisal costs** – are the costs of monitoring operations to make sure that the designed quality is actually achieved – in other words the cost of ensuring process quality. These include sampling, inspecting, testing and all the other elements of quality control. Higher process quality generally needs more effort put into quality control, and this comes at higher costs.

- **Internal failure costs** – are the costs of finding faulty products during the operations, and the associated scrap, repair, rework, test and everything else needed to deal with the defects. Some of these costs come directly from the loss of material, wasted labour, wasted machine time in making defective items, extra testing, duplicated effort, and so on. Others come from the indirect costs of higher stocks, longer lead times, extra capacity to allow for scrap, loss of confidence, etc. Internal failure costs generally fall with higher quality.

- **External failure costs** – are the costs of not detecting faulty units, and delivering them to customers who then find the fault. As well as warranty costs, repairs, etc., they can include liability, loss of reputation, and a range of other direct and indirect costs. These are usually the highest costs and are the ones that organizations should avoid. External failure costs generally decline with higher quality

We can find the total cost of quality by adding these four separate components. Figure 10.6 shows a typical pattern, dominated by high failure costs, and showing the lowest overall cost comes by making products without defects. In other words, operations should make products of perfect quality, where every unit is guaranteed to be fault free. This is the idea of **Total Quality Management (TQM)**.

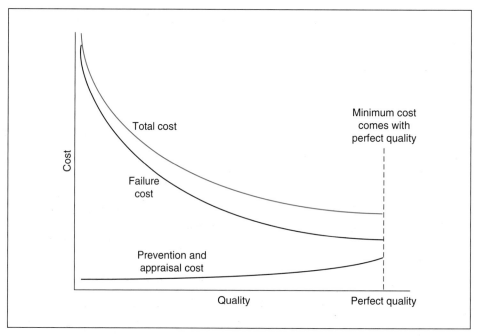

Figure 10.6 Perfect quality gives minimum cost

IDEAS IN PRACTICE B.P. Christofson and Partners

B.P. Christofson and Partners is an independent finance company operating in Scandinavia and the Baltic states. During 2004 Paco Fernandes analyzed the costs of quality in the company. He was particularly interested in monitoring the effects of a new quality management programme that was implemented in 2001. This programme was designed to reverse trends of increasing customer complaints and declining turnover.

Company accounts did not separate the costs of quality, so Paco had to do some special analyses of

transaction records and make a number of assumptions and estimates. Figure 10.7 gives a summary of some key figures. The quality management programme put more emphasis on prevention and appraisal, where costs rose. This improved product quality, giving savings in failure costs. Overall, costs fell significantly. Customers apparently noticed the improvement, as sales reversed their downward trend.

Source: Fernandes P., A case study in controlling quality costs, Finance and Operations, Copenhagen, 2005

Quality Management Programme							
Year	1998	1999	2000	2001	2002	2003	2004
Costs (% of sales)							
Prevention	1.63	1.71	1.56	2.44	3.23	2.91	2.88
Appraisal	3.24	2.71	2.78	4.22	4.65	4.27	4.01
Internal failure	6.93	6.61	7.31	4.35	2.11	1.86	1.72
External failure	5.02	6.13	5.33	3.10	1.37	0.91	0.52
Total (% of sales)	16.82	17.16	16.98	14.11	11.36	9.95	9.13

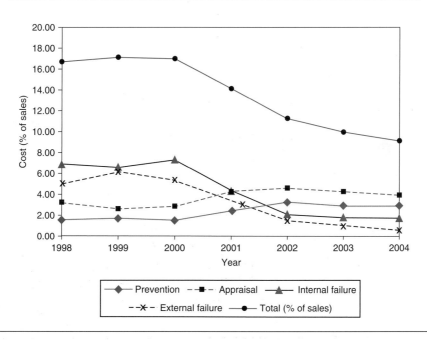

Figure 10.7 Changing costs with quality management programme

TOTAL QUALITY MANAGEMENT

Zero defects

The principle behind TQM is that operations should aim for perfect quality. This means that every unit of a product is guaranteed to be perfect – there are 'zero defects'. This brings obvious benefits to customers, but we have seen that it also brings benefits to operations:

- less waste by eliminating the need to scrap defects
- increased productivity by eliminating work wasted on units that are later found to be faulty
- elimination of procedures for repairing and correcting defects
- lower capacity as scrap, repairs and correction are eliminated
- elimination of the administration needed to deal with customer complaints
- reduction and elimination of warranty costs
- reduced liability and legal responsibility for defects
- lower overall unit costs and improved profitability
- competitive advantage from enhanced reputation
- larger market share with less effort in marketing
- enhanced motivation and morale of employees
- removal of hassle and irritants for managers.

Overriding all of these is the message that high quality is needed to ensure an organization's long-term survival. Deming summarized this in his 'chain reaction' which suggests a sequence of effects, with higher quality products giving lower costs, which give higher productivity, which gives more sales, which allows the organization to stay in business, which creates more and more jobs.

Of course, it is easy to say that operations should aim for perfect quality, but it may be more difficult to see ways of achieving this in practice. In the 1950s the obvious starting point was to get quality control departments to use more rigorous inspections to find the defects. But it soon became obvious that, 'you can't inspect quality into a product'. Operations that were defining new standards of quality would have to use significantly new methods. The strength of TQM is that it not only identified the need for perfect quality, but it also provided a mechanism for achieving it.

- The **mechanism of TQM** is based on the simple observation that the best way to improve quality is not to inspect production and discard defective units, but to make sure that no defects are made in the first place.

You probably think that this is obvious, but this statement laid the foundations for current thinking in quality management and the related philosophy. Its basic premise is that the people responsible for achieving high quality are not the inspectors in a distinct quality control department, but the people in operations who actually make the products. So TQM returns the responsibility for quality to operations.

Obviously, the next job is finding ways for operations to actually make products without defects – and again TQM comes up with a simple mechanism. Suppose you go to a clothes shop to buy a jacket. You will only be satisfied if the jacket is well designed, if it is well made, if there are no faults in the material used, if the price is reasonable, if the salesperson is helpful, if the shop is clean and pleasant, and so on. This means that everyone associated with the jacket – from the person who does the original designs to the person who sells it, and from the person who owns the organization to the person who keeps it clean – is directly involved in the quality of their product. So to get perfect quality, we have everybody in the organization recognizing the importance of quality and doing their own job properly, and cooperating so that their overall effort creates perfect quality.

- **Total Quality Management** has the whole organization working together to guarantee – and systematically improve – quality.
- The **aim of TQM** is perfect quality, making products with zero defects.

Many people had a role in developing this picture of TQM, with a group of leading authors known as the 'quality gurus'. Different people claim to be in this group, but the following six form the core members

- **Edwards Deming,** emphasized the role of management in determining quality and the importance of reducing variability in the process.
- **Armand Fiegenbaum** looked at failure costs, and developed the idea of 'total quality' involving everyone in the organization.
- **Joseph Juran** emphasized the role of senior management and the definition of good quality as satisfying customer demand.
- **Philip Crosby** analyzed the total costs of quality and described straightforward methods for implementing quality management.
- **Genichi Taguchi** showed the importance of product design in allowing high quality, with suitable control of the process.
- **Kaoru Ishikawa** emphasized the contribution of 'workers' to quality and introduced the idea of **quality circles**.

Changes with TQM

TQM has everyone within the organization involved in quality. Senior managers set the scene with strategic policies and goals. Middle managers translate the quality strategy into medium-term tactics and implement the policies. Junior managers make the short-term decisions to monitor and control quality. This gives a general structure for quality management shown in Figure 10.8.

IDEAS IN PRACTICE Patterson's Cake Company

Patterson's Cake Company supply cakes to supermarkets, restaurants, canteens and institutions in the South Eastern States of America. They make a range of products that is fairly standard, but people agree that they taste good for their low price. Over the past thirty years they have developed a solid reputation.

Then in 2002 the company narrowly avoided prosecution by a local Consumer Protection Department, when a customer reported a rusty nail in one of their cakes. The company was not prosecuted and escaped with a warning because of their good record and rigorous quality control procedures. These procedures are carried out by the Quality Control Department, which does a series of inspections and tests to make sure that cakes conform to both legal and company requirements. Ingredients are brought from national suppliers and cause almost no concern. Nonetheless, they are given a visual inspection before being mixed into batches. There are further tests on each batch

after mixing, before baking, after baking, after finishing, and after packing. Most of these tests concern taste and appearance, and make sure the products are consistent and meet design specifications.

Recently the company has been having more difficulties with quality. The number of customer complaints has risen by 18 percent over the past two years, and there are now around 78 complaints per million sales. Most of these complain about taste, but occasionally there are foreign bodies or other serious faults. The company responded by increasing the quality control budget by 25 percent, employing more inspectors and making the inspections more rigorous. Baking staff now joke that they always have an inspector looking over each shoulder.

As an experiment, managers deliberately introduced faults into 40 cakes as they passed through the process. Quality control inspectors only found 14 of these before they were due to leave the bakery.

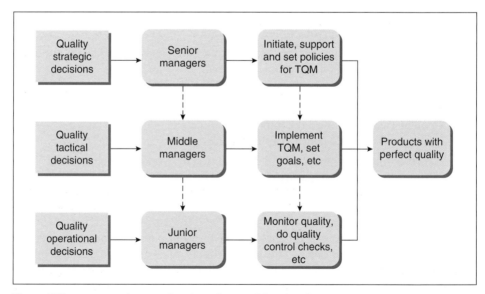

Figure 10.8 TQM needs contributions from all levels of managers

The key point is that quality management stops being a separate function and becomes an integral part of the operations, with everyone taking responsibility for their own quality. This transfer of responsibility to operations does not mean that different people simply do the same inspections, but it shows a fundamental change in attitude towards quality. Each person now becomes responsible for only making products with perfect quality. When they pass on work to following operations, they only pass on units with perfect quality. And if they find a fault they do not pass the work on – but TQM goes further, and says that a fault means something has gone wrong, so everyone has the authority to stop the process, investigate the problem, find the cause of the fault, and suggest ways of avoiding it in the future. This is described as **quality at source**, with job enlargement for each person who is now responsible for both their previous job and an inherent quality management function.

This TQM approach contrasts with traditional practices, where people were judged by their production – often with little regard for the quality – so when they found a fault there was an incentive to hide it and keep up production numbers. The process was only stopped as a last resort, and then the cause of faults goes unnoticed until problems become severe.

Despite the safeguards of quality at source, TQM still has an independent quality control function. But its purpose has changed from inspecting units to find the faults that are known to be there, to confirming that there really are no defects being made. And the focus of their work has moved from inspections of finished products, to earlier in the operations, and in the planning and design stages. Table 10.1 shows some of the changes in operations that come from TQM (Waters).

The effects of TQM can be very broad, expanding far beyond the core concern of quality. To start with, people working with TQM need a new way of thinking and a

Table 10.1 Different attitudes of TQM

Criteria	Traditional attitude	New attitude with TQM
Importance	quality is a technical issue	quality is a strategic issue
Responsibility	quality control department	everyone in the organization
Goal	make acceptably low number of defects	zero defects
Attitude	inspect quality in by finding defects	build quality in and prevent defects from occurring
Inspections	find defective units	check that there are no defects
Main inspection point	final products at the end of operations	during operations and earlier in planning
Cost	high quality costs more	high quality costs less
Problems	left until they become major	identified and solved as soon as possible
People rewarded for	producing more units	producing high quality units
Quality defined by	organization	customers

variety of skills. This needs training, and everyone must understand some statistics so that they can monitor the performance of each operation and see when something is going wrong – and then they must be able to identify, analyze and solve problems as quickly as possible. This can involve huge training programmes, and Ford of America's introduction of TQM started by training 6,000 of their own staff and 1,000 suppliers. The result is a movement of responsibility downwards to people working on the operations, leaving fewer layers of management and flatter organizations. These people are paid differently, with recognition of their increased responsibility, and rewards for high quality. People can also be rewarded for making suggestions for improvement, typically collected through suggestion boxes or informal progress meetings. Other suggestions can be collected in quality circles, which are informal groups of about 10 people who meet regularly to discuss ways of improving their process and raising product quality. These – and all similar initiatives – depend on people who are able and willing to exchange ideas, see themselves as working for the good of the organization, willing to exchange ideas – and who generally share a culture of delivering high quality products.

TQM also affects on deliveries of raw materials from suppliers. Traditionally operations would test all materials arriving before using them, in case there were faults. Then they would order more materials than they actually needed – called overage – to allow for these defects, and they would keep high stocks of raw materials in case there were problems. A house builder, for example, would occasionally reject a whole delivery of cement as faulty, but could continue working normally using their accumulated stocks. These tests, overage and stocks all added unnecessary costs. But when suppliers also adopted TQM, they only sent materials of perfect quality, so the operations no longer had to test them, buy too many, or keep excessive stocks. And the results are lower costs and more efficient material flows through the whole supply chain.

You can imagine another benefit of TQM in a company that makes customized systems from components that are made by different suppliers. Large computer systems were made in this way, and assemblers would collect all the components together, individually test them to find the faults, get replacements for the defects, assemble them, test the complete system – then dismantle it, deliver the parts to the customer, reassemble it, test it again, and hand over the working system. With TQM the assembler knows that all the components will be of perfect quality, so it gets them delivered directly to the customer, assembles the system and hands it over.

We could continue with such arguments, but the message is clear – making products of perfect quality can have a profound effect on an organization. It opens opportunities for new ways of working – such as 'stockless production' as there is no need for stocks to give cover for poor quality; just-in-time operations as operations do not have to be done in advance in case things go wrong (which we describe in chapter 14); lean operations that eliminate waste; fast movement of materials through supply chains; flexible operations that respond quickly to changes without delays caused by poor quality; marketing that does not have to explain why products do not match their specifications. To put it simply, TQM forms the foundations that allow an organization to take advantage of new opportunities, and to use new and better ways of working.

IDEAS IN PRACTICE Total Quality Management

There are many stories about the benefits gained by the first companies to introduce TQM. Most of these are anecdotal, as illustrated in the following examples.

- Xerox Business Products and Systems employ more than 50,000 people. They measure performance using around 250 key indicators of product, service and business quality. In 1989 they won the Malcolm Bradbridge National Quality Award, as in the previous five years their defect rate had fallen from 10,000 parts per million to 300, equipment reliability improved by 40 percent , service response time had improved by 27 percent, the cost of purchased parts fell by 45 percent and manufacturing costs fell by 20 percent (National Institute of Standards and Technology; Gitlow and Loredo).

- In 1984 Ford of America had been running its 'Quality is job one' programme for five years. During this period the number of warranty repairs dropped 45 percent, faults reported by new owners fell 50 percent, their share of the US market rose to 19.2 percent, sales rose by 12 percent in a year, pre-tax profits rose to $4.3 billion, annual operating costs fell by $4.5 billion.

- Japan Steel Work Hiroshima Plant began work on TQM in 1977. Between 1978 and 1981 production rose 50 percent, the number of employees fell from 2,400 to 1,900, the accident rate fell from 15.7 per million man-hours to 2.3, the cost of defects fell from 1.57 percent of sales to 0.4 percent and the number of suggestions per employee rose from 5.6 a year to 17.6.

- Within one year TQM at Hewlett-Packard's Computer Systems Division increased direct labour productivity by 40 percent, faults with integrated circuits fell from 1,950 parts per million to 210, faults with soldering fell from 5,200 parts per million to 100, and faults in the final assembly fell from 145 parts per million to 10.

- DuPont credited TQM for increasing its on-time delivery from 70 to 90 percent, decreasing cycle time from 15 days to 1.5, increasing yields from 72 percent to 92 percent and reducing the number of control tests by a third.

Sources: Websites at www.asq.org; www.qualitydigest.com; www.quality-foundation.co.uk ; www.iqa.org

IMPLEMENTING TOTAL QUALITY MANAGEMENT

Principles for implementation

The ideas behind TQM seem simple enough, but they have widespread effects throughout the whole organization. These include a reorganized quality function, strategic role for quality, involved workforce, quality at source, devolved decisions, quality circles – and a culture based on high quality products, aim of perfect quality, problem-solving, responsibility, improvement, and so on. Changing an organizational culture is notoriously difficult, and superimposing a whole raft of changes on to the organization, practices and performance is going to be very hard. So introducing TQM is not going to be a quick programme for change, but a movement that continues and grows over the long term.

IDEAS IN PRACTICE Deming's 14 principles of TQM

1 Create constancy of purpose towards product quality.

2 Refuse to accept customary levels of mistakes, delays, defects and errors.

3 Stop depending on mass inspection, but build quality into the product in the first place.

4 Stop awarding business on the basis of price only – reduce the number of suppliers and insist on meaningful measures of quality.

5 Develop programmes for continuous improvement of costs, quality, productivity and service.

6 Institute training for all employees.

7 Focus supervision on helping employees to do a better job.

8 Drive out fear by encouraging two-way communications.

9 Break down barriers between departments and encourage problem-solving through teamwork.

10 Eliminate numerical goals, posters and slogans that demand improvements without saying how these should be achieved.

11 Eliminate arbitrary quotas that interfere with quality.

12 Remove barriers that stop people having pride in their work.

13 Institute vigorous programmes of life-long education, training and self-improvement.

14 Put everyone to work on implementing these 14 points.

Deming W.E., Out of the crisis, MIT Press, Cambridge, MA, 1986

There is no shortage of advice about implementing TQM, but it is fair to say that most of this is based on the work of Edwards Deming, who spent 40 years developing his ideas of TQM and compiling a list of 14 'principles' for implementation as shown above.

Deming always emphasized that quality is an aspect of management – with managers in charge of operations and responsible for quality. In effect quality depends on two factors:

1 the *system* that managers design and control, and which contributes 85 percent of the variation in quality

2 *people working with the system*, who contribute 15 percent of the variation in quality.

Improvements in quality come from managers designing better systems rather than people improving their own performance. A person working conscientiously to get high quality in a poor system will get worse results than a careless person working in a better system. And when we have a long wait for a bus or get poor service in a restaurant, it is the manager who designed the system who has done a poor job and not necessarily the person who serves us. This extends to training, where high quality can only be achieved when everybody has been properly trained for their jobs. This seems obvious, but you can visit many shops and find cashiers who know nothing about the products, how to serve customers, or even how to use the till properly. This is not their fault, but a sign that managers have not invested enough in their training.

Steps in implementation

Deming's 14 principles gives general principles for implementing TQM, but managers still have to translate these into positive actions. Normally, there is some kind of 'trigger' that starts them thinking about TQM, and then the whole philosophy develops from this. Four common triggers are:

1 Increasing customer complaints and rejection of low quality products that is causing the organization to decline.

2 A 'quality champion', who is typically a senior manager with the ambition and enthusiasm to drive the organization towards TQM. Unfortunately, this drive can soon falter if the manager moves or hits internal problems.

3 A specific need to improve quality, such as pressure from customers to adopt ISO 9000 standards. This relies less on an individual champion and more on a planned approach to satisfy an identified need.

4 Skills, experience – and training – of people lower down the organization who improve their own work and consequently the product. These activities grow and eventually coalesce into TQM, which emerges as a strategy rather than being imposed by managers.

In practice, the trigger is likely to include some elements of each of these, but it only starts operations organization moving towards TQM. The next stage continues this movement, which can progress in two different ways. Firstly, managers can use shock tactics, exposing the whole organization to the new concepts and practices in virtually a single step. This approach can be very effective if it is well planned and executed, and moves an organization quickly to a new course. Sometimes, existing conditions are so bad that this is the only alternative. However, if there are any problems with the implementation, everyone gets confused, nobody knows what is happening, and quality might even deteriorate.

There are inevitable risks with shock tactics, and most organizations prefer a more measured evolution. A slower, planned approach moves progressively through a series of smaller changes, gradually introducing the whole picture. This allows ideas to evolve and develop naturally, with less risk, problems are overcome one at a time, and any mistakes are quickly rectified. There are many suggestions for organizing this iterative approach, but we can summarize the main stages in seven steps:

1 *Get senior management commitment*. TQM is a strategic issue that relies on direction from senior managers. They must recognize that it gives a way of thinking that affects broad operations and improves long-term competitiveness and performance.

2 *Identify the requirement of products*. Our definition of high quality is based on meeting, or exceeding, the demands of stakeholders, particularly customers and internal operations. But we can only achieve this if we know exactly what they want. With a dominant external view, this means identifying the exact nature of customer demand.

3 *Design products with quality in mind.* Products must have the features demanded by customers and internal operations – giving high design quality – but operations must go beyond this and consider broader quality issues. For instance, there is

always some variation between units, and the product designs must be robust enough to allow for these variations and still give acceptable products.

4 *Design the process with quality in mind.* The process must work efficiently, giving consistent products with minimal variation and guaranteed perfect quality – giving high process quality. (We discuss process design in the next chapter.)

5 *Build teams of empowered employees.* Quality depends on everyone in the organization, so they must all be properly trained, motivated, able and willing to do their job. Their job is essentially to help make high quality products that satisfy the aims of operations, and hence the broader aims of the organization as a whole.

6 *Monitor progress.* Circumstances are continually changing, so operations must monitor the external environment and internal operations, looking for adjustments and improvements.

7 *Extend these ideas to suppliers and distributors.* Organizations do not work in isolation, but are part of a supply chain (which we discuss in chapter 13). The quality of the final product depends on every link of this chain working properly – and there is no point in one company making perfect goods that are broken by the transport company that delivers them, or a transport company guaranteeing delivery within 24 hours when suppliers have a lead time of six weeks.

ISO 9000

It is an important observation that no organization can guarantee high quality by itself. A manufacturer can only make perfect quality goods if its suppliers send perfect quality components and materials; an airline can only give a perfect quality service if it is not let down by airport staff, baggage handlers, flight controllers, connecting transport links, and so on. So TQM can only be achieved when everyone in the supply chain works together. This is the reason why early developers of TQM, particularly companies like Toyota, gave a clear statement that they could only consider suppliers whose view of quality matched their own – and this meant that they also had to introduce TQM. Of course, the car manufacturers are very large companies and they can exert pressure on their suppliers – but it was more difficult for smaller organizations to check the quality credentials of their suppliers. There would certainly be no point in just asking how a supplier felt about quality, as they would all say that it was a prime concern.

The answer to this problem came with the International Standards Organisation's (ISO) 9000 family of standards for quality. ISO defined procedures needed to ensure high quality, and if an organization achieves certain quality standards, it can apply for ISO 9000 certification. Certification is administered by independent third-parties who check that operations:

- says exactly what they are going to do to ensure high quality, describing their procedures, operations and inspections;
- actually do the work in the ways described;
- prove that the work has been done properly by doing audits and keeping appropriate records (Thomas).

People often assume that the ISO standards guarantee high quality. Unfortunately, this is not true, as they only guarantee *consistent* quality. A manufacturer of plastic pipes, for example, might specify the acceptable limits on the diameter of a pipe.

ISO certification means that the pipe is more or less guaranteed to be within these limits, but it does not judge whether the limits are good enough for any particular use.

The ISO 9000 family of standards was launched in 1987, giving generic results that can be applied in almost any type of organization. The standards are reviewed every six years, with the current version having three main parts:

- **ISO 9000:2000, Fundamentals and vocabulary.** This introduces the ISO 9000 standards and lays the foundations for the main standards.
- **ISO 9001:2000, Quality management systems – requirements.** This is the core of the standards and it specifies the requirements of efficient, effective and flexible quality management.
- **ISO 9004:2000 – Guidelines for performance improvement.** This focuses on the systems and methods used to improve performance, emphasizing their relevance to quality management.

One of the useful points of the ISO standard is that it develops the following eight principles that reflect best practice in TQM.

1 *Customer focus.* This emphasizes the external view of quality, with customer requirements the main input to the process and customer satisfaction as the primary aim. Operations must understand the detail of current and future customer needs, convert these requirements into viable products, make these products using efficient processes, and generally strive to exceed customer expectations. Then operations should continually monitor customer satisfaction to see that their requirements are being met, and look for improvements to solve any problems.

2 *Leadership.* TQM needs commitment of top managers to give the strategic direction of quality – establishing the overall aims, commitment policies, structure, systems, culture and organizational structure.

3 *Involvement of people.* By definition, TQM relies on everyone within an organization being involved in the quest for perfect quality – so they should be aware of the importance of meeting customer requirements, and of their responsibilities for this. They should have the appropriate work environment, facilities and infrastructure for doing their jobs – and when there are gaps in their knowledge or skills, they should be given appropriate training.

4 *Process approach.* Recognizing that all the operations used to make a product form a single process, which should be managed as an integrated whole. This includes planning, product design, operations, process control, purchasing, material handling and all other activities that add value.

5 *Systems approach.* Each process in an organisation does not work in isolation, but is a part of the whole picture. Managers have to understand the interactions, moving the whole organization to work effectively and efficiently to meet its aims.

6 *Continuous improvement.* Operations always want to improve, but the emphasis here is on a positive drive forward rather than a vague hope. Everyone should be continuously searching for better ways of doing things, and be willing to adopt new methods.

7 *Factual approach to decision making.* Managers use a range of skills to make their decisions, and intuitive reasoning is certainly one of these. However,

effective decisions are based upon the logical analysis of information, and are based on facts rather than opinions and guesswork.

8 *Mutually beneficial supplier relationships.* We have already said that each organization is a single link in a long supply chain and cannot work in isolation from its suppliers. To get the maximum long-term benefit, there should be mutually beneficial relationships at each point in the supply chain.

This list gives a sound basis for the good practice of TQM, but some people suggest that some other principles should be added, including results orientation (balancing and satisfying the needs of relevant stakeholders), development of people (through education and shared cultural values), continuous learning (encouraging innovation and improvement), and corporate social responsibility.

The main benefits of ISO certification are that it demonstrates an organization's commitment to quality. Perhaps more importantly for the long term, a growing number of organizations will only deal with suppliers who have certification. It must inevitably become increasingly difficult for organizations without ISO certification to compete.

QUALITY CONTROL

We have seen that operations can get considerable benefits from TQM. Some of these are direct benefits, such as lower costs, higher productivity and improved customer satisfaction. Other benefits are less direct, such as the opportunities that come from changing attitudes within the organization. But few managers say that these benefits are easily earned and that TQM is easy to introduce. It needs a sustained effort over many years and – not surprisingly – many organizations fail somewhere on the road. There are many reasons for these failures. Perhaps suppliers cannot guarantee the quality of materials; or managers only give lip service to TQM without really becoming committed; or everyone assumes that someone else is dealing with quality; or administration and bureaucracy get out of hand; or the process cannot reduce the variability enough; or people resist the necessary changes; or they find that they get no personal benefits so the effort is not worthwhile.

Some managers question whether the benefits are worth the sustained effort, especially as the paper trails needed to monitor ISO 9000 certification are notoriously troublesome. Many managers argue that they can get high quality by traditional means, and without all the complex procedures and systems prescribed for TQM. Some go further and argue that TQM puts so much emphasis on the process of delivering high quality, that it actually diverts attention away from the quality of the product. Perhaps the most consistent criticism of TQM is that it raises unrealistic expectations; perfect quality is impossible to achieve in practice, so TQM sets targets that can never actually be reached.

It is worth mentioning again the important point that in a competitive environment, any advantage that operations win is likely to be temporary, and other organizations are always willing to adopt, adapt and improve winning ideas. TQM recognizes that other organizations are continually improving their own products, so any improvement in quality can only give a transient competitive advantage. So a key element of TQM is that it looks for a sustainable advantage by continuing to improve quality. This is the basis of continuous improvement, mentioned as the sixth principle of best practice above, and commonly known by its Japanese name of **'kaizen'**. We will mention continuous improvement is the next chapter, but it has everyone in the organization continuously looking for ways of improving both quality, and every other aspect of operations.

Kaizen raises the question of how managers know that things are improving – and the answer is that they must continually monitor them and measure performance. So TQM assumes that there is a monitoring function that records progress. This is the traditional function of **quality control**.

> ● **Quality control** is the function that uses a series of independent inspections and tests to monitor process quality and make sure that designed quality is actually being achieved.

Of course, with quality at source there should be no defective units made, so the purpose of quality control is not to find faults, but to give independent evidence that the process is working properly and that there really are no defects. And they monitor performance during changes to show that things are actually improving.

The statistical elements of quality control have been an area of continuous interest for almost a century, and most problems here are well understood. Many tools have been developed to help, usually involving some kind of sampling and subsequent statistical analyses. Perhaps the most helpful are process control charts that monitor some aspect of performance over time and quickly highlight any emerging problems. If things are going normally, there should be some minimal variation of performance about a mean value, as illustrated in Figure 10.9. But if performance

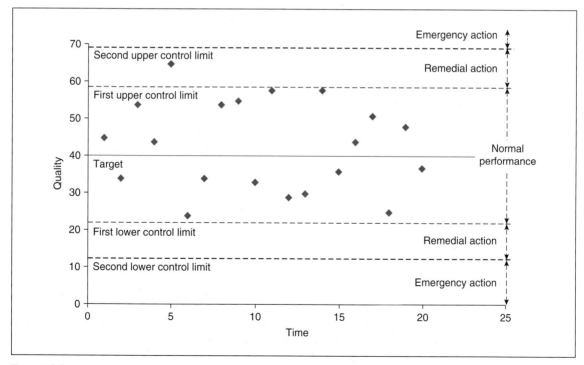

Figure 10.9 Example of a process control chart

IDEAS IN PRACTICE America Online

America Online (AOL) is a leading Internet service provider (ISP). Its ambitious mission is, 'To build a global medium as central to peoples' lives as the telephone or television – and even more valuable.' The company's rapid growth is largely due to its focus of having everyone in the company working towards customer satisfaction by supplying the highest quality service. As they say, 'we are dedicated to the simple premise that our members deserve the best possible – and most valuable – online experience available anywhere'.

AOL have always been more than a basic ISP, and aim at 'making our members' lives better by creating an online experience that helps, informs, and delights them'. To achieve this they created new ways of navigating the Web and searching for content – making on-line communications easier and more interesting.

But this is a dynamic industry, and things move very quickly, so AOL continuously monitor their members' requirements, looking for ways to improve their service, change and refine their offering, and add new capabilities. For example, they led the way in protecting users from spam, viruses, hackers and other dangers; they add a changing mix of original content for their members; instant messaging has evolved into video messaging; animated icons add new capabilities; new services for children (KOL and RED) have state-of-the-art parental controls; AOL for Broadband is expanding the scope for fast connections; AOL Bill Pay allows customers to pay bills on-line; inStore allows on-line shopping; expanding mobile connections give better access to wireless devices.

Source: Website at www.aol.com

---

moves too far away from this mean, performance is deteriorating and managers have to take some kind of remedial action. Process control charts usually have control limits, with any performance outside these considered unacceptable and triggering a response; sometimes a second set of control limits shows performance that is so bad that it needs emergency action. Managers can use control charts to monitor the amount of variation, check that operations remain within acceptable limits, and identify any trends.

Chapter review

- Quality is difficult to define, but it is generally viewed as the ability of a product to meet – and preferably exceed – the requirements and expectations of stakeholders.
- This leads to two basic views of quality: an external view that emphasizes customer satisfaction, and an internal view that emphasizes the requirements of operations. Organizations generally pay more attention to the external view.

- Any judgement of quality must take into account a range of factors, only some of which are quantifiable. The achieved quality depends on both designed quality (satisfying customers) and process quality (matching specifications).

- Quality management is concerned with all decisions that affect product quality. In recent years this has been given much more attention – described as a quality revolution – and has grown into a broader management philosophy.

- High quality brings many advantages, including survival and competitiveness (with quality now a qualifying factor rather than an order winning one) and lower costs (as the high failure costs are minimized with perfect quality or 'zero defects').

- Total Quality Management gives the mechanism for achieving perfect quality. It focuses the effort of everyone in the organization on achieving perfect quality – and makes people working on operations responsible for their own quality through 'quality at source'.

- Perfect quality opens the door for broader changes to operations – such as flatter organizational structures, stockless production, just-in-time, lean operations, and so on.

- Implementing TQM needs changes to culture, operations, methods, ideas – and just about everything else in an organization. These cannot be introduced in a single programme of fixed duration, but evolve over the long term.

- ISO 9000 gives standards for quality and identifies principles of best practice.

- TQM looks for continuous improvement. Quality control monitors process quality and checks that improvements are actually appearing.

CASE STUDY Daxhal Limited

Daxhal Limited moulds and assembles bathroom fitments in its factory in Sheffield. Over the past 10 years, the company has gradually expanded its range into new products, colours and finishes. In 2004 the General Manager retired and was replaced by John Peterson who was keen to improve the long-term prospects of the company.

John identified three significant problems. Despite growing sales, Daxhal's costs were rising steadily and its prices were becoming too high; lead times had been progressively reduced from three weeks to six days, but there was pressure to reduce

these further; although difficult to identify, there was a general feeling that relations within the company had been deteriorating. These problems hid a series of smaller niggles, such as the 3 percent of orders that were delayed, and the need for overtime that was announced at short notice.

It soon became clear that there was no shortage of ideas to solve these problems. In the past employees had been actively encouraged to identify problems and give their ideas for improvement. But hardly any of these ideas got implemented – usually because there was not enough interest from managers, or

(continued)

CASE STUDY Daxhal Limited (continued)

because managers did not know how to move forward with the ideas. Inevitably the ideas dried up, and managers then blamed other employees for their lack of imagination and dedication to the company.

John Peterson started his plans by making a conscious decision to improve internal relations and use this as the basis for improving operations and customer service. As part of this, he returned to the idea of asking employees for their ideas, but this time with support systems in place to make sure that useful ideas are actually implemented. At the heart of this are seven Improvement Teams, each of which is made-up of seven or eight employees, including relevant managers, who can suggest and work on up to four improvement projects at any time. When a project is completed, it is reviewed to assess the potential benefits and to see whether it should be implemented or needs more work.

Within the first few months the benefits of this, and other, initiatives were bearing fruit:

- The layout of a conveyor system was changed to give a smoother flow of materials and more comfortable positions for operators – at virtually no cost to the company.

- An assembly jig was redesigned at a cost of £1,500, but this saves £3,000 a year, speeds up the process, increases machine utilization and improves product quality.

- Suppliers of materials were monitored, and those giving unreliable delivery or high costs have been replaced. Discussions with other suppliers have improved relationships, reduced costs, given lower stocks of raw materials, and improved the quality of delivered materials.

- An unreliable packing machine was replaced by a new one. This came at a high cost, but there are fewer disruptions, lower maintenance costs and no damage to packaged goods.

- Automation is currently being considered to streamline some moulding and assembly operations.

Information about these improvements are regularly passed back to the Improvement Teams, and are discussed – together with broader performance, future plans and financial position – at quarterly employee meetings.

Questions

- John Peterson describes his approach as 'quality improvement'. Do you agree?
- How much progress has the company made?
- What do you think it could have done differently, and what should it do now?
- Is there always a connection between product quality and operations improvement?

Discussion questions

1 There are many different factors to consider in product quality, most of which seem to be subjective and open to discussion. So is it really possible to get a clear view of the quality of anything? And can organizations really define 'high quality products'?

2 What are the consequences of poor quality products? Do these really have a strategic significance for an organization?

3 Of all the possible stakeholders, who is in the best position to judge the quality of a product? What criteria might they use?

4 Something can always go wrong with operations. So is it reasonable for operations to aim for perfect quality?

5 No organization can rely on everyone working together to give perfect quality. The aims of different groups and individuals simply do not coincide. So is TQM founded on a fundamental myth?

6 Do the 'quality gurus' have different ideas, or do they say the same things in different ways?

7 There are now more concerns with the quality of services rather than the quality of goods. Why do you think this is? How can service quality be improved?

8 A local councillor was asked about the quality of the local police force, and replied that 'police spending has increased by 87 percent in real terms over the last five years'. Do you think this was a reasonable answer?

9 What incentive is there for a monopoly supplier to improve the quality of its products?

Useful websites

www.aol.com
www.asq.org (American Society for Quality)
www.avis.com
www.dti.gov.uk/bestpractice
www.iqa.org (Institute of Quality Assurance)
www.iso.org
www.qualitydigest.com
www.quality-foundation.co.uk (British Quality Foundation)

References

Crosby P.B., Quality is free, McGraw-Hill, New York, 1979.

Deming W.E., Out of the crisis, MIT Press, Cambridge, MA, 1986.

DTI, Website at www.dti.gov.uk/bestpractice, Department of Trade and Industry, London, 2005.

Evans J.R. and Lindsay W.M., The management and control of quality (third edition), West Publishing, St Paul, MN, 1996.

Fiegenbaum A., Total quality control, Harvard Business Review, November–December, p 56, 1956.

Fiegenbaum A., Total quality control, McGraw-Hill, New York, 1983.

Garvin D., Managing quality, Free Press, New York, 1988.

Garvin D., Operations strategy, Prentice Hall, Englewood Cliffs, NJ, 1992.

Gitlow H.S. and Loredo E.N., Total quality management at Xerox, Quality Engineering, vol 5(3), pp 403–432, 1993.

Hill T., Manufacturing strategy (4th edition), Palgrave Macmillan, Basingstoke Hants, 2000.

Ho S., Operations and quality management, International Thomson Business Press, London, 1999.

International Standards Organisation, ISO 9000 quality standards, ISO, Geneva, Switzerland, 2000.

Ishikawa K., What is Total Quality Control, Prentice Hall, Englewood Cliffs, NJ, 1985.

Juran J.M., Quality control handbook, McGraw-Hill, New York, 1951.

Juran J.M., Juran on planning for quality, Free Press, New York, 1988.

Kehoe D.F., The fundamentals of quality management, Chapman and Hall, London, 1996.

National Institute of Standards and Technology, Malcolm Baldrige National Quality Award Profile of Winners, Department of Commerce, Washington, 1990.

Parasuraman A., Zeithaml V.A. and Berry L.L., A conceptual model of service quality, Journal of Marketing, vol 49(4), pp 41–50, 1985.

Pirsig R., Zen and the art of motor cycle maintenance, Bantam, New York, 1974.

Radford G., The control of quality in manufacturing, Ronald Press, New York, 1922.

Shewhart W., Economic control of manufactured products, Van Nostrand Rheinhold, New York, 1931.

Taguchi G., Introduction to quality engineering, Asian Productivity Association, Tokyo, 1986.

Thomas K., How to keep ISO 9000, Kogan Page, London, 1996.

Waters D., Operations management (2nd edition), Financial Times Prentice Hall, Harlow, 2002.

Whitford B. and Bird R., The pursuit of quality, Prentice Hall, London, 1996.

Zeithaml V.A., Berry L.L. and Parasuraman A., Communication and control processes in the delivery of service quality, Journal of Marketing, vol 52, pp 36–46, 1988.

CHAPTER 11
Process Planning and Improvement

The process consists of all the operations that combine to make a product. Each product has its own unique process, and in this chapter we see how managers set about planning it. We look at the types of process available and the factors that are important in the choice of best. After the initial design, managers have to continually adjust and improve the process to keep up with changing conditions.

Aims of the chapter

After reading this chapter you should be able to:

- Understand the relationship between a product and the process used to make it
- Explain the role of process planning
- Describe different types of process
- Discuss different levels of available technology
- Consider factors that affect the choice of process
- Understand the need for change and process improvement
- Discuss general approaches to improvement
- Describe different rates of improvement, illustrated by continuous improvement and re-engineering

The key concepts discussed in this chapter are:

Main themes

- **Process**, which consists of all the operations that combine to make a product
- **Process planning**, which considers the best process to make a particular product
- **Process technology**, which describes the level of technology used in a process
- **Process improvement**, which shows how a process evolves and improves over time

PRODUCTS AND PROCESS

Definition of process

The last two chapters have concentrated on products, described the planning and design, and then the broad topic of quality management. In this chapter we look at the fundamental issue of how operations make these products. In other words, we discuss the **process**.

- The **process** consists of all the operations that combine to make a product.

In different circumstances the process might include manufacturing, service, information processing, supply, transport, storage, and all the other operations that combine to supply products to customers. As each product is somehow unique, it follows that every process is also unique – and as an organization makes many products, it will also have many processes. These interact and form a complex network of related activities.

Process planning

Most products can be made in different ways. For example, a news agency can distribute information in a newspaper, by letter, via e-mail, through a Website, over the telephone, on television, on billboards, or a host of alternatives; a chair can be made by skilled craftsmen, assembled from standard parts, made by robots, moulded in plastic, and so on. Operations managers have to consider the features of the product, and then design the best process to make it. In other words, they have to match the process to the features of the product. When product designers specify a standard, low-cost type of shoe that will appeal to lots of people, the best process to make it will have a factory of automated machines rather than a workshop with skilled craftsmen making them by hand. This function of matching the process to the product is **process planning**.

- **Process planning** is responsible for all decisions about a process.
- It describes the type of operations used to make a product.
- Its aim is to find the best type of process for a particular product.

Our model of a process has it transforming a variety of inputs into desired outputs. Process planning adds details to this picture, discussing factors such as the location of facilities, level of technology used, capacity, layout, structure of the supply chain, control mechanisms, and so on. To be pedantic, we should look at process planning and design in the same way that we looked at product planning and design. Then 'planning' is concerned with strategic issues about the type of process, while 'design' looks at the shorter-term detail – such as how a job is done or which machine is used.

Process plans at Amazon.com show how it sells books through the Internet; at CNN they show how it provides a cable news service; at Starbucks they show how it runs coffee shops. The details are added to these broad plans in later tactical and operational aspects of **process design**. In practice, though, we again meet the problem of drawing a line between the two. There is no clear distinction between process plans and design and an apparently small detail in the process can have a strategic impact on the whole organization.

You can see large scale effects of process planning when Nissan build a new assembly line that costs hundreds of millions of euros. Such decisions have long-term effects on profits, production, costs, flexibility, and most measures of performance – and once they are made, organizations have to live with the consequences for many years. Again looking at car manufacturers, there is considerable excess capacity in Europe (and around the world) but it is almost impossible for any company to change its large, automated processes. Even closing down a process becomes difficult with the high financial and social costs involved. The process contains the core activities of an organization, and it cannot change these without overhauling the whole shape of the organization. Lidl operate low cost supermarkets – this defines their processes and these could only be changed by completely revamping the company.

Process centred operations

In principle, customers are more interested in the products they buy, than the processes used to make them. When you buy a jar of coffee, you are interested in its taste, but not really the way that it was made. On the other hand, you would probably be willing to spend more on hand-made clothes than on mass-produced ones. So you are aware that there is a link between the process and the features of the product.

Sometimes, particularly with services, the relationship between process and product is so close that it is difficult to separate the two. The product of a bank is a 'banking service' – and the process used to deliver this is 'banking'. So it is almost impossible to draw a line between the products offered by AOL, MasterCard, The National Theatre, and a taxi service, and the processes used to deliver them. This reasoning shows why managers have to plan their processes carefully. To put it simply, the product must be better than competitors' products – so the process used to make the product must also be better.

Some operations take this reasoning to heart and put so much emphasis on the process that they become **process-centred**. They stress the performance of the process, and adopt strategies based on its distinctive capabilities. They argue that even the best product will soon be overtaken by competitors' designs, improved technology, or changing demands – but the process used to make the product is much more stable. This is why computer manufacturers bring out a new model every few months, but they use the same process for many years – so they should focus on the process of making computers rather than their current models. Similarly, Pfizer make the hugely successful drug Viagra, but it will inevitably be overtaken by other products, so Pfizer should concentrate on the whole process of developing and making new drugs.

Operations that are process-centred consider the whole, integrated process of satisfying customer demand. This is the reverse of specialization, which divides the process into a number of distinct tasks, each of which is largely self-contained. You can see the difference in the way that a customer order is treated. In the traditional organization, everyone does their separate part of the process – manufacturing makes the goods, warehousing adjusts the stocks, transport delivers the goods, accounting sends out the invoices, and so on. Each of these parts essentially works in isolation; the job of the sales department finishes when it collects an order; the job of manufacturing ends when it passes products to the stock of finished goods; the job of the purchasing department finishes when it buys materials. The problem is that no-one looks after the whole process, or integrates the different operations, or even makes sure that customers actually get their products. Process-centred operations have everyone working as a team with the single purpose of supplying products to satisfy customer demand. This removes internal boundaries, expands jobs beyond traditional functions, and has everyone making decisions and dealing with all types of customer issues.

You can see this difference when you contact organizations about a problem. If you walk into a Marks & Spencer store and talk to the first staff member you see, they will usually be able to solve your problem. On the other hand, some organizations keep you at arms' length, and when you eventually find a telephone number, they will repeatedly pass you along a string of different departments, none of whom can really solve your problem.

TYPES OF PROCESS

Five basic types

There are basically three types of process: those that make a single unit of a product; those that make products in batches; and those who make things in continuous flows. Most organisations work with batches, so for convenience people usually divided these into processes that correspond to small, medium and large batches. This gives a spectrum of the five types of process shown in Figure 11.1.

Each of these processes has different requirements and problems. You can imagine this with preparing a meal. You might enjoy cooking for yourself, but this is very different from inviting the boss around for dinner, and even more different from preparing four thousand meals a day in a staff canteen. The following shows some of the main features of each type of process.

Project This is at one end of the spectrum, where the process makes a single unit – such as writing a management report, building a new office block, designing a marketing

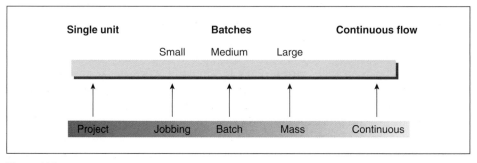

Figure 11.1 Spectrum of processes

campaign, such as satellite manufacturers, or developing a new software package. The product from each project is essentially unique, often tailored to customer specifications – so there is a lot of variety, which needs flexibility, skilled people, and general-purpose equipment.

The main difficulty with projects is that they have a finite life. They typically take a long time, involve a lot of work, are expensive, and involve uncertainty – but after a period of intense activity the product is delivered and the project is over. Operations continually tender for new projects, but they cannot win all of these, and there is inevitably variation in workload. This affects the utilization and planning of resources, and it can be difficult to fit these temporary activities into the permanent structures of the organization.

Jobbing This makes small batches of a wide variety of products (the name comes from job shops in engineering works, which make small batches of products). You can imagine this in a restaurant which serves small batches of meals from its menu, a customized furniture maker that produces a dozen chairs for a customer, or a small baker who makes batches of bread each morning.

Jobbing processes make a narrower range of products than projects, but there is still a lot of variety, with each batch usually made for specific customer orders, so there are no stocks of finished goods. The overall workload varies, depending on the organization's success at winning orders.

Each product goes through a different sequence of operations, and uses a different mix of equipment and resources – so there can be problems in planning, scheduling and keeping track of work. It is difficult to avoid short-term mismatches between workload and capacity, and every time work starts on a new job there are delays for adjustment and set-up. This gives low utilization of resources (typically around 25 percent). Jobbing processes use general purpose equipment, so the capital costs are relatively low, but unit costs are higher.

Batch This is in the middle of the spectrum, with larger batches of similar products made on the same equipment. This might be a printer, a bottling plant, large baker, or a clothes manufacturer – who typically produce a few hundred units at a time. There is less variety in products, which use virtually the same equipment, so after working on one batch for a certain time the whole process switches to a batch of another product. This reduces the delays for set-ups, and units that are not needed for immediate orders are put into a stock of finished goods. The savings from longer production runs, fewer disruptions and higher utilization of resources more than cover the cost of storing finished goods. More standard operations also mean that it is worth having some specialized equipment, so batch processes have somewhat higher fixed costs, but lower unit costs.

Mass This is typical of an assembly or production line that makes large numbers of a standard product. You can imagine this with computers, washing machines and cars moving along a conveyor in a large factory – and you can also imagine it with the processing of credit card transactions. With mass processes there is little variety in the product, except perhaps minor adjustments, so it is worth setting-up a dedicated process designed specially for a product. This usually means specialized equipment, arranged in a line, with units moving down the line from one operation to the next.

The utilization of equipment can be very high, so the high capital cost of expensive facilities is offset by low unit costs.

As the product does not change, there are no set-ups and few problems with planning and control. There is, for example, no need to schedule individual pieces of equipment, or check the progress of individual units through the process. Once the process is working it only needs a small workforce, and in extreme cases can be fully automated. This is fortunate, as people do not like the repetitive and monotonous work on mass processes.

Continuous These are at the other end of the spectrum, and are used for very high volumes of a single product such as electricity, bulk chemicals, insurance cover and petrol refining. The process works continuously with a product emerging as a flow without any interruptions. Continuous processes often use highly specialized

IDEAS IN PRACTICE Bechtel Corporation

Many organizations specialize in a particular type of process. Bechtel Corporation specializes in construction projects, where it is one of the world's leading engineering, construction and project management companies. Its headquarters are in San Francisco, it runs 40 offices around the world, and employs 40,000 people. With annual revenues approaching $20 billion, it has been ranked as America's leading contractor for seven years running.

Bechtel has more than a century of experience in complex projects, and has been involved in 22,000 projects in 140 countries – including construction of pipelines (85,000 kilometres), power stations (420), roads (27,500 kilometres), nuclear power plants (150), railways (10,000 kilometres), chemical and petrochemical plants (375), and mining (350). Among these projects are a number of 'signature projects'. These are typically mega-projects that cost over a billion dollars, are commercially, technically and organizationally complex, take a long time, involve high risk, are difficult to evaluate, are politically sensitive, and include environmental concerns. A selection of signature projects includes building:

- 2000 – one of the world's largest aluminium smelters in Alma, Quebec for Alcan, with a capacity of more than 400,000 tons a year.

- 2004 – the Athens metro for the summer Olympic games.

- 1999 – Ankara-Gerede highway in Turkey, one of the largest highway construction jobs ever at a cost of $1.6 billion.

- 1994 – Channel Tunnel the 32-mile undersea leg between England and France, privately financed at $14.7 billion.

- 2004 – $270 million expansion at the Collhahuasi copper mine in Chile (Bechtel designed and constructed the original $1.7 billion copper concentrator).

- 1998 – new Hong Kong Airport, at a cost of US$20 billion.

- 2004 – 600-kilometre Salah natural gas pipelines in the desert of Algeria.

- 2005 – Jubail Industrial City, Saudi Arabia, recognized as the largest single industrial development project in history with a cost of $20 billion.

Source: Website at www.bechtel.com

facilities with very high capital costs – such as a petrol refinery or steel mill – but efficient operations give low unit costs. They typically need a small workforce and are often automated.

Volume and variety

This classification of process types is useful, but they do form a continuous spectrum and there are really no clear boundaries between them. Doctors, for example, use projects when they give a unique service to each patient, but this becomes a jobbing process when they treat a series of patients with the same illnesses; a knitwear company might make jumpers in a batch process, but move to a mass process when it gets a big order. The important point is not to draw lines between them, but to recognize that different types of process are best suited to different circumstances. We can demonstrate this with the relationship between product variety and production quantity.

Figure 11.2 shows the traditional view. Projects make small numbers of a wide variety of products; the batch processes make medium quantities of products with variety; continuous processes make large quantities of a single product. Reasonable processes appear as a diagonal band across the graph (Hayes and Wheelwright). The traditional view says that processes away from this diagonal cannot be successful. Above the diagonal, area A would make high volumes of a highly variable product. This is a difficult mix to organize, and it needs very flexible operations that come with high unit cost. Moving towards the diagonal would give easier operations and lower unit costs. Below the diagonal, area B would make small numbers of the same product. This suggests missed opportunities and moving towards the diagonal would either increase the volume of a standard product, or allow more customization.

Most operations work on the diagonal, and the main movement has processes that are currently away from the diagonal moving in towards it. But there is a second

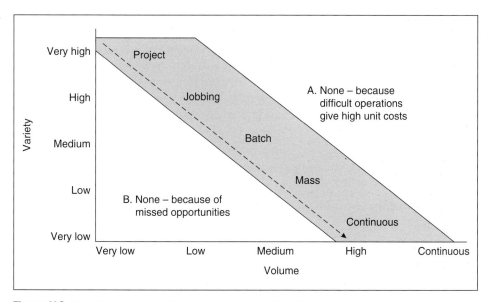

Figure 11.2 Traditional view of process and product features

movement of operations already on the diagonal trying to move further down it, aiming for higher volumes and, consequently, more standard products. A low-volume travel agent, for example, tries to move towards higher volumes of standard holidays; a baker automates its cake production to make large numbers of a few standard products. These movements often change the whole course and culture of the operations, and they do not necessarily go smoothly. You can imagine the problems when, say, a clothes designer such as Pierre Cardin moves from being an exclusive brand to using mass production.

This traditional view is still fairly reliable, but things have changed as improving technology and operations allow more flexibility. Many operations can combine – at least to some extent – both high volumes and product variation. This gives **mass customization** of the type that Dell computers use to tailor products to individual customer specifications.

Process technology

An obvious – perhaps the dominant – feature of the different types of process is the level of technology they use. We can describe three basic levels of technology – manual, mechanized, and automated.

- **Manual processes** – where people have full control over operations that need their constant attention, such as driving a bus. Manual processes have the benefits of flexibility, low capital costs, low risk, imaginative problem solving, and so on. Their disadvantages are high unit cost, need for skilled people, variable quality and low output. If managers want to increase the output from a manual process, they employ more people. But there comes a point when it is cheaper to invest in a mechanized process.

- **Mechanized processes** – have some operations done automatically, so a typical mechanized process has an operator loading a piece of equipment, which can then work by itself until its job is finished, at which point the operator unloads it. Using a DVD player is an example of a mechanized process. Mechanized processes have the advantages of producing higher volumes of uniform products at low unit cost, but the disadvantages of higher capital costs and inflexibility. They still need people to do some of the work and deal with problems. Unfortunately, humans tend to slow down a process, add variability to the quality and increase unit costs. These problems can be overcome by automation.

- **Automated processes** – are a broad category where equipment performs a series of jobs without any operator involvement. A telephone exchange is an example of an automated process.

The level of technology generally rises with production quantities – so a rule of thumb has:

- manual processes for projects and jobbing processes
- mechanized processes for batches
- automation for mass and continuous processes.

Automation in manufacturing

You probably imagine automation in terms of assembly lines making cars, or some other high volume production line. But this is the most sophisticated type of fixed or hard automation, where highly specialized equipment is dedicated to making a single product. Most operations do not have the volumes to support this, so they use flexible or programmable automation. This started in the 1950s with numerically controlled (NC) machines, which are general-purpose machines that can do a series of tasks without needing any involvement of an operator. Such machines have the advantages of giving consistently high quality with low unit costs, and they only need an operator for loading and changing programmes. Paper tapes or cards controlled the early machines, but these were replaced by magnetic tapes and then dedicated microcomputers, to give computerized numerically controlled (CNC) machines. These CNC machines can make even small numbers of units reliably and at low cost, and they have become the most widely used form of automation in manufacturing. Industrial robots began to appear in the 1960s, with computers controlling machines that move materials through a variety of tasks. Systems where computers control manufacturing operations are called computer aided manufacturing (CAM).

As well as controlling production, automation is also used in product design, giving computer aided design (CAD). Now computers design the products (with CAD) and control production (with CAM), so it makes sense to join these two parts into a single CAD/CAM system. This takes the designs from the CAD part and automatically transfers them to the CAM part, and actually makes the products.

The next stage in automated production integrates operations in flexible manufacturing systems (FMS). These combine the separate computers that control each piece of equipment (CNC or robot), so that a single central computer now controls all the machines. This computer coordinates the operations, finds the best schedules for work, and controls the flow of materials. So the four essential parts of FMS are:

1 a central computer to schedule, route, load, and control operations

2 a number of production machines automatically working under the control of the central computer

3 an automatic transport system for moving materials between the machines, typically using wire-guided vehicles

4 automatic loading and unloading stations to transfer materials between the transport system and production equipment.

If we join together the design systems of CAD, the production systems of FMS, and the associated systems for procurement, costing, inventory management and logistics, we get a process that is almost completely automated. This is generally referred to as computer integrated manufacturing (CIM). Then there is really only one more step, and this adds all the remaining systems to give an automated factory. This would work virtually autonomously, with customer requirements entered at the start and finished products delivered at the finish. Computers would plan all the work, order materials, do the operations, deliver products, update bank accounts, and do all the related work without any human intervention. It is fair to say that no company yet has an automated factory, but developments – plotted in Figure 11.3 (Waters) – move inevitably in this direction.

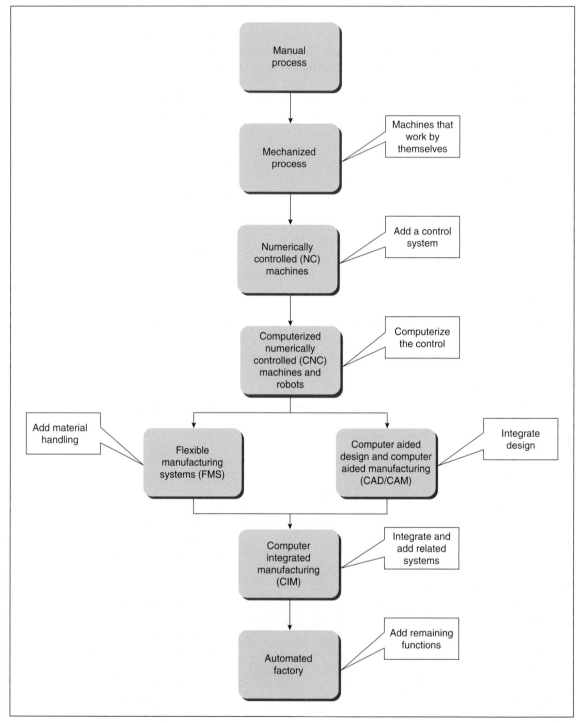

Figure 11.3 Process technology in manufacturing

Automation in services

Automation in manufacturing is obvious, but it is easy to forget the parallel moves in other industries, particularly the services. You can see the effects of automated services all around you, such as automated banking, mail sorting, tax collection, credit card payments, mobile phone operators, Internet service providers, e-business, ordering systems in supermarkets, airline booking systems, and so on. In data communications the past few years have seen progress from stand-alone storage, through distributed processing, local area networks (LANs), electronic data interchange (EDI), the Web, hotspots and mobile access.

The same principles of automation apply to services as manufacturing. But some people argue that the names for different types of process are too closely associated with manufacturing, so we should use other terms for services. There is some disagreement about the best terms, but common ones are:

- **Professional service.** A highly customized personal service – such as doctors, solicitors, consultants, and architects (loosely equivalent to project or jobbing).

- **Service shop.** A higher volume service that still has a lot of personal contact, but less customization – such as hospitals, Hertz car rentals, and large restaurants (equivalent to a batch process).

- **Mass service.** Giving higher volumes of a more general service with less customer involvement – such as a Booker wholesaler, Pickford removals, and football clubs (equivalent to a batch or mass process).

- **Service factory.** Has little customer involvement, and offers large volumes of a standard service, such as the Post Office, electricity suppliers, fire brigades, and Visa International (generally equivalent to a mass or continuous process).

Choosing the level of automation

Automation is often seen as inherently desirable – even the natural way of doing things. But this is not inevitable, and managers have to choose the most appropriate level of automation. If you want a picture of yourself you can use an automatic process, such as the photograph machines in supermarkets, or your mobile phone. But less automated alternatives give different results, including studio photographers and portrait painters. Higher levels of automation bring the advantages of working continuously without tiring, doing operations consistently, always conforming to specifications, being very fast and powerful, working efficiently, increasing productivity, doing tedious and dangerous jobs, storing large amounts of information, and so on. But these do not necessarily give better processes. Each level of technology is best suited to certain types of operations, and it is just as bad to use too much technology as to use too little. Nokayama filling stations installed new pumps that work automatically, offer banking services, show television news channels, give traffic reports, offer e-mail services, and dispense coffee – but the complexity of the pumps meant they were not popular with customers who only wanted to fill-up their cars quickly and get on with their journey. And we have already suggested, higher levels of automation can bring other problems, such as high capital costs and inflexibility. But perhaps the major criticism of automated systems is that they ignore the skills that people can bring to a process, including a personal service, drawing upon varied experiences, using all available information intelligently, being creative, adapting to new and unusual circumstances, using subjectivity and judgement, and generating entirely new solutions.

Automation is often seen as a straightforward replacement of people, rather than a complement to their abilities. When used in this way it often does not give the expected benefits (Brown, 1996). People and machines are better at different jobs, and because automation is better in some circumstances we should not assume that it is better for everything. Despite this warning, it is difficult to overstate the impact of new technology on communications and information management. When Jack Welch was CEO of General Electric he described the impact of the Internet saying, 'I don't think that there's been anything more important or more widespread' and when asked to rank its priority he said, 'It's number one, two, three and four' (Business Week). This view is reinforced by the number of Internet users which passed 400 million in 2001 and continues to climb rapidly. Of course, more sceptical reporters mention that 90 percent of Internet users live in the developed world, and 94 percent of the world's population do not have access. Another concern – which appears with GM crops, human fertility, nuclear power, genetic engineering – is that technology is often capable of things that are not socially acceptable. Grayson and Hodges point out that an organization's ability to do things has , 'less to do with technological constraints and more to do with how far business can win popular support for the use of the new technologies – from both consumers and society in general'.

IDEAS IN PRACTICE Buma Systems SA

A continuing dilemma with housing is that most people want to own their own homes, but the prices are always too high. The reason is that each house is built as a unique, complex project, with a lot of work content, performed at a fixed site, and giving an individual, customized product. This type of process is always expensive.

Over the years, there have been many attempts to solve this problem. The main thrusts have built smaller houses, used cheaper materials, and cheaper construction methods. A common approach has moved from a project to a batch process, giving large numbers of identical houses. Examples of this are the rows of terraced houses from Victorian times, prefabricated houses from the 1940s, estates of semi-detached houses from the 1950s, and tower blocks from the 1960s.

House prices in the UK have risen so sharply that affordable housing is a serious problem in many areas. In 2004 Buma Systems SA introduced a radically new approach to low cost housing in London. Using ready-made units they assembled eight flats on three floors over four days. To achieve this, the company made twenty steel-framed modules in a factory in Krakow, Poland – complete with windows, doors and everything down to carpeting. They transported these modules to London on lorries, where they simply bolted them together on site. The flats in Barling Court have a projected life of 15 years, and are soon to be joined by another 18 flats in Wyndham Road, and more ambitious plans for up to 150 flats a year. Buma's simple idea is to transform a complex, on-site, building project with a batch, manufacturing process done in the controlled conditions of a factory.

Source: Barteczko A., Will Polish homes cure the UK's housing woes?, Warsaw Business Journal, vol 11(15), p 16, 2005

CHOOSING THE BEST TYPE OF PROCESS

Factors in the decision

Managers have to plan the process for a new product, but they also have to review the process whenever there are significant changes to operations, the product, size and nature of demand, costs, competitors' products, objectives, or anything else. These factors are likely to have a significant effect on the choice of process. Sometimes this choice seems fairly clear. For example, the best process for making large numbers of cars is clearly an automated assembly line of the type used by every major manufacturer. But the inflexible and regimented work of assembly lines has inherent problems, and Volvo were continually experimenting with their plants at Kalmar, Gent and Born. In the 1980s they built a plant at Uddevalla, Sweden that had small groups of people assembling separate cars in workshops. This was popular with employees, who had more varied jobs and responsibility, but high costs forced it to close in 1993, and it re-opened in 1996 with a conventional assembly line (Karlsson; Volvo). (Perhaps it is significant that Volvo sold their car division to Ford in 1999.)

Any decision about the type of process should consider the following factors.

- **Overall demand.** We have already seen how the total volume produced can be the central issue for the process. Low volumes use projects or jobbing processes, which have low capital costs but high unit costs; higher volumes use mass or continuous processes that need more capital but have lower unit costs. Figure 11.4 shows a common form of break-even analysis for suggesting the best choice for any particular level of demand.

- **Changes in demand.** The variation of demand also affects the choice of process, with highly seasonal demand – such as hotel bookings – needing more flexible

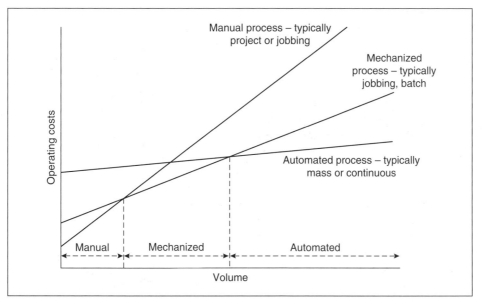

Figure 11.4 Typical break-even analysis for process technology

processes. The aim is to have enough capacity for peak demands, but still work efficiently during slacker periods.

- **Nature of demand.** In Hill's terminology, a mass process is likely to be better when price is the order-winning factor – and when similar products all have the necessary qualifying factors, an efficient process gains an advantage through low prices. And a jobbing process is likely to be better when price is a qualifying factor – so that customers make their final choice from an array of more varied products.

- **Product design.** Sometimes features in the product's design set the best type of process. When assembling electronic equipment, for example, the tolerances are so fine that automation is the only way of achieving them – and when a bespoke tailor makes a high quality suit, the process is fixed as a hand-made project.

- **Variability in design.** When customers are happy with nearly identical products, operations can use mass production to give low unit costs. But when customers want more variety – and are willing to pay for it – a more flexible process is better.

- **Product quality.** The traditional way of getting high quality was to have highly skilled craftsmen making small numbers of a product. These craft processes are still best for many products, but automation is better at guaranteeing high quality – and certainly uniformity – in a wide range of other products.

- **Product flexibility.** This describes the speed at which a process can stop making one product and start making another. If customer demand is likely to change quickly, then a more flexible process is needed.

- **Point in the product life cycle.** In chapter 9 we followed a hypothetical product through its life cycle, and can relate this to the best type of process. The research and development stage might need prototypes that are made by projects. Then during the introduction stage, demand is small and variations are used to test market reaction. These are made by a jobbing process. As the product moves through introduction and into its growth stage, the product becomes more standard by removing variations that customers do not like. The volume of remaining versions increases and a batch process is most effective. As the product moves to maturity, demand is stable and product variation is reduced even more. There is strong competition, so higher efficiency is needed to produce higher volumes at lower costs, and the process moves toward mass production. This simplified example shows that organizations have to adjust both the product and process as they move through the life cycle. In general, the main effort of product planning is near the beginning, as organizations refine their product to the form that customers want. The main effort in process planning comes later in the life cycle, with improvements leading to continually better use of resources (shown in Figure 11.5).

- **Available skills and experience.** Different processes need different types of employees. An automated process might only need a few technical people, while a more flexible process relies on people who are skilled enough to do a variety of different jobs. The choice of process depends on the skills and experiences available, and the training needed.

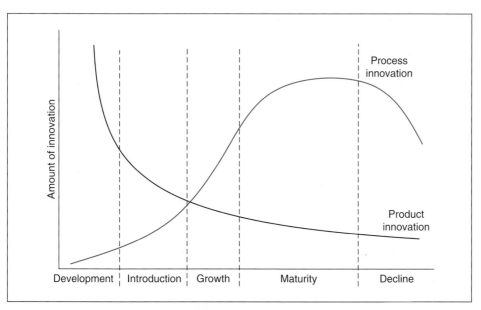

Figure 11.5 Product and process innovation during a life cycle

- **Customer involvement.** Customers are not usually involved in manufacturing, but they can play an active part in services. The process must take account of their knowledge, skills, abilities and needs.

- **Finances.** The costs of alternative processes vary widely, so the choice can be affected by the installation costs and capital available. The choice clearly affects return on investment, net present value, operating costs, unit cost of the product, and other financial measures.

- **Amount of vertical integration.** This affects the security and control of material supply and product demand. Vertical integration gives more stable conditions that encourage investment in higher volume processes – and it allows the higher returns that can justify the investment.

- **Other factors.** In different circumstances many other factors can have a bearing on the choice of process, including the organizational aims, useful lifetime of the process, past experience with technology, activities of competitors, ability to change the process, reliability, support needed, vulnerability of technology, links with other operations, and a whole host of other factors.

Often the actions of competitors drive decisions about the process. When low cost airlines introduced on-line reservations, all competitors had to follow suit; when Federal Express introduced automated systems to track packages and deliver them 'absolutely, positively' the next day, other companies had to introduce equivalent processes. At other times, a final decision is based on the finances – typically looking at the long-term cash flows, payback period (Willis and Sullivan), break-even point (Starr and Biloski), net present value (Hutchison and Holland), return on investment, internal rate of return, opportunity costs, cost-benefit, or whole-life costs (including development work, acquisition, running-in, operating, maintenance and disposal costs). With such financial views, managers really need to ask how much a process will cost, whether the organization can afford this, whether it gives a worthwhile return, and whether they could get a better return by using the money for some other purpose.

As always, these financial analyses have the weakness of relying on assumptions, accounting conventions, parameter values, and forecasts of future conditions – and not giving enough weight to intangible and non-financial measures. And they often omit informed operations managers from the decision making process (Brown, 1998). Another obvious point is that they emphasize the organization's internal view, choosing the process that best suits operations' own aims. We can try to justify this by saying that customers are interested in the products and not the way that they are made, but we have already made the point that you cannot really separate the two, especially with services.

Feasibility of a process

After collecting information about all the factors that can affect the process, operations managers can start looking for the choices that best suit their circumstances. For this they have to identify the requirements of the process, design initial plans to achieve these, check how these perform, add details to the designs and move towards implementation (Figure 11.6 gives a procedure for this).

When checking the performance of plans for the process, managers have to ask three specific questions about the feasibility, benefits and risk (Slack and Lewis).

1 *Is the process feasible?* This asks the basic question of whether the planned process will actually work. Some plans are based on faulty ideas and are simply impossible. But even when the proposal is possible – and even the best option in principle – there can still be practical difficulties, such as untried technology, skills that the organization does not have, need for too much capital, use of too many resources, or introducing too many changes. If such problems are too severe, the process is simply not feasible.

2 *What are the benefits of the process?* This asks if the benefits of the process are high enough, relative to its costs, to justify its use. At the simplest level this makes sure that there is a big enough return on investment, but there may be other, broader benefits. For example, the proposed process might raise productivity and give a more efficient use of resources. Or it might raise performance in terms of the standard competitive features of cost, quality, speed, flexibility, or other features? Of course, there is often a trade-off between these features, so managers have to assess the overall benefit of the process, checking that it will improve overall customer satisfaction.

3 *What are the risks of the process?* The essence of risk is that certain events may happen in the future, and if they do happen, they may have a damaging effect on the organization. If one possible process has a high risk, managers will tend to avoid it – even when it gives clear benefits. An electricity supplier, for example, might be able to reduce costs by using nuclear power stations – but the huge investments needed and long-term uncertainty about waste disposal might deter it from using this process. Sometimes, a risky strategy gives high returns, but on the whole managers are risk avoiders – largely because they are judged harshly for making mistakes. As radical new processes generally come with higher risks, managers tend to prefer smaller adjustments to operations rather than sweeping reforms. Of course, this conservative approach brings its own risk of being overtaken by more innovative competitors.

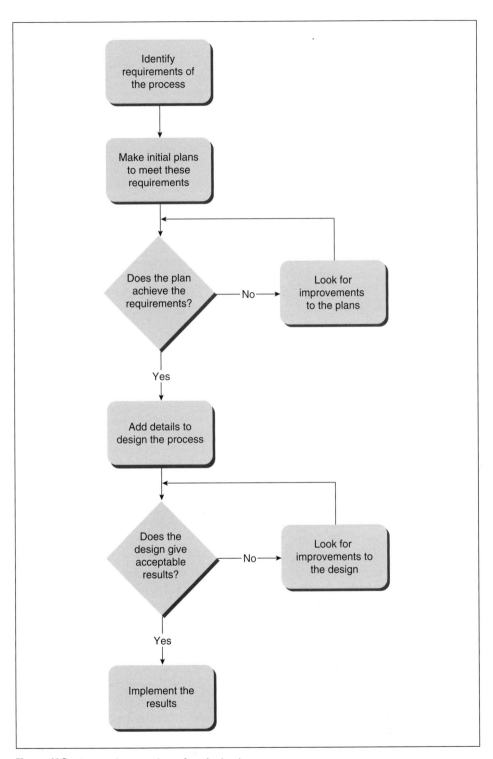

Figure 11.6 General procedure for designing a process

IDEAS IN PRACTICE Martyn Hertzmann

Martyn Hertzmann runs a workshop with 12 craftsmen who make musical instruments. He specializes in making different kinds of historical stringed instruments, particularly the lute family. The output is small, but quality is very high and most customers are successful musicians who want an instrument customized to their needs.

Over recent years the demand for stringed instruments has grown, but this has been largely met by imports from Eastern Europe and Asia. These are virtually mass produced instruments made on an assembly line, which are seen as lower quality than Martyn's, but they sell at a fraction of the price. Martyn has considered gaining a foothold in this growing market by making an additional range of standard quality instruments. He would not make large numbers, so the extra production would use equipment in the workshop more fully and allow the automation of some standard operations. He could hire a few extra people, but existing staff could do most of the work on the new products during slack periods in their traditional work.

After a very brief investigation, Martyn scrapped this idea. His existing employees did not like the move away from a skilled, craft industry to what they considered to be mass production. Nor did they appreciate the implication that they had so much spare time. His existing customers did not want their expensive instruments to be associated with cheaper versions. And the potential new customers were mainly interested in price and would stick to the imported models. There seemed to be insurmountable differences between the two processes for making instruments.

PROCESS IMPROVEMENT

Change is inevitable

There is continual change in all aspects of operations, including products, competitors, costs, markets, locations, employees, customers, state of the economy, business objectives, technology, shareholders, and just about everything else. In response, managers must continually adjust the operations. We saw this in the last chapter, where **continuous improvement** – or **kaizen** – is a central plank of TQM (Imai). This argues that an improved product can only give a temporary competitive advantage, as competitors will improve their own products to at least the same level. Now we can use the same argument for the process. Competitors are always improving their processes, so managers must look for continuous improvement to their operations to remain competitive. If they become complacent and do not look for improvements they inevitably get left behind by more innovative competitors.

Unfortunately, most of us do not really like changes, as they are stressful and uncertain, challenge values and assumptions, imply things were done wrongly before, force us to abandon old and familiar practices, need new skills, use new methods and procedures, form new relationships, and so on. Such hesitation towards change can encourage inertia, with common symptoms including:

- old fashioned products and processes
- falling sales and market share as products are overtaken by new rivals

- increasing customer complaints, particularly about product quality
- reliance on a few customers, especially with long-term, fixed price contracts
- poor industrial relations, low employee morale and high staff turnover
- too much, inflexible top management
- inward-looking managers who are out of touch with customers and operations.

One way of seeing when a change is needed is to use a process control chart, of the type we described in the last chapter. Then when performance moves too far away from the target, control limits give a trigger for remedial action. Being pragmatic, managers can see how urgent changes are by comparing their operations' performance with competitors'. If competitors' operations are already better, there is clearly an urgent need for change – but if they currently have an advantage there is less urgency. Figure 11.7 illustrates this effect, with a diagonal line on the graph showing performance equal to competitors'. Any point below the diagonal shows a need for improvement, and the further operations are below the diagonal, the more urgent the need.

If operations are currently above the diagonal, they are better than competitors and there is less urgency. However, continuous improvement suggests that mangers should still look for changes to maintain their superior performance. As we saw in chapter 5, this can be surprisingly difficult as managers are reluctant to change

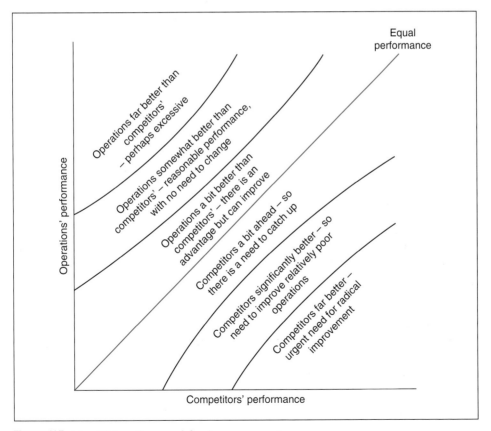

Figure 11.7 Identifying the need for improvement

strategies that have proved successful, so a core capability becomes a 'core rigidity' (Leonard-Barton). At the same time, less successful competitors are very keen to improve their operations and regain the initiative.

The lesson is that managers always have to adapt and adjust their process – even when a process is working very well, there are always opportunities for improvement. Managers should welcome these changes as they create opportunities, improve work conditions, give better operations and performance, and more interesting, better-paid and more secure jobs. This constructive attitude should form part of the organizational culture, helped by:

- commitment to change, accepting that continual change is inevitable, necessary and beneficial
- an experimental approach, encouraging new ideas and practices
- innovative products and processes
- keeping abreast of new developments in the market and industry
- acceptance that not all new ideas will be successful, and willingness to learn from failures
- easy communications, so that everyone knows about changes and why they are needed
- reassurance, guidance and protection of people most affected by changes.

Approach to improvement

When managers want to improve a process – and presumably all changes are aimed at improvements – they have to change some combination of:

- **Operations** – with improved ways of doing activities in the process.
- **Facilities and equipment** – with upgrades, automation, improved layouts, more efficient material flows, new premises, etc.
- **Systems** – providing information, better planning, monitoring performance, setting new standards, etc.
- **People** – through education, training, incentives, participation, work redesign, etc.

They have two options: either they can work harder at what they are already doing, or they can change what they are doing. Needless to say, better results come from changing operations. But change does not inevitably mean improvement, so managers have to positively direct operations towards improvement. In practice, the best place to start looking for this is to see what is going wrong at the moment. According to Townsend, 'All organizations are at least 50% waste – waste people, waste effort, waste space and waste time.' So we can improve the process by identifying this waste and suggesting ways of overcoming it. The Department for Trade and Industry phrases this in terms of four steps:

1 translating broad aims into specific performance goals
2 measuring actual performance
3 identifying the gaps
4 taking actions necessary to plug the gaps.

The difficulty is actually doing these, particularly the fourth step of actually making improvements. Even when the effects of problems are obvious, the real causes or best way to solve them are by no means clear – and presumably if the necessary changes were that obvious they would already have been made. Managers may see that they have a problem with low productivity, but not be able to see the underlying cause or the best way to solve it.

A useful tool for identifying the cause of a problem is an Ishikawa or **fishbone diagram**. Figure 11.8 shows the start of a diagram for a problem of reducing productivity. This might be due to lower output, different measures being used, staff problems, higher use of resources, or changing product mix. If there is a changing product mix it might be because of changing product demand, a backlog of orders, or too low stocks. If the stocks are too low it might be because of seasonality or production problems. After doing a complete analysis of this kind, managers should be able to find the path through the diagram – and hence the fundamental cause of a problem.

Bohn suggests that managers can have eight levels of understanding of the cause-and-effects relationships in a process:

1 *Complete ignorance* – where managers have no idea of the causes, and all effects seem to occur at random. If they make any changes to the process, they are largely tinkering to see what happens.

2 *Awareness* – where managers are aware that certain effects exist and that they are probably relevant to the process, but they do not know anything about the cause-and-effect. Managers try to improve the process by experimenting, developing measures and standards.

3 *Measurement* – where managers can identify the factors that seem to affect operations and can make some relevant measurement, but they cannot control the effects. Managers improve the operations by identifying the causes of largest variations and trying to improve or eliminate them.

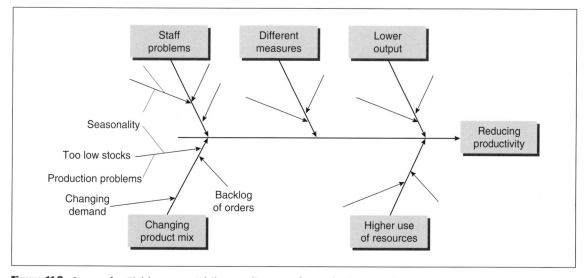

Figure 11.8 Start of a Fishbone or Ishikawa diagram for reducing productivity

4 *Control of the mean* – where managers have some control over the main factors that effect operations. They can control the average level of some variables, but not the variation around this mean. Managers improve the process by identifying the major sources of variation and improving the average performance.

5 *Process capability* – where managers can control both the mean level of the main variables and the distributions around this mean. At this point, managers can control variables to give generally good performance. They improve the process by developing stability and allowing operations to become routine.

6 *Know-how* – where managers know how to control the variables that affect the process, and they can fine tune operations to get the best possible results. Managers improve the process by performing experiments to look for fine adjustments that give optimal results.

7 *Know-why* – where managers have a detailed knowledge of the process and can predict the consequences of any changes and adjustments. This means that the response to any conditions is automatic, and computers can replace managers as the primary means of control. It is difficult to find further improvements to the process, as it is already tuned to give optimal results.

8 *Complete knowledge* – where managers know and understand the effects of every possible variable and condition. They know, in advance, the course of events, and the best option to allow for it. In practice, this idealized state is never reached – and most operations never come anywhere close.

A way of understanding the details of the process is to use 'brainstorming'. This usually means taking a group of analysts to a distant location, locking them in a room, and leaving them until they have thought their way through the details of the process, the nature of the problems, and ideas for solving them. This approach works well when operations have innovative, creative and knowledgeable people who can find dramatically new methods. Usually, though, it is easier and more reliable to ask the people who are actually working on the process if they have any useful ideas. These are the people most closely involved with operations, are the experts in the way that it actually works, and are most likely to know how to make things better. Of course, this assumes that people working on the process are both able and willing to give their opinions. Often they are reluctant to make suggestions – perhaps because they have been so engrossed in the details of their work that they do not notice better options, or else they assume that there is some reason why current methods must be continued. And if they do find improvements, there are the unpleasant suggestions that they have been doing things badly in the past, and that improvements reduce the amount of work and they will lose their job. A more compelling problem is that people have ideas for improvements, but can make no progress with them. They might lack the authority to make changes themselves, find that there is no routine mechanism for assessing new ideas, may never be asked for their opinion by those who could make changes, feel that unsolicited advice is not welcomed, and learn from experience that nobody takes any real notice of their ideas. Faced with such barriers, people normally stop looking for improvements and carry on working in the established way.

A more formal, organizational approach to change can avoid such problems. There are three ways of organizing this.

1 A specialized team of 'improvement staff' who are in a strong position and can, on occasion, dictate requirements to other managers. This works best

when radically new approaches are needed and operations managers do not know how to introduce these or are resisting changes.

2 A specialized team of supporting 'improvement staff' who follow the lead of operations managers and offer assistance, skills, expertise, experience, information and general support when requested. This works best when operations managers are seriously attempting to improve the process but lack some of the specialized skills needed.

3 No special 'improvement staff' at all but everybody has an incentive, knowledge and skills to work towards improved performance. This works best when process improvement has become a part of the operations' culture, and there is no point in having an extra group of people.

Steps in improvement

The first of these is the most radical, with a team of specialists going through the organization and positively searching for improvements. They might approach this using a plan-do-check-act cycle or 'Deming wheel' (shown in Figure 11.9).

- **plan** – looking at existing operations, collecting information, asking for opinions, discussing alternatives, suggesting improvements, planning changes;
- **do** – implementing the improvements, changing operations, adjusting procedures;
- **check** – monitoring operations, checking results, analyzing performance to see if the expected improvements actually appeared, seeing how things have actually changed:
- **act** – if there are real improvements, make the new operations permanent – but if there are no improvements or things are made worse, reverse the changes and return to original methods.

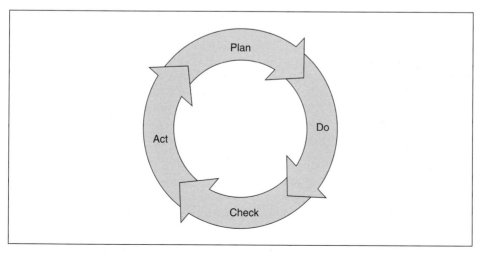

Figure 11.9 Plan-do-check-act cycle for process improvement

We can expand this idea of a formal procedure for improvement, and give the key steps in the following list.

1 *Consider the broad context* – analyzing the industry and markets, examining organizational goals, making sure that everyone is aware of the need for continuous change.

2 *Study the aims of operations* – showing what changes should achieve, why they are needed and the likely effects, and assigning priorities.

3 *Choose the process to be investigated* – identifying core processes and capabilities, their relative performance, priorities and current status.

4 *Describe the current process* – understanding the detailed operations, aims, methods, capabilities, strengths and weaknesses.

5 *Measure performance* – deciding what to measure, defining appropriate measures, recording historical performance.

6 *Identify areas for improvement* – critically analyzing the operations, using benchmarking, value analysis and other comparisons to identify areas that need improving, set challenging but realistic objectives.

7 *Describe new operations* – removing operations that add no value, using the knowledge, skills and experience of everyone concerned to find better ways of doing operations, making it clear how to achieve the objectives.

8 *Plan the implementation* – discussing the new operations widely and getting people committed to the new methods, planning the implementation, anticipating likely problems, making necessary changes to the organization, and giving appropriate training to everyone involved.

9 *Implement the changes* – actually introducing the new methods, perhaps with some specific event to mark the changeover.

10 *Monitor and control the results* – monitoring progress to make sure that objectives are being achieved, giving support and encouragement, having continuing discussions about progress and problems, adjusting the new methods as necessary, accepting that they are only temporary, and continually looking for further improvements.

11 *Remain committed to the new methods* – while they are giving improvements, updating them as necessary, and accepting that they are only temporary until further improvements can be found. This is important as it is common for performance to decline for some time after a change – allowing for adjustments, running-in, correcting errors, and so on – but managers' must expect it to rise to higher levels (as shown in Figure 11.10) (Chew *et al.*).

This is a rather formidable list, and it is clearly designed for major changes. But we saw in the last chapter that continuous improvement looks for a series of small, iterative changes and these can be organized much less formally. Often these minor adjustments are initiated by comments in a suggestion box, and are implemented with almost no formal procedure. So managers do not have to organize a series of major improvement projects, but operations continually evolve and build on experience. This is often described as a **learning organization**, which learns from past experience and applies the lessons to future activities. Garvin defines a learning organization as one that is, 'skilled

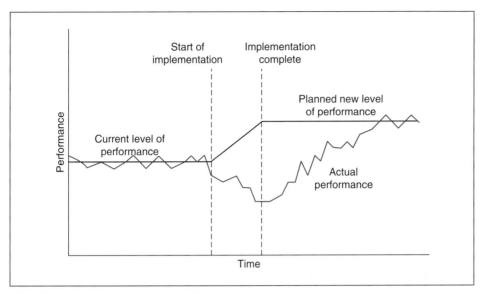

Figure 11.10 Typical pattern of performance during implementation of improvement

at creating, acquiring, and transferring knowledge, and at modifying its behaviour to reflect new knowledge and insights'. Of course, it is not the organization itself that learns but the people within it, and specific mechanisms for learning include training, formal problem-solving methods, rigorous documentation, experimenting with new ideas, analyzing past decisions, benchmarking, learning from others, and so on.

The basic process of learning has managers taking actions, studying the consequences, gaining insight into the relationships between actions and consequences, learning from this and using the results for future decisions. This gives a primary learning loop which continually increases the sum of organizational knowledge (as shown in Figure 11.11). This basic approach focuses on existing operations, and managers can also learn from competitors and other elements in their environment. If a particular action by a competitor leads to success (or failure) then managers should be sensible enough to learn from their experiences without having to go through the procedure themselves. This gives a secondary learning loop, which reinforces the internal one.

Themes for improvement

In our general approach, we have said that managers look for areas of operations to improve. But some specific areas are more prone to poor performance, and managers could save some effort by starting to look at these. For example, operations often have excessive stocks of work in progress, so it makes sense to start looking at this common problem. Over many years of working with continuous improvement, Toyota identified the seven most common problems with a process (Monden). Etienne-Hamilton added more ideas to give 'nine mortal wastes of production', and we extended the list when discussing waste in chapter 6 to include overproduction, waiting, transportation, poor process, work in progress, movement, product defects, overbuying, spare capacity, waste of human resources, bureaucracy, other overheads, equipment and facilities, and stock.

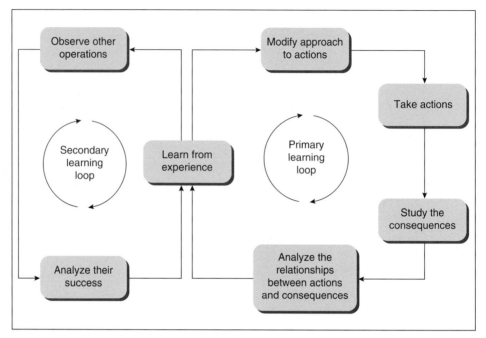

Figure 11.11 Basis of a learning organization

It makes sense to start looking for improvements in these areas. And managers might be able to align an initial search with the focus of the operations strategy. Then an operations strategy that focuses on quality could initially look for improvement in quality; a strategy that included speed could look for improvement in the waiting times, and so on. This reasoning gives themes for improvement, which are loosely based on the focus of the operations strategy, and common themes include quality, cost reduction, lean operations, material management, agility, time compression, world class operations, increasing productivity, human resources, strategic alliances, e-commerce, outsourcing, and so on (Lowson; Cole).

These themes show where managers concentrate their efforts for improving performance. At first sight they all seem to move in different directions, but they often come to the same conclusions. For example, themes of high quality and customer satisfaction would both aim for products with perfect quality, a theme of cost reduction would recognize perfect quality as a way of reducing costs, and a theme of reducing stocks would recognize perfect quality as a way of reducing stock. Whichever theme we start with, it leads to the universal conclusion that operations should aim for perfect quality. In the same way, there are a small number of underlying principles that define 'good operations management'.

In the last chapter we mentioned the features of 'best practice' for TQM, as customer focus, leadership, involvement of people, process approach, systems approach, continual improvement, factual approach to decision making, and mutually beneficial supplier relationships. We have also mentioned the 'seven principles' of lean operations as simplification, integration, standardization, concurrent working, variance control, automation and resource planning (Womack and Jones). Allowing for different

IDEAS IN PRACTICE The EFQM excellence model

In 1992 the European Foundation for Quality Management published its framework for improving performance. This gives guidelines for best practices, and shows managers how they can work towards excellent performance. The model has been used by more than 20,000 organizations, and includes a checklist of five 'enablers' for improvement (leadership, strategy, people, resources and processes) and four result areas (customers, people, society and key performance indicators). The following list shows the type of questions included in this checklist:

Enablers:

1 *Leadership* – do senior managers develop a mission and values that encourage a culture of excellence; are they proactive in introducing new methods; do they encourage continual improvement; do they motivate, support and recognize the achievements of staff.

2 *Strategy* – how are policy and strategy decisions made; how are they translated into action; is the strategy based on long-term expectations of stakeholders; are there regular reviews of strategy to assess progress; is the strategy clearly communicated to employees.

3 *People* – how does the organization get the best out of its employees; are the competencies of each individual noted and developed; does everyone feel involved; is there regular and effective communication; are there recognition and rewards for staff.

4 *Resources* – does the organization manage resources effectively and efficiently; does it

develop external partnerships; how are finances managed; are appropriate levels of technology used; is information used properly.

5 *Processes* – what are the organization's key processes; how are these managed; does the organization monitor performance; does it systematically look for improvements; are products delivered on time; does the organization manage customer relationships.

Result areas:

6 *Customers* – are customer needs and expectations the starting point for product planning; what do customers think of the organization; how satisfied are they with performance.

7 *People* – what do employees think of the organization; do they have high morale and job satisfaction; are conditions monitored and improved.

8 *Society* – how is the organization seen by society; what is its image in the local community; what has the organization done to help the local community or the environment.

9 *Key performance indicators* – does it use the right indicators; does it monitor performance properly; is it hitting performance targets.

Sources: European Foundation for Quality Management, The EFQM Excellence Model, EFQM, London, 1999; British Quality Foundation, The model in practice, BQF, London, 2000. Websites at www.dti. gov.uk/bestpractice; www.qualityfoundation.co.uk

terminology, these two lists have marked similarities. This is not really surprising, and it would be more startling if different approaches to improvement came to completely different conclusions. As always, there is disagreement about what actually constitutes 'best practice' but most people would agree that it includes lean operations and elimination of waste, efficient planning for the longer-term use of resources, quality management with an aim of perfect quality, a focus on customer satisfaction, timely operations, efficient flows of materials through supply chains, partnerships and integration of activities, appropriate use of technology, an emphasis on human resources, flexibility, and a varying list of other issues.

RATE OF IMPROVEMENT

Continuous improvement

We have concentrated on continuous improvement, which usually gives small adjustments to a process. The small, incremental changes have the benefit of being easily absorbed by the process without major disruption – and there is little risk of things going seriously wrong, as it is easy to reverse changes that turnout to be mistakes. Over time these small adjustments build a momentum, and introducing small improvements becomes part of normal operations. In the long term the repeated, iterative adjustment can build-up to give dramatic results.

Of course, all managers are likely to say that they continuously look for improvements – but most of their methods are fairly informal, and Kaizen is a more positive approach that deliberately goes out of its way to look for improvement. This suggests different levels of support for continuous improvement. Brown *et al.* suggest five levels, with Level 1 being the 'natural' or background approach where managers informally look around to see if they can identify improvements. Level 2 has a more structured approach that uses formal methods, such as the plan-do-check-act cycle. Level 3 links formal methods of improvement to the achievement of strategic goals, giving a more coordinated approach. Level 4 adds devolved responsibility so that individuals can experiment and develop their own innovative ideas. Level 5 is a notional end point where everyone is experimenting, learning, sharing ideas and involved in innovative improvements.

Business Process Re-engineering

Continuous improvement is the standard approach for most organizations, but critics say that continually tinkering with a process gives an impression of uncertainty and lack of leadership. It might also move the process in the wrong direction, as a small change might block the way for much bigger gains in another direction. The major criticism, however, is that incremental changes do not get to the root of problems. If you have a fundamentally bad process, then making small adjustments will still leave you with a bad process.

The alternative approach is not to tinker with existing operations, but to start from scratch and design a completely new process. This gives the opportunity to create a dramatically improved – and even the best possible – process. The best known approach of this kind is **business process re-engineering** (BPR).

> ● **Business process re-engineering** is the fundamental rethinking and radical redesign of business processes to achieve dramatic improvements in critical, contemporary measures of performance, such as cost, quality, service and speed (Hammer and Champy).

BPR is a general approach to change rather than a formal procedure, so we cannot say, 'this is how to re-engineer a process'. It does not give new methods – and some people see it as a restatement of Juran's 'breakthrough theory' – but it consolidates several related ideas based on the general principles that:

- a process should be designed from scratch, eliminating functional boundaries and allowing work to flow naturally through the sequence of operations
- managers should strive for dramatic improvements in performance by radically rethinking and redesigning the process
- improved technology – particularly information technology – is a key factor as it allows radical new solutions
- always see things from the customer's point of view
- eliminate all operations that do not add value
- work should be done where it makes most sense, as part of the process rather than in separate functions
- decisions should be made where the work is done, and by those doing the work
- you do not have to be an expert to help redesign a process, and being an outsider without preconceived ideas often helps.

BPR and continuous improvement are not mutually exclusive, and BPR certainly does not replace continuous improvement. Perhaps it is better to imagine the two approaches as the extremes of a spectrum of change – or to have the two approaches working together with occasional, radical redesigns, and between these managers looking for further incremental improvements. Table 11.1 shows a comparison of the key points of continuous improvement and re-engineering.

BPR is an inherently risky approach as it replaces an existing process by a new one. If things go wrong it is very difficult to undo the changes. This is an important point as Hammer admits that three-quarters of BPR implementations do not give the hoped-for improvements. There are many reasons for this, particularly with managers who are

Table 11.1 A comparison of continuous improvement and re-engineering

	Continuous improvement	Kaizen
Size of change	Minor	Major
Effect	Adjustment to existing operations	Dramatic change with new process
Timescale	Short term and continuous	Long term and disruptive
People involved	Everyone	A few champions
Rate of change	Gradual	Abrupt
Theory	Maintain and improve	Scrap and rebuild
Investment	Low, but higher maintenance	High, but lower maintenance
Primary direction	Bottom-up emerging	Top-down design
Risk	Low	High
Correcting mistakes	Easy	Very difficult
Technology	Continues existing levels	Uses the latest technology

nervous about the scope of proposed changes and risks involved. Then they are often tempted to adjust an existing process rather than fundamentally redesign it, settle for minor improvements, stop before all the work is done, and pull back when they meet resistance to change. There are also organizational problems, typically not having anyone to champion the changes, not getting senior management support, not putting enough resources into the BPR, setting up a separate and remote working group, and burying BPR in other programmes and initiatives.

There have been many success stories with BPR, but there have also been some dramatic failures. Some critics say that the whole approach is fundamentally flawed as it:

- always looks for major changes, even when small adjustments would be better
- is virtually impossible to get the dramatic improvements promised
- is very disruptive, introducing sudden, major changes – even if these work as expected the process needs a long time to settle down
- relies on new technology that is beyond the experience and skills of the organization
- is very risky, as problems have a dramatic impact and are difficult to overcome
- is very expensive and puts short-term cost reduction ahead of longer-term interests

IDEAS IN PRACTICE Dell Inc.

In 1984 Michael Dell founded a company to manufacture computer systems, and this has now grown into the world's leading supplier. By 1997 it had delivered its 10-millionth system. By 2000 company sales reached $50 million a day and Dell had also become the world's leading supplier of workstations. By 2005 it had developed into a diversified information-technology supplier, with a product range that included servers, storage, printing and imaging systems, workstations, notebook computers, desktop computers, networking products, software and peripheral products, managed services, professional services, deployment services, support services, training and certification services – and it topped Fortune Magazine's list of 'America's Most Admired Companies'. Its revenue rose from $0.3 billion in 1989, to pass $30 billion in 2001, and $50 billion in 2005.

The enormous success is based on Michael Dell's simple idea of working directly with customers. The company sell computer systems directly to customers usually through their Website. By dealing directly with customers, Dell believes that it can best understand customers' expectations and most efficiently deliver the most suitable results. This direct business model eliminates retailers that add unnecessary time, increase costs, and come as a barrier between Dell and their customers.

The other part of Dell's success is flexible and efficient operations that approach mass-customization. The company builds every system to order, and so eliminates stocks of finished goods. They make a computer system within hours of receiving the orders, and guarantee delivery within a few days (the exact lead time depends on location but is always very short). These efficient operations mean that Dell offer powerful systems at competitive prices. They also mean that stock turns over every four days on average, so Dell can introduce new ideas immediately, without waiting for old stock to work its way through supply chains.

Sources: Websites at www.dell.com; www.dell.co.uk

- emphasizes staff reductions, and becomes an excuse for getting rid of employees, losing their valuable skills and experience
- reduces flexibility and leaves organizations vulnerable to changes in the environment
- is seen as the latest management fad and is not taken seriously.

Ultimately, the difficulty of changing a process depends on how radical the changes are. A process based on radical new ideas will inevitably be more difficult to implement than one based on tried methods – so the expected benefits must be correspondingly greater.

Chapter review

- The process consists of all the operations that combine to make a product. Every product has its own unique process.
- Process planning is the function that is responsible for all decisions about the type of process. It looks for the best match between a product and its process.
- Process planning is a strategic issue which has long-term consequences for the organization. Some operations take this seriously enough to adopt process-centred operations. In principle, process design adds more details to these longer term plans.
- There are essentially five types of process – project, jobbing, batch, mass and continuous. Each of these has different features, problems, requirements and demands on management.
- We can also classify processes according to their level of technology – giving manual, mechanized and automated processes.
- Managers have to consider many factors when choosing the type of process – including the nature of demand, product features, finances, customer requirements, competition, and so on. Planning and design usually involve an iterative procedure that homes-in on an acceptable process.
- Change is inevitable in an organization, and it has to be managed carefully. In particular, managers must look for continuous improvement to the process to remain competitive. We described a general approach to process improvement which contained ten steps.
- Managers often adopt a theme or concentration for improvement that might be aligned to the focus of their operations strategy. Such themes usually come to common conclusions that define good practice in operations management.
- We have concentrated on continuous improvement, which looks for a continuing series of small adjustments to the process, eventually building into a substantial improvement. An alternative looks at radical improvements brought about by complete redesign of the process. This approach is exemplified by business process re-engineering.

CASE STUDY IATA's passenger services

In 2005 people made almost 2 billion plane journeys. Despite this obvious popularity, the industry was not having a smooth time – as it was troubled by rising costs, economic slowdowns, threats of terrorism, areas of conflict, health scares, and so on. The International Air Transport Association (IATA) felt that a way to counteract these negative images was to make airline travelling easier, smoother, simpler, and more convenient for passengers – while saving several billion dollars a year in operating costs.

IATA felt that it could make significant improvement in four areas:

1 *e-tickets*. Traditionally airlines have used paper tickets, but can avoid this by storing all the relevant information about a passenger's journey on their database. The electronic ticket allows passengers to turn up, establish their identity and then check-in. This has the advantage of both lower costs to the airlines (a reduction from $10 to issue and process paper tickets to $1 for the electronic equivalent) and greater convenience for passengers (who no longer have to worry about bits of paper). Globally, electronic ticket use rose from 10 percent of issues in 2001 to 35 percent in 2005, and eliminating paper tickets by 2007 will save almost $3 billion a year.

2 *Boarding passes*. If there is no physical ticket, there is no need for an airline to hand over a boarding card. Instead, passengers can check-in from the Internet, choose their seats, and print their own boarding card (identified by a two dimensional bar-code). Alternatively, they can use a mobile phone to display a code for automatic reading at the gate. Again this gives benefits of both lower costs and greater convenience for passengers.

3 *Automatic check-in*. With automated tickets and boarding passes, there is no need for a passenger to go to an airline's check-in desk. For the past ten years, some airlines have run their own automated check-in machines (as well as

the Internet and phone options). Now IATA is introducing Common Use Self-Service (CUSS) kiosks which allow passengers to check into any flight. These kiosks need not be at the airport, so people can check-in before leaving their hotel, or at a car rental office, railway station, or any convenient point. Most passengers are expected to use CUSS kiosks by 2008, reducing unit handling costs from $3.68 to $0.16.

4 *Baggage handling*. Bags are currently identified by labels containing bar codes. Unfortunately these labels can get crumpled or torn, making them difficult to read and increasing the chance of mistakes. The plan is to replace these with radio-frequency identification (RFID) tags that automatically transmit a burst of data when they pass near to a reader. Supermarkets have used this technology for some time, and it increases the speed and accuracy of reading labels, and reducing maintenance costs. As around 0.7 percent of the 1.5 billion bags carried each year go astray, this could save the industry $1 billion, and a lot of passenger anger. Nonetheless, some further work is needed on the systems, and RFID is unlikely to appear for several years.

Questions

● What problems are currently faced by the airline industry, and why is IATA considering improvements to its operations?

● IATA is looking to improve airline service by introducing high-technology alternatives. Will this necessarily improve passenger service? Are there any viable alternatives?

● IATA is also considering a system of paperless cargo. Are the problems here different to passenger operations?

Source: The Economist Technology Quarterly, March 12th 2005, pp 19–21; Website at www.iata.com

Discussion questions

1 Customers are only interested in the product that they buy and not how they are made. So the process is an internal matter for operations managers. Do you agree with this?

2 Do different types of process need different management skills or types of management?

3 An increasing number of organizations realize that their work really consists of a series of distinct projects. As a result, project management has become much more popular in recent years. Will we reach the stage when all organizations see themselves as doing a series of projects?

4 Technology is improving so quickly that managers can only really imagine conditions over the medium term. Does this mean that the level of technology in an organization is a tactical rather than strategic issue?

5 Some people say that operations can only be automated at the expense of the people working on them. What do they mean by this?

6 How would you set about improving an existing process?

7 When managers have a good process it does, by definition, give the best results. So why do they continually look for further improvements?

8 Any use of Business Process Re-engineering is a result of good marketing by consultants rather than inherent benefits of the method. What do you think of this view?

Useful websites

www.bechtel.com
www.dell.co.uk
www.dell.com
www.dti.gov.uk/bestpractice
www.iata.com
www.qualityfoundation.co.uk

References

Bohn R.E., Measuring and managing technical knowledge, Sloan Management Review, Fall, 1994.

Brown S., Strategic manufacturing for competitive advantage, Prentice Hall, Hemel Hempstead, 1996.

Brown S., Manufacturing strategy, manufacturing seniority and plant performance in quality, International Journal of Operations and Production Management, vol 18(6), pp 565–587, 1998.

Brown S., Lamming R., Bessant J. and Jones P., Strategic operations management, Butterworth Heinemann, Oxford, 2000.

Business Week, Interview with Jack Welch, 28 June, 1999.

Chew W.B., Leonard-Barton D. and Bohn R.E., Beating Murphy's Law, Sloan Management Review, Spring, pp 5–16, 1991.

Cole R.E. Learning from the quality movement, California Management Review, vol 41(1), pp 43–73, 1998.

Department of Trade and Industry, website at www.dti.gov.uk/bestpractice.

Etienne-Hamilton E.C., Operations strategies for competitive advantage, The Dryden Press, Montreal, 1994.

Garvin D., Building a learning organisation, Harvard Business Review, July–August, pp 78–91, 1993.

Grayson D. and Hodges A., Everybody's business, Dorling Kindersley, London, 2001.

Hammer M., Beyond reengineering, Harper Collins, New York, 1996.

Hammer M. and Champy J., Reengineering the corporation, Harper Collins, New York, 1993.

Hayes R.H. and Wheelwright S.C., Restoring our competitive edge, John Wiley, New York, 1984.

Hill T., Manufacturing strategy (4th edition), Palgrave Macmillan, Basingstoke, Hants, 2000.

Hutchison G. and Holland J., The economic value of flexible automation, Journal of Manufacturing Systems, vol 1(2), pp 215–227, 1982.

Imai M., Kaizen – the key to Japan's competitive success, McGraw-Hill, New York, 1986.

Ishikawa K., What is Total Quality Control?, Prentice Hall, Englewood Cliffs, NJ, 1985.

Juran J.M., Juran on planning for quality, Free Press, New York, 1988.

Karlsson C., Radically new production systems, International Journal of Operations and Production Management, vol 16(11), 1996.

Leonard-Barton D., Core capabilities and core rigidities, Strategic Management Journal, vol 13, pp 111–125, 1992.

Lowson R.H., Strategic operations management, Routledge, London, 2002.

Monden Y., Toyota production system, Industrial Engineering and Management Press, Atlanta, GA, 1983.

Slack N. and Lewis M., Operations strategy, Financial Times, Prentice Hall, Harlow, 2002.

Starr M. and Biloski A., The decision to adopt new technology, Omega, vol 12(4), pp 353–361, 1984.

Townsend R., Up the organisation, Coronet Books, London, 1970.

Volvo advertising campaign in the 1990s (for example, Financial Times, 22nd March 1990).

Waters D., Operations management, Financial Times Prentice Hall, Harlow, 2002.

Willis R. and Sullivan K., CIMS in perspective, Industrial Engineering, February, pp 28–36, 1984.

Womack J. and Jones D., Lean thinking, Simon & Schuster, New York, 1996.

CHAPTER 12
Capacity Management

The capacity of a process is the maximum amount that it can produce in a given time. Capacity management is responsible for planning the capacity of a process. Its job is to match the long-term capacity and demand, but this is difficult as both vary over time. Some of the variation follows predictable patterns; the rest is uncertain and needs shorter term adjustments.

After reading this chapter you should be able to:

- Define the capacity of a process and discuss its measurement
- Understand the aims of capacity management
- Describe a general approach to capacity planning
- Consider the timing and size of capacity changes
- Discuss reasons why capacity changes over time
- Appreciate the need for shorter term adjustments to capacity

Aims of the chapter

The key concepts discussed in this chapter are:

- **Capacity**, which is the amount that a process can produce in a given time
- **Capacity management**, which is responsible for all decisions about the capacity of a process
- **Capacity planning**, which looks for a long-term match between the available capacity of a process and the demand for its products

Main themes

MEASURES OF CAPACITY

Definitions

In the last chapter we looked at process planning, which finds the best type of process to make a product. The best process depends to a large extent on the amount of product made – so managers look for a match between the expected demand for a product and potential output from its process. This potential output is defined as the **capacity**.

- The **capacity** of process is the maximum amount of a product that it can make in a given time.

Every process has a limit on its capacity – such as the maximum number of units that a factory can make an hour, the number of passengers that an aeroplane can carry, the maximum number of bottles that a brewery can produce in a day, the number of students in a university's annual intake, the number of customers that a shop can serve, and the maximum weight that a lorry can carry. This capacity is the maximum rate of working, so it always refers to a period of time. Often this is explicit, such as the maximum number of customers that a call centre can help in a day. At other times it is implicit. For example, the number of rooms in a hotel sets the maximum number of guests who can stay each day, the maximum weight of a lorry sets the most it can carry on a single journey.

Sometimes the capacity of a process is obvious – such as the number of seats in a theatre, beds in a hospital, or tables in a restaurant. At other times the capacity is not so clear. How, for example, can you find the capacity of a night club, airport terminal, supermarket, bank, or telephone network? The usual answer gives some kind of surrogate measure, such as a maximum number of people per square metre of floor space in a night club. These limits often come from discussion and agreement rather than any physical ceiling. The maximum size of classes in schools, for example, is set by government policy rather than the physical limits of buildings.

Economies of scale mean that operations often become more efficient with increasing size, so there is an incentive to build the biggest possible car assembly lines, banks, copper mines, call centres, oil tankers, and so on. In practice, managers try to expand the capacity until it reaches a practical limit which might be set by the market size, capital available, or some physical constraints. Sometimes this maximum is an arbitrary limit set by operations policy. Perhaps it is a maximum number of people that managers want working at any single location, so that each site remains small enough for easy communications and teamwork, and managers assume that any bigger capacity would give diseconomies of scale.

Types of capacity

Most operations do not normally work at their full capacity, as this tends to put a strain on both resources and people. Instead they work at a lower level that they can sustain more comfortably over time. So we can define two types of capacity. The first is a **designed capacity**, which is the theoretical limit that can be achieved under ideal conditions with no disruptions or problems of any kind. The second is a more realistic **effective capacity**, which is the maximum output that can be sustained over the long term under normal conditions. This allows for set-up times, breakdowns, stoppages, maintenance, and so on. Now we have:

- **designed capacity**, which is the maximum possible output in ideal conditions
- **effective capacity**, which is the maximum realistic output in normal conditions
- **output** which is the amount actually produced.

The designed capacity of Insulglas double glazing plant is 800 windows a week. They might achieve this for a short period, but after taking into account product changes, workable schedules, staff holidays, defects, and other factors the effective capacity is 650 windows a week. Last year their actual output averaged 570 windows a week.

These two measures reinforce the view that capacity is often not a fixed, absolute value, but is an agreed quantity that can vary according to circumstances. The designed capacity might give a more stable upper limit – but the effective capacity is more variable and depends on prevailing conditions. At one time the effective capacity of a call centre might be 1,800 enquiries a day, and at another time this rises to 2,200 enquiries a day. When the call centre can handle 2,200 enquiries a day, it is clearly working more efficiently – which suggests that managers are doing a better job in organizing the resources. So the effective capacity becomes a measure of management performance.

It might seem strange to describe any capacity as a measure of performance rather than a fixed constraint on output, but there are two arguments for this. Firstly, we can say that the capacity of a process depends not just on the possession of resources, but on the way that they are managed. So two processes can use identical resources in different ways and get different capacities. It is common for virtually identical facilities in different parts of the world to have the same designed capacity – but widely different effective capacities that allow a direct comparison of performance. Secondly, we can point out that the capacity is not fixed but varies over time. Imagine a team of people who are employed to shovel sand. At eight o'clock in the morning they are fresh and working hard; by six o'clock in the evening they are tired and their work rate is much lower. Although the process remains unchanged, its capacity has declined over time.

We can use this observation to define some measures related to capacity. For example, **utilization** shows the amount of the designed capacity that is actually used. If a piece of equipment is available to work for 16 hours a day, but it is only used for 8 hours a day, its utilization is 50 percent. **Efficiency** describes the percentage of possible output that is actually achieved – usually taken as the ratio of output over effective capacity. If people working in an office can process ten forms in an hour, but someone has just spent an hour processing 9 forms, their efficiency is 9/10 = 0.9 or 90 percent. As we saw in chapter 5, efficiency is often confused with **effectiveness**, which measures how well an organization sets and achieves its goals. This is the difference between 'doing the right job and doing the job right'.

If we add productivity, which we described in chapter 5, we get a set of related measures:

- **Capacity** is the maximum output from a process in a given time.
  - **Designed capacity** is the maximum output in ideal conditions.
  - **Effective capacity** is the realistic limit that can be sustained over the long term.
- **Output** or production is the total amount that is actually made.
  - **Productivity** is the amount produced for each unit of resource used.
- **Utilization** is the proportion of designed capacity that is actually used (= output / designed capacity).
  - **Efficiency** shows how well the available resources are used (= output / effective capacity).
  - **Effectiveness** shows how well an organization sets and achieves its goals.

Suppose that a process is designed to make 100 units a day, but unavoidable conditions generally limit the output to 80 units a day. If the process makes 60 units in one day, we can say that:

- Designed capacity = 100 units a day
- Effective capacity = 80 units a day
- Output = 60 units
- Utilization = 60 / 100 = 0.6 or 60 percent
- Efficiency = 60 / 80 = 0.75 or 75 percent

We would need some more information before we could give any useful estimates of productivity.

In this example of Forthright Communications, managers defined more types of capacity, and this idea of dividing designed capacity into productive, non-productive and wasted capacity is quite common (Stratton). A common description has:

- **Designed, or rated capacity** as the total amount of capacity available in any period:

  designed capacity = productive capacity + non-productive capacity + wasted capacity
- **Productive capacity** is the capacity used to make good products.
- **Non-productive capacity** does not make products, but is used for other purposes, such as setting-up equipment, changing products, changeover of shifts, maintenance, time for research and development, standby – plus other legal, contractual or management reasons why it cannot be used. These losses are largely unavoidable, planned losses.
- **Wasted or idle capacity** includes time spent on breakdowns, making units that are later scrapped, bringing faulty units up to standard, waiting for materials, waiting for other resources, or because there is not enough demand to keep facilities busy. These losses occur because of unplanned conditions, but they are largely avoidable by proper management.

IDEAS IN PRACTICE Forthright Communications Inc.

As part of a programme to increase productivity, Forthright Communications collected the following figures for one of their main processes.

- **Designed capacity**

    Two shifts of eight hours for 24 days a month = $2 \times 8 \times 24 = 384$ hours

- **Non-productive use (hours a month) – planned losses**

equipment set-up	12
shift changeover	9
maintenance	10
research and development	12
standby	2
other	3
Total	**48 hours**

- **Wasted capacity (hours a month) – unplanned losses**

no work scheduled	21
breakdowns	7
faulty units	11
other quality failures	7
waiting for materials	4
other	3
Total	**53 hours**

- **Productive capacity**

    = designed capacity – non-productive use – wasted capacity
    = 384 – 48 – 53 = 283 hours

- **Effective capacity**

    = total capacity – non-productive use = 384 – 48 = 336 hours

- **Utilization**

    = productive capacity / designed capacity = 283 / 384 = 0.73 or 73%

- **Efficiency**

    = productive capacity / effective capacity = 283 / 336 = 0.84 or 84%

These figures allowed Forthright to identify areas for improvement, particularly where resources in the process have clearly been wasted. Why, for example did they have to wait for materials to be delivered? And the time when no work was scheduled might suggest declining demand, too much capacity, or seasonal variation. And are the unavoidable losses really unavoidable, or could they be reduced with careful management? Could an increase in the amount of routine maintenance reduce the level of break-down – or is there already too much maintenance?

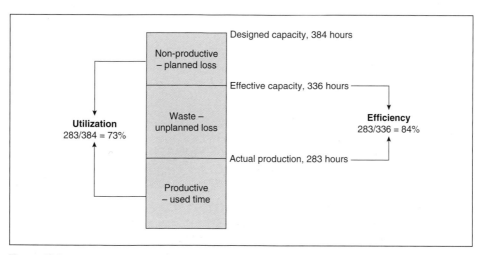

Figure 12.1 Performance figures at Forthright Communications

Bottlenecks

The capacity of a process is not constant throughout all operations, but varies along the length of the process. In a simple form, you can imagine an assembly line, where a product flows down a sequence of machines. It is rare for the line to be perfectly balanced with each machine having exactly the same capacity. Usually the machines have different capacities, and the capacity of the line varies along its length. The capacity of the whole line is clearly limited by the machine with the smallest individual capacity, which forms a **bottleneck**. The kitchens in El Fuento Restaurant, for example, can cook 300 meals in an evening, but the restaurant can only seat 200 customers – so seating is the bottleneck that limits overall capacity.

IDEAS IN PRACTICE SunAlto Orange

SunAlto Orange owns a plant outside Malaga, Spain which produces bottled fruit juice, mainly from local oranges and lemons. During the main citrus season, the plant works at full capacity, and the owners are considering the possibility of expansion.

The main bottling hall has four principal areas (shown in Figure 12.2):

1 Preparation area, with a capacity of 45,000 bottles a day.

2 Bottling area, with a capacity of 55,000 bottles a day.

3 Labelling area, with a capacity of 60,000 bottles a day.

4 Packing area, with a capacity of 42,000 bottles a day.

The bottleneck in this plant is clearly the packing area, which limits production to 42,000 bottles a day. At this point, the main bottling area is only working at (42,000 / 55,000 =) 76 percent utilization. Production from the plant can only be increased by removing the bottleneck, and this means buying more packing equipment. But if the capacity of packing increases beyond 45,000 bottles a day, the bottleneck moves to the Preparation area.

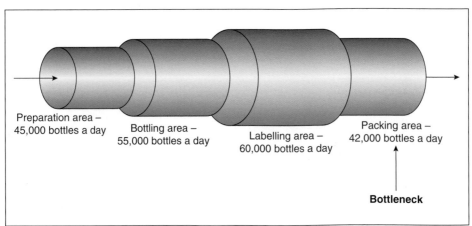

Figure 12.2 Capacity along the process at SunAlto Orange

● A **bottleneck** is formed by the resources or facilities that limit the overall output of a process.

The only way of increasing the capacity of a process is to increase the capacity of the bottleneck (Goldratt and Cox; Schmenner and Swink). El Fuento Restaurant, that we mentioned above, can only increase capacity by adding more seats – but improving the kitchen will have no effect at all. This seems obvious, but you can see many examples where managers have not identified the real bottleneck, and try to increase capacity by adding resources in the wrong area. Companies recruit more managers to give leadership, when they really need more people to make products; services increase the size of customer waiting areas, when they should increase the serving areas; manufacturers recruit more salespeople, when production cannot meet existing demand. You often see one of the most irritating occurrences of this when customers are waiting a long time for service, but there are non-serving staff who are visibly hanging around and not doing anything.

Usually the process is much more complicated than a single assembly line, and several processes run in parallel using the same resources. This is typical of jobbing or batch processes, which make different products on the same equipment. Then each product can follow a complicated route through different types of resource – but one of the resources, perhaps a piece of equipment or department, is fully used and forms a bottleneck. A difficult problem is to allocate the time on this bottleneck to different products so that the overall benefit is maximized. You can imagine this with two products, A and B, using the piece of equipment that forms a bottleneck. The bottleneck limits capacity, so making more of A inevitably means making less of B. Figure 12.3

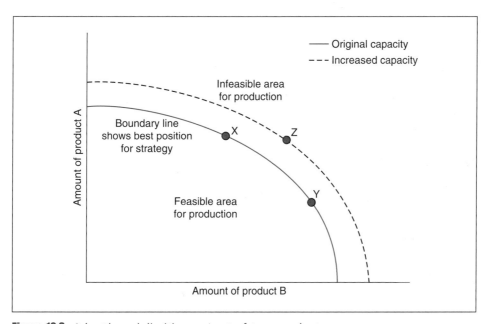

Figure 12.3 A bottleneck limiting output of two products

IDEAS IN PRACTICE Global car sales

In 2000 the global capacity for motor vehicle production was 79.2 million units. This assumes that producers work a standard two-shift, so they could meet high demand for a particular product by hiring more people and moving to three shifts. Conversely, when demand is low they can move to a single shift – but this means laying-off part of the workforce and having hugely expensive facilities lying idle, so a single shift is only economic for the short-term.

Global production in 2000 was 58.8 million units, so there was overcapacity of 20.4 million units, suggesting that average utilization was 74 percent. This is bad news for an industry that must generally achieve utilization of well over 80 percent to be profitable. But things are not really this bad. The installed capacity ranges from modern, state of the art, flexible manufacturing plants, to out-of-date lines for assembling kits or parts. It also ranges from giant new production complexes, to small,

obsolete plants. Old, obsolete and mothballed factories could account for up to 7 million units.

Now if we look at the remaining plants, they rarely run for long periods at more than 90 percent efficiency so the effective capacity falls to $(79.2 - 7) \times 0.9 = 65$ million units.

The forecast demand is also uncertain, and historically global demand has been up to 20 percent above forecasts. Managers allow for sudden growth and forecast errors by some contingency in capacity. A figure of 7.5 percent is reasonable in car manufacturing, so if we add this contingency to current production we get a capacity of $58.8 \times 1.075 = 63.2$ million units.

Now the real overcapacity appears to be closer to $(65 - 63.2 =) 1.8$ million units or only 2.8 percent.

Sources: Pemberton M., Overcapacity – myth or reality, Autolligence Weekly Insight, London, 6th May 2005; Jowit J., Overcapacity costing car sector $130 billion, Financial Times, 19th January, 1999; Websites at www.autolligence.com; www.justauto.com

shows this effect as a boundary, and if we work at point X we can move to another point on the line Y, but cannot move beyond the boundary. The only way of increasing overall output is to increase the capacity of the bottleneck, redefine the boundary and move to another point, say Z.

CAPACITY PLANNING

Approach to planning

Once it is set-up and running, it is difficult to change the capacity of a process. It might need a new building, a new production line, new equipment, an extension to premises, closing an office, or some other kind of major change. Such changes usually come with high costs and take a long time, so capacity decisions are largely strategic. The management function responsible for these is **capacity management** (Menasse; Vollman *et al.*; Klammer and Klammer). At the heart of capacity management is the need to match the capacity of a process to the demand for its products. This is the specific role of **capacity planning**.

- **Capacity management** is responsible for all aspects of operations' capacity.
- **Capacity planning** is the more specific set of activities that match the long-term capacity of a process to the demand for its products.

Any mistake in capacity planning – giving a mismatch between capacity and demand – is likely to have expensive consequences. If capacity is less than demand, the organization cannot meet all demand and it loses potential customers; if capacity is greater than demand, the organization meets all demand but it has spare capacity and under-used resources. You can see these effects clearly when you visit shops. Sometimes there are not enough people serving and you have to wait too long. The capacity of the shop is less than demand, and you probably go to a competitor where the queues are shorter. In other shops there are lots of people waiting to serve you, so there are no queues. But the cost of paying these under-used people is added to your bill.

IDEAS IN PRACTICE KDF Resources GmbH

KDF Resources is expanding its transport and warehousing operations further into Eastern Europe. At present, it meets the demand from its centre in Cologne, Germany, but this is reaching full capacity. The obvious option is to expand the Cologne operations, but KDF quickly discounted this. It already has high operating costs and the facility needs major updating, so any further expansion would have both high capital costs and high operating costs. A more attractive option is to build new facilities in a less expensive area.

KDF estimated that these new facilities would have to handle a future throughput of around €120 million a year. The three main options are to open a single logistics centre to handle all of the new demand, two separate centres for the northern and southern regions, or three smaller ones. Intuitively, a single large centre is most efficient, having both lower construction and operating costs. But this would increase transport costs to individual customers and reduce the speed of delivery. Figure 12.4 outlines some of the main costs. This confirms that the contribution to profit and return on investment

are both highest when KDF build a single logistics centre for the region.

There may be some errors in the forecast demand, as national economies in the area are growing very quickly. The capacity of smaller facilities is more flexible than a single large one. If KDF have under-estimated demand, it will be easier to expand the smaller facilities than to make the single centre even bigger. And if they have been optimistic and over-estimated demand, the cost of a much under-used large facility is far greater than the cost of spare capacity in smaller facilities – and in the worst case they could close-down one of the smaller operations. The last part of Figure 12.4 suggests the expected values with a range of probable throughputs. The single large centre is still the most attractive, but its benefits are clearly declining with uncertainty. If KDF have seriously under-estimated the demand, then opening more facilities would be better – and when it reaches $220 million, it is already better to open two facilities.

Source: Porter M. and Waters D., Capacity planning, Presentation to the East European Business Forum, Warsaw, 2004

(*continued*)

IDEAS IN PRACTICE KDF Resources GmbH (continued)

KDF Resources GmbH Expansion options			
Values are in millions of euros			
Number of centres	**1**	**2**	**3**
Capital cost	30	50	80
Annual figures Costs			
Capital	3	5	8
Operating	4	6	10
Transport	5	4	2
Other	1	1	1
Total	**13**	**16**	**21**
Income			
Throughput	120	120	120
Contribution	**24**	**24**	**24**
Gross profit	**11**	**8**	**3**
Return	**36.7**	**16.0**	**3.8**

Return **Number of centres** **Throughput**	**Probability**	**1**	**2**	**3**
$80 million	0.3	14.5	10.3	2.1
$120 million	0.4	36.7	16	3.8
$180 million	0.2	38.7	28.4	18.2
$220 million	0.1	39.1	41.3	36.1
Expected value		**30.68**	**19.3**	**9.4**

Figure 12.4 Returns for KDF Resources GmbH

If managers know exactly what the demand will be, they can set the capacity to match it exactly. Normally, this is impossible as demand is always uncertain and changing – and we shall see later in the chapter that the capacity is also uncertain and changing. So managers have to steer a careful course.

The example of KDF Resources begins to illustrate a general approach to capacity planning. This finds the capacity needed, compares this with the capacity available, and then develops plans to overcome any differences. To be more specific, we:

1 consider demand and translate this into a required capacity for the process

2 find the capacity already available in the process

3 identify mismatches between capacity needed and that available

4 suggest alternative plans for overcoming any mismatch

5 compare these plans and find the best

6 implement the best.

This standard approach forms the basis for many kinds of planning and is sometimes called **capacity requirements planning**. Although it seems straightforward, there are obvious problem areas. For a start, the future demand is based on forecasts. Capacity planning is a largely strategic issue and needs forecasts of long-term demand – which are notoriously unreliable.

Forecasting demand

The future demand for a product depends on many factors, including the product life cycle, changing customer tastes, fashions, marketing effort, competing products, seasonal variations, state of the economy, business cycle, and a whole host of other things. We cannot analyze all of these, and never know in advance exactly what demand will actually be. The best we can do is make a forecast based on the best available information. Forecasts inevitably contain errors (or else we could become rich by gambling on the stock market or horse races) but they are the best values that we have.

There are many ways of forecasting, with a useful classification shown in Figure 12.5 (Waters, 2001). Here the basic distinction is between qualitative and quantitative methods. If an organization already has records of past demand and knows the factors that affect this, it has the basis of a quantitative forecast. If it does not have any relevant historical records, then it has to rely on qualitative or judgemental methods.

Quantitative forecasts are generally much more reliable, and are the ones which should be used whenever possible. There are two main types of quantitative forecasts.

1 *Projective methods* look at the patterns of past demand and extend them into the future. If demand for a product in the past five months has been 10, 20, 30, 40 and 50 units, then a projective forecast would extend this pattern and suggest that demand next month will be around 60 units.

2 *Causal methods* look at the factors that affect demand and use these to make a forecast. The demand for mortgages in a building society depends on the interest rate they charge – so they can look at their planned interest rates for the future and use these to forecast the demand for mortgages.

Qualitative forecasts are much less formal, and rely on judgement and opinion. Common approaches use:

- *personal insight* – the opinions of a single person who is considered the leading expert in the area
- *panel consensus* – getting an agreed view from a group of experts
- *market surveys* – asking actual and potential customers for their opinions
- *historical analogy* – looking at the demand for similar products in the past
- *Delphi methods* – which use a panel of experts but use posted questionnaires to avoid the problems with face-to-face discussions.

Ideally, managers need forecasts that are accurate, unbiased, responsive, timely and cost effective. There is no single best method of obtaining these, and each method is suited to different conditions.

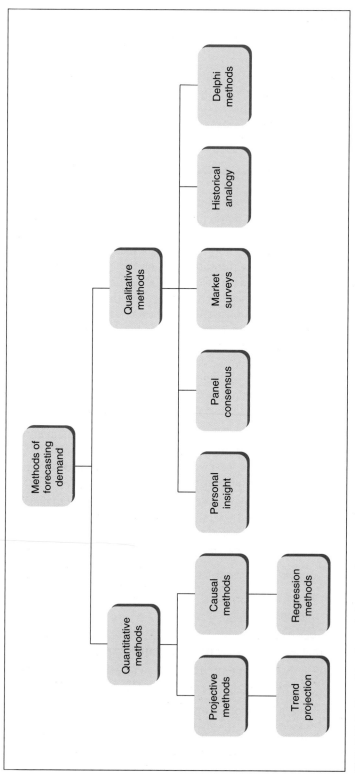

Figure 12.5   Classification of forecasting methods

Alternative capacity plans

Step 1 of our approach to capacity planning takes the forecast demand and translates it into a required capacity for the process. Steps 2 and 3 compare this with the available capacity and identify any mismatch. This brings us to the most difficult part of the procedure, where steps 4 and 5 design alternative plans for overcoming this mismatch and choose the best (as shown in Figure 12.6).

When managers look for a capacity plan, they have to consider more than the potential throughput of operations and extend their thinking to related issues. For example, would it be better to set a lower capacity, and then meet excess demand from back-orders, overtime and sub-contactors? Would it be better to divert capital from other projects and increase capacity, accepting that productivity will be lower in slack periods? Could new products be developed to use spare capacity? How quickly can the capacity be reconfigured to meet changing conditions? What are the bottlenecks and how can they be eliminated? By continuing with such arguments, you can see that capacity planners have to consider a wide range of issues about the nature of facilities, product features, type of process, materials, finance, human resources, and so on. They can generate a large number of possible plans, attempting to balance competing factors. The number of feasible plans is usually so large that it is impossible to list them all, let alone compare them and find the best – so managers usually only consider a few reasonable plans and look at these in more detail. In essence, they give superficial consideration to a long-list of alternatives, but quickly home-in on a shortlist of feasible plans. Then they look at these in more detail and choose the best. The skills, of course, are in choosing the right shortlist, and then selecting the best alternative from this.

There are several broad approaches for generating feasible plans, which we can classify as follows:

1 *Haggling and negotiating.* This recognizes that the circumstances are so complex that any analyses are likely to be of limited use. In particular, it is so difficult to get people to agree on a plan that the only realistic hope is to get them to negotiate and agree a solution. This may not give a solution that is in any way 'optimal' – and may not even be 'good' when judged by rational argument – but it has the support of everyone concerned.

2 *Intuitive or heuristic methods.* These rely on a series of simple rules that in the light of experience seem to give good results. They can start from vague statements, such as 'always consider the most complicated process first', 'add 10 percent of capacity to cover uncertainty', or 'add 20 percent to construction costs for contingencies'.

3 *Adjust previous plans.* Very few processes start entirely from scratch, so an obvious way of planning capacity is to see how an existing process works. Then any problems can be identified, and adjustments made to the new process to cure them. This approach clearly works best in more stable conditions, and when the current results give general satisfaction.

4 *Spreadsheets, graphical methods, etc.* These use appropriate software to do a quick series of 'what-if' analyses. A spreadsheet, for example, can show the results for a process in terms of capacity, facilities, costs, utilization, etc. Managers can quickly adjust features, like the amount of equipment available,

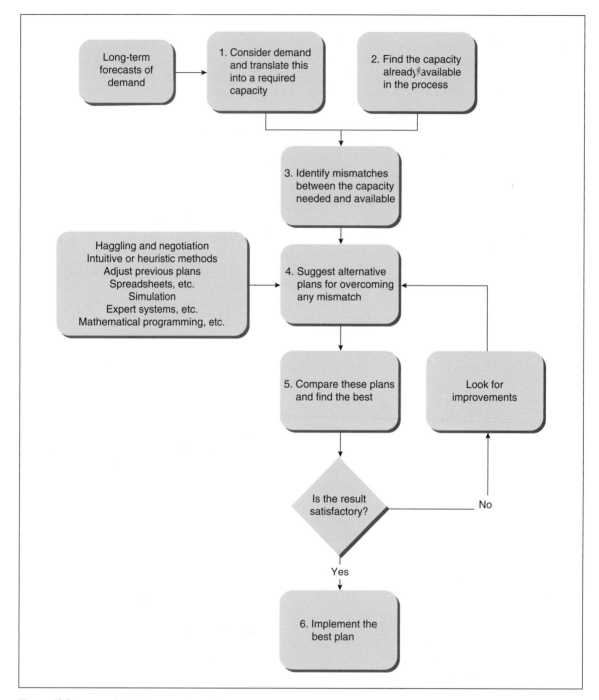

Figure 12.6 Procedure for capacity planning

and check the consequences. Repeating this many times allows them to identify trends and home-in on acceptable solutions.

5 *Simulation.* This extends the basic model presented in a spreadsheet to a fuller simulation of the process, giving a dynamic view that follows operations through a series of typical periods. The result is a very flexible approach, offering a view of how various options for capacity would really work.

6 *Expert systems and artificial intelligence.* These try to include managers' knowledge and judgement in an automated procedure. They use specialized programs that try to make computers duplicate some of the skills of humans. Provided the process is reasonably predictable, these systems can give very good results.

7 *Mathematical programming and other mathematical models.* The previous approaches rely on human judgement (even when automated in expert systems) but the mathematical analyses look for an objective 'optimal solution' that optimize some measure of performance. The most widely used method of this type is linear programming, which – along with its various extensions – builds mathematical models of the process and adjusts parameters until it finds a best solution. Unfortunately, such models tend to be rather complex, and they omit the subjective and non-quantifiable factors.

Having designed alternative capacity plans, the next step is to compare them and choose the best. Even this apparently simple task can be difficult. There are always competing aims, non-quantifiable factors, and different views – so the choice of best is open to debate. As a result, taking the steps in this straightforward sequence does not usually work, and managers usually use some kind of iteration. This designs a plan and sees how close it gets to achieving its objectives; if it performs badly, the plan is modified to find improvements. In effect, steps 4 and 5 are repeated until they give a reasonable solution.

TIMING AND SIZE OF CHANGE

Timing of change

Once the capacity of a process has been fixed it would be comforting to assume that this settles the problem for the foreseeable future. Unfortunately, both the external environment and internal operations change, and if things are left unchecked the process capacity and product demand tend to drift apart. In the short term, managers can make tactical and operational adjustments to overcome any mismatch (which we discuss later in the chapter). In the longer term they have to make adjustments to restore the match. This raises two immediate questions – When should the capacity change? And by how much should it change?

Imagine that you start a new low cost air service between Berlin and Paris, using aeroplanes with 200 seats. While the demand grows from zero to 200 passengers a day, you can meet all demand with a single flight. But when demand goes over 200 passengers a day, you have the choice of losing customers or putting on a second flight. It seems wasteful to put on a flight for a single extra person, so you will probably wait a bit and accept the loss of some customers – but you will not want to wait until potential demand has risen to 400 passengers a day before putting on a second flight. So at what point is it best to increase capacity? Clearly, you could calculate a break-even point for a second plane, and start the service when demand reaches this figure. But you might also ask why the passengers you had turned away would return to your service?

The essential problem with this example – and with almost every other problem of capacity – is that demand comes in small quantities and can take almost any value, while capacity only comes in large, discrete amounts. Typically, operations can increase capacity by opening another shop, buying another vehicle, building another factory, opening a new office suite, and so on. At an extreme you can imagine an electricity company whose generators are all working at full capacity. If it gets another customer, does it have to spend a billion euros on building another power station?

This inherent difference between supply and demand patterns means that there is rarely an exact match between them. And things are really more complicated as both demand and capacity vary over time. So the best that managers can do is look for some level of match that is generally acceptable, and then make short-term adjustments to cover any immediate problems.

Imagine that demand for a product rises steadily over time. At some point managers have to increase the capacity of the process, and this increase comes as a discrete step. It is not possible to exactly match the discrete capacity to the continuous demand, so they have three basic strategies (shown in Figure 12.7).

1 *Capacity more or less matches demand* – sometimes there is excess capacity and sometimes a shortage. This gives a relatively balanced performance that avoids the problems of both excess capacity and too many lost customers. In the best circumstances, short-term differences can be overcome by stocks, which are built-up during periods of excess capacity and used during periods of excess demand. This has the advantages of meeting all – or at least most – demand, maintaining customer satisfaction, and having high utilization of facilities. It has the disadvantages that the stocks come at high costs and if the forecast increase in demand does not materialize the stocks will eventually be scrapped (Waters, 2003). Apart from stock, other mechanisms for improving the match between capacity and demand, include back-orders, queues, sub-contracting – or simply accepting some lost sales.

2 *Capacity leads demand* – so that it is always large enough to meet all demand. This maximizes revenue and customer satisfaction – and there is a capacity cushion to allow for unexpected circumstances. But it needs more investment, utilization is lower, unit costs rise – and there is a risk of having resources that are never used if the long-term forecasts are so optimistic that they never appear.

3 *Capacity lags demand* – with more capacity added only when the extra facilities would be heavily – preferably fully – used. This delays and reduces investment, ensures high utilization, and gives low unit costs. But it restricts output, loses customers, causes delays, lowers customer satisfaction, and has no flexibility to deal with unexpected circumstances.

Each of these strategies is best suited to different conditions. Factors that encourage an early increase in capacity, so that capacity leads demand, are:

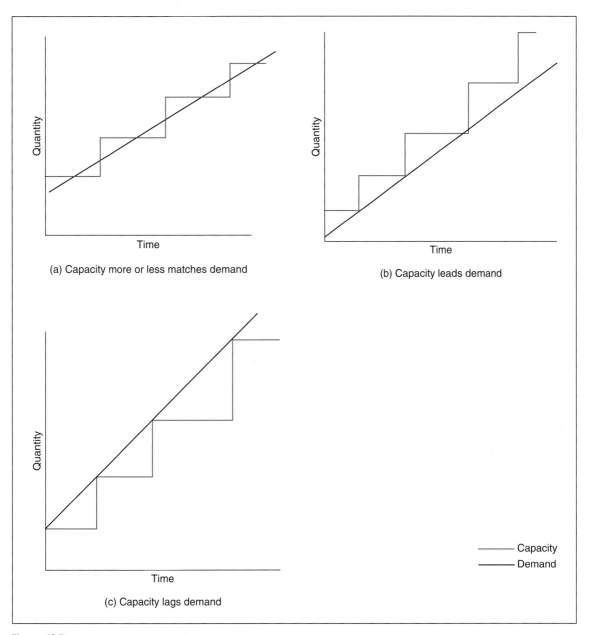

Figure 12.7 Alternative timing of capacity increases

- variable, uneven and uncertain demand
- high profit margins on sales
- high cost of unmet demand, possibly with lost future sales
- low costs of spare capacity, which might be used for other work
- continuously changing product mix
- variable efficiency or other factors that give uncertainty in capacity
- capacity increases that are relatively small.

On the other hand, the main factor that encourages operations to wait as long as possible before increasing capacity – so that capacity lags demand – is the investment cost. Under-used resources can be very expensive, and it is difficult to argue that spare capacity will be needed for higher demand at some point in the distant future.

If you think of a large furniture shop, its capacity to serve customers is largely set by the number of sales people. Because of the nature of the product and its demand, the shop is likely to increase capacity early and make sure there are always enough staff to serve customers. On the other hand, new motorways are expensive and controversial, so expansions are delayed for as long as possible, and the road is crowded immediately it opens.

Sometimes there is some dominant factor in the decisions, such as the position of a product in its life cycle. During introduction and early growth stages, operations are looking forward to growth, so they adopt a capacity leading strategy and build enough capacity for the foreseeable growth. This inevitably increases unit costs, but this is not necessarily a problem as customers are willing to pay premium prices for a new product, and competition is not yet based on cost. During the later growth stage it is more difficult to forecast demand and tell when the product approaches maturity. Operations want enough capacity for current needs, but not so much that they have excess when demand stabilizes, so they try to more or less match capacity to demand. When the product reaches maturity, operations do not want excess capacity, and they are likely to compete on cost, so a capacity lagging strategy is most common.

Several analyses can help with this decision, particularly costing of alternatives. Unfortunately, most of these need a surrogate measure for the cost of lost customers or level of customer service. Hayes and Wheelwright, for example, suggest looking at the relative cost of excess capacity and shortage:

$$\frac{\text{Cost of a unit of capacity shortage} - \text{cost of a unit of excess capacity}}{\text{Cost of a unit of capacity shortage}}$$

When the cost of excess capacity is high, typically with capital intensive industries, this ratio is small; when the cost of capacity shortage is high, typically with high profit margins, this ratio is large. Then a rule of thumb suggests that when the ratio falls below some arbitrary value – say 0.5 – there should be no spare capacity and preferably a shortage; and when the ratio is above this value there should be a positive capacity cushion.

Size of expansion

The other main question about capacity change asks how big the change should be. If you think that demand over the next two years will justify four new offices, should you build them all in one go, or would it be better to add them in four separate steps. Any change to capacity is likely to involve some disruption, so is it better to minimize the disruption by one big change, or is it better to phase the capacity changes over an extended period with a series of smaller adjustments (as illustrated in Figure 12.8)?

There can be benefits to both of these approaches. The usual benefits from a few large increases in capacity include:

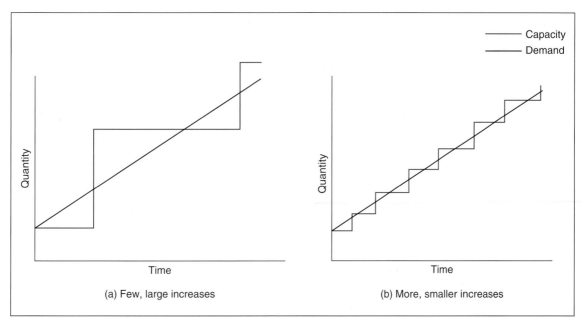

Figure 12.8 Alternative sizes of capacity increases

- capacity stays ahead of demand for a longer time
- extra capacity gives a cushion against unexpected conditions, so fewer sales are lost
- there are fewer disruptions
- bigger expansions give lower costs per unit of expansion
- the expansion might give earlier economies of scale, introducing more efficient processes and reducing unit costs
- it may encourage more demand, particularly with services
- it may give advantages over competitors, such as increased credibility with customers.

On the other hand, the advantages of more, smaller expansions include:

- capacity matches demand more closely
- there may be more disruptions, but each is far less serious
- capital is not tied-up in unneeded capacity
- higher utilization of resources
- there is less risk if demand changes or does not reach expected levels
- smaller expansions can be timed more carefully, so they are more flexible
- the process is less vulnerable to changes – such as new technology – which could leave a large change outdated.

A common rationale for large increases in capacity is that they bring economies of scale faster, spreading fixed costs over more units, using more efficient processes, and

IDEAS IN PRACTICE GlaxoSmithKline

Large capacity can give economies of scale – but it can be difficult to justify, particularly in competitive markets. It is impossible for all organizations to continue expanding, and the need to raise utilization of expensive facilities can drive down prices until operations become uneconomic. In effect, expansion of one organization means contraction of another. To avoid this effect, and still get economies of scale, companies often merge or acquire competitors.

The pharmaceutical industry clearly shows the effects of mergers. The underlying pressure for consolidation is the typical cost of $1 billion to bring a new drug to market – and the observation that bigger companies get considerable economies of scale in research and development. On some scale, this has always been true, and there is a long tradition of mergers in the industry.

In 1830 John Smith opened the first drug store in Philadelphia. Twelve years later Thomas Beecham

launched his famous laxative pill in London. In 1880 Silas Burroughs and Henry Wellcome founded Burroughs Wellcome & Co. In 1906 Glaxo dried milk was established. The connections between these – and thousands of similar events – come clear as the pharmaceutical industry evolves over the next century. In 1989 John Smith's company had become the giant SmithKline Beckman, which merged with the equally big Beecham Group to form SmithKline Beecham. Glaxo and Welcome merged in 1995 to form Glaxo Wellcome, and in 2000 these two companies merged to form GlaxoSmithKline.

GlaxoSmithKline is now one of the world's leading research-based pharmaceutical companies, with annual sales approaching $40 billion and employing 100,000 people. Its annual R&D budget is $5 billion, spent in 24 sites in 11 countries.

Source: Website at www.gsk.com

giving more experience with large-scale operations. But economies of scale are not inevitable, and large expansions might give 'diseconomies of scale', where communications, management and organizational structure needed to support large operations are too complex and inefficient. And the increased capacity might be achieved by means that give short-term benefits, but cannot be sustained over the longer term – for example, by using overtime, which becomes less productive when used over extended periods, or delaying maintenance that increases the longer-term risk of equipment break-downs, or increasing utilization of facilities and uncovering problems that remained hidden by the buffer of spare capacity.

Economies of scale steer organizations towards larger operations, this is not necessarily the best direction. It is a complex decision that includes many factors. One of these is that large centralized facilities are inevitably further away from suppliers and customers, so the logistics costs are higher and the level of service (measured by delivery time, customer contact, etc.) is lower. These questions are considered in supply chain management, which we discuss in the next two chapters.

CHANGING CAPACITY OVER TIME

As we have already suggested, the effective capacity of a process can change quite markedly. Even if there are no changes to the process, there are short-term variations due to staff illness, interruptions, break-downs, weather, holidays, enthusiasm of employees, and so on. And we mentioned the example of people shovelling sand, where tiredness at the end of an eight-hour shift reduces their effective capacity, even though there has been no change in the process. But there are also longer-term variations in the capacity of any process. We can illustrate these by looking at the systematic changes due to learning effects, maintenance, replacement policies and the business cycle.

Learning effects

The more often you repeat something, the easier it becomes and the better your performance. This is why sportsmen and musicians spend a long time practising, so they become more skilful and find it easier to perform at a given level. You see this effect in almost all operations, and it means that the time needed to complete a specific job declines as the number of repetitions increases. Figure 12.9 shows this effect in a graph of a learning curve.

A common shape for learning curves has the time taken to do an operation falling by a fixed proportion every time the number of repetitions is doubled. If someone takes 10 minutes to do a job for the first time, and this declines by 10 percent for every doubling or repetitions – giving a 'learning rate' of 90 percent – the second time takes only 90 percent of this, or 9 minutes; the fourth time takes 90 percent of the time for the second repetition, or 8.1 minutes; the eighth time it takes 90 percent of the time for the fourth repetition, or 7.29 minutes and so on. The obvious effect of the learning curve is that more products can be made in the same time – and the capacity of the process increases. This is an important reason why it is better to continue making the same products for as long as possible, rather than rapidly moving on to new ones.

Maintenance

As facilities and equipment get older, they break-down more often, develop more faults, give lower quality, slow down, and generally wear out (Condra; August; Moubray). Sometimes the changes are slow – like the fuel consumption of a car,

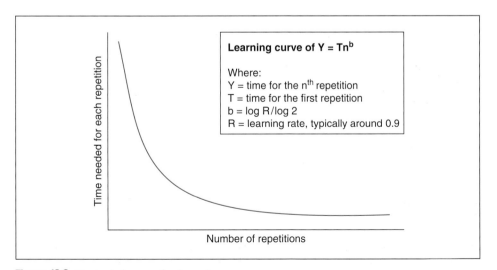

Figure 12.9 Typical shape of a learning curve

which rises steadily with age; sometimes the change is very fast, like a bolt that suddenly breaks. The overall effect, though, is a systematic decline in capacity with age. Sometimes the pattern is more complex, perhaps with an initial running-in period to sort out teething problems before facilities start to work normally.

We can reduce the effects of wear by doing routine or preventive maintenance, which regularly inspects facilities for wear, and replaces vulnerable parts after a certain period of use. This happens when cars have a regular 6,000 km service. By replacing bits that are worn – or are most likely to wear – the facilities are restored to give continuing, satisfactory performance. The problem is deciding how often to do this maintenance. If it is done too often, everything will run efficiently but the maintenance costs are too high; if it is not done often enough, the maintenance cost is low but the equipment still breaks down. Managers have to find the best compromise that gives the minimum overall cost.

Replacement of equipment

Routine maintenance can keep facilities working efficiently – but there comes a point when maintenance and repairs become too expensive and it is cheaper to buy replacements. These replacement decisions can be expensive when, for example, an organization has to consider a new power station, office block, hotel, steel mill, ship and aeroplane. Again, there is the question of when is the best time to replace, and we can repeat the argument used for maintenance. Too frequently gives efficient operations but high replacement costs; too rarely gives low replacement costs but high operating and failure costs. So there is an optimal time for replacement. This leads to a policy of replacing delivery vans every five years, say, or replacing computer systems every three years.

One drawback with this planned replacement is that equipment is routinely replaced when it appears to be working well – in the way that computer equipment, is replaced when it still looks new. As replacement inevitably causes disruptions as people get used to new equipment, it can be difficult to persuade them that this really is better than waiting until the old equipment is obviously not working.

Business cycles

This is more of a response to general economic conditions, where managers try to cut back on capacity during economic downturns and then expand it when the economy improves. A traditional view of a business cycle starts with the industry being optimistic about the future, and expecting sales to rise. So managers increase capacity to match perceived future demand and the economy expands. Actual sales lag behind this increased capacity, and there is a build-up of unused capacity. At some point, industry loses confidence and cuts back on capacity, and the economy contracts. This recession – or at best stagnation – continues until there is again a shortage of capacity and industry again expands (as shown in Figure 12.10). This description gives a convincing argument, but nobody has found a precise cause or explanation for business cycles, and there is a general belief that each cycle is in some ways unique. Nonetheless, they have a significant effect on capacity plans.

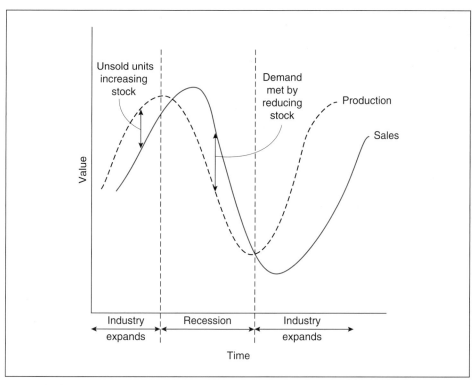

Figure 12.10 Stock levels in a business cycle

Uncertainty

There is always uncertainty surrounding capacity planning. At the heart of plans are the long-term forecasts for demand that inevitably contain approximations and errors. Then there is uncertainty in capacity, caused by systematic variations that we have suggested above and shorter-term variations. And there can be other uncertainty, such as the timing when capacity becomes available, construction delays, feedback from sample markets, problems with product development, installation, teething problems, and so on. Operations managers have the problem of matching a variable and uncertain capacity to a variable and uncertain demand. Not surprisingly, they sometimes make mistakes, and the result is either shortage or spare capacity.

Perhaps the most usual effect has over-optimistic demand forecasts suggesting major expansion. This can be repeated throughout an industry, particularly when a new type of product is widely expected to generate entirely new demand. The result can be excess capacity and falling returns in the whole industry. Mass production industries have a particular problem here, as their processes are largely automated, extra capacity comes in large blocks, it is very expensive, and takes a long time to design and install – and high capacity processes have virtually the same capital cost as lower capacity ones, but the operating costs are much lower. So there is a clear incentive for operations to install higher capacity to give a cushion against unexpected changes – and the new, efficient, low-cost process might attract customers from the older facilities of competitors.

IDEAS IN PRACTICE Wholefood Preparation Ltd

Alex George is the operations manager for Wholefood Preparation Ltd, a vegetable processor based in the East of England. Every year he reviews the performance of the company's production machines so that replacements can be delivered before the end of the financial year.

Alex has calculated some costs for replacing one piece of equipment at different ages (shown in Figure 12.11). This starts with the replacement cost of £210,000, and the residual value of old machines at different ages, which is the amount given by the supplier in part-exchange. The difference between these two gives the total capital cost of the equipment. Alex also has figures for the running cost of the equipment each year. Adding these together gives a total running cost over the lifetime.

If Alex replaced the equipment after four years there would be capital costs of £150,000 and running costs of £36,000, to give a total lifetime cost of £186,000 or £46,500 a year. This option gives the minimum annual cost, and is the one that Alex is considering (after he has taken into account a number of other factors).

Wholefood Preparation Limited						
Age at replacement	1	2	3	4	5	6
Purchase price	£210,000	£210,000	£210,000	£210,000	£210,000	£210,000
Resale value	£160,000	£120,000	£90,000	£60,000	£30,000	£10,000
Capital cost	£50,000	£90,000	£120,000	£150,000	£180,000	£200,000
Running cost in last year	£5,000	£7,000	£10,000	£14,000	£25,000	£38,000
Total lifetime running cost	£5,000	£12,000	£22,000	£36,000	£61,000	£99,000
Total lifetime cost	£55,000	£102,000	£142,000	£186,000	£241,000	£299,000
Average cost each year	£55,000	£51,000	£47,333	£46,500	£48,200	£49,833
				Minimum		

Figure 12.11 Cost of equipment replacement at Wholefood Preparation Limited

Unfortunately, these new processes are inflexible, and cannot respond quickly to changing conditions. If demand falls, there is little that manufacturers can do to respond, except close down the line for periods or leave it ticking-over.

Computer chip manufacturers use large-scale, automated processes and responded to the growing demand in the first half of the 1990s by installing lots of capacity. Then between 1995 and 1996 the industry moved from a 40 percent growth a year, to a 10 percent contraction (Financial Times). A series of decisions by individual companies had led to excess capacity for the whole industry – and this in turn affected prices and the performance of every company. The clear message is that when every organization in an industry acts in its own best interests, there can be problems for the whole industry. The obvious solution is to reduce capacity in the industry and raise returns. But it is expensive to reduce capacity, as whole facilities have to close, staff have to be laid-off, and someone has to pay the high social costs. Any company that contracts, pays all of these costs itself, while the benefits are shared among other companies that remain in the industry. So it is usually better for each company to keep working in the same industry rather than pulling-out – while hoping that declining performance will force competitors to pull out.

DIFFERENT LEVELS OF CAPACITY PLANS

Tactical and operational adjustments

Capacity planning is largely a strategic function. Operations can increase the capacity of a process by opening a factory, designing a new process, opening new offices, or moving to a new location; they can reduce excess capacity by closing offices, shutting down a plant, or transferring facilities to other products. These are strategic decisions with long-term consequences and costs. But demand can change very quickly, by the day or even the hour. So operations need the flexibility to make short-term adjustments

IDEAS IN PRACTICE European car manufacturers

Most car manufacturers use automated assembly lines which cost hundreds of millions of euros to set-up. The high fixed costs give every manufacturer an incentive to build large capacity. Unfortunately, there is not enough demand to keep all the plants busy, and by 2000 there was around 30 percent excess capacity around the world, costing the industry around €70 billion a year.

In Western Europe the market for cars grew healthily from 13.4 million in 1997 to 15 million in 1999. But the motor industry still described itself as being in a crisis. The problem was over-capacity. Despite the strong market growth, production in Western Europe stagnated at about 14.4 million cars a year – while capacity grew to over 21 million cars a year. Western Europe could produce over 6 million more cars a year than it could sell.

The industry started to make fundamental changes – such as the acquisition of Volvo by Ford, joint ventures between Fiat and GM, the merger between Daimler and Chrysler and the integration of Mitsubishi into DaimlerChrysler, the sale of Rover Group by BMW (and its eventual closure), sale of Land Rover to Ford, effective take-over of Nissan by Renault. But five years later – despite the mergers, restructuring, plant closures, tens of thousands of job losses, and broad-ranging cut-backs – there was still too much capacity.

In 2004 European sales were still sluggish, a slump in the value of the dollar made exports to America less valuable, and the falling value of the yen gave Japanese importers another big boost. Ford Europe lost €1.1 billion in the year, Volkswagen reported profits down by half and launched a €2 billion cost-cutting exercise, and General Motors European operations lost €280 million.

Sources: O'Connell D., Carmakers driven to despair, The Times, 7th March, 2004; Jowit J., Overcapacity costing car sector $130 billion, Financial Times, 19th January, 1999; BBC news Friday, 12 May, 2000; Websites at www.bbc.co.uk; www.timesonline.co.uk

to their effective capacity. For instance, an office that gets a sudden surge of work might pay employees to work overtime until the backlog is reduced.

A fairer picture of capacity management starts with strategic capacity plans that give the designed capacity available over the long term, typically setting the number of facilities, the capacity of each, locations, and so on. Superimposed on this are tactical decisions that set the effective capacity over the medium term. These typically adjust the number of people employed, responses to seasonal changes, amount of sub-contracting, leasing additional resources, etc. Then there are operational capacity decisions, which set the effective capacity over the short term. These typically look at employees' work schedules, amount of overtime, assignment of resources to operations, dealing with urgent problems, and so on. The aim of capacity management is not just to match capacity of a process and the long-term demand for its product, but also to allow for shorter-term adjustments.

Alternative approaches

There are several ways that managers can make short-term adjustments to the capacity of a process – they might lease extra space, hire more resources, work overtime, employ temporary staff, sub-contract work, or a host of other alternatives. These all assume that managers set the capacity of a process to match the demand for its products – but they could also adjust the demand to match the process capacity, or they could try to minimize any adjustment (see also Comel and Edson).

Supply management   This is the approach that we have emphasized, with short-term adjustments to the effective capacity to match product demand. This is the usual approach as it changes internal factors that managers can control. The obvious way of doing this is to change the working time, by working overtime to increase capacity or undertime to reduce it. Ways of adjusting capacity include:

- changing the work pattern to match demand
- hiring or firing full-time staff
- employing part-time or temporary staff to cover peak demands
- cross-training employees, so that each can move to the job that is most urgent
- using outside contractors
- sharing capacity between products
- renting or leasing extra facilities
- adjusting the speed of the process or the service time
- rescheduling maintenance periods or other backroom activities
- making customers do some of the work, such as automatic banking or ticket machines, or packing their own bags in supermarkets
- redesigning the operations to make them more efficient, perhaps with more automation or in different locations.

Most of these adjustments are fairly straightforward, but they cannot be made too often or too severely, as they affect employees, operations and customers. For example, changing work schedules every few days would be unacceptable as this interferes with employee's personal arrangements, and frequent changes to working hours would confuse customers.

Demand management   This adjusts demand for a product to match the available capacity of its process. This approach is generally more difficult as it has to adjust external factors that are outside the control of the organization's managers. And it may seem strange to manipulate customer demand, rather than generate as much demand as possible. But in practice, this approach is quite common. Coco Chanel was asked why the price of 'No. 5' perfume was so high, and is reputed to have answered, 'If we lower the price, next week everyone will wear Chanel No. 5 – but next year no-one will wear it.' Changing the price is the obvious way of altering demand, offering discounts to encourage more demand, and charging a premium price when there is a shortage of capacity. There are, though, limits to these adjustments, and prices must be high enough to cover costs, low enough to be competitive, and not change too many times to confuse customers. Ways of adjusting demand, include:

- vary the price
- offer incentives, such as free samples, discounts, or off-peak rates
- change the marketing effort
- limit the customers served, by demanding certain qualifications
- change related products, to encourage substitution
- vary the lead time
- use a reservation or appointment system
- use stocks to cushion demand.

When we think about demand management, our initial concern is usually to increase demand – but when capacity is low and demand is high managers have to actively discourage demand. At first, this seems strange, but it is really quite common. There are many sporting events, like the final at Wimbledon, where there is a huge demand for seats, but only a limited number available. Then the organizers have to find ways of allocating these seats in the most appropriate way. Other examples of demand management include professional institutions which demand qualifications from new entrants, popular restaurants which have queues at busy times, airlines which charge more for executive facilities, specialist cars with long delivery times, artists who produce limited edition prints, fashionable clothes that charge high prices, and so on.

Minimizing the adjustment   This looks for ways of matching capacity and demand without making severe changes to either. This approach has the benefits of keeping the process working smoothly at its most efficient output, and not distorting customer demand or inconveniencing them. The obvious way of arranging this is through stocks – with stocks building-up when capacity exceeds demand and falling when demand exceeds capacity. Of course, the ideal solution is to have spare capacity available, but transferred to other products until it is needed. In practice, this is rarely achievable.

Chapter review

- Every process has a capacity, which is the maximum amount it can produce in a given time. This is sometimes obvious, but it usually needs calculating or agreement. The capacity of the whole process is limited by the amount that can be processed at the bottleneck.
- There are several key definitions for capacity: designed capacity is the maximum output of a process in ideal conditions; effective capacity is the sustainable output under normal circumstances. Related measures consider capacity utilization and efficiency.
- Changes to the process are usually expensive and long term, so capacity is essentially a strategic function.
- Capacity planning matches available capacity and product demand. Any errors are expensive, giving either unmet demand or under-used facilities.
- We described a standard approach to capacity planning with six steps. In practice, this usually involves an iterative method that looks for an acceptable solution that balances competing factors.
- Both demand and capacity change over time. Managers have to continually monitor operations to make sure that there is still a good match between the two. Important decisions concern the timing and size of adjustments to capacity.
- There are systematic variations in capacity, caused by factors like learning effects, maintenance, replacement policies and business cycles. Superimposed on these are shorter-term variations.
- Capacity management is essentially a strategic function, setting the long-term capacity, but it includes both tactical and operational adjustments. These can adjust either the capacity of the process or the demand for products, or look for some approach that minimizes the adjustment.

Discussion questions

1 Why is capacity management a strategic issue? To what extent do tactical and operational factors influence the capacity?

2 Capacity is not really an absolute limit on the output from a process, but it is a measure of management performance. Do you agree with this?

3 You often see notices at the entrance to pubs, clubs, halls and other buildings saying that, 'The capacity of this facility is 200 people'. What does this really mean?

4 Is it always possible to find the capacity of a process? How can you find the capacity of a shopping mall, national park or a shipping lane? Can you give examples where it is difficult to find a capacity, and say how these difficulties are overcome?

5 Is it better to have frequent small changes in capacity, or fewer large ones?

6 Why does capacity change over time?

CASE STUDY Heathrow Airport

The capacity of an airport is usually stated in terms of the number of passengers that can use it in a year. This capacity depends on several factors. The first is the number of runways, which limit the number of time slots available for planes to land and take-off. Any increase in the number of runways comes at very high capital, environmental, and social costs. An alternative is to use existing runways more efficiently, increasing the number of time slots. Safety demands a certain minimum distance between planes, so there is a practical limit on this option. Another alternative is to encourage airlines to use bigger planes, so that more people fit into each time slot. There is a trend towards bigger planes, leading to the 800 seat Airbus A380 which comes into general service after 2006. Of course, rather than use bigger planes, airlines could simply increase the occupancy of each plane, but they have already gone about as far as possible in this direction.

The other major constraint on capacity is the terminal buildings that provide passenger facilities, but which again come at high capital, environmental and social cost.

After considering 52 locations, a decision was made in 1943 to build the main airport for London at Heathrow, and it was officially opened in 1946. By the end of the first year the airport had served 60,000 passengers travelling to 18 destinations. By 2005 this had expanded to 63 million passengers travelling to 170 destinations on 90 airlines. This was at – and arguably well-over – Heathrow's capacity, and continuing growth in passenger numbers had forced many flights to transfer to other airports. Gatwick, Stansted and Luton had grown around London, and these, in turn, had reached their capacity – and needed continual expansion, with passengers moved to more distant airports.

Heathrow had long been arguing for an expansion, and approval was given for a new terminal in 2001, after the longest public inquiry in British history (46 months). The planning process itself cost $120 million over a period of 14 years.

Construction of Terminal 5 started in 2002, with a budget of £4.2 billion sponsored by British Airports Authority (BAA), private finance and the government. The project has two phases. Phase 1, due in April 2008, will provide 47 aircraft stands and will increase capacity by 27 million a year. Phase 2 is due in 2011 and will add another 13 aircraft stands, and will add another 3 million passengers a year. The airport currently employs 68,000 people and this will rise by 16,500 after these expansions.

The building has been designed by Richard Rogers Partnership, with over 60 contractors responsible for different aspects of the building. As well as the terminal building itself and associated aircraft stands and taxiway, the development includes a new control tower, extensions to the Heathrow Express rail link to Paddington, an extension of the Piccadilly underground line, a motorway spur to the M25, a 4,000 space car park, diversion of two rivers, and a water recycling system.

Questions

● How can BAA measure the capacity of Heathrow? What factors affect this capacity?

● For years, Heathrow has been operating beyond its designed capacity. What effects does this have?

● Airports like Heathrow continue to expand. What will eventually limit their capacity?

Sources: Websites at www.BAA.co.uk; www.airport-technology .com

7 Capacity planning is a waste of time. Long-term forecasts of demand are unreliable, and both capacity and demand vary in unknown ways. So organizations should simply get enough capacity to cover likely demand for the future. What do you think of this view?

8 Nobody would seriously consider limiting demand for a product, but would always look for ways of increasing process capacity. Is this true?

Useful websites

www.airport-technology.com
www.apqc.org – American Productivity and Quality Centre
www.autolligence.com
www.baa.co.uk
www.bbc.co.uk
www.gsk.com
www.justauto.com
www.smrp.org – Society for Maintenance and Reliability Professionals
www.sre.org – Society for Reliability
www.timesonline.co.uk

References

August J., Applied reliability centred maintenance, Pennwell, Tulsa, OK, 2000.

Comel J.G. and Edson N.W., Gaining control: capacity management and scheduling, John Wiley, New York, 1995.

Condra L.W., Reliability improvement with design of experiments, Marcel Dekker, New York, 1993.

Financial Times, When the chips are down, 16th July, 1999.

Goldratt M. and Cox J., The goal, North River Press, Boston, MA, 1986.

Hayes R.H. and Wheelwright S.C., Restoring our competitive edge, John Wiley, New York, 1984.

Jowit J., Overcapacity costing car sector $130 billion, Financial Times, 19th January, 1999.

Klammer T.P. and Klammer T., Capacity management and improvement, Irwin, Homewood, IL, 1996.

Menasse D., Capacity planning: a practical approach, Prentice Hall, Englewood Cliffs, NJ, 1993.

Moubray J., Reliability-centred maintenance (2nd edition), Industrial Press, New York, 2001.

Schmenner R.W. and Swink M., On theory in operations management, Journal of Operations Management, vol 17, pp 97–113, 1998.

Stratton A, Capacity management, Canadian Management Accountants Magazine, February 1996.

Vollman T.E., Berry W.L., Whybark D.C. and Jacobs S., Manufacturing planning and control systems (5th edition), McGraw-Hill, New York, 2004.

Waters D., Quantitative methods for business, Financial Times Prentice Hall, Harlow, 2001.

Waters D., Inventory control and management (2nd edition), John Wiley, Chichester, 2003.

CHAPTER 13
Structure of the Supply Chain

Products move through a series of operations in their process. Usually this means that there is a physical flow of materials through related supply chains. In this chapter we look at the structure of supply chains, and the way that their design supports broader operations. Particular concerns are the number and location of facilities, and the relationships between them. In the next chapter, we see how managers control the flow of materials through these supply chains.

After reading this chapter you should be able to:

- Explain the role of logistics – or supply chain management
- Appreciate the role and importance of supply chains
- Describe the structure of a supply chain and the factors that affect its design
- Understand the benefits of integrated logistics within an organization
- Discuss ways to integrate logistics along the supply chain
- Appreciate the importance of location decisions
- Describe methods for finding the best location for facilities

Aims of the chapter

The key concepts discussed in this chapter are:

- The **supply chain**, which is the series of activities and organizations through which materials move on their journey from initial suppliers through to final customers
- **Logistics** or **supply chain management**, which is responsible for the movement of materials through the supply chain
- **Integration** of activities along the supply chain
- **Location** of facilities

Main themes

LOGISTICS AND THE SUPPLY CHAIN

Essential activities

A product moves through a series of operations in its process. This movement is almost invariably associated with a physical flow of materials. This is obvious with goods, when raw materials are physically moved into the operations and finished goods are delivered to customers at the end – but it is also true of services. When you catch a plane, the airline gives you a service, and it also moves a lot of supporting materials, including your luggage; when you eat in a restaurant, someone has to move all the food and associated materials. The function responsible for this movement of materials is **logistics** or **supply chain management** (Waters, 2003b; Coyle *et al.*; Gattorna and Walters; Poitier; Copacino).

> ● **Logistics** – or **supply chain management** – is responsible for all the physical movement of materials.
> ● This includes movement into the process from suppliers, through operations, and then out of the process to customers.

This is an essential function in all operations, and Christopher (1998) says that, 'Logistics has always been a central and essential feature of all economic activity.' Shapiro and Heskett agree, saying that, 'There are few aspects of human activity that do not ultimately depend on the flow of goods from point of origin to point of consumption.' Without logistics, no materials move, no operations are done, no products are delivered, and no customers are served.

Logistics is also expensive, but it is difficult to give an exact figure for the costs. Normal accounting conventions do not separate expenditure on logistics, and there is some disagreement about the activities to include. Few managers can give a precise figure for their logistics costs, but a rule of thumb suggests 15–20 percent of turnover (Waters, 2003a). The UK government says that 12 percent of the GDP comes from wholesale and retail trades and 6 percent comes from transport and storage, implying that overall logistics costs are much higher (Office of National Statistics). This might support an earlier estimate by Childerley that logistics accounted for 32.5 percent of the UK GDP.

When organizing the flow of materials, the broad function of logistics is responsible for a series of related activities (Waters, 2003b), including:

- **Procurement or purchasing** – acquires raw materials from suppliers.
- **Inward transport** – moves the materials from suppliers to operations.
- **Receiving** – checks materials delivered and accepts them into operations.
- **Warehousing or stores** – stores materials until they are needed.
- **Stock control** – sets the policies for inventory levels, orders, etc.
- **Order picking** – finds and removes materials from stores.
- **Material handling** – moves materials during operations.

- **Distribution** – delivers finished goods to customers.
- **Recycling, returns and waste disposal** – to reuse, return, sell or otherwise dispose of materials not needed by the organization.
- **Location** – decides how many facilities there should be, and finds the best locations.
- **Communication** – keeps and reports all records for the logistics system.

Chain of organizations

These activities exist in all operations – but they do not work in isolation. Operations in one organization act as customers when they buy materials from their own suppliers, and then they act as suppliers when they deliver materials to their own customers. A wholesaler, for example, acts as a customer when buying goods from manufacturers, and then as a supplier when selling goods to retail shops. Extending this view, we have materials flowing through a series of organizations as they travel from original suppliers through to final customers. Milk moves through a farm, tanker collection, dairy, bottling plant, distributor, and supermarket before we buy it. A plastic cup starts its journey with a company extracting crude oil, and then it passes through pipelines, refineries, shippers, chemical works, plastics companies, manufacturers, importers, transport companies, wholesalers and retailers before you get it filled with coffee. In previous chapters we described this series of operations as the process, and we know that people use other terms, such as Porter's 'value chain', or 'demand chain'. These different names emphasize different aspects of the process, and when emphasizing the movement of materials, it is usually called a **supply chain**.

- A **supply chain** consists of the series of activities and organizations that materials move through on their journey from initial suppliers to final customers.

The Institute of Logistics and Transport defines logistics as 'the time-related positioning of resources, or the strategic management of the total supply chain' – with a supply chain as, 'a sequence of events intended to satisfy a customer'.

Every product has its own unique supply chain, which exists to overcome the gaps created when suppliers are some distance away from their customers. Supply chains allow for operations that are best done – or can only be done – at locations that are distant from customers or sources of materials. Coffee beans grow in South America, but the main customers are in Europe and North America; the best locations for power stations are away from both their main customers in cities and their fuel supplies. And supply chains also allow for mismatches between supply and demand. For example, the demand for sugar is more or less constant throughout the year, but the supply varies with the harvesting of sugar cane and beet. When there is excess supply, stocks are built-up in the supply chain, and these are used after the harvests finish.

Logistics is clearly a central part of operations, but it did not get much attention until the 1960s when Drucker was able to describe it as, 'the economy's dark continent'. More recently managers have recognized its importance, and are taking a new look at logistics as a way of both improving customer service and reducing costs. They realize that logistics is important because it:

- is essential – all organizations must move materials
- is expensive – the costs can be high, with considerable potential savings
- directly affects profits – as an unavoidable overhead
- forms the main links with suppliers and customers
- determines lead time, reliability and other measures of customer service
- gives public exposure – with advertising on trucks, etc.
- can be risky, with safety considerations
- determines the size and location of facilities
- may prohibit some operations – such as moving excessive loads.

This picture of logistics moving materials along a supply chain emphasizes an important point. All organizations in the same supply chain add value to the same product, so they have a common interest in making sure that the product satisfies final customers. The implication is that they should cooperate to give a smooth and efficient flow of products through to final customers. Competitors are not other organizations in the same supply chain, but organizations in other supply chains who are moving their own products to satisfy the same final customers (Christopher, 1996).

Unfortunately, this picture of cooperation has an obvious flaw. All along the supply chain, buyers pay sellers for their products, and they have fundamentally opposing positions – buyers want to pay as little as possible for expensive materials, while sellers want to charge as much as possible for cheap ones. So there is always some element of competition at the interfaces within a supply chain. And the price paid by the final customer determines the total added value that is shared by organizations along the supply chain – so there is always competition to get a bigger share of this fixed amount.

There is always some competition between organizations that essentially work together – and in the same way there can be cooperation between organizations that are essentially competitors. For example, shops in a mall work together to attract people into the mall, but then compete for their custom. Similarly, organizations work together to form lobby groups that promote their industry, and hotels cooperate when attracting people to a resort, but then compete when people decide where to stay. Brandenburger and Nalebuff include this effect in their description of an organization surrounded by four other players – suppliers, customers, competitors and complementors. Then complementors are organizations that supply complementary products, in the way that finance companies are complementors to vehicle traders, credit card companies are complementors to e-business companies, and DVD manufacturers are complementors to film makers. So competitors can also be complementors.

Structure of a supply chain

The simplest view of a supply chain has a single product moving through a series of organizations, each of which adds value to the product. Along with this flow of materials there are associated flows of information and money – predominantly in the reverse direction. Taking one organization's point of view, activities in front of it – moving materials inwards – are called **upstream**; those after the organization – moving materials outwards – are called **downstream**.

Upstream activities are divided into **tiers** of suppliers. A supplier that sends materials directly to the operations is a first tier supplier; one that sends materials to a first tier supplier is a second tier supplier; one that sends materials to a second tier supplier is a third tier supplier, and so on back to the original sources. Most organizations get materials from many different suppliers, so the supply chain converges as raw materials move in through the tiers of suppliers. Customers are also divided into tiers; one that buys products directly from the operations is a first tier customer; one that gets products from a first tier customer is a second tier customer; one that get products from a second tier customer is a third tier customer, and so on to the final customers. Most organizations sell products to many different customers, so the supply chain diverges as products move out through tiers of customers (as illustrated in Figure 13.1).

Each organization works with many – often thousands – of different products, each of which has its own supply chain. The French company Carrefour is Europe's largest retailer, and this comes at the end of tens of thousands of supply chains; Corus makes steel that is used in countless final products. Some people argue that the term 'supply chain' gives too simple a view and we should really talk about a 'supply network' or 'supply web'. There is little agreement about this, so we shall stick to the most widely used term of 'supply chain'.

IDEAS IN PRACTICE Wal-Mart

In 1962 Sam Walton opened his first discount store in Rogers, Arizona, with an underlying strategy of a wide choice of goods, low prices and friendly service. His store was an immediate success, and he quickly opened more branches. In 1983 he expanded the format to SAM'S CLUB warehouses for members, and in 1988 the first Supercenter selling groceries. In 1991 Wal-Mart started its international expansion, first in Mexico, Puerto Rico and Canada, and then into South America, Asia and Europe.

By 2000 it was the world's largest retailer with 4,000 stores, serving 100 million customers a week, employing 1.2 million staff – or 'associates' – with an annual turnover of US$175 billion. By 2005 this had risen to 5,200 stores (3,600 in the USA and 1,600 in other countries), serving 138 million customers a

week, employing 1.6 million staff and with a turnover of $285 billion.

The logistics operations at Wal-Mart are huge. In the mainland USA they have 61,000 suppliers delivering $3 billion dollars worth of materials a week (supporting another 3 million jobs). This goes to Wal-Mart's 70 main distribution centres, and then on to stores. Operating costs – and therefore profit – depend entirely on the quality of their logistics so, not surprisingly, they use the 'industry's most efficient and sophisticated distribution system'. Their continued success – and strategy of aggressive expansion – depends on the ability of managers to continue moving goods through their supply chains quickly and at the lowest possible prices.

Sources: Websites at www.walmartstores.com; www.walmart.com; www.walmartfacts.com

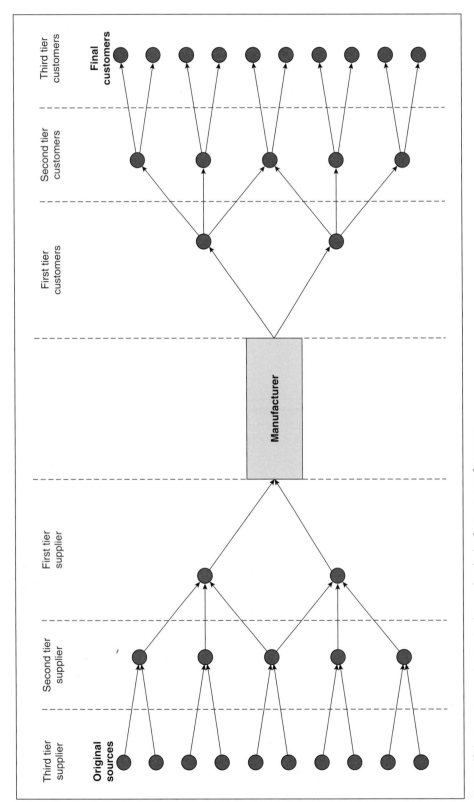

Figure 13.1 Structure of a typical supply chain for a manufacturer

DESIGN OF A SUPPLY CHAIN

Strategic decisions

We can summarize the aim of logistics as moving materials quickly, efficiently and at low cost through the supply chain. This is often described as getting, 'the right materials, to the right place, at the right time, from the right source, with the right quality, at the right price'. This movement does not happen by chance, but needs careful management and, in particular, strategic direction.

Ballou describes four areas needing strategic decisions in the supply chain as customer service, facility location, inventory policy and transport. Helming and Zonnenberg extend this to five strategic areas of supply chain configuration, enabling practices, strategic relationships, organization and application of information technology. They also emphasize the importance of implementation strategy by saying, 'Companies hurl staggering sums of money and human resources at their supply chain infrastructure, only to fail at implementing their supply chain strategy.' A broader view says that every aspect of logistics from procurement through to final delivery can have a strategic impact. As we saw with operations in general, even the smallest detail can, under the right conditions, have a long-term effect on performance.

Here we classify strategic decisions for supply chain managers as of two types. Firstly, there are decisions that design the structure of the chain, showing the facilities, their relationships and locations. Secondly, there is the mechanism for moving material through the chain. We look at the structure in the rest of this chapter, and return to the flow of materials in the next chapter.

The most important decisions about supply chain structure are likely to concern the shape of the chain (setting its width and length), the number of distinct facilities, their function, the size of each, the type of operation at each facility, location of these facilities, capacity at each location, location of stock, customers served from each facility, transport arrangements, relations between organizations, and so on. Of course, these decisions are all interrelated, so that the best number of facilities depends on the capacity of each – and we have already discussed questions of capacity in the last chapter.

Alternative shapes

Every product has its own unique supply chain, and they come in an almost endless variety. Some are very short and simple – such as a cook buying potatoes directly from a farmer. Others are very long and have many tiers of suppliers and customers. The supply chain for Cadbury's starts with cocoa beans growing on farms and ends with the delivery of bars of chocolate to hungry customers; the supply chain for Levi-Strauss jeans starts with cotton growing in a field and ends when you buy them in a shop. Some supply chains are very narrow with hardly any merging or division; others are very wide with many parallel routes. The supply chain for a computer manufacturer, for example, brings together many separate supply chains as Intel provide the processor, Matshita the DVD drive, Agfa the scanner, Hewlett-Packard the printer, Microsoft the operating system, and so on.

Of course, the reason for the different shapes is that each is best suited to different types of product. The main features of a product that influence the design of the supply chain are its value, bulk, perishability, complexity, availability, and profitability.

Building sand has low value, is bulky, and is readily available; most of its cost comes from transport, so it is best to use suppliers as close as possible to the final customer. This gives very short and simple supply chains, and you often buy sand directly from the extractor. Apple iPods are small, expensive, complicated, and are assembled from high technology components in specialized factories. They have a much more complicated supply chain that stretches around the world.

However, it is not just the type of product that determines the shape of the supply chain, as it also depends on the operations strategy. A company that focuses on fast service will use a supply chain with operations near to final customers, so that it can make quick deliveries; a company that focuses on low costs will centralize all operations in a few, large facilities that give economies of scale. Other factors that affect the structure of the supply chain include the type of customer demand, economic climate, availability of logistics services, culture, rate of innovation, competition, market and financial arrangements.

The key features that define the shape of a supply chain are its length and breadth (as shown in Figure 13.2).

- **Supply chain length** is the number of tiers, or intermediaries, that materials flow through between source and destination. You might imagine a supply chain with raw material suppliers, main operations, wholesalers and retailers. Some supply chains are shorter than this when, for example, producers sell directly to final customers through a Website. Usually, though, supply chains are much longer with many intermediaries, perhaps including several stages of manufacturing, and several stages in the distribution of finished products. This can be particularly noticeable when exporters use a series of logistics centres, transport operators, agents, freight forwarders, brokers and agents to move materials through different parts of their journey.

- **Supply chain breadth** is the number of parallel routes that materials can flow through. You can imagine this in terms of the number of routes out to final customers. Cadbury's has a broad supply chain, which means that you can buy their chocolate in a huge number of retailers; Thornton's has a narrower chain, and most of their chocolate sells through their own shops; Pigalle et Fils has a very narrow chain and they only sell their chocolate in two shops in Belgium.

The best choice of length and breadth depends on many factors, with three of the most important being the amount of control that an organization wants over its logistics, the quality of customer service and the cost. A manufacturer delivering directly to its customers has a short, narrow supply chain (like Figure 13.2a). This gives them a lot of control over logistics, but it may be difficult to get either high customer service or low costs. Broadening the chain (Figure 13.2b) gives facilities nearer to customers and improves service, but it increases costs and reduces the manufacturer's control. Making the supply chain long and narrow (Figure 13.2c) uses the expertise of intermediaries to reduce costs, but the manufacturer loses some control and the customer service does not improve. Making the supply chain both long and broad (Figure 13.2d) removes most control from the manufacturer, but customers get good service.

In general, there is a clear trend towards shorter supply chains, as managers realize that they can both reduce costs and improve customer service by moving materials quickly though a shorter chain. This means removing layers of intermediaries, and concentrating operations in fewer facilities. There are many ways of achieving this, such as

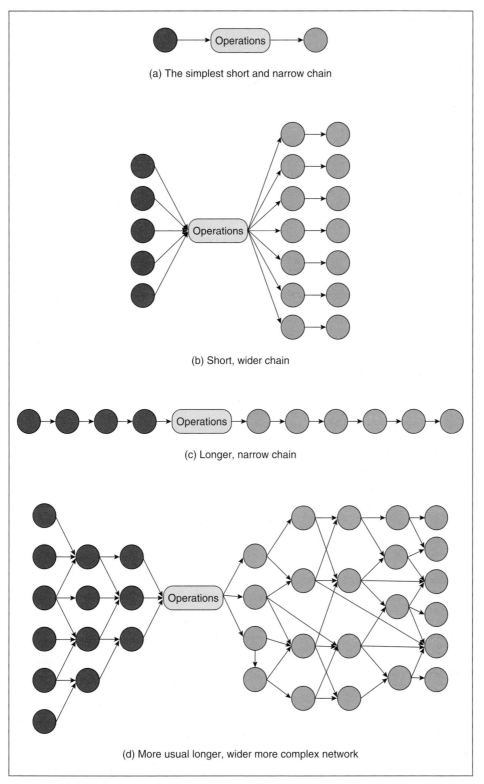

(a) The simplest short and narrow chain

(b) Short, wider chain

(c) Longer, narrow chain

(d) More usual longer, wider more complex network

Figure 13.2 Alternate shapes of supply chains

manufacturers dealing directly with final customers through their Website, or taking advantage of the free movement of materials within the European Union to replace separate national warehouses by a single European logistics centre.

Usually managers do not have to consider all of these questions together or design a supply chain from scratch, but they look for improvements to an existing chain. For this, they can use a variation on our standard planning model, which looks at current operations, sees how well these are performing, and then looks for improvements – as outlined in the following procedure.

Step 1. *Examine the aims of logistics*, finding what logistics should achieve in terms of customer service, costs, speed, etc.

Step 2. *Do a logistics audit,* describing the details of current logistics, including the location of facilities, networks connecting these, measures of performance, and industry benchmarks (an approach to a logistics audit is outlined in the case study at the end of the chapter).

Step 3. *Identify mismatches and problems,* where there are differences between the aims (from step 1) and actual performance (from step 2).

Step 4. *Examine alternatives for overcoming the mismatch*, looking at the general features of the supply chain to see how its structure can be improved.

Step 5. *Add details to the supply chain,* defining the precise facilities needed, their location, size, relationships, etc.

Step 6. *Implement the solutions*, doing whatever is needed to execute the changes.

As with all planning, this is not a straightforward procedure, but can involve a lot of iterations, with final decisions usually based on discussion and agreement.

IDEAS IN PRACTICE ShoeRight Limited

ShoeRight Limited is a manufacturer of shoes based in Lahore, India. Figure 13.3 shows part of their supply chain, describing the distribution of shoes to final customers. This distribution has finished shoes passed to a logistics centre which either prepares them for the domestic market or sends them to a shipper for export. For the domestic market shoes are passed to the final customer either by direct sales (mail order, Websites or factory shops) or to a distributor who passes them to general retailers (specialized shoe shops, clothes shops, supermarkets, large multiple

retailers, small multiple retailers or mixed retailers) or specialist retailers (such as shopping clubs, discount stores, retail warehouses, and door-to-door sales). Then there are other intermediaries, such as wholesalers, buying groups, agents, brokers, cooperatives, etc. And superimposed on the chain are specialized services such as transport, warehousing, finance, freight forwarders, etc. The whole picture becomes very complicated, and a pair of shoes can pass through a surprisingly large number of hands before it reaches the final customer.

(continued)

IDEAS IN PRACTICE ShoeRight Limited (continued)

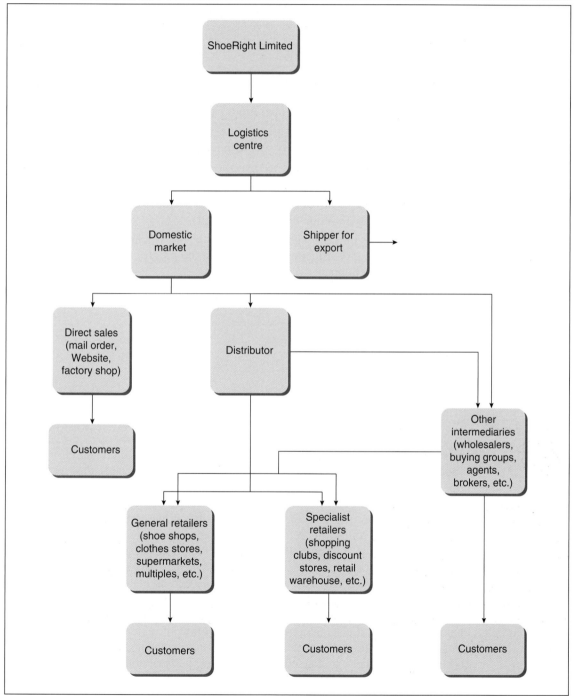

Figure 13.3 Part of the supply chain for ShoeRight Limited

Trends in supply chain management

We have mentioned the trend towards shorter supply chains, but there are many other trends that have a strategic effect on logistics, including:

- integration of supply chains (which we describe in the next section)
- improving communications, which gives greater control of movements throughout the supply chain
- e-business, which allow customers to buy directly from earlier tiers of suppliers
- globalization, reducing the effect of distance and increasing global competition
- outsourcing logistics so that operations can concentrate on their core activities
- improving service, as customers become more demanding they look for better performance in costs, delivery speed, innovation and service level
- reduced number of suppliers, as operations develop long-term relationships and do more business with a smaller set of favoured suppliers
- 'pull' systems such as just-in-time which pulls material through the supply chain (which we describe in the next chapter)
- other methods of reducing the lead-time, such as 'synchronized material scheduling' that coordinates information in the supply chain, and 'cross docking' that eliminates storage in warehouses
- other methods of reducing stock, such as 'vendor managed inventory' where suppliers manage downstream stocks.

INTEGRATING THE SUPPLY CHAIN

Problems with separate activities

We have listed the separate activities that usually form logistics, but if each of them is managed separately they will all have different aims. Transport will try to give fast delivery, inventory control will try to minimize the investment in stock, purchasing will try to reduce material costs, and so on. Although these are all worthy aims, they move operations in different directions – and the activities are so closely related that decisions on one inevitably affect performance in another. For example, reducing the stock of raw materials will reduce the costs of warehousing – but it increases the chance of shortages, and the costs of disruption for operations, emergency orders for purchasing, and urgent deliveries for transport. Purchasing might reduce its administrative costs by sending fewer, larger orders to suppliers – but this increases average stock levels, needs more warehouse space, raises the amount of money tied-up in the warehouse, increases stock administration costs and can cause problems with transport.

When managers from each activity have control over distinct parts of the supply chain, there are artificial barriers to the smooth flow of materials. Imagine a wholesaler that has one fleet of vehicles run by materials management bringing raw materials in from suppliers, and a separate fleet run by distribution to deliver the same goods out to customers. This might work, but you can see the duplication of effort and waste involved in managing two separate vehicle fleets. Another organization might have three stocks – raw materials, work in progress and finished goods – each run by different departments, using different standards and systems that cannot be linked.

The message is that dividing logistics into separate functions leads to duplicated effort and wasted resources. Some of the broader disadvantages include:

- giving different, often conflicting, objectives within operations
- duplicating effort and wasting resources
- giving poor information flows and coordination between the parts
- reducing the speed of movement through the chain
- making planning more difficult
- introducing unnecessary buffers between the parts, such as stocks of work-in-progress, capacity or transport
- increasing uncertainty
- obscuring important information, such as the total cost of logistics.

The way to get around these problems is to look at the supply chain not as a series of distinct activities, but as a single integrated whole. Managers should not focus on their own distinct activities, but should join together to take a broader view of the whole supply chain, looking for the best results for the organization as a whole.

Integration within an organization

The benefits of an integrated supply chain are clear, but it can be difficult to achieve this with widely dispersed activities. The usual approach takes a series of steps, starting by joining together closely related functions. For example, a purchasing department might take over all aspects of receiving materials up to the point when they are delivered to a stock of raw materials. Many organizations moving along this path were tempted to stop when there were two functions left:

- **materials management**, aligned with production and responsible for the flow of raw materials into and through operations
- **physical distribution**, aligned with marketing and responsible for the outward flow of finished goods.

The next obvious step is to combine these two into a single logistics function responsible for all the movement of materials into, through and out of operations. Most operations now use this approach, having travelled through several stages.

Stage 1. Separate logistics activities are not given much attention or considered important.

Stage 2. Recognizing that the separate activities of logistics are important for the success of the organization.

Stage 3. Making improvements in the separate activities, to ensure that each is as efficient as possible.

Stage 4. Internal integration – recognizing the benefits of internal cooperation and combining the separate activities into a single function.

Stage 5. Developing a logistics strategy, to set the long-term direction of logistics.

Stage 6. Benchmarking – comparing logistics' performance with other organizations, learning from their experiences, identifying areas that need improvement and finding ways of achieving this.

Stage 7. Continuous improvement – accepting that further changes are inevitable and always searching for better ways of organizing logistics.

By Stage 4 operations have integrated their logistics, and the last three stages show how the function can be improved. Stage 5 emphasizes the need for a strategic view, Stage 6 looks at other organizations for comparisons and lessons, and Stage 7 recognizes that logistics must continually evolve. But this is not the end of the story. Once an organization has efficient, integrated and strategic logistics, it can start looking at integration along more of the supply chain.

Integration along the supply chain

Each organization accounts for only one step in the supply chain, so when each organizes its own logistics, there is still a fragmented flow of material. Forrester described an interesting consequence of this, that can be illustrated with a retailer noticing that demand for a product has risen by 5 units in a week. When it is time to place the next order, the retailer assumes demand is rising and orders ten extra units to make sure it has enough. The local wholesaler sees demand rise by ten units, and orders an extra 20 units to meet the growth. The regional wholesaler sees demand rise by 20 units, so it orders another 40 units. As this movement travels through the supply chain, a relatively small change in final demand is amplified into a major variation for early suppliers (Lee *et al.*).

Other problems with a fragmented supply chain arise from the traditional view of organizations as adversaries; when a purchaser pays money to a seller it is assumed that one can only benefit at the expense of the other. If the purchaser gets a good deal, it automatically means that the seller is losing out: if the seller makes a good profit, it means that the purchaser pays too much. This adversarial attitude means that there is no cooperation, only short-term concerns, and everyone tries to make as much profit as possible from each deal. Each organization is concerned only with their own objectives and will – when convenient to themselves – change specifications, conditions, suppliers, order patterns, delivery requirements, prices, and just about everything else.

We have described the benefits of integrating logistics within an organization, and can extend these arguments to include further integration along the supply chain. If each organization only looks at its own operations, there are unnecessary barriers between them, disrupting the flow of materials and increasing costs. **External integration** removes these boundaries to improve the whole chain. Christopher (1999) advises this, saying that 'Most opportunities for cost reduction and/or value enhancement lie at the interface between supply chain partners.' Then the benefits of external integration include:

- genuine cooperation between all parts of the supply chain, with shared information, systems, resources, research, development, skills and expertise;

- lower costs – due to balanced operations, lower stocks, less expediting, economies of scale, elimination of activities that waste time or do not add value;
- improved performance – due to more accurate forecasts, better planning, higher utilization of resources, rational priorities, fewer mistakes and problems;
- improved material flow, with coordination giving faster and more reliable movements;
- better customer service, with shorter lead times, faster deliveries, more customization and fewer problems;
- more flexibility, with operations able to react faster to changing conditions;
- standardized procedures becoming routine, with less duplication of effort, information and planning;
- reliable quality with integrated quality management.

Unfortunately, it can be difficult to achieve these benefits. Many managers simply do not trust other members of the supply chain, and they are reluctant to share information let alone work together. Even with sufficient trust, there can be problems with different and competing objectives, different priorities, organizing the exchange of information, incompatible systems, skills needed, security, the complexity of systems, putting too much reliance on one other organization, becoming dependent on their skills and expertise, the time and effort needed, language and cultural barriers, clash of organizational cultures, and so on.

The key point is that organizations must recognize that it is in their own long-term interest to replace conflict by cooperation within a supply chain. They should cooperate with other members of their supply chains, and compete against organizations in other supply chains. This often needs considerable changes of attitude, as suggested in Table 13.1.

Table 13.1 Different views with conflict and cooperation

Factor	Conflict	Cooperation
Profit	An organization only profits at the expense of others	More organizations can share profits
Price	As high/low as possible	Agreed at reasonable level
Relationship	One is dominant	Equal partners
Trust	Little	Extensive
Timeframe	Single order	Long term
Communication	Limited and formal	Widespread and open with shared systems
Information	Secretive	Open and shared
Quality	Blame for faults	Solving shared problems
Contract	Rigid	Flexible
Focus on	Own operations	Final customers

Structures for cooperation

There are several ways that organizations can cooperate, with Lee *et al.* describing three general strategies as:

1 *information sharing* – particularly passing information about final customer demand through the supply chain so that all parts know the exact requirements and can organize their operations accordingly;

2 *channel alignment* – coordinating schedules, material flows, prices and other operations;

3 *operational efficiency* – where parts of the supply chain work together to improve performance, simplify operations, increase the flow of materials and reduce costs.

A starting point for cooperation is the sharing of information between adjacent operations, preferably by directly linking their information systems. You can imagine some benefits of this when a customer is running out of stock of some product. Traditionally the customer notices this, and goes through all the internal procedures to raise an order, sends this to a supplier, who then goes through their procedures for meeting the order. With cooperation and linked information systems, the supplier's system simply notes that the customer is running out of stock and organizes a delivery.

But sharing information is only a starting point for cooperation which can be organized in several ways, ranging from informal arrangements to vertical integration.

Informal cooperation The basic type of cooperation has organizations simply doing business together, and building-up a good working relationship. Perhaps this leads to a designation of preferred suppliers, which can lead to an informal arrangement to coordinate some aspects of operations. This might include EDI links to share information, combining loads to reduce transport costs, agreeing package sizes to ease material handling, joining with other organizations to make joint purchases, and so on. This cooperation can grow to include more functions, with other organizations included in the arrangement. Japanese companies often extend this idea in *Keiretsu* – which are groups of organizations that work together without actually forming partnerships.

Contractual arrangement An informal arrangement has the advantage of being flexible and non-binding. On the other hand, it has the disadvantage that either party can end the cooperation without warning, and at any time that suits them. This is why many organizations prefer a more formal arrangement, with a written contract setting-out the obligations of each party. These are common when organizations see themselves as working together for some time. An electricity company, for example, might agree to supply power at a fixed price for the next three years, provided a customer buys some minimum quantity. More formal agreements have the advantage of showing the details of the commitment, so that each side knows exactly what it has to do. On the other hand, they have the disadvantage of losing flexibility and imposing rigid conditions. In 2001, for example, there were power cuts in California when electricity suppliers found that their long-term contracts with customers specified prices that were too low to cover the rising costs of generation.

A common type of contractual arrangement outsources non-core activities. The essence of **outsourcing** is that some activities are transferred to another organization that can do them more efficiently (Gay and Essinger). For a long time this has been standard practice for ancillary activities, such as legal services, catering, transport, printing, security and transport – but is being used increasingly for more central operations, such as information processing, IT services, warehousing, pension funding, public relations and accounting. In the European Union around 70 percent of transport is now outsourced, along with 45 percent of warehousing, 40 percent of transport management, 25 percent of IT and 10 percent of order processing. There is a clear trend towards outsourcing – particularly logistics – as organizations concentrate on their core activities, look for lower capital costs, reduce operating costs, give better service, use the latest technology, and all the other benefits that can come from outsourcing.

An interesting form of outsourcing occurs when an organization chooses not to do any operations itself, but outsources all operations and coordinates the activities of other organizations. This is the basis of 'virtual organizations'. It is also the usual approach of film makers, where a studio forms a production company specifically to make a particular film. This production company does not make the film itself, but sub-contracts all the work to other companies, sells the end result to the studio, and is then disbanded.

Strategic alliances When organizations are working well together, they may both feel that they are getting the best possible results and neither could benefit from trading with other partners. Then they might look for a long-term relationship which guarantees that their mutual benefits continue. This is the basis of a **strategic alliance** or **partnership**. Ellram and Krause define this as, 'an ongoing relationship between firms, which involves a commitment over an extended time period, and a mutual sharing of information and the risks and rewards of the relationship'.

Partnerships can dramatically change operations. When a supplier knows that it has long-term, repeat business it can invest in improvements to products and operations. The partnership might encourage a supplier to reduce its product range and specialize in one type of product, making it as efficiently as possible and concentrating on giving a small number of customers a very high quality service. At the same time, a customer knows that it has guaranteed – and continually improving – supplies so it no longer has to look around to get the best deals and can reduce the number of suppliers. Japanese companies were among the first to develop strategic alliances, and at the time when Toyota had formed partnerships with its 250 suppliers, General Motors was still working separately with 4,000 suppliers.

The main features of an alliance are:

- organizations working closely together at all levels
- long-term commitment
- openness and mutual trust
- mutual benefits, with agreement on costs and profits to give fair and equitable sharing of rewards
- shared goals, information, expertise, planning, systems and culture
- joint development of products and processes
- continuous improvements in all aspects of the alliance
- flexibility and willingness to solve joint problems
- increasing business between partners with fewer outside relationships.

The majority of major organizations have moved towards partnerships, usually starting with a project team to identify benefits, consider potential partners, define objectives, set timetables, list resource implications, negotiate terms, and so on. When this project team reports, potential partners can be approached and negotiations begin. Some factors that contribute to a successful partnership include management commitment, a high level of achieved service, real cost savings, a growing amount of business, and compatibility of cultures (see also Rowley). Lambert *et al.* summarize these as:

- **drivers**, which are the compelling reasons for forming partnerships, such as cost reduction, better customer service, or security
- **facilitators**, which are the supportive factors that encourage successful partnerships, such as compatibility of operations, similar management styles, common aims, etc.
- **components**, which are the joint activities and operations used to build and sustain the relationship, such as communication channels, joint planning, shared risk and rewards, investment, etc.

Partnerships do not work for every organization – particularly those that only buy a few materials, or do not want to share confidential information, or cannot find reliable suppliers. And some managers are often concerned that terms, particularly price, may not remain competitive, so they prefer a free market approach (Kapoor and Gupta). Another concern is that by concentrating on trade between two partners, both miss opportunities for economies of scale.

Vertical integration If managers want to move beyond partnerships, they really have to own more of the supply chain. A common arrangement has an organization taking a minority share in a major supplier or customer, which gives some say in their operations, but falls short of outright control. A manufacturer, for example, might take a minority share in a wholesaler, to get some influence in the way that its products are distributed. Another option is for two organizations to start a joint venture, where they both put up funds to start a third company with shared ownership. For example, a manufacturer and supplier might together form a transport company for moving materials between the two.

The most common arrangement has one organization simply buying another, thereby increasing the amount of **vertical integration**, which describes the amount of a supply chain that is owned by one organization. If a company buys materials from outside suppliers and sells products to external customers, it does not own much of the supply chain and has little vertical integration. If the company owns initial suppliers, does most of the value adding operations, and distributes products to final customers, it owns a lot of the supply chain and is highly vertically integrated. When an organization owns a lot of the upstream suppliers it has 'backward integration'; when it owns a lot of the downstream customers it has 'forward integration'.

Vertical integration is often the best way of getting different parts of the supply chain to work together. For example, oil companies are generally vertically integrated doing everything from exploring for new oil through to selling to final customers. This brings advantages that include:

- assured and reliable supplies of materials
- easier coordination and greater control of the supply chain

IDEAS IN PRACTICE Petro-Canada

Petro-Canada (PC) is the largest oil company in Canada, originally founded by the Canadian government to compete with major international companies in developing the country's oil assets. It has long been privatized (although the government still owns some shares), and the majority of its income comes from its filling stations.

PC has been forming strategic alliances with its major suppliers since the 1990s. The original impetus was to reduce the cost of acquiring materials that was over $2 billion a year (excluding oil). To form these alliances, they developed an approach by benchmarking other companies with histories of successful partnerships, including Motorola and Dow Chemicals. Pressures to improve performance meant that PC had to get results quickly, and they set targets of reducing costs by 15 percent in a first phase, and eventually 25 percent.

PC began talking to prospective partners, looking initially at the suppliers they did most business with, or whose products were critical. There were already long standing, informal relationships with many of these, and PC extended these to create more formal alliances. Important considerations were that the suppliers were committed to high quality, emphasized customer satisfaction, and had the potential to become 'the best of the best'. This gave PC its

potential partners, and the next stage was to form development teams with members from each company, particularly purchasing and user departments. Because of the time-pressure, these teams looked for quick improvements. Their aim was to get the initiative moving, find some quick returns, generate enthusiasm for the ideas, and then move the partnership forward over the longer term.

We can summarize PC's approach to developing partnerships as follows:

1 prepare the organization for alliances with research, training, systems and practices

2 assess the risk and benefits of partnerships, setting aims and targets

3 benchmark other partnership arrangements

4 select qualified suppliers

5 form joint teams to manage the initiative and move it forward

6 confirm the partnership's principles, commitments, relationships and obligations

7 formalize the terms and conditions

8 continue training and improving.

Source: Internal company reports and Website at www.petro-canada.com

---

- compatible systems and technology, allowing greater sharing of information
- improved material flows
- reducing uncertainty in demand with captive customers
- improved performance and lower transaction costs
- bringing together the work of several suppliers into a single enterprise and giving economies of scale.

Despite such benefits, vertical integration is simply not possible for most organizations. Even a company the size of Heinz cannot buy all the farmers, processors, steel mills, canners, wholesalers, retailers and other organizations in the supply chain for their baked beans. And organizations could find that vertical integration is very expensive, leads to huge organizations that spread their resources too thinly, needs

IDEAS IN PRACTICE Sony

In 1975 Sony launched the first video-cassette recorder that was convenient and cheap enough to use at home. The demand for these was high, and other competitors quickly followed. It became clear, that if videos were to be portable, especially for the growing rental market, the industry would have to adopt a standard format for tapes. Sony proposed its Betamax format, which was arguably technically superior, but other manufacturers preferred the VHS format that was becoming more widely used. VHS had the backing of big Hollywood studios, giving a shortage of movies in Betamax format, and after some dispute this was adopted as the standard.

Sony felt that it would have been in a better position to promote its Betamax format if it had more power over the content of videos – and the way to get this was to move into the movie business, becoming 'content providers'. In 1989 they bought Columbia Pictures to form the core of Sony Pictures Entertainment, which regularly heads box office receipts. Despite this, in 1995 when a standard was needed for the growing DVD market, Sony was again unsuccessful in promoting its standard.

Then in 2005 the problem reoccurred with the high capacity successor to DVD. Sony proposed its Blu-ray technology, this time supported by a consortium with Matsushita, Hitachi and Phillips – while competitors preferred the HD-DVD format backed by Toshiba, NEC and Sanyo.

Rather than help Sony, it can be argued that its dual role as supplier of content and recording technology has actually hindered them. When content producers discuss hardware formats, Sony's media interests make it a rival rather than a partner. This dichotomy was apparent when Sony dominated the portable music market with its Walkman, but delayed marketing an MP3 player because of fears from its music division that it would encourage illegal copying of their material from the internet. Apple did not have to consider this and was seen as a disinterested broker, and its iPod soon became the clear market leader.

Sources: The Economist, March 12th, pp 12, 65-67, 2005; Websites at www.sony.com; www.sony.co.uk; www.sony-europe.com

specialized skills and experience that they do not have, gives unbalanced operations, distracts from core capabilities, reduces flexibility to respond to changing conditions, limits innovation as it is more difficult to change, and so on.

LOCATION OF FACILITIES

Importance of location

We have now looked at the shape of a supply chain and the relationship between members, and can now look at a series of decisions related to the location of facilities. We know that the supply chain for even simple products can be long and complicated. Pharmaceutical companies in Switzerland import raw materials from around the world, and distribute them through their supply chains. Every aspect of the supply chain has to be carefully designed – but you might ask why pharmaceuticals are made in Switzerland when their main market is North America? And if someone wants to buy medicines in New Zealand, why do they travel from Switzerland to the Netherlands, Singapore and Australia before moving to New Zealand? This type of question is considered by **facilities location**.

> ● **Facilities location** finds the best geographic location for operations.
> ● Related decisions include the number of locations, size of facility, type of operation, and so on.

Whenever Toyota build a new assembly line, or Carrefour open a new store, or Burger King open a new restaurant, or Pfizer extend their operations in Eastern Europe, they have to make a decision about the best location. This is an important decision that affects the organization's performance for many years. When Nissan opened a factory in Sunderland, they put a lot of effort into choosing the best site, and now have Europe's most productive car plant. But if they had chosen a poor location, they could have low productivity, unreliable deliveries of materials, poor quality products, and high costs. And if they had made a mistake, they could not simply write-off the investment of several billion euros, close down and move to a better place.

This dilemma affects every organization – if they work in the wrong location their performance is poor, but it can be very difficult to move to a new location. Managers hopefully avoid this problem by putting a lot of care into location decisions – which is why you rarely find night clubs in residential areas full of retired people, big petrol stations on country lanes, factories in city centres, or oil refineries too far away from ports. But this care is not always evident and many organizations locate in the wrong place and quickly go out of business. People sometimes seem reluctant to acknowledge that a location is poor, and you can often find a site where a string of shops has opened, each quickly closing down. Another surprisingly common problem is forgetting that location decisions are for the long term, and then being tempted to choose a location to get short-term benefits, such as development grants, temporary rent reductions, or tax breaks. Such sweeteners can be attractive, but they rarely form the basis of good decisions. And even if organizations make exactly the right location decision, circumstances change – like the petrol station that is left stranded far away from traffic when a new by-pass is built, or the small steel mill that is in an excellent location, but is closed as the industry concentrates in fewer, large facilities.

Alternatives to locating new facilities

Managers have to look for new locations when they expand into new markets, or there are changes in the location of customers or suppliers, changes to operations (such as an electricity company moving from coal generators to gas), upgrading of facilities with new technology, changes to logistics (such as a switch from rail transport to road), changes in the transport network, mergers or acquisitions, a lease expires, or a range of other circumstances. So choosing a good location is a common problem for operations managers. The only real way of avoiding this decision is to outsource logistics and leave the decisions to a third party. You might think that one way of avoiding the problem is simply to alter existing ones – but this is still a location decision, as it assumes the current site is the best available. In practice, when an organization wants to change its facilities – either expand, move or contract – it has three alternatives:

● expand or change existing facilities at the present site
● open additional facilities at another site while keeping all existing facilities
● close down existing operations and move.

A rule of thumb says that around 45 percent of organizations expand on the same site – encouraged by the prospect of economies of scale – a similar number open additional facilities, and 10 percent close down existing operations and move.

A common reason for expansion is entry to a new market, but there are different ways of organizing this, which have different impacts on the location of operations. The following five options are listed in order of decreasing investment.

1 *Full local production* – where a company opens complete new facilities in the new market to make and distribute its product.

2 *Local assembly and finishing* – a company makes most of the product in existing facilities, but opens limited facilities in the new market to finish, assemble or customize.

3 *Local warehousing and sales* – a company makes the product in its existing facilities, but sets up its own facilities and salesforce to handle distribution in the new market.

4 *Exporting* – a company makes the product in its existing facilities and sells it to a distributor working in the new market.

5 *Licensing or franchizing* – local organizations are responsible for all operations to make and supply the product in return for a share of the profit.

Having its own local facilities gives an organization more control over products and the supply chain, higher profits, avoidance of import tariffs and quotas, and closer links with customers. On the other hand they need more investment, and give more complex and uncertain operations. The best choice depends on many factors, such as the capital available, risk the organization will accept, target return on investment, existing operations, time-scale, local knowledge, transport costs, tariffs, trade restrictions and available workforce.

An important question for moving into new markets is how the operations will be organized – and what are the relations with the parent organization? There are three types of alternative here.

- An **international** organization maintains its headquarters in the 'home' country and runs its worldwide activities from there; effectively it continues working in its usual way, but has some transactions across international borders.

- A **multinational** or **multidomestic** organization runs facilities in more than one country, but each has its own subsidiary headquarters and a significant level of independence – essentially the organization has found a pattern that works in one country and transferred it across to other countries.

- A **global** company integrates operations across different countries, viewing the whole world as a single market, using standard products, getting economies of scale.

Some people also describe a 'transnational' company, which tries to combine the benefits of large-scale global operations with local responsiveness (as suggested in Figure 13.4) – but the details of the organization to achieve this are less clear. The United Nations described 7,000 companies as transnational in 1975, but this figure had risen to 60,000 by 2000, and the top 500 of these account for 70 percent of world trade and 30 percent of global GDP (Time).

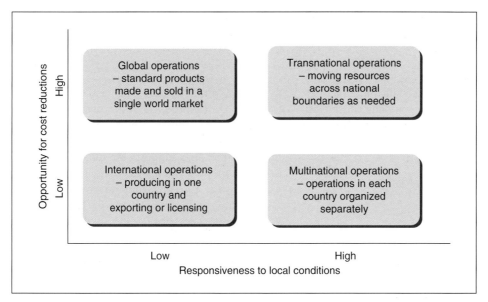

Figure 13.4 Organization for international operations

FINDING THE BEST LOCATION

Choosing a region

Location decisions are invariably difficult. It is difficult for a family to find somewhere to live that satisfies all their needs, but this is trivial compared with a decision about where to open a new logistics centre, hospital, university, amusement park, airport, factory or any other major facility. Managers have to consider many factors, some of which can be measured – or at least estimated – such as operating costs, wage rates, taxes, currency exchange rates, number of competitors, distance from current locations, development grants, population, reliability of supplies. Many other factors are non-quantifiable, such as the quality of infrastructure, political stability, social attitudes, industrial relations, legal system, future developments of the economy, and so on.

There is really a hierarchy of decisions. At the top of this are the broad decisions about which geographic regions to work in. Then more local views consider alternative countries or areas within this region. Then we move to alternative towns and cities within this area. Finally we look at different sites within a preferred town (as shown in Figure 13.6). In 2005, for example, the clothes retailer C&A decided to expand their retail network in central Europe. They looked at various countries and decided to open branches in Poland. Then they looked at cities within Poland and decided to open a branch in Warsaw. After looking at available sites it opened a store in the city centre opposite the Cultural Palace.

The broad decisions about countries and geographical regions to work in are set by the business and operations strategies, with the business strategy playing a bigger role in the higher decisions. An organization with a business strategy of expansion must continually make location decisions for locations in new markets. One clear

IDEAS IN PRACTICE McFarlane and Sons

McFarlane and Sons is a successful manufacturer based in Toronto, Canada. The company considered expansion into the neighbouring US market, and looked at six possible options.

1 open two new small facilities

2 open a new medium-sized facility

3 open a new large facility

4 expand the current facility

5 build a large new facility and close the current one

6 license a local US company.

The costs of these varied, and could be summarized as a fixed annual payment (for rent, electricity, and other overheads) and a variable cost that depends on throughput (handling, depreciation, staff, etc.). Figure 13.5 shows the basic calculations.

The first five options assume that McFarlane is going to continue making its products, maintaining its current profit margin. The last option sells a license to a local producer which gives much lower cost and correspondingly lower margins. The best option clearly depends on expected sales, and a break-even analysis suggests the ranges over which each option gives the lowest costs, so option 4 of expanding the current facility has lowest costs for sales in the range 70,000 units to 130,000 units. With forecast sales of 80,000 this option has the best returns with costs of ($4.1 million + 80,000 × $50 =) $8.1 million and revenue of (80,000 × $120 =) $9.6 million, giving a total contribution of $1.5 million. Although this would also give the company control over its product, they felt that the $1 million a year for licensing was also attractive and considerably less risky. As an experiment, they decided to try a small, experimental licensing scheme with a company in Detroit.

McFarlane and Sons						
Options for expansion						
	Fixed annual cost	Variable cost per unit	Best in range		Cost	Contribution
			From	To		
1. Open two new small facilities	$2,600,000	$80	0	0	$9,000,000	$600,000
2. Open a new medium-sized facility	$1,800,000	$90	0	53,333	$9,000,000	$600,000
3. Open a new large facility	$3,400,000	$60	53,333	70,000	$8,200,000	$1,400,000
4. Expand the current facility	$4,100,000	$50	70,000	130,000	$8,100,000	$1,500,000
5. Build a large new facility and close the current one	$8,000,000	$20	130,000	999,999	$9,600,000	$0
6. License a local US company	$100,000	$1			$180,000	$1,020,000
Forecast sales	80,000					
Gross margin for sales	$120					
Gross margin for license	$15					

Figure 13.5 Expansion options for McFarlane Sons

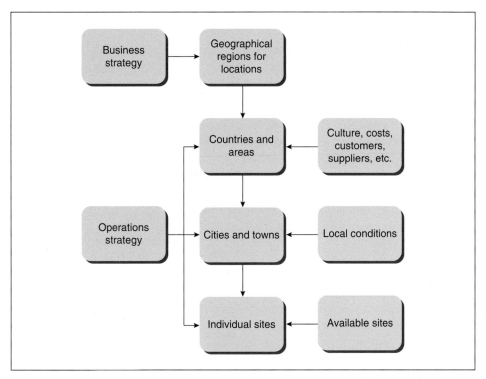

Figure 13.6 Hierarchy of decisions for locations

trend is for organizations to open facilities in countries that have lower operating costs. Efficient transport means that many manufacturers do not have to be close to their final customers, and they are tempted to move to low cost areas. American companies open facilities in Mexico, Japanese companies open factories in China, and German companies open in the Czech Republic. But a problem with this strategy is that costs might not be as low as expected. Transport costs can rise, and they may become more important than operating costs. Large, efficient steel mills in Japan, Taiwan and South Korea, for example, have low operating costs, but importing coal and iron ore is so expensive that their steel is no longer cheap.

Many people assume that low wage rates automatically mean low costs. But this is not necessarily true, as low wages might be accompanied by low productivity – and there is no point in halving wage rates if labour productivity is also halved. And perhaps more importantly, in many operations – particularly large-scale manufacturing – wages form a very small part of overall costs. It makes little sense for a high technology company to move to a low wage economy, when its markets are in industrial centres and wages form a tiny part of its costs. This is the argument that Dell used to justify a new plant in North Carolina, where a spokesman reported that, 'The cost of moving a PC around is much more than the labour cost of building one, so we locate close to customers.'

Of course, cost is only one factor in location decisions, and the strategy may focus on quality, flexibility and speed of response or some other factor. The result is that most organizations prefer to locate in areas that are near markets, have reliable suppliers, good infrastructure, high productivity, guaranteed quality and skilled workforce – even if they appear to have higher operating costs.

The following list includes some of the main considerations when choosing a region.

- **Location of customers.** Services, in particular, must often be close to their customers, which is why shops, buses, libraries, restaurants, solicitors and other services are in town centres. The same arguments hold for some manufacturing operations that need short lead times, which is why there are many local bakers, brewers, builders, etc.

- **Location of suppliers and materials.** This affects the availability of resources and their costs. Manufacturers are more likely to locate near to supplies of raw materials, particularly if these are heavy or bulky. This is why coal-burning power stations are close to coalmines and pulp mills are near to timber forests. Some operations have to be close to perishable materials, which is the reason that fruit and vegetable processors are close to farms, and frozen seafood companies are near to fishing ports.

- **Location of competitors.** This can make a location either more desirable if there is a cluster of similar organizations attracting customers, or less attractive if aggressive competitors are trying to increase their market share.

- **Location of utilities, transport infrastructure, subcontractors, and other facilities.** Again, these can make a location attractive if there are support services, transport links, and other essential facilities – or unattractive if they are absent.

- **Government attitudes.** Perhaps the overriding concerns here are political stability and a welcoming attitude. Government policies fundamentally shape an area's attractiveness – with many offering grants or incentive packages to encourage business, backed-up by quotas and restrictions on imports. Some areas encourage particular types of industry (particularly high technology or finance companies), but are less keen on, say, nuclear, chemical or polluting industries.

- **Prevailing economic conditions.** Organizations also need economic stability – particularly with prices, inflation, tax rates, and movement of money. Some countries make it difficult to move money, and there can be more subtle problems with currency exchange rates.

- **Culture and quality of life.** It is easier to expand into an area that has a similar language, culture, laws, education, health service, and welfare system, than to expand into a completely foreign area.

- **Social attitudes.** Some regions put more emphasis on social welfare than others, with emphasis on individual rather than corporate benefits. Other areas have differing views on a whole range of social factors, including productivity, ethics, absenteeism, technology, and so on.

- **Indirect costs.** Apart from direct operating costs, there are many less obvious costs of working in an area. The usual ones are local taxes and social insurance, but other costs come in many different forms.

- **Climate.** Often something as mundane as the climate can affect the attractiveness of an area. This is obvious when, say, a wine producer is looking to site a vineyard, but is relevant for many other operations.

Choosing a site

After choosing the geographic region and country, managers have to look in more detail at the areas, towns, cities and individual sites. There are several ways they can approach this, generally described as **infinite set** and **feasible set** methods.

Infinite set methods find the best location in principle and then look for an available site nearby. This approach assumes that facilities should be located near the centre of potential demands and supplies, with a rule of thumb saying that a good location is in the centre of highest demand. More usually, geometrical arguments find some kind of 'centre of gravity of demand', which gives a reasonably good starting point to look for locations.

Feasible set approach This assumes that an organization only has a small number of feasible sites and has to choose the best. An obvious way of doing this is to compare the costs, perhaps taking the operating costs, overheads, costs of moving materials inwards from suppliers, and costs of moving products outwards to customers. In general, high operating costs and overheads encourage large centralized facilities that get economies of scale; high costs of inward transport encourage facilities near to main suppliers; high costs of outward transport encourage smaller dispersed facilities near to customers. An obvious problem is that managers do not know the real costs until they open new operations. How, for example, can they know the cost of outward transport when they do not know the actual customers or their demands? An alternative uses a scoring model, which lists relevant factors, gives each a score, and identifies the location with the highest overall score. The important factors and score given to each are largely subjective opinions found by discussion and agreement. Decisions about the location of a new factory, for example, are likely to be dominated by the availability of a skilled workforce, labour relations, closeness of suppliers and services, infrastructure, potential for future expansion, community attitudes, regulations and restrictions, quality of life for employees, and government policies toward industry. On the other hand, services are more likely to emphasize the population density, characteristics of the surrounding population, location of competitors, location of other attractions, convenience for passing traffic and public transport, ease of access, convenient parking, and visibility of the site. The objectives in locating factories and services are clearly different – which is why town centres have shops, but no factories and industrial estates have factories but no shops.

Feasible set and infinite set methods are often used together, with an infinite set approach finding the best location in principle, and then a feasible set approach comparing available sites near to this best location. Then a general approach to finding a site has the following steps:

1 Identify the features needed in a new location, determined by the structure of the supply chain, the business strategy, and any other factors. Look for regions and countries that can best supply these.

2 Use an infinite set method to find the best area for locating facilities.

3 Search around this area to find a set of alternative locations.

4 Use a feasible set method to compare these alternatives.

5 Discuss all available information and come to a decision.

IDEAS IN PRACTICE Walsingham Fetters Ltd

When Walsingham Fetters built an assembly plant, they wanted a site near to its two suppliers and 10 main customers. An initial analysis found the map coordinates of these, estimated the supply and demand, and then calculated the centre of gravity of demand:

$$X_0 = \Sigma X_i W_i / W_i \qquad\qquad Y_0 = \Sigma Y_i W_i / W_i$$

where: X_0, Y_0 are the coordinates of the centre of gravity of demand

X_i, Y_i are coordinates of each customer and supplier, i

W_i is the expected demand or supply at point i

Figure 13.7 shows the centre of gravity is around ($X_0 = 53$, $Y_0 = 43$), and this gave a reasonable point to start looking for locations. Customer 6 was in a nearby industrial estate that had spare capacity, so this is where they eventually built a plant.

IDEAS IN PRACTICE Frances O'Hare

Frances O'Hare describes a location decision where there were eventually five possible alternatives. After many discussions a list of important factors, their relative weights, and scores for each site, were agreed by senior managers (as shown in Table 13.2).

On this evidence, the most important factors in the location decision were operating costs, infrastructure, and closeness to customers, and location C gave the best all-round results. More factors were then widely discussed before a decision was made.

Table 13.2 Scoring model to compare alternative locations

Factor	Maximum score	A	B	C	D	E
Closeness to suppliers	15	11	12	13	18	8
Closeness to customers	20	14	16	11	14	8
Infrastructure	20	12	6	16	8	7
Accessibility	10	6	8	7	9	5
Availability of workforce	5	1	2	4	4	5
Community attitude	10	6	8	7	4	9
Government views	8	2	2	3	4	8
Economic stability	12	10	6	10	5	3
Construction cost	5	3	1	4	2	5
Operating costs	20	12	7	11	9	16
Incentives	4	1	2	2	1	4
Climate	6	3	5	6	4	2
Total	**135**	**81**	**75**	**94**	**82**	**80**

Walsingham Fetters Ltd					
Supplier	X	Y	Weight	X*Weight	Y*Weight
1	89	14	32	2848	448
2	91	31	56	5096	1736
Customer					
1	80	23	25	2000	575
2	87	51	17	1479	867
3	61	89	23	1403	2047
4	15	84	35	525	2940
5	10	17	51	510	867
6	46	51	32	1472	1632
7	22	66	26	572	1716
8	19	52	15	285	780
9	88	24	31	2728	744
10	21	62	19	399	1178
Totals			362	19317	15530
Centre of gravity	53.36	42.9			

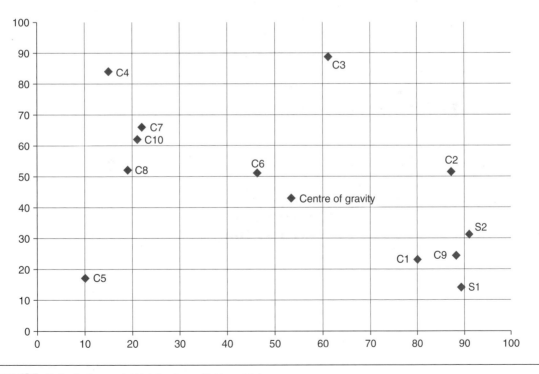

Figure 13.7 Calculations at Walsingham Fetters Ltd

IDEAS IN PRACTICE Intel

Intel Corporation was founded in 1968 and is now the worlds leading producer of semiconductor devices. They are best known for their computer chips, but they make 450 products that earn $35 billion a year. As part of their continuing expansion, Intel was considering a plant in Costa Rica in the 1990s. To encourage them, the government offered eight years free of income tax, followed by four years at half rate, duty free import of materials, and unrestricted movement of money into and out of the country. In addition, they granted more licenses to foreign airlines to increase the number of international flights, built a new power sub-station for the site, reduced their cost of electricity by 28 percent, and reduced the liability for corporation tax.

Intel decided to locate a $300 million semiconductor testing and assembly plant near to San Jose, and by 2000 this was employing more than 2000 people. A spokesman for Intel, said that, 'When we are considering a site we use a multifaceted set of criteria. Incentives are part of this.'

When making location decisions, Deloitte & Touche Fantus found that high-tech industries most often consider:

- **Essential factors:**
  - skilled and educated workforce
  - proximity of research institutions
  - attractive quality of life
  - access to venture capital.

- **Important factors:**
  - reasonable cost of doing business
  - established technology industry
  - adequate infrastructure
  - favourable business climate and regulations.

- **Desirable factors:**
  - established suppliers and partners
  - community incentives.

Sources: Wall Street Journal Special Report, Sept 25, 2000; Websites at www.interactive.wsj.com; www.intel.com; www.deloitte.com

IDEAS IN PRACTICE Location of the 2012 Olympic Games

Nine cities submitted bids for the 2012 Olympic Games – Havana (Cuba), Istanbul (Turkey), Leipzig (Germany), London (United Kingdom), Madrid (Spain), Moscow (Russian Federation), New York (USA), Paris (France) and Rio de Janeiro (Brazil). These 'Applicant Cities' then began the procedure that allows the International Olympic Committee (IOC) to examine each city's ability to host the games, and evaluate the strengths and weaknesses of their plans.

There are two phases in the evaluation. The first phase lasts about ten months, during which the Applicant Cities answer 25 questions that give an overview of their proposals. A working group of IOC administration members and external experts assesses the answers, doing a technical evaluation of the applications. This looks at areas such as government support, public opinion, general infrastructure, security, venues, accommodation and transport. The IOC Executive Board then decides which cities are to be accepted as Candidate Cities.

The five cities that passed this first phase in May 2004 were London, Madrid, Moscow, New York and Paris. These Candidate Cities began the second phase of the procedure, submitting detailed plans within six months. These are studied and analyzed by the IOC Evaluation Commission, which visits each city and reports on its findings. These reports evaluate the bids' performance in a number of areas that are critical to the successful organization of the games.

All relevant information is then considered at the 117th IOC Session in Singapore, where members vote on their choice by a secret ballot. There are successive rounds of voting, eliminating the city with the lowest number of votes in each round, until one candidate receives a majority of the votes. In this case the chosen location was London.

Sources: Websites at www.ioc.com; www.olympic.org

Chapter review

- Logistics is responsible for the flow of materials into, through and out of operations. It consists of a series of related activities that aim at moving materials as efficiently and effectively as possible. This is an essential function in every organization, and often comes at high cost.
- A supply chain consists of all the activities and organizations that materials flow through on their journey from initial suppliers to final customers. Each product has its own unique supply chain.
- These are many different structures for supply chains. Key questions concern its length, breadth, number of facilities, relationships between them, locations, etc. Managers have to design the best structure to fit their needs.
- Logistics consists of a series of related activities. The best results come when these are considered together, giving an integrated function throughout an organization.
- This integration can be extended along the supply chain to give a range of benefits. To achieve external integration, organizations have to work together and cooperate, while competing against other supply chains.
- There are several ways of organizing this cooperation, ranging from informally working together through to vertical integration. One of the most popular options forms strategic alliances.
- Finding the best location for facilities is an important decision with serious consequences for an organization. It is also a complex decision, where many factors have to be considered.
- Location decisions involve a hierarchy of decisions, starting with the best region and moving downwards to identify the best site. A useful approach uses an infinite set method to find the best general area, and then a feasible set method to compare available sites.

CASE STUDY Supply Chain Audit

We have already shown how audits of the environment and operations can give a clear view of their current state – and a supply chain audit can do the same for logistics.

A supply chain audit looks at the details of the supply chain to describe its structure, how it works, its capabilities, strengths, weaknesses, areas that need improvement, performance relative to competitors, costs, and any other relevant information. There are

many ways of conducting an audit, but a useful one concentrates on six key areas.

1 *Supply chain strategy*. This looks at the big picture to check the overall strategy, strategic direction, approach to supply chain design, relationships in the supply chain, risk and flexibility. It sees if the logistics function has a clear idea of its long-term direction, and how

(continued)

CASE STUDY Supply Chain Audit (continued)

this builds on its internal capabilities and external opportunities. It also checks that logistics policies fit into the broader operations, business, and corporate strategies, and easily translate into actual operations.

2 *Structure of the supply chain.* Describes the structure of the supply chain that delivers the strategy. It considers the number, type, size, function and location of facilities, and their relationships with each other. The aim here is to see if the structure of the supply chain is appropriate for achieving its strategy, or whether it needs adjusting and redesigning.

3 *Operations within the supply chain.* This describes the details of activities within the supply chain to see how the movement of materials is actually organized and controlled. The aim here is to assess the quality of the operations – and see if they are compatible with the strategy, make the best use of facilities, and give a competitive advantage. Information from this review can be used to benchmark logistics.

4 *Information.* Operations in the supply chain rely on timely and accurate information, which in turn depends on the information systems. The aim here is to describe the information flows

and see whether they deliver the information that the supply chain needs.

5 *Organizational structure.* This describes the organizational structure of the logistics function, checking the effectiveness of the structure, and the roles and responsibilities of people working in the supply chain. An important question asks whether the structure allows relationships to develop with internal and external partners, encouraging the supply chain to work as a single integrated unit.

6 *Performance measurement.* The aim here is to show how well the supply chain actually works. This measures performance according to a range of different factors and sees if all parts of the supply chain are achieving their goals.

Questions

- What are the benefits of doing a supply chain audit? Who would usually do one, and why?
- Are the six points listed here the most important, or should other factors be considered?
- Describe in detail how you would start doing a supply chain audit for a company.

Discussion questions

1 How much does logistics cost a typical organization? Do you think this is too much?

2 A supply chain really consists of a complex web of interacting buyers and sellers. Does this complexity mean that supply chains are inevitably difficult to organize efficiently?

3 What are the benefits of integrating the separate activities of logistics into a single function? Are these benefits inevitable, or is it sometimes better to break logistics into smaller specialized units?

4 A seller can only ever benefit at the expense of a buyer – and vice versa. So the whole idea of cooperation in a supply chain is based on a myth. Do you think this is true?

5 There is no such thing as a strategic alliance, as stronger partners will always have an advantage over weaker ones, and they will finish the partnership when convenient. What are the consequences of this?

6 Most supply chains cover several countries. What particular problems are there with international logistics?

7 Why is it important to find the best location for facilities?

8 If you decided to start work as an independent management consultant, what factors would influence your choice of location?

Useful websites

www.clm.org – Council of Logistics Management
www.deloitte.com
www.intel.com
www.interactive.wsj.com
www.ioc.com
www.iolt.org.uk – Institute of Logistics and Transport
www.olympic.org
www.petro-canada.com
www.sony.com
www.sony-europe.com
www.walmart.com
www.walmartfacts.com
www.walmartstores.com
www.petro-canada.com

References

Ballou R.H., Reformulating a logistics strategy, International Journal of Physical Distribution and Materials Management, vol 11(8), pp 71–83, 1981.

Brandenburger A.M. and Nalebuff B.J., Co-option, Doubleday, New York, 1996.

Brandenburger A.M. and Nalebuff B.J., How a firm's capabilities affect its boundary decisions, Sloan Management Review, Spring, 1999.

Childerley A., The importance of logistics in the UK economy, International Journal of Physical Distribution and Materials Management, 10(8), 1980.

Christopher M., Emerging issues in supply chain management, Proceedings of the Logistics Academic Network Inaugural Workshop, Warwick, 1996.

Christopher M., Logistics and supply chain management, Financial Times Prentice Hall, Harlow, 1998.

Christopher M., Global logistics: the role of agility, Logistics and Transport Focus, 1(1), 1999.

Copacino W.C., Supply chain management, St Lucie Press, Boca Raton, FL, 1997.

Coyle J.J., Bardi E.J. and Langley C.J., The management of business logistics (6th edition), West Publishing, St Paul, MN, 1996.

Drucker P., The economy's dark continent, Fortune, April, p 103, 1962.

Ellram L.M. and Krause D.R., Supplier partnerships in manufacturing versus non-manufacturing firms, The International Journal of Logistics Management, 5(1), 43–53, 1994.

Forrester J., Industrial dynamics, MIT Press, Boston, MA, 1961.

Gattorna J.L and Walters D.W., Managing the supply chain, Palgrave Macmillan, Basingstoke, 1996.

Gay C.L. and Essinger J., Inside outsourcing, Nicholas Brealey, London, 2000.

Helming W. and Zonnenberg J.P., The five fulcrum points of a supply chain strategy, Supply Chain and Logistics Journal, Winter, 2000.

Institute of Logistics and Transport, Members' Directory, Corby, 2005.

Institute of Logistics and Transport, Website at www.iolt.org.uk.

Kapoor V. and Gupta A., Aggressive sourcing, Sloan Management Review, Fall, 1997.

Lambert D.M., Emmelhainz M.A. and Gardner J.T., Developing and implementing supply chain partnerships, International Journal of Logistics Management, 7(2), 1–17, 1996.

Lee H.L., Padmanabhan V. and Whang S., The bull whip effect in supply chains, Sloan Management Review, Spring, pp 93–102, 1997.

Office of National Statistics, Annual abstract of statistics, HMSO, London, 2004.

Poitier C.C., Advanced supply chain management, Berrett-Kohler, New York, 1999.

Porter M.E., Competitive advantage, Free Press, New York, 1985.

Rowley J., Outsourcing across borders in Europe, Logistics and Transport Focus, 3(1), pp 54–56, 2001.

Shapiro R.D. and Heskett J.L., Logistics strategy, West Publishing, St Paul, MN, 1985.

Time, Supplement to Prince of Wales International Business Leaders Forum, London, 1999.

Waters D., Inventory control and management (2nd edition), John Wiley, Chichester, 2003a.

Waters D., Logistics, Palgrave Macmillan, Basingstoke, 2003b.

Waters D., Global logistics and distribution planning (4th edition), Kogan Page, London, 2003.

In the last chapter we looked at the structure of the supply chain. Here we look at the flow of materials through this chain. This movement is triggered by procurement, which triggers the movement of materials from a seller to a buyer. The flow of materials is unlikely to be completely smooth, and stocks accumulate throughout the chain. These are expensive, and careful management is needed to minimize the associated costs.

After reading this chapter you should be able to:

- Describe the way that traditional planning gives a means of controlling movement in a supply chain
- Appreciate the role and importance of procurement
- Outline the activities involved in procurement
- Discuss the role of stock in supply chains
- Understand the traditional approach to controlling stocks with dependent demand
- Describe the distinctive approach of material requirements planning
- Discuss the features of just-in-time operations
- Appreciate the role of transport in a supply chain

This chapter will emphasize:

- **Procurement**, which organizes the supply of materials
- **Stock**, which forms whenever materials are not used at the time they become available
- **Material requirements planning**, which uses production plans to control the flow of materials
- **Just-in-time**, which arranges all operations to occur at exactly the time they are needed
- **Transport**, which physically moves materials

FLOW OF MATERIALS

The last chapter described the role of logistics and the supply chain in organizing the flow of materials from initial suppliers through to final customers. In particular, we looked at the structure of the supply chain, discussing the number of facilities, their locations, the relationships between them, and so on. In this chapter we look more carefully at controlling the flow of materials (Arnold; Hughes *et al.*; Waters, 2003c; Handfield and Nichols).

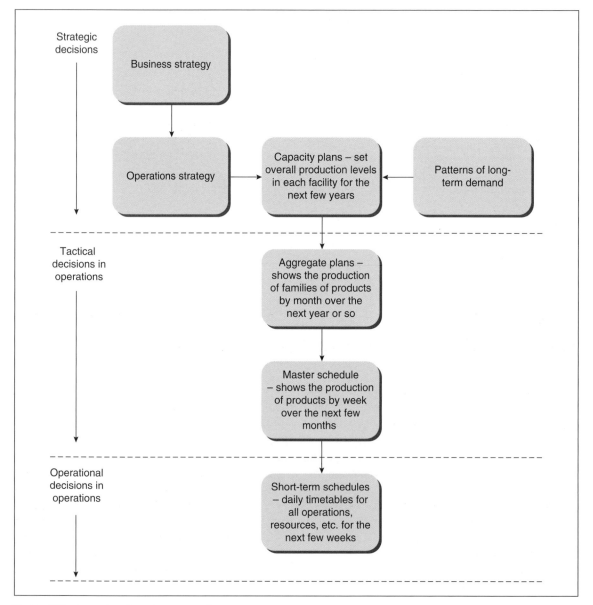

Figure 14.1 Steps in planning procedure

There must always be some mechanism for controlling the flow of materials through a supply chain. The traditional approach uses planned operations, where managers design a detailed schedule for each distinct activity in the chain. By coordinating these schedules, managers control the flow of materials. These schedules are rather like bus timetables: by defining times at which the bus should reach certain points, managers control progress along its route.

To design the schedules, managers start with long-term forecasts of demand and capacity plans, which we described in chapter 12. This sets the overall size of the process and its output. The next steps break this overall figure down into increasingly more detail, until there is eventually a schedule for all operations and resources. This planning is usually described in four steps (illustrated in Figure 14.1):

1 **Capacity plans**, are the strategic plans that ensure capacity meets the long-term demand. These effectively set overall production levels in each facility for the next few years.

2 Managers add details to the capacity plans to give medium term **aggregate plans**, which show the production of families of products, typically by month at each location for the next year or so.

3 Then they add details to the aggregate plans to give the **master schedules**, which show timetables for the production of individual products, typically by week over the next few months.

4 Then they add details to the master schedule to give **short-term schedules**, which show daily timetables for machines, operators and other equipment, typically for the next few weeks.

IDEAS IN PRACTICE Capital Air Service

Capital Air Service operates an executive air service between Ottawa and the main cities of Canada. They use long-term forecasts to show the overall demand for this service, and managers translate this into capacity plans that set the number of aeroplanes, staff and other facilities. These plans cover the next five years in outline, with more details for the next two years, which is about the time needed to make major changes to capacity.

Then managers add details to the capacity plans to give aggregate plans, which show the number of flights each month between the Provinces. These give detailed plans for the next six months, with less detail

for the next year. Details are added to the aggregate plans to form the master schedules, which show the number of flights between cities each day over the next six months or so.

The next stage of planning adds details to the master schedule to give short-term schedules, which show the time of each flight. These daily schedules are finalized three months in advance. The last stage of planning takes the flight information and produces schedules for other operations and resources – including crews, refuelling, meals, maintenance, check-in systems, ticketing arrangements, and overnight stops.

This gives a straightforward top-down approach to planning, but we know that planning is never this straightforward and the actual procedure is likely to be long and complicated. But at the end, managers have detailed timetables for operations, showing what they are doing at any time, what products they are making, and what resources they are using. From a logistics point of view, the key point is that these schedules show when products move forward from one part of the process to another. They also show when materials are needed from suppliers, and hence the timing of deliveries. So the schedules effectively define the flows of materials throughout the supply chain – and when managers know the details of these flows it becomes relatively straightforward to arrange them.

PROCUREMENT

Importance of procurement

Despite the trend towards greater integration, the detailed plans of one organization in a supply chain are rarely known by other organizations. So there must be a mechanism for passing a message backwards to say that operations need materials from a supplier. This is the function of **purchasing** or **procurement**, which is responsible for acquiring all the materials needed by operations (Baily *et al.*; Leenders and Fearon; Saunders). Often people use the terms purchasing and procurement to mean the same thing, but really purchasing refers to the actual buying, while procurement has a broader meaning and includes selecting suppliers, purchasing, contracting, leasing, renting, borrowing, negotiating, agreeing terms, expediting, monitoring supplier performance, and so on.

- **Procurement** is responsible for acquiring all the materials needed by operations.
- It gives a mechanism for initiating and controlling the flow of materials through a supply chain.

You can easily see why procurement is important, as it forms an essential link between adjacent organizations in a supply chain – and it gives the mechanism for coordinating the flow of materials. All operations need materials, and procurement is responsible for acquiring these – so it is clearly an essential function in every organization. In a typical manufacturer, 60–70 percent of costs are spent through procurement. The figure is lower in services, but it still accounts for a significant amount.

Not only is procurement essential, but it can affect broader performance. If it is done badly, materials do not arrive, or the wrong materials are delivered, in the wrong quantities, at the wrong time, with poor quality, at too high a price, with low customer service, and so on. And if procurement is done well, it can save a lot of money. Imagine a company that pays $10 million a year for materials, and sells its products for $11 million. It clearly makes a profit of $1 million a year. If better procurement reduces the cost of materials by 10 percent, they would fall to $9 million, and with the same selling price the company doubles its profits to $2 million a year.

A 10 percent improvement in procurement doubles profit, and to get the same affect from, say, marketing, the company would have to double its sales.

Many organizations were slow to recognize the importance of procurement and often treated it as a clerical overhead – its importance only being noticed when something went seriously wrong. And mistakes in procurement can have serious consequences, stopping processes and preventing anything being done. Kraljic described this in terms of 'risk of exposure' to define different levels of importance for procurement. If we include all the consequences of not having an item in stock when it is needed as a risk, then materials that are cheap and have low risk can be acquired with standard procedures – with operational decisions. On the other hand, materials that are very expensive and have high risk need special arrangements – and strategic decisions (as shown in Figure 14.2).

This is a simplified view, but it does illustrate the different levels of decision in procurement. These are associated with different roles for the function, moving from a clerical role for operational decisions to a strategic role affecting long-term performance. Hayes and Wheelwright suggested a natural progression of operations from playing a minor role to being the source of distinctive capabilities. Reck and Long describe a similar progression with the following steps in procurement:

1 *Passive* – only responds to demand from users, buying materials as directed with no strategic direction.

2 *Independent* – works efficiently and uses best practices, but still a separate function with a strategy that is independent of broader operations.

3 *Supportive* – works to support the operations strategy, with aligned strategies and building distinctive capabilities.

4 *Integrated* – an integrated part of operations, working with other areas to achieve overall success.

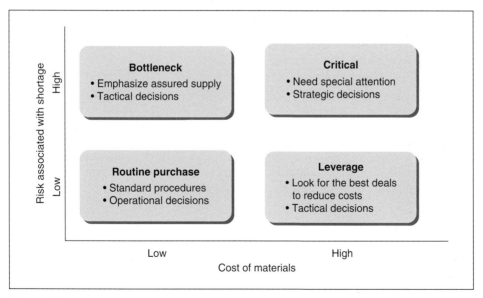

Figure 14.2 Importance of procurement decisions

How procurement works

When you buy something expensive, such as a new computer, you probably approach the purchase in three steps. Firstly, you decide the features you want (in Hill's terminology the qualifying features), then you search for systems that can provide these and identify suppliers (forming a shortlist of options), then you compare offerings in the shortlist and choose the best (based on the order-winning features). Your aim is to find the combination of products and suppliers that best satisfies your needs. The procurement function in an organization essentially works in the same way, but there are obvious variations in the detail. You would not expect an organization such as the US army, which buys millions of items a day, to work in the same way as the directors of Chelsea Football Club when they acquire a new striker. And the US army would not approach its decision to buy pencils in the same way as its decision to buy missiles.

Nonetheless, most procurement follows a series of common steps that starts when a user in operations identifies a need to purchase materials, and ends when the materials are received and paid for (Waters, 2003a). This whole formal procedure is quite complicated and time consuming. Even an apparently simple step, such as comparing the quotations from competing suppliers, is difficult when they describe somewhat different products, prices, delivery, running costs, back-up, maintenance contracts, financing arrangements, trading terms and conditions. It is difficult to compare the deals offered for utilities, such as electricity, credit cards or mobile phones, so it becomes very complicated when there are widely differing products that could serve the same purpose. An important point is that the lowest price is not necessarily the best deal. We saw in chapter 10 that TQM demands some measure of quality when judging suppliers, so the 'right price' is the one that is best for all concerned – buyer, supplier, customers, public, and everyone else. It is certainly not in an organization's long-term interest to save money by substituting cheap materials and hoping that nobody notices the decline in quality. Nor should the organization be so tough in negotiations to force the best possible conditions that the supplier struggles to meet the terms and eventually goes out of business. But this is a complicated issue. Supermarkets in parts of the European Union, for example, have followed consumer pressure to reduce their food prices, and this has meant paying less to farmers who grow the crops, causing a series of well-known consequences.

Similarly, we could look at the procedure to generate a shortlist of suitable suppliers, which seems relatively easy. Most organizations have a list of approved suppliers who have given good service in the past, or who are known to be reliable. If there is no acceptable supplier on file, the organization has to spend time searching for one – and then supplier selection becomes an important decision. Of course, this problem is avoided completely by forming strategic alliances with main suppliers. In many operations, strategic alliances have transformed the way that procurement works, opening the door for a whole series of improvements.

Improving procurement

There are two main concerns with the standard approach to procurement. Firstly, there is the cost – with a guideline suggesting a cost of $80 to process a basic order, and Allen quoting figures of $115 to $150. This is clearly too expensive for very low value items where the procurement would cost more than the materials. Secondly, there is the time that it takes. Paul Sigarro buys material to make designer dresses for l'Haute Vision in Stockholm, and found that a delivery of materials typically took one day to arrive from the supplier in Nice, but administration delayed delivery by more than five weeks. Typically, the delays are longer when there is some kind of problem – such as a mistake in an identifying number, missing delivery details, payment, or some other administrative details. Procurement staff expect to spend a third of their time dealing with such troubles (Cummings).

The problem with the traditional approach is that it is based on a paper system – and even when organizations move to automation, they often automate the same procedures. This has fundamental weaknesses of taking a long time, being expensive, relying on a lot of paperwork, physically moving this paper between locations, having a lot of people doing the administration, being unreliable, introducing errors, having more people to supervise and control the administration, not connecting to other systems such as stock control, and so on. These problems are largely overcome when organizations move to electronic purchasing.

Electronic data interchange (EDI) has allowed automated procurement since the 1980s, but its use is still growing quickly. Automated procurement has an organization linking its information system to a supplier's, and automatically transmitting a signal when it is time to place an order. There are several variations on automated procurement, all of which are considered under the general heading of **e-procurement** (leading to e-business, e-commerce, e-buying and e-just about everything else).

Most organizations already use some form of e-procurement. Surveys suggest that over 60 percent of UK companies used e-procurement by 2002, and 80 percent of European managers soon expect to use it extensively (Cummings; Barclays). As Bill Gates famously said, 'The Internet changes everything', and Andy Grove who was Chief Executive of Intel in 1999 said, 'Any business that is not an e-business within five years simply will not exist' (The Economist). Of course, this is an exaggeration, but it does focus on the advantages of e-business, which include:

- instant access at any time to suppliers anywhere in the world
- a transparent market where products and terms are readily available
- opportunity to buy directly from manufacturers, or earlier tiers of suppliers
- increasing number of specialized Web retailers
- automated procurement using standard EDI procedures
- greatly reducing the time needed for transactions
- reducing costs, typically by 12–15 percent
- outsourcing some procurement activities to suppliers or third parties
- integrating seamlessly with suppliers' information systems.

There are basically two types of e-procurement which are described as B2B (where one business buys materials from another business) and B2C (when a final customer buys from a business). Most of us are familiar with B2C when we buy books, DVDs, holidays or other items from Websites. In the three years to 2002 the number of Internet shoppers in the UK tripled from 2 million to 6 million (Rushe). But most e-procurement is actually B2B where more than three-quarters of organizations already use the Internet for procurement. The Gartner Group have produced the following estimates of B2B trade.

Year	Value of B2B procurement ($ billion)
1998	43
1999	219
2000	433
2001	919
2002	1900
2003	3600
2004	6000
2005	8500

Many people are enthusiastic about the growth of e-procurement, but they often forget an important point. If we organize e-procurement very efficiently, it gives much better communications – but it does not necessarily improve the physical flow of materials. This only happens when organizations in the supply chain use the communications to find better ways of moving materials. As Doerflinger *et al.* say, 'The real barrier to (B2B) entry is the back-end – fulfilment – not the Website itself.'

IDEAS IN PRACTICE Nautilus Software

Nautilus Software installed a new, automated procurement system for a major international client. The core of this system had the client's cash registers linked directly to its main suppliers' delivery system. Then when the client sold an item, an order for a replacement was automatically sent to the supplier, with delivery normally guaranteed before the start of the next working day.

The following figures give an indication of cost savings, with values in euros per transaction. The new system gave a return on investment of almost 400 percent a year.

Source: Bryant E and Singh T., e-business lowers the cost of procurement, Nautilus Software, Mumbai, 2005

Step in procurement	Original cost	Cost with e-procurement
Create detailed requirement	20.6	11.6
Approval process	6.5	3.0
Check requirements	24.3	0
Order processing	65.4	7.8
Receiving	12.6	3.5
Internal delivery	44.1	17.1
Payment process	27.4	0.8
Total	**200.9**	**43.8**

Merrill Lynch give the same type of warning, saying that growing use of the Internet for procurement will change buying patterns and the patterns of logistics, but will probably not generate much new business. For this organizations still have to look for ways of improving customer service.

INVENTORY MANAGEMENT

Models for independent demand

Our ideal picture of a supply chain has materials flowing smoothly between different facilities. In practice, though, this flow is not so smooth. Suppliers send deliveries of conveniently sized loads – perhaps a container, truck or shipfull; operations hold **stocks** of raw materials in case deliveries are delayed; there are stocks of work in progress during the operations; warehouses hold stocks of finished goods to cover for unexpected variations in customer demand. So the true picture has a series of stock-holding points throughout the supply chain, with materials moving in steps between them.

- **Stocks** are supplies of materials that are held by operations until needed.
- They are formed whenever materials are not used at the time they become available.

Stocks give a buffer between unexpected variations in the supply of materials and demand. If a delivery is late, stocks of raw materials mean that a factory can continue working normally; if customer demand is higher that expected, stocks of finished goods mean that it can still meet demand. These stocks bring the following benefits (Waters, 2003b). They:

- allow for demands that are earlier or bigger than expected
- allow for deliveries that are delayed or too small
- give a buffer between adjacent parts of the supply chain
- take advantage of price discounts on large orders
- allow the purchases of materials before an expected price rise
- allow the purchase of materials that are going out of production or difficult to find
- make full loads and reduce transport costs
- give cover for emergencies.

Unfortunately these benefits come at a high cost, which is typically more than 20 percent of the value of stock held. Not surprisingly, organizations attempt to minimize these costs – while maintaining all the benefits that the stocks bring. In the 1920s a standard approach was developed for inventory control, and this remained the best way of managing stocks for most of the century (Harris; Raymond; Wilson).

This is based on a quantitative model that finds the best balance between conflicting costs.

This approach assumes an **independent demand**, where the total demand for an item is made up of lots of separate demands that are not related to each other. The overall demand for bread in a supermarket, for example, is made up of lots of demands from separate customers who act independently. Then managers look for answers to three basic questions.

1 *What items should we stock?* No item, however cheap, should be stocked unless the benefit of holding it is greater than the cost.

2 *When should we place an order?* This depends on the control system used, variability of demand, level of uncertainty, value of the item, lead-time, supplier reliability, and a number of other factors.

3 *How much should we order?* Large, infrequent orders give high average stock levels, but low costs for placing and administering orders: small, frequent orders give low average stocks, but high costs of placing and administering orders.

The first of these questions is a matter of good housekeeping, simply avoiding stock that is not needed. The second two need some calculation – usually based on a variation of the **economic order quantity**. These calculations use a simplified model of operations, and then find the pattern of orders that minimizes the overall cost. As well as giving the size and timing of orders, these analyses give a series of other information, including investment in stock, variation in stock levels, safety stock, probability of shortages, cost, and so on.

IDEAS IN PRACTICE Semple Retail

Semple Retail ran some forecasts which suggested that overall demand for a product would average 4,000 units a year. Holding stock costs $7 a year for each unit in stock, with procurement costing $140 an order, a lead time of one week, and 40 units always held as a safety stock to cover for emergencies. Using a standard inventory control model, they found the following calculations:

- The reorder quantity = $\sqrt{(2 \times \text{reorder cost} \times \text{demand} / \text{holding cost})}$
  = $\sqrt{2 \times 140 \times 4000 / 7}$ = 400 units
- Working stock varies between 0 (just before a delivery) to 400 (just after a delivery), with an average of 200 units

- Safety stock = 40 units
- Average stock = average working stock + safety stock = 200 + 40 = 240 units
- Holding cost = average stock × holding cost = 240 × 7 = $1,680 a year
- Number of orders a year = demand / order size = 4,000 / 400 = 10
- Cost of orders = number of orders × order cost = 10 × 140 = $1,400 a year
- An order is placed when there is one week's working stock left = 4000 / 52 = 77 units

Weaknesses of independent demand models

Independent demand models are still widely used, and they have a number of advantages – as they are easy to understand and use, give reliable guidelines for order size, are easy to automate, encourage stability, and can be extended to cover a wide variety of circumstances. However, they also have a number of weaknesses – as they take a simplified view of inventory systems, use a series of assumptions about operations, use forecasts of demand, consider costs to be known at fixed values, give awkward and varying order sizes, are slow to react to changes, do not deal well with some conditions, and are sensitive to certain parameter values.

But independent demand systems have an intrinsic weakness if demand is not really independent. If you are selling fish and chips, the demand for chips is clearly not independent of the demand for fish, and the basis of the quantitative models breaks down. The immediate effects of this might be small, but in the last chapter we described an effect where small changes in demand are magnified back along the supply chain, giving huge swings in demand for earlier suppliers (Lee *et al.*). The trigger for this instability can be a small adjustment in demand near the end of the chain – but it can also be a faulty forecast, batching of small orders into a reasonably sized delivery, price variations that cause organizations to buy more when prices are low, and a range of other factors that distort demand. Interestingly, price promotions deliberately introduce distortions to demand and can cause such serious consequences that Sellers refers to them as, 'The dumbest marketing ploy'.

In the last chapter we saw that the best way of overcoming these problems is to integrate the supply chain, so that different parts can coordinate their activities. This view has led to new methods of controlling stock, with the two most common methods being material requirements planning and just-in-time operations.

MATERIAL REQUIREMENTS PLANNING

Characteristic approach

Independent demand inventory systems work when the overall demand for a product is made up of individual demands from many customers, and the demands are not related. But there are many situations where demands are clearly not independent. One demand for a product is not independent of a second demand for the product – or demand for one product is not independent of demand for a second product. When a manufacturer uses a set of components to make a product, the demands for all components are related through the production plan for the product. This gives **dependent demand**. A successful way of dealing with this uses **material requirements planning (MRP)** to 'explode' a master schedule to plan the deliveries of materials (Orlicky; Wight, 1974).

> ● **Material requirements planning** uses the master schedule, along with other relevant information, to plan the supply of materials.

The characteristic approach of MRP is that it does not forecast demand for materials from past patterns, but finds demand directly from production plans. It 'explodes' a master schedule to find the times when materials are needed, and then uses this to plan deliveries. You can see the differences between the traditional – independent demand – approach and MRP in the way that restaurant chefs plan the ingredients for a week's meals. With the traditional approach, the chefs see what ingredients they used in previous weeks, use these past demands to forecast demands for next week, and then buy enough ingredients to cover these forecast demands. With the MRP approach, chefs look at the meals they are going to cook each day, analyze these to see what ingredients they need, and then order the ingredients to arrive at the right time.

To illustrate the MRP approach, we can imagine a master schedule that shows operations making 10 chairs in June. A 'bill of materials' shows the materials needed for a product. In this case it lists a seat and four legs, so operations need 10 chair seats and 40 legs ready for assembly at the beginning of June. These are the gross requirements, and operations may not have to order them all if they already have some in stock, or have outstanding orders that are due to arrive shortly. If we subtract these from the gross requirements we get the amount to order:

Amount to order = gross requirements – current stock – stock on order

Now we know the quantities to order and when they should arrive, so the next step is to see when to place the order. For this we need the lead times – and we place each order the lead time before the material is actually needed. If operations buy legs from suppliers who give a lead time of four weeks, they need to place orders at the beginning of May. If they make seats themselves with a lead time of two weeks, they need to schedule the production of these to start in the middle of May.

The last thing to consider is all the other relevant information, such as minimum order sizes, discounts, minimum stock levels, variation in lead time, and so on. When operations take all of this into account they get a detailed timetable for orders. This procedure is shown in Figure 14.3, and this has to be repeated for all materials needed for operations.

Benefits and problems with MRP

Traditional approaches to inventory control forecast likely demand for materials, and then hold stocks that are high enough to meet these. To allow for the inevitable errors in their forecasts and uncertainty in supply and demand, operations hold more stocks than they really need. These extra stocks give a measure of safety, but they also increase the inventory costs. The main benefit of MRP is that it relates the supply of materials directly to the demand, so there are no accumulated stocks of raw materials or work in progress. The associated benefits include:

- lower stock levels, with savings in capital, space, warehousing, etc.
- higher stock turn-over reducing obsolescence and waste
- better customer service – with no delays caused by shortages of materials
- faster delivery times due to improved planning
- less time spent on expediting and emergency orders
- early warning of potential problems with supplies and shortages
- MRP schedules can be used for planning other activities.

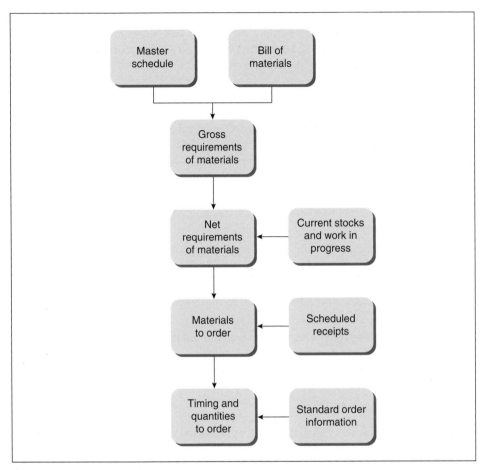

Figure 14.3 Summary of the procedure for MRP

As well as these benefits, there are also problems with MRP, the most obvious being the amount of information and data processing that it needs. The information about schedules, products and materials, comes from three main sources:

1 *master schedules*, give the number of every product to be made in each period

2 *bill of materials*, gives structured lists of the materials needed for each product

3 *inventory records*, show the current state of stocks, lead times, supplier reliability, costs, etc.

Although the calculation that we outlined is simple enough, normal operations make a wide range of products (often hundreds or thousands) from many materials (again, often hundreds or thousands). The MRP calculations are repeated for each material used in each product – and then the various interactions between products, materials, orders, and suppliers are added. The result is a very complex system. Although the principles are straightforward, you hear of many companies that spend millions of dollars and years of effort to get the MRP system working properly. In 1989 Cerveny and Scott reported that 40 percent of companies used some form of MRP, but only 67 percent of these considered it a success. Increasing experience and more sophisticated systems can now considerably increase the success rate, but MRP does not give an ideal solution for all organizations. In fact, it cannot be used at all when there is no master schedule, the master schedule is not designed far enough in advance, it is inaccurate and does not show what actually happens, when plans are frequently changed – or when any of the information needed is unavailable, in the wrong form, or is not accurate enough. In practice, this limits MRP to mass production of complex products in a relatively stable environment.

Some general problems with MRP include:

- it needs a lot of detailed and reliable information about products, plans, operations, bill of materials, suppliers, costs, deliveries, and so on
- the control systems become large and very complex, linking many parts of operations and doing a lot of data analysis
- it is very expensive and time-consuming to implement these systems and get them working properly
- reduced flexibility as materials are only available to make the specified master schedule, and this cannot be adjusted as materials are not available for other schedules
- the order patterns suggested by MRP can be inefficient
- MRP may not recognize capacity and other constraints.

Extending the role of MRP

The basic MRP approach can give significant benefits, but it can only be used in certain circumstances. But one of its major strengths is that the approach can be extended beyond its initial use of controlling stocks. You can imagine this when the MRP schedules show that a lot of one component is needed at a specific time, and there is not enough capacity to make it. Then managers can adjust the plans in some way, either increasing capacity for the component, or adjusting master schedules so that demand for the component is spread over a longer period. In other words, there is feedback between MRP and the planning. MRP uses the master schedule to generate a detailed timetable for acquiring materials, and the consequences are fed-back to planners to make sure that the results are acceptable – and if there are problems, the plans are adjusted. Systems of this kind that include feedback from the MRP to the planning are called **closed-loop MRP** (illustrated in Figure 14.4).

Closed-loop MRP extends the basic approach further into the operations. We started by using MRP to control stocks and schedule the delivery of materials, and now use it more positively in scheduling and capacity planning. But we need not stop here. Materials are only one resource, and organizations have to schedule others, including people, equipment, facilities, finances, transport, and so on. We can use the same MRP approach for these other resources. This thinking has led to a major extension of MRP into **manufacturing resources planning**, or **MRP II**.

Imagine an organization that uses MRP to get a timetable for purchasing materials and preparing materials internally. If it knows when the internal materials have to be ready, it knows when to start preparing them. In other words, MRP schedules the

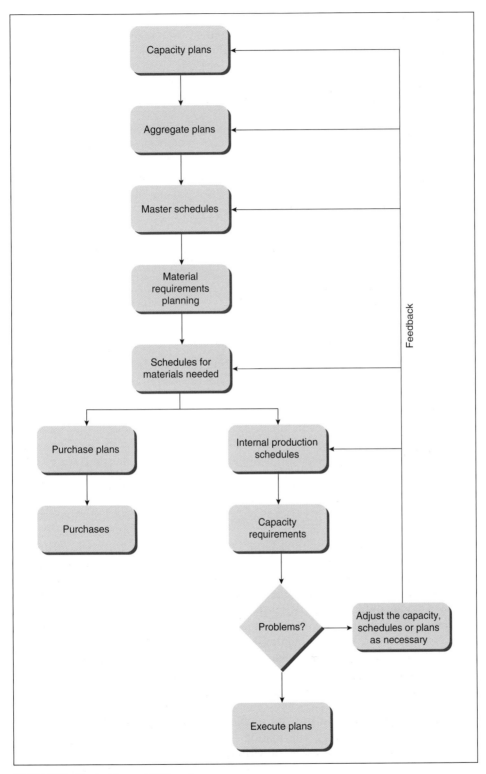

Figure 14.4 Closed-loop MRP system

internal production of components. But we can use these schedules for making components to get timetables for production equipment, people working on it, raw materials, and other resources. And if we know when the raw materials are needed, we can schedule inward transport, drivers, quality checks, and so on. Continuing in this way, we could build an integrated system that would 'explode' the master schedule to give timetables for all the jobs, equipment, operators, machines, and facilities needed to achieve it.

In other words, we could use MRP to schedule all aspects of operations. But there is no reason to stop here, and we could also look at the associated finance, marketing, sales, human resource management, etc. Eventually we would get a completely integrated system that would use the master schedule as the basis for planning all activities and resources in the organization. This is the aim of MRP II.

- MRP II gives an integrated system for synchronizing all activities and resources within an organization.
- These timetables are driven by the master schedule.

MRP II can give very efficient operations, but there can be serious practical difficulties. The main one is, again, the complexity of the systems needed to integrate all functions and activities. As they struggle to get schedules that everyone accepts as being good and workable, many people ask if the rewards from such close integration are worth the effort of achieving them. And MRP II is so inflexible that the whole organization becomes cumbersome, unwieldy, slow to respond to changing conditions. Because of these difficulties, many organizations have moved towards MRP II, but have not implemented complete systems.

Extending MRP along the supply chain

Even when MRP II has generated plans for all activities and material movements within an organization, this is still not the end of the story. Following the trend for integrating the supply chain, we can extend the planning to other organizations. This gives the basis of **enterprise resource planning (ERP)** (Ptak and Schragenheim).

Suppose a manufacturer's MRP system finds that it needs a delivery of 100 units of some material at the beginning of June. It uses this information to schedule its purchases. However, EDI can link the MRP system to the supplier's system, so the supplier knows in advance when it has to deliver this material, and it can start scheduling operations to make sure that it is ready in time. If second tier suppliers are linked to the MRP system of the first tier suppliers, they can also start their preparations. In this way, the message moves backwards through the supply chain, giving integrated planning. Despite obvious problems – with trust, complexity, connecting systems, and the free flow of information – such systems are becoming more common and leading to the next stage of 'virtual enterprise resource allocation' (Brace and Rzevski).

IDEAS IN PRACTICE SAP AG

SAP was founded in Walldorf, Germany in 1972, and is a 'leader in supplying collaborative business solutions for all types of industries and for every major market'. It employs more than 32,000 people in 50 countries and has '12 million users; 91,500 installations; 1,500 partners'.

Forty percent of SAP's income comes from ERP, with its main product mySAP ERP. In 2004, SAP installed 1,335 ERP systems, bringing its total to more than 20,000 around the world, and making it 'undisputed world leader in ERP software'.

ERP systems have only been available since the 1990s, and the market is clearly growing vigorously, passing $10 billion by 2000. Other companies supply large integrated software, including BAAN, JD Edwards, SSA, and PeopleSoft. These have an average installation cost of around $15 million. Of this, 17 percent is for software, 14 percent for hardware, 46 percent for professional services and 23 percent for internal staff costs. The time to get a system working properly varies from under 18 months to over 30 months. After this, benefits begin to appear in about a year and it takes around five years to break even. Peter Burris of META Group makes the comment, 'To say that implementing ERM / ERP solutions requires an enormous commitment is an understatement. They are expensive, are time-consuming, and require change in virtually every department in the enterprise.'

Source: Brace G. and Rzevski G. (1998) Elephants rarely pirouette, Logistics Focus, 6(9), 14–18; Anon (1999) ERM solutions and their value, Meta Group, Stamford, CT; and Websites at WWW.SAP.com and www.metagroup.com

JUST-IN-TIME OPERATIONS

Principles of just-in-time

We have outlined the way that MRP controls material movement, and compared this with the more traditional approach of hierarchical planning. **Just-in-time (JIT)** gives a third option that is particularly useful in certain circumstances. Companies like Toyota spent years developing JIT through the 1970s (Monden; Shingo) and their methods were so successful that all major organizations now use it to some extent.

- **Just-in-time** organizes all activities to occur at exactly the time they are needed.

JIT does not do operations too early (which would leave materials hanging around until they were actually needed) and it does not do them too late (which would give poor customer service) – but at exactly the right time. You can see this effect when you order a taxi to collect you at 12:00. If the taxi arrives at 11:30 you are not ready and it wastes time sitting and waiting; if it arrives at 12:30 you are not happy and will not use the service again. When the taxi arrives at 12:00 – just-in-time for your trip – it does not waste time waiting, and you are pleased that the service arrives exactly when you wanted it.

Just-in-time and stocks

JIT seems a particularly obvious idea – but it can have a dramatic effect on the way that materials are organized. You can see this with stocks of raw materials. The main purpose of material stock is to give a buffer between operations, allowing for mismatches between the supply and demand for materials. If a delivery of raw materials is delayed, or equipment breaks down, or demand is unexpectedly high, or there is some other problem, then operations can still work normally by using the accumulated stocks. The traditional view of managers is that stocks are essential to guarantee smooth operations, so they define stock levels that are high enough to cover likely problems. Unfortunately, with widely varying demand, or serious potential problems, these stock levels can be very high and expensive. MRP reduces the amount of stock by using the master schedule to match the supply of materials more closely to demand. In practice, MRP still adds some safety stock to allow for uncertainty and problems, but it works with much lower stock levels. So the principle is clear – the more closely we can match the supply of materials to demand, the less stock we need to carry. And if we can completely eliminate any mismatch, we can also eliminate the stocks. This is the basis of just-in-time.

You can see an example of these principles with a lawnmower. If a lawnmower has a petrol engine, there is a mismatch between the fuel supply that you buy from a garage, and demand when you actually mow the lawn. You allow for this mismatch by keeping stocks of fuel in the petrol tank and spare can. This is the traditional approach to inventory control, where stocks are high enough to cover any likely demand. The MRP approach would go to the garage to collect some petrol just before you start to mow the lawn. But a just-in-time approach would use a lawnmower with an electric motor, so that the supply of electricity exactly matches demand and there are no stocks of fuel.

But what happens when there really is a mismatch between supply and demand? What does a supermarket do when it sells loaves of bread one at a time, but gets them delivered by the truckload? The traditional answer is to hold enough stock to cover the mismatch – the supermarket puts the truckload of bread on its shelves until it is sold or goes stale. JIT says that this is a mistake. The supermarket should look for a better solution to remove the mismatch – perhaps by opening a small bakery on the premises. This illustrates JIT's views, which we can summarize as follows:

- stock is a waste that serves no useful purpose
- it is held to cover the poor coordination of material flows that give short-term mismatches between supply and demand
- as long as there are stocks, there is no incentive for managers to improve the flow of materials
- so the best way to improve operations is to see why there are differences between supply and demand, take whatever action is needed to overcome the differences – and then remove the stock.

Wider effects of JIT

JIT is much more than a way of controlling stock and – like TQM – it has grown into a management philosophy. It involves a change in the way that managers view their operations, which its supporters describe as 'a way of eliminating waste', or 'a way of enforced problem solving'. In this wider sense, JIT sees an organization as having a series of problems that hinder efficient operations. These problems include long lead times, unreliable deliveries, unbalanced operations, constrained capacity, equipment breakdowns, defective materials, interruptions, unreliable suppliers, poor quality, too much paperwork, too many changes, and many other difficulties. Managers ignore the underlying problems by hiding the symptoms under large stocks, extra capacity, back-up equipment, 'trouble-shooters', and a series of other schemes. But a much more constructive approach is to identify the real problems – and solve them. This approach leads to a number of changes in viewpoint.

- **Stocks.** As we have seen, organizations hold stocks to cover short-term differences between supply and demand. JIT assumes that these stocks actually hide problems. Managers should find the reasons for differences between supply and demand, and then take the action needed to remove them.

- **Quality.** JIT recognizes that all defects have costs, so it supports the view of TQM and says that it is better to find the cause of poor quality, remove it, and make sure that no defects are produced.

- **Suppliers.** JIT relies totally on its suppliers – so it supports the view of customers and suppliers working closely together in long-term partnerships pursuing common objectives.

- **Employees.** JIT argues that an organization's performance depends on the people working for it, so they should all be treated properly.

- **Batch size.** Operations often use large batch sizes to reduce set-up costs and disruptions. But if demand is low, the products made in large batches sit in stock for a long time. JIT looks for ways of reducing the batch size so that it more closely matches demand.

- **Lead times.** Long lead times encourage high stocks, as they have to cover uncertainty until the next delivery. JIT aims for small, frequent deliveries with short lead times.

- **Reliability.** JIT is based on continuous, uninterrupted production, so all operations must be reliable. If, say, equipment breaks down, managers must find the reasons and make sure it does not happen again.

Achieving just-in-time operations

The success of JIT is not based on its development of a simple idea of coordinating activities, but on its description of how to achieve this. In particular, it works by 'pulling' materials through a supply chain. In a traditional process, each operation has a timetable of work that must be finished at a given time. Finished items are then 'pushed' through to form a stock of work in progress in front of the next operation. Unfortunately, this ignores what the next operation is actually doing – it might be working on something completely different, or be waiting for a different item to arrive. At best, the second operation must finish its current job before it can start working on the new material just passed to it. The result is delays and increased stock of work in progress.

JIT uses another approach to 'pull' work through the process. When one operation finishes work on a unit, it passes a message back to the preceding operation to say that it needs another unit to work on. The preceding operation only passes materials forward when it gets this request. You can see the difference in a take-away sandwich bar. With the traditional push system, someone makes a batch of sandwiches and delivers them to the counter where they sit until a customer buys them. With a JIT pull system, a customer asks for a particular type of sandwich, and this is specially made and delivered – thus eliminating the stocks of work in progress. You can also see that there is inevitably some lead time between an operation requesting material and having it arrive. In real JIT systems, messages are passed backwards this lead time before the materials are actually needed. Materials are also delivered in small batches rather than continuous amounts, so JIT still has some stocks of work in progress. These stocks are as small as possible, so it would be fairer to say that JIT minimizes stocks rather than eliminates them.

Now all that we need for JIT is some way of passing a message backwards to the previous operations. The simplest system moves materials between two stages in containers. When a second stage needs some materials, it simply passes the empty container back to the previous stage as a signal to fill it (Figure 14.5). Attached to the container is a card – usually known by the Japanese name of 'kanban' – which give details of the products, quantities, and delivery of materials. In practice, there are many ways of using containers and *kanbans,* which now tend to be electronic messages rather than paper cards – but they work in the same way of sending a message backwards to pull materials through the process.

Benefits and disadvantages of JIT

At a basic level, JIT gives a way of lowering stock, with some companies reducing them by 90 percent (Hay). In general, JIT gives benefits that include:

- lower stocks throughout the process
- related benefits, such as reduction in storage space and overheads
- lower costs for procurement using routine procedures

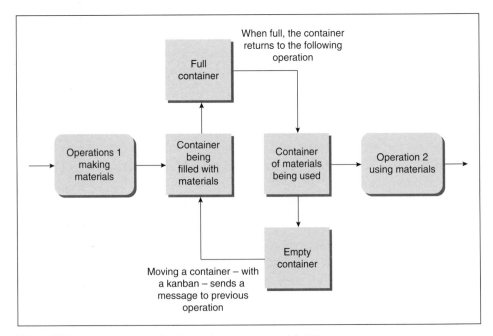

Figure 14.5 Pulling materials through a process with JIT

- faster, coordinated flow of materials giving shorter lead times
- higher productivity, utilization and capacity of resources
- simplified planning and scheduling with less administration
- better quality with less scrap and wastage
- better relations with suppliers
- emphasis on solving problems in the process.

Unfortunately, JIT only works well in certain types of process. The most successful users are large-scale assembly plants, which make virtually identical products in a continuous process. You can see the reason for this by exploring the JIT way of thinking, starting with changes to the process. Every time there are changes to a process, or it switches from making one product to making another, there are delays, disruptions and costs. JIT says that these changes waste resources and should be eliminated. In other words, there should be a stable environment where a process continuously makes large numbers of a standard product. This stable environment encourages low costs through specialized automation, so JIT works best with high volume, mass production. This usually means a well-balanced assembly line, with materials delivered directly to it. In practice, suppliers deliver the smallest batches possible, usually several times a day, and this means short lead times and low delivery costs. So suppliers must be flexible, efficient and located nearby. As there are no stocks to give safety cover, any defects in materials would disrupt production, so suppliers must be completely reliable and deliver materials that are free from defects. If something goes wrong, people working on the process must be able to find the cause, take the action needed to correct the fault, and make sure that it does not happen again. This needs a skilled and flexible workforce that is committed to the success of the organization.

We could continue arguing in this way, but you can see the type of conditions that JIT imposes – and that it involves complete changes in the way that managers think. Then it can bring considerable benefits – but, as always, there can be difficulties. One of the main problems with JIT is its inability to deal with unforeseen circumstances. For example, early in 2001 fuel supplies in the UK were disrupted by industrial action. Companies working with JIT stopped working immediately when their materials were not delivered, while those holding conventional stocks kept working normally. Some specific problems listed by JIT users include the:

- high risks of introducing completely new systems and operations
- high initial investment and cost of implementation
- long time needed to get significant improvements
- inability of suppliers to adapt to JIT requirements and methods
- need for stable production when demand is highly variable or seasonal
- reduced flexibility to meet specific, or changing, customer demands
- difficulty – and high costs – of reducing set-up times
- lack of commitment, cooperation and trust within the organization
- problems linking JIT to other information systems, such as accounts
- increased stress in workforce and inability of people to accept devolved responsibilities.

Extending JIT along the supply chain

Managers can extend JIT principles to other organizations along the supply chain. This extension is known by a variety of names, including **quick response** and more commonly **efficient customer response (ECR)**. Early work in this area was done in the fashion industry, whose traditional planning around four seasons causes severe problems with stocks. At the start of, say, the summer season shops have to be full of new products that reflect the latest styles and give a wide choice. But the summer styles are manufactured some time before the start of a season, and stored in the supply chain. Wholesalers accumulate high stocks to resupply the shops at short notice. But when a style sells well and clears all stocks in the supply chain, it cannot be replaced as the manufacturers have already moved on to making their autumn and winter collections. On the other hand, if demand is lower than expected, no-one can reduce their purchases, as the clothes are already sitting along the supply chain. At the end of each season there are major sales as wholesalers and retailers try to get rid of their less popular items, and major restocking in preparation for the next season.

The industry realized that there were huge potential savings. The way to achieve these is not to have rigid manufacturing pushing huge stocks forward to sit in the supply chain, but to have flexible manufacturing responding to customers pulling items very quickly through the supply chain to retailers. In other words, they introduced JIT principles to the whole supply chain. When a retailer sells an item, their cash register automatically sends a message to the wholesaler requesting a replacement, and the wholesaler's system sends a message to the manufacturer asking for a delivery. The manufacturer is not bogged down in making unwanted products, so it can respond quickly to demands and replace items as they are sold.

In 1985 the US retailer J.C. Penney formed one of the world's first ECR partnerships with Burlington (a fabric manufacturer) and Lanier Clothing (a garment maker). The result was a 22 percent increase in sales and a 50 percent reduction in stock (Karabyus and Croza). As other industries realized the benefits of ECR, Quaker Oats reported a threefold increase in stock turnover, 65 percent lower stocks and 77 percent reduction in paperwork (Boden). Integrated Systems Solutions reported 3–4 percent increase of service level, 40–50 percent reduction in stock and 2–3 times increase of stock turnover (Margulis).

TRANSPORT

Physical movement of materials

We have described three methods for controlling the flow of materials through supply chains – but the materials still have to be physically moved. For this they need **transport**. Apart from intangibles, such as information, software, music, and videos all products rely on transport for delivery. There are several strategic issues for transport, including the ownership and the choice of mode.

> ● Transport is responsible for the physical movement of materials through the supply chain.

An increasingly popular option for logistics is to use third party suppliers. Even when you see lorries driving around in company 'liveries', such as Tesco and Woolworth, these are actually run by a third party transport company. So there are two options for transport:

1 *Private transport*, usually referred to as 'in-house' or 'own-account' transport. This has the advantage of flexibility, greater control, closer integration of logistics and easier communications. Transport can also be tailored to operations' needs, with the best type of vehicles, fleet size, delivery schedule, customer service, and so on. But own account transport can be expensive and operations should only run their own fleet when they have enough work to get economies of scale that reduce their costs below the charges of a specialist third party carrier.

2 *Third party carriers*, which are specialist transport companies, offer a range of services to other organizations. The advantage of this arrangement is that the companies' parties run the transport, leaving the organization to concentrate on its core operations. By using their skills and expertise the transport operators can give better services and lower costs than own account transport. They can get considerable economies of scale and other operational benefits, such as consolidating smaller loads into larger ones, or coordinating journeys to give backhauls, where delivery vehicles are loaded with other materials for the return journey.

   Most third party transport is provided by common carriers, which are companies like TNT and Excel Logistics that move materials on a one-off basis. If you want to send a parcel to Australia, you might use a parcel delivery service such as UPS, which acts as a common carrier. Alternatively, an organization can form a long-term relationship with a contract carrier, which takes-over a part – often most of – the organization's transport for some extended period. Tibbet & Britten, for example, are responsible for all the movement of goods for Wal-Mart in Canada.

There are several factors to consider when choosing the best type of ownership, including capital costs, operating costs, customer service, flexibility and availability of skills. There is a clear trend towards third party carriers with many organizations – including the biggest – reducing their own transport fleets, using more contract operators, and forming alliances. A common option is to use a mixture of own account and third party carriers. Then an organization can use its own transport for core activities, with full utilization giving low costs. Any other transport needs are left to outside operators who deal with peaks and unusual demands.

Mode of transport

Another area for strategic decision concerns the mode of transport, which describes the type of transport used. There are basically five different options – road, rail, air, water and pipeline. Each mode has different characteristics, and the best in any particular circumstances depends on the type of materials to be moved, locations, distance, value, urgency, importance, reliability, and a whole range of other things. Sometimes there is a choice of mode, such as rail or ferry across the English Channel; road, rail or air between Rome and Geneva. Often, though, there is little choice. If you want to deliver coffee from Brazil to Amsterdam, you use shipping; if you want to move oil from Russia to Germany you use a pipeline; if you want an express parcel service across the Atlantic, you use air freight.

In general, water transport is used to ship heavy and bulky goods around the world, but it only serves ports and needs expensive facilities. Many countries have well-developed river and canal routes, such as the US and Canadian use of the St Lawrence Seaway and the Great Lakes. Rail is best for moving heavy and bulky loads over long distances across land, while air is best for light loads over long distances. Road transport is the most flexible, reaching most locations and being best for smaller loads over shorter distances. Pipelines are clearly best for moving large quantities of liquids, but they are expensive, inflexible and slow (typically moving at less than 10 km per hour). The cheapest modes of transport are usually the least flexible, so managers break a long journey into stages to get the best mixture of cost and convenience. They may, for example, use the road to a rail terminal, rail to a port, ship to the nearest port of destination, and so on. These inter-modal journeys rely on an efficient system for transferring materials between modes, usually using containers.

Many factors can be important for a final decision. Operations that routinely use the cheapest mode may be performing badly by some of the other measures.

OPERATIONS IN PRACTICE Christian Salvesen

In 1846 Christian and Theodore Salvesen founded a shipping and fishing company in Norway. The company continued with a general theme of transport, but has undergone a lot of changes over the years. It expanded into several adjacent industries, but in 1997 the owners sold the remaining non-core activities and after restructuring in 1999 focused on their core activities of being a major European logistics business. Their aim is, 'to manage client's supply chains seamlessly across Europe under the single brand of Christian Salvesen'.

Most of the company's business comes from partnership with manufacturers and retailers, using leading-edge systems to control stock levels, and make sure that goods are delivered to customers precisely when they are needed. To support this, they have a fleet of 2,500 vehicles, 5,500 trailers and 14,000 staff working at 160 sites.

One of Christian Salvesen's major contracts is to distribute parts for DaimlerChrysler in the UK. This means that they distribute parts to 300 franchised Mercedes-Benz and Chrysler dealers around the country. It is far too expensive for each dealer to hold in stock all the spare parts that they may possibly need, so DaimlerChrysler hold centralized stocks in their European Logistics Centre at Milton Keynes. Then they use Christian Salvesen to give a guaranteed rapid delivery service to dealers.

At the centre of the distribution operations is Christian Salvesen's SHARP (Shipments Handling And Reporting Programme). Every evening DaimlerChrysler collect the requirements from each dealer and enter the details into the SHARP system. These parts are loaded onto large double-decked articulated trucks at Milton Keynes. These leave between 19:00 and 22:00 and travel to eleven feeder depots around the country. At the feeder depots they have an hour to transfer parts on to 35 local delivery vehicles. Each of these delivers to up to 11 dealers, starting at midnight and finishing by 08:00. For this they need to deliver to unmanned premises with access to dealers' security systems.

When vehicles return to the depot, SHARP records the deliveries, and prepares reports on performance. The system for delivering spares is described as 'highly efficient and completely reliable'.

Source: Website at www.salvesen.com

Transport costs are often a relatively small part of overall costs, and it can be worth paying more to get a rapid and reliable delivery. One of the early studies of logistics by Lewis *et al.* showed that air freight can actually save money. It moves materials through the supply chain so quickly that organizations need fewer warehouses for distribution to customers – by paying more for transport they can reduce overall costs.

Chapter review

- The traditional way of controlling the flow of materials through a supply chain uses detailed schedules for operations. These schedules show the timing for products to be moved out to customers, and materials to be brought in from suppliers. Detailed schedules are designed by progressively adding more details to higher plans.

- Procurement is responsible for acquiring all the materials needed by operations. It consists of all the activities needed to organize an inward flow of materials from suppliers. This is an essential function for all operations and is often responsible for the greatest part of expenditure.

- Procurement sends a signal backwards in the supply chain to trigger a delivery of materials. There are several ways of organizing this. Traditional paper-based methods can be expensive and slow. Most operations have moved towards e-procurement.

- Managers aim for a smooth flow of materials through a supply chain, but there are often interruptions. When materials are not used as soon as they become available, they form stock. These stocks have high costs and need careful management.

- The traditional approach to stock control assumes independent demand for products. Then it uses quantitative models to find order patterns that minimize overall costs.

- Material requirements planning gives an alternative approach which 'explodes' a master schedule to find the requirements for materials and a timetable for delivery. Extension to the basic approach gives feedback to planning (closed-loop MRP) and use for other functions (manufacturing resources planning – MRP II). Enterprise resource planning (ERP) extends the approach along the supply chain to other organizations.

- Just-in-time operations aim at eliminating waste from an organization. They do this by organizing operations to occur just as they are needed. This needs a new way of thinking, which solves problems rather than hides them.

- The key feature of JIT is its 'pull' of materials through the process, rather than the conventional 'push'. Efficient customer response extends the ideas of JIT to other organizations in the supply chain.

- Transport is needed to physically move materials through the supply chain. There are several strategic aspects of transport, including ownership and choice of mode.

CASE STUDY Outsourcing

A survey by Bain & Co. of 25 key management tools identified outsourcing as the fourth most commonly used – with strategic management as the leader. The survey reported 73 percent of companies used outsourcing. Regional differences left 76 percent of companies using outsourcing in North America, 85 percent in Europe, 58 percent in Asia and 72 percent in South America. The average level of satisfaction with outsourcing was 3.98 on a scale of 1 to 5.

The most common area for outsourcing is logistics, particularly transport and warehouse. Third party operators are now responsible for the movement of most products. Fourth party operators are increasingly common, where a management company coordinates the activities of the separate third party companies responsible for different parts of logistics. Other activities that are routinely outsourced include legal services, catering, transport, printing, security and advertising. But outsourcing is becoming more common and moving into more central areas, such as research, design, data processing, information processing, IT services, pension funding, public relations, accounting and human resources. This is collectively known as 'business process outsourcing' and expenditure on this kind of service is estimated to be around $500 billion.

One of the fastest growing areas for outsourcing is IT. Europe is the world's biggest market for IT outsourcing, despite the fact that the biggest six service providers are all American (Accenture, ACS, CSC, EDS, Hewlett-Packard and IBM). The scope of IT outsourcing was demonstrated in 2005 when the British Government awarded the Atlas consortium a $7.6 billion ten year contract to manage 150,000 computers and networking software for the Ministry of Defence.

But there are problems with outsourcing, and some companies are becoming increasingly unhappy with the results. The survey by Bain & Co. found that almost half of large companies found that outsourcing had not met their expectations. Perhaps a problem is that outsourcing has become very trendy and many companies jumped in without enough thought, seeing it as an easy way of passing difficult technical problems to someone else.

Questions

- Why do companies use outsourcing, and what benefits can they expect?

- What activities are outsourced now, and which are likely to be outsourced in the future?

- The British government's record of outsourcing IT development has been very poor, with most systems seeming to be expensive and working badly. What can they do about this?

Source: Rigby D and Bilodeau B., Management tools and trends, Bain & Co., New York, 2005; Gottfredson M., Puryear R. and Phillips S., Survey on outsourcing, Bain & Co., New York, 2005; The Economist, Time to bring it back home?, March 5th–11th, p 63, 2005; Website at www.bain.com

Discussion questions

1 How can the flow of materials be controlled in a supply chain?

2 Why is procurement considered a strategic issue, when it is clearly a routine administrative job?

3 What are the benefits of using e-procurement? How will this affect wider operations?

4 MRP was developed to plan the supply of parts at manufacturers, so it cannot really be used in other types of organization. Do you think this is true?

5 MRP II seems a good idea in theory, but the systems would be so unwieldy that they could never work properly. Even if they did work, operations would be too inflexible to cope with agile competitors. What do you think of this view?

6 If you were in hospital and needing a blood transfusion, would you rather the transfusion service used a traditional system of holding stocks of blood, or a just-in-time system? What does your answer tell you about JIT in other organizations?

7 What are the most significant changes that JIT brings to the operations in an organization?

8 What are the problems of using ECR? How can these problems be overcome?

9 Outsourcing passes a problem to another organization that is less familiar with the context and is not ultimately responsible for the results. And there is no inherent reason why third parties can give better or cheaper results. So why would organizations use outsourcing?

Useful websites

www.bain.com
www.barclaysB2B.com
www.cips.org – Chartered Institute of Purchasing and Supply
www.clm.org – Council of Logistics Management
www.gartner.com
www.iolt.org.uk – Institute of Logistics and Transport
www.metagroup.com
www.salvesen.com
www.SAP.com

References

Allen S., Leveraging procurement: the quiet e-business, Logistics and Transport Focus, vol 3(4), pp 29–30, 2001.

Arnold J.R.T., Introduction to materials management (2nd edition), Prentice Hall, Englewood Cliffs, NJ, 1996.

Baily P., Farmer D., Jessop D. and Jones D., Purchasing principles and management (7th edition), Pitman, London, 1998.

Barclays Bank plc, Website at www.BarclaysB2B.com

Boden J., A movable feast, Materials Management and Distribution, November, pp 23–26, 1995.

Brace G. and Rzevski G., Elephants rarely pirouette, Logistics Focus, vol 6(9), pp 14–18, 1998.

Cerveny R.P. and Scott L.W., A survey of MRP implementation, Production and Inventory Management, vol 30(3), pp 177–181, 1989.

Cummings N., UK leading the world in e-procurement, OR Newsletter, March, p 9, 2002.

Doerflinger T.M., Gerharty M. and Kerschner E.M., The information revolution wars, Paine-Webber Newsletter, New York, 1999.

The Economist, e-business supplement, 24th June 1999.

The Gartner Group, The economic downturn is not an excuse to retrench B2B efforts, The Gartner Group, Stamford, CT, 2001.

The Gartner Group, Website at www.gartner.com

Gates W., Business at the speed of thought, Warner Books, New York, 1999.

Handfield R.B. and Nichols E.L., Introduction to supply chain management, Prentice Hall, Englewood Cliffs, NJ, 1998.

Harris F., Operations and Cost, A. Shaw & Co., Chicago, IL, 1915.

Hay E.J., The just-in-time breakthrough, John Wiley, New York, 1988.

Hayes R.J. and Wheelwright S.C., Restoring our competitive edge, John Wiley, New York, 1984.

Hill T., Manufacturing strategy (3rd edition), Palgrave Macmillan, Basingstoke Hants, 2000.

Hughes J., Ralf M. and Mitchels W., Transform your supply chain, Thomson, London, 1998.

Karabyus A. and Croza M., The keys to the kingdom, Materials Management and Distribution, May, pp 21–22, 1995.

Kraljic P., Purchasing must become supply management, Harvard Business Review, vol 61(5), March–April, pp 109–117, 1983.

Lee H.L., Padmanabhan V. and Whang S., The bull whip effect in supply chains, Sloan Management Review, Spring, pp 93–102, 1997.

Leenders M.R. and Fearon H.E., Purchasing and supply management, McGraw-Hill, New York 1996.

Lewis H.T., Culliton J.W. and Steel J.D.,The role of air freight in physical distribution, Harvard Business School, Boston, MA, 1956.

Margulis R.A., Grocers enter the era of ECR, Materials Management and Distribution, February, pp 32–33, 1995.

Merrill Lynch, e-commerce: virtually there, Merrill Lynch, New York, 1999.

Monden Y.,Toyota production system (2nd edition), Chapman and Hall, London, 1994.

Orlicky J., Material requirements planning, McGraw-Hill, New York, 1974.

Ptak C.A. and Schragenheim E., ERP tools, techniques and applications for integrating the supply chain, St. Lucie Press, Boca Raton, FL, 1999.

Raymond F.E., Quantity and Economy in Manufacture, McGraw-Hill, Chicago, IL, 1931.

Reck R.F. and Long B.G., Purchasing – a competitive weapon, International Journal of Purchasing and Materials Management, Fall, pp 2–8, 1988.

Rushe D., www.basketcase, The Sunday Times, September 2, 2001.

Saunders M., Strategic purchasing and supply chain management (2nd edition), FT Prentice Hall, London, 1997.

Sellers P., The dumbest marketing ploy, Fortune, vol 126(5), pp 88–93, 1992.

Shingo S., Study of Toyota production system from industrial engineering viewpoint, Japanese Management Association, Tokyo, 1981.

Sigarro P., Speed of procurement revisited, Western Operations Seminar, Nice, 2004.

Waters D., Logistics, Palgrave Macmillan, Basingstoke, 2003a.

Waters D., Inventory control and management (2nd edition), John Wiley, Chichester, 2003b.

Waters D., Global logistics and distribution planning (4th edition), Kogan Page, London, 2003c

Wight O.W., Production and inventory management in the computer age, Cahners Publishing, Boston, MA, 1974.

Wilson R.H., A Scientific Routine for Stock Control, Harvard Business Review, No. XIII, 1934.

The first part of this book discussed the broad principles of strategic management. It introduced the idea that organizations have a purpose, and strategic management works to achieve this over the long term. We described four layers of strategic management, with a mission leading to a corporate, business and functional strategies. An operations strategy forms one of the functional strategies.

The second part of the book showed how the general principles developed in the first part can be applied to an operations strategy. If we collect together all the long-term goals, plans, policies, culture, resources, decisions and actions that relate to operations, we get the basis of an operations strategy. This forms the link between higher strategies and more detailed operations. At its core are the decisions that set the long-term direction of operations.

In the third part of the book we looked at some specific areas for strategic operations decisions. These focus on the product, process and supply chain.

Product planning is responsible for ensuring that there is a long-term supply of products that continue to meet customer demands and operations' requirements. Innovative organizations look for new types of products that can help operations achieve their aims. A key part of the product package is its quality. Product plans set the designed quality of a product, and quality management is the function that makes sure this designed quality is actually achieved. TQM is the mechanism that sets the whole organization to making products of perfect quality.

Each product is made by its own unique process. Process planning sets the overall type of process that best achieves operations' aims, with a central question concerning the level of technology. But when the process has been planned and details added to its design, operations managers' job has not finished as they have to keep monitoring the process, looking for continuous improvement.

The capacity of a process has to match the foreseeable demand for its products, and this is the role of capacity management. The main difficulties here are that both the demand and capacity are uncertain and continually changing. The way to deal with this is to set a fixed overall capacity for the long term, and then allow for shorter-term adjustments.

When discussing the process, we concentrate on the operations that make the product – and when we discuss the movement of materials through the process we generally talk about supply chains. There are basically two strategic concerns for the supply chain – what is the best structure (number of tiers, relationships between facilities, locations, etc.) and how do we control the flow of materials (short-term schedules, MRP, JIT, transport, etc.).

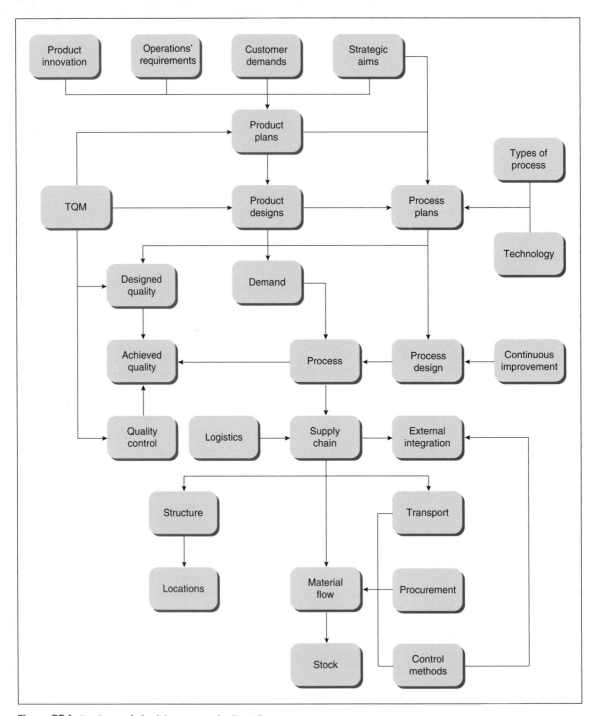

Figure R3.1 Review of decision areas in Part 3

Glossary

Achieved quality how good the delivered product is, defined by how it meets specifications and satisfies customers

Action plan gives a timetable for implementing the operations strategy

Activation translation of higher ideas and decisions into operational activities

Aggregate plans medium term plans which show the production of families of products over the next year or so

Agility flexible operations that can deal efficiently with changing conditions

Analyses for operations gives information about the internal operations

Analyses of the environment gives information about the external environment

Appraisal cost costs of monitoring operations to make sure that the designed quality is actually achieved

Attractiveness the extent to which an industry or market can lead to an organization's success

Automation has operations done by equipment without people taking part (compared with manual and mechanized operations)

Balanced scorecard analysis that gives a broad view of operations performance

Batch process makes a few kinds of products in medium sized batches

Benchmarking analysis of the best operations in an industry, looking for ideas to adopt and adapt

Bottleneck the resource or activity that limits the capacity of a process

Bottom-up design where the strategy emerges from the activities of junior managers and passes upwards through the organization

Business environment complex set of external factors that affect an organization

Business process re-engineering the fundamental redesign of a process to give dramatic improvements in performance

Business strategy strategy for a distinct SBU

Capability operations that an organization does – or can do – particularly well

Capacity of process is the maximum amount of a product that it can make in a given time

Capacity management is responsible for all aspects of operations' capacity.

Capacity planning aims at finding a long-term match between available process capacity and demand for products

Capacity plans strategic plans that ensure capacity meets the long-term demand

Capacity requirements planning standard approach to planning capacity

Change the inevitable alteration of conditions over time

Choice of strategy choosing the best of the set of feasible strategies considered

Closed-loop MRP adds feedback to basic MRP system

Competencies operations that an organization does particularly well

Competition appears when different organizations supply similar products to the same market sector

Competitive advantage features that make customers prefer one supplier over its competitors

Competitive features product features that customers value and which operations can focus on

Concurrent development reduces the time for product development by running stages in parallel rather than series

Continuous improvement acceptance that a process needs to be constantly updated for operations to remain competitive

Continuous process makes one product in a continuous stream

Control adjusting the strategy to correct any problems

Control system monitors the performance of operations and adjustments the strategy to improve its performance

Core capability key operations that an organization does particularly well

Core functions marketing, operations and finance which exist in every organization

Corporate Strategy strategy for a whole diversified corporation

Corporation an umbrella organization for diversified SBUs

Culture values, norms, beliefs and assumptions that influence the way that people think and behave

Customer relationship management collects and analyzes information about customers

Demand the total amount of a product that customers want

Demand management adjusts the demand for a product to match the available capacity of the process

Dependent demand where there are relationships between individual demands for materials

Designed capacity the theoretical limit on output that can be achieved under ideal conditions

Designed quality the quality that a product is designed to have, defined in its specifications

Distinctive capability core operations that an organization does so well that they give a competitive advantage

Downstream organizations later in the supply chain that move materials out of an organization and on towards customers

Economic order quantity order size that minimizes inventory costs

Economic system mechanism for controlling (among other things) the supply and demand of products

Effective capacity the maximum realistic output under normal conditions

Effectiveness shows how well an organization sets and achieves its goals

Efficiency shows how well the available resources are used

Efficient customer response extends JIT to other organizations in the supply chain

Emerging strategy strategy that develops from experience rather than proactive design

Enterprise resource planning (ERP) extends MRP to other organizations in the supply chain

Entry barrier hurdles and costs to an organization of entering a market

Entry strategy point in a product life cycle when operations begin to make a product

Environment the external setting in which an organization works

Environmental scan collects all relevant information about an operations environment

e-procurement a range of methods for automated purchasing

Exit barrier hurdles and costs to an organization of leaving a market

Exit strategy point in a product life cycle when operations stop making a product

Expected value the product of the value of an event and the probability that it occurs

External integration integrating logistics along the supply chain

External view customers' judgement of quality, largely showing how satisfied they are with a product

Facilities location finds the best geographical location for operations

Failure cost costs of making products that are in some way defective

Feasible set method to compare alternative sites for facilities

Feasible strategies strategies that achieve the aims, a relatively small number of which managers consider

Fishbone diagram tool for identifying the cause of a problem

Focus concentration on one aspect of operations

Functional strategy strategy for a function within an SBU

Generic strategy common strategy shared by many organizations

Goals targets for performance expressed in general terms

Human resources the people side of an operations strategy

Implementation turning the aspirations and intents of strategies into positive actions

Independent demand the total demand for an item is made up of lots of separate demands that are not related to each other

Industry a group of organizations making similar or equivalent products

Industry analysis analysis of actual and potential competitors as part of an environmental scan

Infinite set method find the best site for facilities in principle

Infrastructure the organizational structure along with systems, human resources and culture to support it

Innovation doing new and original things rather than continuing with existing practices or adopting the practices of competitors

Inputs all materials and resources used by operations

Integration of the supply chain treating the supply chain as a whole rather than separate activities

Internal integration integrating logistics activities within an organization

Internal view operations judgement of quality, largely defined as meeting specifications

ISO 9000 International Standards Organization standards for quality management

Jobbing process makes a variety of products in small batches

Just-in-time organizes all activities to occur at exactly the time they are needed

Kaizen continuous improvement

Key success factor the factors that customers really value and which an organization must do well

Lean operations aim at doing all operations with the minimum quantity of each resource

Learning organization one that learns from past experience and applies the lessons to future activities

Life cycle standard pattern of demand over a product's life

Logistics is responsible for the movement of materials into a process from suppliers, through operations, and then out of the process to customers

Management all the varied activities done by managers

Management by objectives mechanism for progressively moving objectives downwards through an organization

Management style the way that managers approach decision making

Managers the people who make decisions and run their organization

Manufacturing resource planning (MRP II) extends the MRP approach to all activities and resources within an organization

Marginal analysis identify optimal production levels

Marginal cost cost of producing the last unit of a product

Market customers who buy a particular product

Market analysis analysis of actual and potential customers as part of the environmental scan

Market research collects the views from specific types of customer

Market view of operations strategy emphasizes the environment, and adjusts operations to match the market

Mass customization operations that combine high volumes with significant product variation

Mass process make large numbers of a standard product

Master schedules timetables for the production of individual products over the next few months

Material requirements planning (MRP) uses the master schedule and other relevant information to plan the supply of materials

Materials general term for all inputs delivered to the operations

Materials management is responsible for the flow of raw materials into and through operations

Mission statement of an organization's overall purpose and aims

Monitoring function of the control system in keeping track of operations

Motivation means that people work hard to achieve an appropriate goal

New product development takes initial ideas for products and builds them into new products that are launched on the market

Objectives more specific, preferably quantitative, targets

Operational decisions short-term decisions that have relatively minor consequences for specific activities

Operations activities that make a product

Operations audit gives a detailed description of the operations used by an organization

Operations excellence operations that are done very well, particularly, better than competitors

Operations management the management function responsible for all aspects of operations

Operations managers people who run the operations

Operations mission a statement of purpose setting the long-term direction of operations

Operations purpose long-term aims described in an operations mission

Operations strategy all the long-term goals, plans, policies, culture, resources, decisions and actions that relate to operations

Opportunities conditions in the environment that can be exploited to give benefits

Opportunity cost the reduction in benefit from not buying certain resources

Order-winning features determine which product customers choose from a shortlist

Organization a group of people contributing resources and working together to achieve a specific purpose

Organizational strategy shows what the organization wants to achieve and how it will achieve it

Organizational structure shows how an organization is divided and the relationship between the parts

Output amount actually produced by a process

Outputs all product and by-products created by operations

Outsourcing passing non-core activities to another organization

Package complex combination of goods and services that forms a complete product

Partnership another term for strategic alliance

Performance a measure of how good operations are

PEST analysis examines environmental political, economic, social and technological factors

Physical distribution is responsible for the outward flow of finished goods

Plans and methods needed to achieve the strategic goals and objectives

Positioning delivering products that precisely meet customer demands

Prevention cost costs of preventing defects from occurring

Price elasticity of demand is the percentage decrease in demand that comes from each percentage increase in price

Process consists of all the operations used to make a product

Process-centred has a strategy that emphasizes the superior performance of the process

Process design describes the details of a process

Process planning is responsible for decisions about the process, particularly its strategic direction

Process quality how well the delivered product matches designed specifications

Process technology the level of technology – broadly manual, mechanized or automated – in a process

Procurement is responsible for acquiring all the materials needed by operations

Product general term for the complex package that an organization passes to its customers

Product design describes the details of a product

Product life cycle standard pattern of demand over a product's life

Product planning is responsible for the design and introduction of new products, changes to existing products and withdrawal of old ones

Production possibility curve shows how limited resources define the mix of products that is feasible in particular circumstances

Project makes a wide variety of unique products

Purchasing the actual buying of materials

Purpose the overall aim of an organization

Qualifying features features that a product must have before customers consider it

Quality the ability of a product to satisfy stakeholders – particularly customers and operations

Quality at source has people responsible for passing on work of perfect quality

Quality circles informal groups who meet regularly to discuss ways of improving their process and raising product quality

Quality control function that monitors process quality to make sure that designed quality is actually being achieved

Quality function deployment method of seeing how well the features in product designs meet customer requirements

Quality management is the management function responsible for all aspects of quality

Quick response an alternative name for efficient customer response

Re-engineering business process re-engineering

Resources audit identifies the resources that an organization already has, or could have if needed

Resources view of operations strategy emphasizes internal operations and developing excellent performance

Risk uncertainty about future events

Risk management procedures for dealing with the inevitable risk associated with an operations strategy

Scientific management use of rational analyses to find the 'best' way of doing things

Sector a distinct part of an industry or market segment

Segment a distinct part of an industry or market

Short-term schedules detailed timetables for all resources over the next few weeks

Stakeholders all the people and other organizations that have an interest in an organization

Steps in design details of the procedure for designing an operations strategy

Stock supplies of materials that are stored by operations until needed

Strategic alliance long-term, formal relationship between two organizations

Strategic business unit (SBU) a distinct division of a larger corporation

Strategic decisions long-term decisions that have major consequences throughout the organization

Strategic fit the match of an organization's aims and internal features to its environment

Strategic management the decisions and actions that lead to a strategy

Strategic resources resources that are particularly important to an organization and have a strategic impact

Strategic stretch where operations can adjust their environment, perhaps creating new markets

Strategy shows what the organization wants to achieve and how it will achieve it

Strategy design setting the long-term aims and features of an organization

Strengths things that operations do well

Supply the total amount of a product that is made

Supply chain the series of activities and organizations that materials move through on their journey from initial suppliers to final customers

Supply chain management an alternative name for logistics

Supply management adjusts the capacity of a process to match customer demand

Sustainable competitive advantage superior performance that can persist over the long term

SWOT analysis gives a broad view of operations and their environment, describing their strengths, weaknesses, opportunities and threats

Systems process for delivering information, etc., through the organization and showing how it is used

Tactical decisions medium-term decisions that have consequences for parts of the organization

Threats potentially adverse effects that may hinder the performance of operations

Tiers different levels in the supply chain

Top-down design where senior managers design a strategy and pass it downward through the organization

Total Quality Management has the whole organization working together to guarantee – and systematically improve – quality

Transformed inputs are changed during operations

Transforming inputs are not themselves changed during operations

Transport moves materials between different facilities in the supply chain

Trends in operations general movements that affect the process

upstream organizations earlier in the supply chain that move materials into an organization

Utilization the proportion of designed capacity that is actually used

Vertical integration describes the amount of a supply chain that is owned by one organization

Vision what an organization would ideally like to achieve

Weaknesses things that operations do relatively badly

Zero defects guarantees perfect quality with no defects

Index